THE SOCIETY FOR
MEDIEVAL ARCHAEOLOGY
MONOGRAPH 30

Series Editor
CHRISTOPHER GERRARD

REFLECTIONS:
50 YEARS OF MEDIEVAL ARCHAEOLOGY,
1957–2007

Recent presidents of the Society for Medieval Archaeology, pictured together at the 50th anniversary celebrations in December 2007. Front, from left: Roberta Gilchrist (2005–7), M W Thompson (1993–5), Leslie Webster (2008–10); back, from left: Helen Clarke (1990–2), Charles Thomas (1987–9), Martin Biddle (1996–8), Christopher Dyer (1999–2001). Photograph: Andrew Selkirk

REFLECTIONS:
50 YEARS OF MEDIEVAL ARCHAEOLOGY, 1957–2007

Edited by

ROBERTA GILCHRIST

and

ANDREW REYNOLDS

2009

ISBN 978-1-906540-71-5
ISSN 0583-9106

FRONT COVER
The Seventh Seal (SWD 1957): a knight plays chess with death — using some Lewis-inspired pieces.
(Photograph courtesy of: BFI)

BACK COVER
A reconstruction of the 8th-century phase at the village of Montarrenti, Tuscany, based on excavations by Ricardo Francovich and Richard Hodges (after Cantini 2003).

Published by Maney Publishing, Suite 1C, Joseph's Well, Hanover Walk, Leeds LS3 1AB, UK
www.maney.co.uk

Maney Publishing is the trading name of W. S. Maney & Son Ltd

Typeset, printed and bound in the UK by
The Charlesworth Group

The Society for Medieval Archaeology
dedicates this anniversary volume
to its three founders,
Donald Harden, John Hurst and David Wilson

THE SOCIETY FOR MEDIEVAL ARCHAEOLOGY MONOGRAPHS

ISSN 0583–9106

1 G Bersu and D M Wilson (1966) *Three Viking Graves in the Isle of Man*
2 F W B Charles (1967) *Medieval Cruck-building and its Derivatives*
3 P A Rahtz (1969) *Excavations at King John's Hunting Lodge, Writtle, Essex, 1955–57*
4 A L Meaney and S C Hawkes (1970) *Two Anglo-Saxon Cemeteries at Winnall, Winchester, Hampshire*
5 H E J Le Patourel (1973) *The Moated Sites of Yorkshire*
6 G T M Beresford (1975) *The Medieval Clay-land Village: Excavations at Goltho and Barton Blount*
7 H Clarke and A Carter (1977) *Excavations in King's Lynn, 1963–1970*
8 J G Hurst (general ed) Wharram. A Study of Settlement on the Yorkshire Wolds, vol I: D D Andrews and G Milne (eds) (1979) *Domestic Settlement I: Areas 10 and 6*
9 C M Mahany, A Burchard and G Simpson (1982) *Excavations at Stamford, Lincolnshire, 1963–69*
10 P Mayes and K Scott (1984) *Pottery Kilns at Chilvers Coton, Nuneaton*
11 J G Hurst and P A Rahtz (general eds) Wharram. A Study of Settlement on the Yorkshire Wolds, vol III: R D Bell, M W Beresford and others (1987) *The Church of St Martin*
12 D Austin (1989) *The Deserted Medieval Village of Thrislington, Co Durham: Excavations 1973–1974*
13 V L Yanin, E N Nosov, A S Khoroshev, A N Sorokin, E A Rybina, V L Povetkin and P G Gaidukov (1992) *The Archaeology of Novgorod, Russia*
14 K Parfitt and B Brugmann (1997) *The Anglo-Saxon Cemetery on Mill Hill, Deal, Kent*
15 D Gaimster and P Stamper (eds) (1997) *The Age of Transition: the Archaeology of English Culture 1400–1600*
16 D A Hinton (2000) *A Smith in Lindsey: the Anglo-Saxon Grave at Tattershall Thorpe, Lincolnshire*
17 S Lucy and A Reynolds (eds) (2002) *Burial in Early Medieval England and Wales*
18 S T Driscoll (2002) *Excavations at Glasgow Cathedral 1988–1997*
19 P Mayes (2003) *Excavations at a Templar Preceptory. South Witham, Lincolnshire 1965–67*
20 J Hines, A Lane and M Redknap (eds) (2004) *Land, Sea and Home*
21 W D Klemperer and N Boothroyd (2004) *Excavations at Hulton Abbey, Staffordshire 1987–1994*
22 K Giles and C Dyer (eds) (2005) *Town and Country in the Middle Ages: Contrasts, Contacts and Interconnections, 1100–1500*
23 S M Foster and M Cross (2005) *Able Minds and Practised Hands: Scotland's Early Medieval Sculpture in the 21st Century*
24 A Saunders (2006) *Excavations at Launceston Castle, Cornwall*
25 C Gerrard with M Aston (2007) *The Shapwick Project, Somerset: A Rural Landscape Explored*
26 C Caple (2007) *Excavations at Dryslwyn Castle 1980–95*
27 C Scull (2009) *Early Medieval (Late 5th–Early 8th Centuries AD) Cemeteries at Boss Hall and Buttermarket, Ipswich, Suffolk*
28 G Beresford (2009) *Caldecote. The Development and Desertion of a Hertfordshire Village*
29 N Edwards (ed) (2009) *The Archaeology of the Early Medieval Celtic Churches*

CONTENTS

PART V
SOCIAL APPROACHES TO MEDIEVAL ARCHAEOLOGY

(a)

(b)

(c)

(a) Maurice Beresford (1920–2005) and John Hurst (1927–2003) at Wharram Percy on 18 July 1989 for the presentation of the volume of studies on rural settlements dedicated to them by friends and colleagues. Excavation at Wharram between 1950 and 1992 can claim to be one of the key benchmarks in the making of medieval archaeology, not only for methodological reasons and for its contribution to the understanding of medieval rural settlement and landscape, but for the influence it projected and continues to project well beyond its trenches through the many diggers who participated. (Photograph: Mick Aston).
(b) Professors at Wharram. From left to right: Philip Rahtz (in the hat), Chris Dyer and Dave Austin. Bob Croft (in shorts) explains stratigraphical complexities. (Photograph: Mick Aston).
(c) Wharram Percy. Excavation of the 12th-century camera block discovered beneath House 10, summer 1957. John Hurst, in white shirt (back centre); Maurice Beresford (back left), looking left. Alongside him a domestic mangle has been adapted to raise buckets out of the excavation. (Photograph supplied by Paul Stamper)

(See Chapter 5.)

Drawing reconstruction of the 8th-century phase in Montarrenti, Tuscany. Francovich and Hodges' excavation made clear that a Late Antique and an early medieval village had preceded the medieval castle.

(See Chapter 7.)

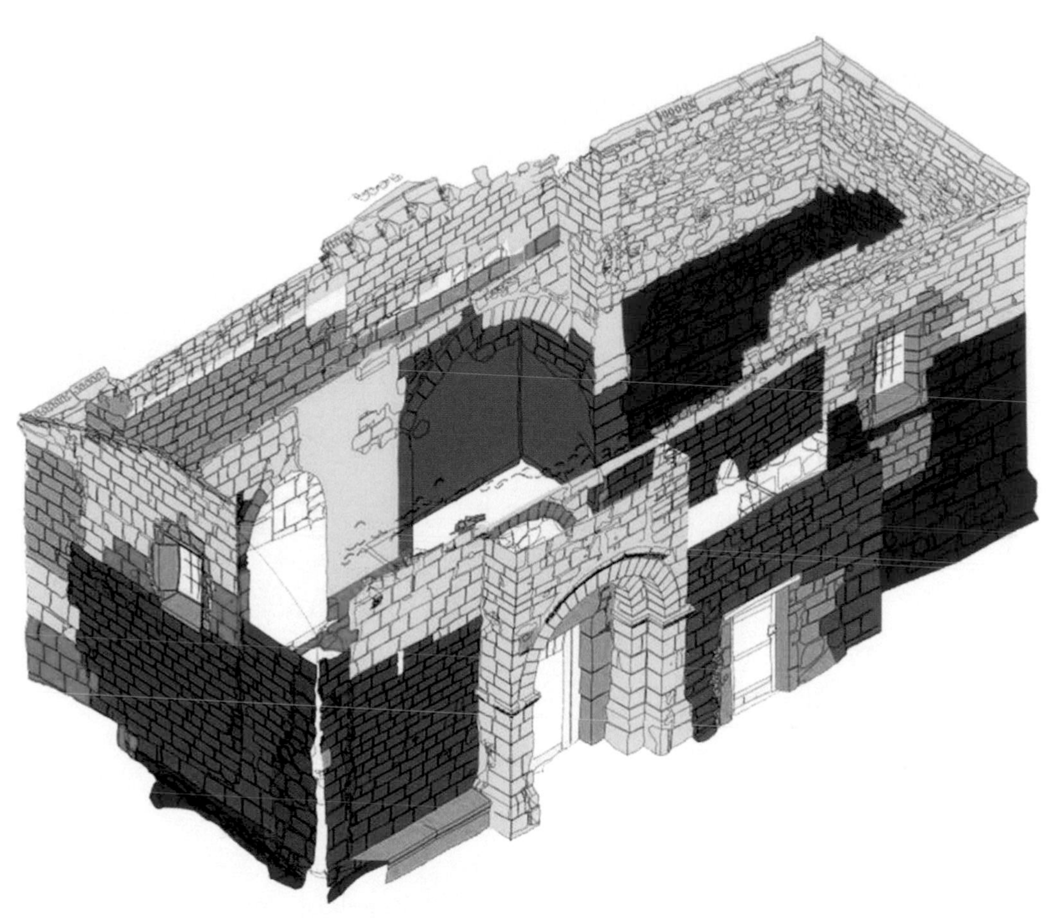

Stratigraphic analysis of San Roman of Tobillas church (Álava).

(See Chapter 9.)

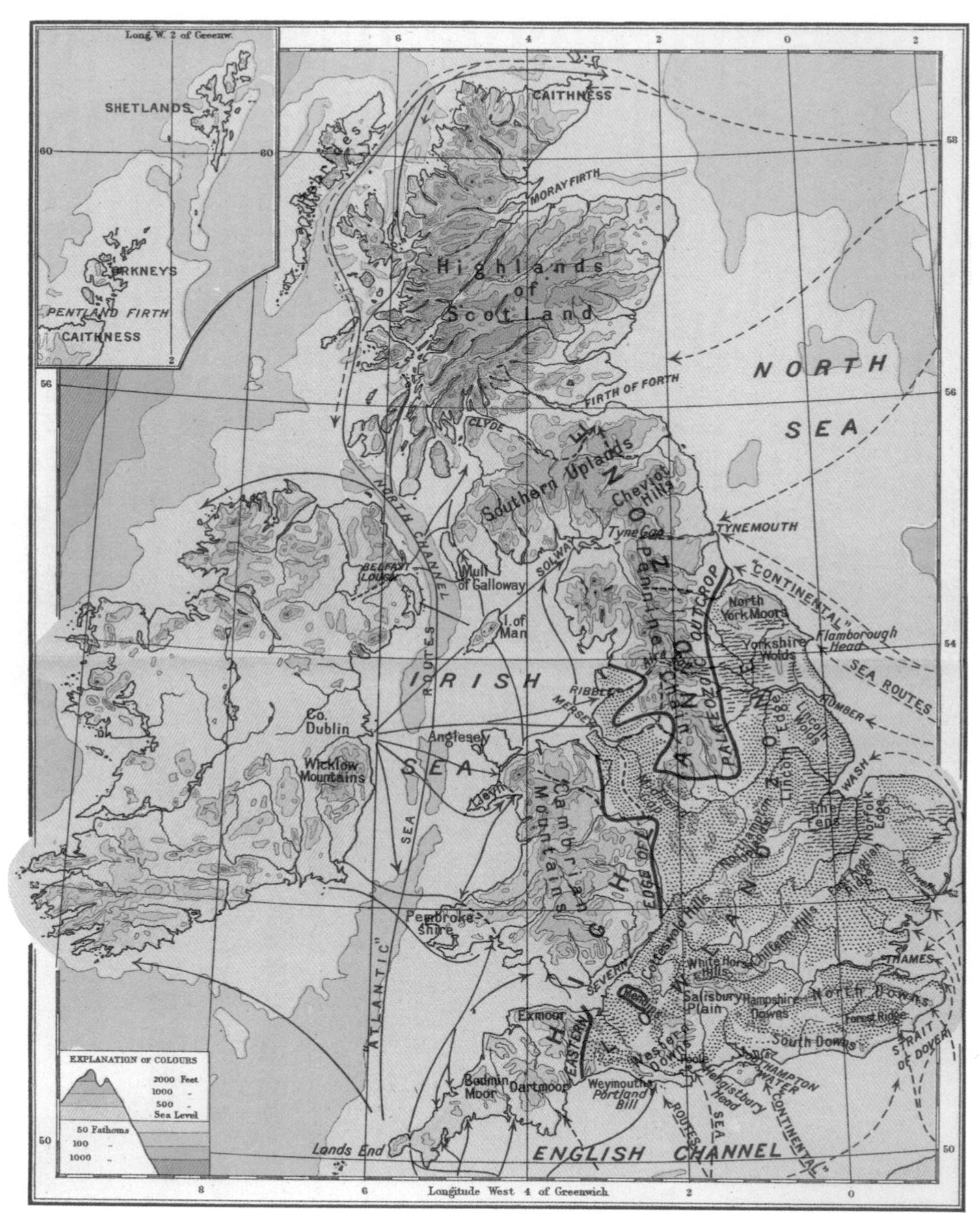

An early depiction of regional variation in landscape character from Cyril Fox's *The Personality of Britain*, that reflects two of the prevailing theoretical perspectives of the time: environmental determinism and the culture-historical approach towards explaining change (after Fox 1932, map B).

(See Chapter 11.)

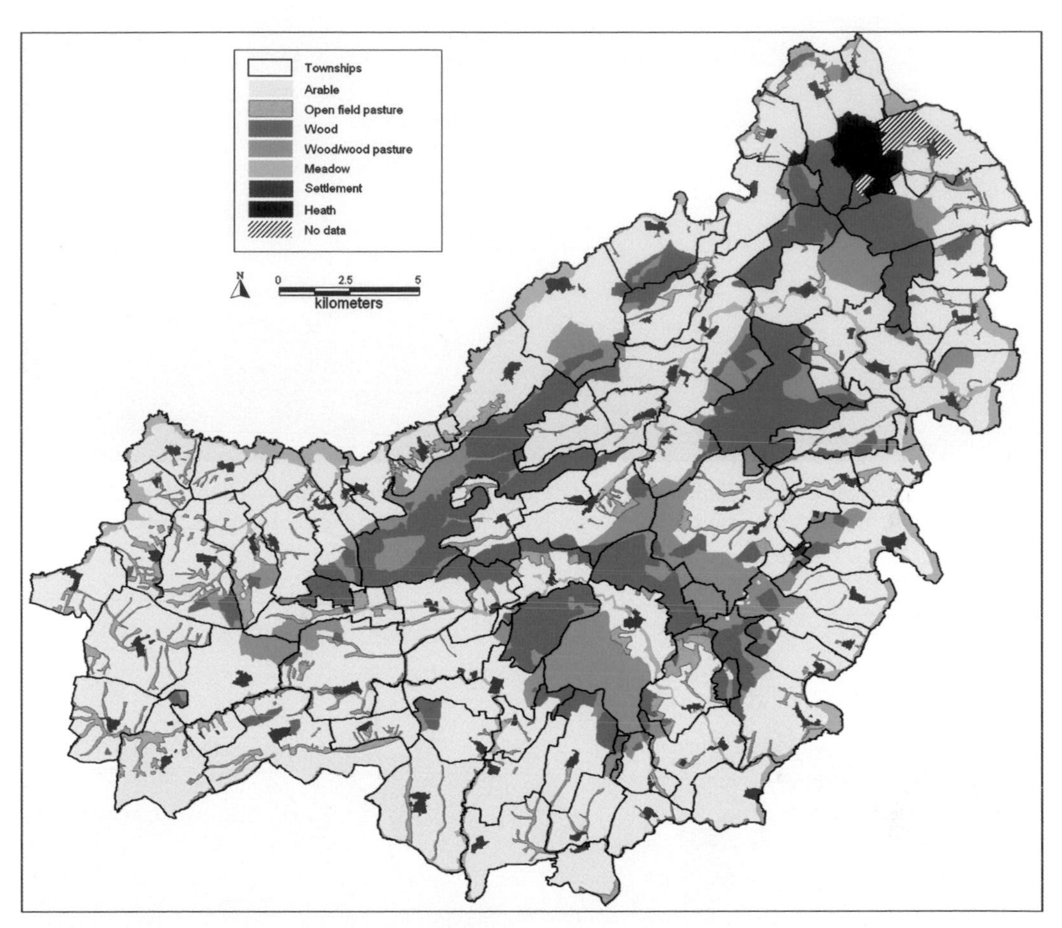

A reconstruction of the medieval landscape of the Rockingham Forest in Northamptonshire by Glenn Foard, David Hall and Tracey Partida. The use of GIS has allowed David Hall's decades of fieldwork and analysis of maps and documents to be plotted in a way that was previously not possible (after Foard *et al* 2005, fig 7).

(See Chapter 11.)

Bodiam Castle, Sir Edward Dallyngrigge's late 14th-century castle is an excellent example of an individual putting his stamp on the landscape. It is also a castle in the centre of a scholarly debate. (Photograph: M Hansson)

Great Chalfield Manor with the church located on the partly moated platform of the residence. (Photograph: M Hansson)

(See Chapter 21.)

Beowulf (US 2007): Grendel, a 6th-century nightmare? (Source: BFI and copyright Warner Brothers)

In Bruges (US/GY/UK 2008): The Church of Our Lady and St John's Hospital — existential angst and moral metaphor in medieval and modern Bruges. (Source: BFI and copyright Universal)

(See Chapter 24.)

INTRODUCTION

'THE ELEPHANT IN THE ROOM' AND OTHER TALES OF MEDIEVAL ARCHAEOLOGY

By ROBERTA GILCHRIST *and* ANDREW REYNOLDS

This volume celebrates the 50th anniversary of the Society for Medieval Archaeology (established in 1957), presenting reflections on the history, development and future prospects of the discipline. The papers are drawn from a series of conferences and workshops that took place in 2007–08, in addition to a number of contributions that were commissioned especially for the volume. They range from personal commentaries on the history of the Society and the growth of the subject (see papers by David Wilson and Rosemary Cramp), to historiographical, regional and thematic overviews of major trends in the evolution and current practice of medieval archaeology.

In order to place British medieval archaeology in comparative perspective, contributions were invited from medieval archaeologists working in southern Europe, a region which has experienced rapid change in disciplinary practice in recent decades. Papers by Andrea Augenti, Gian Pietro Brogiolo, Juan Antonio Quirós Castillo and Florin Curta present critical overviews of the development of medieval archaeology in Italy, Spain and south-eastern Europe. Although very different nationalist frameworks were created by mid-20th-century Fascist and Marxist regimes in the respective countries of southern Europe, some common ground can be found with the character of medieval archaeology that emerged in post-war Britain (see papers by Christopher Gerrard). All of these regions share a long tradition of interest in the medieval past, but the formation of a distinct discipline of medieval archaeology is an invention of the past 50 years, or even more recently in some countries (such as Spain). The Society's future engagement with historiography should seek comparison with the development of medieval archaeology in central and eastern Europe, where the discipline is developing at a swift pace, and with our neighbours in north-western Europe, with whom we share a rich antiquarian heritage.

Wilson and Cramp participated in the birth of the subject first-hand, and their personal perspectives stress the youth and pioneering spirit of the first decades of medieval archaeology across Europe. Cramp underlines the importance of data-gathering in the early years, at a time when the subject was regarded as having very little evidential support. In northern and southern Europe, medieval archaeologists struggled to establish an independent disciplinary identity, and the history of the subject tells of intellectual and methodological wrangles especially with the disciplines of history, art history and classical archaeology. The biographies of medieval archaeology in southern and northern Europe share an uneasy relationship with archaeological theory, and emphasize an initial concern to amass a sound body of evidence that would provide the foundation for the subject. Curta concludes that culture-history remains the dominant approach to medieval archaeology in south-eastern Europe; although the processualism of the 1970s and 1980s by-passed the region, the current generation is more receptive to new theoretical ideas. In contrast, Brogiolo reveals the stubborn resistance to post-processual approaches in contemporary Italian medieval archaeology, despite the strong international character of the subject in Italy. In commenting on the challenges facing medieval archaeology today, there is remarkable unanimity of opinion (see Gardiner and Rippon for the British perspective). In Britain, Italy and Spain, the fragmentary nature of medieval archaeology is considered the major threat to the future of the discipline. Greater co-ordination, communication and confidence are called for in: i) progressing research and teaching in medieval archaeology; ii) gaining research value from developer-funded, rescue and conservation work; iii) enhancing public understanding of the medieval past; and iv) establishing the importance of the study of medieval material culture within the social sciences.

Looking back just 25 years demonstrates that the subject has been transformed in some key respects, while in other ways we continue to display a surprising degree of insecurity as a discipline. The conference proceedings that resulted from the Society for Medieval Archaeology's 25th anniversary contain 15 short contributions on the 'state of the art' as it existed in 1981 (Hinton 1983). With the exception of Richard Hodges's paper, the proceedings lacked any international perspective, with the emphasis placed instead on balancing the Anglo-Saxon, English and 'Celtic' archaeologies of Britain. Rather than thematic overviews, there were reports from the respective interest groups — the Urban Research and Churches Committees (of the Council for British Archaeology), and the Research Groups devoted to the Medieval Village, Moated Sites and Medieval Pottery. There were offerings on 'New Approaches' from veteran archaeologist Philip Rahtz, who had recently established a department of medieval archaeology at the University of York, and 'young turk' Hodges, who was shortly to publish a ground-breaking book on early medieval trade and the origins of towns (Hodges 1982). Although tremendous progress had been made in the first 25 years of the subject (see reviews by Cramp, Gerrard, Rippon), very little interpretative or synthetic work had yet been undertaken. Numerous county-based surveys of medieval archaeology appeared in the late 1970s and early 1980s, but the first national overviews available for students of early medieval archaeology appeared only from the mid-1970s (eg Wilson 1976, Graham-Campbell 1980), with the first digests of later medieval archaeology published nearly a decade later (Clarke 1984; Steane 1985).

In the early 1980s the most vibrant areas of research to emerge were urban archaeology and church archaeology, stimulated by the contemporary climate of rescue and threats to the growing numbers of redundant medieval churches. Twenty-five years later, thematic study in Britain and Ireland has shifted more to landscape and burial archaeology (see papers by Reynolds, Brady, Rippon, Hansson and Hadley), and very significant progress has been made in the archaeology of housing and in the study of medieval material culture (see papers by Roesdahl, Egan and Hinton). Data gathering and analyses have been transformed by the onset of digital technology and computing. Medieval archaeology in southern Europe has seen a similar focus on the study of settlement types — towns, castles, churches, villages and so on — but there are also distinctive sub-disciplines devoted to Late Antique, Byzantine, Early Christian and Islamic archaeology. Landscape and burial archaeology also feature prominently in the recent development of medieval archaeology in southern Europe, as does 'the archaeology of architecture' (termed 'buildings archaeology' in the UK). The fragmentation of interest groups that was obvious in the early 1980s remains a major concern for the coherent intellectual development of the subject across Europe (expressed by Gerrard, Reynolds, Augenti, Brogiolo and Castillo).

The chronological span of the discipline has also increased beyond the traditional confines of the medieval period. In the 1980s, attention was given to the boundary with sub-Roman archaeology, while today the border between later medieval and early modern is the focus of equal attention (eg Gaimster and Stamper 1997; Gaimster and Gilchrist 2003). This broadening of boundaries has fostered a creative new engagement with historical (post-medieval) archaeology — an even younger discipline — but it may have contributed to the disjointedness that has grown up between the sub-disciplines of early and later medieval archaeology. The distinction between early and later medieval archaeology is much less clear-cut than it was perceived to be 25 or 50 years ago, largely owing to the substantial archaeological contribution made to the realization that so many aspects of society and culture can be found either side of the Norman invasion of 1066.

We are more troubled in the 21st century by factors resulting from the professionalization of archaeology — tensions between commercial units and universities, the competing pressures of development and heritage management, and how to harness the research value of developer-led archaeology conducted on medieval sites. It is salutary to recall the warning of Peter Sawyer in the early 1980s that archaeological excavation and analytical techniques were becoming 'so expensive that archaeologists will be reduced to playing with models' (Sawyer 1983, 46). To the contrary, who could have foreseen the explosion of developer-funded archaeology that began in England just seven years later, with PPG16 (1990)? In comparison with 25 or 50 years ago, we enjoy an embarrassment of riches in the form of medieval archaeological data. Have the interpretation and synthesis of these data progressed at a similar pace? Do the strategies employed in developer-funded investigations address coherent research priorities?

The formation of the Society for Medieval Archaeology in 1957 involved substantial negotiation and cooperation between competing disciplines, and there was appropriate attention given to the visibility of the 'Celtic west' (see first paper by Gerrard). At the Society's conference in 1981, a diplomatic fine line was still being brokered with regard to representation. The 1983 proceedings published no fewer than three 'Historians' Views' by Peter Sawyer, Wendy Davies and P D A Harvey.

Today, most medieval archaeologists regard the subject as inherently interdisciplinary, and as possessing its own research agenda which is distinctive from that of medieval history. The historiographical chapters in the present volume highlight the extent to which the first decades of research conformed to an agenda established by medieval history, for example in charting the impact of the Black Death on medieval villages (see paper by Rippon). Although there were no papers commissioned from historians for the 50th anniversary conferences, it might be argued that history remains 'the elephant in the room'[1] for medieval archaeology. Most of the papers in this volume — whether commenting on traditions of medieval archaeology in southern or northern Europe — betray a lingering insecurity regarding the discipline's relationship to history. We are less concerned today with documenting this dialogue than we were during the 'growing-pains' of the 1980s (eg the debate between Driscoll 1984 and Rahtz 1984, or the discussion by Austin 1990). Nevertheless, as Grenville Astill argues in reviewing the study of towns, the long-standing relationship with history is still the dominant influence.

With maturity, medieval archaeology has learned to work in concert with history, providing complementary and alternative approaches, or asking different questions more suited to material data (see papers by Gardiner and Rippon, Gilchrist, Reynolds). Some medieval historians now make full use of archaeology as a complementary source for writing medieval history, or collaborate on an equal basis with archaeologists, although they remain exceptional (eg Astill and Davies 1997; Dyer 1994; Jones, Dyer and Page 2006; Wickham 2005; 2009). One area of discord certainly remains: the disputed role of archaeological theory in the interpretation of medieval archaeology. This long-standing divide was characterized at the 1981 conference as a 'debate between those who favour new approaches and those for whom traditional frameworks remain the best'. There is no doubt that medieval archaeology has since developed its own research agenda, in part through increasing engagement with archaeological theory. Roberta Gilchrist (this volume) argues that over the past 25 years theory has changed the questions that we ask about the Middle Ages, and how we study medieval archaeology. The rise of post-processual approaches may be one reason for the shift away from core topics such as urbanism, towards landscape and burial archaeology. Processualism encouraged grand narratives on themes such as trade and state formation, while the post-processual interest in agency has promoted the study of social identity, gender, religious belief, sensory perception and spatial experience. Studies of churches/monasteries, burials and castles have demonstrated particular theoretical innovation, with the latter attracting dogged resistance from some historians (see the debate between Platt 2007 and Creighton and Liddiard 2008; and Hansson, this volume).

A steadfast antipathy towards theory remains in some branches of the discipline, a resistance explained by Matthew Johnson as 'the discourse of the familiar' (Johnson 2007, and 2008 lecture reported in Gardiner and Rippon). Because we believe that we already understand the social experience of the Middle Ages, we are less inclined to apply anthropological approaches that may yield new perceptions. If 'familiarity' is indeed the primary obstacle to progress, we can take inspiration from the accelerated development of theoretical perspectives in historical archaeology. Just a decade ago, 'the discourse of the familiar' was identified as the main impediment to interpretative maturity in historical archaeology, covering the period from *c*1500 to the present day (Tarlow and West 1999). Today, historical archaeology demonstrates an active dialogue with theory, an interest in narrative approaches of interpretation and a well-connected international network of historical archaeologists. Its source materials include oral history and living cultures, as well as archaeology and documents. The crucial difference seems to be in the active engagement of historical archaeology with *contemporary* experience and practice (for example, the archaeology of the Cold War), promoting more social and interpretative approaches (Hicks and Beaudry 2006). Medieval archaeology is more firmly grounded in antiquity, and the romantic myths and legends of the Middle Ages are thoroughly entrenched in our imaginations. To break down popular and academic preconceptions about the Middle Ages requires more critical engagement with how interpretations of the medieval past impact on contemporary perception (Biddick 1998); medieval archaeology is uniquely placed to bring fresh perspectives to many aspects of medieval society. Mark Hall's paper in this volume is especially welcome for encouraging us to consider the reception and relevance of the Middle Ages today through its portrayal, manipulation and appropriation in films.

The group of papers on scientific developments in medieval archaeology is refreshingly confident in its assertion of progress and innovation, as scientific analysis has 'emerged from the appendices' over the past 25 years. New methods, data and standards for recording have transformed our understanding of medieval health and disease, diet and industry (see papers by Roberts, Müldner, Sykes, Bayley and Watson). These papers survey selective aspects of scientific archaeology, but many other fields have achieved significant contributions to medieval archaeology during this period, notably the dendrochronological dating of timbers from standing buildings and the radiocarbon-dating of skeletal remains from early medieval cemeteries. It is interesting to note that here, too, social perspectives have received particular attention, for example in the harnessing of isotopic analysis to study issues of gender and age in individual life-histories (see Müldner). The study of zooarchaeology has experienced a radical realignment in recent years, with questions coming to the fore of the social meaning of animals, human-animal interactions and the symbolism of food. But these contributions also echo the call for the greater integration of medieval archaeology, and specifically the need for improved communication between medieval archaeologists and scientific specialists (see Sykes, Bayley and Watson).

In addition to surveying the development of medieval archaeology over the past 50 years, these papers outline challenges and priorities for the future of the subject. Specific recommendations are made in the regional and thematic overviews, but a number of overarching points can be identified. There is concern that the complexity and scope of our discipline perpetuate its fragmentation into sub-disciplines and interest groups, perhaps to a greater degree than is experienced in other branches of archaeology. Greater communication and integration is needed to achieve the holistic study of the Middle Ages — spanning the early and later medieval boundary, the social and scientific divide, and the borders between typologies of materials and settlements. A deeper understanding of the formation of academic disciplines and their respective paradigms is required to appreciate the artificial nature of the currently disjointed study of the past (eg Smail 2008). Improved collaboration is needed across Europe to place our regional perspectives within more meaningful frameworks; many pioneering field projects of this nature are already underway and ambitious pan-European syntheses are appearing (eg Graham-Campbell with Valor 2007; Carver and Klapste in prep). Despite this encouraging progress, more regular international (and national) congresses are needed to improve communication and to foster a stronger disciplinary identity. Medieval archaeology faces the same political and funding challenges that beset other areas of the wider discipline, such as the imperative to maximize the research value of developer-funded archaeology, and the real threat to archaeological employment in the face of global economic recession (2009). Great progress has been made in the advancement of new methodologies and in the recording of large corpora of medieval archaeological data. Major challenges remain in the interpretation and presentation of medieval archaeology, and in examining its meaning and relevance to contemporary society. The hurdle to be overcome is not the relationship of medieval archaeology to history, or to archaeological theory. 'The elephant in the room' is medieval archaeology's lack of confidence in our own discipline's ability to write distinctive narratives — archaeological tales that will enhance the social and cultural value of the medieval past to the present.

ACKNOWLEDGEMENTS

The editors would like to thank David Griffiths for his thoughtful comments on the volume. Thanks are also due to many people who assisted with the organization of conferences and workshops in 2007–08, including David Griffiths, Dawn Hadley, Chris King, Carenza Lewis, Steve Rippon, Naomi Sykes, Chris Thomas and Gabor Thomas.

NOTE

[1] 'The elephant in the room' is an English idiom first used in the late 1950s to refer to a controversial issue or obvious truth that is ignored or remains unaddressed, despite the fact that it looms so large that it cannot be overlooked.

BIBLIOGRAPHY

Astill, G and Davies, D, 1997 *A Breton Landscape: from the Romans to the Second Empire in Eastern Brittany*, Routledge, London

Austin, D, 1990 'The "proper study" of medieval archaeology', in D Austin and L Alcock (eds), *From the Baltic to the Black Sea: Studies in Medieval Archaeology*, 9–42, Routledge, London and New York

Biddick, K, 1998 *The Shock of Medievalism*, Duke University Press, Durham NC

Carver, M and Klapste, J (eds), in prep *The Archaeology of Medieval Europe, Vol 2, Twelfth to Sixteenth Centuries AD*, Aarhus University Press, Aarhus

Clarke, H, 1984 *The Archaeology of Medieval England*, British Museum Press, London

Creighton, O and Liddiard, R, 2008 'Fighting yesterday's battle: beyond war or status in castle studies', *Medieval Archaeology* 52, 161–168

Driscoll, S T, 1984 'The new medieval archaeology: theory vs history', *Scottish Archaeological Review* 3.2, 104–108

Dyer, C, 1994 *Everyday Life in Medieval England*, Hambledon, London and Rio Grande
Jones, R, Dyer, C, and Page, M, 2006 'The dynamics of medieval villagescapes', *Internet Archaeology* 19
Gaimster, D and Stamper, P (eds), 1997 *The Age of Transition. The Archaeology of English Culture 1400–1600*, Oxbow, Oxford
Gaimster, D and Gilchrist, R (eds), 2003 *The Archaeology of Reformation 1480–1580*, The Society for Post-Medieval Archaeology Monograph 1, Maney, Leeds
Graham-Campbell, J, 1980 *The Viking World*, Weidenfeld and Nicolson, London
Graham-Campbell, J with Valor, M (eds), 2007 *The Archaeology of Medieval Europe, Vol 1, Eighth to Twelfth Centuries AD*, Aarhus University Press, Aarhus
Hicks, D and Beaudry, M C (eds), 2006 'Introduction: the place of historical archaeology', in D Hicks and M C Beaudry (eds), *The Cambridge Companion to Historical Archaeology*, 1–9, Cambridge University Press, Cambridge
Hinton D A (ed), 1983 *25 Years of Medieval Archaeology*, Department of Prehistory and Archaeology, Sheffield
Hodges, R, 1982 *Dark Age Economics: the Origins of Towns and Trade, AD 600–1000*, Duckworth, London
Johnson, M H, 2007 *Ideas of Landscape*, Blackwell, Oxford
Platt, C, 2007 'Revisionism in castle studies: a caution', *Medieval Archaeology* 51, 83–102
Rahtz, P A, 1984 'The Nuer medieval archaeology. Comment on theory vs history', *Scottish Archaeological Review* 3.2, 109–112
Sawyer, P, 1983 'English archaeology before the Conquest: a historian's view', in Hinton 1983, 44–47
Smail, D L, 2008 *On Deep History and the Brain*, University of California Press, Berkeley/Los Angeles/London
Steane, J, 1985 *The Archaeology of Medieval England and Wales*, Croom Helm, London
Tarlow, S and West, S (eds), 1999 *The Familiar Past? Archaeologies of Later Historical Britain*, Routledge, London
Wickham, C 2005, *Framing the Early Middle Ages*, Oxford University Press, Oxford
Wickham, C 2009, *The Inheritance of Rome*, Allen Lane, London
Wilson, D M (ed), 1976 *The Archaeology of Anglo-Saxon England*, Cambridge University Press, Cambridge

PART I

50 YEARS OF MEDIEVAL ARCHAEOLOGY

CHAPTER I
THE FOUNDATION AND EARLY YEARS OF THE SOCIETY FOR MEDIEVAL ARCHAEOLOGY

By DAVID M WILSON

The Society was conceived as the result of a conversation between John Hurst and me in the old Iron Age Gallery in the British Museum at some time during the autumn of 1956. John had started a very successful newsletter for his Deserted Medieval Village Group and I was organizing informal seminars of professionals interested in the early medieval period in Britain and Western Europe (a seminar which in much altered form survives today as a joint seminar of the BM and University College London). There was good deal of overlap between the two groups, and John Hurst bridged both. My group held monthly meetings, usually on Saturday afternoons in the same disused, dusty and draughty gallery — followed by bring-your-own-bottle parties, fortified by dishes of 'spag Bol' and cheap red wine, in one or other of our very modest flats, to which we invited many of the people involved in John's side of the story. Although we met in London, we drew on postgraduates and young professionals — mostly from Oxford, Cambridge and London — as well as visitors from other parts of the British Isles, the Republic of Ireland and the Continent (for example, Egil Bakka from Bergen was an early member).

At that time, in the United Kingdom as in most of Europe, prehistory and classical studies dominated academic archaeology. There were practically no posts in universities for medieval archaeologists; those who had jobs in medieval archaeology worked either in museums, in the Royal Commissions or in the Ancient Monuments section of the Ministry of Works. One or two aspiring archaeologists held university jobs, but not in archaeology (which they taught on the side). Rosemary Cramp, for example, was an English don at Oxford and Vera Evison was similarly employed at Birkbeck; others were historians or geographers, or were making a living in equally dubious ways outside academe.

John suggested that we did for the generality of medieval archaeology what he had been doing for Deserted Medieval Villages: disseminating information by putting out a cyclostyled newsletter on work in progress. However, I was more interested in producing a journal — more or less on the lines of the *Proceedings of the Prehistoric Society*. I was about to become Director of the British Archaeological Association and, with a group of like-minded young people, intended to reform it (in fact, we did rather a good job). But it was clear that neither it nor the Royal Archaeological Institute, both from their origins strongly grounded in the medieval period, could possibly cope with the increasing interest in the 'dirt archaeology' of that period. Nowadays, of course, societies and journals are founded at the drop of a hat and themed monographs emerge in ever increasing numbers. In the mid-1950s this was not the case. Only the occasional *Festschrift* provided an opportunity for focused publication, and *Festschriften* were few and far between — now one seems to appear every day! One of the best *Festschriften* of the period was a volume dedicated to the memory of E T Leeds, entitled *Dark Age Studies*, impeccably edited by Donald Harden of the Ashmolean Museum. Harden coincidentally was at that time moving from Oxford to become head of the London Museum and was, perforce, giving up the editorship of *Oxoniensia* (then one of the most professional of the local archaeological journals). Although Harden was basically a classicist, *Oxoniensia* included many articles on medieval subjects; we wondered whether he would help us. We approached him and he willingly agreed to edit the sort of journal we had in mind. He was man of some seniority and it was quite a coup to get him on board, as he was a respectable denizen of the corridors of power of the small archaeological world.

We were now well on our way to founding the society. Seldom has an idea been so enthusiastically received. The world of British — and indeed European — archaeology was very small, and almost 19th-century in its organization. Everybody knew, or could easily have contact with, specialists of all periods from the Palaeolithic onwards. John and I were young and enthusiastic and, with Donald's greater experience and wide network of colleagues, we were able to reach out to a large number of people. The great man of the time was Sir Mortimer Wheeler, Secretary of the British Academy and, since 1954, President of the Society of Antiquaries. The three of us went to see him and he agreed to chair a meeting in the Society's rooms. After much preliminary discussion and correspondence we circulated friends and acquaintances and summoned a meeting on 16 April 1957 (see the following paper by Christopher Gerrard). At least 85 people came, all of whom — bar one — approved the idea, and, at a further meeting in June (again chaired by Wheeler) the Society was formally founded. Rupert Bruce-Mitford, Keeper of the Department of British and Medieval Antiquities at the British Museum, was elected President; Donald Harden became Editor, I became Secretary and John became Treasurer. We elected four knights, Cyril Fox, T D Kendrick, F M Stenton and Wheeler as honorary Vice-Presidents (which gave us quite a bit of street-credibility in those hierarchical days). The vice-presidents were W F Grimes, Director of the London Institute of Archaeology, Ralegh Radford (*éminence grise* of medieval archaeology) and Dorothy Whitelock, Elrington and Bosworth Professor of Anglo-Saxon at Cambridge. The Council consisted of Howard Colvin (architectural historian and Fellow of St John's College, Oxford), Gerald Dunning (pottery expert and Inspector of Ancient Monuments), H P R Finberg (Head of the Department of Local History at Leicester University), W G Hoskins (Reader in Economic History, Oxford), Nowell Myres (Anglo-Saxon pottery specialist and Bodley's Librarian), Brian Hope-Taylor (freelance archaeologist), William Pantin (lecturer in medieval Archaeology and

History and University archivist, Oxford) and Robert Stevenson (Keeper of the National Museum of Scotland). Martyn Jope (Reader in archaeology at Queen's University, Belfast) was elected a member of the editorial committee, although he was very much an absentee. This was a very strong field, remarkably so when set against the junior status of John and myself; we could not have achieved it without Harden's influence.

We had no ready source of funds and had to rely on our friends and ourselves to finance the project. A casual conversation with Eric Fletcher (a lawyer, MP and amateur archaeologist) resulted in an anonymous gift of the enormous sum of £250 — the first of his many benefactions to the Society. Christopher Blunt, the numismatist, gave us £25. With a few smaller benefactions we accumulated close to £300 (a sum — labelled 'reserve' — which remained as a separate entry in the accounts for many years). Members were asked to guarantee £5 a head to back any bills in case of problems; otherwise we relied on our subscriptions — £389 in our first year. For the rest we managed on calendarization, publishing the first few volumes in the year following the receipt of subscriptions — a slightly dicey piece of creative accounting. When we went to press with the first volume we had 387 members (of whom 93 were libraries — we had worked hard to get these institutional members), paying a subscription of two guineas (with various adjustments for students and joint members). John Hurst managed our money skilfully (he was paid the princely honorarium of £25) and was much helped by our honorary auditor John Cowen, amateur archaeologist, an executive director of Barclays Bank and later Treasurer of the Society of Antiquaries.

The cost of publication of the first volume exceeded the total assets of the Society for its first year and we had to seek grants from the Council for British Archaeology and various government bodies — the Ministry of Works, the Royal Commission, and the Northern Ireland Finance Ministry — in order to keep solvent. This meant that the Journal's contents were sometimes overbalanced with excavation reports — as was pointed out at the conference celebrating the first 25 years of the Society's existence (Hinton 1983). But we survived; although, due to various complications, including a printer's strike, we had to publish a double volume for 1962–63, which finally enabled us to catch up both in publishing and financial terms. Our ambitions went further. In 1959 Donald Harden persuaded an American friend and amateur archaeologist, J Dunscombe Colt — whose money came from the revolver which bore his name — to give an annual sum to establish a travel fund (initially £100). By 1962 the grant was increased to £300. It continued until Mr Colt's death in 1972. Three years later Eric (now Lord) Fletcher generously replaced it with an annual grant of £500.

From the beginning it was agreed that the Journal should be central to the function of the Society, and I shall discuss this below. We considered that there were already enough lecture meetings in London, so decided to have only one lecture a year, after the Annual General Meeting. This provided a platform over a three-year period for a Presidential lecture, a lecture by a foreigner and a lecture on a major piece of British work. Conferences, however, we considered to be important — both academically and socially. The RAI and BAA conferences had fallen into disrepair and we wanted to have something more academic, to create a greater opportunity to follow up new work and meet our colleagues. All conferences were to be outside London and were to be multi-disciplinary. They were hugely enjoyable and expressed the excitement generated by the new subject, even to me as conference organizer.

I should perhaps provide a little personal background since John Hurst and I were probably more influential than anyone else in leading the Society's activities and direction. John was rather older than me; nevertheless, we overlapped at Cambridge, where we both read archaeology, first under Dorothy Garrod and then under Grahame Clark. After postgraduate work in Sweden, I became Grahame Clark's research assistant and then an assistant keeper in the BM. John meanwhile had moved into the Ministry of Works as an assistant inspector of ancient monuments, where he had a lot of influence, particularly in funding excavations, and had started work at Wharram Percy. Our background in formal archaeology was thus very different from that of most of our fellow medievalists, who had read classics, history or English, although a few had taken the postgraduate diploma at the London Institute of Archaeology. There were few scientists (although Martyn Jope had read biochemistry), but quite a few brilliant amateurs. John had worked with Jack Golson (another Cambridge archaeologist — originally a medievalist) on a number of projects, including excavations on the town walls of Norwich, and in 1952 had started work with Maurice Beresford at Wharram Percy. Although I had published one or two excavations, as a museum curator I was very much an objects man, and indeed was to publish a paper in the first volume of *Medieval Archaeology* on a Merovingian folding-stool. We were much influenced by Grahame Clark's *Prehistoric Europe, the Economic Basis*, which examined prehistory from a completely different angle from that hitherto encountered in the pages of most English archaeological journals (save *PPS* and *Antiquity*). John had produced a great deal of medieval pottery from his excavations at the manorial site of Northolt (excavations which began in 1950), and this led him to establish good contacts with contemporaries in the Low Countries and France, while I was very conscious of ongoing archaeological work in Germany and, more particularly, Scandinavia.

Until the Society's foundation, the sort of thing that interested us had battled for publication space in the main archaeological journals — although the *Archaeological Journal* did admit some 'dirt archaeology' into its antiquarian pages. In view of the increasing amount of excavation — including work on development- and bomb-damaged sites in towns — a vast amount of new archaeological evidence was being produced, which had to be put into context, both economic and chronological. This triggered John's interest in imported pottery, following work by Gerald Dunning, which led to a reassessment of the sort of evidence based on Henri Pirenne, Michael Postan, W G Hoskins and others in the field of economic history. Similarly, Charles Thomas started to publish his work on the imported pottery found on immediately post-Roman sites in western Britain, where Bruce-Mitford had done innovative work at Mawgan Porth in Cornwall. Philip Rahtz was starting to undertake serious excavations for the Ministry of Works and Brian Hope-Taylor beavered away at Yeavering (see Rosemary Cramp's paper in this volume for discussion of these excavations). Medieval numismatics was undergoing a revolution, particularly led by

Christopher Blunt and Michael Dolley, who developed ideas from such influential historians as Sir Frank Stenton. Their work was an essential component of the chronological framework needed for the artefacts found in excavations and hoards, which enabled us to date contexts closely. To the same end, I used numismatic evidence to build up a stylistic chronology of later Anglo-Saxon metalwork, based on the work of Sir Thomas Kendrick.

Cross-disciplinary work was central to much of what we were doing in those stirring times. Numismatists worked with historians and fed the archaeologists, who provided them with new finds. Stylistic studies of manuscript material — pre-eminently those of Francis Wormald, Julian Brown and Rupert Bruce-Mitford — provided further chronological and cultural pointers in the field of Anglo-Saxon studies. Adventurous economic historians — like the formidable Eleanora Carus-Wilson of the London School of Economics (later a president of the Society) — led us into examination of burghal plots and (in our first volume) into the byways of textile production; while Billy Pantin (another president) tied us into vernacular architecture — on which subject the Journal published some of the earliest papers on dendrochronology, as well as Cecil Hewitt's marvellous analyses of medieval carpentry. Rosemary Cramp summarized her BLitt thesis on '*Beowulf* and archaeology', introducing philology to the Society in the first volume. John Dodgson, an enthusiastic proponent of place-name studies and archaeology, attended our conferences and published in the Journal. Leo Biek wrote on the technique of pattern-welding and Bruce Proudfoot on the economy of the Irish rath.

The Journal was designed with some care. Here we had specialist help from Finberg, who in a previous incarnation had been publisher of a small press. He discussed typefaces, measured the length of the lines and decided on the number of lines to the page and the size of the font. Donald Harden drew up the style sheet, which lasted until 2007. The title of the Journal was much discussed. Wheeler insisted that the society should have a snappy title and that we should not get what was then called the 'Dark Ages' into it, or call it 'The Society of post-Roman and Medieval Archaeology' (too negative). So, to emphasize that the medieval period included the period after the end of the Roman Empire, we put a vignette of the Alfred Jewel on the cover. Drawn by my wife, it survives to this day, although now grossly magnified beyond the intended 1:1 scale on the original cover. The contents list was printed on the back page, for ease of use. It was agreed that reviews should be substantial and of international breadth, and we soon recognized that there was need for a reviews editor — a post filled for many years with great energy by Mike Thompson. This attention to detail paid off. The format endures to this day, as do the major elements of its design. The only change made in the first years was in the quality of the card used for the cover. Our debt to Finberg was enormous. Never an easy man, he unfortunately later fell out with the Society and in 1963 resigned in a huff.

The Society would survive or fall on the contents of the Journal and we worked hard at providing a varied menu.[1] Hints of past study inevitably crept in. Out of *pietas* we published in the first volume a posthumous and, it must be admitted, rather old-fashioned article by the doyen of Anglo-Saxon studies, E T Leeds, which was tactfully edited by Sonia Chadwick (soon to be Sonia Hawkes). But in the same volume hints of future developments were present. The Leeds *Festschrift* was reviewed by our first foreign contributor, the Swede, Holger Arbman. Another interesting review was that of Hamilton's major publication of the Pictish and Viking site at Jarlshof by Richard Atkinson, a prehistorian widely held to be the best contemporary excavator in Britain. Our international outlook was boosted by Ralegh Radford, who wrote a good article on the Saxon house, based on the only major rural site then known, Sutton Courtenay, in Berkshire. Radford put this into a European context, introducing many English people to some of the major continental sites — Warendorf, Tofting and so on (his paper coinciding roughly with a similar, but unpublished, lecture by Gerhard Bersu to the British Academy).

John's original newsletter idea was adapted to produce the continuing section on recent work in medieval archaeology, a summary of digs and finds. John and I edited the first few compilations. Later John's wife, Gillian, took over the post-Conquest section, while I survived as compiler of the pre-Conquest section until 1971, when Leslie Webster took it over. This compilation has proved immensely valuable.[2] Two examples from my own field demonstrate this. In the first volume the account of Brian Hope-Taylor's excavations at the Northumbrian royal site of Yeavering remained the only quotable printed account until the publication of the excavations in 1977. Similarly, the account of Old Windsor in the second volume is one of the very few printed sources concerning this enormously important — and still unpublished — site. In those days reviews of books were often rather short and summary; we decided to limit their number and make them longer and less narrative.

It would be tedious to examine the contents of the early volumes in too great a detail. But in order to understand how we tried to fulfil our aims, we might glance at them. Probably because both John and I had missed out on early travel because of the war and currency regulations, we very much wanted to bring in an international dimension, to serve as a model to our elders and betters. We worked hard to achieve this aim. Articles by continental scholars were encouraged. In Volume 2 Günther Haseloff, from Würzburg, published an article on a puzzling Anglo-Saxon hanging-bowl, while in the following volume another German, Fritz Tischler, combined with John Hurst, Myres and Dunning to write up a symposium on Anglo-Saxon pottery which included the first proper summary of imported pottery from English sites. In the same volume, Asbjörn Herteig wrote on the initial excavations on the Norwegian Hanseatic site at Bryggen, Bergen, perhaps the most important waterlogged medieval site ever discovered in western Europe. This was neatly followed in Volume 5 by A van de Walle, who wrote on the Antwerp excavations. This international emphasis was important in a period when travel was expensive and slow (and sometimes constrained by currency regulations), so that personal contact was much more difficult. Involvement with foreign colleagues, quite a few of whom became members, helped our sales to overseas libraries and institutions. Foreign books were particularly sought out and reviewed at some length — a feature still evident today.

Martin Carver in a recent *Antiquity* editorial (vol. 81, 21–24) has criticized the present-day Journal for departing from its internationality. In one sense he is right; but there are now so many involved in the dissemination of European ideas and material in the multitude of co-edited books, that it is surely right that the present officers should continue to give great weight to the British material in *Medieval Archaeology*, a Journal which is read throughout the world.[3] Otherwise it would get too diverse, as indeed has happened with *Antiquity*. Further, as a direct result of our foundation, three European journals were started which to a great extent modelled themselves on *Medieval Archaeology* — namely *Archéologie médiévale*, *Zeitschrift für Archäologie des Mittelalters* and *Archaeologia medievale*, which allow us to keep abreast of much of what is going on in continental Europe.

I have mentioned that in the initial stages of our existence we had to chase grants; so the Journal was perhaps over-weighted with excavation reports, because they often came with a grant for publication. These reports departed from previous models, however, even when reporting on Anglo-Saxon cemeteries, which had been a staple diet of antiquarian journals for more than a century. The report on the Finglesham cemetery, for example, was highly significant in the then current climate. But we turned more and more to economic and settlement archaeology — to the Cheddar royal manor, the Cassington kilns and the Meaux tile-kilns; to town excavations and fortified sites like Lismahon in Co. Down and Corfe Castle in Dorset. Medieval housing and villages got their fair share of space — Garrow Tor in Cornwall, and Riseholme in Lincolnshire, for example, as did churches and monasteries, North Elmham, for example. Sites and subjects like these had previously made appearances in the multi-period journals, but we did our best to make sure that as many as possible were now published in *Medieval Archaeology*. Stuff was pouring in, and the only constraining factor was length, which Harden's brilliant editing and editorial decisions helped to limit.

There were also survey papers — Peter Gelling on shielings in the Isle of Man, the medieval pottery symposium mentioned above, Sonia Hawkes and Gerald Dunning on the post-Roman settlement period, Martyn Jope on the medieval building-stone industry and Charles Thomas on imported 'dark-age' pottery. These in many cases broke new ground and more than balanced out the excavation reports. We published quite a few non-archaeological think-pieces — Nora Carus-Wilson on the trade of the Wash, Billy Pantin on secular housing, Christopher Blunt on coins, John Dodgson on place-names — really contributing to the cross-disciplinary growth of the subject and, at the same time, educating ourselves and our colleagues in neighbouring disciplines in many new areas. Personally, I benefited greatly and in 1960 published, very daringly, the first edition of a now long-forgotten synthetic book called *The Anglo-Saxons*, which ventured into many of these areas in a manner which would now be impossible, and which was completely different from the type of book on the period published earlier. Ignorance and my involvement in the Society certainly gave me courage!

The monograph series was an innovative breakthrough. This was before the days of BAR — and academic publications of digs were sometimes difficult to place. Fortunately for the schema, I had a possible monograph on hand — a report which I had written on Gerhard Bersu's excavations on Viking graves in the Isle of Man. This made a splendid first volume and one which sold out quickly. We had to appoint a paid editor for this project — Ann Morley — who was already indexing the volumes: trained by Donald Harden, she was ideal. The series continues despite all the challenges from other series producers. More than 20 volumes have now been published — not bad considering their cost and consequent outlay in an under-capitalized society.

I have already said that the world of British — and even European — archaeology was very small, and I would like to re-emphasize that statement. By the time John and I had left Cambridge, I would reckon that we had met more than half the professional archaeologists then working in Britain. Having attended the International Congress of Pre- and Protohistoric Sciences meeting in Madrid in 1954, I had met a large number of the active figures in European archaeology — mostly prehistorians, although a few were medievalists — particularly among the Irish, German, Scandinavian and Dutch delegates. Among them were younger colleagues — all, however, somewhat older than me — who were beginning to make a mark in what was basically a new subject — Brian Hope-Taylor, Maire Macdermott (later de Paor), Charlotte and Martin Blindheim and Märta Strömberg, for example — all of whom became involved in one way or another in our Society. The only later medievalist from this country I remember as being present at the Congress was Brian O'Neill — then the senior English specialist on castles and Chief Inspector of Ancient Monuments, who was to die young (49) in the same year.

The annual conference of the Society afforded not only opportunities for networking and getting to know a region, but also to hear lectures relevant to the region, or important updates on major projects. As Secretary, I organized the conferences based on hard work by local secretaries. For the 20 years I ran them, we tended to alternate between the early and later medieval periods, starting with a conference centred at Sheffield in 1958: 120 people attended. It was a real 'rag-bag', based on the theme 'The relationship of archaeology and history in the study of the medieval period'. Based in the university, we were introduced to the region by a group of local scholars, followed by lectures on themes which were to become familiar over the next few years. Brian Hope-Taylor lectured on Yeavering and John Hurst and Maurice Beresford on Wharram Percy. Billy Pantin read a paper on 'monuments and muniments' which was followed by a general discussion in which Christopher Blunt, Gerald Dunning, Arnold Taylor and H P R Finberg were among the participants. An excursion filled most of Sunday, when, *inter alia*, we visited the cruck barn at Cartledge Hall — crucks were all the rage at that time — a Norman ring fort, some Anglo-Saxon carvings and the ruined Wingfield manor-house. The conference fee was 7s 6d (37p). The excursion cost about £1 and accommodation for two nights, together with meals, was £1 4s 6d (rather less than £1.25). We made a profit of some £17 on the event!

The conferences were enormously successful. They were also great fun — the membership of the Society was relatively young — and among all the roistering a great deal of networking was achieved. At Southampton in the following year, a conference on 'The growth of the medieval town' attracted among other things a lecture by Sir Frank Stenton on 'The Anglo-Saxon town', one by John Wacher on medieval Southampton and one by Gerald Dunning on the medieval trade of the south coast. Charles Thomas gave us great publicity by means of a BBC broadcast, and one of our major future supporters, Michel de Bouard, turned up from France.

Two years later we ventured overseas to the Isle of Man, where there were rather more Europeans present, including a lecture by Holger Arbman on the Viking sculpture of Man.

The Kings Lynn conference of 1962 was of exceptional importance as it resulted in the foundation of a committee chaired by Eleanora Carus-Wilson, on which I sat, to excavate medieval sites in the town; excavations which were published by Helen Clarke in our monograph series (Clarke and Carter 1977).

Our first international conference took place at Caen in 1963. Michel de Bouard, then an influential Dean of the Faculty at the university, was the local secretary. David Douglas, a most distinguished Norman scholar, talked on Anglo-Norman relations from 911–1204; de Bouard and Arnold Taylor lectured on castles. P Héliot lectured on the Anglo-Norman Gothic and Adigard des Gautiers lectured on the toponomy and anthropology of England and Normandy in the 10th to 13th centuries — one of the most Delphic lectures I have ever heard! Visits to the Bayeux Tapestry and various churches, mottes and castles were interspersed with good Norman food and drink.

Two years later the conference went to Bergen and Oslo — a really splendid trip. Three lectures by Norwegians — Gerhard Fischer, Asbjörn Herteig and Robert Kloster — introduced a series of visits to sites, churches and museums. It was quite splendid to see how scholars from the two countries reacted with each other. I particularly remember a spirited exchange between the venerable Gerhard Fischer and the deeply learned — if sometimes eccentric — Christopher Hohler on the bases of the columns in Bergen cathedral. There were also memorable receptions and meals.

Conferences in my time included Scottish, Welsh and Irish venues. But perhaps one stands out more than any other, and of this I have been reminded by James Graham-Campbell. I think, more than anything else, it spells out the all-embracing nature of the Society in the archaeological community at a time before 'the end of archaeological innocence' (Clarke 1973). In 1968 James was graduating from Cambridge and came to see me. Let me tell it in his own words:

> I applied to David Wilson at UCL to undertake post-graduate research on the Vikings, but he said: 'Go away to Norway for a year and we can talk about it!' 'But', he added, 'you must come back for the SMA conference in 1969 because it's going to be held in Orkney and Shetland and EVERYONE will be there.' And it wasn't just everyone in Viking studies, it included both the Christopher Hawkeses and both the Graham Clarks of Oxbridge. (J Graham-Campbell, pers comm)

It was indeed an all-embracing conference with people from Scandinavia and from all areas of archaeological and related disciplines. Sverri Dahl from the Faroes lectured on his archaeological work there; Ralegh Radford appeared in Scottish mode to talk on Norse houses in Scotland, Stuart Cruden lectured on St Magnus's Cathedral and (for once) I lectured to the conference — on the St Ninian's Isle Treasure. We visited islands (although the weather was too rough to get to Wyre and Egilsay) and sites on Mainland; we flew to Shetland to have tea with the Provost of Lerwick and looked at sites there. But tea was not the only drink we had. Most memorable was involvement in the late stages of an Orkney wedding which was drawing to a raucous conclusion. But this paper deteriorates into anecdotage and I must draw it to a close.

ENVOI

The Society has helped to mould the study of medieval archaeology both in this country and abroad. The subject has come a long way and the Society has been deeply involved, often in innovatory mode, in its development. From its foundation the Society's work was firmly based in an interdisciplinary approach to the subject, an approach which has led to a vast increase in understanding and interpretation as methods have changed and publication has increased.

Excavation (mostly 'rescue' work, but also of a research nature) has, particularly in the last decades of the 20th century, completely revolutionized the basis of the subject. The method of excavation changed almost as the Society was founded; the grid and trench method initiated by Pitt-Rivers and Wheeler in the late years of the 19th and first half of the 20th century, was varied according to the nature of the sites available. Open area excavation, influenced from Denmark, came to medieval England in the mid-1950s. It had been used on English prehistoric sites before the war, but was probably first used in a modern fashion on a medieval site by Brian Hope-Taylor at Yeavering (from 1953). It soon became almost the norm, often to give a much more coherent view of an excavated site. Excavation, funded on a much grander scale from the late 1960s onwards, produced a vast quantity of finds and different types of site. Few sites were chosen against a planned policy, but enough were sampled to provide a new matrix for an understanding of the totality of medieval Britain, although knowledge is still very patchy.

Thus there developed a need to assemble and order all this new material and set it in a realistic chronological framework. At first there was a great dependence on typology and style-history — methods developed in the first half of the century — and these methods were examined and developed more rigorously as excavators provided the material, particularly metalwork and pottery, and demanded more critical chronological guidelines. Scientific dating methods were introduced gradually. Radiocarbon dating, developed less than a decade before our foundation, was still in its development stages, and was only of general use to medievalists. It was, however, used for very coarse dating. The revolutionary development of an understanding of minting cycles in Anglo-Saxon England enabled students of hoards to date their deposition to within a few years and provided clues to the date of the deposition of archaeological deposits. Rather different, but at least as important, was the development of dendrochronology, first used extensively in the Dublin excavations, but discussed in its early stages of development in our Journal. Residual magnetism and thermoluminiscent dating soon followed, so that by the 1980s there was a firm chronological framework in archaeology for the medieval period.

Influenced at the beginning by a developing interest of economic and social historians in the potential use of archaeological evidence, it became possible to develop a more holistic picture of the medieval period. Archaeology provided industrial sites and analysed processes of extraction and manufacture. The anatomy of towns and rural settlements was greatly boosted. Landscape archaeology was enthusiastically developed. The study of agriculture progressed quickly. The use of flotation provided fresh knowledge about crops to strengthen evidence provided by the examination of grain impressions on pottery and pollen analysis. Developments in the study of both animal and human skeletal material led to population studies and paved the way for applications of DNA and trace element analysis.

The Society and its members have been involved in all these innovations and more; I am confident that it will continue to be as innovative as it was in those early years.

NOTES

[1] Articles mentioned here can be consulted in the online archive of the first 50 volumes, made accessible for the Society's anniversary in 2007 http://ads.ahds.ac.uk/catalogue/library/med_arch/index.cfm?CFID=615449&CFTOKEN=57428789

[2] From Volume 51 (2007), a 'Highlights' section was introduced to cover a selection of major findings or research projects. The full listing is available as an online searchable database with the Archaeology Data Service.

[3] The journal has long had associate editors, many of whom are based in, or represent, other regions of Europe. In 2007, the journal introduced French, German and Italian translations of abstracts.

BIBLIOGRAPHY

Clark, G, 1952 *Prehistoric Europe, the Economic Basis*, Methuen, London

Clarke, D, 1973 'Archaeology: the loss of innocence', *Antiquity* 47, 6–18

Clarke, H and Carter A, 1977 *Excavations in Kings Lynn 1963–1970*, Society for Medieval Archaeology Monograph 7, London

Hinton, D A (ed), 1983 *25 Years of Medieval Archaeology*, Department of Prehistory and Archaeology, Sheffield

Wilson, D M, 1960, *The Anglo-Saxons*, Thames and Hudson, London

CHAPTER 2

THE SOCIETY FOR MEDIEVAL ARCHAEOLOGY: THE EARLY YEARS (1956–62)

By CHRISTOPHER GERRARD

Given the comparative youth of the subject, it is no surprise to find that historiographical studies are still something of a rarity in medieval archaeology. This paper makes use of the original archives of the Society for Medieval Archaeology to tell the story behind the Society's formation, its inaugural meeting in 1957 and the first defining years of its existence. It recounts the dispute over the Society's name, early discussions about the look and academic balance of its Journal and the forbearance of its officers as they battled with printers, finance and the whims and wants of members.

INTRODUCTION

On the afternoon of Tuesday 16 April 1957 at Burlington House, Piccadilly, Donald Harden, newly appointed Director of the London Museum (1956–70), first outlined proposals for what he called a 'society for Dark Age and Medieval Studies'. His handwritten notes for that day have survived.[1] The idea was a simple one; a new society with a new journal, occasional meetings and an annual conference, all to be dedicated to the period 'from the end of the Roman period until the end of the Middle Ages in Britain, but not neglecting the Continent and not being too exclusive in period or subject matter'.[2]

There were precedents, of course. The Society for the Promotion of Roman Studies had been formed in 1911, and the Prehistoric Society of East Anglia of 1908 had become the Prehistoric Society in 1935, so this was the third of the period societies to be established. There was warm support that day among the 77 people present and, under the chairmanship of Sir Mortimer Wheeler (1890–1976), the motion to form the new period society was carried by an overwhelming majority. Rupert Bruce-Mitford (1914–94) was to become the Society's first President. By that time Keeper of British and Medieval Antiquities at the British Museum, Bruce-Mitford curated the post-Roman collections; Sutton Hoo was one of his responsibilities after the finds were retrieved from a disused tunnel of the London underground after the war. But he was also an excavator: Seacourt, outside Oxford (Bruce-Mitford 1940) and Mawgan Porth (Bruce-Mitford 1997) on the north Cornish coast, are among the sites he directed.

THE INAUGURAL MEETING

As David Wilson recounts in his paper, this was not merely a case of coming up with the idea of a medieval society and putting it to the vote. Informal correspondence had been underway for about six months between Harden (1901–94), John Hurst (1927–2003), then a 30-year-old Assistant Inspector of Ancient Monuments at the Ministry of Works and already co-directing excavations at the deserted medieval village at Wharram Percy, and David Wilson, then Assistant Keeper at the British Museum. They had 'agreed to pool plans', as Harden put it in April 1957, 'Hurst from the angle of Medieval Studies, Wilson from the Saxon and Viking standpoint', and Harden, 'who felt lack of Society and journal to carry on British story where the Prehistoric Soc. leaves off'.[3]

The three had begun to talk in the autumn of 1956 and were quickly in 'general agreement on the broad principles',[4] sufficiently anyway for Hurst to solicit views from his colleagues in the archaeological community.[5] Andrew Saunders, for one, remembers lunchtime discussions about a possible Society in the Ministry of Works canteen in the now-demolished Lambeth Bridge House (Saunders, pers comm). Of the 'nearly 100 people' consulted, all gave their support 'wholeheartedly'; only Ralegh Radford suggesting that the time was not yet right to form a new Society.[6] This was perhaps ironic in that he became one of the first three Vice-Presidents and later a President of the Society (1969–71).

With the benefit of these consultations, Hurst now set out his concerns in writing as he saw them in mid-December 1956.[7] The most serious seemed to be financial and, as David Wilson recounts, these worries were allayed somewhat by gifts from Eric Fletcher[8] and Christopher Blunt (1904–87), a former President of the Royal Numismatic Society and a later President of the Society (1978–80).[9] Then Hurst worried how a publisher could possibly be attracted for the Journal if the profits from sales were taken away by the fledgling Society. And if the publisher kept the profits what role could a Society possibly perform? And how to fill the officers' posts? The work would have to be entirely voluntary, that was clear, but no treasurer sprang to mind; in the end Hurst had to fill that post himself. And then there was the problem of secretarial help; all those letters to be answered and subscriptions to be chased. He was right, of course. Once news of the Society was advertised, unsolicited applicants immediately began writing in for non-existent posts: 'I am a high speed Palantype stenotypist of good education and varied reporting experience ...'.[10] One woman looking for work wrote in claiming her interest in archaeology to be 'very deep and abiding. I live in my own house and have no home ties of any kind ...'.[11] One wonders exactly what she thought was involved. Salaries, though not minor honoraria, were out of the question.

The instigators now met to decide upon who should be invited to the inaugural meeting. A copy of the invitation[12] sent out in February 1957 is reproduced in Figure 2.1 but the list of invitees requires further analysis (Figure 2.2). Immediately

Dear

A Proposed Society
for
Dark Age and Medieval Archaeology

A meeting to discuss the formation of a Society which would sponsor a journal covering Dark Age and Medieval archaeological studies in Britain will be held on Tuesday, 16th April, at 2.30 p.m. in the rooms of the Society of Antiquaries, Burlington House, W.1 and Sir Mortimer Wheeler has consented to take the Chair. If you are interested, we very much hope that you will be able to attend. If the project for a Society and Journal is approved in principle by those present, the next step might be to elect a working committee to lay detailed plans.

If you would, in addition, make the existence of this meeting known to any others who might be interested, we should be very grateful. All who would like to take part will be welcome.

Yours sincerely,

D. B. Harden, London Museum

J. G. Hurst, Deserted Medieval Village Research Group

D. M. Wilson, British Museum

February 1957

FIGURE 2.1. Invitation to the meeting on 16 April 1957 to discuss the possible formation of the new period society. Typed on Hurst's trusty typewriter, doubtless with one finger. Hurst brands his allegiance as DMVRG rather than the Ministry of Public Buildings and Works.

Invitees who then attended the 1957 meetings	Attended meeting 16/4/57	Attended inaugural meeting 13/6/57	First annual general meeting 6/12/57	Membership list 1960	Early councils and officers to 1965
ACADEMICS					
H M Colvin, Oxford	√			√	Council 1957–60
R H C Davis, Oxford	letter of support			√	Council 1961–64
W G Hoskins, Oxford				√	Council 1957–58, resigned
J N L Myres, Oxford	telegram of support		√	√	Council 1957–60, President 1963–66
W A Pantin, Oxford				√	Editorial Committee, Council 1957–60, President 1960–63
C Thomas	√				
M M Postan, Cambridge	letter of support			√	
D Whitelock, Cambridge			√	√	Vice-President
E M Carus-Wilson, London				√	Editorial Committee, Council 1960–63, President 1966–68
H C Darby, London	√	√			
J Morris, London	√*			√	
K Sinnhuber, London	√	√		√	
W F Grimes, Director, Institute	telegram of support		√	√	Vice-President
S S Frere, Institute	√			√	
V I Evison, London				√	Council 1961–64
L Edwards, IHR	√	√		√	
E M Jope, Belfast	letter of support			√	Editorial Committee
			R Glasscock, Belfast	√	
G A Webster, Birmingham	√*			√	
L Alcock, Cardiff	letter of support		√	√	Council 1962–65
M Davies, Cardiff	letter of support				
R J C Atkinson, Cardiff	letter of support			√	
R J Cramp, Durham	√			√	Council 1958–63
V B Proudfoot, Durham	letter of support			√	
B R S Megaw, Edinburgh	letter of support			√	
S Piggott, Edinburgh	letter of support				
A L Binns, Hull	letter of support			√	
H P R Finberg, Leicester	√*	√	√	√	Council 1957–61
M W Beresford, Leeds	√		√	√	Council 1958–62
J Thirsk, Leicester		√			
C E P Rosser, Manchester	√	√		√	
F Stenton, Reading				√	Hon Vice-President 1961
F T Wainwright, St Andrews	letter of support			√	
SOCIETIES					
P Corder, Antiquaries	√*	√			
H L Bradfer-Lawrence, Antiquaries	letter of support			√	
M Wheeler, President SoA, and Secretary of British Academy	√	√		√	Hon Vice-President 1961
Miss B De Cardi, CBA	√	√			

Invitees who then attended the 1957 meetings	Attended meeting 16/4/57	Attended inaugural meeting 13/6/57	First annual general meeting 6/12/57	Membership list 1960	Early councils and officers to 1965
MINISTRY OF WORKS					
S Butcher	√		√	√	
D Craig	√	√			
S Cruden, Scotland				√	Council 1961–64
G C Dunning	√	√	√	√	Council 1957–62
B Hope Taylor (and Cambridge)	√	√	√	√	Council 1957–61
J G Hurst (and DMVRG)	√*	√	√	√	Editorial Committee, Treasurer, President 1981–83
Mrs D G Hurst	√			√	
G M Knocker	√	√	√	√	
	W Lee, AML	√		√	
S E Rigold	√*	√	√	√	
Robertson Mackay		√			
P A Rahtz	√			√	
A Saunders	√			√	
A J Taylor	√			√	President 1972–74
M W Thompson	√	√	√	√	Editorial Committee, Council 1962–65, President 1993–95
ORDNANCE SURVEY					
C W Phillips	√	√	√	√	
RCHM					
R M Butler	√	√	√	√	
J T Smith	√			√	
MUSEUMS					
R L S Bruce-Mitford, British Museum	√*	√	√	√	Editorial Committee, President 1957–60, Council 1960–63
R R Clarke, Norwich Museum	telegram of support			√	
E Eames, 'tiles'			√	√	
D Harden, London Museum	√*	√	√	√	Editor, later President 1975–77
	R H M Dolley, British Museum			√	
	J P C Kent, British Museum	√		√	
D Wilson, British Museum	√*	√	√	√	Secretary
R B K Stevenson, National Museum of Antiquities of Scotland				√	Council 1957–61
G Boon, National Museum of Wales	√*	√		√	
H Shortt, Salisbury	√*				
N E W Thomas	letter of support			√	
A H Oswald, Birmingham	letter of support		√	√	
C Gowing, Aylesbury	letter of support			√	

Invitees who then attended the 1957 meetings	Attended meeting 16/4/57	Attended inaugural meeting 13/6/57	First annual general meeting 6/12/57	Membership list 1960	Early councils and officers to 1965
PLACE OR INTEREST ONLY					
P Ashbee, 'barrow excavator'			√		
F Baker, Lincoln	letter of support				
Miss S Chadwick, 'Saxon'	√		√		
Miss J Cook, 'Saxon'	√	√	√	√	
Mrs Joan Clarke			√		
P Gathercole, Scunthorpe	√*	√			
H Hodges, Belfast	√				
Mrs Kaines-Thomas [Margaret Wood], 'architecture'	√			√	
I M Stead, Cambridge		√		√	
M Green, architect	√				
John Harvey, Winchester	√*				
A Steensberg, Copenhagen	√			√	
H Wildgoose, Nottingham	√	√			
OTHERS					
E G Bowen	letter of support				
E M J Campbell	letter of support			√	
J D Cowen	letter of support			√	
Dickinson	letter of support				
Sir Cyril Fox, Past President SoA, sometime Director National Museum of Wales				√	Hon Vice-President
H N Savory, National Museum of Wales	letter of support			√	
R A H Farrar	√	√		√	
E G M Fletcher	√	√		√	Council 1962–65
W Godfrey, National Buildings Record	√*				
J F Head	√	√		√	
A H A Hogg	√*			√	
T Hume	√				
L Grinsell	√				
J Jones, Carisbrooke	√				
C M Mitchell	letter of support				
Miss J Morris	√*				
C A Ralegh Radford, past President Prehistoric Society	letter of support			√	Editorial Committee, Vice-President, President 1969–71
C Rouse	√	√			
L Salzman	√*			√	
N Smedley	√				
A H Smith	√	√		√	
P S Spokes	letter of support			√	

Invitees who then attended the 1957 meetings	Attended meeting 16/4/57	Attended inaugural meeting 13/6/57	First annual general meeting 6/12/57	Membership list 1960	Early councils and officers to 1965
Miss Tudor-Craig	√				
	M Blumstein				
	D Charlesworth	√	√	√	
	P W Curnow			√	
	H R E Davidson			√	
	C H Farthing				
	J Hopkins				
	M R Hull	√			
	E D C Jackson				
	J Johnson	√			
	C Lawrence				
	J Lewis				
	P Lock, Sussex				
	Miss F de M Morgan				
	Mrs Wynn Reeves				
	Mrs Faith Russell-Smith	√			
	Mrs Saunders			√	
	Miss A Savill				
	Dr W Singleton	√			
	T D Tremlett				
		D Britton		√	
		M Deansley			
		J Dodgson		√	
		C Keene	√		
		G H Martin			
			M Gulley		
			M M Harden		
			L G Matthews	√	
			J Shove		
			Mrs J Summerson	√	
			J Wacher	√	
			J Watt	√	
			Mrs A Young	√	

FIGURE 2.2. This list is based on three registers of attendance, the first at the meeting to discuss the formation of the Society on 16 April 1957 (the list of invitees being much longer with only Hurst's invitations formally recorded), the second at the inaugural meeting on 13 June 1957, and the third at the first annual general meeting on 6 December 1957. The practice of recording attendance at meetings was afterwards discontinued. The ticks signify presence, asterisks (*) that they spoke at the meeting; names of later officers are bolded. Names in italics occur on only one of the two lists for the April 1957 meeting and it is now uncertain whether they were present. The names and institutions are taken from Hurst and Harden's own lists, using their own nomenclatures.

noteworthy is the large proportion of men, and the blend of practitioners and academics headed by Cambridge, London and Oxford. The range of fields represented is wide and includes for example, Michael ('Munia') Postan (1899–1981), Chair of Economic History at the University of Cambridge (Miller 1983); Clifford Darby (1909–92), then Professor of Geography at University College London, whose name is associated today with his seven books on the geography of Domesday Book (Williams 1995). There were only three departments in Britain in 1957 teaching a single honours archaeology degree, and of those listed here William ('Billy') Pantin (1902–73) was the only one titled as University Lecturer in Medieval Archaeology and History, while Rosemary Cramp was a Lecturer in Anglo-Saxon Antiquities and Archaeology at Durham. Pantin, Nowell Myres (1902–89), at that time still Bodley's librarian, and economic historian Eleanora Carus-Wilson (1897–1977) later became Presidents. Sir Frank Stenton, the Anglo-Saxon historian born in 1880 and the elder statesman on the list of invitees, was a retired Professor of Modern History at the University of Reading and Vice-Chancellor of that University in the late 1940s. He was to be elected Honorary Vice-President of the Society.

Besides these academics there were also representatives from other societies, including Wheeler himself (he became an Honorary Vice-President in December 1957), as well as the men from the Ministry. This collegial bunch included Hurst (President 1981–83), Michael Thompson (President 1993–95), and Arnold 'Joe' Taylor (1911–2002; President 1972–74), best known for his work on castle architecture and collaborations with architectural historian Howard Colvin (1919–2007) in the *History of the King's Works* (Saunders 2006). Other groups present included the Ordnance Survey, and the Royal Commission and Museums; Bruce-Mitford and Harden were later Presidents of the Society drawn from that group. Next followed a long list of names organized by Hurst according to place or interest (not necessarily correctly): Martin Biddle, 'medieval excavator', was a future President here. Then there was a list of 'others', including Cyril Fox (1882–1967), former President of the Society of Antiquaries, and a later Society President, Ralegh Radford (1900–98). When it came down to it, however, many on this list of notables proved to be busy on the day and nearly half of the people who turned up were not on the list of official invites at all. As likely as not, they were invited verbally. They included, for example, Dorothy Charlesworth (1928–81), Leslie Grinsell (1907–95) and Walter Godfrey (1881–1961), Director and Secretary of the National Buildings Record.

WHAT'S IN A NAME?

It was in front of this assembled multitude that Harden presented a vision for a new Society, but it was at once clear that further discussion would be necessary, and to that end a Steering Committee was created consisting of Harden, Hurst, Wilson and Bruce-Mitford, together with Herbert Finberg (1900–74), Reader and Head of English Local History at the University of Leicester, and Charles Phillips. Phillips (1901–85) had been involved at Sutton Hoo before the war with Stuart Piggott, Grimes, and Crawford whom he had succeeded as Archaeology Officer to the Ordnance Survey in 1947 (Anon 1986; Phillips 1987). Eric Fletcher (1903–90), lawyer,

Labour politician and later life peer, was also co-opted to advise on legal matters[13] and the fund established in his name continues to support research and travel, mainly for younger scholars.

This group of seven met several times at the British Museum during May 1957 but, oddly enough, it was not the format of the new Journal which exercised them but its title. During discussions the previous year Harden had favoured *BRITAIN A.D.* (though this would inconveniently include Roman matters). Wilson, meanwhile, preferred something Latin such as *Acta Archaeologica Medieval*, while Gerald Dunning plumped for the *Journal of English Society*, though others felt that this had too much of a literary flavour. Cambridge Disney Professor of Archaeology Grahame Clark (1907–95) pitched in with the *Journal of Dark Age and Medieval Studies*, but Hurst thought this just too long and was not in any case in favour of the term Dark Age. Hurst's own alternative, the *Journal of Saxon and Medieval Archaeology*, seemed by his own admission to exclude what he called 'the Celtic west' and was therefore considered divisive. Neither was it the 'short snappy title' he was looking for.[14] Soon the picture was confused further by new suggestions: *Alfred* was one, *Monumenta* another and the *Journal of Post-Roman Archaeology* a third.[15]

The name of the Society was proving troublesome, too. At the April 1957 meeting Harden explained that there was opposition to using the term 'Dark Ages' and put forward *The Society for Medieval Archaeology* and the *Society for Historic Archaeology* (in opposition to prehistoric). But, as the meeting progressed, nearly every speaker from the floor of the house pitched in with different suggestions, so the matter was left unresolved and passed on to the Steering Committee to sort out.[16] After discussion they finally settled on the *Society for Dark Age and Medieval Archaeology* as being the best of the bunch, though not ideal; the others were *the New Historical and Archaeological Society* and the *Society of Post-Roman Archaeology*. Herbert Finberg, however, strongly disagreed and now threatened 'a vulgar brawl' were the matter not to be resolved.[17] He found the proposed title 'lamentably imprecise'. He asked 'who will undertake to say when the "Dark Age" ended and the "Middle Age(s)" began?'. The term Dark Age he found 'defeatist and depressing', commenting that, in 'another thirty or forty years' time it may look very silly indeed'; the Renaissance division of the historic process into ancient-medieval-modern he thought obsolete anyway and, as a title for the society, he thought it 'both cumbrous (17 syllables!) and slipshod (an adjective coupled with an adjectival noun)'.

Even Finberg, however, had to confess that he could think of little better. *The Society for the Study of Post-Roman Britain* was his preference, with *LUCERNA, A Review of unwritten evidences of British History since the Roman period* being his choice for a journal title 'with a vignette [on the cover] showing the light we hope to kindle in dark places'.[18] This rejected title he partially recycled in 1964 (Finberg 1964). In spite of Finberg's formidable experience in publishing — he had worked with Basil Blackwell, launched the *Agricultural History Review* and initiated the series of Agrarian Histories of England and Wales (Aim25 2007) — the other six on the Steering Committee resisted him on the grounds that the phrasing 'post-Roman by itself gives a feeling that it will be confined to immediately post-Roman times'.[19] The others felt that Finberg was exaggerating the difficulties of a title approved by the majority, a reaction which Finberg found 'disappointing'.[20] Nevertheless, his point was made with sufficient force that the Steering Committee, probably feeling that their agreed choice of *Society for Dark Age and Medieval Archaeology* would now never pass muster (though various of the draft constitutions bear this name), returned to one of the original suggestions for its name, the snappier *Society for Medieval Archaeology*, and then opted for Martyn Jope's proposal of *Medieval Archaeology* for the journal.

The Finberg incident cannot be allowed to pass without comment because it is symptomatic of what Finberg perceived as an underlying battle between archaeology and history, and because it came to affect the way the Society operated. 'It is a fact', wrote Finberg,

> that every historian I have consulted is unanimous in reprobating the title proposed by the archaeologists on the Steering Committee, and since the success of the Society and its journal will depend to an appreciable extent on the support of historians, and also of librarians, I am confirmed in my feeling that interests other than purely archaeological should be represented on Council by weightier voices than mine.[21]

This was a potential split which the others were keen to heal quickly. After all, one of Hurst's major objectives had been, as he put it, 'cooperation with Historians, Geographers and Architects'. Yet Colvin for one had speculated negatively on how 'orthodox' historians would respond to this invitation[22] and now the dichotomy seemed to be opening up before their eyes. The archaeologists reacted by compromising on the names for both Journal and Society and then strengthened the fledgling Council by adding historians. Indeed, when Bruce-Mitford's term of office ended in December 1959, the new President was Oxford man Billy Pantin. The reasons given in a letter to him were that 'in the interests of the Society an historian should now succeed an archaeologist'.[23] Pantin, one of a generation of life-enhancing academic 'characters' now lost to us, was competent in several areas, but his main interests were monastic history and the investigation of medieval domestic buildings through architecture, archaeology and documents; furthermore he was the Keeper of the Oxford University Archives (Knowles 1975).

THE JOURNAL

As far as the content and tone of the Journal were concerned, Harden, Hurst and Wilson had very firm ideas. Though the early annual conferences are now remembered with enthusiasm, the new Society was originally envisaged as having very few other functions outside an 'annual general meeting with a paper or two to attract [an] audience'. It is worth quoting a letter from Hurst in December 1956 in full:

> I think we are all agreed that the journal should be of a high standard like PPS in quality but not necessarily in format. It would include the Celtic West, Saxon and Medieval periods. I would also agree to Romano-Saxon overlap but both Wilson and I are against anything else Roman. It should go right to 1750 for pottery and excavations but not beyond the renaissance for architecture except for peasant

> houses. The scope should include field work, excavation, the study of museum objects and other things which impinge on the study of Saxon and Medieval settlement as a whole ... The journal should include notes and brief reports on excavations etc carried out during the year. There should be book reviews but not a large bibliography. Advertisements might be admissible on the back cover but not inside.[24]

Not all were in agreement in this. Some, like Stuart Rigold, felt that the Journal should have a certain non-technical bias, others that there were already enough archaeological journals and there was simply not enough academic space for another Society. Hugh Shortt openly stated that 'the field could be more adequately covered by the Royal Archaeological Institute and the British Archaeological Association'. John Harvey expressed worries about detracting support from the county archaeological societies, and urged a 'leavening of architecture', as did Hoskins.[25] Louis Salzman, historian and author of *English Life in the Middle Ages* (1926), 'thought there was no room for the Society and that it would not survive'.[26] He urged 'infiltration' into other publications, though he joined himself in mid-1959 'greatly impressed with the Journal'.[27]

Harden, Hurst and Wilson had predicted dissenters of this kind. Their strategy was to invite the editors of the major societies to support the formation of the new Society formally and ensure an open show of support from the whole archaeological community. Thus, at the Burlington House meeting, it was a Romanist, Graham Webster, who publicly proposed a section in the Journal for work done during the year, while the motion to form the Society was seconded by another Romanist, Sheppard Frere.[28] Though petrol rationing prevented some from attending, prehistorians Stuart Piggott and Richard Atkinson were among those who sent letters of support and later became members. The blessing of the established societies, the use of Mortimer Wheeler as a neutral chair,[29] and the broad interests represented that day were the best kind of reassurance for those who feared the Society might create conflicts of interest. After all, surely the actual editors and presidents of the existing major societies were best placed to judge.

The final look of the Journal was largely down to Donald Harden (editor 1957–74), who had previously been instrumental in the successful launch of *Oxoniensia* in 1936, and a format along the lines of that journal was generally agreed upon.[30] There were early discussions at meetings of the Steering Committee in May 1957, where Finberg and others had an input, just as David Wilson describes. Rough layouts for a possible cover were mocked up by Eva Wilson.[31] But the real decision-making came later on, not always with the expected result. On 2 July 1958 Harden wrote to Headley Brothers (Invicta Press), by then nominated as the Society's publisher, that 'the cover in various guises' would be studied by the Council and Editorial Committee on 21 July.[32] He supplied Headley with a drawing of the Alfred Jewel for the cover with the caveat that 'some of us are not particularly happy about the use of the Alfred Jewel in this way, as it is an awkward shape'. He even sent out two or three other drawings of different objects so that Council and the Editorial Committee could choose between various options. At the meeting the decision was taken to adopt the Jewel and to print the cover in black. No surprise was therefore greater than Harden's to find his copy of the first issue printed in pastel blue. Evidently the final decision had not been conveyed to Headley. 'But I like the blue and the general lay-out very much', wrote Harden to Wilson, 'and wonder whether we could stick to it now . . . For the rest I think it looks lovely and [I] am very pleased with it'.[33] And so the distinctive blue cover format was born.

The Journal was an immediate hit. The volume is 'very excellent', wrote one,[34] 'magnificent',[35] 'a flying start', said another.[36] Articles for the first number had been solicited at an early stage so as to guarantee enough text, but it was also much more the policy then than it is today to prompt individuals to provide material for the Journal.[37] This explains the high proportion of articles by officers and members in volumes I to III. Hurst, in particular, pushed for articles on 'ordinary life' rather than the inhabitants of castles and monasteries. 'We should exclude heraldry, bells, genealogy, ecclesiology', he wrote, 'but of course the dividing line is thin as we would wish to include glazed floor tiles but not stained glass from churches.'[38] Hurst went so far as to insist that the exclusion of Art History was advertised in the prospectus and in doing so was, in a sense, spatially mapping later medieval archaeology in a wider disciplinary landscape. Defending those conceptual boundaries in the early years was down to Harden as editor, and he took great pride in *Medieval Archaeology* being the model for later European counterparts (Hurst 1997, 535).

THE CELTIC QUESTION

Certainly, generating material for the new Journal never proved a problem. A much more serious worry was how to represent geographical interests fairly. The genie escaped from that particular bottle very early on when one senior researcher wrote to demand that 'proportional interest' should be allotted to the Celtic West in each issue.[39] The argument presented was that large Dark Age sites are rather prolific and required fairly lengthy reports and so space should be set aside for their publication. A short time later, another letter from a different Celtic correspondent complained of the 'unfortunate impression' given by the constitution of the Council and warned that 'local interests were being subordinated to those of Southern England'.[40]

These two 'Celtic' correspondents (as they referred to themselves) were right to have their suspicions. At the beginning it was indeed felt that all the Society's officers should be London-based, but they then changed their minds and aimed for wider representation by including Brian Hope-Taylor (1923–2001; at that time working for part of the year at Yeavering in Northumberland, so an honorary northerner!; Graham-Campbell 2001), Maurice Beresford (1920–2005; then a Reader in Economic History at Leeds),[41] Ralegh Radford (1990–99; from Cornwall) and Robert Stevenson (1913–92) from the National Museum of Antiquities of Scotland. Both Ireland and Wales were omitted, since Martyn Jope (1915–96), never the committee man but the obvious academic choice at that time as founder and head of the archaeology department at Queen's University, Belfast, had expressed his unwillingness to sit on the Council.

Some attempt was then made to restore an appropriate disciplinary and geographical balance with the appointment in December 1957 as Honorary Vice-Presidents of historian Sir Frank Stenton and Sir Cyril Fox, whose study of rural houses in Wales had been so influential (Figure 2.3). Stenton's friend Dorothy Whitelock (1901–82), then recently appointed Professor of Anglo-Saxon at Cambridge, became Vice-President. If silence can be deemed as satisfaction then this north–south, east–west, archaeology/history balance might be deemed to have worked, for the trickle of active complaints never became a tide. The constitution of the membership, however, tells a different story. Of the 434 members on 1 December 1960, 16.5% had London addresses and there were more American members (17) than Welsh (14), Scottish (12) or Irish (9).

With a perversity which only academics can muster, another member of Council then objected to the procedures by which Council was selected, finding them to be plain manipulative. Described only as a 'keen socialist', he complained in 1962 that it was undemocratic for Council to perpetuate itself in such an artificial way and that it should, in fact, be elected by the full cohort of members. Hurst was horrified: 'I sympathise with him to some extent but it would be fatal I think if the delicate balance we try to achieve was broken and there were no historians or six or no Scotsmen or six'.[42] In the end, though, it was the historians rather than the Scotsmen who tended to take a back seat. W G Hoskins (1908–92) for one found attendance a struggle, not

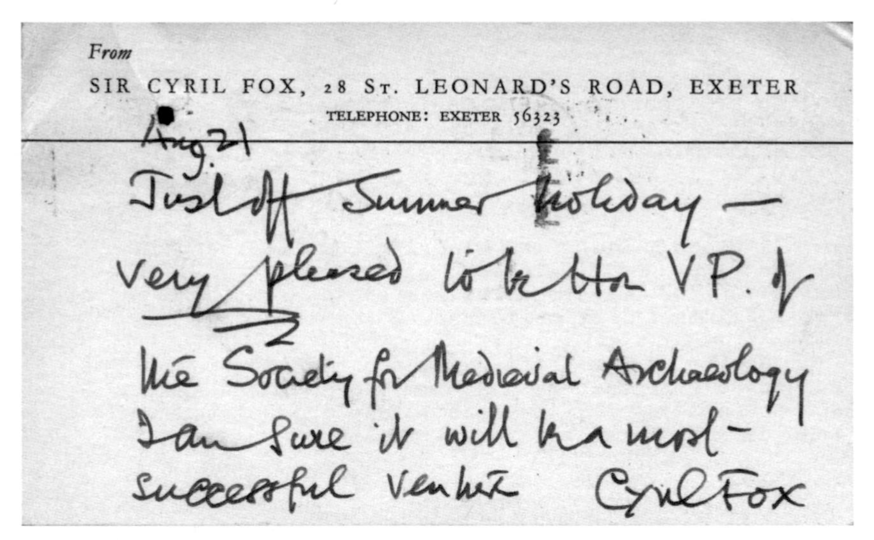

From
SIR CYRIL FOX, 28 St. LEONARD'S ROAD, EXETER
TELEPHONE: EXETER 56323

Aug. 21
Just off Summer holiday —
very pleased to be the VP. of
the Society for Medieval Archaeology
I am sure it will be a most
successful venture Cyril Fox

FIGURE 2.3. Sir Cyril Fox's enthusiasm for the new venture shines through in his acceptance of his post as Honorary Vice-President of the Society. Fox had been a past President of the Society of Antiquaries and successor to Wheeler as Director of the National Museum of Wales from 1926 until his retirement in 1948. Besides Donald Harden, Rupert Bruce-Mitford and David Wilson, others with museum connections on the first list of officers and committee (1957–58) included Sir Thomas Kendrick, Director of the British Museum, and Robert Stevenson, Keeper of the National Museum of Scotland.

helped by him holding a post in Oxford and living much of the time in Exeter from where he commuted on a weekly basis (Beresford 1992). 'I can never get to … meetings', he confessed, 'I feel you should appoint some useful man in my place. I regret this decision but my timetable is so congested that it is forced upon me.'[43] In fact, he was replaced by a very useful woman, Rosemary Cramp.[44] Another historian, Howard Colvin, then wrote to resign shortly afterwards,[45] also feeling he had been 'of very little service to the Society' and had been unable to attend Council, but given the nervousness about losing the support of the historians altogether Colvin was persuaded to see out his term of office and then step down after his three-year term, though he never again came to meetings.

THE EARLY YEARS

It was therefore to a short meeting held on 13 June 1957 at 3.00pm (Figure 2.4), once again at the Society of Antiquaries and under the chairmanship of Sir Mortimer Wheeler, that the final report of the Steering Committee was read. The name of the Society and its Journal were approved and its constitutions adopted. These had been drafted largely by David Wilson (Secretary 1957–76) with useful advice on financial matters from Christopher Blunt, who had been director of a successful merchant

SOCIETY FOR DARK AGE AND MEDIEVAL ARCHAEOLOGY

The second general meeting of those interested in the proposal to form a Society for Dark Age and Medieval Archaeology will be held in the rooms of the Society of Antiquaries, Burlington House, W.1 at 3 p.m. on 13 June 1957. Sir Mortimer Wheeler, P.S.A., has again consented to take the Chair.

At this meeting the Steering Committee appointed by the first general meeting will submit a draft constitution and rules for the new society, and make proposals for appointments of officers and committees.

Copies of the draft rules and constitution, names suggested for officers and committees and an agenda for the meeting will be sent to all those interested some days at least before the meeting.

D. M. WILSON

British Museum, W.C.1

May 1957

FIGURE 2.4. Invitation to the second inaugural meeting on 13 June 1957.

bank. Finberg supplied copies of the constitution of the Agricultural History Society to serve as a basis.[46]

13 June 1957 is therefore the official birthdate of the Society, and in the first 12 months Hurst, as Treasurer (1957–76), was surprised to find enrolments from Dar-es-Salaam to Sinhjukuku and from as far afield as Australia, Canada, India, Mexico, West Africa, and the United States.[47] The BBC publicized the Society through a pamphlet in 1957 on Anglo-Saxon England; *Antiquity*, *The Times*, *The Daily Telegraph*, *Manchester Guardian*, *New Scientist*, *Observer* and *The Scotsman* all published notices of its formation.

Hurst now battled with the ensuing international finance,[48] postage, and journals missing in the post, 'swamped with receipts and invoices',[49] prompting those who failed to pay and targeting those had not subscribed, and offering to meet with Wilson to consider what he termed 'the offenders who really should join' (Figure 2.5). Notepaper and a prospectus were produced to help with recruitment, though the latter caused endless headaches in seeking to provide correct institutional affiliations and titles of officers (Figure 2.6).[50] The archive of letters and cards over the first few years reveals officers already very busy with their own jobs now coping with an additional avalanche of requests, particularly Hurst as Treasurer.[51] On occasions the frequency of contact between Treasurer Hurst and Secretary Wilson by card and

THE SOCIETY FOR MEDIEVAL ARCHAEOLOGY

C/O THE BRITISH MUSEUM · LONDON · W.C.I

President: R. L. S. BRUCE-MITFORD, ESQ.

Secretary: D. M. WILSON, ESQ.

Treasurer: J. G. HURST, ESQ., 67 GLOUCESTER CRESCENT, LONDON, N.W.I

Editor: D. B. HARDEN, ESQ., THE LONDON MUSEUM, KENSINGTON PALACE, LONDON, W.8.

Dear Sir/Madam,

In checking the books, we find that we have no record of your subscription by bankers order, for the year ending 3rd April 195 , actually being paid into our bank.

As we have a record of your intention to pay by bankers order we realise that this mistake could have occured at any stage in the transactions. We would ask you, therefore, if you would be kind enough to check with your bank that this payment has, in fact, been made from your account.

Yours faithfully,

J.G.Hurst
Treasurer.

FIGURE 2.5. An admonishment from the Treasurer.

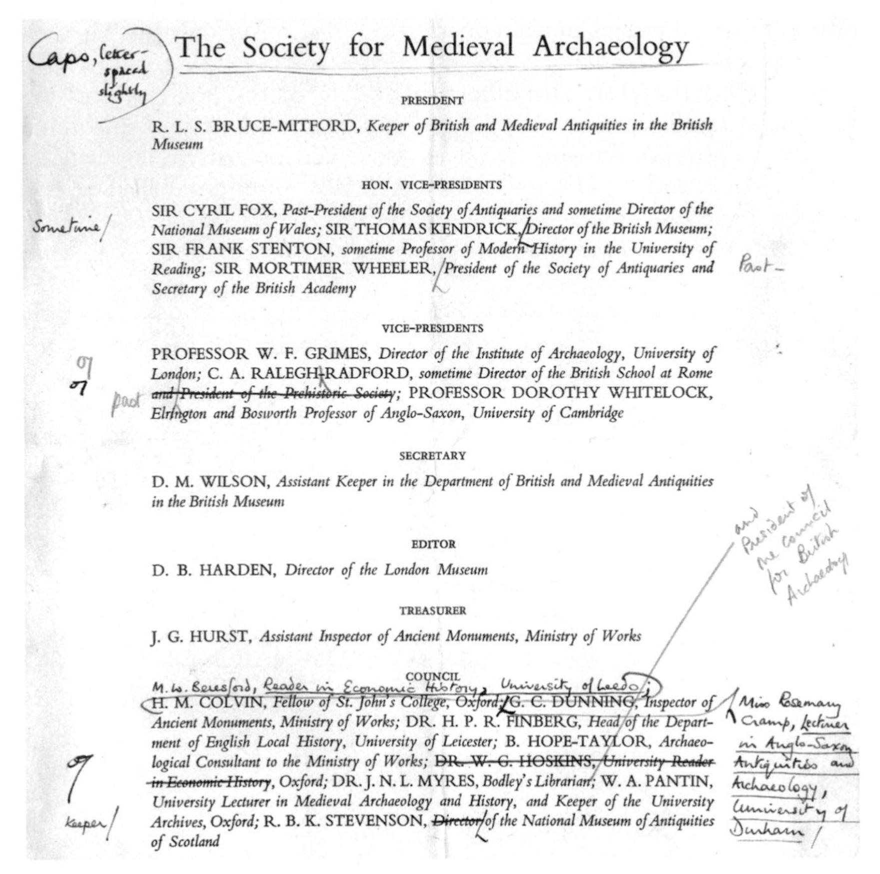

The Society for Medieval Archaeology

PRESIDENT

R. L. S. BRUCE-MITFORD, *Keeper of British and Medieval Antiquities in the British Museum*

HON. VICE-PRESIDENTS

SIR CYRIL FOX, *Past-President of the Society of Antiquaries and sometime Director of the National Museum of Wales;* SIR THOMAS KENDRICK, *Director of the British Museum;* SIR FRANK STENTON, *sometime Professor of Modern History in the University of Reading;* SIR MORTIMER WHEELER, *President of the Society of Antiquaries and Secretary of the British Academy*

VICE-PRESIDENTS

PROFESSOR W. F. GRIMES, *Director of the Institute of Archaeology, University of London;* C. A. RALEGH RADFORD, *sometime Director of the British School at Rome and President of the Prehistoric Society;* PROFESSOR DOROTHY WHITELOCK, *Elrington and Bosworth Professor of Anglo-Saxon, University of Cambridge*

SECRETARY

D. M. WILSON, *Assistant Keeper in the Department of British and Medieval Antiquities in the British Museum*

EDITOR

D. B. HARDEN, *Director of the London Museum*

TREASURER

J. G. HURST, *Assistant Inspector of Ancient Monuments, Ministry of Works*

COUNCIL

H. M. COLVIN, *Fellow of St. John's College, Oxford;* G. C. DUNNING, *Inspector of Ancient Monuments, Ministry of Works;* DR. H. P. R. FINBERG, *Head of the Department of English Local History, University of Leicester;* B. HOPE-TAYLOR, *Archaeological Consultant to the Ministry of Works;* DR. W. G. HOSKINS, *University Reader in Economic History, Oxford;* DR. J. N. L. MYRES, *Bodley's Librarian;* W. A. PANTIN, *University Lecturer in Medieval Archaeology and History, and Keeper of the University Archives, Oxford;* R. B. K. STEVENSON, *Director of the National Museum of Antiquities of Scotland*

FIGURE 2.6. Annotated corrections for a new print run on the opening page of the Society's prospectus, undated but sometime after May 1958 when W G Hoskins resigned.

telephone was three times a week or more during 1958 and 1959. A particular concern was money, for, even with the reserve, finances ran close to the wind. To keep a track of things they maintained an index of 'personal cards'. This no doubt slickly-oiled membership operation is sometimes revealed as having a distinctly *Blue Peter* feel to it: 'I have run out of sticky paper and do not know where to buy it . . .', complained Hurst. 'I don't expect sticky paper is the sort of thing stocked in Camden Town.'[52] Small matters took up inordinate time: 'Cowen [Society auditor] is very cross we have been keeping cash (AGM tea money, odd subs, etc) . . . I will let you have cheque at AGM having lost book at moment'.[53] One letter passed between them has 'Would you hook him?' in the margin. And hook them they did. By August 1958 there were 379 members with numbers increasing by two per week.[54] This rose to 460 members by the end of the first year, 495 at the end of year two, 533 at the end of year three and 600 by February 1960. The number of younger members joining was a particular cause for celebration; one student claiming to be 'at least a prospective specialist in

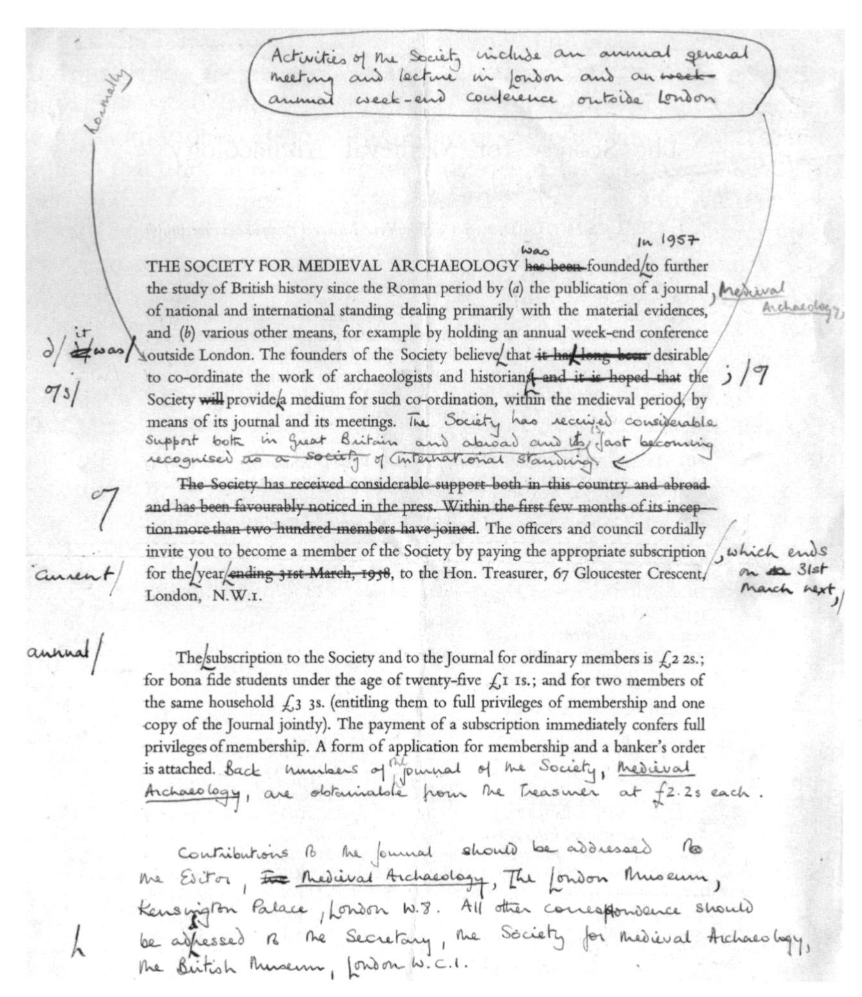

Activities of the Society include an annual general meeting and lecture in London and an annual week-end conference outside London

THE SOCIETY FOR MEDIEVAL ARCHAEOLOGY has been founded to further the study of British history since the Roman period by (*a*) the publication of a journal of national and international standing dealing primarily with the material evidences, and (*b*) various other means, for example by holding an annual week-end conference outside London. The founders of the Society believe that it has long been desirable to co-ordinate the work of archaeologists and historians and it is hoped that the Society will provide a medium for such co-ordination, within the medieval period, by means of its journal and its meetings. The Society has received considerable support both in Great Britain and abroad and is fast becoming recognised as a society of international standing.

The Society has received considerable support both in this country and abroad and has been favourably noticed in the press. Within the first few months of its inception more than two hundred members have joined. The officers and council cordially invite you to become a member of the Society by paying the appropriate subscription for the year ending 31st March, 1958, to the Hon. Treasurer, 67 Gloucester Crescent, London, N.W.1.

The subscription to the Society and to the Journal for ordinary members is £2 2s.; for bona fide students under the age of twenty-five £1 1s.; and for two members of the same household £3 3s. (entitling them to full privileges of membership and one copy of the Journal jointly). The payment of a subscription immediately confers full privileges of membership. A form of application for membership and a banker's order is attached. Back numbers of the Journal of the Society, Medieval Archaeology, are obtainable from the Treasurer at £2.2s each.

Contributions to the Journal should be addressed to the Editor, Medieval Archaeology, The London Museum, Kensington Palace, London W.8. All other correspondence should be addressed to the Secretary, the Society for Medieval Archaeology, the British Museum, London W.C.1.

FIGURE 2.6. Continued

Medieval Archaeology', C P S Platt, wrote to join in January 1960.[55] Among the other students who wrote to join the Society were Cambridge student Max Hebditch,[56] Oxford undergraduate Ann Hamlin[57] and Christopher Taylor, then at the Institute of Archaeology.[58]

However welcome, subscribers could also be demanding: 'we are just unable to understand why a body such as yours should take three weeks to answer a simple letter', wrote one in January 1963. They sometimes subscribed for reasons which were not apparently clear even to themselves. 'I very gladly subscribe even though I can gain nothing by doing so', wrote one;[59] 'I am mainly interested in the origin of experimental sciences' wrote another.[60] A particular grumble was the lateness of the Journal, especially Volume III which was due in March 1960 and had still not appeared by November: 'It is now over a week beyond the date I have promised our keenest critics', wrote Hurst to Wilson, 'there are 12 letters of protest by today's post alone!'.[61]

These irritations were gradually ironed out with the printers, but it was not only the members who caused anxiety for the Society's officers. If anything, letters from council members could be even more trying, ranging from the recalcitrant to plain absent-minded. 'I never quite knew how or why I got on to the organising committee', wrote one, 'and if the committee meets without me I for one shall not repine. Fridays in term-time are anyhow not very easy ... At the moment I am laid up with the prevalent complaint.'[62] 'I'll try to attend your meeting', promised one Vice-President, 'Where is the London Museum nowadays? It used to be near St James's Palace but I've a feeling I last went to it somewhere else.'[63] Others, it seems, merely had better things to do: 'I regret that I have to be so inactive a member in these early stages ... I am going south for a longish holiday'.[64]

From the very start the Society promoted functions other than the production of the Journal: a lecture traditionally held in London in December either at the Institute of Archaeology or the Society of Antiquaries and preceded by tea,[65] and the Annual General Meeting. Two of the first three lectures were given by Bruce-Mitford, one on the miniatures and ornaments of the Lindisfarne Gospels, a second on 'Progress in the

Programme

Friday, 17th April

3.00 p.m. Tour of medieval Southampton conducted by Miss E. M. Sandell, Robert Douch and Norman Cook.

6.45 p.m. INTRODUCTION TO THE REGION: three short papers.
Professor H. Rothwell: *The hinterland of medieval Southampton.*
M. R. Maitland Muller and D. S.Waterman: *Hamwih; the Saxon town.*
J. S.Wacher: *Medieval Southampton.*

8.15 p.m. OFFICIAL RECEPTION by the Lord Mayor of Southampton. (*Informal Dress.*)

Saturday, 18th April

9.30 a.m. LECTURE: M. W. Beresford.
Medieval Town Plantation in Southern England.

11.30 a.m. LECTURE: G. C. Dunning.
Some Aspects of the South Coast Trade in the Anglo-Saxon and Medieval Periods.

2.30 p.m. LECTURE: Sir Frank Stenton.
The Anglo-Saxon Town.

4.15 p.m. SYMPOSIUM on the theme of the Conference. Among those taking part will be Dr. W. G. Hoskins, Mr. R. H. M. Dolley and Dr. A. R. Bridbury.

Sunday, 19th April

9.15 a.m. EXCURSION visiting Corfe Castle, Wareham, Lymington (the medieval bastide) and Christchurch (the Priory and the Norman House). A short description of the excavations at Corfe and Wareham will precede the excursion.

Monday, 20th April

POST-CONFERENCE EXCURSION to the Isle of Wight. Among the places to be visited are Carisbrooke Castle and Museum, the extinct medieval town at Newtown, Chessel Down (the site of the Anglo-Saxon cemetery) and the medieval lighthouse on Chale Down. Intending participants are warned that an early start will be necessary; the excursion will end in time for convenient trains to London.

Please complete this form and return, with the appropriate Conference Fee, to Mr. Robert Douch before 20th March, 1959. (*Cheques should be made payable to 'The Society for Medieval Archaeology'.*)

To Robert Douch Esq., Institute of Education, The University, Southampton.

Name ....

Address ....

....

I wish to attend the Southampton Conference.

I will make my own arrangements for accommodation.

* I wish to stay in one of the University Halls of Residence. (*Dinner, Bed and Breakfast . . . approx. £1 7s. per day.*)

* I wish to take part in the Sunday excursion.

* I wish to take part in the Monday excursion.

† I enclose a Conference Fee of { 7/6 / 12/6 }

* Please strike out where not applicable.

† The Conference Fee, to cover running expenses (not fares for excursions), is 7/6 for members and 12/6 for non-members.

A circular giving fuller details will be issued later.

FIGURE 2.7. Programme for the Society's second Annual Spring Conference in April 1959. The first such conference was held in Sheffield in March 1958, the third at Hereford in 1960, and thereafter on the Isle of Man (1961) and at King's Lynn (1962).

Archaeology of the Anglo-Saxon period since the War'; the other was by Ralegh Radford on his Orkney sites.[66] There was also an annual weekend spring conference held outside London. In 1958 this was held in Sheffield and attracted 80, and in 1959 at Southampton (Figure 2.7). The latter led to a 'steam radio' or Network Three programme about the conference which attracted new members. Later meetings were held in Hereford in 1960 and on Isle of Man in 1961. Though never financially rewarding, they were at least collegial. During one meeting at Caen in spring 1963 the members on the trip apparently behaved so badly that one person suggested that instructions should be issued on how to behave![67]

IN RETROSPECT

What, then, were the 'ground conditions' necessary for a successful new Society? In the year 1957 we have a real sense of a subject 'in the making'. There was a growing platform of medieval projects and discoveries (Gerrard and Rippon 2007), not least through aerial photography (Beresford and St Joseph 1958; Wilson 1995), academic engagement with other more 'senior' disciplines such as history and geography (for example, Postan 1966), and there was popular interest, too, fed by new university extra-mural departments and consolidated by the enormous success of William Hoskins' *The Making of the English Landscape* (1955) and Maurice Beresford's *History on the Ground* (1957). At the same time several younger scholars had established themselves in different institutions and enjoyed passive organizational support enhanced by a common location: London (even if this brought its own challenges). The instigators also had a mission and personal commitment and had been mentored early on in their careers by archaeologists of exceptional talent: Harden by Leeds, Hurst by Clark and so on. All had qualities of personal leadership, tactics and organization which took them to senior positions in their careers and with them, indirectly, went the Society. Finally, and no less important where voluntary cooperation proved a necessity, they were able to activate personal and institutional bonds between the different archaeological 'tribes': Cambridge, the Fenland Research Committee, the Cambridge University Field Archaeology Society, the British Museum, Oxford, the Society of Antiquaries, the Deserted Medieval Village Research Group and the British Association for the Advancement of Science, which Hurst had been attending since the age of 9! These connections between people and places can be mapped like an electrical circuit board. To take one example, in 1951 Hurst attended the British Association meeting in Edinburgh with Jack Golson, who was studying under Munia (Michael) Postan at Cambridge, and there was introduced by Grahame Clark to the Dane Axel Steensberg, a pioneer of open-area excavation. Hurst also knew Harden through the British Association and it was Harden who first asked Hurst to talk about deserted villages in Belfast in 1952, an invitation which led to the formation of the interdisciplinary Deserted Medieval Village Research Group (DMVRG) after discussions at Wharram Percy in August 1952. Several of those who became involved in the Society in its early years, like Sir Cyril Fox and Clifford Darby, were likewise linked to Wharram and the DMVRG. Darby and Clark were both part of the interdisciplinary Fenland Research Committee which was the model for the

DMVRG (Smith 1994; 2006) and both contributed at the moment of the Society's formation.

There have of course been many developments since April 1957, most of them tracked in the pages of *Medieval Archaeology* (see Cramp, this volume). The novelties of dating promoted by Hurst have settled down to become routine and there are new techniques like isotopic studies and research areas in diet and disease which would have pleased Jope. He was also one of the first medievalists off the blocks in arguing for the application of processual approaches and model building in the early 1970s. This was one aspect of archaeology which John Hurst did not anticipate in his original blueprint for the Society and for which, famously, he claimed not the slightest inclination. Today, medieval archaeologists feel more at ease with the cognitive approaches which expose identity, ethnicity, the lived world of experience, the transition from feudalism to capitalism and so on. A key difference since 1957 is that many new practitioners of medieval archaeology trained as archaeologists and engage with the wider ebb and flow of archaeological ideas. Without the generation of 1957, however, we would not be an equal partner technically today and we would lack an understanding of monument classes and artefacts which is so often taken for granted and upon which we continue to build.

ACKNOWLEDGEMENTS

This essay draws largely upon letters and notes in the Society for Medieval Archaeology archive held at the Society of Antiquaries, Burlington House, Piccadilly, London. If any readers have either photographs or further documentation concerning any of the events mentioned here, the Society would be very pleased to obtain copies. I am grateful to Martin Carver, Rosemary Cramp, James Graham-Campbell and Andrew Saunders for their verbal and written comments.

NOTES

[1] Harden notes in blue ink head 'Origin of proposal', no date.

[2] Typed meeting record first draft, 16 April 1957.

[3] Harden notes in blue ink head 'Origin of proposal', no date.

[4] Harden notes in blue ink head 'Origin of proposal', no date. A letter from Hurst to Charles Thomas dated 24 November 1956 places the moment of the decision to go ahead in that month. Subsequently Harden, Hurst, Wilson and Corder met for discussion on 19 December 1956 at Burlington House and for lunch.

[5] These letters and their replies do not survive in the SMA archive but a selection of 10 from Leslie Alcock, Maurice Barley, Maurice Beresford, Grahame Clark, Rainbird Clarke, W G Hoskins, Martyn Jope, William Pantin, John Smith and Charles Thomas are abridged by Hurst in his letter to ?Wilson/Harden, 15 December 1956.

[6] Letter Hurst to ?Wilson/Harden, 15 December 1956.

[7] Letter Hurst to ?Wilson/Harden, 15 December 1956.

[8] Sir Eric Fletcher (1903–90) was a Labour politician who served as Minister without Portfolio in Harold Wilson's first government (1964–66). He was made a life peer in 1970 and maintained a lifelong interest in Anglo-Saxon architecture, writing a dozen or so articles on the subject for the journal of the British Archaeological Association, of which he was President from 1960 to 1963. He addressed the Society at the Poitiers conference in March 1979 (Fletcher 1986).

[9] As David Wilson mentions elsewhere, Fletcher gave £250 and Blunt £25. To put those donations into financial perspective, £300 was about half a lecturer's annual salary in 1957. In 1959 the Society also announced the gift of £100 per annum for three years from Mr H D Colt 'to aid research within the sphere of the Society's interests'; Minute Book 15 December 1959. David Wilson's paper recounts the circumstances.

[10] Accompanied by references from the National Federation of Bedding and the Soroptimists Clubs of Great Britain; letter 1 July 1957.

[11] Letter to Wilson, 31 December 1957.

[12] Of which three versions with carefully different wording were typed up by Hurst.
[13] Letter Harden to Fletcher, 1 May 1957.
[14] Letter Hurst to ?Wilson/Harden, 15 December 1956.
[15] Minutes of Steering Committee meeting, 13 May 1957.
[16] Typed meeting record first draft, 16 April 1957.
[17] Letter Finberg to Harden, 30 May 1957.
[18] Letter Finberg to Harden, 30 May 1957.
[19] Letter Harden to Finberg, 5 June 1957.
[20] Letter Finberg to Harden, 6 June 1957.
[21] Letter Finberg to Harden, 6 June 1957.
[22] Letter Colvin to Wilson, 29 June 1957.
[23] Pantin's acceptance letter to Bruce-Mitford, 26 August 1959.
[24] Letter Hurst to ?Wilson/Harden, 15 December 1956.
[25] Letter Hoskins to Wilson, 28 May 1957.
[26] Typed meeting record first draft, 16 April 1957.
[27] Letter Kenyon to Wilson, 26 April 1959.
[28] Typed meeting record first draft, 16 April 1957.
[29] The CBA was approached originally but did not wish to take part in a formal way; Harden notes in blue ink head 'Origin of proposal', no date.
[30] Letter Bruce-Mitford to Finberg, 25 March 1958. The editorial of volume 1 hoped that an annual volume of 200 text pages could be maintained; in 2007 volume 50 reached 462 pages.
[31] Steering Committee minutes, 13 May 1957.
[32] Letter Harden to Headley Bros, 2 July 1958.
[33] Letter Harden to Wilson, 29 September 1958.
[34] Letter to Bruce-Mitford, 27 September 1958.
[35] Letter to Wilson, 19 November 1958.
[36] Letter to Wilson, 16 November 1958.
[37] There was no 'house style' as there is today. Five words of guidance were provided to those who wished to submit articles for inclusion in the Journal; 'All MSS. should be typewritten' (Harden to Bruce-Mitford 25 July 1958). 15 free copies were provided to each author (letter Harden to Ralegh Radford, probably midsummer 1958, not dated).
[38] Letter Hurst to ?Wilson/Harden, 15 December 1956.
[39] Letter to Hurst, 28 November 1956.
[40] Letter to Wilson, 7 June 1957. Of the 434 members on 1 December 1960, 16.5% had London postcodes.
[41] In accepting his election in July 1958 to Council Beresford stated that 'as John [Hurst] will have explained, I was engaged in practical medieval archaeology of a menial sort on 21 July' (letter Beresford to Wilson, 23 July 1958). Presumably he refers to Wharram Percy.
[42] Letter Hurst to Wilson, 8 December 1962.
[43] Letter Hoskins to Wilson, 19 May 1958. Hoskins seems stressed about his commitments, 'Could you tell me what happened at the Council ... about your proposal that I should read a paper on "Pre-Conquest Exeter"? I should like to know soon as the paper will require a considerable amount of preparation and I am planning my programme of work for the coming winter. — I am well into the first draft of English Local History and toiling away daily, with a day off at great intervals'; letter Hoskins to Finberg, 17 August 1958. In any event, Hoskins was 'not an enthusiastic committeeman' (Wykes 1992).
[44] SMA Minute Book, 5 December 1958. The 1957–58 Council had eight members. Once Hoskins resigned, he was replaced by Maurice Beresford and Rosemary Cramp, taking the total to nine. In 1960 when Pantin became President, past President Bruce-Mitford joined the Council, Colvin stepped down and Eleanora Carus-Wilson came onto Council. Between 1957 and 1961 personnel changes were therefore minimized. Thereafter three-year rotation on Council became the norm.
[45] Letter Colvin to Bruce-Mitford, 7 July 1958.
[46] Christopher Hawkes, the Oxford prehistorian, was among those who commented on the draft constitution; letter Hawkes to Wilson, 11 June 1957.
[47] Several organizations wrote to request the Journal in exchange, a common practice in many countries but something which was not possible in this case, not least because the Society had no library or 'home' and was wholly dependent on the subscriptions of its members.
[48] In 1958 ordinary members and institutions subscription was £2 2s, *bona fide* students under the age of 25 paid £1 1s, two members of the same household £3 3s.
[49] Letter Hurst to Wilson, 7 June 1958.
[50] The trials of officers included envelopes which were too thin, running out of headed paper, ordering more, securing the best price, changing wording and layout for reprints of all printed notices for the AGM, conferences, etc; letter Hurst to Wilson, 13 December 1958. With the exceptions of knighthoods, officers' titles were dropped in the 1961–62 lists.
[51] Only occasionally does the pressure show through; 'I am too busy for this sort of thing. Can you?' (annotation by Hurst to ?Wilson, 25 June 1958 about a request for a speaker), 'I am not sure if this is a crank or an expert' (pencil note by Hurst attached on letter, 16 November 1958).
[52] Letter Hurst to Wilson, 14 April 1958. For the benefit of non-British readers, *Blue Peter* is a BBC television programme aimed at five- to eight-year-olds. An enduring tradition of the programme is the making of 'useful objects', mainly toys, from everyday items such as cereal packets and 'sticky-backed plastic'.
[53] Letter Hurst to Wilson, 9 December 1959.

[54] Letter Hurst to Wilson, 23 August 1958. This was, of course, before the first volume of the Journal had been printed. Wilson had to write on occasions to reassure members and librarians that there would be a product, and soon, particularly since two subscriptions had already been paid; letter to Wilson, 26 August 1958. Some of the complaining cards and letters are Morse-like in their brevity: 'SMA. Have not received journal. Would you kindly enquire into matter. Greetings!' (card to Wilson, 17 November 1958); 'I might just as well not have joined it [the Society] at all . . . but I have not received so much as a cheep form it since I joined! . . . I am probably kicking the wrong person, but perhaps you will pass this on to Wilson with interest if he to blame' (letter to Hurst, 13 May 1958). He was not; there had been a printers' strike.

[55] Letter Platt to Society, 21 January 1960. Later Professor of History at the University of Southampton and author of *Medieval England. A Social History and Archaeology from the Conquest to 1600ad* (1978).

[56] Letter Hebditch to Society, 20 November 1959. Later Director of the Museum of London 1977–97.

[57] Letter Hamlin to Society, 8 December 1959. Later Principal Inspector of Historic Monuments and Director of Built Heritage (Northern Ireland).

[58] Letter Taylor to Society, 14 November 1958. Landscape and field surveyor and author.

[59] Letter to Hurst, 27 February 1958.

[60] Letter to Hurst, 22 September 1959.

[61] Letter Hurst to Wilson, 28 October 1960.

[62] Letter to Wilson, 16 October 1957.

[63] Letter to Wilson, 2 May 1957.

[64] Letter to Wilson, 15 June 1957.

[65] Price 2s 6d on 5 December 1958. The tradition of holding AGMs at these two locations was set early. There were many Antiquaries links and William Grimes, Director of the Institute of Archaeology, was made a Vice-President of the Society at the first AGM on 6 December 1957.

[66] Minute Book, 6 December 1957 (minutes written up and signed at the time of the second AGM, 5 December 1958), 15 December 1959.

[67] Letter to Wilson, 15 April 1963.

BIBLIOGRAPHY

Aim25, 2007 *Finberg, Herbert Patrick Reginald*, accessed 19 December 2007

Anon, 1986 'C W Phillips, OBE, MA, FSA, 1901–1985', *Geographical Journal* 152, 146–147

Beresford, M W, 1957 *History on the Ground*, Lutterworth, London

Beresford, M W, 1992 'Professor W G Hoskins: a Memoir', *Agricultural History Review* 40, 164–167

Beresford, M W and St Joseph, J K, 1958 *Medieval England. An Aerial Survey*, Cambridge University Press, Cambridge

Bruce-Mitford, R L S, 1940 'Excavations at Seacourt', *Oxoniensia* 5, 31–40

Bruce-Mitford, R L S, 1997 *Mawgan Porth, a Settlement of the Late Saxon Period on the North Cornish Coast: Excavations 1949–52, 1954 and 1974*, English Heritage, London

Finberg, H P R, 1964 *Lucerna: Studies of Some Problems in the Early History of England*, Macmillan, London

Fletcher, Lord, 1986 *Random Reminiscences of Lord Fletcher of Islington*, London

Gerrard, C M and Rippon, S, 2007 'Artefacts, sites and landscapes: Archaeology and Medieval studies', in A Deyermond (ed), *A Century of British Medieval Studies*, 525–556, Oxford University Press for the British Academy, Oxford

Graham-Campbell, J, 2001 'Brian Hope-Taylor', *The Independent*, 10 February 2001

Hoskins, W G, 1955 *The Making of the English Landscape*, Hodder and Stoughton, London

Hurst J G, 1997 'Donald Benjamin Harden 1901–1994', *Proceedings of the British Academy* 94, 513–539

Knowles, M D, 1975 'William Abel Pantin 1902–1973', *Proceedings of the British Academy* 60, 447–458

Miller, E, 1983 'Michael Moissey Postan 1899–1981', *Proceedings of the British Academy* 69, 544–557

Phillips, C W, 1987 *My Life in Archaeology*, Alan Sutton, Gloucester

Postan, M M, 1966 *Cambridge Economic History of Europe, Volume 1. The Agrarian Life of the Middle Ages*, Cambridge University Press, Cambridge

Salzman, L, 1926 *English Life in the Middle Ages*, Oxford University Press, London
Saunders, A, 2006 'Arnold Joseph Taylor 1911–2002', *Proceedings of the British Academy* 138, 363–381
Smith, P J, 1994 'Grahame Clark, the Fenland Research Committee and prehistory at Cambridge', unpublished University of Cambridge MPhil thesis
Smith, P J, 2006 'Roots and Origins: archaeology and Wharram. An interview with John G Hurst', *Medieval Settlement Research Group Annual Report* 21, 59–64
Williams, M, 1995 'Henry Clifford Darby 1909–1992', *Proceedings of the British Academy* 87, 289–306
Wilson, D R, 1995 'John Kenneth Sinclair St Joseph 1912–1994', *Proceedings of the British Academy* 87, 417–436
Wykes, D L, 1992 'Professor William George Hoskins (1908–1992) and the Leicestershire Archaeological and Historical Society', *Transactions of the Leicestershire Archaeological and Historical Society* 66, 168–171

CHAPTER 3
MILESTONES IN EARLY MEDIEVAL ARCHAEOLOGY OVER THE LAST 50 YEARS

By ROSEMARY CRAMP

Major changes have been made in the understanding as well as the practice of medieval archaeology over the last 50 years, and this paper provides a personal view of the important discoveries and reassessments in the period up to the Norman Conquest. Specific attention is paid to settlement archaeology with an emphasis on rural settlements, and the irrelevance of the concept of 'type sites' since in both secular and ecclesiastical sites there are significant and ambiguous changes. Current achievements in providing synthetic studies which override the traditional boundaries between urban and rural, site and landscape, or material and spiritual interpretation are also noted.

INTRODUCTION

There is much to celebrate when considering the 50 years of existence of the Society for Medieval Archaeology and its publications. These 50 years have seen medieval archaeology advance from a subject which many of those studying the prehistoric or Roman past considered had no significant evidential support, to one which has produced some of the most exciting new discoveries of our generations. It is difficult to do justice to all the stages and aspects involved in the progress of the research, but it is important to remember how greatly we needed initially a substantial body of archaeological data before we could undertake the theorizing which now underpins current research.

When I went to Durham University in 1955 there was a strong tradition of Roman and prehistoric research in the north, and, as elsewhere, plenty of settlement evidence in the form of visible earthworks, and Roman military works, as well as very striking remains of post-conquest castles and monasteries. I was, however, singled out amongst the archaeologists of that region as 'the girl studying the paper cup culture'. As far as settlement archaeology for the Early Medieval period was concerned there was something to be said for that opinion, although the area was rich in Early Christian churches and monumental sculptures, which should have been a pointer to some foci.

The term Early Medieval can denote a different time-span to different people, and differs also in usage on the continent. I am using Early Medieval or Anglo-Saxon for the period from the 5th through the 11th century and am concentrating on that, leaving others to discuss developments from the 12th century onwards. This largely reflects the division for reports under 'Medieval Britain' in *Medieval Archaeology*. 'Late Antiquity', as used on the continent, has not a wide currency in Britain, but some would see it as applying to parts of Britain at least until the late 6th century (Dark 1994; 2000). In what measure there were dramatically fast or almost imperceptibly slow changes in economic and social life during the relatively long period from the mid-5th to the mid-11th centuries is still nevertheless difficult to chart.

This is an eventful, culturally and politically, diverse period, and there have been substantial changes in interpreting it over the last 50 years, reflecting often the fashionable preoccupations of their day which all archaeologists have derived from contact with other disciplines. Models from anthropology, sociology, economic geography and ecology have all played a part, with a rejection, until comparatively recently, of intellectual links with history or theology. For a full-blooded support for these changes one could cite Dave Austin's 1990 contribution ' "The Proper Study" of Medieval Archaeology', in which one is exhorted to enquire 'into social objectives, strategies and processes, so that we can next enquire into motivation and processes' (Austin 1990, 17). How far we have succeeded in this is considered below and in papers by Roberta Gilchrist and Christopher Gerrard.

The object of the Society, as stated in its first constitution, is 'the furtherance of the study of unwritten evidences of British history after the Roman period' (with no terminal date). I cannot survey the changes reflected in all volumes, but will concentrate on the beginning and the most recent publications. A consideration of the first volume of *Medieval Archaeology* in 1957 reveals a fascinating position in which the subject is poised between new views and old: new techniques in excavation and fieldwork which had hardly entered the general consciousness, and the chewing over of old problems. E T Leeds had died in 1955, but not before he had read the proofs of the volume compiled in his honour and had composed notes on Jutish Kent to answer an article by Christopher Hawkes. This was, as its editor, Sonia Chadwick, put it in Volume 1, 'the last word of the Grand Master of Anglo-Saxon Archaeology' (Leeds and Chadwick 1957, 5). This exposition of the cultural history of Kent 'is expressed in the jewellery and other ornaments recovered from cemeteries'. Thus had the Anglo-Saxons been identified since the time of Sir Thomas Browne.

CEMETERIES

The significance of the grave-goods in these early cemeteries of the 5th to 8th centuries has been explored more widely in later and more extensive cemetery excavations, and there have been advances in seeing the cemeteries within their landscape, as well as more intimately related to their settlements (Powlesland 1986).

Family groups have been identified in Kent, for example at Finglesham (Hawkes and Grainger 2006), whilst the important cemetery at Spong Hill, Norfolk, with *c*2000 cremations and 57 inhumations, is seen as probably serving a large scattered population (Hills 1977; Hills *et al* 1981; 1984; 1987; 1994; McKinley 1994; Rickett 1995). Advances in analysing cremated bone have enabled more precise identification of the contents of urns, both animal and human, and produced a greater understanding of what was considered their appropriate association.

The long-standing and ongoing debate as to who were the Anglo-Saxons, and whether their cultural traits were transported to, or developed in, Britain remains a live issue today (Higham 2007). For Leeds, and others like him, differences in the forms of jewellery and dress fastenings characterized different tribal groupings. Later research has demonstrated, however, that these distinctions are not so clear cut, but the main change in thinking has been the rejection of the idea that it was the presence of North Sea littoral and Scandinavian immigrants in considerable numbers which determined the new 'germanic' fashions. The link between artefacts and identities is now open to question, and alternatives to the view that it was solely population movement which brought about the social and cultural changes in the 5th and 6th centuries AD have been proposed (Lucy 2000, 174–186). A range of social interactions (some of which to do him justice, Leeds also suggested), including diplomacy, trade, movement of peoples and of ideas, is suggested as resulting in the seamless merging of the native with dominant immigrant groups. If one accepts that the same dress fashions and manner of burial as the Germanic immigrants could have been adopted by the native Britons, there has nevertheless to be the desire to emulate such customs. In the light of elite burials such as the Lexden tumulus, dating from the late pre-Roman Iron Age, which has so much in common with elite 'Anglo-Saxon' burials (Foster 1986, fig 9), one has to consider whether there was a coincidental return to pre-Roman customs, which could have affected the different tribal groups living side by side. Certainly excavations at sites such as Dunadd have demonstrated the interest of the British smiths in Anglo-Saxon metalwork (Lane and Campbell 2000, 114–118, 152–153). Recent claims that Old English was spoken in parts of Britain from the Roman period onwards could well be used to explain the change from Latin and Celtic to a Germanic language throughout half of Britain — a linguistic victory not effected by either the Vikings, nor indeed the Norman and Angevin kings. There must, however, have been some significant population change, and modern developments in skeletal research may help here (Budd *et al* 2004), but despite some innovative research we have not yet a wide enough data base for determining the genetic differences between those people who have been excavated in the so-called 'pagan cemeteries' in the eastern areas of England, nor in the cemeteries in the north and west where Irish immigrants lived alongside Britons, Picts and Anglo-Saxons. The detailed study of textile residues and impressions on dress fastenings by the Manchester researchers has provided new insight into changes in dress (Owen-Crocker 1986; 2007), but it is still difficult to compare Germanic and British fashions. By the 8th century folk costume and its embellishments are much less regionalized in Anglo-Saxon England, and probably proclaimed social rather than tribal differences.

The outstanding finds from mound 1 in the Sutton Hoo burial ground were well known in 1957, and its prestige artefacts indicated a wide range of contact for the 7th-century ruler buried there. Subsequently the finds were deeply researched (Bruce-Mitford 1975; 1978; Bruce-Mitford and Evans 1983) and this has provided a touchstone for other elite burials. A major settlement which might be associated with this ruling group has not been discovered, but Martin Carver's immaculate excavations, 1983–93, extended the context of the site within the region and beyond and placed the 7th-century burial ground not only in relation to prehistoric foci, but amongst later graves of what seems to be an execution site (Carver 1998 and 2005). It is now widely perceived that the extravagant furnished burials of the 7th century could be an ideological and political response to the growing power of the Christian religion and its acceptance by some of the rulers. But whether grave contents which include Christian symbols and artefacts are social or religious indicators, or merely additional symbols of power, is still a matter for debate (see Prittlewell - Faulkner 2004; Hirst *et al* 2004).

We know little about the religious beliefs of the incoming 'Anglo-Saxons', but have some hints from literature: there were sacred places such as lakes and woods — even individual trees — and some animals and birds seem to have been protective and prophetic. For the first, migration must have necessitated attachment to new sacred places, and that has been demonstrated in the many cemeteries focused on prehistoric burial mounds, as well as place-names which could indicate pagan religious sites, some of which are on the borders of territories and survived as meeting places (Gelling 1978, 148–162 and fig 11; Morris 1989, 56–92). The role of prophetic birds is well illustrated in the Whitby Life of Gregory the Great. When the missionary Paulinus was about to instruct King Edwin and his household, a crow croaked in an inauspicious part of the sky, which was felt to be a bad omen. But Paulinus told his acolyte to shoot it with an arrow and, the religious instruction over, remarked, 'if that stupid bird was unable to avoid death, then still less could it foretell the future to men who have been reborn and baptized into the image of God, "who has dominion over the fish of the sea and the fowls of the air and every living thing upon earth"' (Colgrave 1968, 99). In missionary conversion here — as with later Scandinavian immigrants — it seems those aspects of the Christian message that resonated with converts' beliefs were stressed. The Cross from the 4th century was seen as a tree, for the Anglo-Saxon a cosmic world tree, and in their monuments and poetry it is celebrated as such, just as the natural created world is benignly linked to mankind and Christ — a relationship explored throughout Anglo-Saxon art.

SETTLEMENTS

By the late 1940s around 1130 cemeteries were known (Meaney 1964) and about half a dozen settlement sites. At least in the last 50 years we have managed to redress the balance and to relate some major cemeteries to settlements. Leeds was one of the few archaeologists who had dug Anglo-Saxon buildings, and he considered the sunken-floored type as typical dwellings. In *Medieval Archaeology* 1, Ralegh Radford analysed Leeds's findings at Sutton Courtenay, the most extensive settlement site which had been excavated, and concluded (as has been later confirmed) that there was evidence not just of sunken-featured, but of rectangular buildings of spaced timbers which could have revealed something like the large halls on the continent, such as Warendorf, if the work had been more extensive. He concluded, 'If criticism is called for it should be directed to the miserably inadequate resources available to scientific British archaeology in the period between the wars' (Radford 1957, 29). How true — we were far behind the Dutch, Germans and Scandinavians in the discovery of settlements of the period, say, 5th–7th centuries, and behind in techniques of excavating timber buildings also. Yet at that time, as acknowledged in the same volume (Radford 1957, 28; Cramp 1957, 71; Wilson and Hurst 1957, 148–149), Brian Hope-Taylor was uncovering, in a meticulous open-area excavation, what he called 'a township' of massive timber buildings at the Northumberland site of Yeavering. Radford dismissed this rather briefly as having given some substance to the literary picture, yet it was archaeologically more important than this.

Archaeology in the landscape had been dominated by visible monuments, of all periods, whilst stone structures, Roman through medieval, were widely researched. But the timber buildings and unenclosed sites of Early Medieval settlements were not so easily visible, and even today there are problems of identification between, for example, Neolithic and Early Medieval. The cropmarks of Yeavering were published originally in a volume of aerial photographs of monastic sites (Knowles and St Joseph 1952, 27, fig 126). The wartime development of aerial photography provided a wider view of unsubstantial earthworks for all periods, but the cropmarkings of the greatly increased ploughed land in England revealed outlines of the timber buildings which were the norm for most people in the Early Middle Ages. The long-term change from stock farming to cereal cultivation in so many parts of England has aided aerial prospection, and, additionally, the massive increase in gravel and sand extraction beginning in the rebuilding after the war, identified many Anglo-Saxon rural sites and buildings to be excavated under rescue conditions. Concurrently, the destruction and then large-scale redevelopment in ancient towns provided the opportunity to investigate their origins and development by professional units, a few of which still operate today.

The 1960s was the decade when Early Medieval settlements in Britain, lay rural and urban, and ecclesiastical, began to emerge into view. Hope-Taylor's pioneering work in open-plan excavation, at Yeavering, 1953–62, probably did not make the widespread impact that it deserved, largely because his definitive report was only published in 1977, but the site was a milestone. It provided an example of a high-status site implanted in an area which had been a tribal and religious gathering-place in early and later prehistory, and was located below the largest hillfort in the region. Important aspects remained matters for discussion for the next 40 years: the apparent attention paid to prehistoric monuments in the landscape, hall buildings on a grand scale several times rebuilt on the same site, and the association of several cemeteries with the settlement. In addition the latest layout included a Christian church, the earliest Anglo-Saxon example in wood. There was evidence for acculturation in the architectural forms: native traditions were apparent in the huge fort; Roman traditions were reflected in the segment of the wooden grandstand/amphitheatre

(Hope-Taylor 1977, figs 12, 55, 57), but how far the architectural traditions of the other buildings were based on Germanic, Roman or native Roman British models has been debated vigorously ever since (Dixon 1982). The debate was revitalized when Martin Millett and Simon James published Cowdery's Down in Hampshire with similar buildings (Millett and James 1983). This type of building with annexes and enclosures has now been identified elsewhere by air photographs in what seem to be central places, such as Sprouston (Smith 1991) and Millfield (Knowles and St Joseph 1952, fig 125; Gates and O'Brien 1988) in the north, where this last was surrounded by sunken-featured buildings. The variety of settlements constructed by rulers in the long pre-Conquest period is only sparsely represented in excavations, although Leslie Alcock's and Philip Rahtz's influential excavations of the enclosed hilltop sites in the west, South Cadbury and Cadbury Congresbury (Alcock 1982, 1995; Rahtz *et al* 1992), and Philip Rahtz's excavation of the late, West Saxon royal vill at Cheddar (Rahtz 1979) greatly extended knowledge in place and time.

Radford's wish in *Medieval Archaeology* 1, that settlements reflecting a wider social structure should be found, has been fulfilled, as large open-area excavations unrolled, and one can only mention a few. Between 1965 and 1977, Margaret and Tom Jones's heroic excavations at Mucking, Essex, on a windswept headland overlooking the Thames, revealed what was to become a normal palimpsest of occupation spanning early Neolithic to medieval (discovered by aerial photography, and excavated in advance of gravel digging). The excavated site covered 18 hectares and work lasted 12 years. It was machine stripped (as has become the norm for such sites since), and about 44,000 features were excavated and recorded, which included 200 sunken-featured buildings, 50 posthole buildings and two associated cemeteries. Sadly, Margaret Jones was not able to synthesize the evidence which she provided in a series of detailed interim reports, but a publication of the Anglo-Saxon settlement was effected by Helena Hamerow in 1993, and publication of other aspects of the site is in preparation. Hamerow proposed, on the basis of the artefactual evidence in the fills of the sunken-featured buildings, a shifting settlement dating between the early 5th and late 7th century when the site was abandoned. Although an alternative model has been suggested by Tipper (2004) — that there were two settlements or clusters of buildings existing contemporaneously in the 6th and 7th — the shift of settlement does seem plausible, and is a phenomenon found elsewhere, as are the boundaries and enclosures separating areas which may have been dedicated to specific functions.

These features, the evidence for the limited life of these settlements, and for the fact that the sunken-featured buildings were the main type of structure rather than the large aisled buildings of the continent, was borne out by another important excavation at West Stow, Suffolk, excavated on a small scale between 1957–61 by Vera Evison, and by Stanley West between 1965–72 (West 1985 and 2001). Settlement spanned a period from the mid-5th to early 7th and comprised 65 SFBs and seven posthole buildings, the development of property boundaries being only in the last phases. West's evidence that floors were suspended over the pits, which were used for storage and then for rubbish disposal, is now widely accepted (Tipper 2004, 84–107). This was a pioneering site in that reconstructions of the excavated houses were built and subjected to research, as well as providing the general public with an experience of Anglo-Saxon lifestyles in a way which has been applied since to other sites.

There were other landmark sites which unfortunately have not been finally published. Chalton, discovered as result of field walking and part of a much wider research survey, produced long, large buildings and small, squarish, ancillary structures. There was only one sunken hut and very little rubbish, and it appeared a well-managed site, but one which moved in the 8th century (Cunliffe 1972; Addyman and Leigh 1973). This was an early example of an Early Medieval landscape project and an attempt to relate topographic and documentary evidence.

In many ways the landscape project of West Heslerton has been the culmination of much of the earlier work. On the south slope of the Vale of Pickering in Yorkshire, Dominic Powlesland and his teams have worked for 30 years excavating an area of over 20 hectares (50 acres) of an Anglo-Saxon burial ground and settlement, and prospecting very much more (Powlesland 1986). The settlement began *c* 5th century, and the cemetery, which contained about 250 people, reused a site with a Neolithic henge and Bronze Age barrows (Haughton and Powlesland 1999). The previous settlement included a Roman cult site with a well and shrine — a stone-based structure dating from post-AD 340. In the 400 years of subsequent occupation, 220 structures were recognized, including many sunken-featured buildings (Tipper 2004, figs C 22–24). There were zones of activity with evidence for grain stores, cooking places, metalworking and weaving. This is now being followed up by an extensive geophysical survey along the valley, the results of which have produced 14 Anglo-Saxon settlements in 11 kilometres amidst a dense ribbon of earlier sites (Powlesland *et al* 2006). The demise of such sites and regrouping into villages, often probably under present villages, may be the result of more stable estate structures, as well as the foundation of centralized churches with the capability to document boundaries and to impose taxes.

Despite considerable new research which has been concerned with the culture of the Viking Age (Wilson 1980; Graham Campbell 1980), including detailed regional studies of place-names and of the distinctive sculpture produced under Scandinavian patronage (Bailey 1980 and 1996, 77–94; Bailey and Cramp 1988; Lang 1991; Coatsworth 2008), it has proved impossible to identify any rural settlement in England as 'Scandinavian' or 'Viking' amongst the new settlement forms and locations of the 9th and 10th centuries. Through study of such topics as ethnicity, Danelaw identities, lordship in the Danelaw, and how the Scandinavians were converted to Christianity and assimilated into society, a picture emerges of gradual and complex interactions and some regional variation in the type of evidence (Hadley and Richards 2000). There is the introduction of Scandinavian-style artefacts, but, as is pointed out also in relation to settlement forms in both country and town, there is evidence of an interaction with existing material culture and the formation of something new which can be identified as Anglo-Scandinavian, an acculturation which can be compared with that in the 5th–7th centuries.

The economic and social impact of the Scandinavians has been most clearly identifiable in urban contexts. When 25 years of Medieval Archaeology was reviewed, Hinton noted particularly the increased activity in urban archaeology (Hinton

1983, 5). Much of this information was published in discrete units, or in compendia of artefacts. The massive input into urban excavation in the 1960s is, however, now bearing fruit, in syntheses such as the wide-ranging assessment of Lincoln (Jones *et al* 2003), or aspects of York (Hall *et al* 2004; Tweddle *et al* 1999), and also in the fascicules, particularly artefact studies, which have flowed from the professional units, especially in York and London. It is now proving possible to take further the pioneering work of those such as Biddle at Winchester (Biddle 1983) and, using excavated data with historical data, to go beyond the development of towns to consider their wider ethos and relationship with their hinterland. An outstanding example of this is the important article by Hutcheson in *Medieval Archaeology* 50 (Hutcheson 2006) which is cloaked in the title 'The Origins of King's Lynn' but which, using the region of western Norfolk, covers landholdings rather than single sites, and multiple tiers of settlements, including productive sites, demonstrating how they are related to the monetary system of Middle Saxon England.

ECCLESIASTICAL ESTABLISHMENTS

Unlike the continent, no continuum of Christian use from Roman to Anglo-Saxon buildings has been credibly established in England, although some Roman buildings survived into the 5th century (Thomas 1981, 155–90; Bell 2005) and many Anglo-Saxon churches occupy Roman sites (Bell 1998). How far there were dedicated dwellings for the clergy is also unknown. In the 6th to 7th centuries a bishop per tribe, peregrinating with the king's retinue between his power centres, rather than a bishop per territory operating from a fixed urban centre, was probably the normal practice in Britain. Pope Gregory's attempt to create fixed episcopal centres based on Roman cities failed, but monasteries fulfilled the need for stable religious communities, and also provided additional meeting places and other resources for the noble donors of their lands. These institutions were frequently linked with landing points, which could be used for exchange and trade of surplus from their often extensive dependent territories (for the processing of possible tribute at Lindisfarne, see O'Sullivan 2001). The monastic community, however, transcended the bonds of secular kinship and lordship being linked to a literate international network, and could draw on its knowledge and resources. Before the full development of urban life, monasteries were the nearest thing to a town, and it would seem that it was only after the development of urban networks in the 10th/11th centuries that some of the earlier functions of monasteries as places of trade and exchange and of craft production were diminished. Earlier monasteries may have helped to maintain some sort of royal presence in towns, for example in the documented but unlocated female establishments at Gloucester and Carlisle.

Although there had been small incursions into several monastic sites by 1957, only Glastonbury in Somerset and Whitby in Yorkshire had been excavated on a sufficient scale to produce site plans. The importance of the former, with its traditional links with the Celtic world, its royal patronage in the 8th century and as a leading reformed house in the 10th, is, however, barely reflected in the confusing archaeological record (Rahtz 1993, figs 44 and 45). St Hilda's monastery at Whitby was the only substantially excavated example of a 'double house' (a community of women with some men for heavy work or to serve as priests). The evidence from the Ministry of Works' clearance of the site was reconsidered in 1976 (Cramp 1976, 223–239; Rahtz 1976b), and Rahtz proposed that the stone-footed buildings on the surviving plans might have succeeded purely timber buildings (Rahtz 1976b, 461). Later excavations at Hartlepool, Hilda's previous house, have supported this sequence, with stone-footed buildings succeeding timber structures in the 8th century (Daniels 1988, figs 21 and 26; Daniels 2007, 60–67). The area excavated at Hartlepool seems to be a craft zone with metal- and stoneworking, but the monastery obviously occupied a much larger area. Recent excavations and field prospection at Whitby have likewise shown activity over the whole headland (Willmott, pers comm). At Whitby, like Hartlepool, the mixed craft activities were to the north of the medieval church, which could show some common planning, and both sites produced evidence of literacy, and fine funerary inscriptions and carving, but no evidence for mortared stone buildings.

Such buildings have, however, been excavated at Wearmouth and Jarrow (Tyne and Wear), thus fulfilling the documented aspiration of the founder to build in the Roman manner, aided by the importation of continental masons and glaziers (Cramp 2005; 2006, 56–161. Both sites of this twin monastery have produced comparable complexes of major stone buildings, between the churches with their cemeteries and the rivers to the south, but here also only an unknown proportion of the sites has been excavated (Cramp 2005, fig 24.3). The influence of such stone buildings on layout has been noted in the Anglian phases of the distant monastery at Whithorn in Galloway (Hill 1997, fig 4.5; Cramp 2005, fig 24.4). Aerial photography and excavations in advance of gravel digging at Hoddom in Dumfriesshire allow us to gain some idea of the potential scale of ecclesiastical sites. Hoddom, occupied between *c*AD 650–850, was already known for a large collection of carved stones around the ruined church near the river. Fieldwork and excavation revealed an area of about 20 acres enclosed by ditches, with some timber buildings near the perimeter, but dominated by stone corn-drying kilns providing important evidence for large-scale processing of grain perhaps from food rents (Lowe 2006, 81–95). Clearly this was a large central place and can be interpreted as a monastery (Lowe 2006, figs 8.11 and 9.1), but the excavator leaves the question open.

Considerable discussion in the last 50 years (Rahtz 1973) as to how one can identify or define a monastery has produced only one generally accepted conclusion — that there was a great variety in types in the pre-10th century, some closely mirroring secular forms. The debate was reactivated by the discovery of 'productive' sites such as Brandon in Suffolk (Carr *et al* 1988), in which a large area of densely packed timber buildings included two churches and cemeteries as well as evidence for extensive craft production, and Flixborough near to the Humber which produced a wealth of finds and ecofactual material as well as a group of timber buildings renewed in several phases (Loveluck 1988; 2001, figs 5.4–5, 5.8–10; Loveluck and Atkinson 2007). This is a high-status site with major changes of lifestyle, one phase of which, in the 9th century, could indicate an ecclesiastical presence.

Changes in the 9th century were observed at the monastic sites at Jarrow and Dacre (R Newman, pers comm) and it is clear that the organization of life inside such settlements could change its nature over time. We have a very poor sample of sites, especially from East Anglia and Wales (but see Knight 2005), but Carver's new excavations at Portmahomack, Tarbat (Carver 2004) have significantly enlarged the evidence from Scotland. However, except for small parts of the New Minster, Winchester (Biddle 1972, fig 7), and Eynsham, Oxford (Hardy *et al* 2003), none of the great reformed houses of England have been excavated in the modern period.

Changes in the 9th century could be connected perhaps with the redistribution of lands during the Viking Age wars, and with wider lay patronage and control. Although there are documentary references to proprietory churches by the late 7th century, it seems that it is not until *c* 10th century that they became common, and parochial, as exemplified in the important report of the Raunds Furnells church and graveyard in Northamptonshire (Boddington 1987).

There has been considerable study of individual churches in this period, fostered by the Taylors's great three-volume work (Taylor and Taylor 1965; Taylor 1978) and their examples of 'structural analysis'. This encouraged detailed analysis of complex churches (supported by limited excavation) at Gloucester (Heighway and Bryant 1999), Deerhurst (Rahtz 1976a; Rahtz and Watts 1997), Brixworth (Parsons 1979; Sutherland and Parsons 1984), Barton on Humber (Rodwell and Rodwell 1982) and Wells (Rodwell 2001), whilst the interior excavation of St Martin's at Wharram Percy formed part of the far-reaching analysis of the whole site (Bell and Beresford 1987; and see Gerrard below). The archaeology of churches has been very substantially supported by historical and landscape study (Morris 1983; 1989; Blair 1992; 2005) which has evaluated and contextualized the disparate archaeological reports. In addition, the later phases of ecclesiastical architectural development have been evaluated within the continental context by Richard Gem, who has taken the study beyond the deceptive boundary of the Norman Conquest (Gem 1993). But all of this work only underlines how much more is to be done. The sequence of ground plans revealed in the outstanding excavations at Winchester Old Minster revealed just how much we have lost of the major churches of the late Saxon period.

The last 50 years have seen the scholarly publications of fundamental data which enrich our understanding of this period, as, for example the British Academy *Sylloge of Coins of the British Isles*, a systematic record of this important body of material. Here the painstaking efforts of scholars such as Michael Dolley in the 1960s produced not only a tight chronology for late Saxon coinage but demonstrated how by a firm control of the metallurgy and weight of the coins the later West Saxon kings could manipulate the economy. A companion Academy series, *The Corpus of Anglo-Saxon Stone Sculpture*, has also served as an essential aid in identifying the presence of early sites, distinguishing their status, and indicating changes of patronage. Additionally, the many modern translations of difficult Latin and Anglo-Saxon texts — laws, letters, saints' lives, chronicles — can provide the authentic voice of the period for those engaged in the reconstruction of the mind-sets of the past. For any rounded study all types of evidence must be taken into account, but the deficiencies and strengths of each subject need to be properly understood.

SUMMARY AT THE PRESENT

If not all the theories which were fashionable in the 1970s have proved useful in Early Medieval archaeology, new attitudes have been shaped, and new priorities embraced, as is evident in the latest volumes of *Medieval Archaeology* and recent monographs. Many of the landmarks mentioned above were recognized as such in the Silver Jubilee volume of the Society's work (Hinton 1983), but what has changed is the quantity of the evidence and nature of the questions now asked of it. It is now possible to recognize Anglo-Saxon settlements and to compare their morphology, crop and animal husbandry with a wider range of continental evidence (Hamerow 2002). But beyond that the greater attention paid to the study of ecofacts in recent publications such as the Flixborough reports enables comparison with crop and animal husbandry not only on the continent but worldwide. The study of human environments, pioneered in the 1980s has indeed now achieved a pivotal position in settlement study. The analysis of whole landscapes rather than individual sites, using a combination of excavation techniques and geophysical survey has opened our eyes to the density of sites in some areas, as the Heslerton project has demonstrated. In addition the combination of documentary, archaeological, and architectural surveys combined with small scale excavations has transformed the understanding of settlement and land use (Gerrard and Aston 2007). But sampling strategies, which are so useful in creating a picture of the large-scale ecology of regions, or even, by test-pitting, the potential of currently occupied rural sites (Lewis 2007), are not as viable in the many areas which were aceramic until the 11th/12th century.

There is now considerable evidence to substantiate shifts in the 8th century, but a generally accepted explanation for this still eludes us. Some sites, both lay and ecclesiastic, have demonstrated changes of layout and status which may be linked to changes in ownership or patronage, but in fact definitions are not as simple as once imagined and the concept of 'type sites', especially in relation to monasteries, is no longer valid.

In 1986, Leslie Webster considered that the desiderata for the future was the excavation of more waterlogged sites and more considered synthesis of existing evidence (Webster 1986, 156). We have had considered syntheses, particularly in relation to urban sites and this can provide new perspectives which have moved from the organization and development of individual towns to wider urban rural links. The centralization of roles originally dispersed in individual sites into a central settlement — a town — for fiscal and administrative purposes is not a new concept, but is given new impetus by the inclusion of archaeological evidence (Hutcheson 2006). On a less positive note the waterlogged wood recovered from urban sites (excluding York, for which see Morris 2000), has been largely wasted for its potential understanding of carpentry and architectural developments between the Roman period and the Norman.

Artefact studies have lost some roles and gained others: the recognition that ethnicity is a complex entity and that artefacts, whether personal or public, cannot be used for a simple distinction between Celts and Saxons or Scandinavians and English may have diminished their role. On the other hand there has been increasing interest in the wider significance of artefacts or individual monuments. Recent volumes of *Medieval Archaeology* clearly reflect the burgeoning interest in discovering symbolism and the intentions behind ritual activities or the fashioning of structures or artefacts. Examples are Helena Hamerow's discussion of 'special deposits' in Anglo-Saxon settlements (Hamerow 2006), and Meggen Gondek's consideration of sculpture in Scotland as 'created monuments related to economic and social investment' which can be quantified, and as symbolic wealth which can create 'landscapes of power' (Gondek 2006, 107, 141). Sometimes this trend can unite the sparse textual evidence and the archaeological with fascinating insight, like Tania Dickinson's analysis (Dickinson 2005) of the apotropaic role of the creatures, including birds, applied to prestige shields, thus providing an archaeological commentary on the attitudes displayed in the Paulinus story quoted above.

Inevitably what I have chosen to emphasize in this paper reflects my own interests, and many important achievements of individuals and groups have been passed over unremarked. But, in a subject which has been so transformed over 50 years, it is impossible to do justice to all the new insights into a period, which followed the collapse of a complex and more centralized political and economic system, and saw far-reaching changes in authority. Fresh starts had to be made in developing social structures, in enlarging small-scale efforts and initiatives, and in providing a legal framework for hierarchies to emerge and even fossilize. And in Anglo-Saxon England a settlement pattern was set for the future. As archaeological evidence grows in mass and understanding over the next 50 years, our comprehension of regional and national frameworks and identities will be radically transformed again.

ACKNOWLEDGEMENTS

I am grateful to Belinda Burke and Derek Craig for their help with the preparation of the text of this paper.

BIBLIOGRAPHY

Addyman, P V and Leigh, D, 1973 'The Anglo-Saxon village at Chalton, Hampshire, 2nd interim report', *Medieval Archaeology* 17, 1–25

Alcock, L, 1982 'Cadbury-Camelot: a fifteen year perspective', *Proceedings of the British Academy* 68, 356–388

Alcock, L, 1995 *Cadbury Castle, Somerset. The Early Medieval Archaeology*, University of Wales Press, Cardiff

Aston, M and Gerrard, C, 1999 '"Unique, traditional and charming": the Shapwick Project, Somerset', *Antiquaries Journal* 79, 1–58

Austin, D, 1990 '"The proper study" of medieval archaeology', in L Alcock and D Austin (eds), *From the Baltic to the Black Sea: Studies in Medieval Archaeology*, One World Archaeology 18, 9–42, Unwin Hyman, London

Bailey, R N, 1980 *Viking Age Sculpture in Northern England*, Collins, London

Bailey, R N, 1996 *England's Earliest Sculptors*, Pontifical Institute of Mediaeval Studies, Toronto

Bailey, R N and Cramp, R, 1988 *Corpus of Anglo-Saxon Stone Sculpture 2: Cumberland, Westmorland and Lancashire North-of-the-Sands*, British Academy, Oxford University Press, Oxford

Bell, R D and Beresford, M W, 1987 *Wharram: a Study of Settlement on the Yorkshire Wolds* 3, ed J G Hurst, *The Church of St Martin,* Society for Medieval Archaeology Monograph 11, London

Bell, T, 1998 'Churches on Roman buildings: Christian associations and Roman masonry in Anglo-Saxon England', *Medieval Archaeology* 42, 1–18

Bell, T, 2005 *The Religious Reuse of Roman Structures in Early Medieval England*, British Archaeological Reports 390, Oxford

Biddle, M, 1965 'Excavations at Winchester 1964', *Antiquaries Journal* 45, 230–261

Biddle, M, 1972 'Excavations at Winchester 1970. Ninth interim report', *Antiquaries Journal* 52, 93–101

Biddle, M, 1976 'Towns', in D Wilson (ed), *The Archaeology of Anglo-Saxon England*, 99–150, Methuen, London

Biddle, M, 1983 'The study of Winchester: archaeology and history in a British town 1961–83', *Proceedings of the British Academy* 69, 93–135

Blair, J, 1992 'Anglo-Saxon minsters: a topographical review', in J Blair and R Sharpe (eds), *Pastoral Care Before the Parish*, 226–266, Leicester University Press, Leicester, London and New York

Blair, J, 2005 *The Church in Anglo-Saxon Society,* Oxford University Press, Oxford

Boddington, A, 1987 *Raunds Furnells: the Anglo-Saxon Church and Churchyard*, English Heritage Archaeological Report 7, London

Bowen, H C and Fowler, P J, 1978 *Early Land Allotment*, British Archaeological Reports 48, Oxford

Bruce-Mitford, R L S, 1975 *The Sutton Hoo Ship Burial: 1 Excavations, Background, the Ship, Dating and Inventory*, British Museum, London

Bruce-Mitford, R L S, 1978 *The Sutton Hoo Ship Burial: 2 Arms, Armour, and Regalia*, British Museum, London

Bruce-Mitford, R L S (ed A C Evans), 1983 *The Sutton Hoo Ship Burial: 3 Late Roman and Byzantine Silver, Hanging-Bowls, Drinking Vessels, Cauldrons and Other Containers, Textiles, the Lyre, Pottery Bottle and Other Items*, 2 vols, British Museum, London

Budd, P, Millard, A, Chenery, C, Lucy, S and Roberts, C, 2004 'Investigating population movement by stable isotope analysis: a report from Britain', *Antiquity* 78, 127–141

Campbell, J (ed), 1982 *The Anglo-Saxons*, Phaidon Press, Oxford

Carr, R D, Tester, A and Murphy, P, 1988 'The Middle Saxon settlement at Staunch Meadow, Brandon', *Antiquity* 62, 371–377

Carver, M O H, 1998 *Sutton Hoo, Burial Ground of Kings?* British Museum, London

Carver, M O H, 2004 'An Iona of the East: The early medieval monastery at Portmahomack, Tarbat Ness', *Medieval Archaeology* 48, 1–30

Carver, M O H, 2005 *Sutton Hoo: a Seventh-Century Princely Burial Ground and its Context*, Reports of the Research Committee of the Society of Antiquaries of London 69, British Museum, London

Coatsworth, E, 2008 *Corpus of Anglo-Saxon Stone Sculpture 8: Western Yorkshire*, British Academy, Oxford University Press, Oxford

Colgrave, B, 1968 *The Earliest Life of Gregory the Great*, University of Kansas, Lawrence

Cramp, R, 1957 'Beowulf and archaeology', *Medieval Archaeology* 1, 57–77

Cramp, R, 1976 'Monastic sites', in D Wilson (ed), *The Archaeology of Anglo-Saxon England*, 201–252, Methuen, London

Cramp, R, 2005 *Wearmouth and Jarrow Monastic Sites* 1, English Heritage, Swindon

Cramp, R, 2006 *Wearmouth and Jarrow Monastic Sites* 2, English Heritage, Swindon

Cunliffe, B W, 1972 'Saxon and medieval settlement-patterns in the region of Chalton, Hampshire', *Medieval Archaeology* 16, 1–12

Daniels, R, 1988 'The Anglo-Saxon monastery at Church Close, Hartlepool, Cleveland', *Archaeological Journal* 145, 158–210

Daniels, R, 2007, *Anglo-Saxon Hartlepool and the Foundations of English Christianity: the Archaeology of the Anglo-Saxon Monastery*, Tees, Archaeology Monograph Series 3, Hartlepool

Dark, K R, 1994 *Civitas to Kingdom: British Political Continuity 300–800*, Continuum International Publishing, Leicester

Dark, K R, 2000 *Britain at the End of the Roman Empire*, Tempus, Stroud

Dickinson, T M, 2005 'Symbols of protection: the significance of animal-ornamented shields in early Anglo-Saxon England', *Medieval Archaeology* 49, 109–163

Dixon, P, 1982 'How Saxon is the Saxon house?', in P J Drury (ed), *Structural Reconstruction: Approaches to the Interpretation of the Excavated Remains of Buildings*, 275–288, British Archaeological Reports 110, Oxford

Faulkner, N, 2004 'Prittlewell: treasures of a king of Essex', *Current Archaeology* 190, 430–443

Foster, J, 1986 *The Lexden Tumulus: a Re-appraisal of an Iron Age Burial from Colchester, Essex*, British Archaeological Reports 156, Oxford

Gates, T and O'Brien, C, 1988 'Cropmarks at Milfield and New Bewick and the recognition of *grubenhäuser* in north Northumberland', *Archaeologia Aeliana* series 5, 16, 1–9

Gelling, M, 1978 *Signposts to the Past*, J M Dent & Sons, London

Gem, R D H, 1993 'Architecture of the Anglo-Saxon church, 735–870: from Archbishop Ecgberht to Archbishop Ceolnoth', *Journal of the British Archaeological Association* 146, 29–66

Gerrard, C and Aston, M, 2007 *The Shapwick Project, Somerset. A Rural Landscape Explored*, Society for Medieval Archaeology Monograph 25, Maney Publishing, Leeds

Gondek, M M, 2006 'Investing in sculpture: power in Early-historic Scotland', *Medieval Archaeology* 50, 105–142

Graham-Campbell, J, 1980 *Viking Artefacts: a Select Catalogue*, British Museum Publications, London

Hadley, D M and Richards, J D (eds), 2000 *Cultures in Contact: Scandinavian Settlement in England in the Ninth and Tenth Centuries*, Studies in the early middle ages 2, Brepols N V, Turnhout

Hall, R A, Rollason, D W, Blackburn, M, Parsons, D N, Fellows-Jensen, G, Hall, A R, Kenward, H K, O'Connor, T P, Tweddle, D, Mainman, A J and Rogers, N S H, 2004 *Aspects of Anglo-Scandinavian York*, The Archaeology of York 8(4), Council for British Archaeology, York

Hamerow, H F, 1993 *Excavations at Mucking. Volume 2: the Anglo-Saxon Settlement. Excavations by M U Jones and W T Jones*, English Heritage, London

Hamerow, H F, 2002 *Early Medieval Settlements: the Archaeology Of Rural Communities in Northwest Europe 400–900*, Oxford University Press, Oxford

Hamerow, H F, 2006 ' "Special deposits" in Anglo-Saxon settlements', *Medieval Archaeology* 50, 1–30

Hardy, A, Dodd, A and Keevill, G, 2003 *Aelfric's Abbey*, Thames Valley Landscapes Monograph 15, Oxbow Books, Oxford

Haughton, C and Powlesland, D, 1999 *West Heslerton: the Anglian Cemetery*, Landscape Research Centre Archaeological Monograph Series 1, Yedingham

Hawkes, S C, 1982 'Finglesham: a cemetery in east Kent', in Campbell (ed) 1982, 24–25

Hawkes, S C and Grainger, G, 2006 *The Anglo-Saxon Cemetery at Finglesham, Kent*, Oxford University School of Archaeology Monograph 64, Oxford

Heighway, C M and Bryant, R, 1999 *The Golden Minster: The Anglo-Saxon Minster and Later Medieval Priory of St Oswald at Gloucester*, Council for British Archaeology Research Report 117, York

Higham, N (ed), 2007 *Britons in Anglo-Saxon England*, Boydell Press, Woodbridge

Hill, P H, 1997 *Whithorn and St Ninian: the Excavation of a Monastic Town 1984–91*, Sutton Publishing, Stroud

Hills, C, 1977 *The Anglo-Saxon Cemetery at Spong Hill, North Elmham: Part I, Catalogue of Cremations nos 20–64 and 1000–1690*, East Anglian Archaeology Report 6, Norfolk Archaeological Unit, Norfolk Museum Service, Gressenhall

Hills, C and Penn, K, 1981 *The Anglo-Saxon Cemetery at Spong Hill, North Elmham: Part II, Catalogue of Cremations nos 22, 41 and 1691–2285*, East Anglian Archaeology Report 11, Norfolk Archaeological Unit, Norfolk Museum Service, Gressenhall

Hills, C, Penn, K and Rickett, R, 1984 *The Anglo-Saxon Cemetery at Spong Hill, North Elmham: Part III, Catalogue of Inhumations*, East Anglian Archaeology Report 21, Norfolk Archaeological Unit, Norfolk Museum Service, Gressenhall

Hills, C, Penn, K and Rickett, R, 1987 *The Anglo-Saxon Cemetery at Spong Hill, North Elmham: Part IV, Catalogue of Cremations (nos 30–2, 42, 44A, 46, 65–6, 2286–799, 3324 and 3325)*, East Anglian Archaeology Report 34, Norfolk Archaeological Unit, Norfolk Museum Service, Gressenhall

Hills, C, Penn, K and Rickett, R, 1994 *The Anglo-Saxon Cemetery at Spong Hill, North Elmham: Part V, Catalogue of Cremations (nos 2800–3334)*, East Anglian Archaeology Report 67, Field Archaeology Division, Norfolk Museums Service, Gressenhall

Hinton, D A (ed), 1983 *25 Years of Medieval Archaeology*, University of Sheffield, Department of Prehistory and Archaeology, Sheffield

Hirst, S M, with Nixon, T, Rowsome, P and Wright, S, 2004 *The Prittlewell Prince: the Discovery of a Rich Anglo-Saxon Burial in Essex*, MoLAS, London

Holbrook, N and Thomas, A, 2005 'An early-medieval monastic cemetery at Llandough, Glamorgan: excavations in 1994', *Medieval Archaeology* 49, 1–92

Hope-Taylor, B, 1977 *Yeavering: An Anglo-British Centre of Early Northumbria*, DoE Archaeological Report 7, Her Majesty's Stationery Office, London

Hutcheson, A R J, 2006 'The origins of King's Lynn? Control of wealth on the Wash prior to the Norman Conquest', *Medieval Archaeology* 50, 71–104

Jones, M and Dimbleby, G (eds), 1981 *The Environment of Man: the Iron Age to the Anglo-Saxon Period*, British Archaeological Reports 87, Oxford

Jones, M J, Stocker, D and Vince, A, 2003 *The City by the Pool: Assessing the Archaeology of the City of Lincoln*, Lincoln Archaeological Studies 10, Oxbow Books, Oxford

Knight, J K, 2005 'From villa to monastery: Llandough in context', *Medieval Archaeology* 49, 93–107

Knowles, D and St Joseph, J K, 1952, *Monastic Sites from the Air*, Cambridge University Press, Cambridge

Lane, A and Campbell, E, 2000 *Dunadd: an Early Dalriadic Capital*, Oxbow Books, Oxford

Lang, J, 1991 *Corpus of Anglo-Saxon Stone Sculpture 3: York and Eastern Yorkshire*, British Academy, Oxford University Press, Oxford

Leeds, E T and Chadwick, S (ed), 1957 'Notes on Jutish art in Kent between 450 and 575', *Medieval Archaeology* 1, 5–26

Lewis, C, 2007, 'New avenues for the investigation of currently occupied medieval rural settlement', *Medieval Archaeology* 51, 133–163

Loveluck, C P, 1998 'A high-status Anglo-Saxon settlement at Flixborough, Lincolnshire', *Antiquity* 72, 146–161

Loveluck, C, 2001 'Wealth, waste, and conspicuous consumption: Flixborough and its importance for mid and late Saxon settlement studies', in H Hamerow and A MacGregor (eds), *Image and Power in the Archaeology of Early Medieval Britain: Essays in Honour of Rosemary Cramp*, 78–130, Oxbow Books, Oxford

Loveluck, C and Atkinson, D, 2007 *The Early Medieval Settlement Remains from Flixborough, Lincolnshire*, Oxbow Books, Oxford

Lowe, C, 2006 *Excavations at Hoddom, Dumfriesshire: an Early Ecclesiastical Site in South-west Scotland*, Society of Antiquaries of Scotland, Edinburgh

Lucy, S, 2000 *The Anglo-Saxon Way of Death: Burial Rites in Early England*, Sutton Publishing, Stroud

McKinley, J I, 1994 *The Anglo-Saxon Cemetery at Spong Hill, North Elmham, Part VIII: the Cremations*, East Anglian Archaeology Report 69, Norfold Archaeological Unit, Norfolk Museum Services, Gressenhall

Meaney, A, 1964 *A Gazeteer of Early Anglo-Saxon Burial Sites*, Allen and Unwin, London

Millett, M and James, S, 1983 'Excavations at Cowdery's Down, Basingstoke, Hampshire, 1979–81', *Archaeological Journal* 140, 151–279

Morris, C, 2000 *Craft, Industry and Everyday Life: wood and woodworking in Anglo-Scandinavian and Medieval York. The Archaeology of York 17, The Small Finds, 13*, Council for British Archaeology, London

Morris, R, 1983 *The Church in British Archaeology*, Council for British Archaeology Research Report 47, London

Morris, R, 1989 *Churches in the Landscape*, J M Dent & Sons, London

O'Sullivan, D, 2001 'Space, silence and shortage on Lindisfarne. The archaeology of asceticism', in H Hamerow and A MacGregor (eds), *Image and Power in the Archaeology of Early Medieval Britain: Essays in Honour of Rosemary Cramp*, 33–52, Oxbow Books, Oxford

Owen-Crocker, G R, 1986 *Dress in Anglo-Saxon England*, Manchester University Press, Manchester

Owen-Crocker, G R, 2007 'British wives and slaves? Possible Romano-British techniques in "women's work" ', in Higham (ed) 2007, 80–90

Parsons, D, 1979 'Past history and present research at All Saints' Church, Brixworth', *Northamptonshire Past Present* 6, 61–71

Powlesland, D, 1986 'Excavations at Heslerton, North Yorkshire', *Archaeological Journal* 143, 53–173

Powlesland, D, Lyall, J, Hopkinson, G, Donoghue, D, Beck, M, Harte, A and Stott, D, 2006 'Beneath the sand: remote sensing, archaeology, aggregates and sustainability. A case study from Heslerton, the Vale of Pickering, North Yorkshire, England', *Archaeological Prospection* 13:4, 291–299, Chichester

Rahtz, P A, 1973 'Monasteries as settlements', *Scottish Archaeological Forum* 5, 125–135, Edinburgh

Rahtz, P A, 1976a *Excavations at St Mary's Church, Deerhurst, 1971–73*, Council for British Archaeology Research Report 15, London

Rahtz, P A, 1976b 'The building plan of the Anglo-Saxon monastery of Whitby Abbey', in D M Wilson (ed), *The Archaeology of Anglo-Saxon England*, 459–462, Methuen, London

Rahtz, P A, 1979 *The Saxon and Medieval Palaces at Cheddar: Excavations 1960–62*, British Archaeological Reports 65, Oxford

Rahtz, P A, 1993 *English Heritage Book of Glastonbury*, English Heritage, London

Rahtz, P A and Watts, L with Taylor, H and Butler, L 1997 *St Mary's Church Deerhurst, Gloucestershire: Fieldwork, Excavations and Structural Analysis, 1971–84*, Reports of the Research Committee of the Society of Antiquaries of London, 55, Boydell, Woodbridge

Rahtz, P A, Woodward, A, Burrow, I, Everton, A, Watts, L, Leach, P, Hirst, S, Fowler, P and Gardener, K, 1992 *Cadbury Congresbury 1968–73: a late/post-Roman Hilltop Settlement in Somerset*, British Archaeological Reports 223, Oxford

Radford, C A R, 1957 'The Saxon house: a review and some parallels', *Medieval Archaeology* 1, 27–38

Rickett, R, 1995 *The Anglo-Saxon Cemetery at Spong Hill, North Elmham, Part VII: the Iron Age, Roman and Early Saxon Settlement*, East Anglian Archaeology Report 73, Field Archaeology Division, Norfolk Museum Services, Gressenhall

Rodwell, W, 2001 *Wells Cathedral: Excavations and Structural Studies, 1978–93*, 2 vols, English Heritage Archaeological Report 21, London

Rodwell, W, and Rodwell, K, 1982 'St Peter's Church, Barton on Humber: excavation and structural study, 1978–81', *Antiquaries Journal* 62, 283–315

Smith, I M, 1991 'Sprouston, Roxburghshire: an early Anglian centre of the eastern Tweed basin', *Proceedings of the Society of Antiquaries of Scotland* 121, 261–294

Sutherland, D S and Parsons, D, 1984 'The petrological contribution to the survey of All Saints' Church, Brixworth, Northamptonshire: an interim study', *Journal of the British Archaeological Association* 137, 45–64

Taylor, H M, and Taylor, J, 1965 *Anglo-Saxon Architecture 1 and 2*, Cambridge University Press, Cambridge

Taylor, H M, 1978 *Anglo-Saxon Architecture 3*, Cambridge University Press, Cambridge

Thomas, C, 1981 *Christianity in Roman Britain to AD 500*, Batsford, London

Tipper, J, 2004 *The grubenhaus in Anglo-Saxon England*, Landscape Research Centre, Yedingham

Tweddle, D, Moulden, J and Logan, E, 1999 *Anglian York: a Survey of the Evidence*, The Archaeology of York AY7(2), Council for British Archaeology, York

Webster, L E, 1986 'Anglo-Saxon England 400–1100', in I Longworth and J Cherry (eds), *Archaeology in Britain since 1945. New Directions*, British Museum Publications, London

West, S E, 1985 *West Stow. The Anglo-Saxon village*, 2 vols, East Anglian Archaeology 24, Ipswich

West, S E, 2001, *West Stow Revisited*, St Edmundsbury Borough Council

Wilson, D M, 1970 revised 1980 *The Vikings and their Origins*, Thames and Hudson, London

Wilson, D M (ed), 1976 *The Archaeology of Anglo-Saxon England*, Methuen, London

Wilson, D M and Hurst, J G, 1957 'Medieval Britain in 1956', *Medieval Archaeology* 1, 147–171

CHAPTER 4
LOOKING TO THE FUTURE OF MEDIEVAL ARCHAEOLOGY

By MARK GARDINER *and* STEPHEN RIPPON

A symposium entitled 'Looking to the Future' was held as part of the Society for Medieval Archaeology's 50th anniversary to reflect upon current and forthcoming issues facing the discipline. The discussion was wide-ranging, and is summarized here under the topics of the research potential of development-led fieldwork, the accessibility of grey literature, research frameworks for medieval archaeology, the intellectual health of the discipline, and relevance and outreach.

INTRODUCTION

Many of the events celebrating the 50th anniversary of the Society for Medieval Archaeology, and the resulting papers in this volume, look back over progress and past achievements. In contrast, the final workshop, 'Looking to the Future', held at the Institute of Archaeology, University College London, on 3 May 2008, reflected upon the current problems and the way in which the subject might develop in the future. The event was not intended to agree a definite road-map for the future, even if such a thing were possible, a subject which was itself debated. Instead, it was designed to stimulate discussion on current questions and it succeeded in that respect. Contributions were made not only by the speakers who provided short introductions to the topics, but also by many of the people who attended and offered comments. There was much vigorous discussion also amongst the break-out groups which met to discuss the formal papers, and by individuals over lunch, during the coffee-breaks and in the reception afterwards. The participants came from across the archaeological profession and included those working in the contract sector, in museums, universities and the state bodies.

It is hardly possible in the present paper to reflect the range of views expressed at that meeting, although a number of themes did emerge very strongly and some degree of consensus was achieved on certain subjects during the course of discussion. It is these which are examined below. It is more than a convention to issue the usual warning that the comments reflect the opinions of the authors and are not necessarily the views of the Society as a whole. Indeed, they are not necessarily even the views of the authors, but reflect their understanding of the mood of the meeting. What we have tried to capture are some of the concerns that were being expressed at the workshop and some possible ways ahead.

THE RESEARCH POTENTIAL OF DEVELOPMENT-LED FIELDWORK

One of the deep rifts which continues to run through the practice of archaeology is the division between academic study and research on the one hand, and contract or development-led survey and excavation on the other. This problem is, of course, not unique to the archaeology of the Middle Ages. There was a strong view at the meeting that this gap was not being bridged, but, if anything, was growing wider. This gulf has become accentuated with the professionalization of archaeology which began in the 1980s. As archaeological units moved from state or local authority support to commercial funding, the money which had been available for undertaking research was eroded. Developers could not be expected to support even those fundamental tasks which were necessary to archaeological research, such as the establishment of ceramic type-series. Intensified commercial competition between units has tended to drive up the efficiency of work in the field, but drive down the scope of the post-excavation process. A developer has an interest in removing the archaeological constraint on building, but most have little interest in the detail of post-excavation work. Planning Policy Guidance note 16 (PPG16) laid the foundations for commercial archaeology in England and established the principle that a developer must pay for the costs of dealing with any archaeological remains that will be damaged or destroyed. It is concerned primarily to ensure that remains are excavated and recorded. It makes little reference to the post-excavation process, referring only to 'a programme of archaeological work in accordance with a scheme of investigation' (Department of the Environment 1990, para 30). The consequence is, as one contributor to the discussion commented, that archaeological units often only regarded pottery as a means of dating: the character of the assemblage, what it might indicate, how it might have formed, and even the fabrics present, are of little concern.

At the heart of this problem are two competing views of archaeological fieldwork. It may be regarded as a routine site operation, comparable to laying a pipeline or constructing foundations. Such operations may, of course, run into problems when unexpected ground conditions are discovered during the works. Generally speaking, such work is straightforward and with proper preparation contractors can complete the work on time and to a budget to fulfil a specification. Archaeological contracting has increasingly adopted such an approach, since it has to be integrated into development project planning. This approach bears little resemblance to the alternative conception of archaeological work which exists, amongst other places, in universities. Excavation or survey is not viewed as a routine operation, but is intended to be an investigation of an original character into a new problem. The aims are fundamentally different. In the first, the central concern is the completion of the task according to a programme. In the second, the character of the task is constantly redefined as the excavation progresses and the only aim is to reveal new information.

A project design for the archaeological contractor is a statement of procedure. On a research excavation, it is a statement of the intellectual aims.

It is quite possible for these two approaches to exist in parallel, as they have done for many years. The excavation units have provided important data through development-led work, and this has allowed insights and the material for new syntheses, for the prehistoric and medieval periods (Bradley 2007; Gilchrist and Sloane 2005; Yates 2007). Yet there is a strong sense that the information obtained in this way is an incidental by-product of the archaeological contracting. It is not central to it. There is also a lurking fear that the information gathered is only a tiny fraction of the evidence which might be found by adopting rather different approaches. One archaeological contractor commented in a reply to a questionnaire sent by Naomi Sykes, 'We are a unit not a research facility — developers don't like to pay, they just want their site cleared of archaeology and to comply with the law'.

This problem, how to add a research-value to development-led fieldwork, is one of the major challenges of our discipline. We should be clear that there is no implicit criticism of archaeological units which are on the whole performing their role very efficiently. The question is whether society should expect developers to pay for units to behave rather more like research facilities. If we decide that this is an unreasonable demand, then we must question why are we asking them to pay for any excavation? Excavation is, or at least it should be, research or it is nothing. It is a particularly pressing question for the Middle Ages, more so even than for the prehistoric and Roman archaeology, because of the quantity of development-led work carried out in still-occupied settlements — both urban and rural — which commonly had medieval antecedents.

STANDARDS, ACCESSIBILITY AND GREY LITERATURE

One crucial result of the expansion in development-led archaeology has been an increase in the amount of fieldwork, and the number of resulting reports. Some projects are seen through to full publication in reports ranging from major monographs to short notes in county-based journals, with the comprehensive archives deposited in museums. In many cases, however, the results of development-led projects are not published. All that is produced is a typescript report placed in the historic environment record. There is now a very considerable body of this so-called 'grey literature' and initiatives such as OASIS: *Online AccesS to the Index of archaeological investigationS* (http://oasis.ac.uk) are beginning to make these reports more accessible to field units and academics alike. We also have a summary list of all archaeological work undertaken from the Archaeological Investigations Project (http://csweb.bournemouth.ac.uk/aip/aipintro.htm). As a profession, however, we have yet to realize the full research potential of this data in the form of synthesis. Much of the data preserved only as grey literature relates to relatively small-scale fieldwork, but cumulatively this has huge potential for research. Even small, unstratified assemblages of material in sufficient numbers can start to shed light on the origins and development of currently occupied medieval settlements.

Concerns were also expressed in the London meeting about the quality of some grey literature, and there is clearly a need for national standards in the content and presentation of reports. Indeed, the matter of standards in professional archaeology was a subject that came up in discussion on several occasions in relation to all stages of development-led work, including the involvement of specialists from the design stage of a project through to its completion, developing approaches for sampling topsoil before it is machined off (including metal-detecting), having a consistent strategy for sieving stratified deposits for both artefacts and palaeo-environmental material, and the quality of reports. There is clearly a role here for specialist groups such as the Medieval Pottery Research Group, who have published their *Minimum Standards for the Processing, Recording, Analysis and Publication of Post-Roman Ceramics* (http://www.medievalpottery.org.uk/occpap2.htm), although national bodies such as the Institute for Field Archaeologists, the Association of Local Government Archaeological Officers (ALGAO), and Cadw, English Heritage, Historic Scotland, and in Ireland, the National Monuments Service and the Institute of Archaeologists of Ireland, also need to take a lead.

RESEARCH FRAMEWORKS

Many research frameworks have been produced in the past by archaeologists in Britain, each seeking to establish an agenda for future study of aspects of the discipline. One recent example is the Medieval Settlement Research Group's policy statement that 'sets out a research and management framework for medieval rural settlement and landscape' (http://www.britarch.ac.uk/msrg/msrgpolicy.htm). English Heritage has recently embarked upon a series of regional research frameworks that comprise a 'resource assessment', summarizing our current state of knowledge, and a 'research agenda' to guide future work (http://www.english-heritage.org.uk/upload/pdf/frameworks.pdf). Most of these regional surveys are now published in various forms (eg http://www.somerset.gov.uk/somerset/cultureheritage/heritage/swarf/publications/). In addition to research frameworks with a geographical emphasis, other examples have a period focus, such as the Prehistoric Society's *Research Frameworks for the Palaeolithic and Mesolithic of Britain and Ireland*. The question of whether medieval archaeology should have such a research strategy was discussed at the London meeting.

There are potentially many benefits to such a project, including the improvement of dialogue between the different sectors of modern archaeology (universities, national government bodies, local authority curatorial staff, field units), the provision of a better rationale for the archaeological work required as part of PPG 16, and the targeting of resources, for example, through doctoral projects and university research. The Society for Medieval Archaeology did attempt a somewhat similar initiative in the mid-1980s when it made recommendations to HBMC, as English Heritage was then known, about priorities and policies for the allocation of grants (Society for Medieval Archaeology 1987). At that time the Society held back from making a more general statement about research priorities and 20 years later the task of agreeing such a thing for medieval archaeology seems even more formidable.

In the last two decades medieval archaeology has greatly expanded its means of investigation and its subjects of study. In addition to the traditional buried or 'dirt' archaeology with which we are all familiar, research resources include documentary and cartographic sources, field- and place-names, and the physical fabric of the historic environment: standing buildings, field boundaries, woodland and so on. Collectively, these form the historic environment. In the 1980s there was little consideration of the questions of gender or of the investigation of perception. Our appreciation of the role of artefacts as symbols has subsequently developed and we regard landscapes in an entirely different way (see papers by Gilchrist, Gerrard, Reynolds and Rippon, this volume). The lateral growth of the scope of medieval archaeology makes it difficult to agree a list of research issues. As a result, there is a very real danger that any such list will reflect the personal enthusiasms of the compilers and command little wider support. Other issues to consider include how to keep research frameworks up-to-date — something that is out-of-date could do more damage than good? — and how to encompass the potentially diverse stakeholders, which might include academics, the curatorial sector, field units, and local communities, in a research strategy project.

It is easier to compile a research agenda for specific sites, areas or problems than to create such a thing for a broad subject such as medieval archaeology as a whole. A narrow research agenda is also likely to be more effective because focused research plans stand a better chance of being realized than airy aspirations. Historic Scotland, for example, has adopted the narrower approach with the creation of research plans for the conservation management and display of individual monuments in care. These identify gaps in understanding, aim to publish the results of backlog project work on the sites, and create programmes for new intervention and recording. In this respect the research agendas for the Scottish properties in care resemble those for World Heritage Sites (WHS) which are increasingly linked to research programmes. Research plays an initial role in the presentation of the case for inscribing a site on the World Heritage List through the establishment of authenticity and integrity. UNESCO also requires that the state of each WHS is monitored to prevent deterioration, something which can only be determined through a study of their baseline condition. Finally, the management guidelines suggest that research should be included in the site management plans of each WHS (Darvill 2007). Specific research programmes linked with sites or small areas are likely to bring real rewards in extending understanding.

In Ireland the approach has been rather different. Instead of establishing a research agenda for contract archaeology, which has expanded massively in the last decade, the Heritage Council has offered substantial grants to synthesize the data produced. The grant scheme known as INSTAR encourages cooperation between archaeological companies, the state sector and higher education, and aims to translate the results of development-led work into 'knowledge about Ireland's past'. Although a number of themes have been identified, the grant scheme is essentially open to proposals for research. This scheme does not set an agenda and is a 'downstream' or post-hoc approach to research. It draws together the results of excavation, rather than informing the process of digging or decisions about what should be dug.

THE INTELLECTUAL HEALTH OF THE DISCIPLINE

The impact of theoretical approaches has been considerably less far-reaching in the archaeology of the Middle Ages than in prehistory. This has been a cause of disquiet for those who have argued for a more theoretically aware approach to the medieval period (see Gilchrist, this volume). Theoretical developments in the humanities have sometimes been assimilated into our subject in an implicit rather than explicit manner. Matthew Johnson made the point at the London meeting that there was no such thing as a-theoretical archaeology. All archaeology has a theoretical stance, even if that position is taken for granted rather than explicit. His concern was that familiarity with the subject breeds an acceptance of the terms of the debate, rather than a critical re-examination of them. We do not consider our position in relationship to the material we are studying, but take it as read. Johnson contrasted the more abstract formulations of early medieval archaeology with the more material subjects which are studied by later medievalists (Figure 4.1). Put simply, the later Middle Ages seems much more familiar to us, while the pagan world of peoples in the 5th and 6th century does not. Questioning the basis of what we take for granted may yield new insights. The difference in perspectives on the early and later medieval periods, however, is not just a product of our familiarity or our desire to examine the basis of our knowledge, but is also the result of a greater abundance of written evidence. We are able to move beyond simple abstractions to deal with the details of people's lives in the 14th and 15th centuries in a way that is not possible in earlier periods.

The relationship between archaeological and written evidence still remains a source of some concern, to judge from the discussion in London. A number of contributors expressed an uncertainty about the role of material culture in the study of a period for which there are also numerous documents. This seemed to be a curious return to the fear expressed in the 1970s that archaeology was merely there to provide illustrative material to a narrative which was being written by historians. Strangely enough, this does not seem to be a significant concern for post-medieval archaeologists who are working within a period when there is an even greater quantity of written evidence. They have embraced the alternative perspectives provided by material culture to present views which may examine aspects of the past not revealed by written sources, and even to challenge the documentary record (see, for example,

Early Medieval Archaeology	Later Medieval Archaeology
Race	Church
People	Village
Tribe	Field
Migration	Castle
Invasion	Landscape

FIGURE 4.1. Contrasting subject matter in early and later medieval archaeology (after Matthew Johnson).

various papers in Tarlow and West 1999). Of course, some medieval archaeologists have done exactly the same, and the academic skirmishes which have become known as 'the Battle for Bodiam' exemplify this point (Goodall 1988; see also Hansson, this volume). The argument has been not just about whether Bodiam was simply a military structure. It also concerns how far we can accept at face value the written statement in the Patent Rolls of the purpose and intentions of Sir Edward Dallingridge, the builder of the castle. The rolls state that the castle was licensed to be built as a defence against the French. Archaeological opinion has largely accepted that the building had a strongly symbolic purpose. There is still much fight left in the defenders of the older view that it was a primarily a defensive building, as the latest contribution to the affray indicates, but most have concluded that the Battle for Bodiam has been won and have moved on to consider other fortifications (Platt 2006).

Bodiam Castle is an instance in which medieval archaeology has set the agenda, not merely followed that provided by historians. The recent study of castles has opened up new perspectives on elite culture, so that it has become necessary to look afresh at the symbols by which the gentry and nobility sought to display their status. The subject of dining, for example, has benefited from studies of the spaces in which it took place and the rituals of meals, as well as the types of food consumed (Brears 2008; Sykes 2004). In this area, it has not been a matter of contrasting the material and written sources of evidence, but of combining them to provide a deeper understanding of the social role and symbolism of food and eating (see also papers by Müldner and Sykes, this volume). Archaeology and history are not competing to provide an interpretation of the past, but should be seen as offering alternative and preferably complementary routes to it.

The problem of fitting archaeology into the wider agenda was highlighted by a number of contributors at the London meeting, particularly those working in commercial archaeology. The difficulties of moving beyond the business of excavation to the wider study of archaeology have already been discussed. The problem of integrating knowledge about the past into a wider synthesis is even bigger still. Terry O'Connor has noted that 'historians have continued to write as if for other historians, and ... there is little indication that the archaeologists will hasten to cross (let alone demolish) the disciplinary fence ... There is a sense of two cultures talking together, but not necessarily *to* each other' (quoted at the London meeting by Naomi Sykes, from O'Connor 2008). Very few would now advocate that we should practise medieval archaeology as if it was the study of a period without documents, forging a view of the past which was independent of history and ignored written sources entirely. Our view of, for example, the late medieval landscape is infinitely more detailed than is possible for any prehistoric period. Not only do we have an abundance of surviving remains, but also written evidence, later maps, place-names and even folklore to draw upon in understanding the landscape of the past (on folklore, see Franklin 2006; Phythian-Adams 1999). The sheer quantity of the evidence is actually part of the problem. It is often hard to see how archaeology fits into this immensely complex picture and be sure that we not only know about evidence from other disciplines, but understand its limitations. We are asking medieval archaeologists to be experts in their own field, and also to have more than a passing acquaintance with numerous other disciplines. Few other subjects make such a demand upon their practitioners, and it is hardly surprising that we often are reluctant to demolish those disciplinary fences.

During the course of her presentation in London, Naomi Sykes noted that the application of scientific investigation is less common for the later medieval period than the early Middle Ages, and *much* less common for the medieval period than prehistory. The assumption seems to be that, for periods in which written sources are more abundant, scientific analysis can contribute little. This cannot be correct. Although we have written evidence for the European trade in stockfish in the late Middle Ages, for example, this does not mean that isotopic sourcing of the catch-sites of the fish is superfluous and can contribute no new information (Barrett *et al* 2008). Equally, we have a better understanding of the problems, particularly the difficulties of communication, which may have led to the sinking of the *Mary Rose* now that isotopic studies have demonstrated that a third or a half of the crew were of foreign origin (Bell *et al* 2008). This observation augments our knowledge of the tragedy and helps us to interpret the historical record anew. These examples are chosen from some of the more recently published work.

It is difficult to take a dispassionate view of the intellectual health of the medieval archaeology. Measured in one way, there are considerable grounds for optimism. There is an almost overwhelming stream of articles and books about the medieval period. The reading lists which we give to our undergraduate students bear very little resemblance to those which we received when we first studied the subject. There are numerous signs that there is immense activity in almost all branches of the subject. Yet, in spite of this, there are some nagging doubts that all is not entirely rosy. Too often the contributions have been made by individuals who are working entirely on their own in the pursuit of a particular subject of research. We lack the size of community to ensure that there are a number of researchers applying themselves to the same or similar problems and willing to debate interpretations. The Battle for Bodiam is one of a fairly small number of examples of a subject which has been fiercely, though constructively, contested. Understanding does not only advance in that way, of course, but critical engagement is a sure sign of the intellectual liveliness of a subject area. There is a concern too that medieval archaeology may be splintering into separate areas — artefacts, landscapes, religion — each with its own pre-occupations aired in their specialist journals, and that the subject lacks a coherent vision of the past as a whole.

Finally, there is the problem that we began with. It is entirely unsatisfactory for the subject to be divided into those who gather evidence (the contract archaeologists) and those who analyse it (generally, the university archaeologists). The process of excavation is not neutral activity of observation and recording; it is an active engagement with soils and walls. Excavation is informed by our assumptions and what we expect. We record what seems significant: interpretation takes place at the trowel's edge, to use Ian Hodder's term (Hodder 1999, 92). The idea that we will gather the information now and interpret it at some time in the future is unrealistic. Of course, it is possible to reinterpret excavation records, but too often the things we wish had been examined have remained unconsidered and unrecorded. It may seem unrealistic to say this in the world of competitive tendering, but should not all excavation be committed to the wider enterprise of understanding the past?

RELEVANCE AND OUTREACH

Many of the topics discussed above touch upon the central issue of relevance and accessibility, including the need to make the results of archaeological research in the medieval period relevant to scholars working with other source material and in other disciplines. With large sums of public and private money now spent on studying medieval archaeology we have a responsibility to make the results of our research available to as wide an audience as possible. In part, this means publishing the results of fieldwork through a variety of media and for a number of audiences in different forms, ranging from scholarly monographs through to popular booklets and websites. Museums have been fulfilling part of this role by providing the interface between people and the past for several centuries through traditional galleries containing artefacts, and more recently by means of open-air museums containing vernacular buildings. The presentation of archaeological sites that are accessible to the public is another way that we can reach out to the public. Some rural sites may be seen without requesting prior permission because they are in the ownership of a local authority or the National Trust, and others because they are crossed by a public footpath or are in areas in England and Wales covered by the 'right to roam' under the Countryside and Rights of Way Act (Dyer 1989, 1990). However, archaeological earthworks are not readily comprehensible to the non-specialist and information panels may be a useful aid to interpretation. Presenting complex information derived from a multi-disciplinary subject, such as archaeology, is in itself a specialist task that has to take into account factors such as the National Curriculum for schools, access for those with difficulties with mobility, and social agendas such as social inclusion. As such, museums will continue to be at the forefront of making research into medieval archaeology relevant.

Like any academic discipline, one of the most important ways that we can reach out to the wider public is through involving them in practical work, but in recent decades this has proved very difficult to do within the context of development-led work, such are the constraints of tight schedules, health and safety, and insurance concerns. University-led research projects have more scope for involving members of the local community although these will always be relatively few in number, and may involve considerable travel time and cost. There are, however, other ways that professional archaeology can promote community involvement, of which Carenza Lewis's Higher Education Field Academies are a fine example. The HEFA involves digging small test-pits within the gardens and other open spaces of rural villages and hamlets, a straightforward task that is ideal for people with no previous experience. Each 1m square pit is dug in 10cm layers, the spoil is sieved for finds and tested for geochemical indicators of historic occupation, and the details of each layer are recorded. In addition to introducing 14- to 15-year-old pupils to archaeology, and increasing their confidence and aspirations to continue in education, the results of

20 or so test-pits in an average-sized village can reveal important information about these currently occupied medieval settlements, within which archaeological research is otherwise rarely carried out (Lewis 2007).

CONCLUSION

This summary has sought to reflect the mood of the London meeting which was quietly reflective rather than celebratory of the 50 years of achievement. Delegates to the symposium were cautious about the future. Uncertainties about funding and employment in the commercial sector and in museums, together with crises in the teaching of archaeology and funding of research in universities, produced a sombre and reflective air. The sense of excitement and even confidence which had accompanied first the discovery and later the publication of such remarkable sites as Sutton Hoo, Yeavering and Cheddar palace seemed to belong to a different era. There was a sense of considerable uncertainty about directions in which medieval archaeology might develop. It is not clear whether the allegiances of medieval archaeology should belong to a study of the past represented by history and historical geography, or to the broader social sciences and their concern with critical theory.

Yet this tentative view of the subject reflected at the London meeting seems remarkably distant from the perception held by the wider public, who see archaeology as an exciting and vibrant discipline. Medieval archaeology, in particular, is perceived as dealing with interesting and relevant subjects, including Vikings, castles and parish churches. There is a very strong desire among the public to know about and make sense of the remains of the past which they can see around them, a desire which stems from a need to understand their position in the present. Reflecting upon the last 50 years of medieval archaeology should also encourage us to look more positively to the future. There has never been a Golden Age when there were sufficient funds for all the work we wanted to do. Archaeologists have muddled through and, in spite of all the problems and obstacles, it has been a most remarkable half-century of discovery. Is there any real reason to think that the next 50 years will not be quite as extraordinary?

BIBLIOGRAPHY

Barrett, J, Johnstone, C, Harland, J, Van Neer, W, Ervynck, A, Makowiecki, D, Heinrich, D, Hufthammer, A K, Bødker Enghoff, I, Amundsen, C, Christiansen, J S, Jones, A K G, Locker, A, Hamilton-Dyer, S, Jonsson, L, Lõugas, L, Roberts, C and Richards, M, 2008 'Detecting the medieval cod trade: a new method and first results', *Journal of Archaeological Science* 35, 850–861

Bell, L S, Lee Thorp, J A and Elkerton, A, 2008 'The sinking of the Mary Rose warship: a medieval mystery solved?', *Journal of Archaeological Science* 36:1, 166–173

Bradley, R, 2007 *The Prehistory of Britain and Ireland*, Cambridge University Press, Cambridge

Brears, P, 2008 *Cooking and Dining in Medieval England*, Prospect Books, Totnes

Darvill, T, 2007 'Research frameworks for World Heritage Sites and the conceptualization of archaeological knowledge', *World Archaeology* 39:3, 436–457

Department of the Environment, 1990 *Planning Policy Guidance: Archaeology and Planning (PPG 16)*, Her Majesty's Stationery Office, London

Dyer, C C, 1989 'Medieval settlement sites which are accessible to the public', *Medieval Settlement Research Group Annual Report* 4, 17–19

Dyer, C C, 1990 'Medieval settlement sites which are accessible to the public (part 2)', *Medieval Settlement Research Group Annual Report* 5, 8

Franklin, L, 2006 'Imagined landscapes: archaeology, perception and folklore in the study of medieval Devon', in S Turner (ed), *Medieval Devon and Cornwall: Shaping an Ancient Countryside*, 144–161, Windgather Press, Macclesfield

Gilchrist, R and Sloane, B 2005 *Requiem: the Medieval Monastic Cemetery in Britain*, Museum of London Archaeology Service, London

Goodall, J, 1998 'The Battle for Bodiam Castle', *Country Life* 116 (16 April 1998), 58–63

Hodder, I, 1999 *The Archaeological Process: an Introduction*, Blackwell, Oxford

Lewis, C, 2007 'New avenues for the investigation of currently occupied medieval rural settlements: preliminary observations from the Higher Education Field Academy', *Medieval Archaeology* 51, 133–163

O'Connor, T, 2008 'Review of C M Woolgar, D Serjeantson and T Waldron (eds), *Food in Medieval England: Diet and Nutrition*', *Environmental Archaeology* 13, 89–90

Phythian-Adams, C, 1999 'Environments and identities: landscape as cultural projection in the English provincial past', in P Slack (ed), *Environments and Historical Change: the Linacre Lectures*, 118–146, Oxford University Press, Oxford

Platt, C, 2006 'Revisionism in castle studies: a caution', *Medieval Archaeology* 51, 83–102

Society for Medieval Archaeology, 1987 'Archaeology and the Middle Ages. Recommendations to the Historic Buildings and Monuments Commission for England', *Medieval Archaeology* 31, 1–12

Sykes, N, 2004 'The dynamics of status symbols: wildfowl exploitation in England AD 410–1550', *Archaeological Journal* 161, 82–105

Tarlow, S and West, S (eds), 1999 *The Familiar Past?: Archaeologies of Later Historical Britain*, Routledge, London

Yates, D, 2007 *Land, Power and Prestige: Bronze Age Field Systems in Southern England*, Oxbow Books, Oxford

WEBSITES

http://oasis.ac.uk
http://csweb.bournemouth.ac.uk/aip/aipintro.htm
http://www.medievalpottery.org.uk/occpap2.htm
http://www.britarch.ac.uk/msrg/msrgpolicy.htm
http://www.english-heritage.org.uk/upload/pdf/frameworks.pdf.
http://www.somerset.gov.uk/somerset/cultureheritage/heritage/swarf/publications/
http://www.arch.cam.ac.uk/aca/fa/index.html

PART II

REGIONAL TRADITIONS IN MEDIEVAL ARCHAEOLOGY

CHAPTER 5
TRIBES AND TERRITORIES, PEOPLE AND PLACES: 50 YEARS OF MEDIEVAL ARCHAEOLOGY IN BRITAIN

By CHRISTOPHER GERRARD

This paper considers the development of medieval archaeology in Britain since the formation of the Society for Medieval Archaeology. While progress in the 1930s is acknowledged, the main focus is upon key projects, personalities, sponsorship, societies and influential institutions such as universities and the Council for British Archaeology, as well as technical and conceptual initiatives since 1957. Among the characteristics of the British discipline, it is argued, are its many research groups, the intellectual diversity of their participants, the range of research publications, the underlying quality of database and fieldwork, the impact of 'rescue archaeology' in the 1970s and 1980s and of developer funding today. An uneasy relationship with archaeological theory is highlighted and particular use is made of postgraduate thesis data to quantify past and present subject trends. Methodological initiatives and the contribution of works of corpus and catalogue are stressed.

INTRODUCTION

This essay provides a background to recent developments in medieval archaeology in Britain and raises themes to be discussed in greater detail by other contributors to this volume. Four sub-sections below consider organizations and infrastructure, funding, methods and ideas, all with reference to personalities and projects, making use of evidence taken from autobiographies, obituaries, textbooks, reviews, interviews and contemporary archives. The venture is a risky one, not least because many of the actors are still alive and a lack of historical distance invites partisan bias (Söderqvist 1997), but also because the weight of evidence can seem unremittingly English. There are, however, compelling reasons to attempt it. The last half-century in medieval archaeology represents not merely an additional accretion of 50 years of further practice, it has also been a time of foundational contributions, institutional innovation and the development of powerful new techniques. One simple but quantifiable

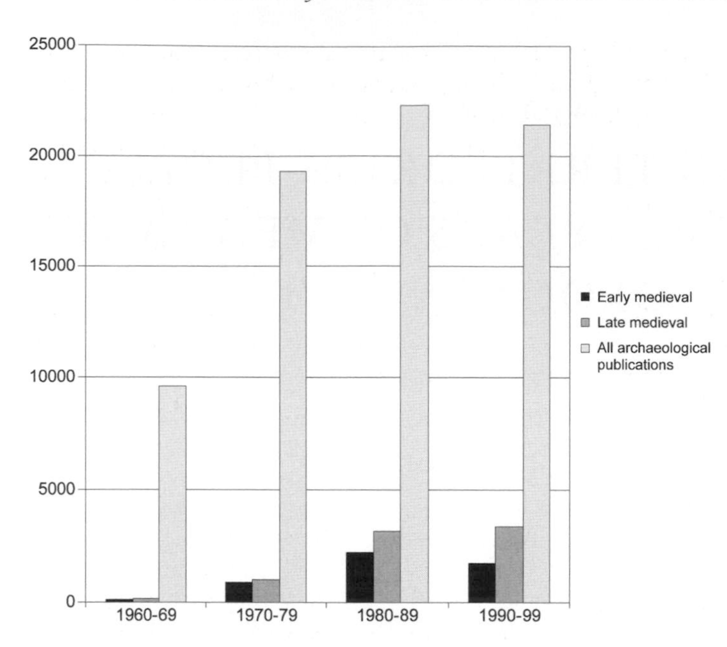

FIGURE 5.1. Numbers of publications in medieval archaeology by decade 1960–2000. These statistics are taken from the British and Irish Archaeological Bibliography (BIAB) by totalling 'migration and early medieval' and 'medieval' publications and calculating these as a percentage of the total number of publications. The figures are not comprehensive but likely to reflect the broad trends. Later medieval publication topics now double those for the early medieval period.

measure of this is the number of publications being produced within the subject area, over 5000 in the 1980s and again in the 1990s, while medieval archaeology's 'market share', the number of medieval publications as a percentage of all archaeology outputs in Britain and Ireland, has surged from just 3% in the decade 1960–69 to 24% in 1990–99 (Figure 5.1).

DEVELOPMENTS BEFORE 1957

Any review of this kind must first acknowledge the long, if rather weak, roots of the subject in the foggy indifference of earlier centuries (Gerrard 2003) and then its strengthening framework during the first half of the 20th century, particularly for Anglo-Saxon archaeology, by Gerard Baldwin Brown, Tom Kendrick, Thurlow Leeds and others. Interest in later medieval archaeology was a little slower in maturing; deprived of an early and enduring fascination with cemetery sites, momentum came from different directions. After the First World War and especially during the 1920s, the priority lay in the clearance and consolidation of standing architecture of the later medieval State and Church. Among the endeavours of the day were the restoration of castles like Beaumaris in North Wales, where the moat was partially cleared and flooded again, and abbeys like Rievaulx in North Yorkshire, where spoil and fallen masonry were pick-axed, trenched and trucked away on a light railway constructed for the purpose (Fergusson and Harrison 1999). The motive for these gargantuan projects was architectural display and education for a public now absorbed in rambling guides and, for the more privileged, motoring into the countryside. Academic direction was rarely strictly archaeological, at least as we might define it today.

The term 'medieval archaeology' is thought to have first been used by W G Hoskins in a lecture title at Vaughan College, Leicester, in April 1937 (Beresford 1992), and there is convincing evidence of a shift in attitude during that decade. Excavation targets became more diverse, showing that there was more to medieval archaeology than standing structures (eg Jope and Threlfall 1958), and there were innovations, too, in the study of finds. The *London Museum Medieval Catalogue* illustrated 'a typical cross-section of medieval practice and craftsmanship, both rich and poor' (Ward Perkins 1940), grouping objects by function for the first time and making explicit use of archaeological objects such as those recovered by Pitt Rivers from his excavations at Caesar's Camp near Folkestone in 1878. Archaeology at this time was also gaining in credibility with more established disciplines like history (eg Stenton 1943), particularly economic history (eg Postan 1973; Miller 1984; Bentley 2005)[1] and geography, which was by then emerging as an independent field. Geographical techniques like distribution maps quickly found their way into the writing of the culture-history of the Middle Ages (eg Jope 1952).

After the war, interest accelerated. Anglo-Saxon archaeology had been 'very largely a museum study' until that point (Wilson 1965), centred on objects and the cemeteries from which they came, but now fieldwork came into its own at Thetford, Yeavering and elsewhere, while the pre-war excavations at Sutton Hoo did much to stimulate public interest through its spectacular grave goods. William Grimes with the Roman and Medieval London Excavation Council excavated monastic sites and bomb-damaged churches like St Bride's in the capital, the first sustained campaigns of urban archaeology (Grimes 1968; Milne 1997). Other cities followed suit. Popular interest in local history, fed by new university extra-mural departments, typified a more multi-disciplinary approach and was consolidated by the enormous success of W G Hoskins' *The Making of the English Landscape* (1955) and Maurice Beresford's *History on the Ground* (1957). Their fusing of landscape and documents into a new kind of forensic history was to prove hugely influential on later practitioners and, in the year 1957, we have a real sense of a subject 'in the making'. Certainly it was genuinely innovative in its methods, particularly in its use of aerial photography, and especially the obliques taken by Kenneth St Joseph flying Austers and Cessnas out of Cambridge airport after 1945. This brought many new discoveries, the Northumbrian royal sites at Millfield and Yeavering among them. The volume *Medieval England: an Aerial Survey*, on which St Joseph collaborated with Maurice Beresford, first appeared in 1958.

ORGANIZATIONS

Societies and research groups

It was precisely 20 years after Hoskins had first used the term 'medieval archaeology' that the Society bearing that name was formed. The year 1957 was therefore not so much a true beginning as a moment of consolidation, a recognition of past achievements and an anticipation of what was to come. A small group with similar goals already existed and now set about formalizing their links, principally with a view to improving dissemination of ideas and information. There is no doubting either the value of the Society's Journal and monographs as a vehicle for publication, or the role it has performed in bringing people together through meetings and conferences in order to share values, expertise and standards. The Society is not above criticism, however. Its original vision might be taken to task for not engaging with a wider public (although this is only in many ways a recent development), and perhaps too for not promoting European themes with sufficient vigour (though see Wilson, this volume). Even within the terms of its own remit there has been a lack of thorough engagement with parts of its constituency, with younger scholars certainly, and with Welsh and Scottish medievalists (who have inclined towards journals with a regional or national identity, such as *Archaeologia Cambrensis*). In the 1980s and 1990s there was a particular sense that the Journal content did not accurately reflect the conceptual trends of the day. Richard Hodges saw 'a distinct danger of medieval archaeology becoming an academic backwater' (Hodges 1982, 11) and complained of the 'dinosaur-like mood' at Society meetings (Hodges 1989). Peter Ucko (1990, xii) went further: 'it seems at least questionable whether it [medieval archaeological enquiry] should really remain accepted within the mainstream of the archaeological discipline'. Senior historians meanwhile directly accused processual archaeologists of 'status-seeking' when they stressed the scientific nature of the discipline (Hobsbawn 1979), while others were taken aback by their appetite for fashionable language. 'If this is the way forward in archaeological reporting', wrote Colin Platt (1978), 'it is clearly time for some of us to get off.' Clearly, in such an atmosphere, the Society ran the risk of alienating a sizeable and influential part of its membership, precisely that part it had striven to bring into the fold from the beginning (Gerrard, this volume). Yet in failing to attract publication on these debates (the medieval contributions to the 1986 TAG conference appeared elsewhere, for example), the Society also came to be regarded by some as overly 'conservative' in tone, too 'old guard'. Likewise, the Journal has never attracted many 'crossover' articles from archaeological scientists, who mostly favour a more technically minded readership in international science journals. This both limits the appreciation of new scientific approaches by those who consider themselves first and foremost as social scientists, and hinders wider discussion. Whatever the reasons, successive Journal editors would all agree that synthetic articles, critical reviews and thematic material have generally been harder to come by (Dickinson 1983, 37), whereas there has always been a steady diet of excavation accounts, often with funding attached.

Of course, the Society is far from the only publication portal for medieval archaeologists. Numismatics and place-name studies are rare visitors to the pages of *Medieval Archaeology* and a peculiar characteristic of the subject is that overlaps are encouraged with other subjects. Relevant articles are to be expected in the *Agricultural History Review* or *Vernacular Architecture*, for example. Shorter items of international relevance may be directed to *Antiquity*, theory to *Archaeological Review from Cambridge*, groups of thematic papers towards *World Archaeology*, pottery to *Medieval Ceramics*, landscapes to *Landscape History*, architecture to the *Journal of the British Archaeological Association* and so on; while large fieldwork projects may find a multi-period readership more readily in the *Archaeological Journal* or the *Antiquaries Journal*. Even this list is far from exhaustive; there are also county journals which may carry articles of national and international importance, while edited volumes of papers, books and monographs complete the more traditional 'research outputs'. By comparison, the diversity of format and delivery which is a hallmark of our subject would be inconceivable in the sciences, where short, multi-authored articles, often electronically delivered, are now much more the norm.

Another outcome of working in a field with fuzzy, ill-defined disciplinary edges with varied methodologies is a tendency for interests to fracture along thematic lines and for practitioners to seek out more comfortably defined 'knowledge domains'. An unusual feature of medieval archaeology (particularly the later medieval period) has been the contribution of its 'groups', for example, the Medieval Pottery Research Group (since 1974; Blake 2000) and the Castle Studies Group (since 1987). These introduce finely meshed sets of concepts and methods, and thereby form a tight focus for debate and publication on specific topics,[2] not to mention field trips and workshops which the period Society promoted with lesser frequency and sometimes greater cost. Members of the Medieval Settlement Research Group, and its original guise the Deserted Medieval Village Research Group (DMVRG) which was established in 1952, form an especially cohesive multi-disciplinary research cluster. They have had a real and practical impact on the distribution map of known desertions, doubling their number over a 25-year period as well as influencing the selection of sites to be dug (Beresford *et al* 1980) (Figure 5.2).[3] There have never been any formal ties between the period Society and the various research groups (and in the case of the Society for Church Archaeology, another society altogether, formed in 1996); the groups are not sub-sets of the period Society, as some people outside the medieval world naturally assume. One reason for this is that the DMVRG preceded the formation of the period Society by five years, a second being that the revenue so generated would be insufficient for such a broad umbrella of activities, while yet a third is that the model of the interdisciplinary research group is ultimately derived from the Fenland Research Committee in the 1930s, which itself claimed no patronage from any one society in its day (Smith 2006, 109).

This range of possible affiliations and the segmented feel it gives to the discipline, not to mention the diversity of individual experience represented in the membership (archaeologists, architects, historians, etc) perhaps explains why we do not easily fall victim to 'disciplinary socialization' (Becher and Trowler 2001, 41–103). This is a popular notion with historians of science but, in fact, observation suggests that there is little 'community of practice' or consensus of identity among us (for example in clothing, speech patterns, etc), at least in a way routinely expressed by other professionals. For archaeologists in academic life, for example, these hidden rules of behaviour (where they can be said to exist at all) tend to be constituted through their employing university and mainly through individual departments, and the same may well be true of other employing institutions. Unlike some science subjects where research is a team effort, archaeology is frequently conducted by individuals who operate independently and seek recognition in a multiplicity of different ways, so they are in no sense 'socialized' into a uniform code of behaviour.

FIGURE 5.2. Members of the Medieval Settlement Research Group visiting the AHRC-funded Whittlewood Project at Akeley, Buckinghamshire, in February 2002. From left to right: Harold Fox, Christopher Taylor, Anthony Fleming, Mark Page, Carenza Lewis, Paul Blinkhorn, Stephen Coleman, Christopher Dyer, Mark Gardiner, Richard Page, Mike Thompson, John Hurst, Mick Aston, Sandy Kidd, Stephen Rippon. The Barbour and fleece as expressions of disciplinary socialization? (Photograph: Teresa Hall)

The institutional matrix

The achievements of the past half-century must be assessed within a wide matrix of heritage initiatives and institutions. Among these are the revival of the archaeology branch of the Ordnance Survey under Charles Philips from 1947, which accurately located and characterized so many of our field monuments (until its demise in 1978), and the local authorities who developed the old OS cards into Sites and Monuments Records (now Historic Environment Records). Many counties, such as Durham and Somerset, have abridged versions of these databases available online and they can be formidable tools for development-control and research. Another important innovation is the Portable Antiquities Scheme, a collaborative and sometimes controversial project led by the British Museum to seek out and record archaeological objects found by members of the public (often metal-detectorists). Some 300,000 finds of all periods have been recorded to date, a selection appearing each year in *Medieval Archaeology*, and the patterning of discoveries has already changed our concept of inland markets and trading sites between the 7th and 9th centuries (Ulmschneider and Pestell 2003). Earlier initiatives include: the National Buildings Record, which

a

b

FIGURE 5.3. (a) An event at Worcester Cathedral during National Archaeology Week. In July 2008 there were 430 events to choose from, including opportunities for excavation, guided tours, exhibitions and workshops. Scotland has an Archaeology Month during September. (b) Chris Gaffney demonstrating the use of geophysics at Shapwick, Somerset, to enthralled children. (Photographs: Mick Aston)

gave us a reliable description of the medieval building stock for the first time after 1940 and led to the introduction of 'listing'; the opening up of national and county record offices which provide unprecedented access to maps and original documents;[4] the evolving standards of the Victoria County History[5] and the various Royal Commissions for Historic Monuments whose excellence in field archaeology set the bar so high. It was work by the Commission, for example, which led to the discovery of the earthwork remains of later medieval gardens and unsuspected ornamental landscapes (Everson 1998). This brief round-up must also include the Council for British Archaeology, so often at the forefront of research policy over the past 50 years from its earliest period-based committees to the more specialist thematic groups of the later 1960s to the mid-1990s. Of the latter, two of the most productive were for churches (Butler 1983; Morris 1983; Blair and Pyrah 1996) and urban research (eg Heighway 1972; Barley 1975; Schofield and Leech 1987; for waterfront archaeology, Milne and Hobley 1981). Part of their success was the rotating constituency which brought together otherwise dispersed expertise (Heyworth 2006). Today the CBA is not only a notable publisher but remains at the forefront of wider engagement, including National Archaeology Weeks (Figure 5.3a and 5.3b) and Young Archaeologists Clubs. This mission has also been helped along in recent years by free entry to national museums, including engaging and attractive displays like those at the National Museum of Scotland and Sutton Hoo, and the popularity of television archaeology (Aston 2000, 26–42).

Universities

Since 1957 there has been a huge overall expansion in the number of students and universities, matched both by increases in academic staff in archaeology departments and the overall number of other institutions who teach archaeology.[6] If the 533 staff returned in the 2008 Research Assessment Exercise within the archaeology subject area can be taken as a guide to overall numbers today, then that figure is more than twice the 211 full-time academic archaeologists counted 20 years ago (Austin 1987). Of those 533 individuals, there were 51 academic staff with medieval interests in 25 Archaeology departments in Britain, of which 13 are professorial grade.[7] Without dwelling on the historical development of those posts, almost all departments today contain one or more medieval archaeologists working in Britain with major groupings (in 2008) at York (6), Durham (4), Glasgow (4) and Reading (4). These numbers would rise considerably if all staff working on medieval archaeology on a global scale were to be counted; UCL would include at least 6 members of staff on that basis. Even so, medieval archaeologists with north-west European interests must represent around 10% of the total number of academic archaeologists in British universities.

Universities offer a healthy range of postgraduate programme options; medieval doctoral projects are regular funding winners and several reach publication (eg Devlin 2007). For further detail, an analysis of postgraduate theses in British and Irish universities over the past 40 years can compare between numbers of students undertaking medieval topics against those for other periods or working in different regions of the globe (Figure 5.4). The absolute dominance of foreign topics, regularly reaching

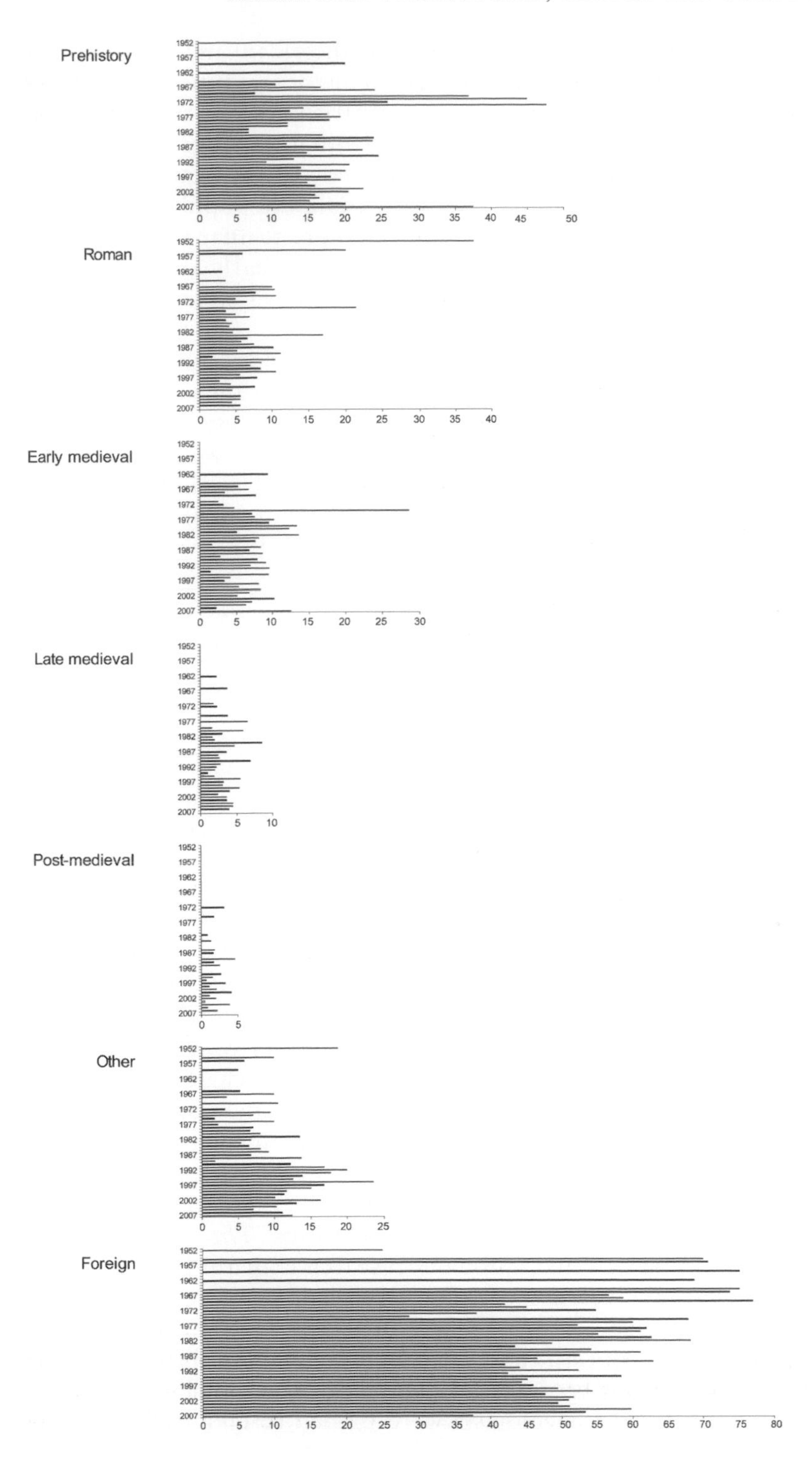

FIGURE 5.4. Doctoral and MPhil theses by decade and subject. The statistics from which these graphs are generated are taken from the online *Index to Theses*, 'a comprehensive listing of theses with abstracts accepted for higher degrees by universities in Great Britain and Ireland'. The data have been 'cleaned' to remove duplicate entries, the later deposition date being registered. Not all universities are represented, but most are and no thesis is knowingly excluded, so the broad patterns are probably representative. Some completions may have been absorbed into other subject areas, particularly architecture, geography, history and theology.

over half the total number of successfully examined theses in any one year, is especially striking. Within the range of British topics prehistory dominates, routinely producing between 15–20% of the total; early medieval topics are the next most popular, with Roman and later medieval more or less of equal standing and numbers of post-medieval theses trailing behind. Among the trends in the figures could be noted a faltering enthusiasm for Roman topics after *c*1990; the popularity of early medieval topics in the second half of the 1970s, and the more regular appearance of later medieval topics after 1980, with an intriguing lapse in the early 1990s. Overall, however, the relative proportions have changed little in 40 years, something of a surprise in itself.

Major funds are provided directly to individual archaeology projects by the Research Councils (especially AHRC and NERC) including, over the past five years, four projects costed at over £300,000[8] and another eight over £40,000 (all to be spent over several years). Information is not released to show just how many applicants there are in any one year specifically for medieval archaeology projects; only successful applications are named. Nevertheless, there are sufficient data to demonstrate that medieval archaeology holds its own against prehistorians and Romanists, though it does rather less well for science-based projects.

Significant monies for research are also provided by charities (including the Leverhulme Trust) and local and national societies, not least the Society of Antiquaries and the Society for Medieval Archaeology. Many activities, however, have no obvious funding streams attached, in particular those of a more synthetic kind engaged in by lone university scholars. Time to pursue these ventures is, in effect, funded by most universities from the Government income granted on the basis of qualitative judgements on the 'outputs' from university departments. These assessments of the research performance of UK universities have been undertaken since 1992 by the Universities (now Higher Education) Funding Council in order to reward quality. This is not the place for a detailed dissection of the culture of audit on archaeological research (such as Norris and Oppenheim 2001). All would agree, however, that the impact on universities has been far-reaching. Research is now more 'managed' and 'impact-seeking' and far greater importance is attached both to place of publication and to deadlines, the inevitable product of any cyclic assessment exercise. Among the less predictable side-effects is the disincentive for academic authors to write textbooks, even to experiment with the latest portable digital technologies which will presumably provide e-textbooks to the next generation (Walford 2000). In the current climate, some consider products like this frivolous, a trend which explains why so many US and Australian archaeology textbooks are being adapted to the British market, though there are some welcome exceptions (eg Graham-Campbell and Valor 2007). Some ask how the vivid writing and general readership of W G Hoskins' *The Making of the English Landscape* (1955) would be rated in today's research climate? How many of the essential tomes on library shelves, some of them a decade or more in maturing, might today be deemed an indulgence?

Another specific cause for concern, and one not unrelated to the pressure to deliver publications, is the faltering tradition of fieldwork. The 'golden' age in the 1960s and 1970s when university archaeologists were funded to take on large-scale research excavations, as were Peter Addyman at Ludgershall Castle and Rosemary Cramp at Wearmouth and Jarrow (Figure 5.5), has long gone. Archaeology departments can struggle to justify high quality practical training against a background of declining undergraduate income for teaching. In turn, this shifts the burden of vocational skills training onto employers, mostly the commercial units; a trend which is perhaps illustrative of the increasingly narrow base from which archaeological education is now delivered. Medieval archaeology owes more than is often given credit to an army of 'extra-mural' departments headed up by the likes of Mick Aston, Phil Barker, Tony Brown, David Hill, David Parsons, Trevor Rowley and a host of others. Their engagement with the amateur sector, local societies and the Workers' Educational Association cannot be overlooked, even if it is a shrinking and disfavoured sector today.

The role of the State

One organization which has had direct but untrumpeted impact on the development of medieval archaeology in Britain is the Ancient Monuments and Historic

FIGURE 5.5. Rosemary Cramp guides a site visit at Jarrow in 1966 with David Wilson (far right), Sir Eric Fletcher (later Lord Fletcher of Islington) (in glasses), Eric Parsons and Harold Taylor (to his left). (Photograph courtesy of Rosemary Cramp)

Buildings Directorate, in its various incarnations. Many inspectors developed medieval specialisms, as Bryan O'Neil did for fortifications (eg O'Neil 1946) and Gerald Dunning for artefacts (for an appreciation, see Hurst 1982), and this tradition continued in the 1960s and 1970s with John Hurst for pottery (eg Hurst 1962–63), Stuart Rigold for architecture (eg Rigold 1967) and Roy Gilyard-Beer for monasteries (eg Gilyard-Beer 1955). Patrick Faulkner, whose concepts on spatial planning in medieval castles and houses became influential (eg Faulkner 1958), was an architect with Ancient Monuments. From being a body primarily concerned with the preservation of Guardianship sites, the numbers of inspectors grew rapidly after 1947 in order to cope with the scheduling programme, advice on grant-aiding and threats posed to field monuments. John Hurst was in charge of developing a policy for medieval archaeology, identifying key sites for excavation, finding directors for projects and disposing of limited funds. It must be remembered that Brian Hope-Taylor's excavations at Yeavering in Northumberland (Hope-Taylor 1977), like those at early medieval rural settlements such as West Stow (West 1985), investigated types of site which were quite unknown in their day, and much of this should be attributed to John Hurst's astute selection of sites (Andrew Saunders, pers comm). It is easy to forget just how recent is our understanding of some major medieval monument classes. Surprising though it may seem, there were still only two published modern excavations of deserted medieval villages as late as 1970, at Hangleton in Sussex (Holden 1963) and Upton in Gloucestershire (Hilton and Rahtz 1966). By 1991, some 2400 excavations had taken place on early medieval sites, with 6500 excavations on later medieval sites, about 35% of all excavations then recorded (RCHME 1991).

Later developments at the Ministry included the Ancient Monuments Laboratory, the Central Excavation Unit and the appointment of full-time digging inspectors like Brian Davison who, for the first time, combined post-excavation work into their job description. Significant initiatives since the 1980s include the backlog publication programme (which allowed work to begin in earnest on many significant sites), the writing of national and regional research frameworks (eg Petts and Gerrard 2006) and the Monuments Protection Programme. The latter has accelerated the process of protecting important medieval archaeological remains and led to important research in its own right, most notably the mapping of rural settlement from 19th-century series of 6-inch to 1 mile maps (Roberts and Wrathmell 2000).

Overall, while there are undoubtedly many more archaeologists involved with medieval archaeology than there were in 1957, precise numbers are not easily calculated.[9] Museum staff, local government posts, commercial units and self-employed pottery and small finds specialists have varied duties and their job titles are not especially revealing. The 'boilerhouse' of British medieval archaeology, particularly those professional archaeologists who undertake much of the excavation and fieldwork, certainly generates the most funds, but they often have little freedom to determine the direction of their day-to-day research interests, still less time to pursue them freely and they are often less vocal both in publication and through representation on committees.

THREATS AND RESPONSES

In the 1950s the bomb-damaged city centres of several medieval towns were investigated with limited public and charity money. But far greater damage came with urban regeneration schemes in the mid-1960s at which point more generous State funds began to be deployed. The predicted UK population growth led planners to believe that a city the size of Leeds would need to be built every year for the next 40 years (Lane 1966). In response, there was a predictable onslaught on historic towns: a fifth of the centre of Worcester was removed without recording in the 1960s, Gloucester lost a quarter of its 603 listed buildings between 1947 and 1971 (Aston and Bond 1976, 214), Scottish cities like Aberdeen, Dundee and Stirling were heedlessly redeveloped, and many other cases could be cited. But with this loss came opportunity, and by the late 1960s some 60 English towns had seen sustained archaeological excavation, among them Southampton, where a large port settlement of 8th to 9th-century date was discovered on the west bank of the river Itchen (Morton 1992); King's Lynn, where the first timber waterfront was exposed in 1964 (Clarke and Carter 1977), and Winchester, where 'rescue' became subordinate to 'research' in a long-term programme which saw 2% of the walled area of the town being examined in all (Biddle 1983). That work first began in 1961 and proceeded on an essentially voluntary basis, working for part of the year only, until the founding of the Winchester Research Unit in October 1968 (Figure 5.6). The Unit, fully funded for five years and with permanent paid staff, was the first of its kind in the UK and proved an important model for British archaeology as a whole, not least because excavation was carried out without period bias. It is perhaps not well enough appreciated that the Unit was set up on the explicit model of the urban teams then operating in all the main towns of Poland, which Birthe and Martin Biddle had visited at the invitation of the Polish Institute for the History of Material Culture in the summer of 1966.

Archaeology in the countryside was also under threat. The deep ploughing of land had begun in earnest during the war, and the drive towards improving farm productivity continued with the introduction of the Common Agricultural Policy. Fixed price levels for farm products proved an understandable temptation to larger farmers who now intensified production by draining pasture and converting to arable with well-documented consequences for archaeological landscapes. Other immediate threats came from motorways (Figure 5.7), new towns and quarrying. The largest excavation ever conducted in Europe in its day, 18 hectares in all, was at Mucking between 1965 and 1978, in advance of gravel extraction (Hamerow 1993).

In countering these threats, Ancient Monuments legislation offered far less effective protection than it does today. The most satisfactory option was 'Guardianship', in which the responsibility for maintenance and management of an archaeological monument was transferred to the State. This provided opportunities for excavation in advance of scheduling or conservation work, designed to make sites more visible and understandable. Launceston Castle, excavated by Andrew Saunders, was one site which benefited from this policy (Saunders 2006). Otherwise, the scheduling of a monument in the 1970s merely provided for a window of three months for negotiation and action once the landowner advised of a threat. For selected sites

FIGURE 5.6. Martin Biddle's excavations at Wolvesey Palace in Winchester in August 1970. West Hall, looking south-east. The work was funded throughout by the Ancient Monuments Inspectorate in its various guises. Wolvesey was only one of four major and a number of smaller excavations in progress at the same time in Winchester, all staffed each summer by about 200 volunteers, both students (from 25 different countries) and more senior people on leave from universities and other jobs for the summer or part of it. For an account of principles and procedures see Biddle 1990, 9–23, with Table 2. (Photograph: Martin Biddle)

there might be some payment of compensation which then delayed destruction and permitted 'rescue' excavation. The inadequacies of the process were well understood but those who had drafted the 1931 Act, at a time of agricultural depression it must be remembered, simply did not envisage threats to preservation from the plough, nor could they have anticipated the significance placed by archaeologists on field monuments rather than the structures and more readily appreciable earthworks which were the focus of their own interests. It was not until later that the *Ancient Monuments and Archaeological Areas Act 1979* finally bolstered protection for sites on the schedule. By 1995, a total of 14,478 monuments were protected by scheduling in England, of which 333 (2.3%) were early medieval and 3500 (24%) later medieval (Darvill and Fulton 1998, 193–195; no figures available outside England). Inevitably, some classes of monuments are better represented than others; 89% of all Welsh castles are scheduled, for example (Avent 2000).

As a result of high-profile events such as the destruction at New Palace Yard at Westminster in 1972 and the formation of the organization RESCUE, in which

FIGURES 5.7a and 5.7b Rescue excavation at Sadler's Wood (Oxon) on the M40 corridor in 1972. Earthwork survey and subsequent excavation revealed a substantial mid 13th–14th century farmstead. The work was confined to the width of the new road and the full plan of the site was not recovered (Chambers 1974). (Photographs: Mick Aston)

medieval archaeologists were prominent campaigners, there was a marked rise in income for archaeology (Heighway 1972). Most of the major units came into being in the early 1970s: Norwich in 1971; York and Lincoln a year afterwards. In England the total rescue archaeology budget rose from £150,000 in 1967 to 7 million 20 years later (Wainwright 2000). Sites like Coppergate in York, which unearthed the best-preserved evidence of Viking Age urban life in the Danelaw (Hall 2004), were funded in part from that rescue budget, as well as by interested individuals and companies (Figure 5.8). In London alone there was a 300% rise in the numbers of urban excavations between 1970 and 1990 so that analysis and publication inevitably fell behind. Even when core funding was withdrawn from the units in the early 1980s, excavators could take advantage of money and labour from job creation programmes. Excavations at the High Street in Perth (Bogdan and Wordsworth 1978) and at Hulton Abbey in Staffordshire (Klemperer and Boothroyd 2004) were among those funded in

FIGURE 5.8. Richard Hall, Director of Archaeology at the York Archaeological Trust, and Peter Addyman, former Trust director, explain the 16–22 Coppergate excavations (1976–81) in York to the Prince of Wales. The well-preserved archaeological evidence for trade, industry and housing at Viking Age urban centres, like York and Flaxengate in Lincoln, has captured the imagination of the public and transformed our understanding of the Scandinavian presence in the 9th and 10th centuries. Together the Jorvik Viking Centre, DIG (formerly the Archaeological Resource Centre) and Barley Hall have attracted 14 million visitors since their opening. (Photograph: York Archaeological Trust)

this way. By the late 1980s, however, it was the major developers who were already making the significant donations towards costs, particularly in the larger cities and towns. The vast majority of medieval sites, however, remained vulnerable, as events at the Rose Theatre illustrated, and this brought about a momentous change in policy guidance in February 1990 (Biddle 1989).

Planning Policy Guidance Note 16, which placed the burden on developers to fund archaeological fieldwork, has had a tremendous impact on the way in which all archaeology is undertaken in Britain (Biddle 1994). On the positive side, more money now finds its way into archaeology, strategies for sampling are now more sophisticated, and the geographical range and variety of sites under excavation is extensive. Recent excavations in small towns in Wales in advance of redevelopment are one example of the broadening agenda (Marvell 2001). Under exceptional circumstances, small-scale work can also broaden into a fruitful research project, as it did at Llandough near Penarth, where over a thousand early medieval burials were excavated in 1994 by Cotswold Archaeology (Figure 5.9) (Holbrook and Thomas 2005).

FIGURE 5.9. In 1994, 1026 7th- to early 11th-century inhumations were excavated at Llandough, near Penarth (Glamorgan), by Cotswold Archaeology in advance of development. The excavation was sponsored by Ideal Homes Wales Ltd (now part of Persimmon Homes) with Cadw funding the stratigraphic analysis of the site and the National Museums and Galleries of Wales co-ordinating reports on the artefacts. The early medieval monastic cemetery, the largest early medieval population so far excavated in Wales, was the subject of a PhD project at the University of Bristol. This is an excellent example of collaborative funding from private and public sectors to achieve a published result.

On the negative side, not all parts of our medieval heritage are subject to the familiar controls. Ecclesiastical buildings, for example, have long lain outside the secular system of listed building consent (Bianco 1993), and even elsewhere there are frustrations when commercial interests so rarely match academic priorities as to where and what to dig. Few recently excavated rural sites have produced lengthy structural sequences, for example, though this need not always be the case, as Raunds demonstrates (Boddington 1996). Nevertheless, the scale of individual excavations has generally shrunk, while the number of interventions has risen. Particularly worrying is the severely limited finds analysis for some sites and the restricted circulation of results. A vast body of data now exists which is not available to the discipline, and some worry that this may never be so.

METHODS

The fact is that, for many of us, time travel even back as far as 1957 would be a startling experience, not least because of the revolution in office technology during the intervening decades. No one now will admit to being impressed with the photocopier or microfiche reader, those forgotten innovations which pre-date the onslaught of the personal computer (in the early 1980s), the internet and the digital image; even the term 'software' is itself one year younger than the Society for Medieval Archaeology. We live now among the Google generation in a globalized academic landscape in which, to take one mildly eyebrow-twitching example, the major works of Gerard Baldwin Brown (1849–1932) are most easily accessed as 'flip books' through the Canadian Library services (Baldwin Brown website). Such digital eccentricities are barely worthy of comment for those who routinely navigate the delights of COPAC, ADS and the abstract service British and Irish Archaeological Bibliography (BIAB). Among the online resources now available to the medievalist are volumes 1–50 of *Medieval Archaeology* through the Archaeological Data Service, dendrochronological dates for vernacular buildings (Vernacular Architecture Group 2000), the database of excavated monastic cemeteries (Gilchrist and Sloane 2005), the digital archive for the Whittlewood settlement project including images and video clips (Dyer *et al* 2005) and POTWEB which shares the Ashmolean Museum's ceramic collections over the internet (Haslam *et al* 2001). Not all digital initiatives are without their controversy, however, as scepticism in some quarters at the seductive visual appeal of Historic Landscape Characterization (HLC) demonstrates (eg Williamson 2007).

By 1995 the national archaeological database in England had registered around 3000 monuments of early medieval date (1% of the total) against 60,000 of later medieval date, the latter representing about 21% of all the known monuments (Darvill and Fulton 1998, 195; no figures available outside England). These figures reflect advances in prospection techniques and improvements in coverage. Geophysics, pioneered at sites such as South Cadbury by Leslie Alcock in the late 1960s, was still limited on large-scale projects as late as the early 1990s, and even then only rarely integrated fully into research methodology (Gaffney *et al* 2007). In part this was due to the limited technology available at the time. Though early medieval timber buildings can still be elusive, nowadays much larger areas can be revealed using magnetic techniques, new technology which has been accelerated due to the need for rapid and extensive results for PPG16-type surveys. Other new tools of prospection over the last half-century include test-pitting, soil chemistry and fieldwalking; the latter it seems first applied to a medieval landscape project by the Oxford University Archaeology Society in 1964. Technology now extends the possibilities of remote sensing across previously unresponsive soil types using infrared and ultraviolet frequencies and LiDAR, which effectively scans the ground surface using laser technology to produce extremely detailed elevation models. The latest prospection tools incorporate both high-resolution GPS and Geographical Information System (GIS) for modelling landscapes and site surveys (eg Chapman and Fenwick 2002).

On site, there is now greater sophistication in every aspect of excavation, from recording systems to trenching strategies and materials collection. As late as 1970 it was common enough for only a selection of animal bones to be retained for further study. Environmental sampling, too, was the exception, but now our interpretation of the historic landscapes is greatly changed; gone are the impenetrable forests of Anglo-Saxon settlers. These methodological developments have affected British archaeology as a whole, of course, but where medieval archaeology can lay some claim to leading the way is in its adoption of open-area excavation. Though Gerhard Bersu introduced open-area excavation to British medieval archaeology with his excavations at the Viking site of Vowlam on the Isle of Man (Bersu 1949), 30 years later Hurst (1971, 86) pointed out how 'prehistorians and Romanists have been slower to see its potential'. The technique had already been in use for some years in Denmark and Holland before it made its debut at the deserted medieval village of Wharram Percy (Figures 5.10a and 5.10b), a reminder of the many ways in which internationalism has been a force for change (for additional detail, see Dickinson 1983, 38). Philip Rahtz was among the first to try out open-area excavation at Chew Valley Lake in 1953–55 (Rahtz and Greenfield 1977), as was Hope-Taylor at Yeavering in 1953–62 (see Cramp, this volume). The technique only became common in the 1960s and was trialled on a large scale during urban excavations at the Old Minster and Lower Brook Street in Winchester where the development of the town was unpicked from the Iron Age to the late medieval period (Biddle and Kjølbye-Biddle 1969). With it came other novelties, among them the extremely precise recording of pebble scatters and shallow post-sockets at Hen Domen castle under Phil Barker's direction (Higham and Barker 2000) and the use of a vertical tripod-mounted camera to produce a composite mosaic of photographs at the Templar preceptory at South Witham in 1967 (Mayes 2002).

More recently, on-site recording of excavation pushed forward again in the 1990s, notably at West Heslerton (Powlesland 1996) where clickable plans, section drawings and videoclips of excavations at the early Anglo-Saxon settlement are managed within GIS. Likewise, digitized photogrammetry, such as that used at Wardour Castle (Reilly 1998), has transformed the recording of historic buildings and builds upon the 'structural criticism' advocated by Joan and Harold Taylor for Anglo-Saxon architecture (Taylor 1972) and by Warwick and Kirsty Rodwell at Barton-upon-Humber, Rivenhall and elsewhere (eg Rodwell and Rodwell 1982). Major

a

b

c

FIGURE 5.10. (a) Maurice Beresford (1920–2005) and John Hurst (1927–2003) at Wharram Percy on 18 July 1989 for the presentation of the volume of studies on rural settlements dedicated to them by friends and colleagues. Excavation at Wharram between 1950 and 1992 can claim to be one of the key benchmarks in the making of medieval archaeology, not only for methodological reasons and for its contribution to the understanding of medieval rural settlement and landscape, but for the influence it projected and continues to project well beyond its trenches through the many diggers who participated. (Photo: Mick Aston). (b) Professors at Wharram. From left to right: Philip Rahtz (in the hat), Chris Dyer and Dave Austin. Bob Croft (in shorts) explains stratigraphical complexities. (Photo: Mick Aston). (c) Wharram Percy. Excavation of the 12th-century camera block discovered beneath House 10, summer 1957. John Hurst, in white shirt (back centre); Maurice Beresford (back left), looking left. Alongside him a domestic mangle has been adapted to raise buckets out of the excavation. (Photograph: Paul Stamper)

advances in dating include the systematic application of dendrochronology, especially to waterfronts and roof types where it has hugely strengthened the study of medieval buildings (Hillam 1998; for recent Scottish applications, see Crone 2000), work recently complemented by new luminescence methods of dating brick (Bailiff 2007). The discovery of radiocarbon dating has had greatest impact on early medieval chronologies, though less so here than in prehistory.

In the same way, many aspects of the post-excavation process have been refined; the Harris matrix was invented during analysis of site records at the Winchester Research Unit (Harris 1975). Almost every category of find is now more rigorously understood. Medieval pottery, for example, now benefits from new techniques of fabric analysis from petrology to ICP, radiography to investigate the forming processes of pottery, and the analysis of organic residues. Detailed ceramics analysis of this kind builds upon extended regional and national sequences, surveys of imports, and profitable linkage with the written record, linking place-names with production sites and use-wear with culinary practice (Hughes and Evans 2000). Among the novel analytical techniques of the moment are stable isotope analyses whose applications now range from medieval dietary reconstruction (Müldner and Richards 2005) to the identification of sources of cod catches from bone collagen (Barrett *et al* 2008); and ancient DNA methods which have been applied to leprosy cases (Taylor *et al* 2006), among others.

Special acknowledgement should be made of works of classification and chronology, the printed corpus and catalogue where only the very highest standards are tolerated. They must include works by the Taylors for Anglo-Saxon church architecture (eg Taylor and Taylor 1966), Rosemary Cramp's team for Anglo-Saxon stone sculpture (eg Cramp 2006), as well as core artefact studies such as Nowell Myres for early Saxon pottery vessels (eg Myres 1969), Donald Harden for glass (eg Harden 1972) and Michael Dolley for coins (see Cramp, this volume). For the later period there is William Pantin for medieval domestic buildings (eg Pantin 1962–63), David Gaimster for German stonewares (eg Gaimster 1997), and Geoff Egan and others for London metalwork finds (eg Egan 1998). These essential systematic studies of material culture and monuments continue to furnish the groundwork for all medieval research illuminating not only technology, trade and patterns of consumption, but also influencing the dating and interpretation of sites (Figures 5.11a and 5.11b).

DIRECTIONS OF RESEARCH

The analysis of theses topics is one means by which the direction of research in medieval archaeology can be mapped over the past 50 years.[10] From this exercise it emerges that recent postgraduate research into early medieval archaeology remains dominated by artefact, sculpture and cemetery studies with notable lacunae in urban themes and buildings (Figure 5.12). Theses in later medieval archaeology are dominated by artefacts and landscape themes with a burst of castle projects over the past decade (nine in all between 1997 and 2005). Urban and monastic topics suffer by comparison. The main 'winner' in recent years in both early and medieval

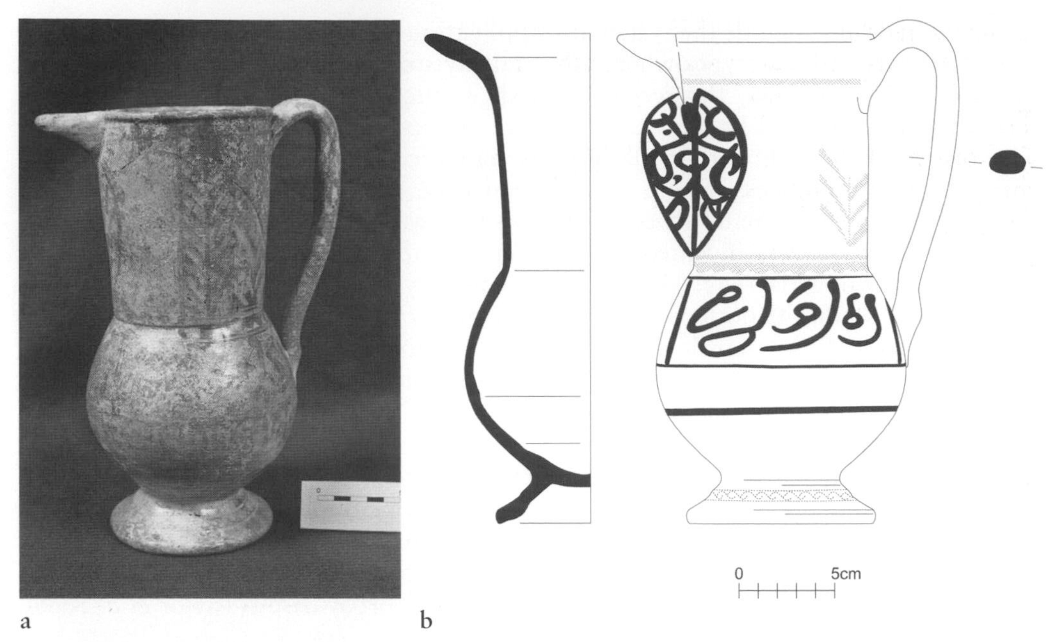

FIGURES 5.11a and 5.11b Malaga lustreware jug of 14th-century date from the manor house at Micheldever (Hants), country retreat for the abbot of Hyde, the wealthy Benedictine abbey in Winchester. In the first half of the 20th century there was only one published Spanish later medieval pot, the Pithay dish from Bristol. The first summary of foreign imports was collated by Gerald Dunning (1961) and in 1964 John Hurst travelled to Spain to collect further identifications (Hurst 1977; Hurst *et al* 1986). Following these pioneering studies, and in line with methodological and theoretical developments paralleled in many other categories of medieval artefact, more recent studies include both compositional analyses (eg Hughes 2003) and detailed consideration of colour, decorative symbolism and religious associations (Gutiérrez 2000). (© Winchester Museums Service; drawing: Alejandra Gutiérrez)

archaeology, however, is science. Dendrochronology, analytical investigations and conservation projects all figure here, but human health and environmental archaeology (including both animal and plant remains) currently dominate. Since *c*2000 the combined total of science-led medieval theses is 23, as against buildings with five and urban themes with just two. This skewing is partly a question of funding streams, partly to do with the novelty of the applications and, to some extent, a matter of individual and institutional leadership. On this evidence, medieval archaeology is fast becoming more science-based and looking away from the humanities.

Among the other key changes seen in the theses data over the past half-century is the move away from the study of individual monuments towards the investigation of whole landscapes, which are often picked apart by multi-disciplinary teams (Johnson 2007). Stephen Rippon's recent overview of historic landscapes in the North Somerset Levels is one of a series of regional landscape and settlement analyses over a long chronology (eg Jones and Page 2006), in this case providing a full account of the transformation of wetland there from the late prehistoric to the post-medieval

Early medieval

	Crafts, artefacts, sculpture	Countryside, landscape	Burials, grave goods, cemeteries	Churches, Christianity	Science	Towns	Buildings	Trade	Shore forts	Transition Roman-early medieval	Theory
2006					1						1
2005	1	1		1	3					1	
2004	2	2	1	1	2		1				
2003	4	2	1	1	2	1					
2002	1			1	3						
2001			2	1						1	
2000	3	1	3	2			1	1			
1999	1	1			1	1			1		
1998	5		1								
1997		1	1		1						
1996	1		1		1						
1995	2	3	2		1			1			
1994					1						
1993	2	2	2	1							
1992	3		1	1							
1991	3	1	1		1						
1990	4	2									
1989	2										
1988	2	1		2							
1987	1	3	1								
1986	2	1	1				1				
1985						1					
1984	2	1			1						
1983	2	1	1		1						
1982	1	2		2							
1981	1			1	1						
1980	1	1	3								
1979	1	1	2	1							
1978	1	1	1		1						
1977	2	2									
1976			2	1							
1975	3	1									

Later medieval

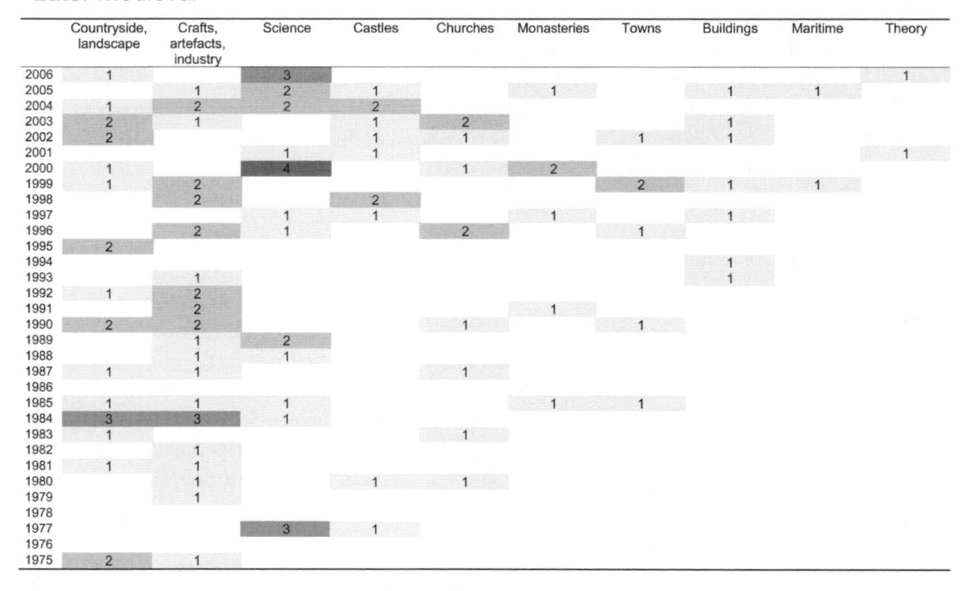

	Countryside, landscape	Crafts, artefacts, industry	Science	Castles	Churches	Monasteries	Towns	Buildings	Maritime	Theory
2006	1		3							1
2005		1	2	1		1		1	1	
2004	1	2	2	2						
2003	2	1		1	2			1		
2002	2			1	1		1	1		
2001			1	1						1
2000	1		4		1	2				
1999	1	2					2	1	1	
1998		2		2						
1997			1	1		1		1		
1996		2	1		2		1			
1995	2									
1994								1		
1993		1						1		
1992	1	2								
1991		2				1				
1990	2	2			1		1			
1989		1	2							
1988		1	1							
1987	1	1			1					
1986										
1985	1	1	1			1	1			
1984	3	3	1							
1983	1				1					
1982		1								
1981	1	1								
1980		1		1	1					
1979		1								
1978										
1977			3	1						
1976										
1975	2	1								

FIGURE 5.12. Thesis topics in early and later medieval archaeology since 1975. Data taken from the online *Index to Theses*. The statistics refer to all higher degrees accepted by universities in Great Britain and Ireland; shading indicates peaks of activity. In the early medieval table, 'artefacts' includes glass, coins, pottery and ironwork, while 'science' includes disease, isotopes, faunal remains, etc. Authors may rightly protest that their work falls into more than one of the categories, especially since judgement on content is based on the thesis title alone.

period and seating within that landscape study a more detailed account of fieldwork and excavation at the marshland settlement at Puxton (Rippon 2006). Through a succession of parish- and multi-parish sized projects like this, medieval archaeology has made a distinguished contribution to the development of 'landscape archaeology', a term apparently first coined in Mick Aston's front room in the early 1970s (Mick Aston, pers comm) and gradually accommodating an ever-expanding range of monument types. Martin Carver's Sutton Hoo work shows how different scales of landscape investigation can be played out in a fieldwork project (Carver 2005) in order to pursue a deeper understanding of choices and actions by local communities responsible for the funerary record there, a very different set of research questions to those which inspired pre-war excavation of the 6th- and 7th-century barrow burials on the same site (Figure 5.13). Some later medieval projects would do well to follow Carver's example in examining the wider European context.

It is unhelpful that medieval archaeologists have acquired a reputation for resistance to the latest theoretical developments. This resistance is not due to the

FIGURE 5.13. Excavations at Sutton Hoo in 1988. An overview photograph looking east, taken by a camera on a kite (one string is visible, centre left). The right-hand area (Sector 44) is just being opened with the eroded surfaces of Mound 6 and 7 under the pastry strips of the modern ground. Well-soaked in the lower foreground is the site where the burials of Mound 17 will appear, a young man and his horse in adjacent pits. The pale grey markings in this Sector (Sector 48) are ditches of the Neolithic and Bronze Age, examples of which have been fully excavated centre left (Sector 41). (Photograph by permission of Martin Carver)

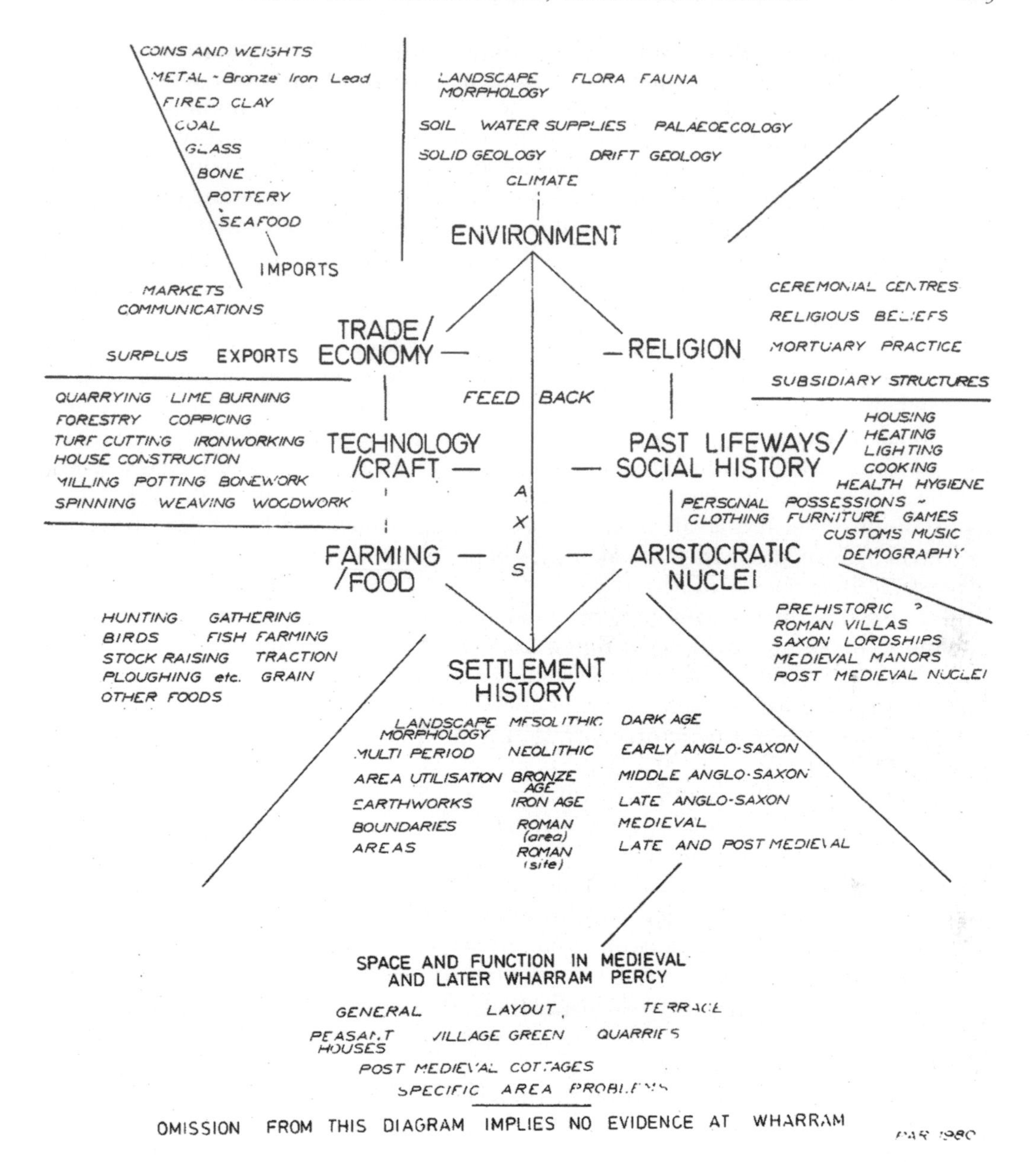

FIGURE 5.14. Philip Rahtz's 'data sheets' for Wharram Percy (Yorks) published in 1980 and 1981. Rahtz's intention was to suggest 'ways in which the mass of data from some 40 years of work could be ordered and analysed in a more holistic way' (Rahtz 2001, 142). He promoted a similarly explicit processual approach to his work at the reoccupied Iron Age hillfort at Cadbury Congresbury (Somerset).

inherent nature of the topic, but may be best explained by its comparative youth and a lack of self-confidence, in particular the belief, a strongly felt one until a decade ago, that to command the respect of the wider intellectual community explicit statements of theoretical orientation should await the accumulation of more data. Until the 1970s, most work took a 'common sense' or 'functionalist' approach and, as the fledgling subject expanded its excavations, establishing functions and chronologies for monuments and objects, it inevitably tended towards detail rather than longer-term trends. In that cumulative venture there was deemed to be a 'correct' way of working, one that demanded detailed verification with no adherence to the whims of theoretical 'fashion'.

In the 1970s and 1980s processual archaeology sought to generalize rather than particularize, and a more scientific approach was advocated in pursuit of laws of human behaviour, one which favoured numerical and quantitative techniques such as locational modelling and the trade and exchange models employed by Richard Hodges in his *Dark Age Economics* (Hodges 1982). In her review of Helen Clarke's synthesis *The Archaeology of Medieval England* (1984), Kathleen Biddick (1985) called upon later medieval archaeologists to experiment with similar strategies, as David Austin did with central place theory (Austin 1986). Good examples of processual archaeology in action are Philip Rahtz's data sheets for Wharram Percy (Rahtz 1985), which promoted the technique of systems analysis through flow diagrams, breaking down society into components, examining each in turn in a structured way (Figure 5.14). Other medieval archaeologists remained theoretically inert to these overtures, even antagonistic to what was referred to at the Cambridge conference in 1981 as 'incomprehensible jargon', 'playing with models in Legoland' (Hurst 1983).

'Soft-processualism' still permeates more writing than is realized, but today's cognitive approaches emphasize culture and the role played by ideas in shaping human behaviour. In modelling individual or collective behaviour, systems approaches like that advocated by Philip Rahtz for Wharram Percy generalize broadly about social groups and tend to obscure the role of the individual. The recent *Perceptions of Medieval Landscapes and Settlements* (POMLAS) workshops run by the Medieval Settlement Research Group, on the other hand, were directly concerned with medieval people's view of themselves and their environment, the 'lived world of experience' (for an example of this approach in history, see Kleinschmidt 2000). Several studies now emphasize these more anthropological aspects, among them Matthew Johnson in his dissection of the cultural dimension of housing (Johnson 1993) and David Stocker who, in the context of 'designed' landscapes, is aware of just how deeply symbolism and imagery are embedded in later medieval culture (Stocker and Stocker 1986). For artefacts, where this approach is less well advanced, the placement of dress accessories on clothing and the colour, texture and decoration on glass and pottery are now taking centre stage as we strive to understand how objects might have carried meaning and impacted on social behaviour. Exploring the medieval sensory environment is yet another possible avenue for future research, including smells and acoustics in domestic and ritual spaces such as churches and monasteries, both in different regions and for successive architectural periods (Giles

2007; Graves 2007). Such approaches show no disrespect for the observations of earlier researchers, but they do offer an evolution in the types of questions being asked.

Another arena for research, also visible in the theses data, has been ethnicity and identity (see Cramp, this volume). This is of obvious relevance for the early medieval period where interest in origins, artefacts, family groups and status is triggered by the analysis of large cemeteries like Spong Hill in Norfolk (Hills 1977; Hines 1997). Among the many questions raised are the level of interaction between migrants and resident groups, impacts on cultural continuity, indeed the extent to which material culture is any guide at all to ethnic or racial groupings, however we choose to define them (Lucy 2002; Hills 2003). Recent authors tend to affirm that dress styles are part and parcel of the construction of social status and an active element in its negotiation (eg Mytum 2003 for a Viking example). Identity is of interest too for later periods, for example in determining how pottery imports relate to the documented presence of foreign merchants in medieval Southampton (Brown 1997), while Roberta Gilchrist's examination of the lives of religious women in medieval England pioneered a broadening of feminist archaeology into a wider project, the archaeology of gender (Gilchrist 1994).

Quite why medieval archaeologists have sought out certain themes for investigation and not others depends upon a wide variety of factors, among them influences from elsewhere in archaeology (especially prehistory), training, mentors, institutional objectives and funding.[11] Political ideology, too, may have had its part to play. For example, we might ask to what extent research into 'ordinary peasant life' has been driven by individuals with a strong social conscience or should we see this interest merely as a corrective against the perceived imperfections of the pre-war obsession 'with the upper classes ... with the castles, abbeys and churches', as Hurst himself put it (Smith 2006, 104)? My answer would be that the 'invisible college' of medieval archaeology, that unofficial professional network which has been silently created over the past 50 years and which is one of the greatest achievements of those decades, is broad in its political persuasions.[12] Our natural tendency is mild anarchy, not ideological consensus.

ACKNOWLEDGEMENTS

I am especially grateful to Mick Aston, Martin Biddle, Martin Carver, Rosemary Cramp, Richard Hall, Neil Holbrook, Alejandra Gutiérrez and Paul Stamper for providing the images for this article, and to Martin Biddle, Martin Carver, Rosemary Cramp, Margarita Díaz-Andreu, Andrew Saunders and Paul Stamper for their suggestions for improvements to the text.

NOTES

[1] For example, the first full-time lecturer in economic history was at the London School of Economics in 1904. In 1970 there were 30 chairs and nearly 200 teachers in universities (Harte 1971).

[2] Part of the appeal of the groups is therefore that they conceptually 'tidy' up the pluralism of medieval archaeology.

[3] John Hurst and Maurice Beresford visited some 2000 deserted medieval village sites personally over a 20-year period (Smith 2006, 105).

[4] Until about 1930 there was one well equipped County Record Office, 11 more appeared in the 1930s and another 13 immediately after the war (Bentley 2005, 207).

[5] Early (pre-1960s) VCH volumes stand accused of containing 'much fluff with an occasional article from an Oxford graduate needing work' (Bentley 2005, 138).

[6] As far as I can determine, William ('Billy') Pantin (1902–73), University Lecturer in Medieval Archaeology and History at the University of Oxford (and Keeper of the University Archives), was the first academic to have the words 'Medieval Archaeology' incorporated into the title of his post, immediately after the war. Before that he had been a Lecturer in Ecclesiastical Institutions since 1937, so the change in emphasis is significant in terms of disciplinary identity. Rosemary Cramp at Durham was the first full-time Anglo-Saxon archaeologist to be appointed in any British university as a Lecturer in Anglo-Saxon Antiquities and Archaeology in 1955. Other active academics in the late 1950s had more generic titles or their interests were developed in other departments. Martyn Jope was a Reader in Archaeology at Belfast in 1957, for example, while Howard Colvin was a Fellow of St John's College, W G Hoskins was a Reader in Economic History, both at Oxford, Frank Stenton was a Professor of Modern History at Reading, while Herbert Finberg was Head of the Department of English Local History at Leicester. During the 1960s named posts increased: David Wilson became a Reader in Archaeology of the Anglo-Saxon period at University of London, as was Vera Evison; Martin Biddle took up a Lectureship in Medieval Archaeology in Frank Barlow's Department of History at Exeter in 1963, while Philip Rahtz was a lecturer in Medieval Archaeology at the University of Birmingham in 1964. As late as the mid-1970s, however, in the eight Scottish universities only one member of staff specialized in post-Roman archaeology.

[7] This RAE list may exclude 'affiliated staff' such as research or visiting fellows, any member of staff not indicated as having a recognized academic title (eg Lecturer, Reader, etc), emeritus staff, and anyone who might be working on medieval archaeology employed outside a department or division which includes Archaeology (eg a School of Education or Department of History). A worrying feature of the list is the number of staff aged over 40, while only 14 women feature on the list of 51 staff. Of those departments who returned archaeologists in RAE 2008, only Liverpool, Central Lancashire and Nottingham Trent failed to return a medievalist (Gilchrist, pers comm).

[8] The four most generous recent awards by AHRC are for the Corpus of Anglo-Saxon stone sculpture (Principal Investigator: Rosemary Cramp, Durham), Medieval Settlements and Landscapes in the Whittlewood area (Chris Dyer, Leicester), South Cadbury Environs Project (Gary Lock, Oxford) and the Wallingford *Burh* to Borough Project (Neil Christie, Leicester). The first two projects have received more than one round of funding.

[9] There were estimated to be 4425 professional archaeologists in the UK in 1999 (Aitchison 1999).

[10] No single measure is entirely satisfactory for this purpose, but the theses examination is in essence an exercise in academic 'gate-keeping' and community building, especially today when successful completion is a pre-requisite for academic posts. Books reviewed in *Medieval Archaeology* or articles published in that journal might also be quantified and it has also been suggested to me that conceptual interests could also be mapped through old university examination questions, but I am more realistic about the attention span of the reader!

[11] There are topics in medieval archaeology which have not sustained their interest and while it is usually possible to understand their initial popularity, it is often much more difficult to understand why they have been abandoned. Lack of innovation and progress is one reason, absence of leadership another, competing opportunity a third. Boredom should not be under-estimated.

[12] For further discussion of the concept of the 'invisible college' in the context of Gordon Childe and other prehistorians, see Díaz-Andreu 2007.

BIBLIOGRAPHY

Aitchison, K, 1999 *Profiling the Profession. A Survey of Archaeological Jobs in the UK*, Council for British Archaeology, English Heritage and Institute for Field Archaeologists, York

Aston, M A, 2000 *Mick's Archaeology*, Tempus, Stroud

Aston, M A and Bond, C J, 1976 *The Landscape of Towns*, Dent, London

Austin, D A, 1986 'Central Place Theory and the Middle Ages', in E Grant (ed), *Central Places, Archaeology and History*, 95–104, University of Sheffield, Sheffield

Austin, D A, 1987 'The future of archaeology in British universities', *Antiquity* 61, 227–238

Avent, R, 2000 *CADW and castle conservation*, Castle Studies Group Newsletter 1999–2000

Bailiff, I K, 2007 'Methodological developments in the luminescence dating of brick from English late medieval and post-medieval buildings', *Archaeometry* 49:4, 827–851

Baldwin Brown website, www.archive.org/details/artsinearlyengla/browuoff (accessed April 2008)

Barley, M W (ed), 1975 *The Plans and Topography of Medieval Towns in England and Wales*, Council for British Archaeology Research Report 14, London

Barrett, J, Johnstone, C, Harland, J, Van Neer, W, Ervynck, A, Makowiecki, D, Heinrich, D, Hufthammer, A K, Enghoff, I, Amundsen, C, Christiansen, J, Jones, A, Locker, A, Hamilton-Dyer, S, Jonsson, L, Lõugas, L, Roberts, C and Richards, M, 2008 'Detecting the medieval cod trade: a new method and first results', *Journal of Archaeological Science* 35, 850–861

Becher, T and Trowler, P R, 2001 *Academic Tribes and Territories*, 2nd edn, Society for Research into Higher Education, Buckingham

Bentley, M, 2005 *Modernizing England's Past. English Historiography in the Age of Modernism 1870–1970*, Cambridge University Press, Cambridge

Beresford, M W, 1957 *History on the Ground*, Lutterworth, London

Beresford, M W, 1992 'Professor W G Hoskins: a memoir', *Agricultural History Review* 40, 164–167

Beresford, M W, Hurst, J G and Sheail, J, 1980 'MVRG: The First Thirty Years', *Medieval Village Research Group Annual Report* 28, 36–39

Beresford, M W and St Joseph, J K, 1958 *Medieval England: an Aerial Survey*, Cambridge University Press, Cambridge

Bersu, G, 1949 'A promontory fort on the shore of Ramsey Bay, Isle of Man', *Antiquaries Journal* 29, 62–79

Bianco, C, 1993 'Ecclesiastical buildings in use', in J Hunter and I Ralston (eds), *Archaeological Resource Management in the UK. An Introduction*, 89–99, Alan Sutton, Stroud

Biddick, K, 1985 'Review of Helen Clarke, The Archaeology of Medieval England', *Speculum* 61, 395–396

Biddle, M, 1983 'The study of Winchester: archaeology and history in a British town, 1961–1983', *Proceedings of the British Academy* 59, 93–135

Biddle, M, 1989 'The Rose reviewed: a comedy (?) of errors', *Antiquity* 63, 753–760

Biddle, M, 1990 *Object and Economy in Medieval Winchester*, Winchester Studies 7ii, Clarendon Press, Oxford

Biddle, M, 1994 *What Future for British Archaeology?*, Oxbow Lecture 1, Oxford

Biddle, M and Kjølbye-Biddle, B, 1969 'Metres, areas and robbing', *World Archaeology* 1, 208–219

Blake, H, 2000 'The formation of the second generation: a documentary version of the origin and early history of the MPRG', *Medieval Ceramics* 24, 12–22

Blair, J and Pyrah, C (eds), 1996 *Research Designs for Church Archaeology*, Council for British Archaeology Research Report 104, York

Boddington, A, 1996 *Raunds Furnell. The Anglo-Saxon Church and Churchyard*, English Heritage, London

Bogdan, N Q and Wordsworth, J W, 1978 *The Medieval Excavations at the High Street, Perth, 1975–76: an Interim Report*, Perth High Street Excavation Committee, Perth

Brown, D H, 1997 'The social significance of imported medieval pottery', in C G Cumberpatch and P W Blinkhorn (eds), *Not so Much a Pot, More a Way of Life*, 95–112, Oxbow Books, Oxford

Butler, L A S, 1983 'Church archaeology and the work of the Council for British Archaeology's Churches Committee', in Hinton, D (ed), 1983 *25 Years of Medieval Archaeology*, Department of Prehistory and Archaeology, University of Sheffield, Sheffield, 117–126

Carver, M O H, 2005 *Sutton Hoo: a Seventh-Century Princely Burial Ground and its Context*, British Museum, Reports of the Research Committee of the Society of Antiquaries of London 69, London

Chambers, R A, 1974 'A deserted medieval farmstead at Sadler's Wood, Lewknor', *Oxoniensia* 38, 146–167

Chapman, H P and Fenwick, H, 2002 'Contextualising previous excavation: the implications of applying GPS survey and GIS modelling techniques to Watton Priory, East Yorkshire', *Medieval Archaeology* 46, 81–89

Clarke, H and Carter A, 1977 *Excavations in Kings Lynn 1963–1971*, Society for Medieval Archaeology Monograph 7, London

Clarke, H, 1984 *The Archaeology of Medieval England*, British Museum Press, London

Cramp, R, 2006 *Corpus of Anglo-Saxon Stone Sculpture. Volume vii: South-West England*, Oxford University Press, Oxford

Crone, A, 2000 'Native tree-ring chronologies from some Scottish medieval burghs', *Medieval Archaeology* 44, 201–216

Darvill, T C and Fulton, A, 1998 *MARS: The Monuments at Risk Survey of England. Main Report*, Bournemouth University and English Heritage, Bournemouth and London

Devlin, Z, 2007 *Remembering the Dead in Anglo-Saxon England. Memory Theory in Archaeology and History*, British Archaeological Reports 446, Oxford

Díaz-Andreu, M, 2007 'Internationalism in the invisible college. Political ideologies and friendships in archaeology', *Journal of Social Archaeology* 7:1, 29–48

Dickinson, T, 1983 'Anglo-Saxon archaeology: twenty-five years on', in Hinton, D (ed), 1983 *25 Years of Medieval Archaeology*, Department of Prehistory and Archaeology, University of Sheffield, Sheffield, 33–43

Dunning, G C, 1961 'A group of English and imported medieval pottery from Lesnes Abbey, Kent and the trade in early Hispano-Moresque to England', *Antiquaries Journal* 41, 1–12

Dyer, C, Jones, R and Page, M, 2005 *The Whittlewood Project: Medieval Settlements and Landscapes in the Whittlewood Area*, found at ads.ahds.ac.uk/catalogue/archive/whittlewood_ahrb_2006

Egan, G, 1998 *Medieval Finds from Excavations in London 6. The Medieval Household: Daily Living c1150–c1450*, Her Majesty's Stationery Office, London

Everson, P, 1998 '"Delightfully surrounded with woods and ponds": Field evidence for medieval gardens in England', in P Pattison (ed), *There by Design. Field Archaeology in Parks and Gardens*, 32–37, British Archaeological Reports 267, Oxford

Faulkner, P A, 1958 'Domestic planning from the twelfth to the fourteenth centuries', *Archaeological Journal* 115, 150–183

Fergusson, P and Harrison, S, 1999 *Rievaulx Abbey. Community, Architecture and Memory*, Yale University Press, New Haven and London

Gaffney, C, Gater, J and Shiel, D, 2007 'Geophysical survey Part 2', in C M Gerrard with M Aston (eds), *The Shapwick Project, Somerset. A Rural Landscape Explored*, Society for Medieval Archaeology Monograph 25, The Society for Medieval Archaeology, London, 213–227

Gaimster, D, 1997 *German Stoneware 1200–1900. Archaeology and Cultural History*, British Museum Press, London

Gerrard, C M, 2003 *Medieval Archaeology. Understanding Traditions and Contemporary Approaches*, Routledge, London

Gilchrist, R, 1994 *Gender and Material Culture: the Archaeology of Religious Women*, Routledge, London

Gilchrist, R and Sloane, B, 2005 *Medieval Monastic Cemeteries of Britain (1050–1600): a Digital Resource and Database of Excavated Examples*, found at ads.ahds.ac.uk/catalogue/archive/cemeteries_ahrb_2005

Giles, K, 2007 'Seeing and believing: visuality and space in pre-modern England', *World Archaeology* 39:1, 105–121

Gilyard-Beer, R, 1955 *Gisborough Priory, Yorkshire*, Her Majesty's Stationery Office, London
Graham-Campbell, J and Valor, M, (eds), 2007 *The Archaeology of Medieval Europe. Volume 1, Eighth to Twelfth Centuries AD*, Aarhus University Press, Aarhus
Graves, C P, 2007 'Sensing and believing: exploring worlds of difference in pre-modern England: a contribution to the debate opened by Kate Giles', *World Archaeology* 39:4, 515–531
Grimes, W F, 1968 *The Excavation of Roman and Medieval London*, Routledge and Kegan Paul, London
Gutiérrez, A, 2000 *Mediterranean Pottery in Wessex Households (13th to 17th Centuries)*, British Archaeological Reports 306, Oxford
Hall, R A, 2004 '*Jórvík*': a Viking-age city', in J Hines, A Lane and M Redknap (eds), *Land, Sea and Home*, 283–296, Society for Medieval Archaeology Monograph 20, Maney Publishing, Leeds
Hamerow, H, 1993 *Excavations at Mucking 1: the Anglo-Saxon Settlement*, English Heritage, London
Harden, D B, 1972 'Ancient Glass, III: Post Roman', *Archaeological Journal* 128, 78–117
Harris, E C, 1975 'The stratigraphic sequence: a question of time', *World Archaeology* 7, 109–121
Harte, N B, 1971 'Introduction: the making of Economic History', in N B Harte (ed), *The Study of Economic History*, xi–xxxix, Routledge, London
Haslam, J, Mellor, M and Moffett, J, 2001 'Potweb: museum documentation — a world vision', *Medieval Ceramics* 25, 99–107
Heighway, C, 1972 *The Erosion of History*, Council for British Archaeology, London
Heyworth, M, 2006 *A Brief History of the CBA*, available at www.britarch.ac.uk/cba/history.html
Higham, R A and Barker, P, 2000 *Hen Domen, Montgomery: a Timber Castle on the English-Welsh Border*, University of Exeter, Exeter
Hillam, J, 1998 *Dendrochronology: Guidelines on Producing and Interpreting Dendrochronological Data*, English Heritage, London
Hills, C, 1977 *The Anglo-Saxon Cemetery at Spong Hill, North Elmham, Norfolk, Part 1*, Norfolk Archaeological Unit, Gressenhall
Hills, C, 2003 *The Origins of the English*, Duckworth, London
Hilton, R H and Rahtz, P A, 1966 'Upton, Gloucestershire, 1959–1964', *Transactions of the Bristol and Gloucestershire Archaeological Society* 85, 70–146
Hines, J (ed), 1997 *The Anglo-Saxons from the Migration Period to the Eighth Century: an Ethnographic Perspective*, The Boydell Press, Woodbridge
Hinton, D (ed), 1983 *25 Years of Medieval Archaeology*, Department of Prehistory and Archaeology, University of Sheffield, Sheffield
Hobsbawn, E, 1979 'An historian's comments', in B C Burnham and J Kingsbury (eds), *Space, Hierarchy and Society*, 247–252, British Archaeological Reports International Series 59, Oxford
Hodges, R, 1982 *Dark Age Economics: the Origins of Towns and Trade, A.D.600–1000*, Duckworth, London
Hodges, R, 1989 'Parachutists and truffle-hunters: at the frontiers of Archaeology and History', in M Aston, D Austin and C Dyer (eds), *Rural Settlements of Medieval England: Studies Dedicated to Maurice Beresford and John Hurst*, 287–306, Blackwell, Oxford
Holbrook, N and Thomas, A, 2005 'An early medieval monastic cemetery at Llandough, Glamorgan: excavations in 1994', *Medieval Archaeology* 49, 1–92
Holden, E W, 1963 'Excavations at the deserted medieval village of Hangleton, part 1', *Sussex Archaeological Collections* 101, 54–181
Hope-Taylor, B, 1977 *Yeavering: an Anglo-British Centre of Early Northumbria*, Her Majesty's Stationery Office, London

Hoskins, W G, 1955 *The Making of the English Landscape*, Hodder and Stoughton, London

Hughes, M J, 2003 'Chemical analyses of Spanish ceramics from the Studland Bay Wreck by ICP-AES and neutron activation', in A Gutiérrez, 'A shipwreck of Sevillian pottery from the Studland Bay wreck, Dorset, UK', *International Journal of Nautical Archaeology* 32:1, 37–41 (24–41)

Hughes, M J and Evans, J, 2000 'Fabrics and food: 25 years of scientific analysis of medieval ceramics', *Medieval Ceramics* 24, 79–90

Hurst, J G, 1962–63 'White Castle and the dating of medieval pottery', *Medieval Archaeology* 6–7, 135–155

Hurst, J G, 1971 'A review of archaeological research (to 1968)', in M Beresford and J G Hurst (eds), *Deserted Medieval Villages*, 76–144, Lutterworth Press, London

Hurst, J G, 1977 'Spanish pottery imported into medieval Britain', *Medieval Archaeology* 21, 68–105

Hurst, J G, 1982 'Gerald Dunning and his contribution to Medieval Archaeology', *Medieval Ceramics* 6, 3–20

Hurst, J G, 1983 'Medieval archaeology twenty-five years on: summing up', in Hinton, D (ed), 1983 *25 Years of Medieval Archaeology*, Department of Prehistory and Archaeology, University of Sheffield, Sheffield, 132–135

Hurst, J G, Neal, D S and van Beuningen, H J E, 1986 *Pottery Produced and Traded in North-West Europe 1350–1650*, Rotterdam Papers 6, Rotterdam

Johnson, M, 1993 *Housing Culture. Traditional Architecture in an English Landscape*, Smithsonian Institution Press, Washington DC

Johnson, M, 2007 *Ideas of Landscape*, Blackwell Publishing, Oxford

Jones, R and Page, M, 2006 *Medieval Villages in an English Landscape. Beginnings and Ends*, Windgather Press, Macclesfield

Jope, E M, 1952 'Regional character in West Country pottery', in H E O'Neil, 'Whittington Court Villa, Whittington, Gloucestershire', *Transactions of the Bristol and Gloucestershire Archaeological Society* 71, 61–97

Jope, E M and Threlfall, R I, 1958 'Excavation of a medieval settlement at Beere, North Tawton, Devon', *Medieval Archaeology* 2, 112–140

Kleinschmidt, H, 2000 'Space, body, action: the significance of perceptions in the study of the environmental history of early medieval Europe', *The Medieval History Journal* 3:2, 175–221

Klemperer, W D and Boothroyd, N, 2004 *Excavations at Hulton Abbey, Staffordshire 1987–1994*, Society for Medieval Archaeology Monograph 21, The Society for Medieval Archaeology, London

Lane, L, 1966 'A plan for a new metropolitan city. Humber. Counter-magnet to London and showcase for Britain', *Architects Journal* 19, 168–216

Lucy, S, 2002 'Burial practice in early medieval eastern Britain: constructing local identities, deconstructing ethnicity', in S Lucy and A Reynolds (eds), *Burial in Early Medieval England and Wales*, Society for Medieval Archaeology Monograph 17, The Society for Medieval Archaeology, Leeds, 72–87

Marvell, A G, 2001 *Investigations along Monnow Street, Monmouth*, British Archaeological Reports 320, Oxford

Mayes, P, 2002 *Excavations at a Templar Preceptory. South Witham, Lincolnshire 1965–67*, Society for Medieval Archaeology Monograph 19, Maney Publishing, Leeds

Miller, E, 1984 'Michael Moissey Postan 1899–1981', *Proceedings of the British Academy* 69, 544–557

Milne, G, 1997 *St Bride's Church, London. Archaeological Research 1952–60 and 1992–5*, English Heritage Archaeological Report 11, London

Milne, G and Hobley, B (eds), 1981 *Waterfront Archaeology in Britain and Northern Europe*, Council for British Archaeology Research Report 41, London

Morris, R, 1983 *The Church in British Archaeology*, Council for British Archaeology Research Report 47, London

Morton, A D, 1992 *Excavations at Hamwic. Vol. 1, Excavations 1946–83, excluding Six Dials and Melbourne Street*, Council for British Archaeology Research Report 33, London

Müldner, G and Richards, M P, 2005 'Fast or feast: reconstructing diet in later medieval England by stable isotope analysis', *Journal of Archaeological Science* 32, 39–48

Myres, J N L, 1969 *Anglo-Saxon Pottery and the Settlement of England*, Clarendon Press, Oxford

Mytum, H, 2003 'The Vikings and Ireland: ethnicity, identity and cultural change', in J H Barrett (ed), *Contact, Continuity and Collapse: the Norse Colonization of the North Atlantic*, 113–37, Brepols, Turnhout

Norris, M and Oppenheim, C, 2001 'Citation counts and the Research Assessment Exercise V', *Journal of Documentation* 59, 709–730

O'Neil, B H St J, 1946, 'The castles of Wales', in V E Nash-Williams (ed), *A Hundred Years of Welsh Archaeology*, Cambrian Archaeological Association, Centenary Volume 1846–1946, 129–140, Gloucester

Pantin, W A, 1962–63 'Medieval English town-house plans', *Medieval Archaeology* 6–7, 202–239

Petts, D with Gerrard, C M, 2006 *Shared Visions: the North East Regional Research Framework for the Historic Environment*, Durham County Council, Durham

Platt, C, 1978 Review of 'Excavations in King's Lynn 1963–1970', by Helen Clarke and Alan Carter, *Medieval Archaeology* 22, 201–203

Postan, M M, 1973 *Essays on Medieval Agriculture and General Problems of Medieval Economy*, Cambridge University Press, Cambridge

Powlesland, D, 1996 'West Heslerton, North Yorkshire, Anglo-Saxon settlement: a new approach to post-excavation analysis', *English Heritage Archaeology Review 1996–97*, 4.20.31 (www.eng-h.gov.uk/archrev/rev96_7/whes.htm)

Rahtz, P A, 1985 'Wharram Percy research strategies', in D Hooke (ed), *Medieval Villages*, Oxford, 205–213

Rahtz, P A, 2001 *Living Archaeology*, Tempus, Stroud

Rahtz, P A and Greenfield, E, 1977 *Excavations at Chew Valley Lake, Somerset*, Her Majesty's Stationery Office, London

RCHME, 1991 'Excavations and medieval England: The Excavation Index', *Medieval Archaeology* 35, 123–125

Reilly, S, 1998 'Old Wardour Castle, Wilts', *Central Archaeological Service News* 9, 2–3

Rigold, S E, 1967 'Fourteenth-century halls in the East Weald', *Archaeologia Cantiana* 82, 246–256

Rippon, S, 2006 *Landscape, Community and Colonisation. The North Somerset Levels during the 1st and 2nd Millennia AD*, Council for British Archaeology Research Report 152, York

Roberts, B K and Wrathmell, S, 2000 *An Atlas of Rural Settlement in England*, English Heritage, London

Rodwell, W J and Rodwell, K A, 1982 'St Peter's Church, Barton-upon-Humber: Excavation and Structural Study, 1978–81', *Antiquaries Journal* 62, 283–315

Saunders, A D, 2006 *Excavations at Launceston Castle, Cornwall*, the Society for Medieval Archaeology Monograph 24, The Society for Medieval Archaeology, Leeds

Schofield, J R and Leech, R, (eds) 1987 *Urban Archaeology in Britain*, Council for British Archaeology Research Report 61, London

Smith, P J, 2006 'Roots and origins: archaeology and Wharram. An interview with John G Hurst', *Medieval Settlement Research Group Annual Report* 21, 59–64

Söderqvist, T (ed), 1997 *The Historiography of Contemporary Science and Technology*, Harwood Academic, Amsterdam

Stenton, F, 1943 *Anglo-Saxon England*, Clarendon Press, Oxford

Stocker, D and Stocker, M, 1996 'Sacred profanity: the theology of rabbit breeding and the symbolic landscape of the warren', *World Archaeology* 28:2, 265–272

Taylor, G, Watson, C, Bouwman, A, Lockwood, D and Mays, S, 2006 'Variable nucleotide tandem repeat (VNTR) typing of two palaeopathological cases of lepromatous leprosy from medieval England', *Journal of Archaeological Science* 33, 1569–79

Taylor, H M, 1972 'Structural criticism: a plea for more systematic study of Anglo-Saxon buildings', *Anglo-Saxon England* 1, 259–272

Taylor, H M and Taylor, J, 1966 *Anglo-Saxon Architecture i–ii*, Cambridge University Press, Cambridge

Ucko, P, 1990 'Foreword', in D A Austin and L Alcock (eds), *From the Baltic to the Black Sea. Studies in Medieval Archaeology*, ix–xii, Routledge, London

Ulmschneider, K and Pestell, T, 2003 'Introduction: early medieval markets and "productive" sites', in T Pestell and K Ulmschneider (eds), *Markets in Early Medieval Europe*, 1–10, Windgather Press, Macclesfield

Vernacular Architecture Group, 2000 *Dendrochronology Database*, found at ads.ahds.ac.uk/catalogue/specColl/vag_dendro

Wainwright, G J, 2000 'Time please', *Antiquity* 74, 909–943

Walford, L, 2000 'The Research Assessment Exercise: its effect on scholarly publishing', *Learned Publishing* 13, 49–52

Ward Perkins, J B (ed), 1940 *London Museum Medieval Catalogue 1940*, London Museum, London

West, S, 1985 *West Stow: the Anglo-Saxon Village*, Suffolk County Planning Department, Ipswich

Williamson, T, 2007 'Historic Land Characterisation: some queries', *Landscapes* 8:2, 64–71

Wilson, D M, 1965 *The Anglo-Saxons*, Penguin, London

CHAPTER 6

ETHNICITY AND ARCHAEOLOGY IN LATER MEDIEVAL IRELAND: THE CHALLENGE OF THE GAEL

By NIALL BRADY

A consideration of the material representation of the Gaelic population in later medieval Ireland must engage directly with an academic conservatism that is associated with 20th-century scholarship. Fresh insight is being provided by recognizing what was accepted in the previous century, and engaging in new fieldwork that focuses on Gaelic lordships in their own right, rather than as elements that occupy the fringes of the colonized Anglo-Norman lands. The examples in this paper are drawn from north Roscommon within the lordship of the O'Conor, and are the result of research being conducted in the Discovery Programme's Medieval Rural Settlement Project module.

INTRODUCTION

Discussion of the archaeology of later medieval Ireland has traditionally been informed by the cultural assemblages associated with the Anglo-Normans and their descendants (Barry 1987). Whether considering urban landscapes or the countryside, artefacts or written sources, the dominance of the colonist is striking. More recently, a national programme of archaeological research has identified the study and understanding of Gaelic Ireland as the single most useful area for further examination in the broader canvas of the period *c*1170–1650 AD (O'Conor 1998, 144). Since 1998 the impetus has been to focus on discrete landscape studies which seek to reveal the nature and development of settlement within Gaelic lordships, recognizing the fact that the Irish, like the Anglo-Norman, represent considerable internal variety (for example, Duffy *et al* 2001; Breen 2005; Doran and Lyttleton 2007).

In many respects, the empirical emphasis of this research has been dictated by the fundamental difficulty of recognizing the indigenous dweller(s) in the archaeological record. In a general sense, the ethnicity of the Irish is clear and distinct, and this is perhaps manifest in the use of the Irish language in the written sources. Yet, the archaeological narrative of the Gael is strangely absent. The 'invisibility' of the Gael is especially potent during the transitional period of the 12th–13th centuries, in the years immediately following the Anglo-Norman incursion to Ireland in 1169. Even in those areas of the country where Gael and Gall co-existed cheek by jowl, such as throughout much of the eastern half of the country where Anglo-Norman manors appear on former Irish-held estates, it seems that the great bulk of data reflect the outsider(s). It would be naïve to suggest that the ethnicity of the Irish, in terms of its archaeological expression, is wholly absorbed by the Anglo-Norman assemblages. The distributions of Anglo-Norman fortifications and artefacts such as pottery reveal gaps in what are known to have been Irish lands. In promoting a solution to this issue, researchers are beginning to express an open-minded attitude to the interpretation of archaeological data as it emerges. This is seen, for instance, in relation to questions of continuity from the early medieval period. The present paper explores some of the issues and draws its examples from research being conducted by the Discovery Programme's Medieval Rural Settlement Project in the central north midlands of Ireland. The questions related to Ireland in the later medieval period are not exclusive to the island. They have obvious comparisons not only with those parts of Britain where the king's rule was less direct, and perhaps most notably Scotland, but also with areas on the continent where local culture becomes the quiet, yet dominant, factor throughout the period (Govan 2003).

AT THE HEART OF THE MATTER: 'ARCHAEOLOGICAL VISIBILITIES'

In any discussion of early medieval Ireland there is rarely a problem in identifying a rich and varied archaeological signature. Throughout the period before *c* 1000 AD, medievalists are content to discuss the dispersed settlement pattern that is richly endowed with a consistent range of primary settlement forms. Enclosed earthworks known as ringforts dominate the settlement record; so-called because of the characteristic earthen bank and ditch that defines their perimeter, these sites number some 45,000 examples and include a range of subtypes identified largely by the nature of their bank construction and the number of enclosing elements (Stout 1997). Ringforts functioned as residences for freemen and nobility. So too did crannogs, artificial islands that served a similar function to ringforts but whose more complex lacustrine locations suggest added defence and prestige, as well as the ability for their inhabitants to interact directly with water systems as the most advantageous communications medium (Wood-Martin 1886; O'Sullivan 1998; Fredengren 2002). Individual church sites and ecclesiastical enclosures form the third most visible early medieval settlement form in Ireland. While many were small sites on a par with the ringforts and crannogs, others were far larger and served as proto-towns (Doherty 1980; King 1998; McErlean and Crothers 2007). Centres such as Clonmacnoise in the central midlands on the River Shannon served such a role, as did the equally impressive site of Glendalough in the Wicklow mountains, and the monastery of Nendrum in Co Down, where recent excavation of the site's tidal watermill has brought renewed focus to the importance of early monasteries as economic hubs. There were more formal urban sites as well, championed by the Hiberno-Norse port towns of Dublin, Waterford and Cork. Within the countryside there are also souterrains, or underground passages and chambers which can occur within ringforts and ecclesiastical enclosures or may be the only obvious element of settlement sites whose perimeters were not defined in a way that has survived (Clinton 2001).

Regardless of where one looks in Ireland, the symphony of these main elements is clearly apparent in an early medieval context (Figure 6.1). There is an understanding that chronological limitations make it difficult to recreate the settlement density in any particular century or part thereof, and discussions have instead focused on the spatial patterns that sites form in relation to one another. It may come to pass that future narrative of early Irish society sees the 9th century as a time of particular expansion (McCormick and Murray 2007, 108–115). This is entirely in keeping with an emerging view of early medieval society across much of Europe, and it is interesting to note that the 8th–10th centuries are where scholars are increasingly happy to see the emergence of villages in the English countryside (Reynolds 2003; Gardiner and Rippon 2007, 1). The cultural dynamic in Ireland may not be unique, and the distinctions may rest in regional differences.

The picture of a densely settled, busy countryside is manifestly different when considering the later medieval landscape (Figure 6.2). Medievalists wrestle with a traditional classification system of field monuments that really does not easily recognize 'native' forms of settlement, other than the more obvious documented continuities witnessed in larger monasteries and in port towns. The picture is

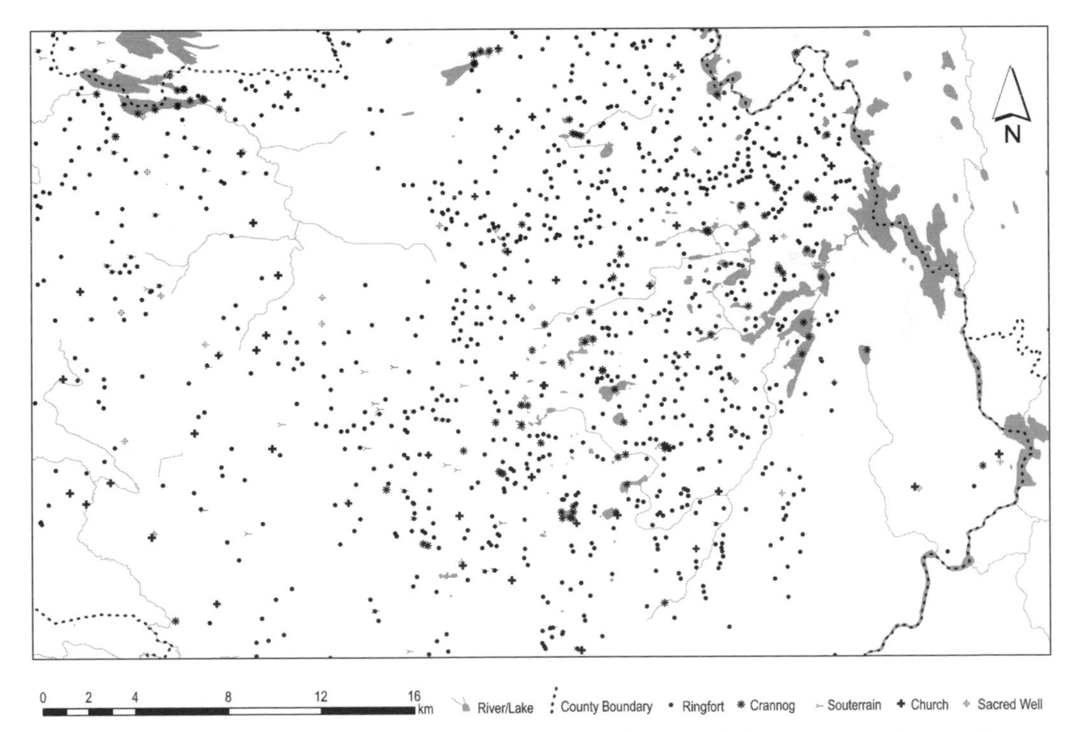

FIGURE 6.1. Distribution of early medieval settlement in north Roscommon. (Source: the Discovery Programme)

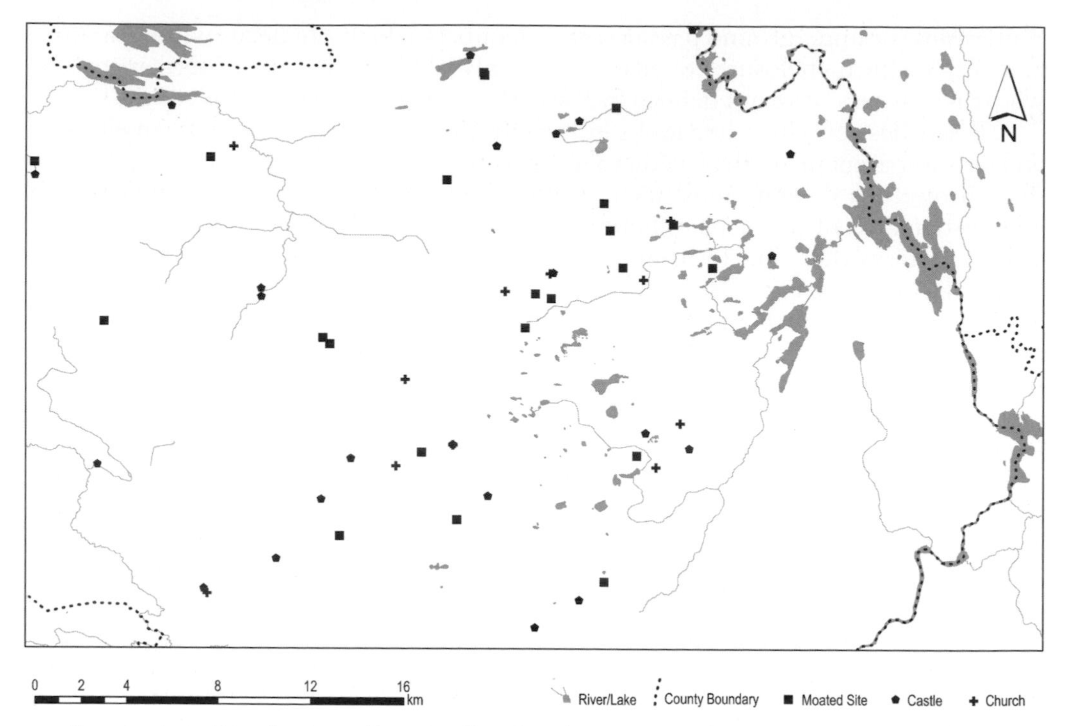

FIGURE 6.2. Distribution of later medieval settlement in north Roscommon. (Source: the Discovery Programme)

dominated by new site types introduced by continental orders and then by the Anglo-Normans: ordered and planned monasteries and bishoprics; formal urban landscapes; motte-and-bailey earthwork castles; and large-scale stone castles typify the settlement forms of the late 12th–14th centuries, with the increasing appearance of villages; while moated sites are seen largely during the 14th century. By and large, but not exclusively, these structures are built by the newcomers. By the 15th century, tower house castles, with or without associated bawns, or associated defended enclosures, occur across the island and are being built by lords regardless of their cultural origins. When considering later medieval Ireland from the perspective of the Anglo-Norman, this situation is hardly a cause for concern since there is a wealth of archaeology to reflect upon. There is also an impressive corpus of written sources that help to illuminate the manorial economy within which many of these sites operated (Down 1987). Difficulty arises, however, when one tries to look at the indigenous Irish, especially in the transitional centuries between the early and later medieval periods; namely the late 12th–early 14th centuries (Barry 1985, 51, 200; O'Keeffe 1996, 143–146; O'Conor 1998, 73–94). The numbers of settlement sites that can be associated with the Irish are few and need to be argued for almost on a case-by-case basis.

To take the example of north Roscommon in the north central midlands of Ireland, this is a landscape that was politically relatively stable throughout much of the medieval period up to the late 1500s. The native kings' rule endured, whether they were the O'Conors to the south or the McDermotts to the north. The king's interests are apparent, either directly by his own hand, with the construction of Roscommon Castle, or through his barons, such as Richard deBurgh's building of Ballintober Castle at the start of the 14th century. Yet the heartlands of the Irish territories remained under direct control of the indigenous kings. To trace the disposition of later medieval sites within these lordships can be a frustrating exercise (Figure 6.2). It is possible to identify who occupied the landscape from the range of written sources that survive, but it is very difficult to 'see' these people in the archaeological record (Connon 2005). The absence of sites across the interior of the O'Conor lordship is striking. When one understands that the distribution indicated is an amalgamation of site types over four centuries, the dearth is even more apparent. The moated sites and 'castle' sites which do much to fill out the 'later medieval settlement pattern' belong largely to the 14th and 15th centuries. The transition period of the 12th–13th centuries presents little physical remains. Opinion has differed on how we should approach a solution to what must be an artificial absence of evidence. Already in the 1980s, it was suggested that we should consider the continuation of earlier settlement forms into the later period (Graham 1988, 29–32). Continuity has raised a guarded response from some quarters, cautious that it may be interpreted as cultural stagnation in contrast to the progressive nature of Irish society seen in other areas (O'Keeffe 1996, 145). That the Irish built castles regularly during the period is a preferred view, thereby demonstrating the emerging cosmopolitan nature of Gaelic Ireland in the high Middle Ages (O'Keeffe 2000, 26–29). However, the evidence for widespread construction of castles by the Irish remains small-scale, despite arguments to the contrary (McNeill 1997, 72–74, 157–164; O'Conor 1998, 75–77; Barry 2007; Kenyon 2007, 126–127; O'Conor 2008).

The picture is further compounded by artefact assemblages from the later period. Ceramics are common throughout much of the medieval west, but the absence of local wheel-thrown potteries is a distinguishing characteristic of Gaelic society. Imported wares are mostly found in the east and south of the country, close to the port towns through which the ceramics would have arrived. Locally made wares based on English and continental forms extend this distribution inland but do not occur in large numbers on Gaelic lands. The degree to which pottery can be used as a cultural indicator has been questioned recently in relation to the Hansa in Finland, where it is suggested that a wider spectrum of interacting factors must be accounted for to explain a particular sequence of distributions (Immonen 2007). Such discussion could usefully be applied to consider the 'ethnicities' of the Anglo-Norman lands, where such pottery is commonplace. Yet the stark contrast in pottery distributions between those lands and the predominantly Gaelic territories must reflect a cultural nuance to some degree. Certain pottery is associated with Gaelic lands, especially those in the north midlands and south Ulster area, where primitive hand-made cooking wares known as 'everted rim ware' and 'souterrain ware' occur. The suggested regionality associated with this crude pottery is deserving of its own study. Overall, however, pottery was not used in any significant way by Gaelic society. Leather, wood and metal would have served in its place as containers and cooking/

eating implements. Such material does not survive well on dryland sites and this adds to the 'invisibility' in the archaeological record.

Current opinion on how to resolve 'invisibility' issues is increasingly disposed towards Graham's view for continuity of settlement form from the preceding early Middle Ages. The emerging results of research into the O'Conor lordship presented below supports the view that continuity is a positive aspect of Irish society and not culturally regressive. Yet the solution is not necessarily straightforward, as the study is revealing a complex mixing of elements which include the absorption of new ideas as well as the adaptation of existing patterns of behaviour. The range of information suggests a vibrant and no doubt varied Gaelic identity that continued through a period marked elsewhere by colonization. It supports the view of a culture that is very much in tune with developments across Europe, but one that is adapted to its own particular regional strengths.

NORTH ROSCOMMON AND THE LORDSHIP OF THE O'CONOR

The Discovery Programme, Ireland's archaeological research institution, has selected the O'Conor lordship in north Roscommon as a study area in which to examine the landscape of a Gaelic territory through the later medieval period (Brady 2003, 7–21). The boundaries of the lordship are more or less coterminous with those of the present-day barony of Roscommon (McNeary and Shanahan 2005, 3 n2). The area occupies a mixed topography, the eastern perimeter of which is delineated by the River Shannon, Ireland's primary river, which affords access to a network of inland lakes across the Irish midlands as well as to the sea via Limerick far to the south (Figure 6.3). The central area of the lordship is divided between a drumlin landscape in the eastern half, filled with small lakes and localized bogland partly associated with the Shannon's floodplain, and a series of limestone ridges in the west which generate excellent grazing potential for livestock and for which the area is renowned. These ridges, which form the core of a limestone plain known as *Magh nAí*, support a rich prehistoric landscape of burial monuments and enclosures centred around Rathcroghan, the ancient heart of the wider region of Connacht, Ireland's north-west province. It is from Rathcroghan that the mythological ruler Queen Maeve controlled her dominion, and it is here that the medieval epic focused on the northern half of Ireland, the *Táin Bo Cualigne*, began. The very western edge of the later O'Conor lordship is defined by peat and bogland, and includes Ballintober, the site of DeBurgh's magnificent castle.

In unravelling the later medieval narrative of this landscape, documentary analysis has proved to be an important asset. The absence of formal manorial accounts and related factual documents on Gaelic estates has led historians to rely heavily on chronicles, genealogies and praise-poems, and these sources do not lend themselves to providing the type of insight to land-holding that archaeologists find most useful. The relict nature of the north Roscommon landscape, however, presents a complex platform onto which toponymic detail can be overlaid, which in turn provides a sense of its historical development (Connon 2005). It is possible to reconstruct medieval parish boundaries, which allows for consideration of the

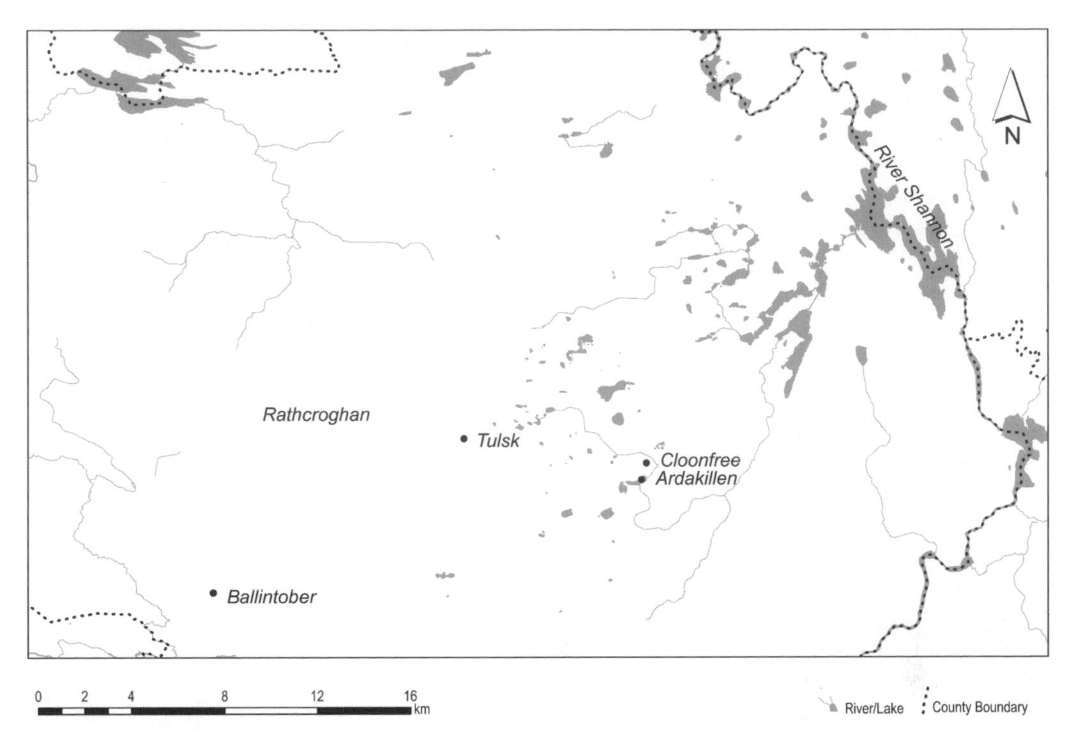

FIGURE 6.3. Sites mentioned in the text. (Source: the Discovery Programme)

disposition of monuments within the parishes, and perhaps affords a good opportunity to consider the nature of the later medieval imprint. It has been suggested that the relative disposition of monuments within medieval estate holdings is a key to understanding the medieval settlement pattern in Gaelic lands, regardless of the early/later medieval origins traditionally assigned to those monuments (Duffy *et al* 2001, 58–60). The Roscommon module is exploring this thesis further using medieval parish boundaries as an overarching framework.

One location where excavation has taken place within the O'Conor lands prior to the present research project is at Ardakillen Lake in the drumlin area, close to Strokestown (see Figure 6.3). The lake was once larger than it is today, and it is filled with archaeological sites, including crannogs located on the old lake bed, a series of earthwork sites and the medieval parish church on and adjacent to the former shoreline. In 1368, Tadhg O'Conor was taken prisoner by Rory O'Conor, king of Connacht, in his own *longphort*-stronghold at Ardakillen (*AC*, 334–335.15). In 1388, Domnaill O'Conor burned the fort of Ardakillen and the adjacent islands (*AU*, 19–21), while in 1467 the *insi*-islands of Ardakillen Lake were taken by O'Conor Don (*AC*, 538–539.10). Drainage works during the 19th century cut through a large crannog on the lake and revealed a settlement whose origins lay in the early medieval period but which also retained a distinct horizon of later medieval activity (Wood-Martin 1886, 236–239; Whitfield 2001). An early timber post palisade is replaced by a stone-wall perimeter, and the range of artefacts recovered echo the two principal occupation horizons. Ham Green pottery, imported from the Bristol area, is 12th–13th century in date and is present among the artefacts recovered from the 'Strokestown crannogs' (O'Sullivan 2001, 406). More detailed survey of the lake area and the adjacent lands is ongoing and should reveal further the extent of the later medieval settlement.

In the 19th century, Ardakillen presented evidence for the continuation of early medieval occupation sites in the later period, yet the acceptance of this as reflecting a more widespread pattern of usage has been slow (Brady and O'Conor 2005). This part of the study area has also produced another challenge to archaeologists who wish to understand the material culture of Gaelic society. The O'Conor lands retain 22 moated sites. Until recently, moated sites in Ireland were widely regarded as being English in origin, representing a later stage of settlement onto the margins during the agricultural expansion experienced before the calamities of the mid-14th century (Barry 1977). The moated site at Cloonfree, close to Ardakillen, reveals a more complex story (Figure 6.4) (Finan and O'Conor 2002). The site is referred to in the chronicles as the residence of Aodh O'Conor which was burned in 1306, and two praise-poems exist from 1300–06 and 1309 respectively which describe the site as the

FIGURE 6.4. Cloonfree moated site, view from the south-east across the ditch. (Source: the Discovery Programme)

exotic construction of Aodh, more wondrous than Cruachan, Tara and Cashel. The sense of exaggeration is part and parcel of this literary genre, but the poems state clearly that the moated site was designed and built by the Irish lord. The poems also describe the residence as a 'four ridged rath' and as a 'stately four-squared rath' respectively (Quiggan 1914, 337; McKenna 1923, 641). In doing so, they present compelling evidence for the conscious decision by Aodh O'Conor to build something novel on his lands, buoyed up by the use of 'foreign arches' whose style is described as 'strange'. Yet Cloonfree is not built classically as a moated site. While it conforms in shape to moated sites more generally, it is not situated adjacent to flowing water which would fill its moat permanently. The site is built on a slight elevation and is more in keeping with the location for a traditional ringfort. Indeed, the references to a four-ridged rath suggest that the novelty of its design lay mostly in its squared shape. Aodh's innovations, it seems, were tempered by a need to retain a sense of what he and his builders were accustomed to. Whether this translates as cultural identity or simply knowing the limitations of his artificers is perhaps a moot point.

Ardakillen crannog and Cloonfree moated site demonstrate indigenous settlement in the later medieval period within the O'Conor lands, if from different perspectives. The extent to which ringforts in the lordship could retain similar evidence for occupation in the later period is a question which the present study addressed directly by selecting a site for investigation at Tulsk (Figure 6.5). Tulsk today is a small village located in the centre of the study area (Figure 6.6). It serves as the junction for what is believed to be a series of ancient routeways running

FIGURE 6.5. Tulsk Fort, view from the south-west. (Source: the Discovery Programme)

FIGURE 6.6. Orthoimage showing aerial survey of Tulsk village and the primary monuments indicated. (Source: the Discovery Programme)

east–west and north–south, connecting Rathcroghan with the River Shannon on the one hand, and the important medieval centres of Boyle to the north and Roscommon to the south respectively. The village is the focal point for a series of townlands and there is a small scattering of archaeological sites in the village. A stone-filled earthen mound in Castleland townland is considered to be the site of Tulsk Castle, noted in contemporary chronicles as being built in 1406, destroyed in 1407, and repeatedly rebuilt, captured and/or destroyed throughout much of the following centuries. It is not a large site, and at 24m × 26m in diameter it is a discretely sized mound lying 112m north of the Dominican Priory, founded in 1448 (Brady *et al* 2005, 41). The priory is in the neighbouring townland of Tulsk, separated from Castleland by a narrow stream, the Ogulla River. The presence of the priory suggests that a larger settlement existed here, but the evidence for this is not forthcoming (Bradley nd). While it is possible that the settlement lies under the modern village, the presence of a large earthen ringfort, known as Tulsk Fort, 98m north-east of the priory and 60m east of Tulsk Castle, presents itself as an anomaly in this otherwise later medieval landscape. The ringfort, which is also in Tulsk townland, is closer to the crossroads of the ancient routeways than either of the other two monuments, at least in terms of the modern alignment of the roads.

The dominant position of the ringfort in the settlement's wider topography suggests that this was a location of primary importance throughout the medieval period. Tulsk Fort is not an ordinary ringfort, whose internal spaces are generally at the same height as that of the surrounding landscape, or at least represent the natural rise of the topography. Tulsk Fort has been described as a rath whose appearance was 'decidedly Norman' (Knox 1911, 225–228). It is perhaps more accurately classified as a raised ringfort/rath. Raised ringforts, or 'platform ringforts' are formed by an enclosing element of bank and external fosse surrounding an interior higher than the surrounding landscape. It is thought that these sites occur late in the series and may owe their origins to ordinary ringforts whose interiors were subsequently raised in height. Few platform ringforts have been investigated, and the majority of those that have are located in the north-east, in Co Down (O'Conor 1998, 90). The example in Tulsk presented an opportunity to extend the enquiry into the north central midlands of Ireland.

The site at Tulsk occupies a slight elevation between the priory and a broad expanse of bogland to the north of the settlement. The mound is egg-shaped in plan with the long axis aligned east to west. It measures 36m east–west by 27m north–south across internally. The banks rise sharply to a height of *c*1.5m above the surrounding field, except in the north-west quadrant where the land falls away some 5.3m towards a small seasonal spring that empties into the Ogulla River. Several relict field banks and associated features are evident in the field around the site. The interior of the site reveals very little insight to the casual observer. Individual stones stand out above the grass but there is little to suggest the presence of significant stone alignments. The most striking feature is an open D-shaped setting built into the northern perimeter. Geophysical survey confirmed the presence of a surrounding fosse or ditch and added further detail to the relict field boundaries that surround the site (Figure 6.7) (Brady and Gibson 2005). The survey also presented a complex of

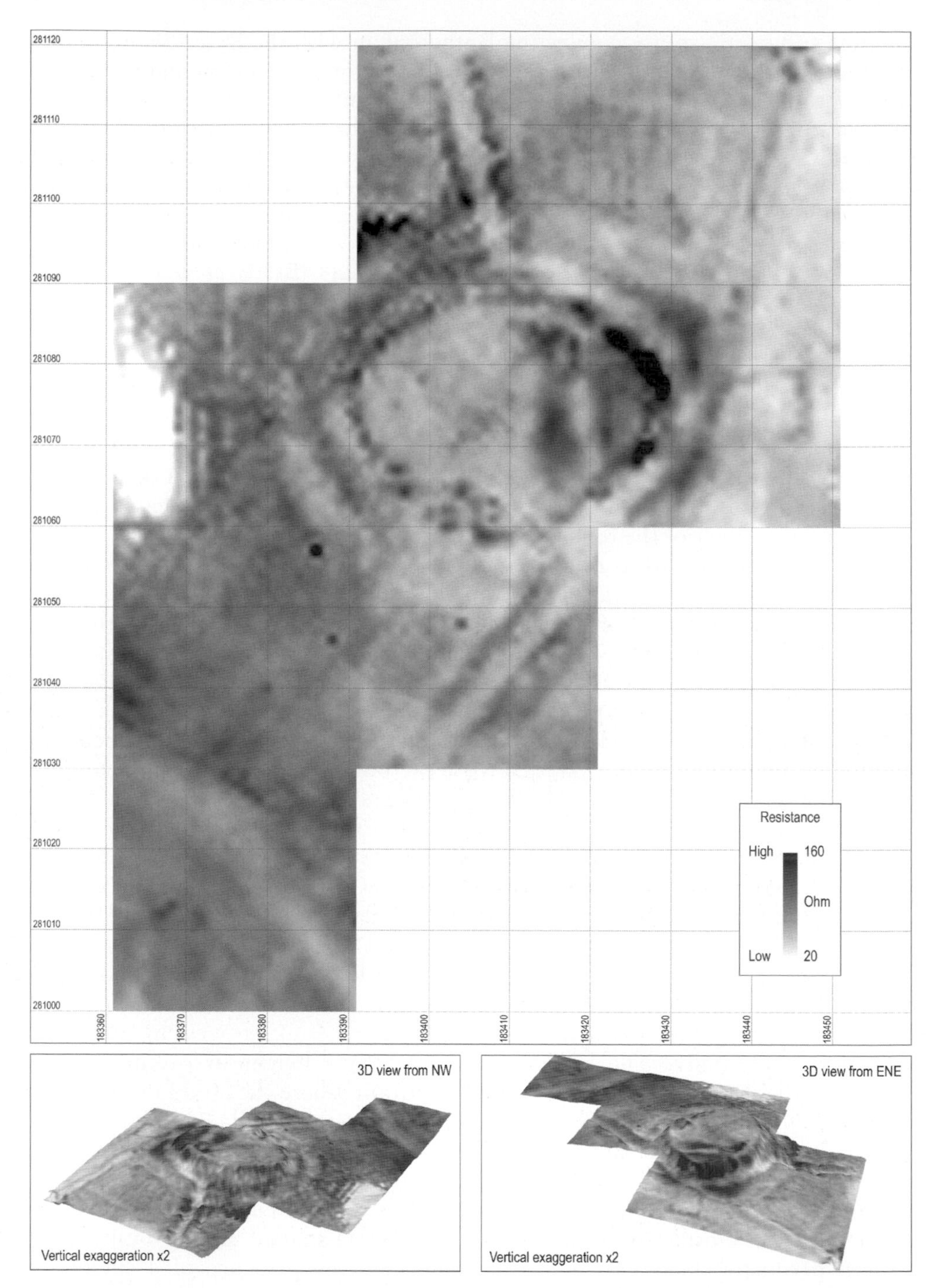

FIGURE 6.7. Resistance Survey, Tulsk Fort. Line-drawing based on GIS-generated map. (Source: the Discovery Programme)

anomalies within the mound's interior, especially along the eastern perimeter where a series of impressive features were indicated, extending across the ditch and further east of the mound. With the hindsight of excavation, much of this complexity can be understood but at the outset the data simply indicated a concentration of contexts and served to suggest where the excavations should focus. It was decided to open a section across the site's interior to achieve an insight to the stratigraphic record. In doing so, a cutting 55m long by 6m wide was opened, and this has subsequently been extended in the eastern half to reveal more fully the north-east quadrant of the site (Figure 6.8).

The excavations have revealed a sequence of five main horizons of activity, two of which appear to be early medieval in date when the site served as a ringfort, and two horizons are later medieval and early modern/Elizabethan in date respectively. The fifth and lowest horizon is prehistoric in date and pre-dates the construction of the ringfort. The earliest medieval stratum seems to belong to the 10th–11th centuries, based on small finds including lignite bracelet fragments, bone pins, copper alloy and iron ringed pins, glass beads and a gaming piece. The assemblage suggests the presence of a reasonably affluent family and is typical of many ringfort excavations. The base of a corn-drying kiln and a series of other burning events and associated ash spreads over the occupation level produced the bulk of the small finds. The bottom of

FIGURE 6.8. Photograph of the Tulsk Fort excavations, 2008, looking north-east from the top of the site, showing the masonry stonework of the medieval tower. (Source: the Discovery Programme)

the ringfort bank and a deep v-shaped fosse associated with it has also been identified. The bank is constructed from boulder clay and is supported by a drystone revetment on its interior. The western part of the site has revealed a sequence of clay deposits introduced to raise the interior surface, and to transform the site into a platform. A depth of *c* 1.2m of these clays survives, but no occupation levels have been associated with the raising event as the uppermost levels were truncated by later activity.

A series of trenches were cut through the introduced clays to accommodate massive rubble foundations which extend in places to more than 2.5m in depth. The foundations supported a masonry tower and this sequence of events represents the first clear appearance of the later medieval horizon. The tower is aligned north-northwest/south-southeast and explains many of the geophysical anomalies on the eastern side of the site. It retains battered external walls with a rounded north-east corner; the only corner exposed by excavation. At this stage, the tower measured 20m long by 10m wide externally. A garderobe set into the wall fed directly into the external fosse. The interior space appears to be divided into a main chamber and a narrow north chamber. There is no obvious entrance to the tower and it remains possible that this lies in the unexcavated southern half. In creating the tower, the builders modified other parts of the ringfort. They recut the external ditch to make a broader but shallower fosse. They also cut a ditch internally to separate the tower from the wider interior of the site, thereby creating a bawn area from the larger ringfort space. In time the tower collapsed, or was collapsed, and a period of rebuilding occurred that included a 15m long by 9m wide extension to the tower on its eastern side. The extension effectively transformed the site by filling in the fosse at this location and adding what was probably a fortified house or hall to that side of the tower.

All of these events occurred before the mid-1500s, it seems, because at that stage the ruined, encastellated ringfort enjoyed one last horizon of activity when it was reoccupied to serve as part of garrisoning works associated with the queen's governor to Connaught, Sir Richard Bingham. Bingham visited Tulsk in the 1590s and his presence had already been suggested by the reworking of the chancel end of the priory as quarters for his cavalry (O'Conor *et al* 1996, 68). The discovery of what appear to be padstones to support timber-framed buildings on top of the former ringfort, along with a stone-lined cellar and small finds dominated by musket and pistol shot, and silver coin, indicate that Bingham's works extended to what would have been a very suitable platform from which to protect his northern flank.

The excavations at Tulsk Fort roundly inform issues surrounding continuity of ringforts beyond the 1st millennium. The results have not yet revealed continuous settlement from the early medieval period into the later medieval period because each new significant building horizon effectively truncated the upper levels of preceding deposits with the resultant loss of contextual information. There are some indications for continuity from the small finds recovered, but these matters need to be teased out in greater detail. In the meantime, the presence of the medieval tower, which is probably 15th-century in date, demonstrates a desire to occupy older settlement types and thereby maintain a link with the past. The complexity of the site also calls into question the association of the historically referenced Tulsk Castle with the mound in the adjacent Castleland townland. That site has yet to be investigated, but it is relatively slight in comparison. It is perhaps worth suggesting that the ringfort may have served as the castle site. The foundation of a castle in Tulsk in 1406 must be associated in some way with the emergence of the O'Conor Roe as a separate and distinct line of the O'Conors, following a schism in 1385 which resulted in their line and that of the O'Conor Don, whose primary base lay in Ballintober, to the west. Tulsk became a principal residence of the O'Conor Roe and it is therefore quite appropriate to consider the ringfort in this context.

Among the artefacts recovered is a plough pebble. These modest little stones were used in timber ploughs to prevent wear, and over time the stones are worn back and fall off the plough. Plough pebbles are also found in Britain, Denmark and France, where they were used over several centuries but are for the most part medieval in date. In Ireland, they are exclusively 13th-century in date and are found in the east of the country, associated with Cistercians and Anglo-Normans during a time of great agricultural enterprise (Brady 1988; Brady in press). Plough pebbles in Ireland therefore represent the use of progressive ploughing technology and the associated economic dynamic that goes with it. The discovery of a pebble at the heart of a Gaelic lordship raises some rather interesting possibilities.

The difficulties associated with identifying an archaeological representation of Gaelic society in terms of settlement form only scratches the surface of our understanding of Gaelic society more generally. There is little direct written information concerning the economic basis, and what is available has not helped to counter the disdain with which foreign observers such as Giraldus Cambrensis and Stephen of Lexington held Ireland. The dominance of cattle in Irish documentary sources coupled with the sense to which the Anglo-Normans settled much of the best agricultural land has led inevitably to a tacit understanding that the Gaelic economy was largely pastoral in nature and small in scale. There is little evidence for grain production, aside from the recovery of hand-querns, and there is no real insight to how land was managed or produce stored, processed and distributed. The plough pebble from Tulsk offers some hope of delving more deeply into issues concerning the economic basis of daily life in Gaelic Ireland. What it suggests is that the lands at Tulsk were being ploughed in a very progressive manner and that land productivity was taken seriously. The fact that the Cistercian abbey of Boyle is a mere 35km to the north may suggest the immediate source of this knowledge. The presence of relict fields across this part of north Roscommon has been noted previously and the suggestion was made that the fields retain elements that are later medieval in date (Herity 1988). The present study is beginning to take this work further by conducting a widespread mapping programme of the relict boundaries, which is supported by a series of focused investigations (Shanahan and McNeary 2007). The results so far have shown a multi-layered pattern of land division of which the later medieval period is but a part.

CONCLUSIONS

The Discovery Programme's current research into Gaelic landscapes presents a deep understanding of the archaeology and historical development of the O'Conor

Roe lordship. It advances discussions since the 1980s by exposing new data through focused field assessment and excavation. The emerging results help to distinguish more clearly the material cultural expressions of the native Irish at this time. At certain levels, these data indicate the retention of values that distinguish the Irish from their Anglo-Norman neighbours. There is clear evidence for the occupancy of older settlement forms, such as crannogs and ringforts. The range of finds recovered from the Strokestown crannogs include artefacts from the transitional phase, and, while important late 12th- and 13th-century levels appear to have been truncated at Tulsk, there are some artefacts recovered from disturbed later contexts that fit neatly into the gap.

There is not enough evidence yet to speak with confidence on the question of continuity of use (for a related perspective from art historical circles, see Hourihane 2007). The experimentation with moated site construction, if that is what lies behind the design of Cloonfree, suggests a willingness to absorb mainstream ideas, while still holding on to what is tried and tested. If correctly interpreted, this aspect shows a conservative optimism, and begs a greater question in terms of the extent to which the Irish perceived themselves as being different. The use of plough pebbles reveals a new perspective and shows the presence of rational economic minds, as one sees on the Anglo-Norman manors. The fact that north Roscommon is favoured more as a region for livestock than cultivation perhaps only emphasizes the commitment to enhancing productivity. The pebble opens up an area of research that has been pursued too narrowly, and it may come to pass that archaeology has something useful to contribute to discussions that deal with the economy in Gaelic Ireland. The range of features identified by sinking oneself into the empirical world of field survey and excavation reveals the complexity of any investigation that seeks to identify an ethnicity of one cultural group over another. Shades of grey abound. There is little that seems to be absolute. Ethnicity indeed may be a concept that interests modern-day researchers rather more than it did the Irish in the Middle Ages.

ACKNOWLEDGEMENTS

I wish to thank Terry Barry, Thomas Finan, Kieran O'Conor, Jimmy Schryver and John Soderberg for ongoing conversations and discussions on the various topics addressed in this paper. I would also like to acknowledge my colleagues in the Discovery Programme with whom I continue to enjoy investigating the north Roscommon landscape, especially Anne Connon, Anthony Corns, Rory McNeary, Michael Potterton, Brian Shanahan, Robert Shaw and Ingelise Stujits.

BIBLIOGRAPHY

Annals of Connacht, 1944, ed and trans A M Freeman, Institute for Advanced Studies, Dublin

Annals of Ulster, ed and trans W M Hennessy and B MacCarthy, 1895, vol III AD 1379–1541, Stationery Office, Dublin

Barry, T B, 1977 *Medieval Moated Sites in Ireland*, British Archaeological Reports 35, Oxford

Barry, T B, 1987 *The Archaeology of Medieval Ireland*, Methuen, London and New York

Barry, T B, 2007 'The origins of Irish castles: a contribution to the debate', in Manning (ed) 2007, 33–39

Bradley, J, nd 'The Urban Archaeology Survey: Roscommon', unpublished report commissioned by the Office of Public Works

Brady, N, 1988 'The plough pebbles of Ireland', *Tools and Tillage* 6, 47–60

Brady, N, 2003 *Exploring Irish medieval landscapes: the Discovery Programme's Medieval Rural Settlement Project, 2002–2008*, Discovery Programme, Dublin

Brady, N, in press 'Just how far can you go with a pebble? Taking another look at ploughing in medieval Ireland', in J Fenwick (ed), *Lost and Found, ii*, Wordwell, Bray

Brady, N and O'Conor K D, 2005 'The later medieval usage of crannogs in Ireland', *Ruralia* 5, 127–136

Brady, N, and Gibson, P, 2005 'The earthwork at Tulsk, Co. Roscommon: topographical and geophysical survey and preliminary excavation', *Discovery Progamme Reports* 7, 65–75

Brady, N, Connon, A, Corns, A, McNeary, R, Shanahan, B, and Shaw R, 2005 'A survey of the priory and graveyard at Tulsk, Co. Roscommon', *Discovery Progamme Reports* 7, 40–58

Breen, C, 2005 *The Gaelic Lordship of the O'Sullivan Beare: a Landscape Cultural History*, Four Courts Press, Dublin

Clinton, M, 2001 *The Souterrains of Ireland*, Wordwell, Bray

Connon, A, 2005 'Vernacular Gaelic sources for rural settlement in medieval Roscommon 1100–1650 AD: a preliminary study', *Discovery Progamme Reports* 7, 23–31

Doherty, C, 1980 'Exchange and trade in early medieval Ireland', *Journal of the Royal Society of Antiquaries* 110, 67–89

Doran, L and Lyttleton, J (eds), 2007 *Lordship in Medieval Ireland: Image and Reality*, Four Courts Press, Dublin

Down, K, 1987 'Colonial Society and Economy', in A Cosgrove (ed), *A New History of Ireland. ii. Medieval Ireland 1169–1534*, 439–491, reprint, Oxford University Press, Oxford

Duffy, P J, Edwards, D, and FitzPatrick, E, 2001 'Introduction: recovering Gaelic Ireland, c.1250–c.1650', in Duffy *et al* (eds) 2001, 21–73

Duffy, P J, Edwards, D and FitzPatrick, E (eds), 2001 *Gaelic Ireland, c.1250–c.1650: Land, Lordship, and Settlement*, Four Courts Press, Dublin

Finan, T and O'Conor, K D, 2002 'The moated site at Cloonfree, Co. Roscommon', *Journal of the Galway Archaeological and Historical Society*, 54, 72–87

Fredengren, C, 2002 *Crannogs*, Wordwell, Bray

Gardiner, M and Rippon S, 2007 'Introduction: the medieval landscapes of Britain', in M Gardiner and S Rippon (eds), *Medieval Landscapes. Landscape History after Hoskins, Volume 2*, 1–8, Windgather Press, Macclesfield

Govan, S, 2003 *Medieval or Later Rural Settlement in Scotland: 10 Years On*, Historic Scotland, Edinburgh

Graham, B J, 1988 'Medieval settlement in Co. Roscommon', *Proceedings of the Royal Irish Academy* 88c, 19–38

Herity, M, 1988 'A survey of the royal site of Cruachain in Connacht — IV: ancient field systems at Rathcroghan and Carnfree', *Journal of the Royal Society of Antiquaries of Ireland* 118, 67–84

Hourihane, C P, 2007 'Continuing the tradition: insular influences in Irish manuscripts of the late medieval period', in R Moss (ed), *Making and Meaning in Insular Art*, 317–330, Four Courts Press, Dublin

Immonen, V, 2007 'Defining a culture: the meaning of *Hanseatic* in medieval Turku', *Antiquity* 81, 720–732

Kenyon, J R, 2007 'Irish castle studies: a view from across the sea', in Manning (ed) 2007, 123–130

King, H, 1998 *Clonmacnoise Studies volume 1*, Dúchas the heritage service, Dublin

Knox, H T, 1911 'Some Connacht raths and motes', *Journal of the Royal Society of Antiquaries of Ireland* 41, 205–240, 301–342

Manning, C (ed), 2007 *From ringforts to foritified houses. Studies on Castles and Other Monuments in Honour of David Sweetman*, Wordwell, Bray

McCormick, F and Murray, E, 2007 *Knowth and the Zooarchaeology of Early Christian Ireland*, Royal Irish Academy, Dublin

McErlean, T and Crothers, N, 2007 *Harnessing the Tides. The Early Medieval Tide Mills at Nendrum Monastery, Strangford Lough*, The Stationery Office/ Environment and Heritage Service, Belfast

McKenna, L, 1923 'Poem to Cloonfree castle', *Irish Monthly* 51, 639–645

McNeill, T, 1997 *Castles in Ireland: Feudal Power in a Gaelic World*, Routledge, London and New York

McNeary, R and Shanahan, B, 2005 'Medieval settlement, society and land use in the Roscommon areas, an introduction', *Discovery Progamme Reports* 7, 3–22

McNeary, R and Shanahan, B, 2008 'Settlement and enclosure in a medieval Gaelic lordship: a case study from the territory of the O'Conors of North Roscommon', in R Compatangelo-Soussignan, J Bertrand, J Chapman and P Laffont (eds), *Landmarks and Socio-Economic Systems: Constructing of Pre-industrial Landscapes and their Perception by Contemporary Societies*, 187–197, Presses Universitaires de Rennes, Rennes

O'Conor, K D, 1998 *The Archaeology of Medieval Rural Settlement in Ireland*, Discovery Programme Monographs 3, Royal Irish Academy, Dublin

O'Conor, K, 2008 'Castle studies in Ireland — the way forward', *Château Gaillard* 23, 329–339

O'Conor, K D, Keegan, M, and Tiernan, P, 1996 'Tulsk abbey', *Roscommon Archaeological and Historical Journal* 6, 67–69

O'Keeffe, T, 1996 'Rural settlement and cultural identity in Gaelic Ireland, 1000–1500', *Ruralia* 1, 142–153

O'Keeffe, T, 2000 *Medieval Ireland. An Archaeology*, Tempus, Stroud

O'Sullivan, A, 1998 *The Archaeology of Lake Settlement in Ireland*, Discovery Programme Monographs 3, Royal Irish Academy, Dublin

O'Sullivan, A, 2001 'Crannogs in late medieval Gaelic Ireland, c.1350–c.1650', in Duffy *et al* (eds), 2001, 397–417

Quiggan, E C, 1914 'O'Conor's house at Cloonfree', in E C Quiggan (ed), *Essays and Studies Presented to William Ridgeway on his Sixtieth Birthday, 6 August, 1913*, 333–352, Cambridge University Press, Cambridge

Reynolds, A, 2003 'Boundaries and Settlements in later sixth to eleventh century England', in D Griffiths, A Reynolds and S Semple (eds), *Boundaries in Early Medieval Britain*, 98–136, Oxford, Anglo-Saxon Studies in Archaeology and History 12

Stout, M, 1997 *The Irish Ringfort*, Four Courts Press, Dublin

Turner, D, 1998 'Peasant housing and holdings in a marginal area-medieval settlement in the west highlands and islands of Scotland: some problems', *Ruralia* 2, 71–77

Whitfield, N, 2001 'A filigree panel and a coin from an Irish crannog at Alnwick Castle, with an appendix on the discovery of crannogs at Strokestown, Co. Roscommon', *Journal of Irish Archaeology* 10, 49–72

Wood-Martin, W G, 1886 *The Lake-Dwellings of Ireland or Ancient Lacustrine Habitations of Erin Commonly Called Crannogs*, Hodges Figgis, Dublin

CHAPTER 7
MEDIEVAL ARCHAEOLOGY IN ITALY: FROM THE ORIGINS TO THE PRESENT DAY

By ANDREA AUGENTI

In Italy medieval archaeology was practised at least since the 19th century, but it was only after the Second World War that a mature concept of the discipline began to take shape. This paper looks at the evolution of medieval archaeology in the peninsula, mainly through the analysis of the work of some individual scholars and by presenting some key experiences and main tendencies. Finally, it is argued that Italian medieval archaeologists need to let their own work be more coordinated and 'visible', in order to gain a more systematic flow of information and also to prevent the destruction of medieval remains.

INTRODUCTION

In 1967 David Whitehouse wrote that: 'Medieval archaeology in the sense of a field study involving controlled excavation is in its infancy in Italy' (Whitehouse 1967, 63). It was surely true, at the time, but the full picture was not captured by that sentence. The biography of medieval archaeology in Italy is a long and complex story, including a false start, progressive development and a promising current phase.[1] It is also the story of the evolution of many fields of interests and approaches, of different traditions of study that gave birth to one of the most active sectors of Italian archaeology. It is a story that deserves to be investigated and told, which is the aim of this paper. The narrative offered here is articulated in four sections, starting with the first experiences of excavations of medieval sites and then following the progressive growth of the discipline up to present day. Attention is given to the contributions of individual scholars as much as to general trends and developments. Finally, a critical discussion of the present state of the art shows current tendencies and possible new directions for the future.

I CONCEPTION (1870–1950): A DIFFICULT START

In the second half of the 19th century Italy was crowded with local historians interested in the reconstruction of local history on the model of the *longue durée.*

Most of them were amateurs, people deeply embedded in the local context, people whose social position and jobs could be varied (noblemen, bourgeoisie; doctors, pharmacists, lawyers, engineers; and priests, obviously, in Italy!); most of them were persuaded that history could also be written from archaeological evidence. It is not my intention to provide a complete list of all these characters, and I am quite sure that future research will reveal many more names than those we know of at the moment; nevertheless, at least some of them deserve to be mentioned, to give an idea of the wide geographical spread of this phenomenon.

Paolo Vimercati Sozzi (1801–83), for instance, was a count, a member of the lay nobility of the city of Bergamo (Lombardy), and a lawyer; he was a collector, too, very much devoted to gathering evidence related to the history of his own territory. Vimercati Sozzi also carried out excavations on different sites between 1834 and 1869, and wrote many manuscripts (among them is worth citing the *Spicilegio archeologico*) illustrated by objects he either saw or found, dated from the pre-Roman up to early medieval period (Figure 7.1). His work is still of great value for those interested in the archaeology of that specific area (Calderini Mazzucchelli 2004).

Moving to Piedmont, the cemetery of Testona is considered to be the first 'scientifically' explored early medieval Italian necropolis (1878). The site was excavated by Claudio and Edoardo Calandra, father and son; they were not professional archaeologists: Claudio was a politician, while Edoardo was a painter. They both collected ancient arms, and were fascinated by the Lombards (this can be also seen in

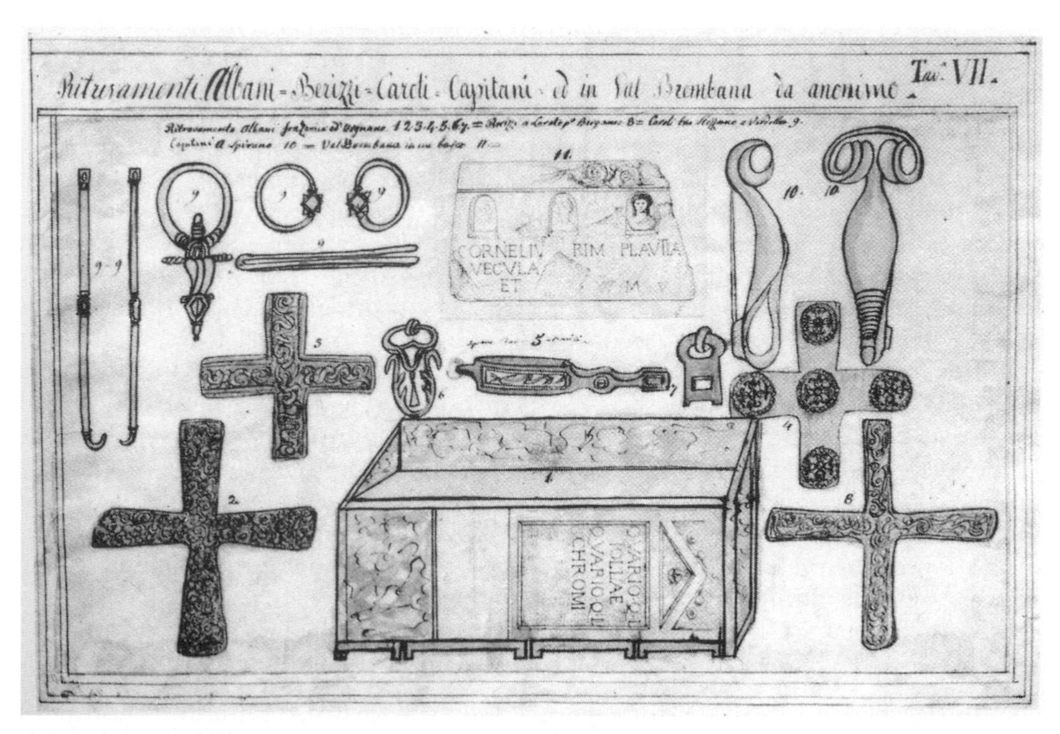

FIGURE 7.1. P Vimercati Sozzi, Spicilegium Archaeologicum. Roman and early medieval objects.

a painting by Edoardo depicting King Alboin and Princess Rosmunda: La Rocca 2004, 178–182) (Figure 7.2). In fact, the work of the Calandras can be placed in a sort of middle ground between the work of local historians and amateurs on one side, and that of professional archaeologists and historians on the other. In this phase, both categories found themselves dealing with early medieval and medieval archaeological horizons.

The profile of Gaetano Chierici (1819–86) is slightly different. Chierici was a priest, and a high school professor in Reggio Emilia (Emilia-Romagna). His main interest was prehistoric archaeology, but he sometimes found himself unintentionally digging medieval sites. This was the case, for example, with S. Ilario d'Enza, an important parish church where he wanted to excavate prehistoric remains, but where he also found (unsurprisingly) early medieval evidence. Chierici published the excavation, in a report that includes what is so far considered to be the oldest section drawing with archaeological stratigraphy and structures published in Italy (1882) (Gelichi 1997a, 23–27). Thus, we can ascribe to Chierici the title of 'accidental medieval archaeologist', something which he could share with many others. He was also a local historian, however, and on this basis he dug certain relevant medieval monuments of the Reggio Emilia district, including the castle of Canossa. Chierici stands in the middle ground between the amateurs and professionals, like the Calandras; perhaps a step forward, according to the quality of his excavations and documentation.

We can now add to this context the work of the professionals. During these years one can observe in action professional archaeologists who mainly belonged to different fields of research, and who, for one reason or another, found themselves excavating medieval remains (sometimes even without noticing). This happened, for instance, to the most distinguished prehistorian of the time, Luigi Pigorini. In 1865 Pigorini thought he had brought to light a prehistoric settlement at Fontanellato, near Parma, but only 20 years afterwards he realized that instead he had found an early medieval village (Gelichi 1997a, 19–21).

Other individuals like Angiolo Pasqui, Raniero Mengarelli and Roberto Paribeni are involved in this history in a different way. They were mainly Classical archaeologists who took charge of the excavations — initially started by local amateurs — of two of the most important early medieval cemeteries discovered in Italy: Nocera Umbra and Castel Trosino.[2] These archaeologists understood the relevance of such discoveries, and briefly dedicated themselves to the study of the Middle Ages. When we look at these scholars' activities, the impression is that in Italy the Middle Ages were broadly considered part of the historical game, and thus were important, alongside the main attraction of 'barbarian' cemeteries. But the main focus stayed on the prehistoric and Roman phases.

Not all archaeologists working in this period were engaged with the Middle Ages, though. It is possible to identify a small group of professional scholars who were deeply interested in the matter, and who pursued a systematic and mature archaeological approach to the post-Roman period. Alfredo D'Andrade (1839–1915), a Portuguese architect, was very active in Piedmont, Liguria, Val'Aosta and Sardinia between the end of the 19th century and the beginning of the 20th. From 1885 he was

FIGURE 7.2. Gepid princess Rosmunda is forced by the Lombard King Alboin to drink from the skull of her own father, according to the writer Paul the Deacon. (Painting: E Calandra 1880)

chief of the Office for the preservation of monuments of Turin, so that he attended to all the excavations and restoration within the city. This was accomplished by giving equal importance to the Roman and medieval remains, a sort of urban archaeology *ante litteram*. No wonder: D'Andrade had mainly trained himself by studying the works of Viollet-le-Duc and Arcisse de Caumont, so that his interests were half-way between architectural restoration and archaeology, and the Middle Ages firmly attracted his attention (he was a close friend of the Calandras, too). He restored many medieval castles, and created himself a medieval 'borgo' for the *Esposizione Generale Italiana* in 1884, based on a detailed knowledge of their archaeological remains (Cerri, Biancolini Fea, Pittarello 1981; Torsello 1997, 96). This is the main reason why D'Andrade has been termed 'a sort of sub-alpin Viollet-Le-Duc' (Settia 1984, 21). One of the most impressive products of D'Andrade is the unpublished *Archaeological Map of Turin* (Figure 7.3), in which Roman and medieval remains are included and given the same degree of importance (Mercando 2003). This work of D'Andrade is quite similar to that of the great Rodolfo Lanciani, who between 1893 and 1901 published the *Forma Urbis Romae*, the gigantic archaeological map of Rome (Palombi 2006, 285–294); it must be said that the two scholars knew each other, and exchanged opinions quite frequently.

Another architect with a pronounced interest in archaeology was Giacomo Boni (1859–1925). Boni started his career in 1885, directing the first medieval excavation

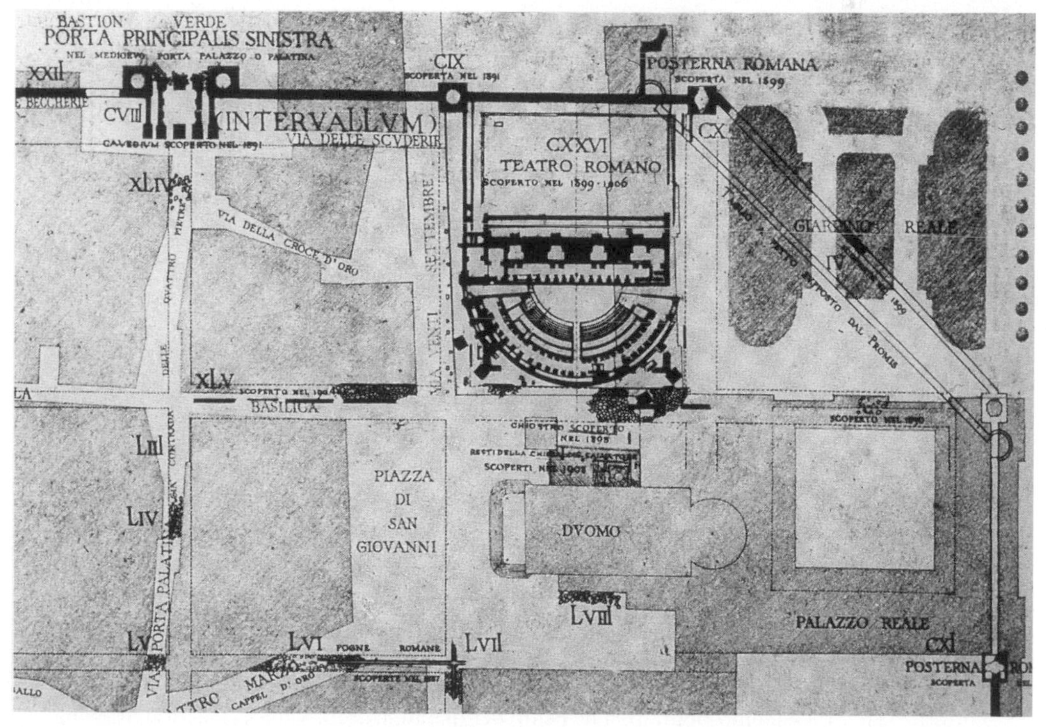

FIGURE 7.3. Late 19th-century archaeological map of Turin (after A D'Andrade).

carried out in Italy not concerned solely with the discovery of a cemetery or a monument, but undertaken to understand how a particular monument had been constructed. The monument in question was the bell-tower of San Marco in Venice, which had collapsed after being struck by lightning (Figure 7.4). Boni understood that the only possibility to reconstruct the tower was to establish by excavation how the foundations had been laid. After this exploit he took charge as a state inspector of medieval monuments in southern Italy, and spent time working in Apulia, Basilicata and Calabria. During his lifetime Boni was in close contact with John Ruskin, Philip Webb and other members of the *Society for the Protection of Ancient Buildings*, so that he knew perfectly the principles that inspired that vision of conservation, and he considered the Middle Ages as the focus of his research activity. From 1895 he was responsible for the archaeology of the central area of Rome, where he excavated several sites. He is considered to be the pioneer of stratigraphical excavation in Italy (he also wrote a short handbook about this, in 1901); a lone pioneer, though, since stratigraphical method started to spread only from the 1970s in historical archaeology. After 1901 Boni became less and less interested in the Middle Ages, and turned his attention to the ancient and archaic history and archaeology of Rome (Augenti 2000).

Thus, medieval archaeology was in the air, and certain scholars practised it with a degree of conviction. The first person to describe medieval archaeology in a

a

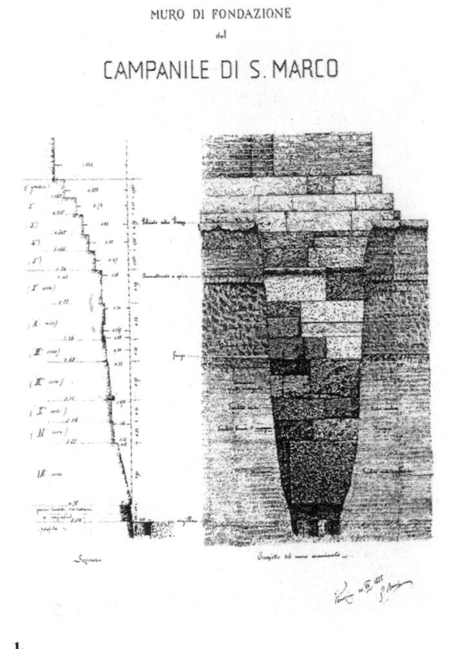

b

FIGURE 7.4. (a) Giacomo Boni. (b) The belltower of San Marco, Venice. (Section drawing: G Boni)

programmatic way was Paolo Orsi (1859–1935), a distinguished archaeologist who worked for most of his life in Sicily. In 1887 Orsi published an article about gold foil crosses of the Lombard period kept in some Italian museums, where he stressed the importance of a discipline that did not exist in Italy: the archaeology of the Middle Ages. Such a field of study — he wrote — was intensively practised in France and Germany, but only sporadically in Italy. If an analysis of objects is fundamental in order to understand past societies, then this is obviously valid also for the centuries after the fall of the Roman empire; and inscriptions should be studied, too, at least until the year AD 1000, 'so to link up classical Romanness with the bourgeoning spring of the true Italian essence' (Orsi 1887, 334; Gelichi 1997a, 33–36). During his years in Sicily, Paolo Orsi directed several excavations of Byzantine villages and cemeteries. He also carried out architectural analysis of standing buildings (mainly churches) (Figure 7.5) and studied in detail objects in museums and from excavations, providing a great and still unsurpassed contribution to the knowledge of the island in the Middle Ages (Orsi 1942). Unfortunately, his call for an Italian medieval archaeology was left almost unheard for many years, with one notable exception.

Ugo Monneret de Villard (1881–1954) can be considered the only scholar who responded from an institutional point of view to Orsi's lament about the lack of medieval archaeology in Italy. Monneret was very much devoted to oriental archaeology, but he was also active in Italy, mainly in Lombardy, where he excavated a number of churches (Figure 7.6). In all this experience he put the Middle Ages at the centre of his interests; and, most importantly, he was the first Italian university

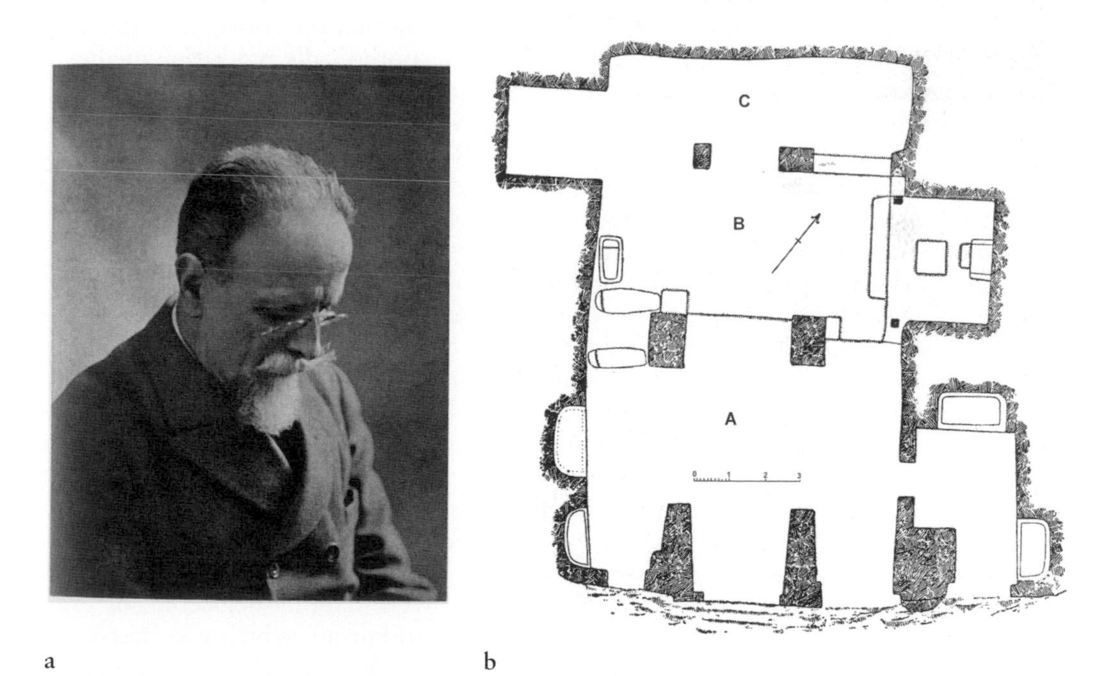

a b

FIGURE 7.5. (a) Paolo Orsi. (b) Buscemi, church of St Peter, Sicily. (Plan drawing: P Orsi)

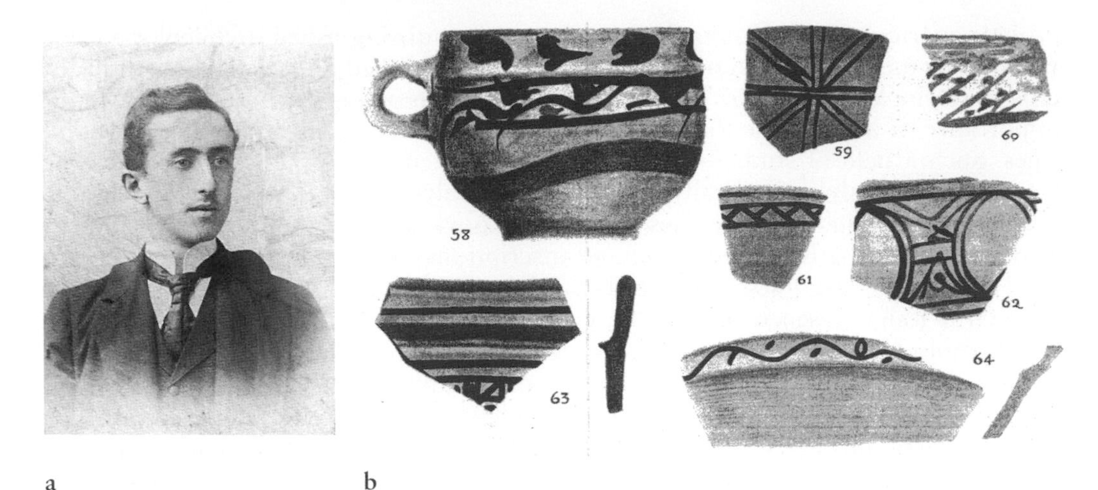

a b

FIGURE 7.6. (a) Ugo Monneret de Villard. (b) Medieval pottery drawn and studied by U Monneret de Villard.

professor of medieval archaeology: in the years 1913–23 he taught the subject in the Politecnico of Milan (Augenti 2001). Unfortunately this experiment was left unrepeated for some decades, but it is the proof that at that time the importance of medieval archaeology was beginning to be recognized.

To sum up, in the time between the birth of the nation (1861) and the first decades of the 20th century, we can see many people sporadically practising medieval archaeology in Italy. Some of them were amateurs, others were professionals who accidentally found themselves excavating medieval horizons; some were scholars systematically involved in the study of the post-Roman period, although somehow they remained isolated within the national archaeological milieu. Thus, the idea of medieval archaeology existed, although most of what happened in the field seems to be linked to the initiative of individuals.

The story of this phase of the development of the discipline is also the story of failure: the Middle Ages were never considered as a milestone of Italian national identity, and thus could easily be dismissed as a subject of study. Take the case of the historian Carlo Cipolla, who started looking at early medieval cemeteries in order to identify the characteristics of the true 'Italians'; when the results of skeletal analysis gave him no suitable answers, he abandoned his archaeological interest (La Rocca 1993). The melting pot represented by early medieval Italy was evidently not the right context to find the roots of purity in the 'Italian race'. During this period the Italian archaeological tradition was dominated by Classics and mostly ancient art history. With the coming of fascism, the Roman empire increasingly became the real focus of research, while other periods and their remains were happily neglected, or even demolished (eg the church of St Hadrian in the Roman Forum, which was destroyed to bring to light the seat of the Roman senate where the church had been set up in the 7th century) (Cederna 1981, 197–208).

Nonetheless, in this phase the three main traditions of study in Italian medieval archaeology were already visible: i) 'barbarian' archaeology; ii) the archaeology of standing monuments; and iii) the archaeology of settlements.

II THE BIRTH OF A DISCIPLINE (1950–73)

Starting in the 1950s, a number of individuals promoted a new awareness of the importance of medieval archaeology in different parts of the nation. Much of the impulse that allowed medieval archaeology to consolidate as a discipline came from Gian Piero Bognetti (1902–63). Bognetti was an eminent legal historian, particularly interested in the Lombard period, who also worked in Venice for some years, where he was involved in the study of the famous medieval town. From these interests sprang the will to excavate two very important sites of early medieval Italian history: Torcello, one of the islands of the Venetian lagoon, and Castelseprio, a Late Antique hillfort and then a small town of Lombardy, where early medieval frescoes had been recently discovered by Bognetti himself in the church of S. Maria *foris portas* (Figure 7.7).

By initiating these two excavations, Bognetti was giving concrete form to his idea that archaeology was a means to solve precise and relevant historical problems. According to his own words, 'it is a historical problem the element that pushes towards archaeological investigation; and it is historic awareness the element that provides, in most cases, the principal criteria for evaluation of the archaeological discoveries' (Bognetti 1961, 67). Bognetti was not an archaeologist. But he showed himself very aware of the methodology, and alert to the possibilities offered by the international scene. In fact, he went for the appropriate method, and chose for both sites to collaborate with a Polish équipe (one of the best European schools for fieldwork, at the time). Stratigraphical excavation was being employed again in an Italian historical context, some decades after Boni's excavations. Unfortunately

a

b

FIGURE 7.7. (a) Gian Pietro Bognetti. (b) Castelseprio, church of Santa Maria foris portas.

Bognetti died before he could see the results of the excavations he promoted, but — mostly thanks to him — Torcello and Castelseprio are still considered key sites of Italian medieval archaeology.

One of the main characteristics of this phase is the growing interaction between Italian scholars and foreign individuals, groups and traditions of study. First we can see engagement with individual German scholars, like Joachim Werner, Fuchs, and then Otto Von Hessen and Volker Bierbrauer. This tradition of study pays much attention to artefacts, mainly from cemeteries and museum collections (see, for instance, Fuchs and Werner 1950; Von Hessen 1968) (Figure 7.8). Fibulae, belt-buckles, weapons, pottery and many more items are considered, but seen as exclusively 'Germanic' objects (this starts from the assumption that objects are markers of ethnicity — an intensely debated issue nowadays). The goal of these scholars was evidently to seek the traces of those Germanic ancestors — mainly Goths and Lombards — who came to Italy between the 3rd and the 6th century. On the other hand, very few excavations were carried out by the 'German school'; the most important is probably Invillino, a Lombard castle of Friuli mentioned by the early medieval writer Paul the Deacon. Unfortunately, no 'Lombard' evidence (cemeteries or objects) came to light during the investigations, and that was the last important German medieval excavation in Italy (Bierbrauer 1987).

Scandinavians played their part, too. Two Swedish teams excavated castles in South Etruria, and started to expand our knowledge of that particular type of settlement (Tordeman and Thordeman 1967; Stiesdal 1962). But the most active foreign group was without doubt the British. Interest in the Middle Ages came first of all during the fieldwork activity of the South Etruria Survey project, led by John Brian Ward-Perkins. In this framework excavations were carried out at different sites such as the papal estates of Santa Cornelia (1960), Santa Rufina (1965), the castles of Castel Porciano (1966) and Mazzano (1971), the city of Tuscania (1971) and others (it is interesting to note that these sites cover a very extended time-span, running from late antiquity to the medieval period) (Christie 1991; Wallace-Hadrill 2001, 107–109). In this context David Whitehouse — who was selected for this purpose by the late John Hurst — started studying the medieval pottery of central and southern Italy, thus picking up the thread of an established tradition of pottery studies which stretched back to scholars like Gaetano Ballardini and Giuseppe Liverani (Whitehouse 1967; Gelichi 1997a, 51–70). With his own work, Whitehouse gave a great and renewed impulse to this fundamental sector in Italian studies. According to Richard Hodges, 'Whitehouse's ground-breaking work became the cornerstone of medieval archaeology in Italy' (Hodges 2006). Certainly, as Chris Wickham has recently argued, scientific medieval archaeology, in English on Italy, begins here (Wickham 2001, 39).

But the time was ripe also for the Italians, and British scholars found in Italy a very fertile context for carrying out medieval archaeology. This was not only due to Bognetti, whose leading role remains nevertheless unquestioned. Nino Lamboglia was born and raised in Liguria, where he worked until his premature death. Lamboglia was a very active scholar, who cultivated different fields of interests. He was a brilliant ceramicist and a scholar much interested in methodology: he is widely considered the man who brought stratigraphic excavation back to the attention of the

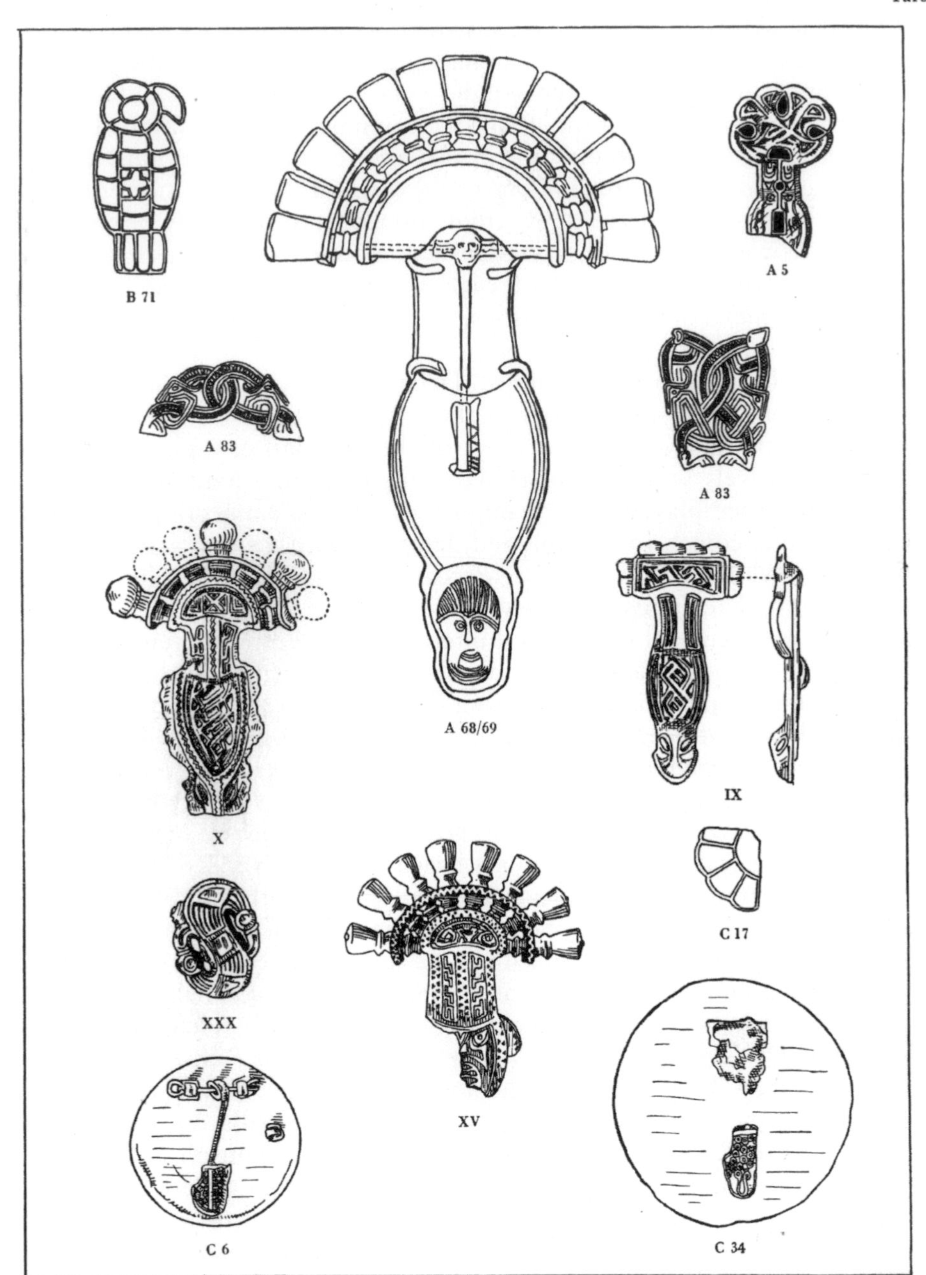
Tafel A
B 71
A 5
A 83
A 83
X
A 68/69
IX
C 17
XXX
XV
C 6
C 34
A 5 Cividale. A 68/69 Nocera Umbra, Grab 2 (vgl. Taf. 13). A 83 Nocera Umbra, Grab 162 (vgl. Taf. 20). B 71 Cividale. C 6 Castel Trosino, Grab 168 (vgl. Taf. 36). C 17 Nocera Umbra, Grab 87. C 34 Castel Trosino, Grab H (vgl. Taf. 43). IX Keszthely (Ungarn). X und XXX Pallersdorf-Bezenye (Ungarn), Grab 20. XV Unbekannter ungarischer Fundort. B 71, C 17 und IX Maßstab 1 : 1. A 83 Maßstab 4 : 5. Alles übrige Maßstab 2 : 3.

FIGURE 7.8. Fibulae of the Lombard period (after Fuchs and Werner 1950).

Italians (after Giacomo Boni's long-forgotten exploit) (Manacorda 1982, 104–109). Lamboglia was mostly devoted to the reconstruction of the history of his own region and, although he was trained in Roman archaeology, he practised fieldwork at many sites of different periods, including the Middle Ages (Varaldo 1997–98). He was also interested in the accurate restoration of ancient monuments, and examined medieval structures in order to distinguish building phases and recent interventions. Thus, one can say that he picked up the thread of one of the original three traditions of study of Italian medieval archaeology cited above, that connected to the study of monuments (a tradition that was never really extinguished, if one takes a look at Richard Krautheimer's drawings at the end of each volume of the *Corpus Basilicarum Christianarum Romae*). For all these reasons, we can consider Lamboglia another key scholar of the time.

Lamboglia selected one of his pupils, Tiziano Mannoni, for the study of the medieval pottery of Liguria (the book was then published in 1975: Mannoni 1975), and it was Mannoni, and with him the rest of the Ligurian group, who started to interact more intensively with British scholars, in particular David Whitehouse and Hugo Blake (the latter played a very important role in connecting the different regional groups: Francovich 1975, 399); and, later on, with a small group of Tuscan historians among whom one can include Riccardo Francovich and Guido Vannini, who soon became archaeologists themselves.

One can find evidence of this fruitful interaction between different groups, and also with French archaeologists, who started to excavate medieval sites in Sicily and Calabria from 1974, by simply browsing the proceedings of what is considered to be 'the founding conference of Italian medieval archaeology', held in Scarperia (Florence) in 1972 (*Archeologia e geografia del popolamento* 1973). Human geographers and medieval historians were also involved in that event, which sparked a dialogue that characterized the evolution of the discipline for many years thereafter.

In the meantime, other Italian scholars based at the University of Salerno were trying to establish a tradition of medieval archaeology in southern Italy. A group led by Paolo Delogu and Paolo Peduto (with a Polish team, again) started excavations in Capaccio (1973), an abandoned city within the ancient Greek colony of *Paestum* (Figure 7.9). In 1974 a Centre for Medieval Archaeology was established, based in the same university (Delogu 1975). At the same time, another research group was established at the University of Palermo (Sicily), the *Group for Research in Medieval Archaeology* (Gruppo Ricerche di Archeologia Medievale). Since 1966 medieval archaeology has been taught in Italy (after Monneret de Villard's long-forgotten achievement), and archaeology posts multiplied all over the peninsula.

And then came the journals. The first, a partial attempt to publish a journal concerning early medieval archaeology, came in the form of *Alto Medioevo* (1967). This publication is important, but it clearly had two main biases. First of all, the limited span of time which it covered: it is archaeology until the year 1000 (possibly a remnant of an old tradition, already seen in Orsi's view). Secondly, there was little space in the journal for 'proper' archaeology, with most of the articles concerning sculpture, and very much linked to art history. The journal died after only two volumes. Nevertheless, the demand for a periodical publication entirely dedicated to

FIGURE 7.9. Excavations in Capaccio (Paestum), 1970s. Wheeler's box-excavation technique is recognizable

medieval archaeology was evident. In 1971 the first number of the *Notiziario di Archaeologia Medievale* (*NAM*) appeared, a newsletter published in Genova by the Ligurian Group, and in the same year the Palermo group gave birth to the *Gruppo Ricerche di Archeologia Medievale*, a similar attempt centred on regional scale.

The same period witnessed the birth of a new museum in Rome: the *Museo dell'Alto Medioevo* (1967). Conceived in order to house finds dated from the end of the Roman empire down to the year 1000 (again!) this museum was the first to consider archaeology as a means to shed light on the early Middle Ages. Thus, this was the first experiment of its kind in Italy. The museum, which remains open today, offers to the public an interesting collection, mainly centred on the Lombard period, through finds gathered mainly from the cemeteries of Noncera Umbra and Castel Trosino (Melucco Vaccaro 1983).

To sum up, this was a very fertile phase in the history of Italian medieval archaeology. In general terms we can still consider this as a protohistoric phase, if one thinks of the general state of research, but the foundations for the birth of the discipline were laid. Certain regional groups carried out intensive fieldwork, and among these the Ligurian group is surely the most structured, the most methodologically advanced, and the most aware of the possibilities offered by the new discipline and its goals. Tuscan and Campanian groups are starting to take shape, and will soon emerge into the field. Interaction with foreign scholars and institutions is now intense, and one of the results of this is the general growth of medieval archaeology. As for chronological concerns, the focus is still mainly on the early Middle Ages, as demonstrated by excavations, journals, and also by the curriculum in university courses (Francovich 1975, 404–407).

As for the contents, the three cited traditions of study of Italian medieval archaeology are still there, but the study of settlements is becoming stronger than before (a minor emphasis on cemeteries can be pointed out during this phase). The study of material culture is assuming a greater importance, above all since the study of pottery on a scientific basis is gaining more and more attention.

III INFANCY (1974–1993)

1974 represents a major turning point in Italian medieval archaeology, being the year of publication of the first volume of the journal *Archaeologia Medievale*, which was mainly the result of the collaboration between the Tuscan and the Ligurian groups. The cultural matrices of the journal are different, and part of this can be detected also in the subtitle 'Material Culture, Settlements, Territory' (*Cultura Materiale, Insediamenti, Territorio*). On one hand, a clear debt is stated towards the historians of the French tradition, since the structure of the subtitle clearly echoes that of the famous journal *Annales: économies, sociétes, civilisations*. On the other hand, the stress on material culture — a concept prioritized in the subtitle of the Italian journal — can possibly be interpreted as a reflection of that particular field in Eastern European archaeology; therefore, it is perceived to play an ideological role.

An influx of other traditions is also detectable in the contents of the journal as much space is devoted, in the early volumes, to the issue of lost villages. This subject was already very popular among historians, geographers and archaeologists in Britain and France, and is now approached by Italians as well. Most research is concentrated on a particular type of abandoned settlements: castles. Another major issue is evidently the study of artefacts, their production and classification.

Another new development is closer attention to stratigraphic and typological methodology. This is not an isolated attitude in the Italian scene: in fact, the 1970s are the years in which these methodologies reappear, thanks to the efforts of scholars such as Nino Lamboglia and Andrea Carandini (in 1981 the latter published the first Italian excavation manual written after Boni's, entitled 'Histories from the Earth' (*Storie dalla terra*) as a tribute to R E M Wheeler's 1954 *Archaeology from the Earth*). More generally, Italian historical archaeology is now slowly casting aside the burden of its marriage with art history. The concept of material culture is therefore expanding, in objects as much as in time, and many other archaeologies are now possible; medieval archaeology is obviously included.

Last but not least, a shift in chronology can be perceived, with many papers and excavation reports dedicated to the later medieval period. Italian medieval archaeology is now taking a fuller shape, also making clear the methods and issues by and on which it will work in the future. Many of these aspects are visible also in the increasing number of conferences concerning the methods and goals of medieval archaeology, the most important ones being the *Colloquio internazionale di archeologia medievale* (Palermo-Erice 1974); the *Tavola rotonda sulla archeologia medievale* (Rome 1975); and *Archeologia medievale nell'Italia settentrionale* (1981).[3]

The leading figure of this period and for the last 30 years is surely Riccardo Francovich (1946–2007) (Figure 7.10), who founded the journal *Archeologia Medievale* at the age of 28 (with his own money). Trained as an historian at the University of Florence by Elio Conti, he taught medieval archaeology in Siena for his entire academic career. A restless scholar, his interests were manifold: the archaeology of rural settlements (castles and villages), study and classification of pottery, archaeology of power, archaeometallurgy. Following the words of Bognetti, he used to start investigations from an historical problem, interrogating sites and territories for a solution and in his way. This is how his major excavations took shape, as at Scarlino and Montarrenti, both conceived in order to understand the roots of medieval

FIGURE 7.10. Riccardo Francovich and Richard Hodges.

landscape, or Rocca San Silvestro, carried out to seek the material traces of mineral extraction and to explore feudal means of controlling metal production when linked to a settlement.

Another important issue for Francovich was the use of technology in archaeological investigation. For example, he was one of the first Italian scholars to appreciate the potential of GIS analysis as computer-aided research, but also geophysical survey, aerial photography and remote sensing. Francovich engaged with all of these important tools, in order to gain precise and relevant information from a quantitative standpoint. In fact, one of the first applications of this approach was the creation of a database including written and archaeological evidence, plus aerial photographs, of the hilltop settlements of medieval Tuscany. Francovich was also very much concerned with problems related to the restoration of medieval monuments, and with politics and ethics, too. Throughout his life, he struggled to protect medieval cultural heritage, and therefore he tried hard to assess and make clear the responsibilities and the duties of the state service for archaeology (*Soprintendenze*) and those of the universities, in order to prevent the former abusing the latter.

As a tireless cultural promoter he organized dozens of conferences, seminars, congresses, schools, and trained three generations of archaeologists. He has been without any doubt one of the greatest European archaeologists of the 20th century, and the motor shaping Italian medieval archaeology from the 1970s. This influence included continuing collaboration with geographers and mostly with historians, which Francovich pursued until his very last days, and also by fostering collaboration and dialogue with foreign scholars and institutions. In the case of Francovich this was sealed by the long-lasting, deep friendship with Richard Hodges, which gave life to the joint excavation of Montarrenti in the 1980s (Figure 7.11).[4]

Again, during this phase much activity was carried out by foreign institutions. The British School at Rome, first under the direction of David Whitehouse (1974–84), and then of Graeme Barker (1984–88) and Richard Hodges (1988–95), has played a key role in the upgrading of Italian medieval archaeology (Wickham 2001, 35–44; Wallace-Hadrill 2001, 120–144). Apart from the excavation of Montarrenti, emphasis must be placed on the project on Farfa Abbey and on the massive investigation of the early medieval monastery of San Vincenzo al Volturno.[5]

The Ecole Française has also been involved in such developments, with teams excavating at the castles of Latium (Caprignano, for example) in order to test archaeologically the historical theories of Pierre Toubert (Hubert 2002). The fruitful dialogue between Italian scholars and these 'schools' is evidenced by the 1989 volume of *Archeologia Medievale*, entirely dedicated to the issue of incastellamento (one of the major topics of Italian medieval archaeology).

Many people are now active in medieval archaeology, in Italy, with the Ligurian and Tuscan groups remaining the largest and most advanced. There are groups and university courses in many regions, while the state service for archaeology began to employ the first medieval archaeologists in the *Soprintendenze* in 1980, although this experiment remains almost unrepeated. And the first chairs of medieval archaeology were also instituted in the universities in 1980. Thus, this period may be considered one of expansion and consolidation, even from an institutional point of view.

FIGURE 7.11. Drawing reconstruction of the 8th-century phase in Montarrenti, Tuscany. Francovich and Hodges' excavation made clear that a Late Antique and an early medieval village had preceded the medieval castle. (After Cantini 2003).

One of the major new achievements of Italian archaeology is now the incorporation of the concepts and methods of urban archaeology. The first such experiment was carried out in Pavia by a British archaeologist, Peter Hudson, followed by the excavation of the *Crypta Balbi* in Rome and the investigation of the major cities of Lombardy (Brogiolo 2000a). The influence of the British tradition is evident in this sector (from Wheeler to the work of M O H Carver). Since urban archaeology is not focused on a specific period, but tries to examine all the evidence from the foundation of a town to the present day, a renewed stress is given to medieval archaeology, especially concerning the transition from Antiquity to Late Antiquity and then the early Middle Ages.

A general shift in interest from the later to the early Middle Ages can be perceived during these years. Proof of this is the subject of the conference held in Pontignano in 1992, *The History of the Early Middle Ages in the Light of Archaeology* (6th–10th centuries) (Francovich and Noyé 1994). The need to understand long-term processes and phenomena by stepping backwards in time is evident. And so, too, is the need to expand the analysis of the context to types of settlement rarely considered before; this is the case for key sites such as Monte Barro (Lombardy) and Perti (Liguria), both Late Antique strongholds.[6]

IV YOUTH AND BEYOND (1994–)

We now enter the youth of medieval archaeology in Italy, in other words the last 15 years. One of the major events during these years is the birth of the Society of Italian Medieval Archaeologists (*SAMI*, 1994). The society — initiated by Francovich — promotes the development of research and organizes national conferences of medieval archaeology, every three years (Gelichi 1997b; Brogiolo 2000b; Fiorillo and Peduto 2003; Francovich and Valenti 2006).

New directions are being undertaken. The boom of research in the field of the archaeology of standing buildings has stimulated the birth of a new journal, *Archeologia dell'architettura* (1996). This is one of the most promising fields for medieval archaeologists, connected with restoration and preservation (and it represents the consolidation of one of the above-cited original three traditions of study of Italian medieval archaeology, which in fact has witnessed a constant growth during these decades).

New issues — or, I should say, old issues under a new light — are also under investigation: cities, for instance.[7] In the last few years a new emphasis has been placed on the study of the cities of the Adriatic Sea. The reason for this development is quite simple, in that in this area a significant body of Italian history was made starting from Late Antiquity to the Middle Ages. In archaeological remains researchers look for the end of the Roman world (Ravenna and Classe, Grado), the shaping of a new urban landscape in the early Middle Ages (Comacchio) and the birth and triumph of one of the most important and powerful European cities, Venice.[8] An insight into the transformation of production and commerce is also provided by this context, facilitating a connection with the international debate on the birth of European economy that was stimulated by Michael McCormick (McCormick 2001).

Ethnicity is also now a much-discussed theme. The situation has radically changed since the 1970s and the 1980s, when a very simplistic attitude led scholars to identify ethnic groups according to the style and form of artefacts and the assortments of grave goods. It was easier then to recognize a Lombard warrior or a Roman lady. But was it? Following the impact of scholars such as Guy Halsall and Walter Pohl (among many others — Halsall 1995; Pohl 1998 and 2000), and after the extraordinary discovery of the *Crypta Balbi* was made, ethnicity is much more debated in Italy. In the *Crypta Balbi* (an ancient monument in the very centre of Rome) a dump was found, with many metal, bone, antler and wooden objects, all traces of intense production. This evidence has been connected with a workshop linked to a monastery, which evidently produced items and weapons used both by Romans and Lombards. In fact, objects from this workshop have been found in the Lombard cemetery of Nocera Umbra (Arena *et al* 2001). In a world where artefacts easily crossed frontiers and whose people could articulate many different concepts through the use of material culture, it seems much more complicated now to establish an individual's ethnic identity, but much more interesting too (see, for instance, Barbiera 2005).

And then there is epigraphy. One hundred years after Orsi's statement about the importance of inscriptions, the project of a corpus was launched in 2002. The volumes of the *Inscriptiones Medii Evi Italiae* are meant to include all Italian inscriptions from the 5th up to the 12th century. One volume has been published so far (Cimarra *et al* 2002); many others are due to appear.

Certain other subjects are also being reconsidered from a different angle, and on a different scale. Such is the case of lost villages (perhaps the backbone of European medieval archaeology). Here a holistic approach towards the medieval landscape is being experimented with, in contrast with the past, when mostly castles were the object of study. Catalogues of sites are now available on a territorial scale, at least for the regions of Apulia and Sardinia (Milanese 2006).

Generally speaking, though, it is possible to identify only one comprehensive project entirely dedicated to the medieval archaeology of an Italian region: that is 'Archaeology of Medieval Landscapes' (*Archeologia dei paesaggi medievali*), concerning Tuscany in the Middle Ages, directed by Riccardo Francovich and carried out by a team of researchers from the University of Siena (Francovich and Valenti 2005). All the elements of the medieval landscape are considered by the project design: cities, castles, villages, churches, monasteries and many other site types. A massive work of cataloguing has been achieved, and many of these sites are being excavated, while aerial and field surveys are undertaken across vast territories. Here we have a good example of archaeological research intelligently aided by new technologies, so as to record and process a massive amount of data. This project is — and will remain without any doubt for a long time — a model for many other similar investigations, in Italy and abroad.

In a nutshell, and surely with many omissions, this is the state of the art of Italian medieval archaeology at the present time. All in all, can we consider the current situation a phase of maturity? My personal view is no, and youth is for me the best metaphor for the current state of the discipline. Italian medieval archaeology is certainly very active and thriving, and a long tradition can be charted, but further strategic direction is needed, if improvement and thus a mature status is to be achieved for the field. I suggest here only some possible directions.

What is necessary for the future is mainly a better balance in the research agenda. First of all, we need to balance our research on geographical grounds. Francovich's project on the Tuscan landscapes stands alone in the national scene. We need more equal coverage of investigation in our regions, some of which are left almost completely untouched by a programmatic research design (for example, Umbria, Marche, Basilicata and others). Such a goal could be achieved gradually, by selecting in advance site-types such as cities, castles, villages or monasteries, or types of artefacts such as pottery or metal finds and exploring them in a systematic way. But the necessity now of an overall regional approach is very urgent.[9]

Then there is the problem of the relationship between medieval archaeology and art history. Here medieval archaeologists have to be brave — as suggested long ago by Andrea Carandini — and to tackle the problem by focusing many more excavations and stratigraphical analyses of the standing structures within important monuments. This is the only way to shed light on the unity of the original context, in a country were the medieval period left such an enormous monumental inheritance. These buildings seem now frozen in the moment in which they were constructed or decorated with frescoes, and they stand completely detached from their original context. Rather, they were frequented daily and utilized by huge numbers of people, and exhibit long histories of restoration, alteration and reconstruction. To write such intense and articulated histories in detail is without doubt one of the principal future goals of medieval archaeology.

A chronological balance is also badly needed in our research agenda. As we have seen, in the 1970s Italian medieval archaeology was very much oriented towards the Middle Ages. Since the 1980s things started to change, and attention expanded to the early medieval period. This shift can be seen not only by browsing the pages of *Archeologia Medievale*, or by considering the subjects of major congresses and seminars held in recent years, or those of the recently published books;[10] a further illustration can be found in the titles of the exhibitions. It is worth noting that, out of the last ten major exhibitions organized in Italy about the medieval period, only two were dedicated to the Middle Ages. Again, a balanced look at the 1000 years or so that we call the medieval period would allow us to see things in perspective and to achieve a better understanding of long-term processes concerning, for instance, the shaping of landscapes and the transformations of material culture.

This leads to my very last point. One of the most important lessons to be learnt from the work of Riccardo Francovich is that we must communicate medieval archaeology to a wider public through books, obviously, but also through museums, exhibitions and archaeological parks. We need to state in many different ways how active and how important our discipline is and can be in our country. This is an urgent priority in a nation where archaeology is mainly a stronghold of the classical scholarly tradition. Culturally, this is not surprising. Italy's past obviously owes very much to the pre-Roman and Roman periods, therefore it is no wonder that it attracts such academic (and popular) attention. The real issue, in this case, is both ethical and political. Because of this general predilection for a selected element of the past, in Italy archaeological remains of the early and later medieval period are constantly at risk. A more coordinated, systematic, communicated and thus visible medieval archaeology is more likely to succeed in challenging this trend, and to provide an overall view of another consistent slice of our past, as interesting, valid and as fundamental as the classical one.

ACKNOWLEDGEMENTS

I would like to thank the editors for their generous assistance with the English text.

NOTES

[1] An overall history of Italian medieval archaeology has not been written yet. Short synthesis and discussions are Delogu 1986; Francovich 1987; Gelichi 1997a; Wickham 1999; La Rocca 2000; Augenti 2005.

[2] New editions of these excavations are now available: Rupp 2005 (Nocera Umbra); Paroli and Ricci 2005.

[3] *Colloquio*; *Tavola rotonda*; *Archeologia medievale nell'Italia settentrionale*.

[4] Hodges 2007; Augenti 2007. A complete bibliography of Francovich's writings is now available in *Archeologia Medievale* 24, 2007, 6–16.

[5] Montarrenti: Cantini 2003; Farfa: McClendon 1987; San Vincenzo al Volturno: Hodges 1993, 1995.

[6] Synthesis on Italian Late Antique and early medieval fortifications: Brogiolo and Gelichi 1996.

[7] A survey including the most recent data is Augenti 2006.

[8] Ravenna, Classe and Grado: Augenti and Bertelli 2007; for Comacchio: Gelichi 2006a; for Venice: Gelichi 2006b; Gelichi 2008.

[9] Also more cities should be taken as objects of study: those that have been selected for an exhaustive monograph so far are few indeed, if one considers the incidence of the urban phenomenon in the peninsula. Plus, the cities of the central and southern area have been much neglected, in comparison with those of the north.

[10] For instance, while a synthesis concerning early medieval towns has been published (Brogiolo and Gelichi 1998 — English-speaking readers are referred to Gelichi 2002), nothing similar for the medieval towns is available yet.

BIBLIOGRAPHY

Anon 1973 'Archeologia e geografia del popolamento', *Quaderni Storici* 24, 689–1016

Anon 1976 *Tavola rotonda sulla archeologia medievale* (Rome 1975), Istituto Nazionale di Archeologia e Storia dell'Arte, Rome

Anon 1983 'Archeologia medievale nell'Italia settentrionale: il prossimo decennio (Pavia, 1981)', *Archeologia Medievale* 10, 43–316

Anon 1978 *Atti del colloquio internazionale di archeologia medievale* (Palermo-Erice, 1974), Istituto di Storia Medievale, Università di Palermo, Palermo

Arena, M S, Delogu, P, Paroli, L Ricci, M, Saguì, L and Vendittelli, L (eds), 2001 *Roma dall'antichità al medioevo. Archeologia e storia nel Museo Nazionale Romano*, Crypta Balbi, Electa, Milan

Augenti, A, 2000 'Giacomo Boni, gli scavi di Santa Maria Antiqua e l'archeologia medievale a Roma all'inizio del Novecento', *Archeologia Medievale* 27, 39–46

Augenti, A, 2001 'Per una storia dell'archeologia medievale italiana: Ugo Monneret de Villard', *Archeologia Medievale* 28, 7–24

Augenti, A, 2005 'Medieval Archaeology in Italy: Current Patterns and Future Perspectives', in P Attema, A Nijboer and A Zifferero (eds), *Papers in Italian Archaeology*, VI. *Communities and Settlements from the Neolithic to the Early Medieval Period, vol. i*, 44–51, British Archaeological Reports International Series 1452, Oxford

Augenti, A (ed), 2006 *Le città italiane tra la tarda Antichità e l'alto Medioevo, Atti del convegno (Ravenna 2004)*, All'Insegna del Giglio, Florence

Augenti, A, 2007 'Per Riccardo Francovich', *Antropologia Museale* 16, 75

Augenti, A and Bertelli, C (eds), 2007 *La croce, la spada e la vela: l'alto Adriatico tra V e VI secolo*, Skira, Milan

Barbanera, M, 1998 *L'archeologia degli Italiani*, Editori Riuniti, Rome

Barbiera, I, 2005 *Changing Lands in Changing Memories. Migration and Identity During the Lombard Invasions*, All'Insegna del Giglio, Florence

Bierbrauer, V, 1987 *Invillino-Ibligo in Friaul I. Die römische Siedlung und das spätantik-frümittelalterliche Castrum*, Beck, München

Bognetti, G P, 1961 'I rapporti pratici tra storia e archeologia', *Bollettino dell'Istituto di Storia della Società e dello Stato Veneziano* 3, 67–76

Brogiolo, G P, 2000 'Urbana, archeologia', in Francovich and Manacorda (eds) 2000, 350–355

Brogiolo, G P (ed), 2000b *II Congresso Nazionale di Archeologia Medievale* (Brescia 2000), All'Insegna del Giglio, Florence

Brogiolo, G P and Gelichi, S, 1996 *Nuove ricerche sui castelli altomedievali dell'Italia settentrionale*, All'Insegna del Giglio, Florence

Brogiolo, G P and Gelichi, S, 1998 *La città nell'alto medioevo italiano. Archeologia e storia*, Laterza, Rome-Bari

Calderini Mazzucchelli, S, 2004 *Paolo Vimercati Sozzi (1801–1883): collezionista e antiquario*, Civica Biblioteca e Archivi Storici 'Angelo Mai', Bergamo

Cantini, F, 2003 *Il castello di Montarrenti — lo scavo archeologico (1982–1987). Per la storia della formazione del villaggio fortificato in Toscana (secc. VII–XV)*, All'Insegna del Giglio, Florence

Cederna, A, 1981 *Mussolini urbanista. Lo sventramento di Roma negli anni del consenso*, Laterza, Rome-Bari

Cerri, M G, Biancolini Fea, D and Pittarello, L (eds), 1981 *Alfredo D'Andrade: tutela e restauro*, Vallecchi, Florence

Christie, N (ed), 1991 *Three South Etrurian Churches: Santa Cornelia, Santa Rufina and San Liberato*, The British School at Rome, London

Cimarra, L, Condello, E, Miglio, L, Signorini, M, Supino, P and Tedeschi, C, 2002 *Lazio — Viterbo, 1* (*Inscriptiones Medii Aevi Italiae*, 1), Centro Italiano di Studi sull'Alto Medioevo, Spoleto

Delogu, P, 1975 'Lo statuto del centro per l'archeologia medievale dell'Università di Salerno', *Archeologia Medievale* 2, 409–410

Delogu, P, 1986 'Archeologia medievale: un bilancio di vent'anni', *Archeologia Medievale* 13, 491–505

Fiorillo, R and Peduto, P (eds), 2003 *Atti del III Congresso Nazionale di Archeologia Medievale* (Salerno 2003), All'Insegna del Giglio, Florence

Francovich, R, 1975 'Archeologia medievale e istituzioni (nota informativa)', *Archeologia Medievale* 2, 399–408

Francovich, R, 1987 'Premessa', in R Francovich (ed), *Archeologia e storia del medioevo italiano*, 9–20, La Nuova Italia Scientifica, Rome

Francovich, R, 2006 'Una nota su Tiziano Mannoni e l'archeologia postclassica', in N Cocuzza and M Medri (eds), *Archeologie. Studi in onore di Tiziano Mannoni*, 9–12, Edipuglia, Bari

Francovich, R and Manacorda, D (eds), 2000 *Dizionario di archeologia*, Laterza, Rome-Bari

Francovich, R and Noyé, G (eds), 1996 *La storia dell'alto Medioevo italiano (VI–X secolo) alla luce dell'archeologia*, All'Insegna del Giglio, Florence

Francovich, R and Valenti, M (eds), 2005 *Archeologia dei paesaggi medievali. Relazione progetto (2000–2004)*, All'Insegna del Giglio, Florence

Francovich, R and Valenti, M (eds), 2006 *IV Congresso Nazionale di Archeologia Medievale* (Abbazia di San Galgano 2006), All'Insegna del Giglio, Florence

Fuchs, S and Werner, J, 1950 *Die langobardischen Fibeln aus Italien*, Mann, Berlin

Gelichi, S, 1997a *Introduzione all'archeologia medievale. Scavi e ricerche in Italia*, Carocci, Rome

Gelichi, S (ed), 1997b *I Congresso Nazionale di Archeologia Medievale* (Pisa 1997), All'Insegna del Giglio, Florence

Gelichi S, 2002 'The Cities', in C La Rocca (ed), *Italy in the Early Middle Ages 476–1000* (*Short Oxford History of Italy*), Oxford University Press, Oxford

Gelichi, S, 2006a '"... Castrum igne combussit ...": Comacchio tra Tarda Antichità e Alto Medioevo', *Archeologia Medievale* 33, 19–48

Gelichi, S, 2006b 'Venezia tra archeologia e storia: la costruzione di un'identità urbana', in Augenti (ed) 2006, 151–183

Gelichi, S, 2008 'Flourishing places in North-Eastern Italy: towns and *emporia* between late antiquity and the Carolingian age', in J Henning (ed), *Post-Roman Towns, Trade and Settlement in Europe and Byzantium*, 1, 77–104, Walter de Gruyter, Berlin–New York

Halsall, G 1995 *Settlement and Social Organization. The Merovingian Region of Metz*, Cambridge University Press, Cambridge

Von Hessen, O, 1968 *Die langobardische Keramik aus Italien*, Steiner Verlag, Wiesbaden
Hodges, R (ed), 1993 *San Vincenzo al Volturno*, I, The British School at Rome, London
Hodges, R (ed), 1995 *San Vincenzo al Volturno*, II, The British School at Rome, London
Hodges, R, 2006 'John Hurst and Fifty Years of the Society for Medieval Archaeology', *Society for Medieval Archaeology Newsletter* 36, 2
Hodges, R, 2007 'Riccardo Francovich (1946–2007)', *Medieval Archaeology* 51, 203–206
Hubert, E, 2002 *L'«incastellamento» en Italie centrale. Pouvoirs, territoire et peuplement dans la Vallée du Turano au Moyen Âge*, École Française de Rome, Rome
La Rocca, C, 1993 'Uno specialismo mancato. Esordi e fallimento dell'archeologia medievale italiana alla fine dell'Ottocento', *Archeologia Medievale* 20, 13–43
La Rocca, C, 2000 'Storia, archeologia e — Medioevo', in Francovich and Manacorda (eds) 2000, 305–311
La Rocca, C, 2004 'L'archeologia e i Longobardi in Italia. Orientamenti, metodi, linee di ricerca', in S Gasparri (ed), *Il regno dei Longobardi in Italia. Archeologia, società e istituzioni*, 173–233, Centro Italiano di Studi sull'Alto Medioevo, Spoleto
Manacorda, D, 1982 'Cento anni di ricerche archeologiche italiane: il dibattito sul metodo', *Quaderni di Storia* 16, 85–119
Mannoni, T, 1975 *La ceramica medievale a Genova e nella Liguria*, Istituto Internazionale di Studi Liguri, Genova
McClendon, C B, 1987 *The Imperial Abbey of Farfa. Architectural Currents of the Early Middle Ages*, Yale University Press, New Haven–London
McCormick, M, 2001 *Origins of the European Economy. Communication and Commerce AD 300–700*, Cambridge University Press, Cambridge
Melucco Vaccaro, A, 1983 'Matrici culturali e struttura del Museo dell'Alto Medioevo in Roma', *Archeologia Medievale* 10, 7–18
Mercando, L (ed), 2003 *Archeologia a Torino. Dall'età preromana all'Alto Medioevo*, Umberto Allemandi & C, Turin
Milanese, M (ed), 2006 *Vita e morte dei villaggi rurali tra medioevo ed età moderna*, All'Insegna del Giglio, Florence
Orsi, P, 1887 'Di due crocette auree del Museo di Bologna e di altre simili trovate nell'Italia superiore e centrale', *Atti e memorie della Reale Deputazione di Storia Patria per le Province di Romagna* V, 333–414
Orsi, P, 1942 *Sicilia bizantina*, Edizioni Clio, Rome
Palombi, D, 2006 *Rodolfo Lanciani. L'archeologia a Roma tra Ottocento e Novecento*, L'Erma di Bretschneider, Rome
Paroli, L and Ricci, M, 2005 *La necropoli altomedievale di Castel Trosino*, All'Insegna del Giglio, Florence
Pohl W, 1998 'Telling the Difference: Signs of Ethnic Identity', in W Pohl and H Reimitz (eds), *Strategies of Distinction: the Construction of Ethnic Communities*, 300–800, 17–70, Brill, Leiden-Boston-Köln
Pohl W, 2000 *Le origini etniche dell'Europa. Barbari e Romani tra antichità e medioevo*, Viella, Rome
Rupp, C, 2005 *Das langobardische Gräberfeld von Nocera Umbra*, I, All'Insegna del Giglio, Florence
Settia, A A, 1984 *Castelli e villaggi dell'Italia padana*, Liguori, Naples
Stiesdal, H, 1962 'Three Deserted Medieval Villages in the Roman Campagna', *Analecta Romana Istituti Danici* 2, 63–100
Thordeman, B and Thordeman, B H (eds), 1967 *San Giovenale*, VI, CVK Gleerup, Lund
Torsello, P, 1997 *Restauro architettonico. Padri, teorie, immagini*, Franco Angeli, Milan

Varaldo, C, 1997–98 'Lamboglia e l'archeologia medievale', *Rivista di Studi Liguri* 63–64, 69–95

Wallace-Hadrill, A, 2001 *The British School at Rome. One Hundred Years*, The British School at Rome, London

Whitehouse, D, 1967 'The Medieval Glazed Pottery of Lazio', *Papers of the British School at Rome*, 35, 40–86

Wickham, C, 1999 'Early Medieval Archaeology in Italy: the Last Twenty Years', *Archeologia Medievale* 26, 7–20

Wickham, C, 2001 'Medieval Studies and the British School at Rome', *Papers of the British School at Rome* 69, 35–48

CHAPTER 8

ITALIAN MEDIEVAL ARCHAEOLOGY: RECENT DEVELOPMENTS AND CONTEMPORARY CHALLENGES

By Gian Pietro Brogiolo

This paper provides an overview of the recent development of medieval archaeology in Italy. Following a review of current knowledge of rural settlement, urbanism, fortified settlement, trade, burial archaeology and churches, the paper moves on to consider contemporary concerns regrading the role, practice and future of the discipline.

INTRODUCTION

There is no clear continuity between Italian medieval archaeology as it developed between the end of the 19th and the beginning of the 20th century, and the discipline defined since the 1970s (Gelichi 1997; Francovich and Brogiolo 1998; Terrenato 1998; Wickham 1999; Augenti 2003), born in the lively cultural context following 1968, animated by a strong will of social and political change. From 1966 a parliamentary committee of inquiry capsized the idealistic concept, then still dominating in Italy, of the heritage as constituted only by artefacts of art-historical interest and of archaeology as ending in the 6th century AD. The necessity of a systematic knowledge not just of artefacts or sites, but also of their context was developed, covering even the medieval period, proposing a preservation program that was not based on fortuitous discoveries, with episodic and often illogical intervention of preservation. This public engagement was connected to the reception of the historiographical interest in daily life and material culture spread by the School of the *Annales*, in accordance with a mainly Marxist approach.

These ideas were expressed in the editorial of the first number of the review *Archeologia Medievale* (1974), which proposed an archaeology of the lower classes, in accordance with some of the theoretical tenets of the Institute for Material Culture of Warsaw, and claiming the necessity of public engagement for the preservation of heritage. The aim was to increase knowledge of material culture, in particular of its more humble expressions, through a systematic application of stratigraphic archaeology. Stratigraphic techniques were acquired by Italian medieval archaeologists thanks to a collaboration with prehistoric and British archaeologists who conducted several campaigns in Italy during the 1960s and 1970s. Italian medieval archaeology was attracted to some of the historiographical problems raised by the study of written sources, such as that of *incastellamento*, analysed by Pierre Toubert (1973) in his work on Southern Sabina.

In the meantime, the contribution of Italian medieval archaeologists to international theoretical debate, in which the lion's share was dominated in the 1970s by the New Archaeology, and in the two following decades by post-processualism, was limited. Notwithstanding the interest with which prehistorians and classical archaeologists welcomed the New Archaeology, this made its first appearance in the field of medieval archaeology only in 1982, thanks to a paper by Richard Hodges. Ten years later (1991), again a British archaeologist (John Moreland) presented to his Italian colleagues post-processualism, which gained just a small number of followers. In part, this could be explained in the light of the marginal role of medieval archaeology in the scientific and academic life of the 1970s and of the 1980s, then dominated by an art-historical and philological approach to the study of the classical past. The study of Late Antiquity was still anchored to the (particularly strong) tradition of Early Christian archaeology, while medieval archaeology was represented by a few groups of ground-breaking specialists mainly based and operating in Milan, Siena and Genoa. At the beginning of the 1980s, the medieval archaeologists working for the *Soprintendenze* were just a dozen, whose engagement in fieldwork prevented them from a steady involvement in research, even if they played a fundamental role in the diffusion of the stratigraphic methodologies applied to rescue excavations. The same is true for the professional archaeologists, who gave birth to cooperative societies such as the *Cooperativa archeologica lombarda* and *Società lombarda di archeologia*, founded in 1981 by people mainly interested in the archaeology of the Middle Ages and working on urban digs in Brescia and Milan. In that period, the most important problem to solve was that of the development of an archaeological discipline interested not just in the study of artefacts of art-historical relevance, but aimed at the reconstruction of complex stratifications through a multi-disciplinary approach.

British Archaeology offered a model that took two decades to take root in Italy, and that sometimes produced an uneasy relationship with Early Christian archaeologists (*infra*). In this sense, medieval archaeologists contributed to the renewal of the discipline more from a practical point of view than from a theoretical one: good examples are the remarkable achievements of Riccardo Francovich and his team at the Siena University in the application of information technologies to archaeology, and of Tiziano Mannoni in the field of archaeometry, of Lanfredo Castelletti of the Musei Civici di Como in that of zooarchaeology and palaeobotany, and of Francesco Mallegni in the study of human remains. Rescue Archaeology represents one of the most important areas in which medieval archaeologists have been involved. In Italy, except for the *regioni a statuto speciale* (Trentino-Alto Adige, Valle d'Aosta, Sicilia), salvage archaeology is an exclusive prerogative of the State. Even in this field, the British theoretical debate exercised a positive influx on Italy, where — not by chance — Martin Carver's pamphlet (2003) *Archaeological Value and Evaluation*, summarizing the debate, was published.

Nonetheless, Rescue Archaeology acquires scientific value only if part of wider research projects (such as those devoted to the reconstruction of the history of a town or of a territory), and only through a rapid publication of its results (or their dissemination through other means). The current situation in Italy does not allow any of these conditions: from a scientific point of view, the results of Rescue Archaeology are often disappointing in comparison with the investment of human and financial resources it involves. However, it has offered a lot of job opportunities for those archaeologists who would be otherwise unemployed. Currently, the archaeologists employed in institutions are 750 (350 in the *Soprintendenze*, and 400 in the universities), but many of them come from an art-historical background, and cannot be considered archaeologists in a full sense.

Italian medieval archaeologists engaged themselves also in the establishment of the archaeology of architecture, the methodological and epistemological basis of which was discussed for the first time in 1987, after a decade of seminal experiences, during the *Summer School on Archaeology* organized by Siena University (Francovich and Parenti 1988). Since then the discipline made its way in the field of archaeology as well as in that of architectural restoration, fostering a lively debate among the scholars of the two disciplines (Mannoni 1995; 1996; 1997; Tagliabue 1993), meeting each other on the occasion of several congresses (Della Torre 1996; De Marchi *et al* 1998; Brogiolo *et al* 1999; Biscontin and Driussi 1996; Cavada and Gentilini 2002), and through the review *Archeologia dell'Architettura*, founded in 1996.

This debate resulted in new methodological approaches, and the discipline has seen an undeniable growth since the pioneer stage of the 1980s (D'Ulizia 2005), but it is affected by a plurality of languages, methods, and research interests that hinder the finding of a common ground by the several scholars working in the field, mainly based in Siena, Genoa, Venice, Brescia, Rome, Milan, Padua, and so on. At the present time, they agree just on the name of the discipline, the 'archaeology of architecture': a denomination that has prevailed over other ones, such as the archaeology of historic buildings, or building stratigraphy.

In general, in the last two decades Italian medieval archaeologists have focused their attention mainly on important historiographical themes, testing their veracity through an analysis of the material evidence. I am going to present here the state of research, illustrating also immediate aims for the future where these can be identified.

Rural settlement

The first experiences in the study of rural settlement are represented by the excavation of several 'second-generation' castles dating to the 10th to 11th century, carried out in southern Tuscany first by Riccardo Francovich and then by Marco Valenti, that offered the opportunity to verify the models elaborated by Pierre Toubert (1973) for the Sabina, and by Chris Wickham (1985) for northern Tuscany. In the beginning these researches were aimed at the reconstruction of the birth and development of these hilltop sites, but later their attention shifted to the evolution of the settlement dynamics in Tuscany between the 6th and the 7th century. The excavations at Scarlino, Montarrenti, Poggibonsi and Mirandolo have brought to light the traces of the early medieval occupation of these sites, attesting the precocious formation of a new nucleated form of settlement on hilltop locations from the end of the 6th and the beginning of the 7th century (Francovich and Hodges 2003; Valenti 2004; 2007). The debate on the genesis and on the characteristics of the medieval rural landscape has found its privileged areas of interest at one end, in the transformation of the countryside during Late Antiquity and in the end of the Roman villas (Brogiolo *et al* 2005; Volpe and Turchiano 2005), and, at the other, in the origin of the new villages, as illustrated by the examples offered by Collegno (province of Turin: Pejrani 2004), Geridu in Sardinia (Milanese 2001), Quattro Macine in Apulia (Arthur 1996), Poggibonsi and Miranduolo in Tuscany (Francovich and Valenti 2007; Nardini and Valenti 2005) and Piadena, Sant'Agata di Castel Bolognese, and Nogara in the Po valley (Gelichi 2005). At the moment, a more traditional approach characterizes research devoted to the castles of southern Italy (cf the proceedings of the congresses in Fiorilla and Peduto 2003; Francovich and Valenti 2006).

Urbanism

Our knowledge of the early medieval town has changed significantly since the 1980s, when the results of the first excavations at Brescia, Verona and Milan allowed a reconstruction of the evolution of urbanism not based exclusively on the documentary record. Notwithstanding the homogeneous picture offered by different sites, there has been a debate (see Ward Perkins 1997 for a synthesis; new researches in Augenti 2006) among those scholars who argued a traumatic fracture in the material fabric of towns (Brogiolo 1984; 1987; Brogiolo and Gelichi 1998), and those who argued a more positive continuity (Ward Perkins 1984; La Rocca 1986). In the course of the second half of 1990s this sharp opposition started fading, substituted by a general consensus on the fact that early medieval urbanism was marked by the coexistence of aspects of continuity and discontinuity, from a material point of view as well as from the institutional one. The cases of Siena (Francovich *et al* 2006), Florence (Cantini *et al* 2007), Naples (Arthur 2002), Rome (Paroli and Vendittelli 2004) and Canosa (Volpe 2007) should be listed among the most interesting researches carried out so far, while the excavations of Rome (*Crypta Balbi*: Arena *et al* 2001) and Brescia Santa Giulia (Brogiolo 1999; Brogiolo *et al* 2005) and the Capitolium (Rossi 2002) have been extensively published.

Fortified settlements

The 'first-generation' rural fortresses, that is to say those built between the 5th and the 7th century AD, have been the subject of interest from historians since the beginning of the 20th century, and Giampiero Bognetti (1948) considered them expression of a militarization of society, affecting and profoundly transforming settlement patterns. This hypothesis has been partly confirmed by the archaeological investigation of several fortresses of northern Italy, such as Castelseprio (Brogiolo and Gelichi 1996), Monte Barro (Brogiolo and Castelletti 2001), Monselice (Brogiolo 1994), Sant'Andrea di Loppio (Maurina 2005), Sant'Antonino di Perti (Murialdo and Mannoni 2001). More recently, in southern Italy certain fortresses (Vaccarizza, Mercato San Severino, Amendolea: Fiorilla and Peduto 2003), placed in the area of the changing frontiers between the Dukedom of Benevento and the Byzantine territories have been the subject of similar research. Moreover, as in the case of Garda, excavation of the fortress went hand in hand with the archaeological investigation of its territory, showing the relevance in the landscape of a number of regions of these fortified settlements, built by the imperial authorities in the 5th century, then by the Goths and the Byzantines in the 6th, and again by the Byzantines and the Lombards between the 7th and the 8th centuries.

Trade

The reconstruction of Mediterranean trade patterns between Late Antiquity and the early Middle Ages, to which archaeologists like John Hayes (1972) and Clementina Panella (1989), down to Simon Keay (1984) and Paul Reynolds (1995), devoted their studies, has recently relied on the exceptional context of the 7th century brought to light at the *Crypta Balbi* in Rome (Paroli and Vendittelli 2004), as well as on the works of Paul Arthur on southern Italy (Arthur 2002), of Federico Cantini on Tuscany (Cantini *et al* 2007), and of the 'Gruppo Ceramis' in northern Italy (Brogiolo and Olcese 2001; Curina and Negrelli 2002; Gelichi and Negrelli 2007). For a general synthesis see Saguì 1998. Meanwhile, the current researches at Comacchio and Nonantola are shedding new light on the vitality of exchange between the Byzantines and the Lombards between the end of the 7th and the 8th century (Gelichi 2007). The study of pottery is of course one important aspect of the archaeology of craft activities, such as metallurgy (for the Lombard period: La Salvia 2007). This has been investigated in its productive aspect (mines, furnaces, and forges), but also — for example, in Tuscany — as a factor affecting the occupation of hilltop sites from the 7th century (Francovich 1993).

Burials

As far as funerary archaeology is concerned, the excavation of cemeteries with grave goods predominated down to the 1990s (Paroli 1997; Brogiolo and Cantino Wataghin 1998), though — even if at a slow pace — interest has been slowly shifted to a study of the ethnic, ritual, social and demographic aspects of burials (La Rocca 1997; Daim 1999; Paroli 2007; Barbiera and Dalla Zuama 2007). Several scholars have affirmed the existence of an evolving aristocracy, in which the ethnic dichotomy between Germans and Romans had no relevance (Barbiera 2005). However, a similar interpretation seems to under-estimate the significance of other tomb typologies, exploring just a single class of burials (those with grave goods in open field cemeteries) and considering only a short chronological span and a limited geographical area, corresponding to the Lombard period and territories. To achieve a better understanding of the different ideologies and funerary rites, the social status of the dead, and aspects of the complexity of the period between the 6th and the 7th century, research should consider also those tombs placed near residential and religious buildings (Brogiolo 2002; Chavarría 2007). Death rituals were managed by restricted social groups, each possessing its burial spaces and expressing local attitudes towards more widely shared beliefs. A similar situation persisted down to the Carolingian period, when burial practices were absorbed under the control of the Church, that tried to impose, not always successfully, a ritual homogeneity and specific inhumations areas next to places of worship (Treffort 1996).

Churches

Church buildings, one of the most important aspects of a society as deeply Christian as that of the Middle Ages, have been the subject of exclusively art-historical and liturgical interest. Only in the last decade have Italian medieval archaeologists studied them systematically, focusing their attention on the origins of the parish (Pergola 1999; Fiocchi Nicolai and Gelichi 2001), and on the different typological and functional aspects of funerary, martyrial, pilgrimage, monastic and hermitage churches (Cantino Wataghin *et al* 2000; Cantino Wataghin 2000; Brogiolo 2001; Brogiolo *et al* 2002). However, the most fruitful approach has been the investigation of the relationship between religious buildings, settlement patterns, and cemeteries (Brogiolo 2003; Brogiolo and Chavarría 2008; Volpe 2008; Gelichi 2008). This requires large numbers of excavations and sample digs, the stratigraphic analysis of the standing fabric of churches, and systematic surveys of the neighbouring territories, in order to obtain an articulated and reliable, even if partial, picture.

During its first 30 years, Italian medieval archaeology privileged a thematic and settlement-based approach to research, focusing on topics such as castles, villages, towns, and burials. Moreover, if the first experiences were devoted initially to the study of the late medieval period, nowadays attention is concentrated on Late Antiquity and on the early Middle Ages. This choice has been inspired by the great urban excavations of the 1980s, as well as by the influence exerted by the project *The Transformation of the Roman World*, financed by the European Science Foundation from 1994 to 2000. In the same context, should be placed the museum exhibitions (and the related catalogues) devoted to Charlemagne and the origins of Europe (among which, that held at Brescia 2000: Brogiolo and Bertelli 2000a, b), and the more recent ones as such that of Turin (Palazzo Bricherasio, 2007: Brogiolo and Chavarría 2007b) and of Venice (Palazzo Grassi, 2008) on Rome and the Barbarians (Roma ei Barbari 2008).

This approach has limits that I will analyse in the conclusion. But first, we must dwell on the most recent developments. Recent years have represented a critical phase for Italian medieval archaeology, the consequences of which are not yet fully apparent.

BETWEEN SUCCESS AND CRISIS

The development of Italian medieval archaeology reached its acme in the second half of the 1990s, marked by contradictory signs of success and crisis. An undeniable success has been represented by the recognition of the discipline by public opinion and by institutions: at Genoa (where Tiziano Mannoni and his team worked mainly in the field of the archaeology of architecture); at Siena (where the local tradition has been consolidated through the organization of the *Summer Schools* at Pontignano and of great symposia, as well as through publishing activity and a great effort in the application of new technologies); in the North (with the seminars on Late Antiquity and the early Middle Ages, colloquia, and the archaeological investigation of castles, villages, churches and cemeteries: Brogiolo and Castelletti 1992; Brogiolo 1994; 1995; 1996a; 1996b; Brogiolo and Gelichi 1996; Brogiolo 1999; Brogiolo and Olcese 2001; Brogiolo 2003; Brogiolo *et al* 2005; Brogiolo and Delogu 2005; Brogiolo and Chavarría 2007a), as well as in the south of Italy where a leading role has been played by the Department of Archaeology at Foggia University, under the scientific direction of Giulio Volpe, promoter of a series of researches focusing on rural settlement and on the religious architecture of Late Antiquity and the early Middle Ages, as well as of congresses devoted to specific themes of southern Italian relevance (on the countryside, Volpe and Turchiano 2005, and on the towns, in press). Thanks to the resources now available, southern Italy appears a privileged area of research, even if not always linked to the most recent and innovative historiographical debate. This is demonstrated by the papers appearing in the proceedings of the colloquia of the *Società degli Archeologi Medievisti Italiani* held at Salerno (2003) and San Galgano (2006), and of the congresses organized at Foggia on Late Antiquity (in 2004 on the countryside, and in 2006 on urbanism), and by prestigious projects such as those of Segesta in Sicily (A Molinari, F Cambi), San Vincenzo al Volturno (F Marazzi, following the excavations directed by R Hodges), Salerno (P Peduto), in Salento (P Arthur), in Calabria (G Noyé), and in the province of Foggia at San Giusto, Herdonia-Ordona, Canosa, and Faràgola (G Volpe). An important role in the success of the early 1990s should be attributed to the *Società degli Archeologi Medievisti Italiani*, founded in 1994 (http://archeologiamedievale.unisi.it/New Pages/SAMI/home.html), that promoted, every three years, the national congresses of Medieval Archaeology at Pisa (1997), Brescia (2000), Salerno (2003), San Galgano (Siena) (2006), Foggia-Manfredonia (2009).

However, the symptoms of a crisis have marked the last decade. This is in part due to the lack of innovative ideas and to the dispersion of medieval archaeologists in a variety of research interests and approaches, but also to the imposition within universities and *Soprintendenze* between 'medieval' and 'Early Christian' archaeologists. Currently, 75 professors are teaching medieval archaeology in universities, but just one-fifth come from the generation of scholars who developed the discipline in Italy, and they are mostly based in southern Italy and in single centres: 32 in the south, 24 in the north (9 working at Bologna University) and 19 in the central regions of the country (9 at Rome). The problem is not just an academic one (these people will develop the next generation of university teachers), but it also has an epistemological nature: what will the discipline of the future be like?

At the moment, 'Early Christian' and 'medieval' archaeologists are separated by different approaches to research, as clearly attested by confronting the proceedings of the last SAMI congress (held in 2006), with the proceedings of the *Convegno nazionale di Archeologia Cristiana* which appeared in 2007 (Bonacasa Carra and Vidale 2007). We are facing the birth of a new generation of scholars (a third of professors will retire in the next ten years), and the discipline has lost its most prestigious figure, Riccardo Francovich, who died tragically in March 2007.

This uncertainty is sharpened by a distinct, epistemological crisis of the discipline, caused by a plurality of factors, and primarily by the disenchantment regarding collaboration with historians, a collaboration that inspired a great part of the research interests of the last 30 years. This union revealed itself to be unfruitful: the archaeologists, following an agenda set by historians, did not follow their own lines of research (*infra*). A similar failure marks even the archaeology of architecture: collaborating with architects, many archaeologists abandoned their interests to support restoration programmes.

Equally important is the retreat of Public Archaeology, caused by a chaotic flood of laws, and by the monopoly of the *Soprintendenze* on Rescue Archaeology, probably the most important area of intervention in the 1980s and in the 1990s of 'medieval' archaeologists, who saw their professional ambitions frustrated by endless precariousness, and excluded from any possibility of evaluation and publication of their data.

Italian medieval archaeology suffered from the fragmentation of its scientific agenda, due to the complete overlap of research interests with the material record (towns, 'first and second generation' castles, villages, churches, cemeteries), often not linked to any wider historiographical and interpretative background (*infra*). This fragmentation gave rise to the appearance of new research areas, embodied by the publication of reviews such as *Archeologia dell'Architettura* (1996) and *Archeologia postmedievale* (1997). Medieval archaeologists played a role of primary importance in the definition of these disciplines, losing their ties with medieval archaeology (Brogiolo 2006; Gelichi and Librenti 2007). In the meanwhile, Islamic archaeology and Byzantine archaeology reclaimed their dignity as autonomous disciplines.

This external and internal crisis coincides with a wider crisis of identity that archaeologists are suffering, wondering what is their public role. At the beginning of the 3rd millennium, in the context of a globalization that is rapidly destroying local and national identities, and challenging the ideas and opinions of those who study the past, a lot of archaeologists feel an urgent need to be an active component of contemporary society. The study of the past has a political significance, especially for the defence of local cultures, made up by landscapes, architecture, and traditions, characterizing territories and distinguishing them from each other.

DEBATING OURSELVES

In a situation such as the current one, marked by growing uncertainty, it is necessary to take sides, avoiding internecine wars and friendly fire, and seeking common ground as much as possible. Obviously, this implies a rethinking of medieval archaeology in the legislative and institutional context, preserving its own identity, acquired over more than 30 years of experience. The challenge is to achieve public recognition, also from an economic point of view, as a group of people whose work has social significance.

At the end of a phase lasting more than 30 years, Italian medieval archaeology must fight for its survival, redefining its theoretical and methodological basis. This process must involve a dialogue with the archaeologists of early Christianity in order to find common ground, to construct a new discipline, linked to international trends in archaeology, exploring new topics, as well as other disciplines linked to the study of the Middle Ages.

In Italy, medieval archaeology defined itself as ancillary to the stratigraphic method, aimed — according to some archaeologists — at the reconstruction of sequences of excavated sites, eventually comprising a wide range of technical and scientific analyses. It is indeed an instrument for the recovery and organization of data, but this organization should not be considered as neutral, because it depends on specific theoretical assumptions, influencing the way in which the data are recovered.

In its problematic relationship with scholars of written sources, Italian medieval archaeology limited its intervention to comparing the available data with existing historiographical theories, in particular with those linked to the tradition of the *Annales* or of neo-Marxism/neo-positivism. With rare exceptions, it had no connection with post-processualism. This is not a negative factor, if one considers how post-processualism proposed an uncritical multiculturalism, denying *a priori* the existence of differences among cultures; an over-valuation of ideas as factors for change, to the detriment of the role of the economic, political, and military ones; a superficial approach, by non-archaeologists, of 'second-hand' material data, in order to construct interpretative models. These resulted in inconsistent interpretations deconstructing the data offered by the written record as well as those offered by archaeology. Italian medieval archaeology, remaining without connection to post-processualism, must renew itself and confirm its disciplinary autonomy, asserting:

(a) the centrality of archaeology in the construction of historical models for the post-classical period, rejecting any subordination to scholars of written sources, and creating autonomous research interests, as — for example — palaeo-environmental reconstruction (currently pursued by various scholars based in Milan, Padua, and Siena), in order to evaluate the impact of climatic change between Late Antiquity and the early Middle Ages, but also the form of exploitation of the territories around the settlements of the period; the study of human remains (for which Pisa University is still the most important centre), in order to compare the results of analysis carried out by physical anthropologists with the theories of cultural ones;

(b) the role of the *longue durée*, according to the tradition of the *Annales* (Bintliff 1991), and a comparison with medieval archaeologists operating on a diachronic approach;

(c) the uniting of the several, divided research fields, in the light of the experience of 'global archaeology' proposed by Tiziano Mannoni in the 1980s (Mannoni 1994), and of the so-called 'archaeology of complexity' (Brogiolo 2007). The aim is an interdisciplinary approach, exploiting the contribution of ethno-archaeology, through the analysis of traditional economies and societies in rural areas (Vidale 2004). Reconstructed through the written sources or directly observed 'in action', material culture can provide useful models for the interpretation of the societies of the past. The aim is that of overcoming processualist and post-processualist theories, often characterized by a marked determinism or by fanciful reconstructions (Giannichedda 2002). This will allow the reconstruction of a general sequence, between micro and macro-history, comprising technological and economic aspects, as well as those pertaining to the sphere of society and ideology (Trigger 1996). Three important areas of research are: the territories of farming, pasture, and transhumance, of metallurgy and of other pre-industrial craft-activities, and of hydraulic systems; living spaces, comprising scattered settlements and nucleated ones; and ideological spaces, rich in symbolic significance (churches in the first place, but also caves, 'witch trees', and the scene of traumatic events such as battlefields, which remained alive in collective memory).

These intertwined areas of research should be investigated through a plurality of sources, exploring their inter-relations, but through different interpretative readings: (a) in a physical network (the communication systems), connecting a web of different places; (b) in their economic and social relations, determined by functions or by the movement of wealth (investment, revenue, gift); (c) in their symbolic network, linking different sections of a territory, such as the processions which, still during the Modern period, were organized and performed at abandoned settlements or at the sites of important events.

In many areas, as for example in the mountains, there is extraordinary evidence of satellite-sites gravitating around settlements: caves and shelters inhabited by hermits, hunters and shepherds, production-installations exploiting water-power, pastures and slopes used in the context of pastoral activities; mines. Nowadays these are marginal sites, but in the past, down to the second half of the 20th century, they were of primary importance for the local economies. These are complex and stratified landscapes, evolving through mutually integrated structures (settlements, productive and symbolical spaces), each with its own rhythm and duration: settlements that often survived crisis and the abandonment of single production centres, reconverting their economic basis, as occurred in several areas after the closure of metallurgical installations. In the same way, places of worship sometimes survive the disappearance of the settlements they served, and — even if losing their economic and social function — acquired a wide symbolic significance. These different rhythms cannot be compressed into rigid chronological phases, clearly separated from each other, but should be considered in the context of multi-phase sites, sometimes changing their function and significance, but also remaining unaltered through time, as in the case of the shelters used by shepherds since the Bronze Age to the first half of the 20th century. The last surviving shepherds could describe in detail the ancestral practices linked to these sites.

The work of the archaeologist must not be limited to the reconstruction of the evolution of the countryside. Italy has a long urban history, starting at the beginning the 1st millennium BC: at the origins of urbanism are aristocratic and patronage societies that founded proto-urban settlements and then real towns, extending over their territories a close net of economic, social and ideological relations. The reconstruction of this net is the primary aim of our research, collecting the evidence and recomposing it, in order to identify the transformations of the ties between the *central places* and the countryside.

In the context of a similar perspective, archaeological research devoted to the post-classical period should be limited to a precise chronological span or to a specific thematic and methodological issue (as, for example, building and craft activities, the landscape and settlement history, or religious buildings), but must also try to draw wide pictures. In the last years, Medieval Archaeology segmented into a variety of approaches, all with their own label (*Historical Archaeology*, *Industrial Archaeology*,

Ethno-archaeology, Contemporary Archaeology, Landscape Archaeology, Material Culture Studies, Rescue Archaeology). A more interesting approach is perhaps that of an *Archaeology of Complexity and of Relationships*, the chronological and spatial limits of which can not be determined *a priori*, depending of the nature and quality of the available sources as well as on the duration of the single phenomenon (Brogiolo 2007).

It is necessary to pass from a *conjunctural* archaeology, one that classifies sites, architectural heritage, and landscapes on the basis of their dimensions and function, even if in a reconstructed sequence, to a *diachronic* archaeology, trying to define the transformations of social and cultural contexts, from their first evidence to the pre-Industrial age, to reconstruct the evolution of the identity of a territory and of the communities inhabiting it through time. The aim is not that of a *local* archaeology, but the insertion of local history in the context of a web of relations: 'dig locally, think globally', to use the words of Orser (Orser 2007).

For this reason, it is necessary to widen and recompose the knowledge of single scholars, modulating it on the basis of the object of research and applying to it new methodologies and techniques. The development of a new epistemological approach is needed, overcoming the interpretation of the material world as the exclusive product of the mind (Hodder 1992; 1999), and these all-too-successful attempts to clear away positivist research methods (Tilley 1991). Economic and social history should retake the centre-stage, not by reproposing obsolete historiographical themes, but through a refoundation of Italian medieval archaeology, rethinking its methodologies, research interests and chronological limits.

At the same time, a reflection of the social significance of the work of the archaeologist is necessary. Archaeological research played a role of first importance in the construction of national identities, as clearly attested by the use of the medieval past during the Risorgimento and by the exploitation of the idea of the Roman Empire by the Fascists. After World War II, Italian archaeology gave up the political use of history, but now it is necessary to rethink this choice, in the face of globalization. Archaeologists should not be neutral before the demolition of all the values on which Western society rested since the Renaissance, ignoring a consumerism that flattens our values and lives, except for economic differences, and which deadens democratic institutions. In Italy the Catholic Church is trying to reassert a vision of the world as having its roots in the Middle Ages, and the lay parties define themselves simply as 'progressive', in the name of a mistaken multiculturalism, and do not oppose the loss of our cultural traditions. Archaeologists of the post-classical period, who investigate the origins of the contemporary world, should not renounce the possibility of holding a public role. The past was not always a peaceful meeting place between cultures, as it appears in the politically correct visions of some post-modernists as underlined by Liebeschuetz (2001), but was often a place of violent conflict and of the usurpation of the rights of the people. In the reconstruction of this past, not only the cult of saints must play a central role, but also social and economic history, following in the tradition of that rational analysis of reality that runs through the West from Copernicus to Bertrand Russell.

BIBLIOGRAPHY

Arena, M S, Delogu, P, Ricci, M, Saguì, L and Vendittelli, L, 2001 *Roma dall'Antichità al Medioevo. Archeologia e storia nel Museo Nazionale romano Crypta Balbi*, Electa, Milano

Arthur, P, 1996 'Masseria Quattro Macine — A deserted medieval village and its territory in Southern Apulia: an interim report on field survey, excavation and document analysis', *Papers of the British School at Rome* 64, 181–237

Arthur, P, 2002 *Neaples. From Roman Town to City State*, Archaeological Monographs of The British School at Rome 12, Austin and Sons Ltd, Hertford

Augenti, A, 2003 'Archeologia medievale in Italia. Tendenze attuali e prospettive future', *Archeologia Medievale* 30, 511–518

Augenti, A (ed), 2006 *Le città italiane tra la tarda Antichità e l'alto Medioevo, Atti convegno (Ravenna 2004)*, All'Insegna del Giglio, Firenze

Barbiera, I, 2005 *Changing Lands in Changing Memories. Migration and Identity during the Lombard Invasions*, Biblioteca di Archeologia Medievale 19, All'Insegna del Giglio, Firenze

Barbiera, I and Dalla Zuanna, G, 2007 'Le dinamiche della popolazione nell'Italia medievale. Nuovi riscontri su documenti e reperti archeologici', *Archeologia Medievale* 34, 19–42

Bintliff, J (ed), 1991 *The* Annales *School and Archaeology*, New York University Press, New York

Biscontin, G and Driussi, G (a cura di), 1996 *Dal sito archeologico all'archeologia del costruito, Atti del convegno (Bressanone)*, Arcadia Ricerche, Padova

Bognetti, G P, 1948 'S. Maria foris portas di Castelseprio e la Storia religiosa dei Longobardi', in G P Bognetti, G Chierici and A De Capitani d'Arzago, *Santa Maria di Castelseprio*, 11–51, Fondazione Treccani per la storia di Milano, Milano, rist. in Bognetti G P, *L'età longobarda*, III, Milano 1966.1

Bonacasa Carra, R M and Vidale, E (eds), 2007, *La cristianizzazione in italia fra tardoantico ed altomedioevo: aspetti e problemi*, Atti del IX Congresso nazionale di Archeologia Cristiana (Agrigento 20–25 novembre 2004), Saladino, Palermo

Brogiolo G P, 1984 'La città tra tarda antichità e Medioevo', in G P Brogiolo (ed), *Archeologia urbana in Lombardia*, 48–56, Panini, Modena

Brogiolo, G P, 1987 'A proposito dell'organizzazione urbana nell'altomedioevo', *Archeologia medievale* 14, 27–46

Brogiolo, G P, 1994 'Ricerche archeologiche su Monselice bizantina e longobarda', in A Rigon (ed), *Monselice. Storia, cultura e arte di un centro 'minore' del* Veneto, 46–63, Canova Treviso

Brogiolo, G P (ed), 1999 *S. Giulia di Brescia. Gli scavi dal 1980 al 1992. Reperti preromani, romani e alto medievali*, All'Insegna del Giglio, Firenze

Brogiolo, G P, 2002 'Oratori funerari tra VII e VIII secolo nelle campagne transpadane', *Hortus Artium Medievalium* 8, 8–31

Brogiolo, G P, 2006 'Ha un futuro l'archeologia dell'architettura?', in N Cucuzza and M Medri (eds), *Archeologie. Studi in onore di Tiziano Mannoni*, 437–439, Edipuglia, Bari

Brogiolo, G P, 2007 'Dall'Archeologia dell'architettura all'Archeologia della complessità', *Pyrenae* 38:1, 7–38

Brogiolo, G P (ed), 1994 *Edilizia residenziale tra V e VIII secolo*, Atti 4° seminario sul tardoantico e l'altomedioevo in Italia centrosettentrionale (Monte Barro 1993), Società archeologica padana, Mantova

Brogiolo, G P (ed), 1995 *Città, castelli, campagne nei territori di frontiera (secoli VI–VII)*, Atti 5° seminario sul tardoantico e l'altomedioevo in Italia centrosettentrionale (Monte Barro 1994), Società archeologica padana, Mantova

Brogiolo, G P (ed), 1996a *Early Medieval Towns in the Western Mediterranean*, Atti conv. internaz. (Ravello 1994), Società archeologica padana, Mantova

Brogiolo, G P (ed), 1996b *La fine delle ville romane: trasformazioni nelle campagne tra Tarda Antichità e Alto Medioevo*, Atti convegno (Gardone Riviera 1995), Società archeologica padana, Mantova

Brogiolo, G P (ed), 1999 *Le fortificazioni del Garda e i sistemi di difesa dell'Italia settentrionale tra tardo antico e alto medioevo*, 1–167 (Gardone Riviera 1998), Società archeologica padana, Mantova

Brogiolo, G P (ed), 2001 *Le chiese rurali tra VII e VIII secolo in Italia settentrionale* (Garda 2000), Società archeologica padana, Mantova

Brogiolo, G P (ed), 2003 *Chiese e insediamenti nelle campagne tra V e VI secolo, Atti 9° seminario sul tardo antico e l'alto medioevo* (Garlate 2002), Società archeologica padana, Mantova

Brogiolo, G P, Bellosi, G and Doratiotto, L (eds), 2002 *Testimonianze archeologiche a S. Stefano di Garlate*, Stefanoni, Lecco

Brogiolo, G P and Bertelli, C (eds), 2000a *Il futuro dei Longobardi. L'Italia e la costruzione dell'Europa di Carlo Magno*, catalogo della mostra (Brescia 2000), Skirà, Milano

Brogiolo, G P and Bertelli, C (eds), 2000b *Il futuro dei Longobardi. L'Italia e la costruzione dell'Europa di Carlo Magno. Saggi*, Skirà, Milano

Brogiolo, G P and Cantino Wataghin, G (eds), 1998, *Sepolture tra IV e VIII secolo*, 7° seminario sul tardo antico e l'alto medioevo in Italia centrosettentrionale (Gardone Riviera 1996), Società archeologica padana, Mantova

Brogiolo, G P and Castelletti, L (eds), 1992 *Il territorio tra tardoantico e altomedioevo. Metodi di indagine e risultati*, Atti 3° seminario sul tardoantico e l'altomedioevo (Monte Barro 1991), Biblioteca di Archeologia Medievale, All'Insegna del Giglio, Firenze

Brogiolo, G P and Castelletti, L (eds), 2001 *Archeologia a Monte Barro II – Gli scavi 1990–97 e le ricerche al S. Martino di Lecco*, Consorzio Parco Monte Barro, Oggiono

Brogiolo, G P and Chavarría, A, 2005 *Aristocrazie e campagne nell'Occidente mediterrraneo da Costantino a Carlomagno*, All'Insegna del Giglio, Firenze

Brogiolo, G P and Chavarría Arnau, A (eds), 2007a *Archeologia e società tra Tardo Antico e Altomedioevo*, Atti 12° seminario sul Tardo Antico e l'Altomedioevo (Padova 2005), Società archeologica padana, Mantova

Brogiolo, G P and Chavarría Arnau, A (eds), 2007b *I Longobardi. Dalla caduta dell'Impero all'alba dell'Italia*, catalogo della mostra, Silvana, Milano

Brogiolo, G P and Chavarría Arnau, A, 2008 'Chiese, territorio e dinamiche del popolamento nelle campagne tra tardoantico e altomedioevo', *Hortus Artium Medievalium* 14, 7–29

Brogiolo, G P, Chavarría, A and Valenti, M (eds), 2005 *Dopo la fine delle ville: evoluzione nelle campagne dal VI al IX secolo*, 11 Seminario sul Tardo Antico e l'Alto Medioevo (Gavi 2004), Documenti di Archeologia 40, Società archeologica padana, Mantova

Brogiolo, G P and Delogu, P (eds), 2005 *L'Adriatico dalla tarda antichità all'età carolingia*, Atti convegno (Brescia 2001), All'Insegna del Giglio, Firenze

Brogiolo, G P, De Marchi, M and Della Torre, S (eds), 1999, *I metodi dell'archeologia e il progetto d'intervento sull'architettura* (Atti del convegno, Brescia 1996), New Press, Como

Brogiolo, G P and Gelichi, S, 1996 *Nuove ricerche sui castelli altomedievali in Italia settentrionale*, All'Insegna del Giglio, Firenze

Brogiolo, G P and Gelichi, S (eds), 1996 *Le ceramiche altomedievali (fine VI–X secolo) in Italia settentrionale: produzioni e commerci*, Atti 6° seminario sul tardoantico e l'altomedioevo in Italia centrosettentrionale (Monte Barro 1995), Società archeologica padana, Mantova

Brogiolo, G P and Gelichi, S, 1998 *La città nell'alto medioevo italiano*, Laterza, Bari (5.a ed. 2005)

Brogiolo, G P, Morandini, F and Rossi, F (eds), 2005, *Dalle* domus *alla corte regia. S. Giulia di Brescia. Gli scavi dal 1980 al 1992*, All'Insegna del Giglio, Firenze

Brogiolo, G P and Olcese, G (eds), 2001 *Produzione ceramica in area padana tra il II secolo a.C. e il VII d.C.* (Desenzano 1999), Società archeologica padana, Mantova

Cantini, F, Francovich, R, Cianferoni, C and Scampoli, E, 2007 *Firenze prima degli Uffizi*, All'Insegna del Giglio, Firenze

Cantino Wataghin, G, Destefanis, E and Uggé, S, 2000 'Monasteri e territorio: l'Italia settentrionale nell'alto medioevo', Atti del II Congresso Nazionale SAMI, 311–316 (Brescia 2000), All'Insegna del Giglio, Firenze

Cantino Wataghin, G, 2000 'Monasteri tra VIII e IX secolo: evidenze archeologiche per l'Italia settentrionale', in Brogiolo and Bertelli (eds) 2000b, 129–141

Carver, M O H, 1998 *Sutton Hoo: a Burial Ground of Kings?*, British Museum Press, London

Carver, M O H, 2003, *Archaeological Value and Evaluation*, Società archeologica padana, Mantova

Cavada, E and Gentilini, G (eds), 2002 *Il progetto di restauro architettonico. Dall'analisi all'intervento* (Trento 2000), Provincia autonoma di Trento, Trento

Chavarría, A, 2007 '*Splendida sepulcra ut posteri audiant.* Aristocrazie, mausolei e chiese funerarie nelle campagne tardoantiche', in Brogiolo and Chavarría Arnau (eds)2007a, 127–146

Curina, R and Negrelli, C (eds), 2002 *1° Incontro di studio sulle ceramiche tardoantiche e altomedievali*, Atti del Convegno (Manerba 1998), Società archeologica padana, Mantova

Daim, F, 1999 'Archaeology, ethnicity and the structures of identification: the example of the Avars, Carantanians and Moravians in the eighth century', in W Pohl and H Reimitz (eds), *Strategies of Distinction. The Construction of Ethnic Communities, 300–800*, 71–93, Transformation of the Roman World 2, Brill, Leiden–Boston–Köln

Della Torre, S (ed), 1996 *Storia delle tecniche murarie e tutela del costruito. Esperienze e questioni di metodo* (Brescia 1995), Guerini Studio, Milano

De Marchi, M, Mailland, F and Zavaglia, A (eds), 1998 *Lo spessore storico in architettura tra conservazione, restauro, distruzione* (Milano 1995), Regione Lombardia, Milano

D'Ulizia, A, 2005 'L'Archeologia dell'architettura in Italia. Sintesi e bilancio degli studi', *Archeologia dell'architettura* 10, 9–41

Fiocchi Nicolai, V and Gelichi, S, 2001 'Battisteri e chiese rurali (IV–VII secolo), in L'edificio battesimale in Italia. Aspetti e problemi', Atti dell'VIII Congresso Nazionale di Archeologia Cristiana (Genova, Sarzana, Albenga, Finale Ligure, Ventimiglia, 1998), 303–384, Istituto internazionale di studi liguri, Bordighera

Fiorilla, R and Peduto, P (eds), 2003, *III congresso di Archeologia medievale* (Salerno 2003), All'Insegna del Giglio, Firenze

Francovich, R (ed), 1993 *Archeologia delle Attività Estrattive e Metallurgiche* (Pontignano 1991), All'Insegna del Giglio, Firenze

Francovich, R and Parenti, R (eds), 1988 *Archeologia e Restauro dei Monumenti, I ciclo di lezioni sulla ricerca applicata in Archeologia* (Certosa di Pontignano 1987), All'Insegna del Giglio, Firenze

Francovich, R and Brogiolo, G P, 1998 'Some problems in the medieval archaeology of Italy', in H Hundsbichler *et al* (eds), *Die Vielfalt der Dinge. Neue Wege zur Analyse mitellalterlicher Sachkultur* (Krems an der Donau 1994), 117–141, Österreichen Akademie der Wissenschaften, Wien

Francovich, R and Hodges, R, 2003 *Villa to Village: the Transformation of Italian Rural Settlement*, Duckworth, London

Francovich, R and Valenti, M (eds), 2006 *IV congresso di Archeologia medievale* (San Galgano 2006), All'Insegna del Giglio, Firenze

Francovich, R, Valenti, M and Cantini, F, 2006 'Scavi nella città di Siena', in Augenti (ed) 2006, 273–298

Francovich, R and Valenti, M (eds), 2007, *Poggio Imperiale a Poggibonsi. Il territorio, lo scavo, il parco*, Silvana editoriale, Milano

Gelichi, S, 1997 *Introduzione all'archeologia medievale. Scavi e ricerche in Italia*, Carocci, Roma

Gelichi, S (ed), 2005 *Campagne medievali. Strutture materiali, economia e società nell'insediamento rurale dell'Italia settentrionale (VIII–X secolo)*, (Nonantola-S. Giovanni in Persiceto 2003), Documenti di Archeologia, 37, Società archeologica padana, Mantova

Gelichi, S (ed), 2007 'Comacchio e il suo territorio tra la Tarda Antichità e l'Alto Medioevo', in F Berti, M Bollini, S Gelichi and J Ortalli (eds), *Uomini, territorio e culto dall'Antichità all'Alto Medioevo*, 365–689, Corbo Editore, Ferrara

Gelichi, S, 2008 'Costruire territori. Il monastero di Nonantola e le sue terre nell'altomedioevo', *Hortus Artium Medievalium* 14, 65–79

Gelichi, S and Librenti, M, 2007 *Constructing Post-Medieval Archaeology in Italy: a new agenda, Proceedings of the International Conference* (Venice 2006), All'Insegna del Giglio, Firenze

Gelichi, S and Negrelli, C, 2007 *La circolazione delle ceramiche nell'Adriatico tra Tarda Antichità e Altomedioevo* (3° incontro di studio Ceramis), Documenti di Archeologia, 43, Società archeologica padana, Mantova

Giannichedda, E, 2002 *Archeologia teorica*, Carocci, Roma

Hayes, J W, 1972 *Late Roman Pottery*, London, British School at Rome

Hodder, I, 1992 *Leggere il passato. Tendenze attuali dell'archeologia* (orig edn *Reading the Past. Current Approaches to Interpretation in Archaeology*, Cambridge 1986), Einaudi, Torino

Hodder, I, 1999 *The Archaeological Process, An Introduction*, Blackwell, Oxford

Hodges, R, 1982 'Method and theory in medieval archaeology', *Archeologia Medievale* 8, 7–37

Keay, S J, 1984, *Late Roman Anphorae in the Western Mediterranean: a Typology and Economic Study. The Catalan Evidence*, 2 vols, British Archaeological Report International Series 196, Oxford

La Rocca, C, 1986 '*Dark ages* a Verona. Edilizia privata, aree aperte e strutture pubbliche in una città dell'Italia settentrionale', *Archeologia Medievale* 13, 31–78

La Rocca, C, 1997 'Segni di distinzione. Dai corredi funebri alle donazioni "post obitum" nel regno longobardo', in Paroli (ed) 1997, 31–54

La Salvia, V, 2007 *Iron Making During the Migration Period: the Case of the Lombards*, British Archaeological Reports International Series 1715, Oxford

Liebeschuetz, W, 2001 'Late Antiquity and the concept of decline', *Nottingham Medieval Studies* 45, 1–11

Mannoni, T, 1994 *Archeologia dell'urbanistica*, Escum, Genova

Mannoni, T, 1995 'Lo stato dell'archeologia del costruito in Italia. Prima parte', *Notiziario di Archeologia Medievale* 66, 25–27

Mannoni, T, 1996 'Lo stato dell'archeologia del costruito in Italia. Seconda parte', *Notiziario di Archeologia Medievale* 67, 7–11

Mannoni, T, 1997 'Lo stato dell'archeologia del costruito in Italia. Terza parte', *Notiziario di Archeologia Medievale* 68, 10–11

Maurina, B, 2005 'Insediamenti fortificati tardoantichi in area trentina: il caso di Loppio', in no ed, *Romani e Germani nel cuore delle Alpi tra V e VIII secolo. Saggi*, 351–371, Athesia, Bolzano

Milanese, M, 2001 (ed), *Geridu. Archeologia e storia di un villaggio medievale in Sardegna*, Delfino, Sassari

Moreland, J, 1991 'Method and Theory in Medieval Archaeology in the 1990s', *Archeologia Medievale* 18, 7–42

Murialdo, G and Mannoni, T, 2001 *S. Antonino. Un insediamento fortificato nella Liguria bizantina*, Istituto internazionale di studi liguri, Bordighera

Nardini, A and Valenti, M, 2005 *Il castello di Miranduolo. Guida breve allo scavo archeologico (anni 2001–2004)*, All'Insegna del Giglio, Firenze

Orser, C, 2007 'The global and the local in modern-world archaeology', in Gelichi and Librenti (eds) 2007, 25–33

Panella, C, 1989, 'Gli scambi nel Mediterraneo occidentale dal IV al VII secolo dal punto di vista di alcune merci', in *Hommes et richesses dans l'empire byzantin, tome I: IV–VII siècle*, 129–141, Paris

Paroli, L (ed), 1997 *L'Italia centro-settentrionale in età longobarda*, All'Insegna del Giglio, Firenze

Paroli, L, 2007 'Mondo funerario', in Brogiolo and Chavarría Arnau (eds) 2007b, 203–209

Paroli, L and Vendittelli, L (eds), 2004 *Roma dall'antichità al medioevo II. Contesti tardo antichi e altomedievali*, Electa, Milano

Pejrani Baricco, L (ed), 2004 *Presenze longobarde. Collegno nell'alto medioevo*, Soprintendenza per i Beni Archeologici del Piemonte, Torino

Pergola, P (ed), 1999 *Alle origini della parrocchia rurale (IV–VII sec.)*, Atti della giornata tematica dei Seminari di Archeologia Cristiana (École française de Rome,19 marzo 1998), Sussidi allo Studio delle antichità cristiane pubblicati a cura del Pontificio Istituto di Archeologia Cristiana 12, Città del Vaticano

Roma e i Barbari. La nascita di un mondo nuovo, Catalogo della Mostra (Venezia-Palazzo Grassi 2008), Electa, Milano

Reynolds, P, 1995, *Trade in the Western Mediterranean ad 400–700: the Ceramic Evidence*, British Archaeological Report International Series 604, Oxford

Rossi, F (ed), 2002 *Nuove ricerche sul Capitolium di Brescia. Scavi, studi e restauri*, Edizioni ET, Milano

Saguì, L (ed), 1998 *Ceramica in Italia: VI–VII secolo*, All'Insegna del Giglio, Firenze

Tagliabue, R, 1993 *Architetto e Archeologo. Confronto tra campi disciplinari*, Guerini Studio, Milano

Terrenato, N, 1998 'Fra tradizione e trend. L'ultimo ventennio (1975–1997)', in M Barbanera (ed), *L'archeologia degli italiani. Storia, metodi e orientamenti dell'archeologia classica in Italia*, 175–192, Editori riuniti, Roma

Terrenato, N (ed), 2000 *Archeologia teorica. X ciclo si lezioni sulla ricerca applicata in archeologia* (Pontignano 1999), All'Insegna del Giglio, Firenze

Tilley, C, 1991 *Material Culture and Text. The Art of Ambiguity*, Routledge, London

Toubert, P, 1973 *Les structures du Latium médiéval. Le Latium méridional et la Sabine du IX.e siècle à la fin du XII.e siècle* (BEFAR, 221), Ecole Française de Rome, Roma

Treffort, C, 1996 *L'église carolingienne et la mort: Christianisme, rites funéraires et pratiques commémoratives*, Presse Universitaire de Lyon, Lyon

Trigger, B G, 1996 *A History of Archaeological Thought*, 2nd edn, Cambridge University Press, Cambridge

Valenti, M, 2004 *L'insediamento altomedievale nelle campagne toscane: paesaggi, popolamento e villaggi tra VI e X secolo*, Biblioteca del Dipartimento di Archeologia e Storia delle Arti — Sezione Archeologica Università di Siena 10, All'Insegna del Giglio, Firenze

Valenti, M (ed), 2007 *Poggio Imperiale a Poggibonsi: dal villaggio di capanne al castello di pietra, I. Diagnostica archeologica e campagne di scavo 1991–1994*, 159–218, All'Insegna del Giglio, Firenze

Vidale, M, 2004 *Cos'è l'etnoarcheologia?*, Carocci, Roma

Volpe, G, 2007 'Architecture and Church power in Late Antiquity: Canosa and San Giusto (Apulia)', in L Lavan, L Özgenel and A Sarantis (eds), *Housing in Late Antiquity*, 131–168, Late Antique Archaeology 3.2, Brill, Leiden

Volpe, G, 2008 'Vescovi rurali e chiese nelle campagne dell'Apulia e dell'Italia meridionale fra Tardoantico e Altomedioevo', *Hortus Artium Medievalium* 14, 31–47

Volpe, G and Turchiano, M (eds), 2005 *Paesaggi e insediamenti rurali in Italia meridionale fra Tardoantico e Altomedioevo*, Atti del 1° Seminario sul Tardoantico e l'Altomedioevo in Italia Meridionale (STAIM, 1), (Foggia 2004), Edipuglia, Bari

Ward Perkins, B, 1984 *From Classical Antiquity to the Middle Ages. Urban Public Building in Northern and Central Italy ad 300–850*, Oxford University Press, Oxford

Ward Perkins, B, 1997 'Continuists, catastrophists and the towns of post-Roman northern Italy', *Papers of the British School at Rome* 65, 157–176

Wickham, C, 1985 *Il problema dell'incastellamento nell'Italia centrale*, All'Insegna del Giglio, Firenze

Wickham, C, 1999 'Early medieval archaeology in Italy: the last twenty years', *Archeologia Medievale* 26, 7–20

CHAPTER 9
MEDIEVAL ARCHAEOLOGY IN SPAIN

By JUAN ANTONIO QUIRÓS CASTILLO

As in other countries in southern Europe, medieval archaeology in Spain is a young discipline. The predominance of prehistoric and Classical archaeology in academe has conditioned the study of medieval societies on the basis of the archaeological record. It is only in the last 30 years that medieval archaeology has undergone a significant quantitative and qualitative development. This paper presents a brief analysis of the discipline's historiography and of the main subjects studied, and considers the main challenges currently posed by the development of the subject.

INTRODUCTION

As in other parts of southern Europe, the archaeology of medieval societies in Spain is a discipline of very recent creation, despite the fact that its antecedents can be traced back to the 19th century. In spite of this, the discipline has undergone a spectacular development in the last few decades. As the field currently stands, there have never before been so many active archaeological projects or such systematic investigations of medieval sites. There is now an impressive number of published monographs and related studies. As discussed later in this paper, however, this explosion in professional interest and output contrasts with a negligible presence in academic institutions. This has led to the existence of several 'medieval archaeologies'; an absence of methodological and epistemological reflection can be observed, and the results obtained by archaeology have been marginalized in historical syntheses devoted to the medieval period.

This paper is not a summary of the recent academic results of medieval archaeology in Spain. A book on this topic has recently been published (Quirós Castillo and Bengoetxea 2006). The aim here is to provide a critical review of the state of the discipline from different points of view, as well as an overview of the different subjects dealt with in recent years. First, a brief analysis of the history of medieval archaeology in Spain is provided, followed by a consideration of the current situation. In conclusion, the paper will outline the challenges which will ideally be addressed in coming years.

HISTORIOGRAPHY OF MEDIEVAL ARCHAEOLOGY IN SPAIN

Despite the fact that the antecedents of medieval archaeology in Spain can be traced in various ways since the 19th century, it is only from the 1980s that medieval archaeology developed in modern terms. Various schools emerging in the previous century have had considerable influence on the discipline's construction. In general terms, three main lines of enquiry have influenced the formation of the discipline.

A first tendency or school is linked to the archaeological study of the Middle Ages, understood as the study of monumental material evidence. From the beginning of the 20th century, a monumentalist school which defined 'Visigothic', 'Mozarab' and 'Asturian architecture' linked the history of art with archaeology and developed around people like M Gómez Moreno. On the basis of such studies, several authors and their associated 'schools', from Spain (eg Puig i Cadafalch, Camps Cazorla, Palol) and other countries (particularly Germans like Schlunk and, subsequently, Hauschild) carried out intensive work on medieval structures, and established architectural and stylistic periods between the end of the Roman world and the Romanesque (Preromanic). This work involved dating buildings according to stylistic attributes defined in the absence of precise chronological indicators, thus creating a major corpus of monumental remains. The earliest studies (Gómez Moreno 1919) explored the singularity of what defined 'Hispanic' in Hispanic architecture under Byzantine influence, and the enduring nature of what was Roman. Some even denied the existence of a Visigothic style (Torres Balbás), while in the 1940s the existence of Visigothic art and architecture was defined (Schlunk) and took root in the succeeding decades. Following this scheme of styles, from the 1970s onwards, a 'Christian archaeology' was articulated which, from the end of the 1970s and practically up to the present, has organized national congresses, although on an irregular basis. 'Christian Archaeology' is dominated by a focus on remains of a monumental and mono-thematic nature.

Apart from this monumentalist approach, archaeological study of the Middle Ages developed throughout the 20th century from the point of view of 'Visigothic archaeology'. In Spain, as in other parts of Europe, the archaeological study of Germanic peoples underwent an early development via culture-historical approaches. It was during the 1930s, and the early years of Francoism in particular — when relations with Nazi Germany were more intense — when the development of an archaeology of the Goths was fomented in Spain. During the 1930s and 1940s, German authors like H Zeiss and W Reinhart and Spanish archaeologists were highly influenced by Nazi archaeology (Zeiss 1934). Among the latter, of particular significance is Julio Martínez Santa-Olalla who was one of the most important scholars of his day working on the Visigothic period. Excavations of important cemeteries like Castiltierra or Herrera del Pisuerga are attributable to Santa-Olalla (1933). Whereas these authors emphasized links between Spain's early history and Germanic peoples, other scholars were far removed from this philo-Germanic current, and re-emphasized the importance of the Classical, early Imperial substratum of the Visigothic world. In this vein, the works of J Supiot (who excavated the Espirdo-Veladiez cemetery) or those of C de Mergelina (who had already investigated the Carpio de Tajo cemetery in the 1920s) are particularly worthy of mention. In the mid-1940s, at the end of the Second World War and following a certain distancing from the Francoist regime, philo-Germanic studies of an ethnic and migrationist nature gradually began to give way to new studies that reassessed the older stylistic approaches (Molinero Pérez 1948). The concept of Hispanic-Visigothic art was introduced as the result of a more conservative approach. This led to the development of new syntheses and allied studies that limited the presence of the 'Visigoths' to specific parts of the pensinsula, depending on the distribution of cemeteries and artistic styles (Palol and Ripoll 1988), and thus, scholarly attention became focused on monumental remains.

A second area which has had a notable influence on the development of the discipline is the study of Andalusi material. Here, too, the most immediate precedents must be sought in the Romanticist antiquarian movement from the end of the 19th century. The first archaeological research carried out at complexes like Madīnat Elvira, Madīnat al-Zahrā' or Bobastro reveals unequivocal attention to material evidence of a monumental nature. Throughout the 20th century, in the context of the restoration of monuments, there were interventions in palatial complexes (like the Alhambra) and large and impressive sites (like the Cordoba mosque). In the 1930s, the al-Andalus journal began to publish Spanish archaeological material and provided the basis for systematic archaeological analysis of themes such as cities, cemeteries, architecture and prestigious ceramics. It is important to point out that it was precisely because of Andalusi archaeology that medieval archaeology was first incorporated into Spanish universities, with the creation in 1912 of the Chair of Andalusi Archaeology held by M Gómez Moreno.

A third influence on the creation of medieval archaeology was the activity carried out in the 1960s outside academic circles, mainly in museums. Exceptions were A Del Castillo and M Riu, who, under the auspices of the Chair of Medieval History of the University of Barcelona, were involved in major research on regional territorial archaeology. A number of individuals were prominent in this field (Zozaya, Rosselló, García Guinea, etc), which included areas of enquiry that had begun to be explored elsewhere in Europe (such as the excavation of deserted villages or the systematization of 'common' ceramics), although the interpretative frameworks used were determined by the dominant historiography of the time. Thus, in the 1970s, when historical archaeology was being consolidated as an academic discipline in Spain, only a few groups were working on the medieval period, and these were working, in the main, outside the university sector. This initial stage of the development of medieval archaeology in Spain perhaps ended with the appendix written by M Riu with the translation into Spanish of the *Manual of Medieval Archaeology. From Prospection to History* by Michel de Boüard (1977). In this text, Riu assembled an exhaustive bibliographic compilation of many works carried out to date in the field of archaeological research on the Spanish Middle Ages, classified according to subject matter. In the same year, the National Archaeology Congress included in its programme a session devoted exclusively to medieval archaeology. Also at that time, the French school, under the direction of Pierre Guichard (1976), started its activities, and, from the Casa de Velázquez, would play a fundamental role in putting new energy into the discipline.

Only after the 1980s, however, was there a true explosion and development of medieval archaeology in Spain, which established the basis for the discipline as it currently stands. In 1980, the first meeting on a national level took place in Toledo, and the following year the second international congress on Medieval Ceramics in the Western Mediterranean was held in the same city. In 1983, the first congress on Spanish medieval archaeology was held in Huesca with the participation of over 400 scholars. This event resulted in the first syntheses of studies carried out up to 1983, providing regional reviews of the state of medieval archaeology across Spain at that time. The congress was organized by the Spanish Association of Medieval Archaeology, founded in 1982, which has promoted the publication of a journal (since 1986) and has organized a number of national congresses (Huesca 1983, Madrid 1987, Oviedo 1989, Alicante 1993, Valladolid 1999).

It was at the first conference in 1983 that the main approaches considered so far in this paper converged and that the real situation of the discipline could be gauged. Inertia in the development of theoretical frameworks initially led this convention to divide its sessions into 'Visigothic Archaeology', 'Archaeology of the Christian Kingdoms' and 'Al-Andalus Archaeology'. This division, which more or less reflected former traditions, was only interrupted in the congresses held in the 1990s, although it has survived to a certain extent to the present. This situation ensures that it is still very common to find works and syntheses that conclude with the feudal invasion (11th–15th centuries) and which are limited to a dogmatic thematic framework. On the contrary, reflections that contemplate diachronic processes in all their complexity are less frequent.

Moreover, it must be pointed out that the Law on Spanish Historical Heritage was passed in 1985, which enabled the transfer of the management of heritage to regional governments, and created a new management model for archaeology. This development led to a major increase over the last 30 years in the number of archaeological interventions carried out within the framework of urban expansion and its infrastructure, which have mostly affected medieval and post-medieval archaeological contexts. This administrative framework has entailed the emergence of new players who participate in the management of archaeological heritage (for example, commercial archaeologists and local authority archaeologists).

Paradoxically, this exponential growth of archaeological activity on medieval sites did not bring with it a consolidation of the discipline or a reinforcement of methodological, conceptual or theoretical approaches. There are several reasons for this situation that nowadays influence Spanish medieval archaeology. In the first place, there has been no consolidation of Spanish medieval archaeology in the academic sphere. Indeed, it was from the 1980s onwards that staff numbers rose in universities in Spain but, due to the policy of those running Departments of Archaeology and Medieval History, as well as to the conceptual and methodological vacuum of medieval archaeology, the subject failed to benefit from this period of growth. At the present time, only 12 of the 74 universities in Spain have teachers with academic qualifications in medieval archaeology. Accordingly, the number of teachers of medieval archaeology in Spain is very small (scarcely a dozen), and they are distributed in two areas. The greater numbers of teachers are based in Andalusia and the Mediterranean, with a few working in the Meseta region (except for Madrid) and in the north of Spain. This academic geography is and has been of significant importance in the development of the discipline. Current reforms of university studies, however, will entail in many cases the elimination of medieval archaeology as a degree course and its inclusion, where appropriate, in postgraduate courses.

In the face of an almost total absence of formal training and research programmes arranged by universities, the demand for experts to work in the field of management archaeology — which to a large extent concerns medieval sites — has been met by graduates in prehistory or Classical archaeology. The fracture between academe, the business world and local authorities is manifested in terms of operation, training and scientific approach. This disjointedness among the principal players has had a very negative effect on the development of the discipline, with the result that very few professional archaeological projects have resulted in publications or ended up being referenced in academic work.

Nor did the Spanish Association of Medieval Archaeology succeed in becoming, as in other countries like Britain or Italy, a polarizing element to solve the situation described above. Having failed to include university lecturers, CSIC (Consejo Superior de Investigaciones Científicas) researchers, experts and administrators, the influence of the Spanish Association gradually decreased to a marginal presence after the 1990s. Furthermore, national congresses were not held on a regular basis and the resulting *Gazette* itself failed to include the most important works carried out in the discipline. Indeed, a congress devoted to the problems of medieval archaeology in Spain was held in Jaén in 1993, and it was then that the new review *Arqueología y Territorio Medieval* (Archaeology and Medieval Territory) published by the University of Jaén was conceived. Unlike the already-mentioned journal, this latter review has been published regularly and has managed, to a certain extent, to include the academic output generated by academe.

Due to its originality and significance, it is also worth mentioning the initiative carried out in Catalonia by the ACRAM (Catalan Association for Research on Medieval Archaeology). This association, made up only of commercial archaeological contractors, organizes congresses on medieval and post-medieval archaeology on a regular basis in Catalonia, and publishes the *Medieval Archaeology* journal, three issues of which have been published to date. It is important to point out that this activity is promoted and financed by the contractors themselves, and neither the universities nor research centres have managed to lead or promote a similar arena for voicing and exchanging ideas.

It should not surprise us that the first work of reference following the 1985 legislation was that written by M Barceló, under the provocative title *Arqueología Medieval. En las afueras del medievalismo (Medieval Archaeology. In the suburbs of medievalism)* (Barceló Perelló 1988). In this book, which the author defines as a 'methodological reflection', Barceló gives his full attention to theoretical and conceptual aspects relating to the growth of medieval archaeology, while paying only secondary attention to the discipline's methodological aspects. This book denounces how archaeology is placed outside 'medievalism', the latter being understood as the academic dimension of medieval history, being relegated to a mere auxiliary function or for illustrating historical narratives. Barceló proposes a highly conceptual research programme, in which there is space for the use of archaeological and written record within the context of a specific interpretative framework.

Naturally, this kind of proposal gained supporters among the emerging field of medieval archaeology linked to medieval history, although it also gave rise to considerable antagonism within the discipline of medieval archaeology itself, which felt threatened by a reflection of this nature on the relationship between archaeology and medieval history. To date, the main syntheses and reflections on the role of medieval archaeology had been based essentially on subjects already touched on by medieval history, but without questioning basic aspects like the construction of the archaeological record. We thus arrive at the paradox where some historians called for a greater participation of archaeology in furthering knowledge of the Middle Ages (possibly to supply empirical data to fill gaps), but, at the same time, vacant positions for lecturers in medieval archaeology were not being filled.

The situation did not change much during the 1990s, at least in relation to the greater part of the historiography of medieval studies. The most recent syntheses of Spanish and general medieval history fail to mention even a single European or peninsular archaeological site. Medieval archaeology is evidently still considered by many historians solely as a source for illuminating specific aspects of daily life in medieval society.

Despite the fact that this is the standard outlook, it is also true that one cannot generalize completely. One cannot tackle the history of the Islamic presence in the Iberian Peninsula, for example, without recourse to archaeological studies, and soon it will not be possible to speak of the Late Middle Ages without making use of the numerous advances being made by archaeology. Many of these results have not yet been used in modern syntheses, but this will surely happen.

To support Barceló's affirmations it must be pointed out that medieval archaeology has not only been left out of 'medievalism', but also remains on the fringe of archaeology. Although in recent years greater attention is being paid by universities and research centres to the medieval period, archaeologists are still in the minority.

MEDIEVAL ARCHAEOLOGY IN THE PRESENT

As discussed above, it is only in the last 25 years that medieval archaeology has been systematically developed in Spain (Figure 9.1). A bibliometric analysis of the main publications over this period helps us to understand the evolution of the discipline and the changing nature of the different subjects with which the discipline has been concerned (Figure 9.2).

During the second half of the 1980s, when the basis of medieval archaeology as currently practised was laid, considerable work was done on the creation of chronological and analytical methods and frameworks (the study of ceramics in particular underwent major development); while, at the same time, new areas of research were

FIGURE 9.1. Main sites mentioned in the text.

explored, such as the study of irrigated cultivation systems, the organization of rural space, castles and cemeteries. It was probably the study of the Late Middle Ages that underwent the most thorough renewal in this period, with critical review of monumental constructions, such as churches, as well as in the analysis of ceramics of the Visigothic period.

Since the 1990s, however, there has been a significant growth in archaeological engagement with medieval material, taking in very different subjects and contexts. Although settlement and territorial studies, based on prospection and the gathering of data from archaeological interventions, have been at the core of new developments in terms of quantity and quality, there has also been a great increase in work carried out in the context of monumental restoration and urban archaeology. Thanks to these developments the discipline as a whole has undergone a profound renewal, while one of the subjects that has developed most in these years is urban archaeology (Figure 9.3). Excavations carried out in 'living cities' (notably Mérida, Valencia, Zaragoza, Toledo, Córdoba, Barcelona, Tarragona, Cartagena, San Martí de Ampurias,

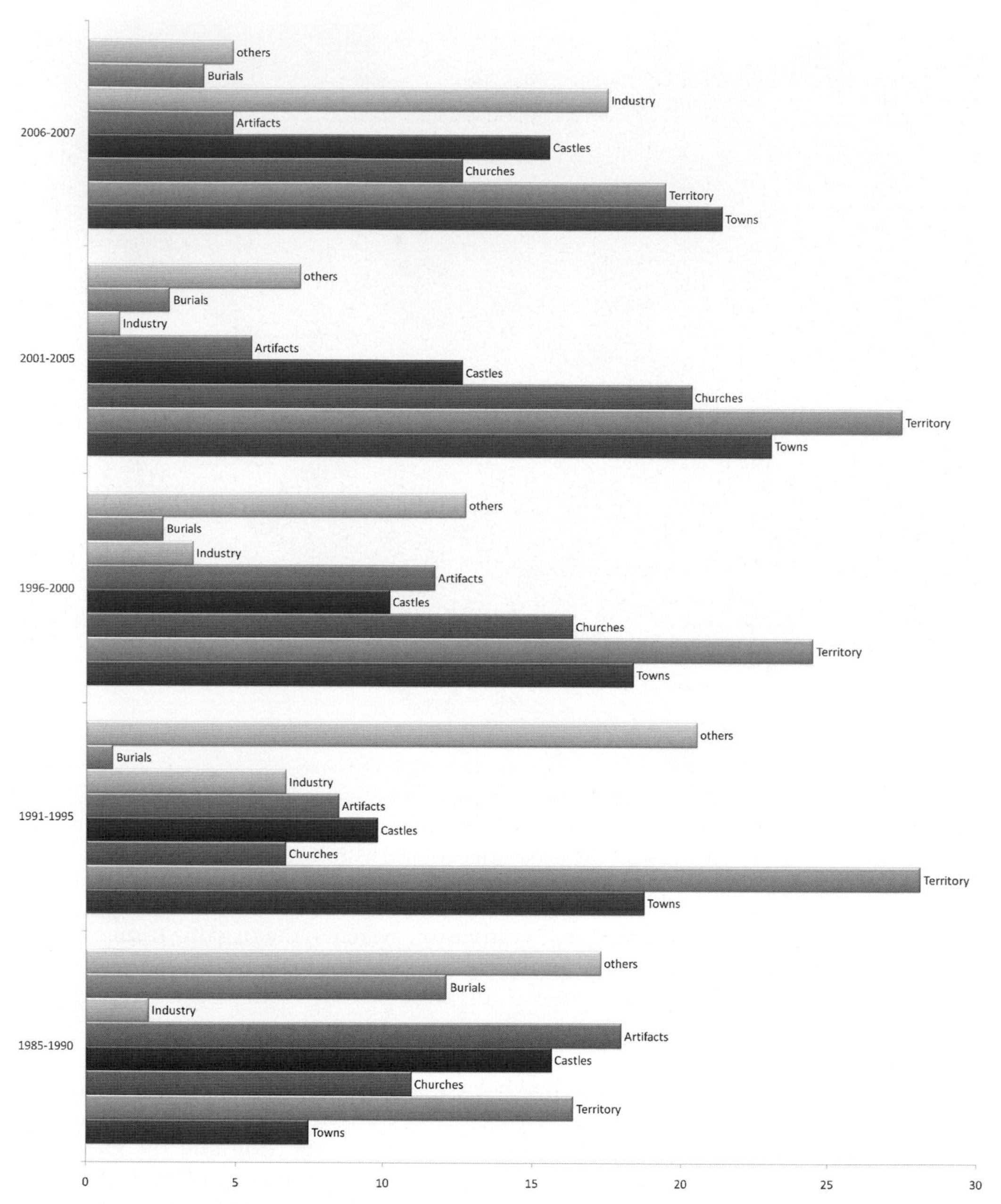

FIGURE 9.2. Bibliometric analysis of medieval archaeology in Spain 1985–2007. (From *Arqueología y Territorio Medieval*; *Boletín de Arqueología Medieval*; *Arqueologia Medieval. Revista Catalana d'Arqueologia Medieval*; *Congresos de Arqueología Medieval Española*; *Congressos d'Arqueologia Medieval i Moderna a Catalunya*)

FIGURE 9.3. Episcopal area of the city of Valencia in early medieval period.

Granada, Denia and León) as well as in deserted villages (such as Recópolis and Tolmo de Minateda) have revealed the deep transformations experienced by urban centres in the Early Middle Ages and the bases upon which renewal or the development of a new urban network occurred at the end of this period. As in other European countries, including Britain, it has not been possible to process or synthesize into narrative accounts even a tiny proportion of the number of interventions carried out, largely due to the failure of heritage management models to deal with such a large number of archaeological investigations.

In conceptual terms, debate about the urban phenomenon in the Early Middle Ages has depended on external traditions, based for example on Italian models, where cities of the early medieval period (5th–10th centuries) have been analyzed using paradigms created by recent history using written documents. Indeed, this is one of our discipline's pending matters: the historical exploitability of urban archaeology (Díaz Martinez 2000).

Likewise, during the 1980s and 1990s, the first excavation works were carried out in rural settlements (for example at Cerro Peñaflor, El Cañal de Pelayos, El Bovalar, Navalvillar and Vilaclara de Castellfollit), although based on approaches far different from those applied to deserted villages elsewhere in Europe (Figure 9.4). Indeed, the archaeology of rural spaces has given priority to extensive rather than intensive studies, which has frequently raised plausible interpretative proposals compatible with a limited knowledge of rural medieval settings. Rural studies also

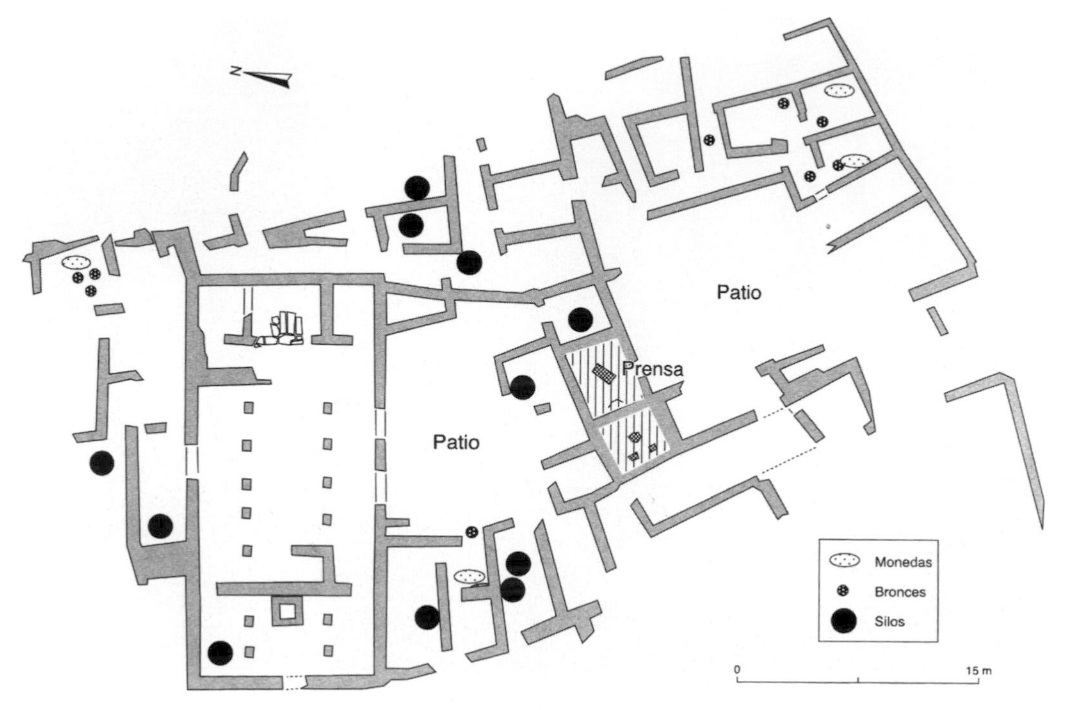

FIGURE 9.4. Plan of the village of Bovalar (Lleida).

engaged with varying historiographical traditions. To give just one example, during the 1990s, a series of doctoral theses of a micro-territorial or sub-regional nature were carried out in the north of the peninsula which, for the first time, aimed to integrate material records in the interpretation of medieval landscapes (Escalona Monge 2002; Fernández Mier 1999; García Camino 2002). The limited quality of available records and the initial historiographical approaches used led to conflicting interpretations of the same territories (eg in Castile).

The 1990s likewise saw a rise in the number of interventions concerned with churches and monumental complexes in the context of restoration work. A qualitatively significant contribution was the introduction and development of the so-called 'Architectural Archaeology' (Caballero Zoreda and Escribano Velasco 1996) under the strong influence of Italian archaeology (Figure 9.5). Stratigraphic readings of architectural fabrics enabled methodologically rigorous analyses of buildings which facilitated refinements of chronology (in the study of early medieval ecclesiastical architecture) as well as encouraging research in neglected regions (for example, Barcelona and Álava).

The archaeology of castles, which had been relatively more important in the 1980s, did not succeed in generating an archaeology of *incastellamento* or of territorial powers, but frequently ended up being limited to an archaeology of monuments, with specific exceptions (for example, the case of the Kingdom of León).

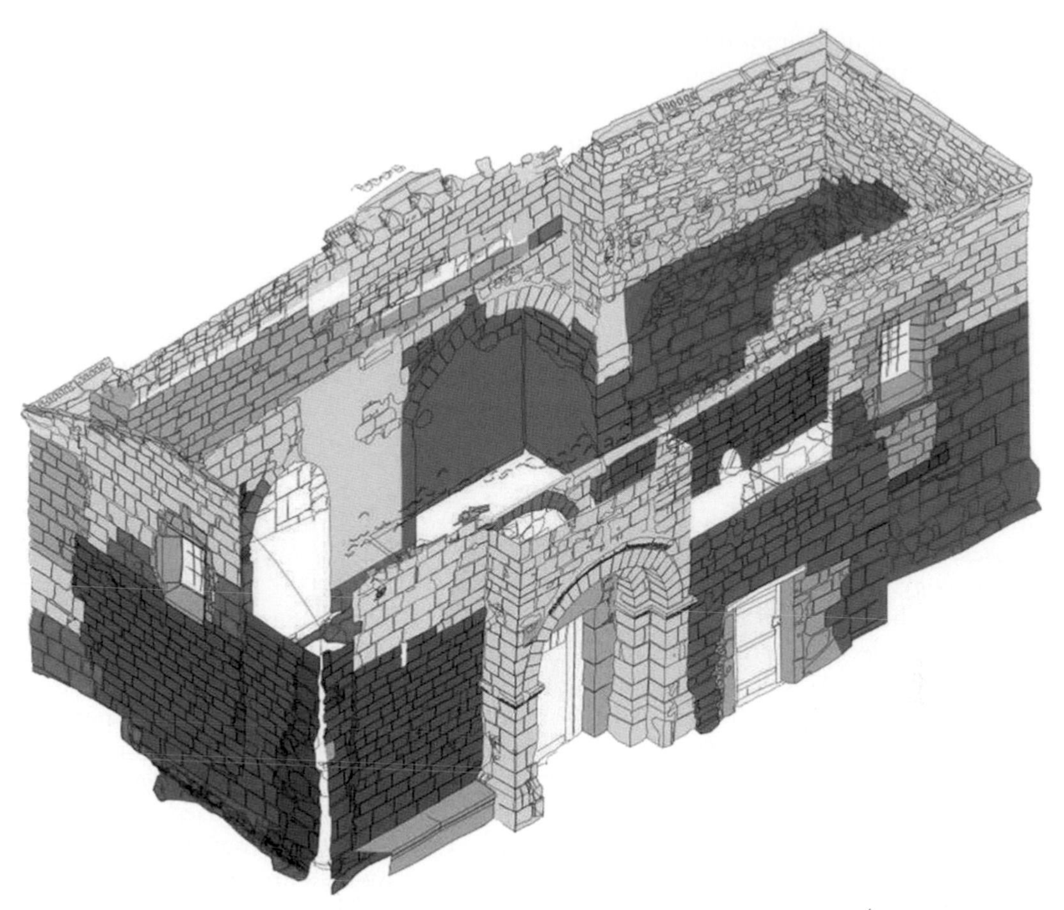

FIGURE 9.5. Stratigraphic analysis of San Roman of Tobillas church (Álava).

There is no doubt, however, that it was Andalusi archaeology which underwent the most significant development during the 1990s, as can be appreciated by its unquestionable presence in congresses and scientific meetings and its gradual incorporation into university teaching. This renewal of studies was articulated around two main issues: broadening the chronological scope (paying special attention to the emiral and caliphal period), and widening thematic scope. If the focus during the 1970s and 1980s was exclusively on monuments, decorated ceramics, epigraphy and numismatics, other aspects such as deserted villages or the material culture of these periods being unknown, from then on, the situation was to change thanks to the dating of the first emiral ceramic finds from the south and south-east of al-Andalus. Using these materials, archaeology contributed decisively to the re-conceptualizing of Islamic societies and to the study of complex phenomena such as the shaping process of Islamic social training or to the explanation of Andalusi landscapes (ie Acién Almansa 1994). Progress made on material culture (for example, in the south-east), rural deserted villages (like Cerro Miguelico), hydraulic networks (especially in the Balearic islands), monumental complexes (like Madinat al-Zahra': Vallejo Triano 2004) and Andalusi territorial structure by French and Spanish authors has helped us to identify the structure of Andalusi rural settlement, of the *husun* or *castillo*, as well as the role of the state and tribal groups in the shaping of the landscape. The most important territorial studies, some of which were carried out as doctoral theses (for example, by J C Castillo, S Gutiérrez and A Gómez), took in, above all, Andalusian, Levantine and Balearic regions (Bazzana 1992; Bazzana, Cressier and Guichard 1988; García Porras 2001; Gómez Becerra 1998; Gutiérrez Lloret 1996; Malpica Cuello 2003). Other archaeological records, such as ceramic, numismatic, architectonic and decorative materials, were systematized in a parallel fashion. Andalusi cities perhaps provoked the least theorizing in the 1990s, despite the fact that many historic centres were intensively excavated in advance of architectural restoration.

The importance of the research carried out in the late medieval and Islamic world in these territories was considerable, with the result of many European scholars showing an interest in their findings, and solid relations were forged with other archaeological traditions like the French tradition, through the *Castrum* congresses, or the Italian tradition, through the Hispano-Italian congresses on medieval archaeology.

With the advent of the new millennium many of the tendencies documented in the previous decade were maintained, although new developments have been made. The classification of ceramics and the creation of standard archaeological indicators (Gerrard *et al* 1995), although still few in quantity, are now available for periods like the Late Middle Ages (13th–15th centuries), although primary study of certain categories of archaeological materials is still required. Regional studies are still important, although the need is evident to go beyond such broadly based approaches and carry out extensive excavation projects. The importance of urban archaeology is growing in terms of the communication of discoveries, which are not always accompanied by an archaeological conceptualization of the city. Monumental archaeological remains are now governed by very elaborate protocols with regard to archaeological intervention, mainly due to the growth of architectural archaeology and widespread restoration of monuments (Caballero Zoreda and Mateos Cruz 2000).

A new phenomena in recent years is the development of the serious archaeological study of the medieval peasantry through open area excavation of rural sites. This development has allowed archaeologists to overcome the division between archaeology of dwellings and that of agricultural landscapes (Figure 9.6). In the case of the Madrid region such work has produced startling results, revealing early medieval settlements and their associated landscapes on a scale not previously realized (Quirós Castillo and Vigil-Escalera Guirado 2006). The study of processes like the demise of Roman towns or villae (Chavarria Arnau 2007), the creation of early medieval networks of villages or the organization of Andalusi and the nature of early medieval territories provide major avenues for research in this field.

The archaeology of fortifications is likewise another subject undergoing a significant growth (Barceló Perelló and Toubert 1998). Leaving behind the more monumental and descriptive traditions, recent years have seen an increase in studies which analyze such architecture in social terms (Gutiérrez González 1995; 2006),

FIGURE 9.6. Early medieval village of Zaballa (Álava), 6th–12th centuries.

following the lead established in the previous decade (for example, at Peñaferruz). Within this framework, Andalusi as well as feudal fortifications take on a new meaning as centres for territorial articulation.

The wide acceptance of architectural archaeology has allowed a broadening of subject matter (archaeology of building techniques; archaeology as applied to restoration) and the formation of consolidated research groups whose work can be found in the new journal, *Arqueología de la Arquitectura*, in which the majority of modern studies of medieval buildings are now published.

Two spheres in which important contributions are now being made are cities and funerary rituals. While the management of the findings of urban archaeology is still a matter pending for all of European archaeology, in recent years some significant steps have been taken in Spain, and, indeed, specialists in al-Andalus are actively re-addressing the role and significance of cities in Islamic social formations. Recent interventions in Saqunda (Cordoba) and Vega Baja (Toledo) have clearly evidenced the kind of conflicts that this type of intervention generates in terms of heritage management.

Lastly, with regard to the study of cemeteries and other kinds of burial sites, progress is being made to move beyond the historical approaches that limited the interpretation of burials exhibiting certain rituals or containing certain grave goods as indisputably 'Visigothic'. This is perhaps one of the clearest cases where the absence of explicit methodological and theoretical frameworks ensures the continued use of categories and concepts that are quite obsolete (Ripoll López 1998; Azkarate Garai-Olaun 2002).

More recently, significant steps have been taken to engage a wider public with the creation of museums, archaeological parks and exhibition projects. In fact, medieval archaeology has become a powerful tool for creating local and cultural identities. It nevertheless remains the case that most interpretations neglect to include evidence drawn from medieval archaeology, with the exception of the occasional image or illustration.

CHALLENGES POSED

To conclude, it is useful to draw attention to certain of the main challenges facing medieval archaeology in the coming years. In the first place, there is an urgent need for interventions giving priority to creating high-quality field records. Over the last few decades, extensive archaeological fieldwork has revealed a series of important sites upon which the main paradigms have been built. Yet, excavations are largely concerned with small areas and, of the materials recovered, the study of ceramics (Caballero Zoreda *et al* 2003) and structures far outweighs the emphasis placed upon bioarchaeological remains and archaeometric approaches. It is therefore necessary to re-orient research priorities, particularly in problematic areas such as urban archaeology, and to place a greater stress on the importance of generating qualitatively superior records, with a fuller appreciation and application of environmental archaeology and archaeological science more broadly. This latter aspect forms the second major challenge confronting medieval archaeology in Spain. The lack of specialist laboratories and sampling strategies makes it currently difficult to achieve these objectives.

A third challenge for the coming years is to develop an integrated medieval archaeology in Spain. Much activity is carried out within the framework of so-called professional or commercial archaeology and, in quantitative terms, is still mainly undertaken independently from academic and other research centres. This unnecessary division between both spheres can be overcome by integrating professional activities in academic work and by the collaboration, but not supplantation, of university teams in the management of heritage.

Making the results of archaeological fieldwork available to a wider public is yet another current problem. Very few archaeological interventions result in publications and the scarcity of editorial initiatives in Spain devoted to medieval archaeology is partly to blame. Basic priorities are the use of digital resources, publication by the different authorities of reports and papers on excavations on the internet and the creation of high-quality monograph series (such as the French series *Documents d'Archéologie Française*) which outline the findings of the excavations.

Equally important is the attainment of a more academically integrated approach to medieval archaeology. In fact, this is perhaps the most complex challenge to be tackled. The impermeability of academic institutions, the situation of the discipline in the universities throughout Spain and the process of integration into the EHEA (European Higher Education Area) does not appear to augur a very bright future for these aspirations. Will there be a day when medieval archaeology is no longer in the suburbs of 'medievalism' or in the suburbs of archaeology?

Finally, it is particularly important that the discipline moves forward in terms of theoretical and methodological reflection. Medieval archaeology in Spain, as in many other parts of Europe, is frequently practised without explicit theoretical and conceptual approaches, with the result that it does not generate new models or paradigms, but continues to follow those formulated by historians or other related traditions. Indeed, the methodological and conceptual dependence of Spanish medieval archaeology at the beginning on the French tradition, and then upon the Italian, has been and still is considerable. It is necessary now to foster debate and to bring about frameworks to build a conceptually robust discipline (Malpica Cuello 1993).

However, all these above-mentioned challenges are not intended to detract from the fact that the growth and maturing of medieval archaeology in Spain has been extraordinary in recent years; within a few years, no serious scholar of the medieval period will be able to neglect material records in writing the history of the Spanish Middle Ages.

ACKNOWLEDGEMENTS

I am grateful to Alfonso Vigil-Escalera and Lorena Elorza for their critical comments.

BIBLIOGRAPHIC NOTE

The most important review published in Spain dedicated to medieval archaeology is *Arqueología y Territorio Medieval* published by the University of Jaén. Likewise, worthy of mention is the review *Arqueología Medieval* published in Barcelona by the ACRAM and the *Boletín de Arqueología Medieval*, which has resumed publication. The only conference devoted to late medieval archaeology held on an irregular basis is the 'Visigodos y Omeyas' (Visigoths and Omeyas), in Mérida. There are no editorial series expressly devoted to medieval archaeology in Spain.

BIBLIOGRAPHY

Acien Almansa, M, 1994 *Entre el feudalismo y el Islam. 'Umar Ibn Hafsun en los historiadores, en las fuentes y en la historia*, Universidad de Jaén, Jaén

Azkarate Garai-Olaun, A, 2002 'De la tardoantigüedad al medievo cristiano. Una mirada a los estudios arqueológicos sobre el mundo funerario', in D Vaquerio (ed), *Espacios y usos funerarios en el Occidente romano*, 115–140, Universidad de Córdoba, Córdoba

Barceló Perelló, M (ed), 1988 *Arqueología Medieval. En las afueras del 'medievalismo'*, Crítica, Barcelona

Barceló Perelló, M and Toubert, P, 1998 *L'incastellamento. Actas de las reuniones de Girona (26–27 noviembre 1992) y de Roma (5–7 mayo 1992)*, Escuela Española de Historia y Arqueología en Roma, Roma

Bazzana, A, 1992 *Maisons d'Al-Andalus: hábitat medieval et structures du peuplement dans l'Espagne orientale*, Casa de Velázquez, Madrid

Bazzana, A, Cressier, P and Guichard, P, 1988 *Les châteaux ruraux d'al-Andalus. Histoire et Archéologie des Husun du Sud-Est de l'Espagne*, Casa de Velázquez, Madrid

Bolós Masclans, J, 2004 *Els origens medievals del paisatge catalá. L'arqueologia del paisatge com a font per a conèixer la historia de Cataluna*, Publicacions de l'Abadia de Montserrat — Institut d'Estudis Catalans, Barcelona

Caballero Zoreda, L and Escribano Velasco, C (eds), 1996 *Arqueología de la Arquitectura. El método arqueológico aplicado al proceso de estudio y de intervención en edificios históricos*, Junta de Castilla y León, Valladolid

Caballero Zoreda, L and Mateos Cruz, P, 2000 *Visigodos y Omeyas. Un debate sobre la Antigüedad Tardía y la Alta Edad Media*, CSIC, Madrid

Caballero Zoreda, L, Mateos Cruz, P and Retuerce, M, 2003 *Cerámicas tardorromanas y altomedievales en la Península Ibérica*, Archivo Español de Arqueología, Madrid

Chavarria Arnau, A, 2007 *El final de las villae en Hispania (siglos IV–VII D C)*, Brepols, Turnhout

Díaz Martinez, P C, 2000 'City and territory in Hispania in Late Antiquity', in G P Brogiolo, N Gauthier and N Christie (eds), *Towns and Their Territories Between Late Antiquity and Early Middle Ages*, 3–35, Brepols, Leiden

Escalona Monge, J, 2002 *Sociedad y territorio en la Alta Edad Media castellana. La formación del Alfoz de Lara*, British Archaeological Reports International Series 1079, Oxford

Fernández Mier, M, 1999 *Génesis del territorio en la Edad Media. Arqueología del paisaje y evolución histórica en la montaña asturiana*, Universidad de Oviedo, Oviedo

García Camino, I, 2002 *Arqueología y poblamiento en Bizkaia, siglos VI–XII. La configuración de la sociedad feudal*, Diputación Foral de Bizkaia, Bilbao

García Porras, A, 2001 *La cerámica del poblado fortificado medieval de 'El Castillejo' (Los Guájares, Granada)*, Athos-Pérgamos, Granada

Gerrard, C M, Gutiérrez, A, and Vince, A 1995 *Spanish Medieval Ceramics in Spain and the British Isles*, British Archaeological Reports International Series 610, Oxford

Gómez Becerra, A, 1998 *El poblamiento altomedieval en la costa de Granada*, Universidad de Granada, Granada

Gómez Moreno, M, 1919 *Iglesias mozárabes. Arte español de los siglos IX a XI*, CSIC, Madrid

Guichard, P, 1976 *Al Andalus. Estructura antropológica de una sociedad islámica en Occidente*, Barcelona

Gutiérrez González, J A, 1995 *Fortificaciones y feudalismo en el origen y la formación del reino leonés (siglos IX–XIII)*, Universidad de Valladolid, Valladolid

Gutiérrez González, J A, 2006 'Sobre la transición del sistema antiguo al feudal: una revisión arqueológica del Altomedievo hispano', *Territorio, Sociedad y Poder* 1, 53–78

Gutiérrez Lloret, S, 1996 *La Cora de Tudmir de la Antigüedad Tardía al mundo islámico. Poblamiento y cultura material*, Casa de Velázquez, Madrid

Gutiérrez Lloret, S, 1997 *Arqueología. Introducción a la historia material de las sociedades del pasado*, Universidad de Alicante, Alicante

Malpica Cuello, A, 1993 'Historia y Arqueología medievales: un debate que continua', *Problemas actuales de la Historia*, 29–47, Universidad de Salamanca, Salamanca

Malpica Cuello, A, 2003 *Los castillos en al-Andalus y la organización del territorio*, Universidad de Granada, Granada

Molinero-Pérez, A, 1948 *La necropolis visígoda de Duratón (Segovia)*, Segovia

Palol, P and Ripoll López, G, 1988 *Los godos en el Occidente europeo. Ostrogodos y Visigodos en los siglos V–VIII*, Encuentro, Madrid

Palol, P, 1999 *Del Romà al Romanic: histórica, art i cultura de la tarraconense mediterrània entre els segles IV i X*, Enciclopedia catalana, Barcelona

Quirós Castillo, J A and Bengoetxea, B, 2006 *Arqueología (III). Arqueología Postclásica*, Universidad Nacional de Educación a Distancia, Madrid (2ª ed 2008)

Quirós Castillo, J A and Vigil-Escalera Guirado, A, 2006 'Networks of peasant villages between Toledo and Velegia Alabense, northwestern Spain (V–Xth centuries)', *Archaeologia Medievale* 33, 79–128

Ripoll López, G, 1998 'The arrival of the Visigoths in Hispania: population problems and the process of acculturation', in W Pohl and H Reimitz (eds), *Strategies of Distinction. The Construction of Ethnic Communities, 300–800*, 153–185, Brepols, Turnhout

Riu Riu, M, 1977 'Arqueología medieval en España', apéndice a M De Boüard, *Manual de Arqueología Medieval. De la prospección a la historia*, Teide, Barcelona

Roselló Bordoy, G, 1978 *Ensayo de sistematización de la cerámica árabe en Mallorca*, Museo de Palma, Palma de Mallorca

Santa-Olalla, M, 1933 'Zur Tragweise der Bügelfibeln bei den Westgoten', *Germania* 17, 47–50

Torres Balbás, L, 1985 *Ciudades hispanomusulmanas*, Instituo Hispano-árabe de Cultura, Madrid

Vallejo Triano, A, 2004 *Madinat al-Zahra. Guía oficial del conjunto arquitectónico*, Junta de Andalucía, Sevilla

Zeiss, H, 1934 *Die Grabfunde aus dem spanische Westgotenreich*, Berlin

WEBSITES (consulted in January 2009)

Journal 'Arqueología y Territorio Medieval' (Archaeology and Medieval Territory): http://www.ujaen.es/revista/arqytm/

Asociación de Arqueología Medieval Española (Spanish Association of Medieval Archaeology): http://aeam.es/

Portal Arqueología Medieval (Medieval Archaeology Portal): http://www.arqueologiamedieval.com/

CHAPTER 10
MEDIEVAL ARCHAEOLOGY IN SOUTH-EASTERN EUROPE

By FLORIN CURTA

Medieval archaeology developed in earnest in south-eastern Europe only after the implementation of the Communist regimes under Soviet aegis. Despite the general ideological alignment to dialectical materialism, as well as more recent claims to the contrary, the impact of Marxism on the research agenda and interpretations applied to the material culture of the Middle Ages was not very significant. Through the analysis of two key sites — Pliska (Bulgaria) and Kranj (Slovenia) — this paper demonstrates that the culture-historical paradigm was by far more powerful, the general lines of which had been established before 1945. In the case of Pliska, the only critical reaction to the culture-historical paradigm was Marxist, but an alternative interpretation failed to take into consideration the chronology of the site and its relatively long history. In south-eastern Europe, the theoretical strength of the culture-historical paradigm has less to do with the appeal of nationalism and much more with the strong links long established between historiography and medieval archaeology. If there is currently a search for new theoretical models in the medieval archaeology of the south-east European countries, it is not so much in reaction to Marxism, as to the remarkably resistant tradition of culture-history.

INTRODUCTION

Despite some pioneering work in the late 19th century, medieval archaeology in south-eastern Europe began to develop into a serious discipline only 60 years ago (for a useful survey of the early history of Yugoslav archaeology, see Gunjača 1956).[1] The main catalyst for the sudden rise of medieval archaeology was the post-war shift in emphasis from traditional political and constitutional to social and economic history. In south-eastern Europe (with the obvious exception of Greece), the rise of medieval archaeology thus coincides in time, and was ultimately caused by, the imposition of Communist regimes under Soviet aegis, if not control.[2] As a consequence, archaeology was organized along the lines of Soviet multidisciplinary studies of 'material culture history' (a phrase in which the key component is *history*) (for Soviet archaeology, see Trigger 1989, 207–243, and Klein 1997; for Soviet-style archaeology in Romania, see Dragoman and Oanţă-Marghitu 2006). The discipline received a degree of institutional attention it had never before experienced. Considerable long-term investments, with no parallel at that time in western Europe, made possible large-scale excavations, following the principles first championed by the Soviet school of archaeology. During the 1950s and 1960s the research agenda was tied to the new requirements of the cultural policies promoted by the Communist regimes and to the predominantly Marxist philosophy, which had inspired them. The conclusion of the First Congress of Yugoslav Archaeologists, which took place in 1950 in Niška Banja, was that 'archaeology as a social-historic discipline has to be directed into research of material and spiritual culture entirely on the basis of historical materialism' (cited in Slapšak and Novaković 1996, 286–287 with n 50; for the congress in Niška Banja, see Korošec 1950 and Novaković 2002, 342). Economic and social issues were now to be preferred to any of the traditional topics of historical enquiry, especially political and church history. In addition, a new emphasis on economic and social history encouraged the use of archaeological evidence, instead of, or in combination with, written sources. That evidence derived first and foremost from the excavation of cemeteries, the first archaeological sites to be published as monographs (Korošec 1947; Kastelić 1950; Stanchev and Ivanov 1958; Beslagić and Basler 1964).[3] Cemeteries were also preferred because of the firm belief that the analysis of grave goods would produce conclusions about social structures, which could in turn serve for the writing of the new social history. The use of archaeological sources also encouraged a shift in emphasis from the later to the early Middle Ages, particularly the centuries of the so-called 'Great Migration' or 'barbarian invasions' which had until then been almost completely neglected (Kovačević 1960; Tăpkova-Zaimova 1966).

By directing the attention of archaeologists to how ordinary people lived, the Marxist paradigm eventually led to the development of settlement archaeology, and contributed to the gradual shift of emphasis away from an exclusive preoccupation with excavating cemeteries. Embracing the principles of 'horizontal' excavation of large areas, in order to expose as many settlement features and relationships between them as possible, a number of early medieval villages were excavated completely, such as Garvan in Bulgaria and Dridu in Romania (Văzharova 1986; Zaharia 1967) (Figure 10.1). In Yugoslavia, settlement sites were excavated in the 1970s and 1980s as part of micro-regional studies, the purpose of which was to generate a long-range diachronic view of settlement history, from prehistory to the early modern age (Stanojev 1996).

The growth in the 1960s and 1970s of cemetery archaeology, especially in Hungary and Yugoslavia, led to a rapid increase in the volume of data, to such an extant that by 1990 entire chronological gaps in the knowledge of the early Middle Ages had been almost completely bridged primarily because of archaeological research. One of the earliest books dedicated to the Avars was almost exclusively based on archaeological evidence (Kovačević 1977; for an excellent survey of cemetery archaeology in Hungary, see Tomka 1992).[4] Gyula László famously attempted to reconstruct the structure of the Avar society on the basis of an analysis of excavated

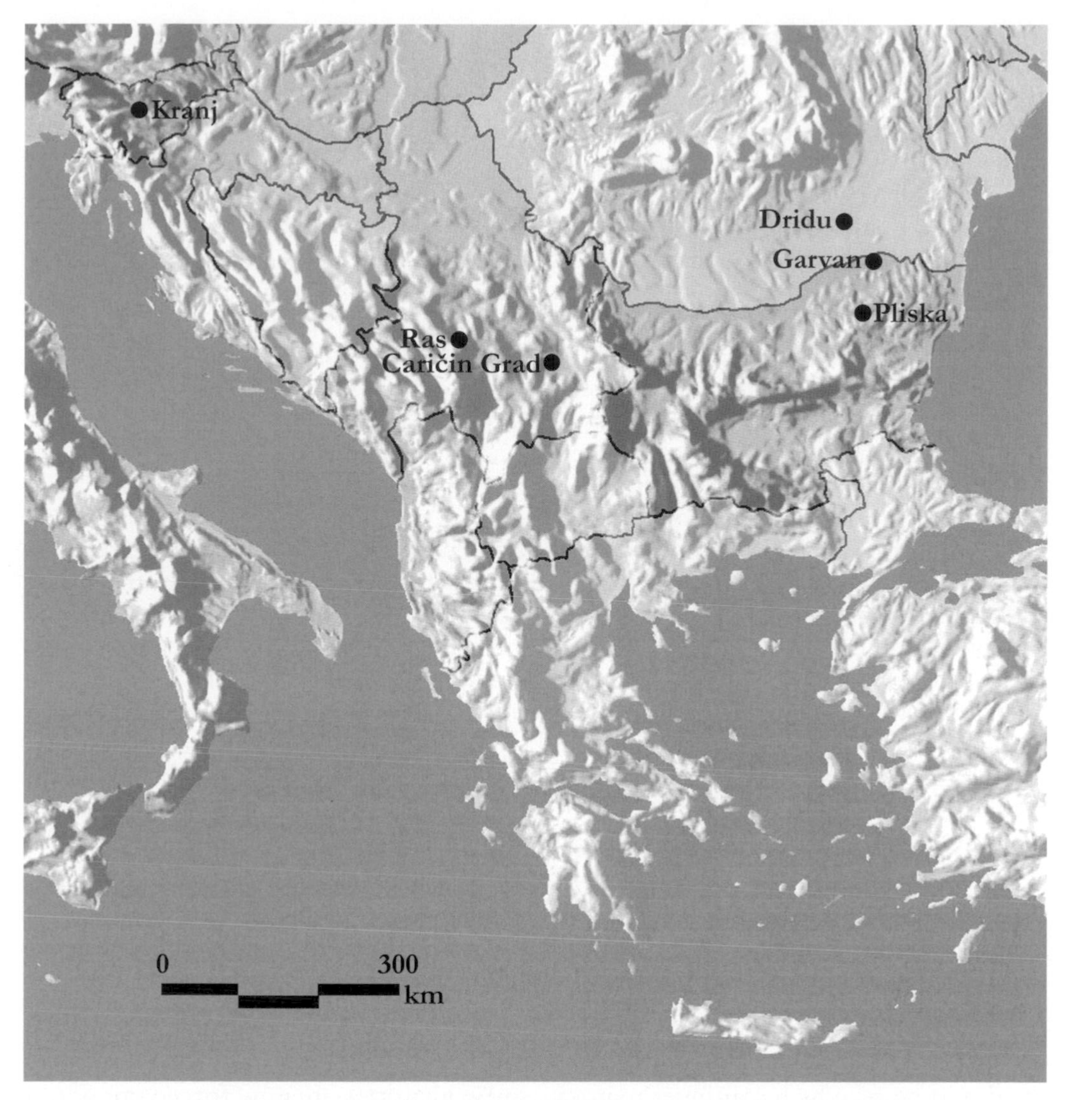

FIGURE 10.1. Distribution of the main sites mentioned in the text.

cemeteries that was sophisticated for its time (László 1955). László's book was very influential and for a long time remained the only work of social analysis in Avar archaeology (Erdélyi 1981; Szenpéteri 1985; 1986, Čilinská 1991; Zabojník 1995; Daim 1996). However, most other scholars continued to rely on written sources for writing social history (Grafenauer 1960; Cankova-Petkova 1962; Angelov 1967; 1973; Koledarov 1969).

The leading role taken by history in establishing national priorities for archaeological work provided the stimulus for excavation agendas on such high-status sites as Pliska and Preslav. Similarly, the identification with Iustiniana Prima

(Emperor Justinian's foundation) of the 6th-century site excavated since 1912 in Caričin Grad, in central Serbia, is based exclusively on written sources, for no inscription has been found that contains the name of that city (Bavant 2007, 337–338; Bavant and Ivanišević 2003). Historical questions about political power combined with an interest in early urban development in the medieval Balkans have motivated the work of Marko Popović at Ras, an 11th- and 12th-century Byzantine border fortress that subsequently became one of the earliest capitals of Nemanjid Serbia (Popović 1999; for Ras as a capital, see Kalić 1997). The tendency to use archaeology to illustrate what was already known from documentary history has been a salient feature of the archaeology practised in south-eastern Europe during the post-war decades. Despite a strong emphasis on the Marxist interpretation of history, archaeologists in the region have worked within a 'culture history' framework. Recent studies have shown that, with very few exceptions, Marxist ideas in the archaeology practised behind the Iron Curtain never had more than a superficial influence, considerably diminished by a strong undercurrent of culture-history tradition (see especially Bejko 1998; Novaković 2002, 340–343; Anghelinu 2007). Needless to say, most practitioners of this kind of archaeology had little understanding of, or even interest in, the processualist ideas that had transformed the discipline of archaeology since the 1960s. A survey of the archaeological literature will produce no evidence of the concept of 'culture as system'. Nor was there any reaction to the structuralist idea that, instead of being a direct reflection of social processes, material culture, like language, was used actively in the past to construct and categorize the world and, as a consequence, to negotiate and create cultural identities. To the best of my knowledge, 1990 is the date of the earliest reaction to New Archaeology in the medieval archaeology of former Yugoslavia, the country in south-eastern Europe which was by far more open to developments in the West than Albania or Romania (Stevanović 1990).[5]

Things have changed dramatically during the last 15 years. First and foremost, the predominant tendency has been one of increasing regionalism. Despite earlier and tentative attempts to describe political and cultural interactions within the region, studies of medieval archaeology in south-eastern Europe have by now taken different paths in different countries, with little, if any, relation to each other. Ever since the war in Yugoslavia, there has been an increasing body of literature on the archaeology of ethnogenesis, which continues to grow as new identities are now forged out of old languages and historical traditions (Janković 1995; Babić 1997; Trifunović 1997; Šlaus and Filipec 1998). At the same time, somewhat paradoxically, the field is moving toward more complex interpretative methodologies, and increasing attention is paid to questions of power and gender (Stepanov 1999; Kostova and Popkonstantinov 2005). The word 'identity' is also more often employed recently for titles of archaeological studies (eg Milinković 2004). There is also a shift in emphasis from the early to the late Middle Ages, even to the Ottoman period. With drastic cuts in state funding following the collapse of the Communist regimes, and with the concomitant development boom in both urban and rural contexts, rescue archaeology (especially in connection with the building of motorways and pipelines) has now become the predominant *modus operandi*. Gone are the days of multi-year, massive excavations of a single site, with generous funding and hundreds of workers at hand. Even older sites of national importance on which generations of archaeologists have already invested a great deal of energy and resources can only avoid a complete shut-down of archaeological research with outside funding. These dramatic changes demand a reconsideration of the goals and results of archaeological research on the Middle Ages (Stanilov 2001).

In dealing with a region as large and diverse as south-eastern Europe, one is always faced with the risk of denying local diversity and dynamic political change (for a definition of south-eastern Europe, see Curta 2006, 2–5).[6] As a result of such a 'melting pot' approach, some have concluded that 'in the Balkans, archaeology is one of the means of uncovering and presenting the symbolic resource of the past and, as such, it is used in the quest for political legitimacy' (Kaiser 1995, 133; the phrase 'melting pot' approach is that of Halsall 1995, 1). Perhaps because of the supposedly unique qualities of Balkan archaeology, Bailey (1998) regards Bulgaria as an 'exotic' case. For a critique of Bailey's approach and much more balanced views, see Nikolov (2002). That such a (mis)use of the archaeological research is not at all unique to the Balkans hardly needs any further emphasis. It is perhaps less evident that the Balkans are often used as a stereotypical 'other' meant to assume all the negative qualities that the (West) European 'self' rejects in its own image.[7] There seems to be a firm belief that 'in the Balkans, the relationship between past and present has been a reflexive one conditioned by several factors: ethnicity, nationalism, and (until 1989) Marxism' (Kaiser 1995, 99). Just as it has frequently been said about the archaeology practised in the south-east European countries that it was used to justify claims to territory and political influence, so it has also been maintained that 'in Southeast Europe from 1945 to 1989, Marxist ideology also figured prominently in theories of the prehistoric and protohistoric past' (Kaiser 1995, 110). Like Kaiser, many assume that Marxism has truly informed the kind of archaeology practised in Eastern Europe under Communism. Others have vehemently rejected the idea of a genuine 'Marxist archaeology' under Communism and argue instead for 'residual Marxism' (for Poland, see Barford 1995; 2002; Lech 1997; Milisauskas 1997–98; Lech 2002). Of course, this contradiction produces a picture of a truly exotic scholarly landscape, one which, unlike the rest of Europe, accommodated both culture-history and Marxism, despite their radically different approaches. One is thus led to believe that in the Balkans anything goes, as long as archaeological research is geared toward serving the political agenda of the present.

My study seeks to shed light on this heretofore neglected aspect of research on the history of medieval archaeology by focusing on two particularly illuminating case studies: Pliska, one of the earliest high-status sites in south-eastern Europe to become the object of archaeological research; and Kranj, the largest 6th-century cemetery so far excavated in the region. By comparing the two histories of archaeological research and interpretation, my intention is to show that in each case archaeological practice was meaningfully constituted and historically contingent. However, in both cases, archaeologists chose from a restricted set of interpretative models those that best suited their general understanding of the history of which the sites were supposed to speak. Instead of a direct reflection of the political agenda of the present, medieval archaeology, in both cases, served as a touchstone for ideas first put forward by historians. If the culture-history paradigm was eventually preferred, it was not so much because of a nationalist agenda, but because Marxism (or its rather vulgar version adopted during the Communist regimes) had failed to produce a paradigm that could successfully compete with, or much less replace, the models of historical development advanced by local historians.

THE TOWN

The main residence of the first Bulgar rulers at Pliska, in north-eastern Bulgaria, is surrounded by embankments with a total length of 12 miles forming an irregular quadrangle of more than nine square miles (Rashev *et al* 1995, 254–255; Squatriti 2005, 71–74; Kirilov 2006, 127). The ruins of the buildings within that quadrangle have been robbed of stone for centuries, and many of the architectural and sculptural elements have meanwhile been swallowed by limekilns (Krăndzhalov 1966, 440). Many of the standing structures in the archaeological park opened in the 1960s are in fact churches built after the conversion of Bulgaria to Christianity in 864. The middle of the area enclosed by embankments, the so-called Inner Town includes the palatial compound and covers two square miles (Rashev and Dimitrov 1999, 71; Ivanov 2004).

The first to notice the ruins of a large city in what was then the Ottoman beyerlik of Rumelia was the German traveller Carsten Niebuhr.[8] During a 1767 visit to Preslav, he learned from locals about the remains of what 'must have been in older times a big city' (Niebuhr 1837, 173). More than a century later, but only a few years before the Russo-Turkish war of 1877, the Viennese artist and amateur ethnographer Felix Kanitz visited and described the ruins of the Inner Town.[9] To him, those ruins did not look very different from those of a Roman camp, an observation which would have a particularly influential role in the history of the subsequent research on the site (Kanitz 1880, 254–256). Kanitz found an inscription of the Bulgar ruler Malamir (AD 831–836) in the ruins of what would later be called the Great Basilica. On this basis he (wrongly) identified the site as the 'fortress of Burdizon', mentioned in the text as having been destroyed by Malamir 'in the lands of the Greeks' (Kanitz 1879, 241–243 and 356). The inscription has been published by Beshevliev (1963, 179–180). Some time later, in 1884, the Czech historian Konstantin Jireček also visited the site. He had been for a few years the head of the ministry of national education in one of the first cabinets of the autonomous Principality of Bulgaria created after the Congress of Berlin (1878). It was the historian Jireček who first identified the site with the 'city called Pliskova' mentioned by Leo the Deacon as having been conquered in 971 by Emperor John Tzimiskes (Talbot and Sullivan 2005, 184; Jireček 1886, 194–196).[10] The ruins on the outskirts of the village of Aboba also attracted the attention of another Czech, Karel Škorpil, who together with his brother had arrived in Bulgaria from Bohemia at the invitation of their slightly older cousin, Konstantin Jireček, to help with the modernization of the country.[11] The two brothers started to work as teachers of mathematics and natural science, respectively, devoting their free time to the identification and study of antiquities. On the basis of an inscription of the Bulgar ruler Omurtag (AD 814–831), Škorpil identified the ruins in Aboba with the residence of the Bulgar rulers. The inscription had been carved on a column recycled as spolium in the Church of the Forty Martyrs, which was erected in 1230 in Veliko Tărnovo, 129km south-west from Aboba. Correctly surmising that the column (and inscription) had been brought to Veliko Tărnovo from Aboba, Škorpil noted that the text of the inscription mentioned a new 'house', which Omurtag had apparently built on the bank of the Danube, at a distance said to have been 40,000 fathoms (ie 85.3km) from his 'old home' at an un-named location. A second inscription found in 1905 in Chatalar (present-day Khan Krum), some 16 miles to the south-west from Aboba, specifically mentioned Omurtag to have lived in 'the camp of Pliska', a detail which Škorpil used to locate in Aboba the 'old home' mentioned in the inscription of the Church of the Forty Martyrs.[12] Škorpil's reading of the inscription from the Church of the Forty Martyrs has recently been challenged by Georgiev (2004; 2005). By 1925, his interpretation of the site had gained so much acceptance that the name of the village of Aboba officially changed into Pliskov in 1947.

Škorpil was also the first to excavate the site. To be sure, the initiative had come from the founder and director of the Russian Archaeological Institute in Constantinople, the prominent Byzantinist, Fedor I Uspenskii, who conducted excavations in Pliska between 1899 and 1900. The results of those excavations, complete with a detailed plan of the entire site (Figure 10.2) and a photo album of 117 plates, were published in the 10th volume of the Institute's annual reports.[13] The main focus of research was of course the Inner Town, the stone enclosure which, on the basis of the two inscriptions he had discovered, Škorpil dated to the reign of Omurtag. Guided by his firm conviction that he had revealed an unknown page of history, Škorpil followed his intuition in positioning his spade. He dug in search of walls and architectural or sculptural remains. When he found a wall, he followed it as far as he could; when he turned up a courtyard or pavement, he cleared as much of its surface as possible. The numerous graves he encountered when removing the first layers above what he called the Court Basilica were carefully excavated and the precise location or depth of each one of them were duly recorded (Figure 10.3).

Activity resumed on the site only 30 years later, as Krăstiu Miiatev reopened excavations in the Inner Town between 1931 and 1937 (Karasimeonoff 1940–41; for Miiatev's life and activity, see Doncheva-Petkova 1993b). Miiatev's idea was to continue where Škorpil had stopped, and in the course of six years, he re-excavated the 'Throne Palace'. Underneath the building excavated by Škorpil, he found a much larger one of rectangular form (Figure 10.4). Since it pre-dated the Throne Palace, which Škorpil had dated to Omurtag's time, and since he had discovered traces of destruction by fire, Miiatev dated the large rectangular building to the reign of Omurtag's predecessor, Krum (*c*803–814). He named the building 'Krum's Palace' and believed it to be the building from which Emperor Nicephorus I is said to have looked over Pliska from the balcony in 811, before setting fire to the capital city of his arch-enemy, Krum (Miiatev 1936; 1940–41; for the military conflict between Nicephorus I and Krum, see Curta 2006, 149–150).

New excavations in Pliska only began after the imposition of the Communist regime under Soviet protection in 1945 (Ivanova 1947; Mavrodinov 1948; Mikhailov 1948). Initially, the excavators distanced themselves from the old interpretation of the

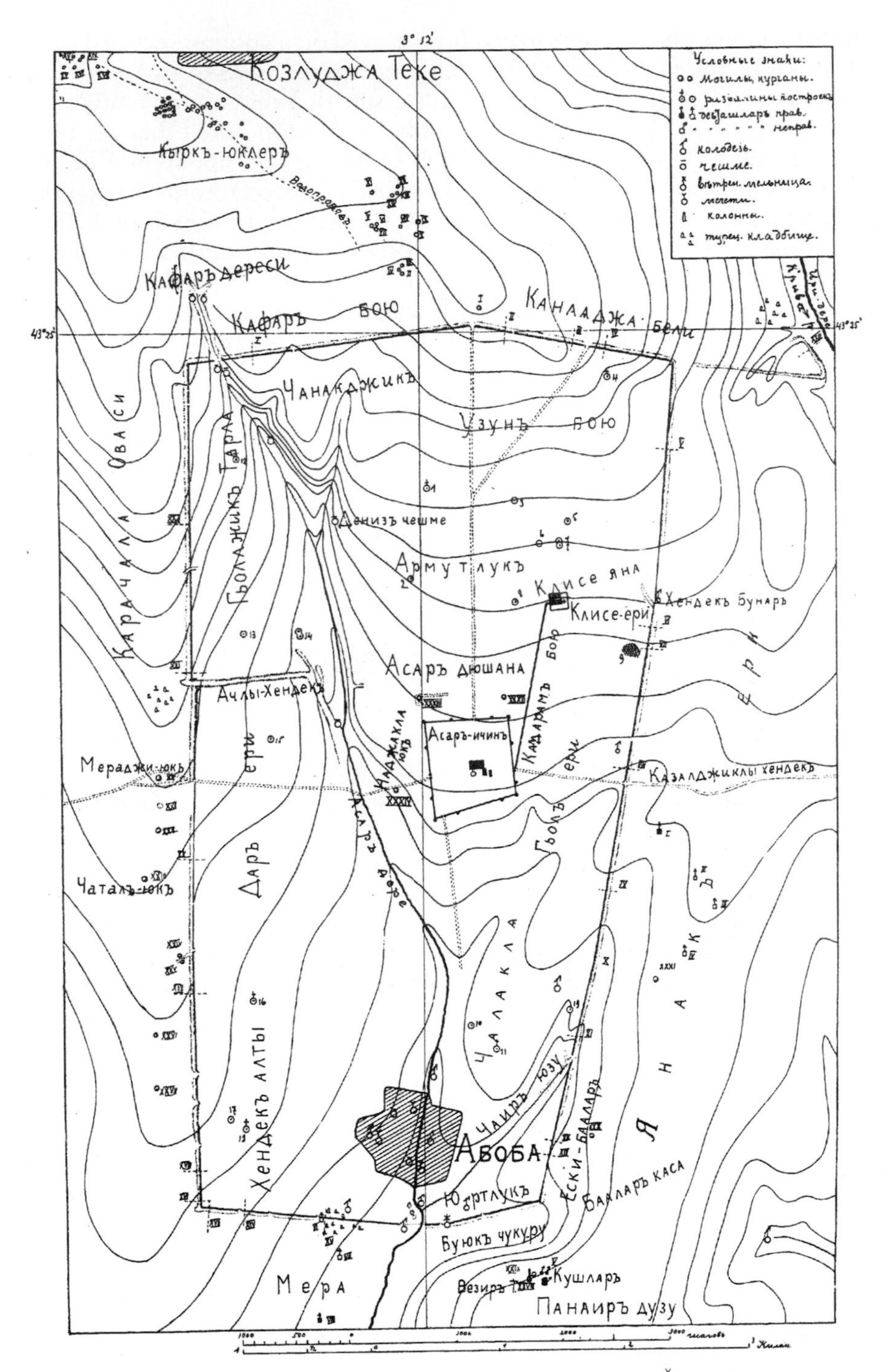

FIGURE 10.2. Aboba-Pliska. (Site plan drawn by Karel Škorpil 1905)

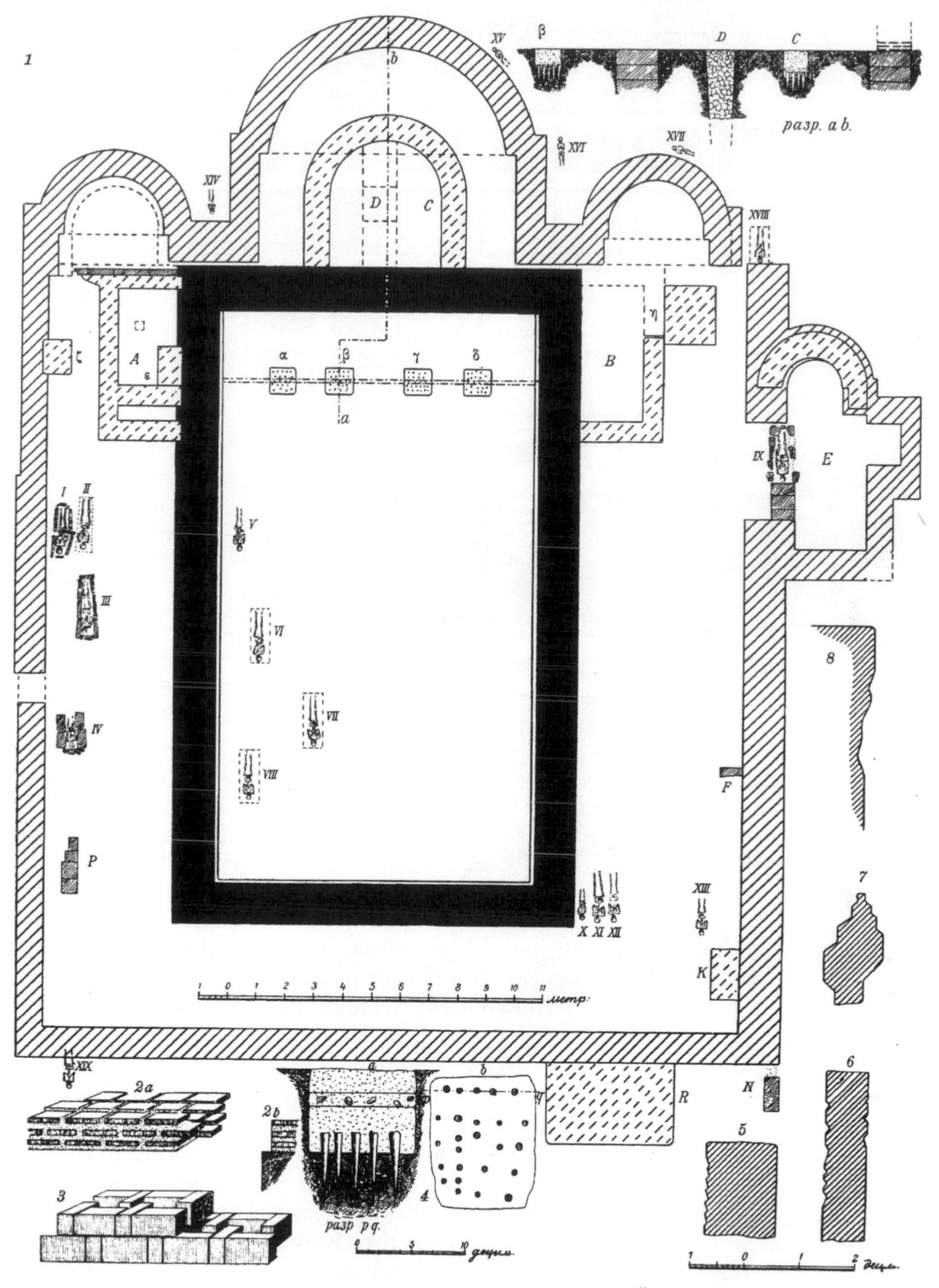

FIGURE 10.3. Pliska, Court Basilica, excavated by Karel Škorpil, 1899–1900.

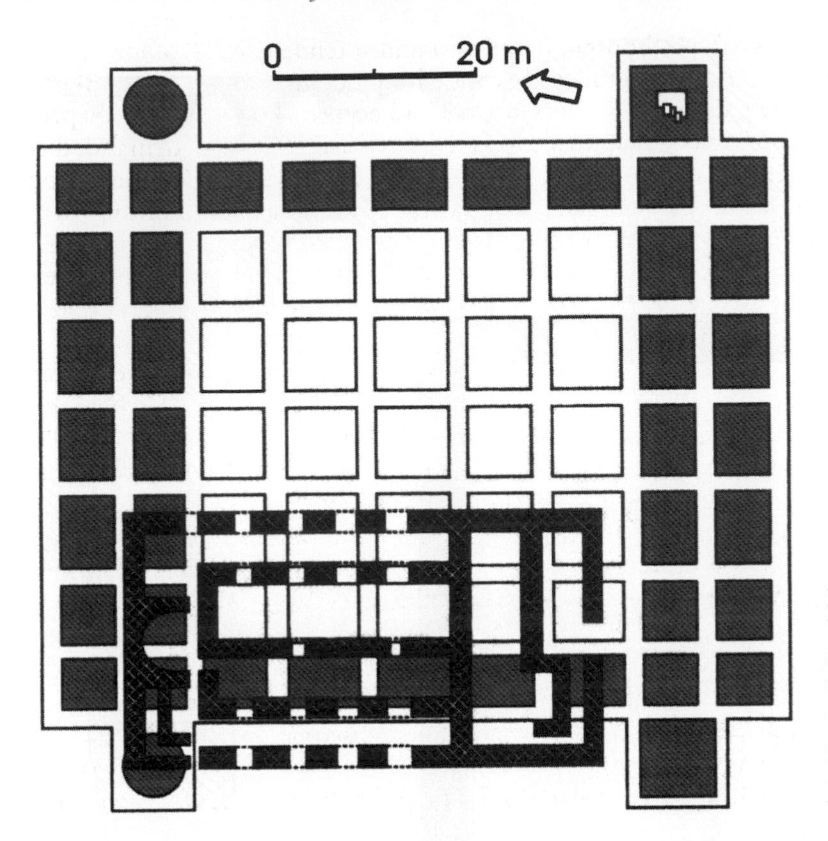

FIGURE 10.4. Pliska, Throne Palace, excavated by Karel Škorpil, 1899–1900, and Krum's Palace, excavated by Krăstiu Miiatev, 1931–37 (after Stanilov 2003).

site. For example, Stamen Mikhailov, the main excavator between 1945 and 1955, insisted upon the century-long gap between the Throne and Krum's Palace, thus suggesting a much earlier date for the latter, possibly of Roman origin (Mikhailov 1972; for the idea that Pliska had Roman origins, see also Mikhailov 1960). The discovery of a hypocaust in the so-called Palatial Compound to the north from Krum's Palace seems to have planted serious doubts in the minds of the post-war excavators of Pliska about the medieval origin of the site. Coins minted between the 2nd and the 4th century, a fragment of a Greek inscription mentioning Emperor Commodus, and several spolia from clearly Roman monuments fuelled further suspicions that Škorpil and Miiatev had been completely wrong. The most devastating critique in that respect came from Dimităr Krăndzhalov, who strongly believed that the sole reason for identifying the ruins near the village of Aboba with Pliska was Bulgarian national pride (Krăndzhalov 1964; 1966; 1971).[14] He even accused the excavators at Pliska of falsifying their data and hiding evidence in order to promote what he saw as the myth of Bulgar Pliska. Following Felix Kanitz's suggestion, Krăndzhalov thought that Pliska was in fact a Roman camp. Although later criticized for his exaggerations and obstinate focus on the 'Roman thesis', even when the evidence pointed to the contrary, Krăndzhalov certainly succeeded both in fostering scepticism about Pliska's Bulgar origins and in injecting among Bulgarian scholars a grain of self-consciousness about 'bourgeois and nationalist tendencies'. Krăndzhalov's idea may have gained initial acceptance, because he paid lip service to the party apparatchik Vălko Velev Chervenkov, who in 1948 had accused historians of the pre-war period of 'methodological helplessness and backwardness' and demanded a thorough application of Marxism to the study of Bulgarian history (Krăndzhalov 1948; for Chervenkov's life and activity, see Ivanov *et al* 2000). By pointing to a Roman date, Krăndzhalov's goal was to shift the emphasis to the 'slave-owning stage' of the Marxist sequence of modes of production. Only Roman slaves could have been responsible for the enormous amount of work that went into the building of ramparts for both the Outer and the Inner Town.

The reply came in the 1960s from Stancho Stanchev-Vaklinov, who, after hesitatingly accepting Krăndzhalov's ideas, boldly took advantage of the changing tide in culture politics introduced by Todor Zhivkov,[15] to insist upon the specifically Bulgar character of the architecture at Pliska (Stanchev 1962). He drew many comparisons to monuments of stone architecture in Persia, Armenia, and even the Islamic Near East, in order to demonstrate the medieval origin of the site (Vaklinov Stanchev 1967–68, 133–145; Vaklinov Stanchev 1968, 245–249, 252, 260, 262–264; Vaklinov 1977, 92–96). Stamen Mikhailov had re-excavated the so-called Court Basilica, first discovered by Karel Škorpil, and had identified three building phases, the first of which consisted of two rectangular enclosures (Mikhailov 1955) (Figure 10.5). Stancho Vaklinov now regarded the enclosures as a pre-Christian Bulgar temple, an interpretation which would become the point of reference for the subsequent definition of a particular type of Bulgar sacral architecture, later identified at other sites (Brentjes 1971; Aladzhov 1985, 73–74; Bonev 1989; Teofilov 1993; Ovcharov and Doncheva 2004, 91–92).

An even stronger emphasis on the pre-Christian, specifically Bulgar past of Pliska became evident in the years prior to the 1981 jubilee of Bulgaria's 1300 years of existence, which was organized by the newly appointed minister of culture, Liudmila Zhivkova, the daughter of the Communist strongman in Sofia (Zhivkov and Zhivkova 1981; for Liudmila Zhivkova's life and activity, see Raionov 2003). The 1961 excavation of a cistern to the north of the Inner Town had produced a rosette with runic inscription, the deciphering and interpretation of which is by far the most popular subject of current debate in Bulgarian medieval archaeology (Georgiev 1995; Mikhailov 1995; Ovcharov 1995; Sidorov and Keledzhiev 1999; Zhdrakov *et al* 2002). By the late 1970s, attention shifted to traces of timber buildings in the central area of Pliska. In 1981, Rasho Rashev excavated one such building between Krum's Palace and the Court Church. This was a circular feature, with a diameter of 14m, the remains of which consisted of three circles of postholes in a concentric arrangement. Under the assumption that the Bulgars were nomads, the feature was quickly dubbed the Large Yurt (Rashev 1983, 257–259; Rashev and Docheva 1989; Georgiev 1997). Reconstructions advanced by the excavator and by others show a platform with a ramp or a flight of podia and a pavilion or tent on top, but little evidence exists for this interpretation (Figure 10.6). According to Rashev, the building must be one of the earliest in Pliska dating back to the late 7th or early 8th century. However,

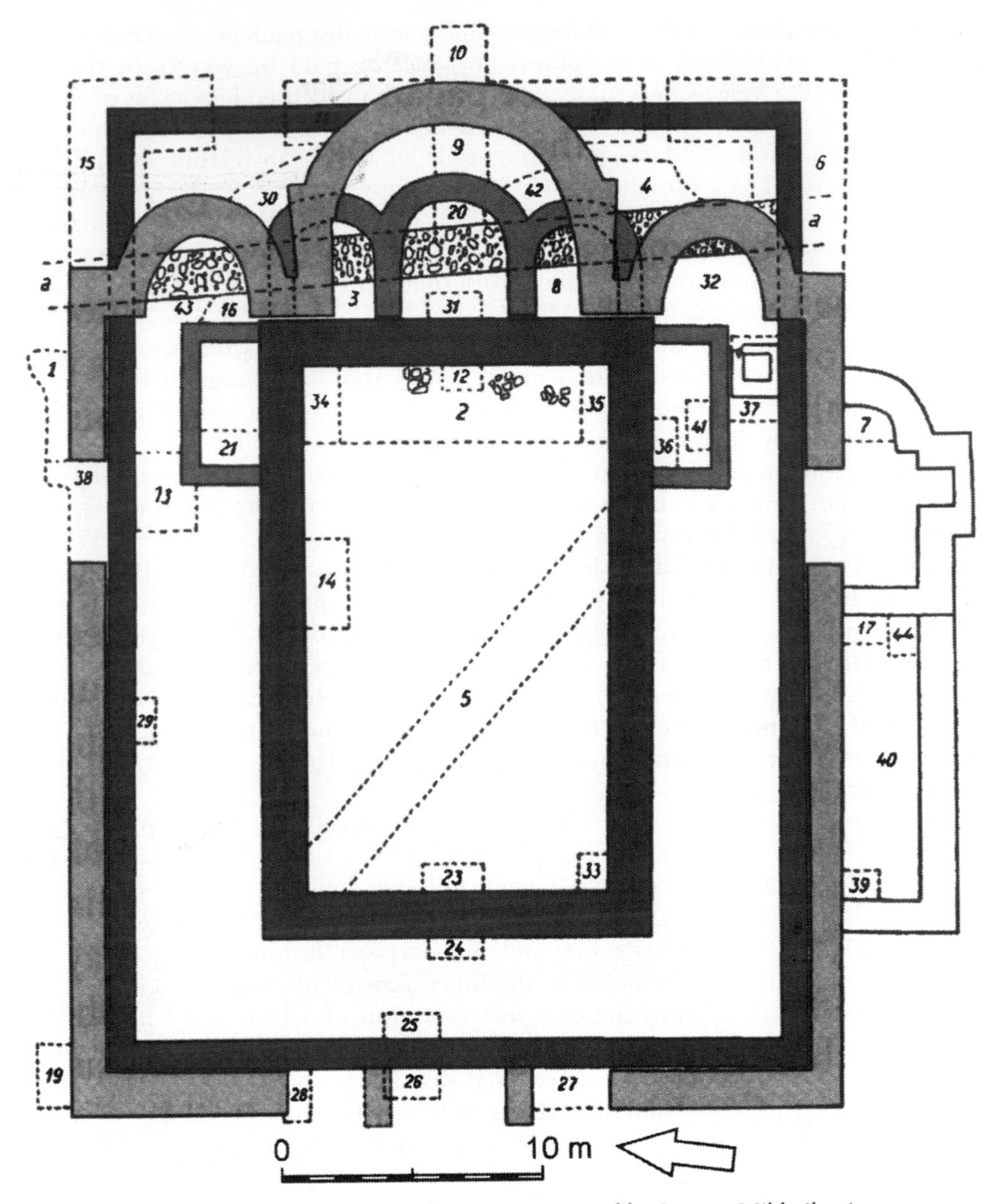

FIGURE 10.5. Pliska, Court Basilica, (re-)excavated by Stamen Mikhailov in 1949 (after Mikhailov 1955).

several small finds associated with the 'Large Yurt' point to a later date within the 9th century. Such a dating suggests that the source of inspiration for this building was the architecture of the Chrysotriklinos in Constantinople (Rashev and Docheva 1989, 301–303, 309; Georgiev 1997, 297–298; Fiedler 2008, 186).

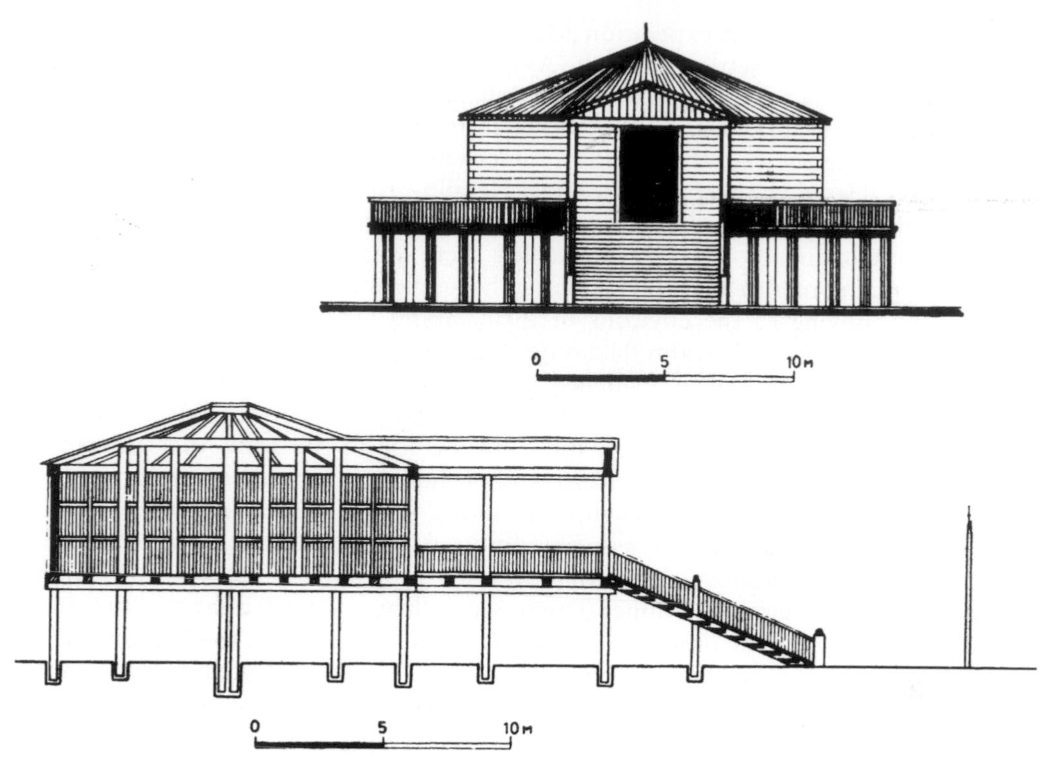

FIGURE 10.6. Pliska, Large Yurt, reconstruction (after Rashev and Docheva 1989).

The Large Yurt came to light only one year after a Soviet-Bulgarian joint expedition had finished opening up a relatively large area in the southern part of the Inner Town. Instead of yurts, Soviet and Bulgarian archaeologists stumbled upon 17 sunken-featured buildings dated to the 10th and 11th century (Pletneva 1990; Dimitrov 1994, 47–48). Though by no means unique, the discovery raised some key questions about the nature of the settlement in Pliska after the capital of medieval Bulgaria moved to Preslav and during the early years of the Byzantine occupation. Moreover, the work of the Soviet-Bulgarian expedition highlighted the importance of understanding relations between the inhabitants of the high-status site in the Inner Town and those of the surrounding countryside. Rasho Rashev plotted on a map of Pliska all known areas of settlement within the Outer Town. He concluded from their distribution that most settlements could be dated to the 10th and 11th centuries, with only five small clusters of 8th- to 9th-century sites (Rashev 1995). Between 1989 and 1991 over 27 miles of drainage ditches were dredged in the Outer Town. The results of the accompanying archaeological survey confirmed Rashev's conclusion (Georgiev 2000, 21, fig 3).[16] No stone buildings have so far been found between those settlements, which consist only of sunken-featured buildings. As a consequence, some have advanced the idea that sites within the Outer Town were service settlements similar to those known from medieval Poland and Bohemia (Henning 2000, 78; 2005, 43).

A joint German-Bulgarian expedition led by Joachim Henning excavated between 1997 and 2002 one such settlement in the Asar Dere area, to the west from the western rampart of the Inner Town. A Marxist archaeologist most famous for his book on agriculture and agricultural implements in the late antique and early medieval Balkans, Henning viewed the palatial compound in Pliska as a large centre of consumption (Henning 2000; 2007; see also Henning 1982; 1987). According to him, the decision of the Bulgar rulers to establish a centre of power in Pliska created a considerable demand of victuals, for which there was no pre-existing settlement infrastructure. In order to meet that demand, those rulers therefore created settlements *ex nihilo* by moving to the environs of their capital large groups of people from various other parts of their realm (Henning 2005, 42–43).

Judging from the published evidence, there can be no doubt about the agricultural character of the sites located within the Outer Town of Pliska. But Pliska also produced evidence of industrial activities. On the site of the 10th- to 11th-century commercial quarter, next to the western wall of the Inner Town, Bulgarian archaeologists have found a number of smelting furnaces, which they dated to the 9th and 10th century on the basis of the associated pottery (Doncheva-Petkova 1979; 1980; 1985; 1993a; 1995; Antonova and Vitlianov 1985; see also Vitlianov 1993; for other industrial activities within the Inner Town, see Milchev 1975; Balabanov 1981). An important discovery of the most recent excavations at Pliska is that the relatively large industrial area located to the west from the palatial compound included not only a metalworking production centre, but also workshops producing vessel and window glass, evidently for the palace (Doncheva-Petkova and Zlatinova 1978; see also Dzhingova and Kuleff 1992; Wedepohl 2007).

Finally, it is important to note that the archaeological excavations in Pliska have so far produced some 400 burials within the Inner Town and about 500 within the Outer Town area. All of them post-date the conversion to Christianity and no burial is known that could be dated before that (Fiedler 2008, 188; Kirilov 2006, 138). This intriguing situation has led some to introduce interpretations emphasizing the symbolic use of the landscape. Uwe Fiedler has advanced the idea that the absence of burials in Pliska may be due to the fact that the palatial compound grounds were viewed as sacred. This interpretation, enthusiastically accepted by some Bulgarian archaeologists and rejected by others, has received further substantiation from the discovery of a number of barrows of prehistoric origin on the western side of the Outer Town, outside the precinct. Some of them were used for sacrifices during the 9th century, as indicated by a 12m deep sacrificial pit containing the skeletons of two horses, two dogs, and a cat (Fiedler 2007; Rashev and Stanilov 1998). Meanwhile, having noticed that the execution of neither earthworks surrounding the Outer Town, nor Inner Town stone walls can be justified in military terms, Paolo Squatriti has proposed that they were in fact an expression of the power of the Bulgar rulers over their subjects: the embankments offered 'a unique occasion for rulers to exercise power over the bodies of those whom they ruled by having them handle the soil' (Squatriti 2005, 90).

Without any explicit reference to post-processualist approaches to material culture, the most recent interpretations of Pliska emphasize the symbolism of the site, while de-emphasizing the traditional interpretation of its political role. Pavel Georgiev has recently suggested that during the first few decades after the arrival of the Bulgars to Bulgaria in AD 680, Pliska served only as a seasonal residence (Georgiev 2003; for the beginnings of Pliska, see also Rashev 2007). As a consequence, its timber buildings could only have been temporarily occupied. Pliska became a permanent residence with its specific architecture and triple enclosure no earlier than the mid-8th century (Georgiev 2002; 2007); now, even that interpretation has been abandoned. Instead, the idea has been put forward that, much like the Ottonian kings of later times, the rulers of early medieval Bulgaria initially had no fixed residence, but travelled from one residence to another. Pliska became their main residence in the early 800s, while a new and fixed residence was established only after 900 in Preslav (Kirilov 2006, 174–179).

THE CEMETERY

The first excavator of the very large cemetery discovered in Krainburg (now Kranj, in northern Slovenia), at the foot of the Karawanken Mountains, was the local miller, Thomas Pavšlar. He owned a large piece of property on the narrow strip of land between the Sava and the Kokra Rivers, at a place known as 'Na Lajhu'. The first graves were accidentally found there in 1898, but over the next few years Pavšlar is said to have unearthed between 200 and 250 burial assemblages. He later donated the grave goods from some 71 graves to the Provincial Museum in Ljubljana, but nothing is otherwise known about the rest of his discoveries (Stare 1980, 7).[17] By 1900, however, in charge of the excavations at Kranj was Joseph Szombathy, newly appointed custodian of the anthropological and prehistoric collection of the Hofmuseum in Vienna, a clear indication of the great significance attributed to the Kranj finds in the very capital of the Empire.[18] Szombathy was a trained archaeologist most famous for his discovery a few years later of the Palaeolithic female figurine now known as the 'Venus of Willendorf'; he proceeded rigorously and in just two weeks excavated 66 graves to the west and north from Pavšlar's property. The news about the rich finds from Kranj quickly reached Ljubljana, where the local saving bank placed 600 crowns at the disposal of the regional museum, whose director, Alfons Müllner, appointed Franz Schulz to lead the excavations at Lajh. Within a few weeks in 1901, Schulz dug up another 58 graves between what are now the Savska Cesta and the Sejmišče Street (Šmid 1907, 55: more excavations were carried out in 1905 by the Regional Museum in Ljubljana as work began on the enlargement of the street going through the cemetery). Meanwhile, a local gymnasium teacher named Jakob Žmavc began the excavation of the central and northern part of Pavšlar's property. Žmavc drew up a general plan of his excavations of 1903–04, on which he carefully marked the orientation of each grave, the depth of the grave pit, as well as the position of the arms and legs of the skeleton (Stare 1980, 12) (Figure 10.7). He also drew individual grave plans, on which he indicated the position of the grave goods in relation to the skeletons (Figure 10.9). The fourth and last major excavation at Lajh took place in 1905 and was carried out by the newly appointed director of the Regional Museum in Ljubljana, Valter Šmid.[19] Unlike all his predecessors, Šmid excavated a very large

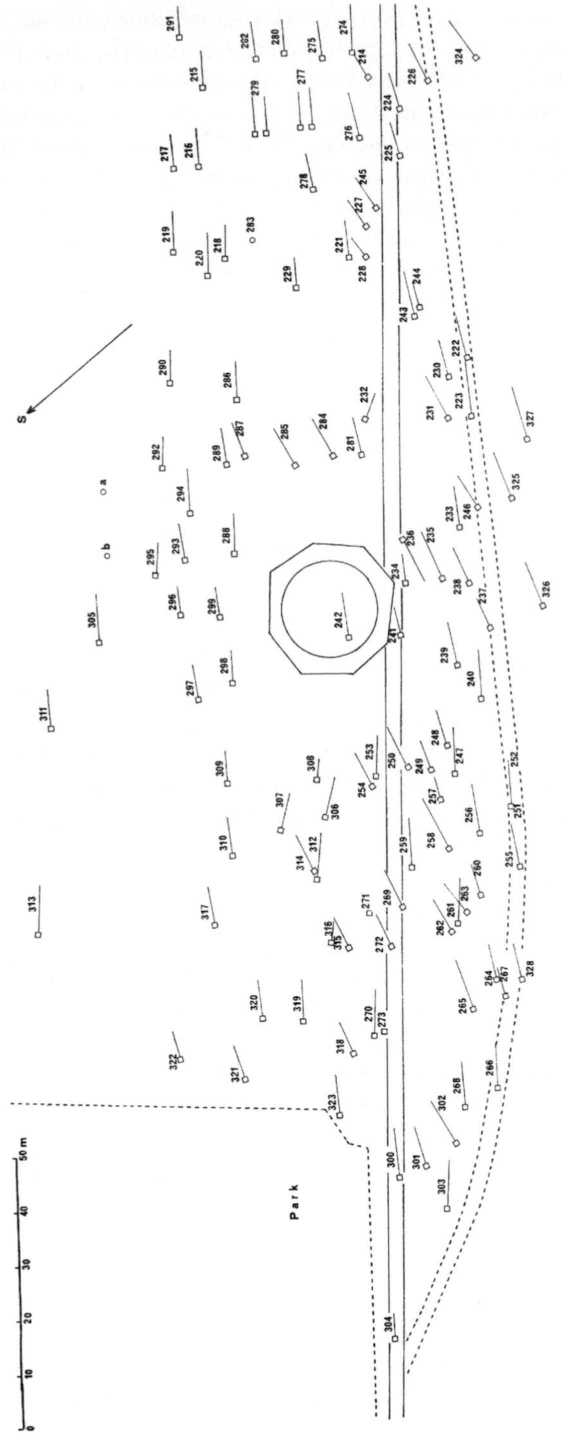

FIGURE 10.7. Kranj-Lajh. Jakob Žmavc's excavations of 1903, plan reconstructed by Vida Stare (after Stare 1980).

number of graves (213), which he published together with a plan of his excavations (Šmid 1907). The total number of graves known to have been excavated in Kranj between 1898 and 1905 is 647 (Stare 1980). His comparatively more attentive method of excavation revealed interesting details such as remains of burial shrouds, which he promptly placed for analysis under the microscope of the local pharmacist (Šmid 1907, 56). Besides the fact that the shrouds were all made of wool, nothing else is known about the analyses. Šmid noticed that rich burial assemblages were consistently found in relatively deep grave pits, but drew no conclusion from that concerning the social structure of the community using the cemetery (Šmid 1907, 56–57). His concern was of a different nature. Šmid regarded archaeology as a historical science: his goal was to discover in the archaeological record the major events and processes known from written sources. As a consequence, when pointing to analogies between grave goods found in Kranj and artefacts from burial sites in Italy attributed to the Lombards, Šmid aimed at something more than just ethnic attribution. According to him, the cemetery was abandoned in the mid-7th century, an indication that the community in Kranj had been wiped out by some catastrophe. Šmid linked the Avar victory over the Friulan Duke Lupus, mentioned by Paul the Deacon in his *History of the Lombards*, with the annihilation of the population in Kranj and the subsequent abandonment of the cemetery (Paul the Deacon, *History of the Lombards* V, 18–21; Šmid 1907, 75–77).

In 1909, Šmid lost his position as director at the Regional Museum in Ljubljana, and moved to Graz (for the political circumstances surrounding Šmid's removal from the Museum, see Slapšak and Novaković 1996, 282; Novaković 2002, 332). Following World War I and the creation of the kingdom of Yugoslavia, he continued to excavate on sites throughout Slovenia, including Ljubljana, although Šmid never returned to Kranj (he believed the cemetery had been completely excavated: Šmid 1907, 55). In fact, work resumed there only in 1977, when salvage excavations across the Sava River from Lajh, between the railroad station and the Iskra factory, led to the discovery of another small cemetery, including six walled burial vaults (Sagadin 1987). For more than 70 years between 1905 and 1977, Kranj was often mentioned in archaeological literature, especially in studies dedicated to artefacts — primarily brooches, pins, and buckles — of the so-called 'Great Migration' period. Most such studies embraced Šmid's interpretation of the site as Lombard and accepted his chronology extending into the first half of the 7th century. After all, the First Congress on Yugoslav Archaeologists in Niška Banja (1950) had already set as a goal for future research the study of the ethnic groups which had lived in the Balkans at the time of the arrival of the Slavs (Korošec 1950, 214; Novaković 2002, 342). Twelve years later, however, the German archaeologist Joachim Werner noted that the Kranj cemetery was unlike any of those in Hungary or northern Yugoslavia, which had been attributed to the Lombards. According to him, the only possible explanation for that was the dominant presence of the native Romanized population (Werner 1962, 126–127).[20] Werner may have been encouraged to think of 'natives' by the changing tide in Yugoslav archaeology of the 1950s. Thirty-three graves excavated in Mihaljevići in the district of Sarajevo (Bosnia-Herzegovina) and dated to the 5th and 6th century had already been attributed to the local Balkan population (Miletić 1956;

1961; 1969). The idea of a native, Romanized population in the Balkans, the material culture of which was similar to that of sites in the Italian and Austrian Alps has been also advanced by Vinski (1954 and 1956). Among historians who embraced the idea, mention must be made of Milko Kos (1955, 22). Werner's interpretation of the Kranj cemetery triggered a dramatic shift of emphasis in the interpretation of that site, as well as of other cemeteries (Bled-Pristava, Ptuj, Kašić, Knin, and Rakovčani), on which excavations had been carried out. In 1951, the Slovenian historian Bogo Grafenauer sharply criticized the culture-historical approach, and without mentioning Gustaf Kossinna's name, rejected the idea that certain types or groups of artefacts could be directly associated with particular ethnic or linguistic groups (Grafenauer 1951). Thirteen years later, however, he embraced Werner's idea, while still insisting upon a 'Germanic' component within the population of the Kranj cemetery (Grafenauer 1964, 216).[21] The Croatian archaeologist Zdenko Vinski went even further. Drawing comparisons with artefacts from other cemetery sites in Croatia, Slovenia, and Bosnia, Vinski concluded that the core of the Kranj cemetery comprised a numerous group of graves, which he attributed to the ancient Romanized population of the South-eastern Alps (Vinski 1970, 151; 1971a, 255).[22] Nonetheless, on the basis of the plan of Žmavc's excavations of 1903 (Figure 10.7), he regarded Kranj as a typical *Reihengräberkreis* cemetery, with characteristic inhumations on a west-east orientation.[23] From the relatively small number of male and the comparatively higher number of female and child burials, he concluded that Kranj was the cemetery of the population living in the Late Roman fort of Carnium (Vinski 1971a, 257). No proper anthropological sexing has been done on any group of skeletons from Kranj, except that available to István Kiszely (1970); see also Barbiera 2007. In tune with the prevailing interpretation of burials with no grave goods, Vinski also advanced the idea that many of those who were buried in Kranj must have been Christian (Vinski 1971a, 257; 1971b, 384).[24] Against Šmid, Vinski restricted the chronology of the entire cemetery to the 6th century, but still linked its end to the invasion of Avars and Slavs (Vinski 1971a, 257, 261; 1971b, 384–385; 1971c, 56). Vinski's restricted chronology is based on his interpretation of ten coins found in different burial assemblages. The earliest of them was, according to him, a solidus struck in Ravenna for Odoacer, and the latest, a bronze coin minted for Emperor Justin II. Among the latest assemblages in Kranj, he listed grave 331, which produced a silver belt buckle with triangular plate with a close analogy in Cividale-San Giovanni (Italy). Vinski's conclusion was that the artefacts found in the latest graves at Kranj were the 'prototypes' of Lombard dress accessories in Italy (Vinski 1971a, 260–261; 1971c, 57). For grave 331, excavated at some point between 1901 and 1904 by Pavšlar, see Stare (1980, 118). In other words, before entering Italy in 568, the Lombards or, at least some of them, briefly stopped and lived for while in the fort at Carnium. Judging by the small number of graves with weapons, the Lombard garrison must have been quite small. Most other male burials had either very few, or no grave goods at all, a further indication (to Vinski) of their local origin (Vinski 1971a, 261; 1971b, 385). Marijan Slabe (1978, 68–69) pointed to artificially deformed skulls as signalling the presence of 'foreigners' of Germanic origin. What, then, was the main occupation of all these men? Vinski interpreted grave 185 to be that of a comb-maker, but he was not at all interested in the social analysis of the cemetery (Vinski 1971a, 261; Stare 1980, 113). Vinski's interpretation of grave 185 was most likely based on the presence of tools, including a wimble (a tool for boring) among the associated grave goods. There are, however, no bone or antler artefacts in that burial assemblage) (Figure 10.8). Subsequent commentators also seem to have been concerned more with the ethnic attribution of

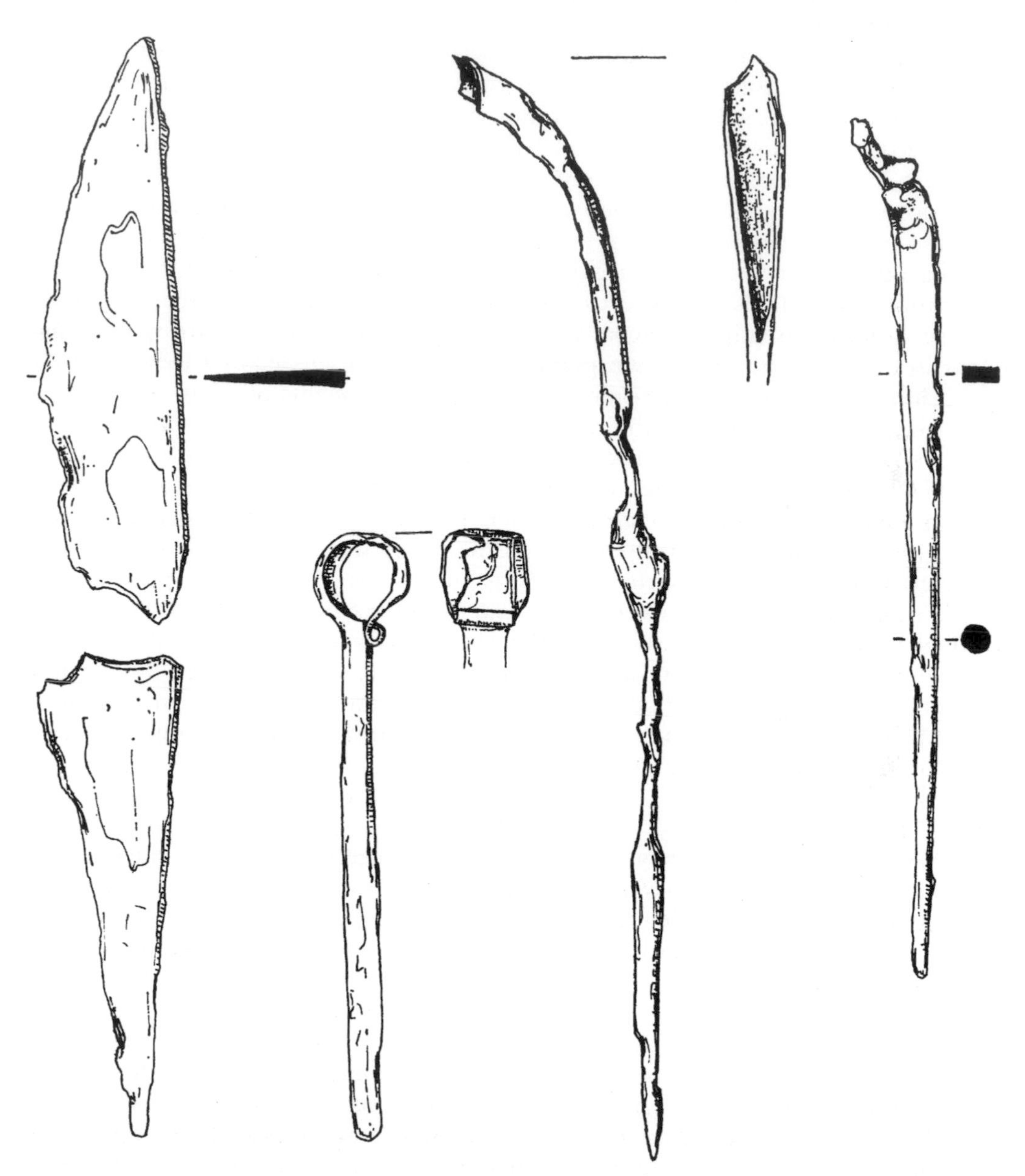

FIGURE 10.8. Kranj-Lajh, tools from grave 185 (after Stare 1980).

the finds. For example, Davorin Vuga noted that the presence of a 4th-century crossbow fibula (*Zwiebelknopffibel*) in grave 327, which he interpreted as the tomb of a 'magnate', indicated that 'the natives were neither ethnically nor socially subordinate to Germanic federates' (Vuga 1980, 20; see Stare 1980, 118). No anthropological sexing of the skeleton in grave 327 has ever been performed, but judging from the presence of a pin and a comb, this may have well been the tomb of a woman (Figure 10.9). The analysis of what he viewed as coins struck in a Lombard mint after 650 led Peter Kos to the conclusion that there must have been enclaves of native Romanized populations in the Cisalpine region as late as the second half of the 7th century (Kos 1981; Kos's interpretation of the artefacts as coins has now been challenged by Martin 2000, 194–196). Relying on Zdenko Vinski's analysis of the cemetery, Lujo Margetić however argued that the Lombards had come to Kranj from Italy, not from Pannonia. The Lombard garrison in Carnium was in fact an advanced position of the Lombard kingdom in Italy (Margetić 1992; for a view of Margetić's conclusion as 'hasty', see Ciglenečki 1999, 296). By contrast, in a thorough examination of male burials with short daggers of the *sax* type, Max Martin concluded that such burial assemblages signal the presence in Kranj *c*550 of a group of Gepids (Martin 2000, 180; graves with weapons have also been discussed by Knific 1995).

Only recent salvage excavations, which revealed elements of a Late Antique and early medieval settlement to the north from Lajh, have slowly begun to shift the emphasis to social issues. The discovery within what seems to be the fort of Carnium of a glassmaking workshop, as well as of a basilica with baptistery underneath the present-day parish church in downtown Kranj has only recently begun to raise questions about the relationships between the newly discovered settlement and the cemeteries at Lajh and Iskra crossroads (Ciglenečki 2005, 266–267; see Sagadin 1991; 1995; Valić 1991). So far, however, no attempt has been made to undertake analysis of the Lajh cemetery with the aim of establishing the sequence of development of the burial ground and its organization, in order to assess the relative status within the community of the individuals buried in each generation. The social interpretation of the Kranj cemetery remains a task for future generations of archaeologists.

CONCLUSION

What does the town have to do with the cemetery? What do they have in common? At first glance, they do not belong in the same category. The town was excavated continuously during the last 60 years or so; the excavation of the cemetery ceased completely before World War I and, although adjacent areas were opened up again during the last few decades, no further exploration of the cemetery is known to have taken place. Yet, examined more closely, the boundaries between the town and the cemetery begin to blur. The archaeological study of Pliska began with a series of attempts to identify in the landscape a site otherwise known from historical sources and inscriptions; the archaeological interpretation of the cemetery site in Kranj conjured up the gloomy picture of Paul the Deacon's account in the *History of the Lombards*. The desire to write national history, or at least to illustrate it with finds from the 'first capital of Bulgaria' long obscured the chronology of the site and

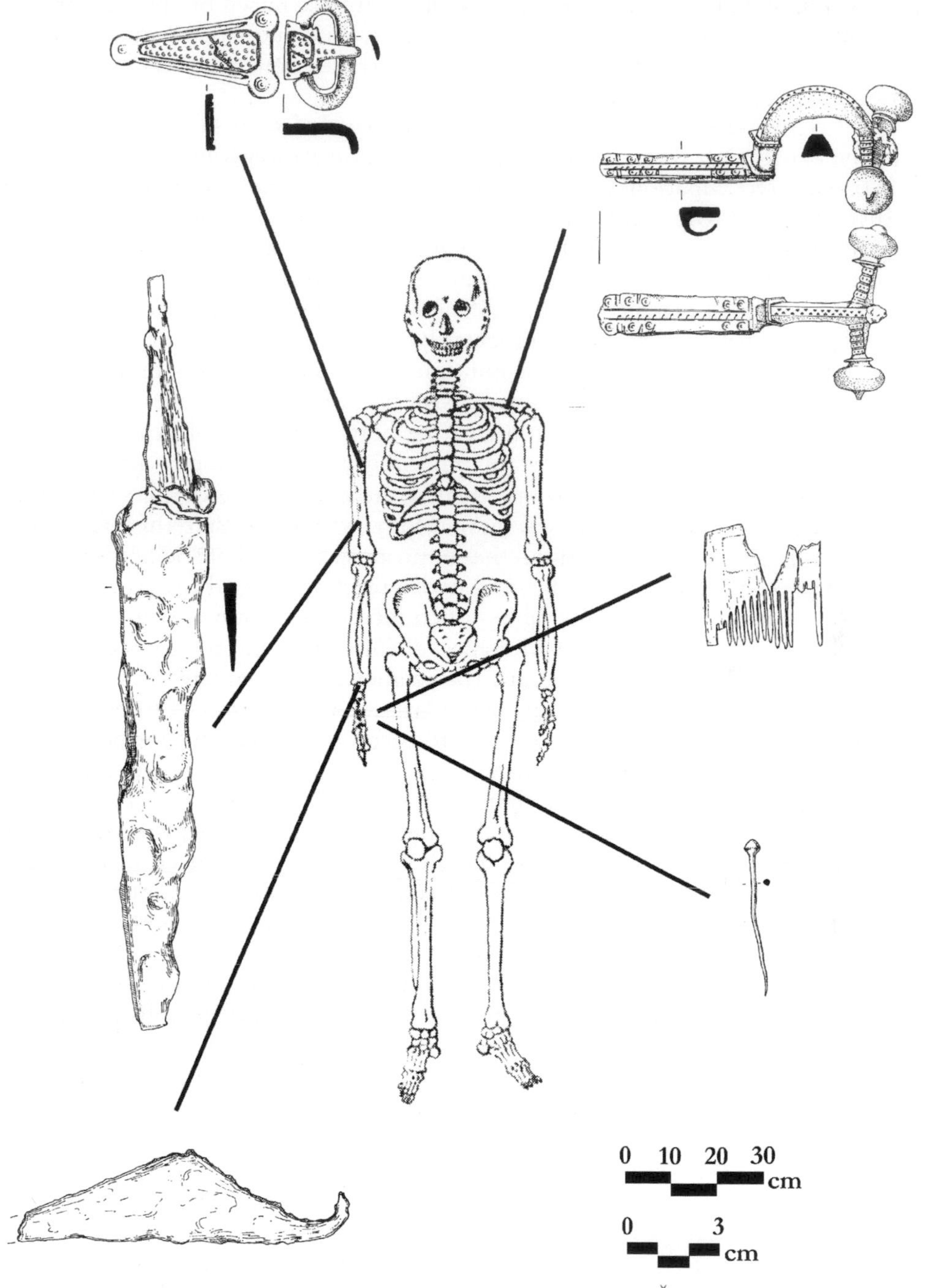

FIGURE 10.9. Kranj-Lajh, grave 327: skeleton drawing by Jakob Žmavc, with the positions of some of the associated grave goods. Scale for skeleton (above) and for grave goods (below) (after Stare 1980).

effectively prevented a realistic approach to the problems raised by the interpretation of the abundant archaeological data, the very issue which now confronts any scholar interested in the study of the Kranj cemetery beyond the ethnic attribution of its burial assemblages.

Not to overstretch the comparison, established discourse about Pliska was met in the 1960s with sharp criticism for its alleged nationalist bias, as well as with an obstinate preoccupation with pushing the origin of the site back into Roman antiquity. There is no equivalent to that for the cemetery in Kranj. Dimităr Krăndzhalov's criticism seems to have been inspired by a genuine desire to apply to Pliska an interpretative model of Marxist inspiration, one which favoured a slave-based mode of production capable of mobilizing workers and resources for the erection of Pliska's long embankments. By contrast, there is not a single whim of dialectical materialism in any of the multiple contributions to the understanding of the Kranj cemetery. Marxism is conspicuously absent from the medieval archaeology of Tito's Yugoslavia, a phenomenon indicating both a lack of political pressure and the general 'policy of the Yugoslav state, especially after the conflict with the Soviet Union under Stalin, to tolerate and marginalize rather than overtly persecute' (Babić 2002, 315; see also Novaković 2002, 343). Many will argue that this difference in attitude towards Marxism is essential, that to propose a model of social organization, even if based on a faulty chronology and understanding of the history of the site, is entirely different from not advancing any such model or from not even needing one. Such claims are justified, yet those differences themselves point to a set of similarities that cast doubt on assumptions about the medieval archaeology of south-eastern Europe being essentially Marxist during the last 50 years or so. For in both cases — Bulgaria and Yugoslavia — Marxism failed to become a paradigm, irrespective of the quantity and frequency of citations from Marx and Engels. For over 50 years, in both Bulgaria and Yugoslavia (and, for that matter, all of south-eastern Europe under Communist regimes) Marxism occupied a theoretical space otherwise neglected in contemporary archaeological practice. Highly simplistic and in need of compulsion in order to gain acceptance, dialectical materialism, basically a rudimentary version of Marxism, did not offer any alternative to the historical narratives that guided the work of archaeologists. Such an explanation takes into account that the theoretical strength of the culture-historical paradigm has less to do with the appeal of nationalism and much more with the strong links long established between historiography and medieval archaeology. If there is currently a search for new theoretical models in the medieval archaeology of the south-east European countries, it is not so much in reaction to Marxism, as to the remarkably resistant tradition of culture-history.

NOTES

[1] Among the pioneers of medieval archaeology in south-eastern Europe, mention must be made of Lujo Marun's excavations of the episcopal church of St Mary in Biskupije (Radić 1895a; 1895b; 1895c; 1896a; 1896b; 1897; Marun 1898), József Ujfalusi's excavations of the cathedral in Alba Iulia (Transylvania, Romania; Ujfalusi 1903), and Miloje Vašić's first publication of early medieval pottery from Serbia (Vašić 1906). For Lujo Marun, see Jurišić (1979). For an assessment of contemporary developments in the medieval archaeology of the Yugoslav lands, see Reinecke (1897).

[2] No survey exists of the history of Communism in south-eastern Europe; however, for Romania, see Tismăneanu 2003; for Communism and archaeology, see Kaiser 1995; Nikolov 2002; Babić 2002; and Novaković 2002.

[3] The fact that the first two major cemeteries to be published in Yugoslavia as monographs were from Slovenia (Bled and Ptuj) may be attributed to post-war concerns with correcting the errors of the past. Excavations on the cemetery site in Bled were financed and encouraged by the Nazis along the lines of Hitler's declared intention 'to make this land German again'. The Austrian archaeologists responsible for the excavation sought to prove an early Germanic presence south of the Alps. In response, excavations were reopened in Bled after the war, with the specific purpose of demonstrating the presence of the early Slavs in the area. See Slapšak and Novaković (1996, 287–288) and Novaković (2002, 338–339).

[4] The Late Avar period (*c*700 to *c*800/20) is almost completely devoid of written sources, yet can now be studied in detail on the basis of archaeological excavations of both settlements and cemeteries (Fülöp 1991).

[5] To be sure, in 1985 and 1986 Lewis Binford gave a series of lectures at the Department of Archaeology of the University of Ljubljana. However, according to Predrag Novaković, 'the cultural historical approach is still deeply rooted in Slovene archaeology, and processual and post-processual issues only ocasionally appear in contemporary archaeological practice and debate in Slovenia' (Novaković 2002, 348).

[6] It is, for example, very difficult to lump together developments in archaeology taking place in Tito's Yugoslavia with those characterizing the discipline during the regimes of Nicolae Ceauşescu in Romania or Enver Hoxha in Albania. The matter is one of institutional history, but also of political context.

[7] For an excellent critique of that stereotype, see Todorova 1997.

[8] A surveyor and geographer in the service of the Danish crown, Carsten Niebuhr (1733–1815) joined the expedition sent by King Frederick V of Denmark to Egypt, Syria and Arabia. He was the only surviving member of the expedition, and on his way back to Denmark from Constantinople, Niebuhr travelled across the Balkans in 1767.

[9] Felix Philipp Kanitz (1829–1904) was a Viennese artist, who developed an interest in the Balkan provinces of the Ottoman Empire. He travelled across the region many times between 1856 and 1900, especially after being appointed first curator of the Anthropology and Prehistory Museum in Vienna in 1870 (Paskaleva 1996, 93).

[10] Regarding Konstantin Jireček's life and activity, see Dorovský 1983.

[11] For the relations between the Škorpil brothers and Jireček, see Miiatev and Iantarski 1961. The two brothers co-authored an article on Bulgar antiquities (Škorpil and Škorpil 1921). For Karel Škorpil's life and activity in Bulgaria, see Stoianov 1933; Miiatev 1961; Velkov 1961; Rashev 1998; Doncheva-Petkova 1999; Rashev 2000.

[12] Both inscriptions have been published by Beshevliev (1963, 246–250). For Škorpil and the Bulgar inscriptions, see Beshevliev 1961.

[13] For a thorough description of the site, see Shkorpil 1905c; for small finds, see Shkorpil 1905b; for barrows and 'megaliths', see Shkorpil 1905a; for coins and seals, see Panchenko 1905; for inscriptions, see Uspenskii 1905.

[14] Dimităr Krăndzhalov (1907–71) was a Bulgarian Slavist, born in Romania, with studies in Iaşi and Prague. He first moved to Bulgaria in 1940, where he initially worked as teaching assistant at the University of Sofia. During the war and the Bulgarian occupation of what is now (the Republic of) Macedonia, he was the head of the department of Bulgarian History at the University of Skopje. He remained in Skopje until 1945 when he returned to the University of Sofia, where he became assistant professor in 1946. He occupied that position until 1949, when he became professor of east and south-east European history at the University of Olomouc in Czechoslovakia. He became head of the Department of History at that university in 1951 (and again, in 1968), dean of the Philosophy Faculty there in 1957 (and again in 1961) and president of the university in 1968.

[15] As a protégé of Nikita Khrushchev, Zhivkov emerged as the new leader of Communist Bulgaria at the same time as Chervenkov was ousted from his position of power.

[16] The results of the fieldwork were the basis for Ianko Dimitrov's still unpublished dissertation.

[17] Pavšlar's 'private excavations' apparently produced a large quantity of artefacts, which he initially refused to show to Simon Rutar, the conservator for Carniola of the *k.u.k Zentralkommission* in Vienna, which had been established in 1850 for the study and protection of art and historical monuments. Despite the quite elaborate structure of the commission, until 1918 there was in fact no legislation for the protection of historical monuments and/or archaeological sites, which may well explain Pavšlar's attitude (Slapšak and Novaković 1996, 278–279; Novaković 2002, 329).

[18] Joseph Szombathy (1853–1943) was custodian of the *k. u. k. Naturhistorisches Hofmuseum* in Vienna, which had been created in 1876 by Emperor Franz-Joseph. He was appointed chief curator of the archaeological and prehistoric collection in 1882. His excavations in Kranj were

funded by the Viennese Anthropological Society (Kiszely 1970, 66).

19 A Catholic priest since 1898, Valter Šmid (Walter Schmid) (1875–1951) was in 1905 a fresh graduate in history, archaeology and geography from the University of Graz, the Austrian town to which he would later return to become first the head of the prehistoric, numismatic and early medieval departments of the Provincial Museum for Styria (Joanneum), then a professor of archaeology at the university (Novaković 2002, 332–333). A native of Slovenia fluent in both German and Slovenian, Šmid was the first to study systematically the early medieval cemeteries of the region (Šmid 1908).

20 For the influence of the German archaeological school upon Yugoslav archaeologists, see Novaković 2002, 347.

21 A professor of Slavic history at the University of Ljubljana, Bogo Grafenauer (1916–95) first published his *History of Slovenians* in 1954. However, his remarks about Kranj are to be found only in the second edition of his book, published in 1964.

22 In the 1970s, Zdenko Vinski (1913–96) was the undisputed doyen of Yugoslav medieval archaeology, a subject he had already taught for some years at the University of Ljubljana. He first dealt with Kranj in a paper dedicated to cross-shaped brooches in Yugoslavia, which he attributed to the local, pre-Slavic population. Within his catalogue of finds, there is also a specimen from grave 104 in Kranj, which Vinski promptly attributed to a Lombard woman, because of the associated S-shaped fibulae. According to him, the Lombards adopted the dress with cross-shaped fibulae from the native, Romanized population of the western Balkans (Vinski 1968, 136).

23 The allegedly consistent west–east orientation of graves on the old plans may, however, be the result of inaccurate observation (see Stare 1980, 12; Vuga 1980, 19).

24 Originating in Germany, the idea that burials with no grave goods were Christian was shared by many in Eastern Europe at that time (eg Bóna 1961). See also Bierbrauer (1984, 53, 55). Slightly more than a quarter (26%) of all burial assemblages excavated in Kranj produced no grave goods whatsoever.

BIBLIOGRAPHY

Aladzhov, Zh, 1985 'Die Religion der heidnischen Protobulgaren im Lichte einiger archäologischer Denkmäler', *Prähistorische Zeitschrift* 60, 70–92

Angelov, D, 1967 'Die bulgarischen Länder und das bulgarische Volk in den Grenzen des byzantinischen Reiches im XI. und XII. Jahrhundert (1018–1185)(Sozial-ökonomische Verhältnisse)', in J M Hussey (ed), *Proceedings of the XIIIth international Congress of Byzantine Studies, Oxford 5–10 September 1966*, 149–166, Oxford University Press, London/ New York

Angelov, D, 1973 'Génèse et développement du régime féodal en Bulgarie (VIIe–Xe siècles)', *Etudes Balkaniques* 9:3, 37–58

Anghelinu, M, 2007 'Failed revolution, Marxism and the Romanian prehistoric archaeology between 1945 and 1989', *Archaeologia Bulgarica* 11:1, 1–36

Antonova, V and Vitlianov, S, 1985 'Pliska. Zapadna krepostna stena — sektor sever (Arkheologicheski razkopki 1973–1975 g.)', *Pliska-Preslav* 4, 46–78

Babić, B, 1997 'Sloveni severno i zapadno od Dunava — nijhova penetracija i naseobinska stabilizacja na Balkanskim prostorima u svetlosti arheoloških i pisanih istorijskih izvora u periodu VI–IX veka', in V V Sedov (ed), *Etnogenez i etnokul'turnye kontakty slavian*, 7–20, Institut Arkheologii RAN, Moscow

Babić, S, 2002 'Still innocent after all these years? Sketches for a social history of archaeology in Serbia', in P F Biehl, A Gramsch and A Marciniak (eds), *Archäologien Europas. Geschichte, Methoden und Theorien*, 309–321, Waxmann, Münster

Bailey, D W, 1998 'Bulgarian archaeology. Ideology, sociopolitics and the exotic', in L Meskell (ed), *Archaeology under Fire. Nationalism, Politics, and Heritage in the Eastern Mediterranean and Middle East*, 87–110, Routledge, London/New York

Balabanov, T, 1981 'Zhelezarska i mednikarska rabotilnica v Pliska', *Muzei i pametnici na kulturata* 21:4, 34–39

Barbiera, I, 2007 'Il sesso svelato degli antenati. Strategie funerarie di rappresentazione dei generi a Kranj Lajh e Iskra in Slovenia (VI–XI secolo)', in C La Rocca (ed), *Agire da donna. Modelli e pratiche di rappresentazione (secoli VI–X). Atti del convegno (Padova, 18–19 febbraio 2005)*, 23–52, Brepols, Turnhout

Barford, P M, 1995 'Marksizm w archeologii polskiej w latach 1945–1975', *Archeologia Polski* 40, 7–75

Barford, P M, 2002 'Reflections on J Lech's vision of the history of "Polish" archaeology', *Archaeologia Polona* 40, 171–184

Bavant, B, 2007 'Caričin Grad and the changes in the nature of urbanism in the Central Balkans in the sixth century', in A G Poulter (ed), *The Transition to Late Antiquity on the Danube and Beyond*, 337–374, Oxford University Press, Oxford

Bavant, B and Ivanišević, V, 2003 *Iustiniana Prima-Caričin Grad*, Centre Culturel Français/Institut Archéologique, Belgrade

Bejko, L, 1998 'Vështrim mbi mendimin arkeologjik shqiptar dhe kontekstin e tij social', *Iliria* 28: 1–2, 195–208

Beshevliev, V, 1961 'Karel Shkorpil kato epigraf', in K Miiatev and V Mikov (eds), *Izsledvaniia v pamet na Karel Shkorpil*, 25–27, Izdatelstvo na Bălgarskata Akademiia na Naukite, Sofia

Beshevliev, V, 1963 *Die protobulgarischen Inschriften*, Akademie Verlag, Berlin

Beslagić, S and Basler, Đ, 1964 *Grborezi, srednjovjekovna nekropola*, Zavod za zaštitu spomenika kulture, Sarajevo

Bierbrauer, V, 1984 'Jugoslawien seit dem Beginn der Völkerwanderung bis zur slawischen Landnahme: die Synthese auf dem Hintergrund von Migrations- und Landnahmevorgängen', in K-D Grothusen (ed), *Jugoslawien. Integrationsprobleme in Geschichte und Gegenwart. Beiträge des Südosteuropa- Arbeitskreises der Deutschen Forschungsgemeinschaft zum V. Internationalen Südosteuropa Kongreß der Association Internationale d'Études du Sud-Est-Européen Belgrad, 11.–17. September 1984*, 49–67, Vandenhoeck and Ruprecht, Göttingen

Bóna, I, 1961 'Fünf Jahre Langobardenforschung in Pannonien (Neue Beiträge zu der Archäologie und Geschichte der Langobarden)', *Régészeti Dolgozatok* 3, 36–43

Bonev, S, 1989 'Za arkhitekturniia oblik na prabălgarskite ezicheski khramove', *Problemi na prabălgarskata istoriia i kultura* 1, 328–337

Brentjes, B, 1971 'On the prototype of the Proto-Bulgarian temples at Pliska, Preslav and Madara', *East and West* 21, 213–216

Cankova-Petkova, G, 1962 'Gesellschaftsordnung und Kriegskunst der slawischen Stämme der Balkanhalbinsel (6.–8. Jh.) nach den byzantinischen Quellen', *Helikon* 2, 264–270

Ciglenečki, S, 1999 'Results and problems in the archaeology of the Late Antiquity in Slovenia', *Arheološki vestnik* 50, 287–309

Ciglenečki, S, 2005 'Langobardische Präsenz im Südostalpenraum im Lichte neuer Forschungen', in W Pohl and P Erhard (eds), *Die Langobarden. Herrschaft und Identität*, 265–280, Verlag der Österreichischen Akademie der Wissenschaften, Vienna

Čilinská, Z, 1991 'Soziale Differenzierung und ihre Spiegelung im Bestattungsritus des 7.–8. Jahrhunderts in der Slowakei', *Acta Archaeologica Carpathica* 30, 187–212

Curta, F, 2006 *Southeastern Europe in the Middle Ages, 500–1250*, Cambridge University Press, Cambridge/New York

Daim, F, 1996 'Repräsentationsmittel im Symbolssystem der awarischen Gesellschaft. Grenzen der Aussage archäologischer Funde', in F Daim, K Kaus and P Tomka (eds), *Reitervölker aus dem Osten. Hunnen + Awaren. Burgenländische Landesausstellung 1996. Schloß Halbturn, 26. April–31. Oktober 1996*, 339–341, Amt der Burgenländischen Landesregierung, Eisenstadt

Dimitrov, Ia, 1994 'Stratigrafiiata na Pliska i prouchvaneto na ruskata ekspediciia prez 1977–1980g.', *Arkheologiia* 36: 3–4, 37–51

Doncheva-Petkova, L, 1979 'Zapadnata krepostna stena v Pliska (Prouchvaniia na iuzhniia sektor prez 1973 i 1974 g.)', *Pliska-Preslav* 1, 81–97

Doncheva-Petkova, L, 1980 'Za metalodobiva i metaloobrabotvaneto v Pliska', *Arkheologiia* 22:4, 27–36

Doncheva-Petkova, L, 1985 'Razkopki na zapadnata krepostna stena v Pliska (Prouchvaniia na iuzhniia sektor prez 1973–1977 g.)', *Pliska-Preslav* 4, 91–116

Doncheva-Petkova, L, 1993a 'Novi prouchvaniia krai zapadnata krepostna stena na Pliska', *Pliska-Preslav*, 79–84

Doncheva-Petkova, L, 1993b 'Ucheniiat Krăstiu Miiatev', in D Ovcharov and I Shtereva (eds), *Prinosi kăm bălgarskata arkheologiia. Dekemvriiski dni na bălgarskata arkheologiia 'Prof. dr. Stancho Vaklinov'*, 7–17, Arges, Sofia

Doncheva-Petkova, L, 1999 'Karel Shkorpil i istoriiata na prouchvaniiata na Pliska', in J Henning (ed), *Zwischen Byzanz und Abendland. Pliska, der östliche Balkanraum und Europa im Spiegel der Frühmittelalterarchäologie*, 7–12, Johann Wolfgang Goethe Universität, Frankfurt

Doncheva-Petkova, L and Zlatinova, Zh, 1978 'Stăklarska rabotilnica krai zapadnata krepostna stena v Pliska', *Arkheologiia* 20:4, 37–48

Dorovský, I, 1983, *Konstantin Jireček, život a dílo*, Univerzita J. E. Purkyne, Brno

Dragoman, A, and Oanţă-Marghitu, S, 2006 'Archaeology in Communist and post-Communist Romania', *Dacia* 50, 57–76

Dzhingova, R, and Kuleff, I, 1992 'An archaeometric study of medieval glass from the first Bulgarian capital, Pliska (ninth to tenth century AD)', *Archaeometry* 34:1, 53–61

Erdélyi, I, 1981 'Einige Bemerkungen über die Awaren-Gesellschaft im Lichte der archäologischen Quellen', *Veröffentlichungen des Museums für Völkerkunde zu Leipzig* 33, 227–238

Fiedler, U, 2007 'Ein Hauptstadt ohne Gräber? Pliska und das heidnische Bulgarenreich an der unteren Donau im Lichte der Grabfunde', in J Henning (ed), *Post-Roman Towns, Trade, and Settlement in Europe and Byzantium*, 273–292, De Gruyter, Berlin/New York

Fiedler, U, 2008 'Bulgars in the Lower Danube region. A survey of the archaeological evidence and of the state of current research', in F Curta (ed), *The Other Europe in the Middle Ages. Avars, Bulgars, Khazars, and Cumans*, 151–236, Brill, Leiden/Boston

Fülöp, Gy, 1991 'La basse époque avare en Hongrie', in G Donnay (ed), *L'art des invasions en Hongrie et en Wallonie. Actes du colloque tenu au Musée royal de Mariemont du 9 au 11 avril 1979*, 151–154, Le Musée, Morlanwelz

Georgiev, P, 1995 'The bronze rosette from Pliska. On decoding the runic inscriptions in Bulgaria', *Byzantinoslavica* 56, 547–555

Georgiev, P, 1997 'Krăglata dărvena postroika v Pliska (Prinos za izuchavane na bălgarskiia dvorcov ceremonial ot nachaloto na IX v.)', *Problemi na prabălgarskata istoriia i kultura* 3, 296–312

Georgiev, P, 2000 'Selishtnata struktura na Aboba-Pliska', *Arkheologiia* 41:3–4, 16–30

Georgiev, P, 2002 'Za khronologiiata i kharaktera na dărveneto stroitelstvo v Pliska', *Izvestiia na Istoricheski muzei Shumen* 10, 73–85

Georgiev, P, 2003 'Nachaloto na Aboba-Pliska', in V Giuzelev, K Popkonstantinov, G Bakalov and R Kostova (eds), *Studia protobulgarica et mediaevalia europensia. V chest na profesor Veselin Beshevliev*, 175–182, Centăr za izsledvaniia na bălgarite TANGRA TanNakRa IK, Sofia

Georgiev, P, 2004 'Arkheologicheskite realii v Tărnovskiia nadpis na khan Omurtag (chast I)', *Arkheologiia* 45:3–4, 27–36

Georgiev, P, 2005 'Arkheologicheskite realii v Tărnovskiia nadpis na khan Omurtag (chast II)', *Arkheologiia* 46:1–4, 55–65

Georgiev, P, 2007 'Periodisierung und Chronologie der Besiedlung und des Baugeschehens im Gebiet um die Große Basilica von Pliska', in J Henning (ed), *Post-Roman Towns, Trade, and Settlement in Europe and Byzantium*, 361–372, De Gruyter, Berlin/New York

Grafenauer, B, 1951 'O arkheologiji in zgodovini', *Zgodovinski časopis* 5, 163–173

Grafenauer, B, 1960 'Zgodnjefevdalna družbena struktura Jugoslovanskih narodov in njen postanek', *Zgodovinski časopis* 14, 35–95

Grafenauer, B, 1964 *Zgodovina slovenskega naroda*, Državna zalžba Slovenije, Ljubljana

Gunjača, S, 1956 'O srednjovjekovnoj arheologiji u Jugoslaviji', *Starohrvatska prosvjeta* 5, 181–199

Halsall, G, 1995 *Settlement and Social Organization. The Merovingian Region of Metz*, Cambridge University Press, Cambridge/New York

Henning, J, 1982 'Die Entwicklung der Landwirtschaftstechnik und gesellschaftliche Veränderungen im Übergang von der Antike zum Mittelalter im unteren Donaugebiet', in J Herrmann and I Sellnow (eds), *Produktivkräfte und Gesellschaftsformationen in vorkapitalistischer Zeit*, 525–547, Akademie Verlag, Berlin

Henning, J, 1987 *Südosteuropa zwischen Antike und Mittelalter. Archäologische Beiträge zur Landwirtschaft des I. Jahrtausends u. Z.*, Akademie Verlag, Berlin

Henning, J, 2000 'Vom Herrschaftszentrum zur städtischen Großsiedlung mit agrarischer Komponente. Archäologische Nachweise der Landwirtschaft aus dem frühmittelalterlichen Pliska', *Pliska-Preslav* 8, 74–86

Henning, J, 2005 'Ways of life in Eastern and Western Europe during the early Middle Ages, which way was "normal"?', in F Curta (ed), *East Central and Eastern Europe in the Early Middle Ages*, 41–59, University of Michigan Press, Ann Arbor

Henning, J, 2007 'The metropolis of Pliska or, How large does an early medieval settlement have to be in order to be called a city?', in J Henning (ed), *Post-Roman Towns, Trade, and Settlement in Europe and Byzantium*, 209–240, De Gruyter, Berlin/New York

Ivanov, S, 2004 'Nabliudeniia vărkhu stroitelnite osobenosti na kamennata krepost v Pliska', *Pliska-Preslav* 10, 212–228

Ivanov, V, Ganchovska, V and Vasilev, K, 2000 *Vălko Chervenkov prez pogleda na negovi săvremennici*, Evropresa, Sofia

Ivanova, V, 1947 'Les fouilles du Musée National de Sofia à Preslav et Pliska', *Byzantinoslavica* 9, 315–323

Janković, Đ, 1995 'The Serbs in the Balkans in the light of archaeological findings', in J Ilić, D Hadži-Jovančić and I Grdović (eds), *The Serbian Question in the Balkans*, 125–146, Faculty of Geography, University of Belgrade, Belgrade

Jireček, K, 1886 'Archäologische Fragmente aus Bulgarien', *Archäologisch-epigraphische Mitteilungen aus Österreich-Ungarn* 10, 43–104 and 129–209

Jurišić, K, 1979 'Fra Lujo Marun osnivac starohrvatske arheologije', *Kačić. Zbornik Franjevačke provincije Presvetoga Otkupitelja* 11, 1–124

Kaiser, T, 1995 'Archaeology and ideology in southeast Europe', in P Kohl and C Fawcett (eds), *Nationalism, Politics, and the Practice of Archaeology*, 99–119, Cambridge University Press, Cambridge

Kalić, J, 1997 'Srpski drzhavni sabori u Rasu', *Saopshtenja* 29, 27–33

Kanitz, F, 1879 *Donau-Bulgarien und der Balkan. Historisch-geographisch-ethnographische Reisestudien aus den Jahren 1860–1879*, 3, Fries, Leipzig

Kanitz, F, 1880 *Donau-Bulgarien und der Balkan. Historisch-geographisch-ethnographische Reisestudien aus den Jahren 1860–1879*, 2nd edn, vol 3, Fries, Leipzig

Karasimeonoff, P, 1940–41 'Neue Ausgrabungen in der Residenz von Pliska', *Izvestiia na Bălgarskiia arkheologicheski institut* 14, 136–168

Kastelić, J, 1950 *Slovanska nekropola na Bledu. Arheološko in antropološko poročilo za leto 1948*, Slovenska Akademija Znanosti in Umetnosti, Ljubljana

Kirilov, Ch, 2006 *Die Stadt des Frühmittelalters in Ost und West. Archäologische Befunde Mitteleuropas im Vergleich zur östlichen Balkanhalbinsel*, Habelt, Bonn

Kiszely, I, 1970 'Short anthropological characterization of the Langobard-age grave-yard in Kranj', *Glasnik Antropološkog Društva Jugoslavije* 7, 65–79

Klein, L S, 1997 *Das Phänomen der sowjetischen Archäologie. Geschichte, Schulen, Protagonisten*, Peter Lang, Frankfurt/New York

Knific, T, 1995 'Vojščaki iz mesta Karnija', *Kranjski zbornik*, 23–40

Koledarov, P, 1969 'Settlement structure of the Bulgarian Slavs in their transition from a clan to a territorial community', *Byzantinobulgarica* 3, 125–132

Korošec, J, 1947 *Poročilo o izkopavanju na Ptujskem gradu, leta 1946*, Akademija znanosti in umetnosti, Ljubljana

Korošec, J, 1950 'Prvo posvetovanje jugoslovanskih arheologov', *Zgodovinski časopis* 4, 212–215

Kos, M, 1955 *Zgodovina slovencev od naselitve do petnajstega stoletja*, Slovenska matica, Ljubljana

Kos, P, 1981 'Neue langobardische Viertelsiliquien', *Germania* 59:1, 97–103

Kostova, R, and Popkonstantinov, K, 2005 'Women and monasticism in Bulgaria, 9th–10th c. according to the archaeological and epigraphic data', *Godishnik na Sofiiskiia Universitet — Centăr za slaviano-vizantiiski prouchvaniia "Ivan Duichev"* 93, 267–275

Kovačević, J, 1960 *Arheologija i istorija varvarske kolonizacije južnoslovenskih oblasti (od IV do početka VII veka)*, Vojvodanski muzej, Novi Sad

Kovačević, J, 1977 *Avarski kaganat*, Srpska književna zadruga, Belgrade

Krăndzhalov, D, 1948 *Zemleni ukrepitelni săorăzheniia na Balkanskiia poluostrov i falshivata prabălgarska teoriia*, Universitetska pechatnica, Sofia

Krăndzhalov, D, 1964 'Sur la théorie erronée de l'origine protobulgare de la cité près d'Aboba (Pliska)', in *Actes du XIIe Congrès international d'études byzantines. Ochride, 10–16 septembre 1961*, 193–203, Comité yougoslave des études byzantines, Belgrade

Krăndzhalov, D, 1966 'Is the fortress at Aboba identical with Pliska, the oldest capital of Bulgaria?', *Slavia Antiqua* 13, 444–445

Krăndzhalov, D, 1971 'Le système de défense du limes romain sur le Bas-Danube et le rôle de la forteresse d'Aboba- Pliska', *Acta Universitatis Palackianae Olomucensis, Facultas Philosophica. Historica* 15, 13–44

László, Gy, 1955 *Etudes archéologiques sur l'histoire de la société des Avars*, Akadémiai kiadó, Budapest

Lech, J, 1997 'Between captivity and freedom, Polish archaeology in the 20th century', *Archaeologia Polona* 35–36, 25–222

Lech, J, 2002 'On Polish archaeology in the 20th century, remarks and polemic', *Archaeologia Polona* 40, 185–252

Margetić, L, 1992 'Neka pitanja boravka langobarda u Sloveniji', *Arheološki vestnik* 43, 149–173

Martin, M, 2000 'Mit Sax und Gürtel ausgestattete Männergräber des 6. Jahrhunderts in der Nekropole von Kranj (Slowenien)', in R Bratož and H-D Kahl (eds), *Slovenija in sosednje dežele med antiko in karolinško dobo. Začetki slovenske etnogeneze*, 141–198, Narodni muzej, Ljubljana

Marun, L, 1898 'O najznamenitijim starohrvatskim grovobima na groblju odkrivene biskupske bazilike S. Marije u Biskupiji kod Knina', *Starohrvatska prosvjeta* 3–4, 113–118

Mavrodinov, N, 1948 'Razkopki i prouchvaniia v Pliska', *Razkopki i prouchvaniia* 3, 159–170

Miiatev, K, 1936 'Der grosse Palast in Pliska und die Magnaura von Konstantinopel', *Izvestiia na Bălgarskiia Arkheologicheski Institut* 10, 136–144

Miiatev, K, 1940–41 'Krumoviiat dvorec i drugi novootkriti postroiki v Pliska', *Izvestiia na Bălgarskiia arkheologicheski institut* 14, 73–135

Miiatev, K, 1961 'Nauchnoto delo na Karel Shkorpil', in K Miiatev and V Mikov (eds), *Izsledvaniia v pamet na Karel Shkorpil*, 5–14, Izdatelstvo na Bălgarskata Akademiia na Naukite, Sofia

Miiatev, P and Iantarski, G, 1961 'Korespondenciia na Khermengild i Karel Shkorpil s Konstantin Irechek (1881–1899)', in K Miiatev and V Mikov (eds), *Izsledvaniia v pamet na Karel Shkorpil*, 29–48, Izdatelstvo na Bălgarskata Akademiia na Naukite, Sofia

Mikhailov, S, 1948 'Razkopki v Pliska prez 1945–1947 godina', *Razkopki i prouchvaniia* 3, 171–225

Mikhailov, S, 1955 'Dvorcovata cărkva v Pliska', *Izvestiia na Arkheologicheskiia Institut* 20, 229–264

Mikhailov, S, 1960 'Za proizkhoda na antichnite materiali ot Pliska', *Arkheologiia* 2:1, 15–22

Mikhailov, S, 1972 'Koia sgrada e Krumoviiat dvorec v Pliska', *Izvestiia na Arkheologicheskiia Institut* 33, 279–283

Mikhailov, S, 1995 'Kăm tălkuvaneto na bronzovata sedmolăcha rozeta ot Pliska', *Palaeobulgarica* 19:2, 94–101

Milchev, A, 1975 'Zaniatchiiski i tărgovski pomeshteniia severno ot iuzhnata porta na vătreshniia grad na Pliska', in G Kozhukharov (ed), *Arkhitekturata na părvata i vtorata bălgarska dărzhava. Materiali*, 398–407, Izdatelstvo za Bălgarskata Akademiia na Naukite, Sofia

Miletić, N, 1956 'Nekropola u selu Mihaljevićima kod Rajlovca', *Glasnik zemaljskog muzeja Bosne i Hercegovine u Sarajevu* 11, 9–39

Miletić, N, 1961 'Nekropola u selu Mihaljevićima kod Rajlovca', *Glasnik zemaljskog muzeja Bosne i Hercegovine u Sarajevu* 15–16, 249–257

Miletić, N, 1969 'Novi prilozi poznavanju autohtonih kulturnih elemenata u Bosni u doba doseljenja Slovena', in A Benac (ed), *Simpozijum Predslavenski etnički elementi na Balkanu u etnogenezi južnih Slovena, održan 24–26. oktobra 1968 u Mostaru*, 233–238, Akademija nauka i umjetnosti Bosne i Hercegovine, Sarajevo

Milinković, M, 2004 'Arkheologija mode kao arkheologija identiteta — nekoliko primera', in M Rakocija (ed), *Niš and Bzyantium. II Symposium, Niš, 3–5 June 2003. The Collection of Scientific Works* 2, 185–196, Prosveta, Niš

Milisauskas, S, 1997–98 'Observations on Polish archaeology 1945–1995', *Archaeologia Polona* 35–36, 223–236

Niebuhr, C, 1837 *Reisebeschreibung nach Arabien und anderen umliegenden Ländern, iii. Niebuhr's Reisen durch Syrien und Palästina, nach Cypern und durch Kleinasien und die Türkey nach Deutschland und Dänemark*, Perthes, Hamburg

Nikolov, V, 2002 'Die bulgarische Archäologie im letzten Jahrzent des 20. Jahrhunderts', in P F Biehl, A Gramsch and A Marciniak (eds), *Archäologien Europas. Geschichte, Methoden und Theorien*, 303–307, Waxmann, Münster

Novaković, P, 2002 'Archaeology in five states. A peculiarity or just another story at the crossroads of "Mitteleuropa" and the Balkans, a case study of Slovene archaeology', in P F Biehl, A Gramsch and A Marciniak (eds), *Archäologien Europas. Geschichte, Methoden und Theorien*, 323–352, Waxmann, Münster

Ovcharov, D, 1995. 'Otnovo za bronzovata sedmolăcha rozeta ot Pliska (Po povod tălkuvaneto na Stamen Mikhailov)', *Palaeobulgarica* 19:4, 114–115

Ovcharov, D, and Doncheva, S, 2004 'Monumentalnite preslavskite baziliki — genezis, arkhitekturen tip, razvitie', *Preslav. Sbornik* 6, 91–106

Panchenko, B A, 1905 'Vizantiiskiia pechati i monety', *Izvestiia Russkogo arkheologicheskogo instituta v Konstantinople* 10, 291–300

Paskaleva, V, 1996 'Felix Kanitz, die bulgarische Länder und die Bulgaren', *Bulgarian Historical Review* 24:2, 93–102

Pletneva, S A, 'Stratigraficheskie issledovaniia v drevnei bolgarskoi stolice — Pliske', in V I Guliaev and G E Afanas'ev (eds), *Problemy izucheniia drevnikh poselenii v arkheologii. Sociologicheskii aspekt*, 99–127, Institut Arkheologii Akademii Nauk SSSR, Moscow

Popović, M, 1999 *Tvrđava Ras*, Arheološki institut, Belgrade

Prezelj Mirnik, I, 2000 'Re-thinking ethnicity in archaeology', in R Bratož and H-D Kahl (eds), *Slovenija in sosednje dežele med antiko in karolinško dobo. Začetki slovenske etnogeneze*, 581–603, Narodni muzej Slovenije, Ljubljana

Radić, F, 1895a 'Hrvatska biskupska crkva sv. Marije u Biskupiji i kaptolska crvka sv. Bartula na sadašnjem Kapitulu kod Knina', *Starohrvatska prosvjeta* 1:1, 35–39

Radić, F, 1895b 'Hrvatska biskupska crkva sv. Marije u Biskupiji i kaptolska crvka sv. Bartula na sadašnjem Kapitulu kod Knina', *Starohrvatska prosvjeta* 1:2, 90–96

Radić, F, 1895c 'Hrvatska biskupska crkva sv. Marije u Biskupiji i kaptolska crvka sv. Bartula na sadašnjem Kapitulu kod Knina', *Starohrvatska prosvjeta* 1:3, 150–156

Radić, F, 1896a 'Grobna raka u starohrvatske biskupske bazilike s. Marije u Biskupiji kod Knina i u njoj nađeni mrtvački ostanci', *Starohrvatska prosvjeta* 2:2, 71–86

Radić, F, 1896b 'Srebrne ostruge i saponi iz starohrvatskog groba u biskupskoj bazilici S. Marije u Biskupiji kod Knina', *Starohrvatska prosvjeta* 2:1, 5–9

Radić, F, 1897 'Mrtvački ostanci iz triju starohrvatskih grobova uz ruševine biskupske bazilike kod Knina sv. Marije u Biskupiji kod Knina', *Starohrvatska prosvjeta* 3, 31–38

Raionov, B, 2003 *Liudmila: mechti i dela*, Kameliia, Sofia

Rashev, R, 1983 'Pliska — the first capital of Bulgaria', in A G Poulter (ed), *Ancient Bulgaria. Papers Presented to the International Symposium on the Ancient History and Archaeology of Bulgaria, University of Nottingham, 1981*, 255–267, Department of Classical and Archaeological Studies, University of Nottingham, Nottingham

Rashev, R, 1995 'Pliskovskiiat aul', *Pliska-Preslav* 7, 10–22

Rashev, R, 1998 'Karel Shkorpil i starite bălgarski stolici', in *Chekhi v Bălgariia i bălgari v Chekhiia*, 273–278, Svetlana, Shumen

Rashev, R, 2000 'Karel Shkorpil — izsledovatel na rannosrednovekovnata bălgarska kultura', in D Ovcharov (ed), *Kulturnata integraciia mezhdu chekhi i bulgari v evropeiskata tradiciia, materiali ot VII liatna nauchna sreshta, Varna, 25–27 iuni 1999 g.*, 146–152, Arges, Sofia

Rashev, R, 2007 'Der Beginn von Pliska und der bulgarischen Landnahmezeit', in J Henning (ed), *Post-Roman Towns, Trade, and Settlement in Europe and Byzantium*, 449–462, De Gruyter, Berlin/New York

Rashev, R and Dimitrov, Ia, 1999 *Pliska. 100 godini arkheologicheski razkopki*, Svetlana, Shumen

Rashev, R and Docheva, V, 1989 'Iurtoobrazna postroika v Pliska', in *Problemi na prabălgarskata istoriia i kultura* 1, 291–313

Rashev, R and Stanilov, S, 1998 'Kenotaf für einem Herrscher bei der ersten bulgarischen Hauptstadt Pliska', *Das Altertum* 44, 67–72

Rashev, R, Georgiev, P, Iordanov, I, Apostolov, K, Atanasov, G, Bonev, S, Dăanev, G, Dimitrov, M, Dimitrov, Ia, Iotov, V, Konakliev, A, Petrova, P, Pletn'ov, V and Stanchev, D, 1995 'Materiali za kartata na srednovekovnata bălgarska dărzhava (teritoriiata na dnesna severoiztochnata Bălgariia)', *Pliska-Preslav* 7, 157–332

Reinecke, P, 1897 'Slavische Gräberfunde im kroatischen und slovenischen Gebiete', *Verhandlungen der Berliner Antrhopologischen Gesellschaft*, 362–367

Sagadin, M, 1987 *Kranj. Križišče Iskra (nekropola iz časa preseljevanja ljudstev in staroslovanskega obdobja)*, Narodni Muzei, Ljubljana

Sagadin, M, 1991 'Kranj-Pungart', *Varstvo spomenikov* 33, 221

Sagadin, M, 1995 'Poselitvena slika rimskega podeželja na Gorenjskem', *Kranjski zbornik*, 13–22

Shkorpil, K, 1905a 'Megaliticheskie pamiatniki', *Izvestiia Russkogo arkheologicheskogo instituta v Konstantinople* 10, 372–384

Shkorpil, K, 1905b 'Oruzhie', *Izvestiia Russkogo arkheologicheskogo instituta v Konstantinople* 10, 38–321

Shkorpil, K, 1905c 'Ukrepleniia Abobskoi raviny', *Izvestiia Russkogo arkheologicheskogo instituta v Konstantinople* 10, 62–152

Shkorpil, H and Shkorpil, K, 1921 'Drevnebălgarski pametnici', *Izvestiia na Varnenskoto arkheologichesko druzhestvo* 7, 9–27

Sidorov, M and Kelevdzhiev, E, 1999 'Opit za identifikaciia i datirane na rozetata ot Pliska', *Palaeobulgarica* 23:2, 78–88

Slabe, M, 1978 'Künstlich deformierte Schädel der Völkerwanderungszeit in Jugoslawien im Lichte ihrer Aussagekraft', in D Dimitrijević, J Kovačević and Z Vinski (eds), *Problemi seobe naroda u Karpatskoj kotlini. Saopštenja sa naučkog skupa 13.–16. decembre 1976*, 67–73, Matica Srpska, Belgrade

Slapšak, B and Novaković, P, 1996 'Is there national archaeology without nationalism? Archaeological tradition in Slovenia', in M Díaz-Andreu and T Champion (eds), *Nationalism and Archaeology in Europe*, 256–293, Westview Press, Boulder/San Francisco

Šlaus, M and Filipec, K, 1998 'Bioarchaeology of the medieval Đakovo cemetery, archaeological and anthropological evidence for ethnic affiliation and migration', *Opuscula Archaeologica* 22, 129–139

Šmid, W, 1907 'Reihengräber von Krainburg', *Jahrbuch für Altertumskunde* 1, 55–77

Šmid, W, 1908 'Altslovenische Gräber Krains', *Carniola. Zeitschrift für Heimatkunde* 1, 17–44

Squatriti, P, 2005 'Moving earth and making difference, dikes and frontiers in early medieval Bulgaria', in F Curta (ed), *Borders, Barriers, and Ethnogenesis. Frontiers in Late Antiquity and the Middle Ages*, 59–90, Brepols, Turnhout

Stanchev, S, 1962 'Pliska-Théories et faits', *Byzantinobulgarica* 1, 349–365

Stanchev, S and Ivanov, S, 1958 *Nekropolăt do Novi Pazar*, Izdatelstvo za Bălgarskata Akademiia na Naukite, Sofia

Stanilov, S, 2001 'Bălgarskata arkheologiia prez posledneto desetiletie na XX vek, srednovekovna arkheologiia', *Arkheologiia* 42:3–4, 95–99

Stanojev, N, 1996 *Srednjovekovna seoska naselja od V do XV veka u Vojvodini*, Muzej Vojvodine, Novi Sad

Stare, V, 1980 *Kranj. Nekropola iz časa pereseljevanja liudstev*, Narodni muzej, Ljubljana

Stepanov, C, 1999 *Vlast i avtoritet v rannosrednovekovna Bălgariia (VII–sr. IX v.)*, Agató, Sofia

Stevanović, M, 1990 '"Nova arkheologija", da li ona ima buduchnost?', *Balcanica* 21, 185–200

Stoianov, I, 1933 'Karel Shkorpil i bălgarskata arkheologicheska i istoricheska nauka (po sluchai negovata petdesetgodishna deinost v Bălgariia)', *Byzantinoslavica* 5, 183–234

Szentpéteri, J, 1985 'Gesellschaftliche Gliederung des awarenzeitlichen gemeinen Volkes von Želovce I. Die führende Schicht der Bevölkerung (Bewaffnete und umgegürtete Personen)', *Acta Archaeologica Academiae Scientiarum Hungaricae* 37, 79–110

Szentpéteri, J, 1986 'Gesellschaftliche Gliederung des awarenzeitlichen gemeinen Volkes von Želovce II. Innere Gruppen der Bevolkerung (Schmuck und sonstige rangbezeichnende Beigaben)', *Acta Archaeologica Academiae Scientiarum Hungaricae* 38, 147–184

Talbot, A-M and Sullivan D, 2005, *The History of Leo the Deacon. Byzantine Military Expansion in the Tenth Century*, Dumbarton Oaks Research Library and Collection, Washington

Tăpkova-Zaimova, V, 1966 *Nashestviia i etnicheski promeni na balkanite prez VI–VII v.*, Izdatelstvo za Bălgarskata Akademii na Naukite, Sofia

Teofilov, T, 1993 'Ot kapishte kăm cărkva', *Godishnik na muzeite ot Severna Bălgariia* 19, 73–92

Tismăneanu, V, 2003 *Stalinism for All Seasons: A Political History of Romanian Communism*, University of California Press, Berkeley

Todorova, M, 1997 *Imagining the Balkans*, Oxford University Press, New York

Tomka, P, 1992 'Awarische Grabsitten — Abriß der Forschungsgeschichte bis 1963', in F Daim (ed), *Awarenforschungen*, 969–1023, Institut für Ur- und Frühgeschichte der Universität Wien, Vienna

Trifunović, S, 1997 'Slovenska naselja V–VII veka u Bačkoj i Banatu', in V V Sedov (ed), *Problemy slavianskoi arkheologii*, 173–185, Institut Arkheologii RAN, Moscow

Trigger, B G, 1989 *A History of Archaeological Thought*, Cambridge University Press, Cambridge

Ujfalusi, J, 1903 *A gyulafehérvári székesegyház, alapittatásának 900-ik évfordulója alakalmbó*, Schäser Ferenc Könyvnyomdája, Gyulafehérvár

Uspenskii, F I, 1905 'Nadpisi starobolgarskiia, kolonny s imenami gorod; nadpisi s fragmentami dogovor; nadpisi istoricheskago soderzhaniia; fragmenty nadpisei raznago soderzhaniia i proiskhozhdeniia', *Izvestiia Russkogo arkheologicheskogo instituta v Konstantinople* 10, 173–242

Vaklinov, S, 1977 *Formirane na starobălgarskata kultura, VI–XI vek*, Izdatelstvo za Bălgarskata Akademiia na Naukite, Sofia

Vaklinov Stanchev, S, 1967–68 'Istokăt v starobălgarskoto izkustvo ot VII do XI vek', *Trudove na Visshiia pedagogicheski institut 'Bratia Kiril i Metodii' — Veliko Tărnovo* 5, 125–162

Vaklinov Stanchev, S, 1968 'L'Orient et l'Occident dans l'ancien art bulgare du VIIe au Xe siècle', *Corso di cultura sull'arte ravennate e bizantina* 15, 241–285

Valić, A, 1991 'Osmerokotna stavba pri farni cerkvi v Kranju', in T Knific and M Sagadin (eds), *Pismo brez pisave. Arheologija o prvih stoletjih krščanstva na Slovenskem*, 33–35, Narodni Muzej, Ljubljana

Vašić, M, 1906 'Starosrpska nalazishta u Srbiji. Prilozi za poznavanje stare srpske kulture', *Starinar* 1, 39–88

Văzharova, Zh, 1986 *Srednovekovnoto selishte s. Garvăn, Silistrenski okrăg (VI–XI v.)*, Izdatelstvo za Bălgarskata Akademiia na Naukite, Sofia

Velkov, V, 1961 'Bibliografiia na trudovete i statiite na Karel Shkorpil', in K Miiatev and V Mikov (eds), *Izsledvaniia v pamet na Karel Shkorpil*, 73–85, Izdatelstvo na Bălgarskata Akademiia na Naukite, Sofia

Vinski, Z, 1954 'Ein völkerwanderungszeitlicher Goldschmuck aus der Herzegovina', *Germania* 32, 307–313

Vinski, Z, 1956 'Körbchenohrringe aus Kroatien', in J Haekel, A Hohenwart-Gerlachstein and A Slawik (eds), *Die Wiener Schule der Völkerkunde. Festschrift, anlässlich des 25 jährigen Bestandes des Institutes für Völkerkunde der Universität Wien (1929–1954)*, 564–568, Ferdinand Berger, Vienna

Vinski, Z, 1968 'Krstoliki nakit epohe seobe naroda u Jugoslaviji', *Vjesnik Arheološkog Muzeja u Zagrebu* 3, 103–166

Vinski, Z, 1969 'Autochtone Kulturelemente zur Zeit der slavischen Landnahme des Balkanraums', in A Benac (ed), *Simpozijum "Predslavenski etnički elementi na Balkanu u etnogenezi južnih Slovena", održan 24–26. oktobra 1968 u Mostaru*, 171–199, Akademija nauka i umjetnosti Bosne i Hercegovine, Sarajevo

Vinski, Z, 1970 'Kranj i horizont groblja na redove 6. stoljeća u zapdanoj Jugoslaviji', *Arheološki vestnik* 21–22, 151–152

Vinski, Z, 1971a 'Die völkerwanderungszeitliche Nekropole in Kranj und der Reihengräberfelder-Horizont des 6. Jahrhunderts im westlichen Jugoslawien', in G Novak (ed), *Actes du VIIIe Congrès international des sciences préhistoriques et protohistoriques. Beograd, 9–15 septembre 1971*, 253–265, Comité National d'Organisation, Belgrade

Vinski, Z, 1971b 'Haut Moyen Age', in G Novak, A Benac, M Garašanin and N Tašić (eds), *Epoque préhistorique et protohistorique en Yougoslavie — Recherches et résultats*, 375–397, Société archéologique de Yougoslavie, Belgrade

Vinski, Z, 1971c 'Rani srednji vijek u Jugoslaviji od 400. do 800. godine', *Vjesnik Arheološkog Muzeja u Zagrebu* 5, 47–73

Vitlianov, S, 1993 'Metalografski izsledvaniia na kovashka produkciia ot Pliska i Preslav', *Izvestiia na Istoricheski muzei Shumen* 8, 309–320

Vuga, D, 1980 'A study of burying methods in the period of the great migration (5th to 6th century) in the south-eastern Alpine and Cisalpine world', *Balcanoslavica* 9, 17–25

Wedepohl, K H, 2007 'Soda-Kalk-Glas des 8. und 9. Jahrhunderts von Asar-dere in Pliska (Bulgarien) im Vergleich mit frühmittelalterlichem Glas in Westeuropa', in J Henning (ed), *Post-Roman Towns, Trade, and Settlement in Europe and Byzantium*, 351–360, De Gruyter, Berlin/New York

Werner, J, 1962 *Die Langobarden in Pannonien. Beiträge zur Kenntnis der langobardischen Bodenfunde vor 568*, Verlag der Bayerischen Akademie der Wissenschaften, Munich

Zábojník, J, 1995 'Soziale Problematik der Gräberfelder des nördlichen und nordwestlichen Randgebietes des awarischen Kaganats', *Slovenská Archeológia* 43, 205–344

Zaharia, E, 1967 *Săpăturile de la Dridu. Contribuţii la arheologia şi istoria perioadei de formare a poporului român*, Editura Academiei RSR, Bucharest

Zhdrakov, Z, Boiadzhiev, A and Aleksandrov, S, 2002 'Kăm interpretaciia na sedmolăchata zbezda ot Pliska', *Palaeobulgarica* 26, no. 4, 33–54

Zhivkov, T and Zhivkova, L, 1981, *13th Centennial Jubilee of the Bulgarian State*, Sofia Press, Sofia

PART III

MEDIEVAL LANDSCAPES, SETTLEMENTS AND MATERIAL CULTURE

CHAPTER 11
UNDERSTANDING THE MEDIEVAL LANDSCAPE

By STEPHEN RIPPON

Fifty years ago the study of the medieval countryside — as opposed to individual sites — was just beginning, and since then major advances have been made in both the techniques at our disposal, and the greater understanding they have provided for how the historic landscape has developed. This paper reviews the history of research into the medieval landscape across mainland Britain beginning with a series of pioneering studies in the late 19th/early 20th century, through the emergence of 'landscape archaeology' as a recognized discipline in the 1970s, to some current debates.

The increased interest in landscape has been one of the major trends within medieval archaeology in the past 50 years. In this short paper it is impossible to discuss all the developments and practitioners, but an attempt will be made to provide a broad discussion that reviews trends in interpretative traditions, new methods and some current debates. The focus will be on England, where the greatest amount of work on the medieval countryside has been carried out, though comparisons will be made with Scotland and Wales where important initiatives are now underway.

INTRODUCTION

The medieval landscape: early interest

In the first half of the 20th century it was historians who dominated the study of landscape, working within the culture-historical paradigm dominant at that time. Some of the first works to discuss such mundane matters as the rural countryside — as opposed to the great historical topics such as constitutional and religious history — were Seebohm's *English Village Community* (1892), Vinogradoff's *Villainage in England* (1892), and Maitland's *Domesday Book and Beyond* (1897). In his *English Field Systems* (1915), Gray went significantly further in appreciating regional variation in landscape character by describing a series of distinctive patterns of land management, the origins of which he attributed in part to the impact of different waves of settlers who had sailed across the English Channel in the 5th century AD. In *The Personality of Britain* (1932), Fox also developed the concept of regional variation in landscape character — most famously his distinction between the upland and the lowland zones — and, while his history of the people that populated Britain was similarly written in terms of migrations, this seminal study also reflects another dominant paradigm of that time: environmental determinism (Figure 11.1).

By the 1950s historians were starting to explore landscapes in the field and through their depiction on early maps, with pioneering studies including Orwin and Orwin's *The Open Fields* (1938) and Beresford's *History on the Ground* (1957). In 1952, W G Hoskins wrote that

> The great Cambridge historian, Maitland, regarded the Ordnance map of England as one of the finest records we have, if only we could learn how to decipher it, and indeed it is. But the landscape itself is an equally revealing document, equally full of significant detail, and difficult to interpret it aright. (Hoskins 1952, 289)

It was also during the 1950s that the interests of historians and archaeologists came together in the study of deserted medieval villages, though in these early years the agenda behind excavating such sites — and it was a very 'site-based' agenda — was to use archaeology to test ideas that had already emerged from historical documents, such as the impact of the Black Death on rural settlement (Beresford and Hurst 1990, 27–28). In these early years of medieval archaeology there were also pioneering projects that looked at landscapes characterized by more dispersed settlement patterns such as Fox's work at Gelligaer Common in Glamorganshire and on Dartmoor in Devon (1939; 1958), and Leeds's work on 'Early Saxon' sites near Oxford (1947), but the agenda was soon dominated by the English village.

THE LANDSCAPE IN THE EARLY YEARS OF *Medieval Archaeology*

The early volumes of *Medieval Archaeology* give a clear impression of the interests that concerned the founders of our discipline. Deserted medieval villages make an early appearance in Thompson's (1960) report on Riseholme (Lincolnshire) and occasionally other papers plotted the distribution of sites against a background of the natural topography, such as Proudfoot's study of Irish raths (1960), and Gelling's report on shielings on the Isle of Man (1961). In the first 10 volumes of *Medieval Archaeology*, however, just 10% of papers were on rural settlement, compared to 30% on artefacts and around 40% on high-status sites (castles, manor houses, monasteries and towns). Comparison with the last 10 years of *Medieval Archaeology* (1998–2007) is not easy, as fewer papers have such a narrow emphasis on specific types of artefact or the excavation of individual sites, but perhaps up to a quarter of contributions have a broadly landscape focus (a trend that is also reflected in the increased numbers of rural settlements whose investigation is registered in *Medieval Archaeology*: Gerrard 2003, fig 4.3). Returning to the early volumes of *Medieval Archaeology*, however, it is noticeable that while an explicit focus on the landscape is rare, the breadth of some papers is impressive, with notable examples of interdisciplinary research including Dodgson's study of *–ingas* and *–inga* place-names

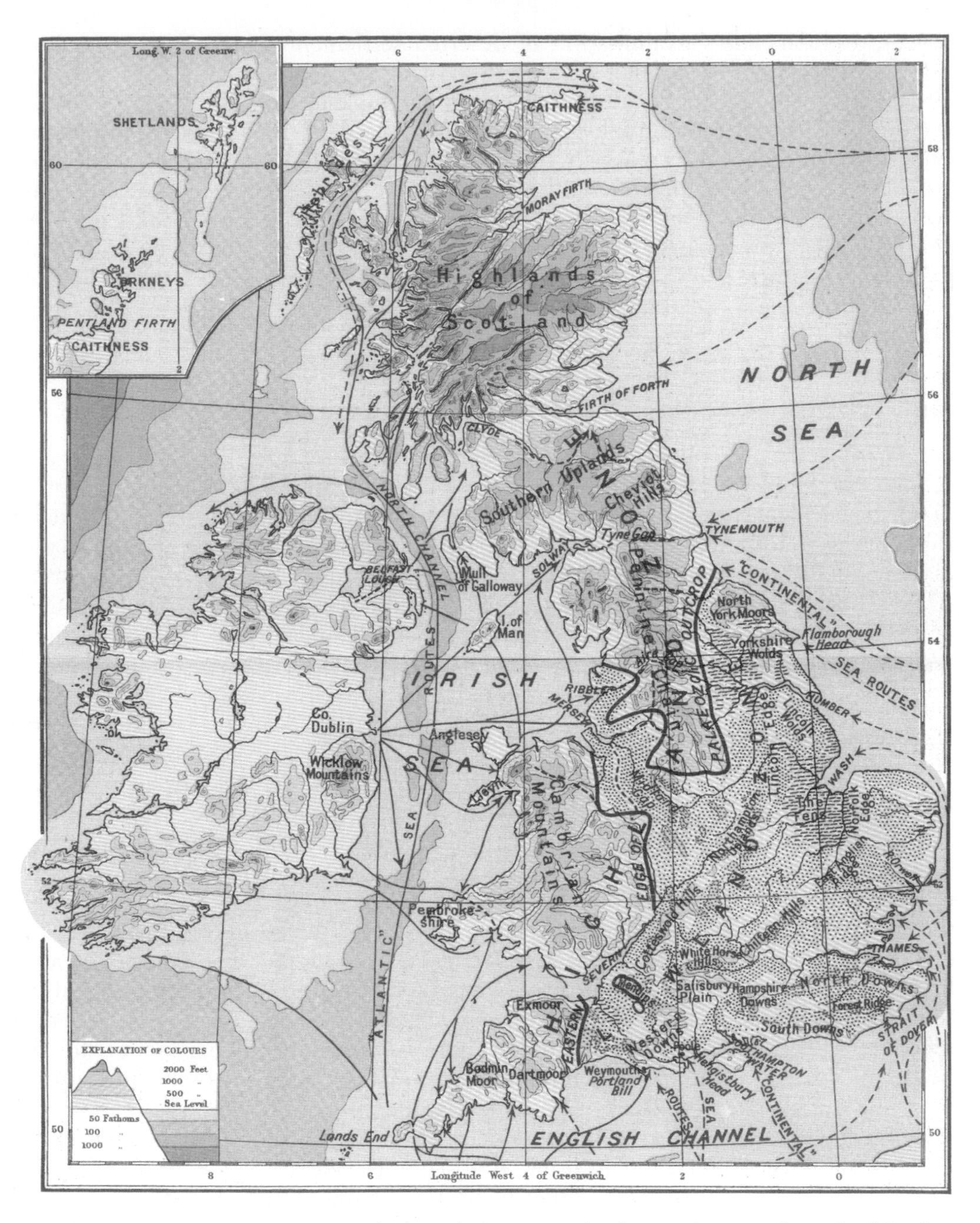

FIGURE 11.1. An early depiction of regional variation in landscape character from Cyril Fox's *The Personality of Britain*, that reflects two of the prevailing theoretical perspectives of the time: environmental determinism and the culture-historical approach towards explaining change (after Fox 1932, map B).

(1966), and Linehan's examination of deserted settlement and rabbit warrens on Dartmoor (1966). The latter is a remarkable paper that plotted 126 sites and used documentary sources, alongside ground survey and the mapping of earthworks shown on the RAF aerial photography from the late 1940s. It reconstructed individual buildings within a wider context of similarly abandoned trackways, crofts, and lynchets, as well as the still-functioning field boundary pattern that in these moorland fringes is also medieval in date (what we would now call the 'historic landscape'). All this is a clear precursor to the better known work on Dartmoor by Austin at Okehampton Park (1978), and Fleming and Ralph at Holne Moor (1982), both of which are classic examples of what emerged during the 1970s as 'landscape archaeology'.

THE STUDY OF LANDSCAPE IN RELATED HISTORICAL DISCIPLINES

Within the disciplines of history and historical geography there were also scholars studying the landscape in one form or another. Britain has a long tradition of detailed historical studies of particularly well-documented medieval estates — notably those of the major monastic houses — and some historians did at least attempt to give documented places a spatial context, such as Finberg's (1951) study of Tavistock Abbey (Figure 11.2). H P R Finberg was the second director (Hoskins being the first) of the Department of English Local History at the University of Leicester, whose members — including more recently, Alan Everitt, Charles Phythian-Adams, Harold Fox, and Christopher Dyer — have promoted a distinctive form of landscape research, with a strong emphasis on local *pays*, that has become known as the 'Leicester approach' (Tranter *et al* 1999).

The middle decades of the 20th century also saw the growth of historical geography with its clear focus on the landscape both at the local scale — for example, the analysis of village plans (eg Thorpe 1949) — and the mapping of historical data sets such as Domesday (eg Darby 1952; 1977). These regional Domesday Geographies remain an invaluable resource for the landscape archaeologist and historian, both for the analysis of the Domesday evidence itself, and the introduction they provide to the distinctive districts within each English county. Indeed, while best known as a historical geographer, Darby was also a landscape historian somewhat ahead of his time, for example through his work on medieval Fenland (Darby 1940; 1983). Another reflection of the value he placed upon collaborative research was his support for the Medieval Village Research Group (Gerrard 2003, 130). Other important contributions to giving documentary sources a spatial/landscape dimension were the mapping of early medieval estates from the boundary clauses of Anglo-Saxon charters, begun by Grundy in the 1920s but put on a firmer footing by Hooke (eg 1978; 1981; 1985), and Jones (1972) who reconstructed earlier territorial arrangements in Wales. The work of botanist Rackham (1986) has also been instrumental in providing a succinct summary of the major landscape character zones in Britain, and the history of woodland management. Other historical resources that were developing at this time, and have become so important to landscape archaeologists, include the revival of the Victoria County Histories, the county-based volumes of the English Place-Names

FIGURE 11.2. An early attempt at reconstructing a medieval landscape, from H P R Finberg's *Tavistock Abbey* in Devon. A comparison with more recent work shown in Figure 11.4 reflects the remarkable progress in the techniques of landscape reconstruction that has been made in recent years (after Finberg 1951).

Society, the *Agrarian History of England and Wales*, and the work of the many county Records Societies and other publishers such as the British Academy in making historical sources available in transcribed and often translated form. For Glastonbury Abbey, for example, we have published editions of the Great Chartulary (Watkin 1947; 1952; 1956), 13th-century Custumals of Abbots Michael de Glastonbury and Roger de Ford (Elton 1891), a 14th-century Feodary of Abbot Walter Monington (Weaver 1910), the chronicle of John of Glastonbury (Carley 1985), and the late 12th-century surveys of Hilbert the Precentor, Henry Sully and Reginald de Fontibus

(Stacey 2001), all of which contain a wealth of topographical detail and have been of great importance in understanding the monastic landscape (eg Abrams 1996; Rippon 2004; in press; Gerrard with Aston 2007).

THE FIELD SURVEY TRADITION

There has been a long tradition of field survey within British archaeology, started by the antiquarian interest in sites such as abbeys and castles (Gerrard 2003, 5–55), and put on a more systematic footing by pioneering figures such as Toms (Bradley 1989) and Allcroft (1908, 552) — whose surveys included a deserted medieval village at Bingham in Nottinghamshire 'said to have been destroyed by a hurricane'. Crawford (1953) also included medieval sites in his *Archaeology in the Field*. Although their emphasis in this early work was very much on recording sites, not whole landscapes, it laid the foundations of the British field survey tradition later developed by the Royal Commissions. By the 1960s the careful survey of earthworks was being developed by the likes of Bowen, whose *Ancient Fields* (1970) was an important step forward in the identification of medieval as well as 'celtic' field systems. This field survey tradition was developed by the Royal Commission on the Historical Monuments of England (RCHME), with some of the most notable work being carried out by Taylor and his colleagues. Taylor's (1967) reconstruction of the changing settlement patterns, field systems and land-uses in Whiteparish, Wiltshire, for example, went significantly beyond what Finberg had achieved in Tavistock as a piece of landscape reconstruction with a strong historical geography influence. Long-term research projects, such as Fowler's work in Fyfield and Overton (2000), also in Wiltshire, set new agendas in landscape-scale research and inspired projects along similar lines elsewhere (eg Drewett 1982).

In the 1960s and 1970s there was also a transformation in the scale at which both survey and excavation were undertaken. The Jones's work on the early medieval settlement at Mucking is a notable example where the concept of digging a discrete 'site' was replaced by the investigation of entire landscapes (see Hamerow 1993 and Rippon 2008 for interpretations of this site). Four books demonstrate this increasing emphasis upon investigating whole landscapes. The first two are the collections of papers published in *Archaeology and the Landscape* (Fowler 1972) and *Recent Work in Rural Archaeology* (Fowler 1975a) which reflect a moment when traditional ground-based field survey was being joined by aerial photography, fieldwalking and palaeoenvironmental analysis to study archaeological remains on a scale previously unseen. Aerial photography for archaeological purposes was not in itself new — Crawford and Keiller (1928), for example, included medieval strip lynchets and a shrunken medieval settlement in their *Wessex from the Air* — but its growing popularity transformed understanding of the density of past settlement, revealing the extent of cropmarks in the arable lowlands that complemented the already well-known earthwork complexes that survived in pastoral areas (Beresford and St Joseph 1958; RCHME 1960; Benson and Miles 1974; Leech 1977). Increased urban and industrial expansion, including the growing demand for sand and gravel by the construction industry, led to rescue excavations on a previously unseen scale, with linear infrastructure developments such as the M4 and M5 motorways leading to archaeological investigations revealing unsuspected densities of sites in areas that had seen hardly any work in the past (Fowler 1979). Another innovation was fieldwalking that once again transformed our understanding of the density and nature of settlement in those areas with extensive arable cultivation and a good ceramic sequence. While some early studies may have had methodological problems — such as Wade-Martins's study of the Launditch Hundred (1980), where walking was restricted to areas around known deserted or still-occupied medieval settlements — whole-parish studies in the East Midlands and East Anglia were soon revealing the development of complete settlement patterns (eg Foard 1978; Davison 1990; Rogerson *et al* 1997; West and McLaughlin 1998). Alongside the continued results from earthwork surveys by the Royal Commissions in England, Scotland, and Wales (eg RCHME 1972; 1982; RCAHMS 1980; RCAHMW 1982), the dynamic and regionally varied medieval landscape that Taylor was able to describe in *Village and Farmstead* (1983) was far more complex than if he had been writing 20, possibly even 10, years earlier.

Two other seminal books of the 1970s were Aston and Rowley's *Landscape Archaeology: An Introduction to Fieldwork Techniques on Post-Roman Landscapes* (1974), and Taylor's *Fieldwork in Medieval Archaeology* (1974). These were innovative in a number of ways, not least their focus on the medieval and post-medieval periods (at a time when so much fieldwork was focused on the prehistoric and Roman periods), and their extensive use of maps and plans of the modern landscape, alongside aerial photography and earthwork survey, to try and understand the origins of what today we call 'the historic landscape': the present pattern of settlements, roads, fields and land-uses. It was the whole landscape — both urban and rural — which was being studied as opposed to the traditional focus on individual sites, and, whilst elite landscapes continued to receive attention, there was also a growing interest in the ordinary villages, hamlets and farmsteads within which the vast majority of the medieval population made their living. This approach was consolidated in Aston's *Interpreting the Landscape* (1985), which remains one of the best books on the subject.

The growth of landscape archaeology in the 1970s was not just about new techniques and the scale at which they were used: there was also a new agenda. One paper in *Recent Work in Rural Archaeology* provides an example: Fowler's (1975b) 'Continuity in the landscape: a summary of some local archaeology in Wiltshire, Somerset and Gloucestershire'. The traditional view of the origins of the medieval landscape, in the champion countryside of England's central zone at least, was that villages and open fields were introduced by the Anglo-Saxon settlers of the 5th and 6th centuries and that they replaced a sparsely settled and well-wooded country: a classic example of the culture-historical approach followed by the likes of Gray (1915), Fox (1932) and Hoskins (1955), whereby change in the landscape was brought about by invasion and migration. The increasing scale of aerial photography, fieldwalking and rescue archaeology, however, had revealed a Romano-British countryside that was far more densely settled than was previously thought: in the Nene Valley, for example, the number of known settlements in a study area of some

1000 square kilometres increased from 36 in 1931 to 434 in 1972 (Taylor 1975, 113). Fieldwalking and excavation were also suggesting that the 5th- and 6th-century settlement pattern was dispersed, with farmsteads and small hamlets spread across the areas covered by later parishes, rather than lying in the compact villages that are so characteristic of the later medieval period. Where medieval villages had been deserted, and so could be excavated, there was also no evidence that they dated back much before the Norman Conquest: rather than seeing the end of Roman Britain as a major discontinuity in the landscape, archaeologists such as Fowler were increasingly seeing continuity in settlement, land-use and even the estates into which the landscape was divided. Other examples of this emerging paradigm of continuity in the early post-Roman centuries include Jones's (1979; 1981; 1985) suggestion that territorial structures documented in later medieval Welsh law books might date back to the Roman period or earlier and that similar 'multiple estates' could be recognized in England (but see Gregson 1985). Likewise, Bonney (1979) argued that a relationship between Early Anglo-Saxon burials and parish boundaries meant that the latter were Roman or earlier in date (but see Goodier 1984 and Reynolds 2002), while Rodwell (1978) claimed that whole field systems may have survived in use since the Roman period. One example both of the impact that the 'New Archaeology' had on medieval scholarship, and the emerging trend towards seeing continuity in the landscape, is the use of techniques of spatial analysis borrowed from geography (eg Figure 11.3; Burrow 1982, fig 31). Thiessen polygons, for example, were used to try and reconstruct the territories associated with hillforts reoccupied in the early medieval period that seemed to show a close relationship with later parish boundaries. It is probably fair to say that theoretical archaeology has not had the same impact on the study of the medieval landscape as has been the case in the prehistoric period, though notable exceptions include Jope's (1972a; 1972b) work published at the height of interest in the 'New Archaeology', and subsequent studies have continued to show the potential for more processual and post-processual approaches (eg Rahtz 1983; Austin and Thomas 1990; Johnson 1996; 2002; and see Chris Gerrard this volume).

In 1979 the Society for Landscape Studies was founded, as a reaction against the highly empirical tradition that had developed within medieval archaeology, and reflecting the desire of many to develop a more holistic approach towards landscape research. By the 1980s the interdisciplinary principles and a larger-scale vision of landscape archaeology were becoming more commonplace in the study of all periods, though the approaches in the prehistoric and historic periods were somewhat different. A tradition of large-scale programmes of archaeological survey and excavation with a largely prehistoric and Romano-British focus developed in the heartland of British field archaeology — central southern England and in particular the chalk downs (eg East Hampshire Survey: Shennan 1985; East Berkshire Survey: Ford 1987; Maddle Farm Project: Gaffney and Tingle 1989; Stonehenge Environs Project: Richards 1990; Cranborne Chase: Barrett *et al* 1991; Vale of the White Horse Survey: Tingle 1991; Linear Ditches Project: Bradley *et al* 1994; Danebury Environs Project: Cunliffe 2000). Those with a greater interest in the medieval period tended to focus on smaller-scale parish surveys that integrate the study of maps, documents, and even standing buildings with programmes of archaeological survey,

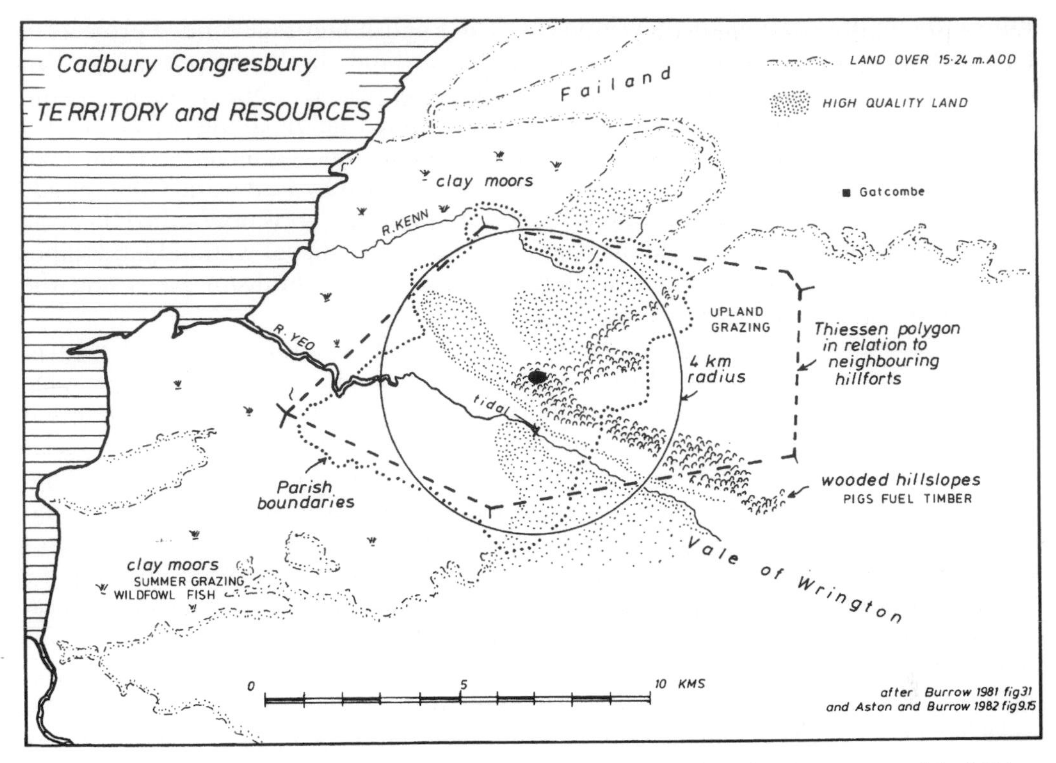

FIGURE 11.3. Possible early estates associated with the early medieval reoccupation of the hillfort at Cadbury Congresbury in Somerset. Ideas such as Thiessen polygons, borrowed from another discipline (geography) were typical of the 'New Archaeology' that came rather late to the study of the medieval period (after Rahtz *et al* 1992, fig 162).

and sometimes excavation. Such surveys were occasionally driven by threats from development, such as the urban expansion of Milton Keynes in Buckinghamshire (Croft and Maynard 1993) and gravel extraction around Raunds in Northamptonshire (Parry 2006), but more often they were research led as at Wharram Percy in Yorkshire (Hall 1982, fig 32; Hurst 1985, 204), Puxton (Rippon 2006) and Shapwick (Gerrard with Aston 2007) in Somerset, Hales, Lodden (Davison 1990) and Barton Bendish (Rogerson *et al* 1997) in Norfolk, and Walsham-le-Willows in Suffolk (West and McLaughlin 1998). One reason why medievalists work on a smaller scale, of course, is that in addition to the field evidence they work in a period for which some places have a large body of documentary material and its integration with evidence on the ground was a key character-defining feature of the emerging discipline of landscape archaeology (eg Aston and Rowley 1974; Taylor 1974; Moorhouse 1979).

Whilst these surveys were on a relatively modest scale, on the Continent far more ambitious projects were shedding new light on the long-term development of larger-scale landscapes in areas such as East Brittany (Astill and Davies 1997) and the Biferno Valley in southern Italy (Barker 1995). In Britain, the largest-scale surveys were on the major wetlands areas in response to a variety of threats such as agricultural improvement, desiccation and development. The English Heritage funded projects in the North-West (eg Hodgkinson *et al* 2000) and around the Humber estuary (Van de Noort 2004) yielded modest results for the medieval period, while those of Fenland produced a remarkable series of studies that integrated fieldwalking, aerial photography and the analysis of historical maps and documents (eg Silvester 1988; Hall 1996). The Gwent Levels Historic Landscape Study, funded by Cadw and Countryside Council for Wales, was one of the pioneering examples of what is now called 'historic landscape characterization' (Rippon 1996), while other medieval wetland landscapes that have seen extensive research include Romney Marsh (Eddison 2000) and the North Somerset Levels (Rippon 2006).

It is clear from the examples given above that archaeologists in England had enthusiastically embraced the ideas of landscape archaeology, but there were some significant differences elsewhere in Britain. By the 1990s it was clearly recognized that the state of research into medieval settlement and landscape in Scotland and Wales was falling well behind that in England, with the publication of work in Scotland 'limited to say the least' and that in Wales 'even bleaker' (Atkinson *et al* 2000, vi; and see Morrison 2000). Part of the problem is that in Scotland the historic landscape of today is largely a post-medieval creation. Whereas in large parts of England the patterns of fields, roads and settlements that are depicted on 19th-century maps contain many elements that are medieval in date — especially away from the areas of Parliamentary Enclosure of former open field — in Scotland this is not the case. Here, the modern settlement patterns and field systems were largely created in the last two and a half centuries (eg Dixon 2002; 2007a; 2007b; Macinnes 2003), and with relatively scarce medieval documentary sources it is not surprising that in Scottish historical geography too the emphasis in 'medieval or later rural settlement' is largely on the 'later' (eg Dodgshon 2000; Fenton 2000; Whyte 2000; Lelong 2003).

Intensive agriculture in the Scottish lowlands also means that there are few upstanding remains of any pre-modern landscapes — in sharp contrast to the numerous deserted medieval villages that have dominated research in the central parts of England — and although the uplands contain a wide range of well-preserved relict landscapes, pre-18th-century buildings are extremely rare (eg Wickham-Jones 2001; Boyle 2003; Halliday 2003). Whilst there are a few notable examples of the familiar techniques of landscape archaeology being used on medieval sites in lowland Scotland, such as aerial photography and fieldwalking that led to the discovery of the deserted settlement at Rattray, in Aberdeenshire (Murray and Murray 1993), and the RCAHMS's continued landscape-scale field surveys (RCAHMS 1990; 1994; 1997; 2007), the amount of excavation of medieval rural sites in Scotland remains 'pitifully small' (Dixon 2000, 260; and see Lelong 2003). Progress is, however, now being made, and while there is still no equivalent development-led work to the Raunds Project, there are now some excellent multi-disciplinary research programmes including the University of Sheffield's research in the Hebrides (Sharples and Parker Pearson 1999; Branigan 2005), and the Ben Lawers Historic Landscape Project in the central Highlands (Boyle 2003; Turner 2003).

In Wales, the study of medieval rural settlement has been described as 'marginal', both in the sense of the best preserved remains usually being in upland areas, and in terms of the relatively limited attention that it has received (Thompson and Yates 2000, 37). As Edwards (1997b, 5) has observed: 'medieval settlement archaeology in Wales has received surprisingly little attention when compared with the amount of research, survey and excavation which has been carried out on both rural and urban settlements of the same period in England over the last fifty years'. Early work focused on post-Roman high status sites — such as Dinas Powys — and deserted rural settlement in upland areas where a lack of dating evidence was a common problem (eg Fox 1939; Butler 1971; Edwards 1997b, 2–5). In recent decades the bias towards upland areas has remained, although some excellent work has been done here (eg Cefn Graenog in Caernarfonshire: Kelly 1982, and see Ward 1997; Browne and Hughes 2003). But themed projects funded by Cadw are now targeting previously neglected topics such as later medieval royal courts (eg Longley 1997; Johnstone 1997), and lower-status rural settlement (eg Thompson and Yates 2000, 38; Roberts 2006), in an effort to redress the bias in excavation towards high-status sites such as castles and towns. While there is also a strong tradition of standing building survey in Wales (eg Fox and Raglan 1951; RCAHMW 1988; Smith 1988; Suggett 2005), there is a desperate need for more interdisciplinary landscape-based projects akin to Wharram Percy, Raunds, Whittlewood and Shapwick, that embrace the entire medieval landscape of settlement, communication systems, field systems and associated land-uses, something that the work of David Austin and Andrew Fleming at Strata Florida should achieve (Austin 2004).

NEW TECHNIQUES AND NEW DIRECTIONS

In recent years the range of techniques available to the landscape archaeologist has increased dramatically. Geophysical survey is becoming quicker and more sophisticated, allowing the coverage of ever-greater areas, and GPS (Global Positioning System) makes accurate but rapid earthwork survey possible across large areas (eg Chapman and Fenwick 2002). Development-led survey and excavation is adding enormously to the volume of data on medieval settlement, both deserted and, perhaps more importantly, still occupied. The application of PPG-16 (Planning Policy Guidance Note 16: advice from government to local authorities on how archaeology should be dealt with in the planning process) means that there are now increasing numbers of excavations within currently occupied settlements that are starting to shed light on their origins, and in areas as far apart as Gloucestershire and Cambridgeshire it is the Middle Saxon period that is emerging as the foundation date for many villages (eg Taylor *et al* 1994; Mortimer 2000; Reynolds 2003; Cessford 2004; 2005; and see Rippon 2008). In many villages, of course, there are no vacant plots to be developed, but even here archaeologists have started to make headway in testing the conclusions of plan analysis through the digging of large numbers of small test-pits (Rippon 2006; Page and Jones 2007; Gerrard with Aston 2007; Lewis 2007).

Another area that has seen recent advances is palaeoenvironmental sampling. On-site work is now routine, and we have increasing numbers of large, well-dated assemblages of both crop remains and animal bone, though more work is needed on rural settlements. There is also a need for more off-site work, to complement the large numbers of well-dated sequences we have for the prehistoric period (Bell 1989; Dark 2000). In the past, attention has focused on upland peat bogs that are of little value in the medieval period, lying well beyond areas of settlement and presenting at best a broad regional picture due to their vast catchment areas. Increasingly, however, attention is shifting to the potential of small valley mires that occur within areas that were settled and farmed throughout the medieval period and these are addressing issues such as the absence of a widespread woodland regeneration in lowland areas in the early post-Roman period, and the intensification of agriculture around the 8th century that is now being identified as far afield as Devon (Rippon *et al* 2006) and East Anglia (Murphy 1996, 29; Rippon 2008). Preliminary work on the sediments filling small valleys in the East Midlands show the potential to address similar issues, though better dating is required (eg around Whittlewood: Page 2006, 52–53, 56, 86; Branch *et al* nd).

In the past two decades the British tradition of detailed local case-studies has continued, though an increase in the resources that are sometimes available, the use of GIS (Geographical Information Systems), and a change in philosophy with regard to the most appropriate scale at which landscape should be studied, have contributed to a move away from individual parishes towards studying larger districts. Notable examples include the Clwydian Hills in Wales (Brown 2004), Swaledale in Yorkshire (Fleming 1998), Whittlewood in the East Midlands (Jones and Page 2006), and the North Somerset Levels (Rippon 2006). The work of Glenn Foard and David Hall in particular, in reconstructing the medieval landscape across the whole of Northamptonshire will be a remarkable achievement (see Foard 2001, and Foard *et al* 2005 for the Rockingham Forest area pilot study: Figure 11.4). The survey team within English Heritage (the former RCHME) have also shifted their focus, from attempting to produce definitive county gazetteers of archaeological sites towards more focused projects on individual distinctive districts (eg *The Field Archaeology of Exmoor*: Riley and Wilson-North 2001; *The Malvern Hills: An Ancient Landscape*: Bowden 2005; *The Historic landscape of the Quantock Hills*: Riley 2006; *The Malvern Hills: An Ancient Landscape*: Bowden 2005; note how the titles of these volumes reflect the more holistic view of landscape shifting from field archaeology to the historic landscape as a whole). In Scotland and Wales the production of county-based inventories by the Royal Commissions there has similarly been replaced by thematic volumes focusing on particular regions (eg RCAHMS 2007), previously neglected subjects such as rural settlement (eg Boyle 2003; Roberts 2006), and particular types of standing buildings (eg Suggett 2005).

A growing appreciation that individual medieval sites can only be properly understood when placed in their wider landscape context is seen in many area of medieval archaeology, reflected in recent books on *Monasteries in the Landscape* (Aston 2000), *Monastic Landscapes* (Bond 2004), '*Landscapes of Lordship*': *Norman Castles and the Countryside* (Liddiard 2000), *Castles and Landscapes* (Creighton 2002), and *Castles in Context: Power, Symbolism and Landscape* (Liddiard 2005). There are even entirely new facets to the medieval countryside that are being discovered, such as the extent to which some high status sites were associated with parks, gardens and planned landscapes sometimes with deeply embedded meaning

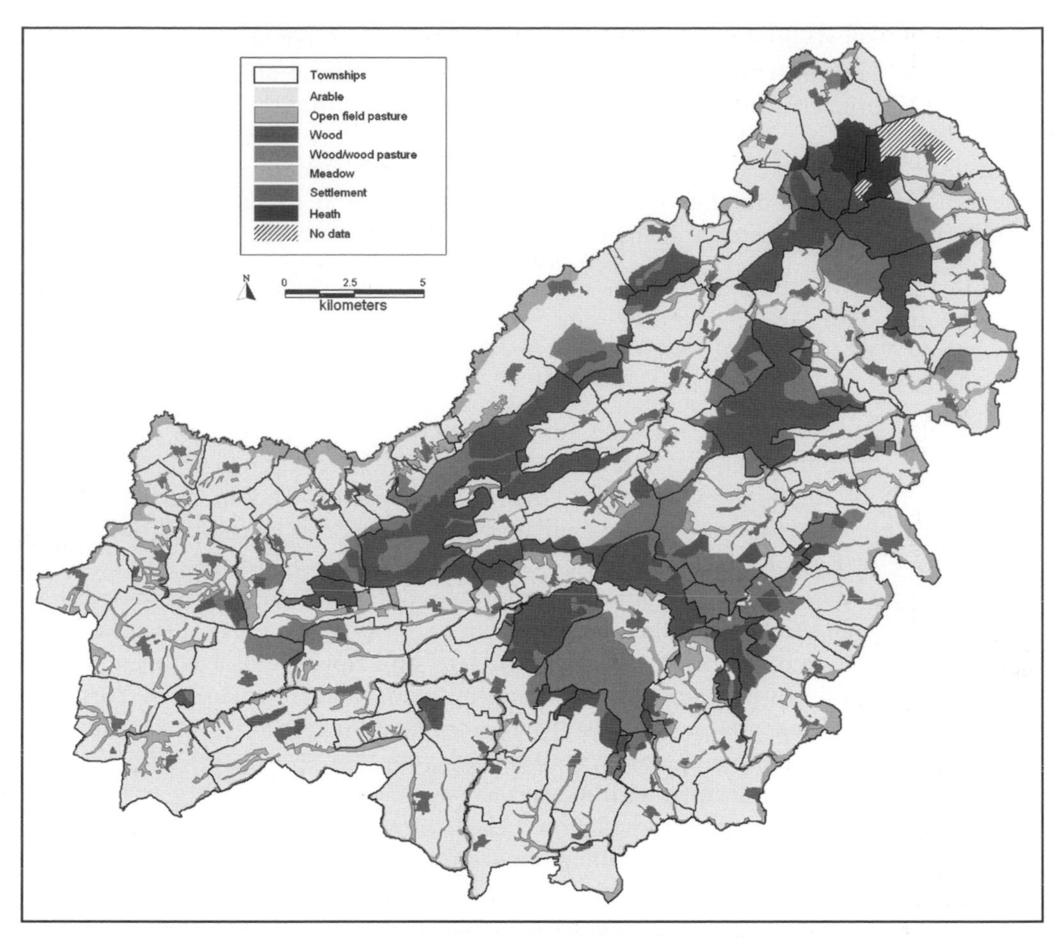

FIGURE 11.4. A reconstruction of the medieval landscape of the Rockingham Forest in Northamptonshire by Glenn Foard, David Hall and Tracey Partida. The use of GIS has allowed David Hall's decades of fieldwork and analysis of maps and document to be plotted in a way that was previously not possible (after Foard *et al* 2005, fig 7).

and symbolism (Harvey 1981; Gilchrist 1999, 111; Richardson 2005; Liddiard 2007; Creighton 2009). Another area in which the agenda of landscape research has moved on is the concept of marginality. It is striking how many of the pioneering projects referred to in this paper were in locations that would traditionally have been regarded as 'marginal' such as the uplands and wetlands (see Postan 1972). Traditional views of marginality have, however, changed radically, and we should now see various environments as offering different potential for human communities that will not always be based on cereal production (eg Bailey 1989; Fox 1996; Rippon 2000, 3–6). The study of specialist settlements adds much to the richness and texture of our countryside, and has also increased in popularity in recent years, such as seasonal settlements in the uplands, and the fishing villages of south-west England that were a surprisingly late addition to the distinctive landscape character of this region (eg Fox 1996; 2001). This more holistic approach to studying the landscape is also reflected in a growing appreciation of the need to understand towns within their rural hinterlands (Giles and Dyer 2005; see Astill, this volume). Industrial archaeology, however, remains a subject that is somewhat detached from the wider world of landscape research, although a number of projects are now seeking to integrate the understanding of industrial sites and their fuel supply with their wider landscape context (eg Astill 1993; Foard 2001; Atkinson 2003; Rippon *et al* 2009).

REGIONAL VARIATION IN LANDSCAPE CHARACTER: A MIDLAND-CENTRIC DEBATE

Whilst there has been research into the medieval landscapes in all parts of Britain, there remain areas that are subject to much debate, such as the origins and development of regional variation in landscape character, and in particular why the 'aberration' (Taylor 1983, 125) of villages and open fields developed only in the central zone of England. As far back as Gray's *English Field Systems* (1915), it has been recognized that the champion countryside that stretched from North-East England, through the East Midlands, and down to Wessex, was very different to the areas either side, and the origins of these villages and open fields has been studied through detailed local projects in places ranging from Wharram Percy in Yorkshire (Beresford and Hurst 1990), Raunds (Parry 2006), Whittlewood (Jones and Page 2006), and Milton Keynes (Croft and Mynard 1993) in the East Midlands, and Shapwick in Somerset (Gerrard with Aston 2007).

A trilogy of three major studies (Lewis *et al* 1997; Roberts and Wrathmell 2002; Williamson 2003) has recently examined the origins of regional variation in landscape character, focusing on the Midlands and East Anglia. Lewis, Mitchell-Fox and Dyer (1997) have provided what can be regarded as the currently dominant view, that areas which were to acquire champion countryside were the most developed regions of England and that the countryside here was reordered from around the 10th century, although this model does not fit comfortably with the results of recent survey and excavations in areas such as Northamptonshire, Lincolnshire and Norfolk that seem to suggest that settlement started to nucleate before the mid-9th century (Hayes and Lane 1992, 48; Lane and Hayes 1993, 69; Steedman 1994; Brown and Foard 1998; Rippon 2009). Roberts and Wrathmell (2000; 2002) have used a variety of mapped data-sets to suggest that the origins of the champion countryside in what they term England's 'central province' lay in the Roman or even late prehistoric period, this being the area most extensively cleared of woodland. There is, however, no correlation between the density of population in Domesday and those parts of England that saw the transformation of their landscape through the creation of villages and open fields. Williamson (2003; 2007a) has suggested a very different explanation: that the physical form of the terrain, which affects the extent of meadow, and the characteristics of particular soils in relation to when they can be ploughed, determined the form taken by settlement patterns and field systems.

This suggestion that the natural environment may have had a greater part to play in shaping human behaviour appears in a number of other recent studies by younger scholars and is a direct challenge to the post environmental-deterministic paradigm of social agency being the over-riding cause of variation in landscape character. Draper (2006, 112), for example, suggests that the physical landscape is 'fundamental to understanding settlement and society', contrasting the very different patterns of settlement and agriculture in the chalk downland and clay vales of Wiltshire, while in his study of Somerset, Corcos (2002, 190) states:

> it must now be clear that a common thread is the importance of ecology and natural environment as important considerations in shaping the nature of medieval settlement, and by extension, the nature of human communities ... This is not a 'deterministic' conclusion, but one which accepts and indeed celebrates the extraordinary adaptive abilities of pre-industrial societies, and the symbiotic relationship between them and their ecological resource base.

It is difficult to disagree with Johnson's (2007, 145) assertion that 'the landscape archaeologist ... is examining the effects of real people leading real lives, and, further, doing so in active ways', and Lewis *et al* (1997, 186) are right to remind us that 'human ingenuity is not *always* constrained by physical conditions' [my italics]. However, such is the fear of being accused of environmental determinism that there could be a tendency to overlook the possibility that the inherent properties of soil and topography do influence landscape character. Indeed, in another challenge to current orthodoxy, Martin (2006) has recently returned to the issue of the impact that migration might have had on the landscape, by suggesting that Scandinavian colonization contributed to a profound variation in landscape character either side of the Gipping and Lark valleys in Suffolk, a difference that Williamson (2006, 29–30) attributes to the effect that topography had on social interaction and trade/exchange networks. I have also examined the impact that the Anglo-Norman Conquest had on the landscape of southern Wales, identifying not just very 'English' landscapes of villages and open fields that contrast with adjacent 'Welshries' that had very dispersed settlement patterns and predominantly enclosed fields, but also distinctive planned settlements that could have been created by Flemish colonists (Rippon 1996, 63–64; 1997; 2008).

In a further contribution to the debate over the origins of regional variation in landscape character, I have tried to shift the focus away from Midland England towards regions to the east and west of the central zone, and ask why these areas did not see the development of villages and open fields (Rippon 2007a; 2008). Any notion that areas such as the South-East and the South-West were somehow backward and remote is rejected, and it is argued that the 'long eighth century' (the late 7th through to the early 9th centuries: Hanson and Wickham 2005) saw widespread agricultural intensification in the countryside right across southern England, but that the landscape developed in different ways in different areas. The South-West, for example, saw the development of a form of rotational agriculture, known as convertible husbandry, but little settlement nucleation. In the southern and eastern Midlands and East Anglia, palaeoenvironmental sequences similarly show an intensification of agriculture and here dispersed settlement patterns do appear to have been replaced by nucleated villages, but 'divergent developments' — a term developed by Alan Lambourne (2008) — saw this pattern fossilized in the Midlands, whereas in East Anglia there was a subsequent trend towards settlement dispersion as farmsteads migrated towards greens and commons.

Even after 50 years of medieval archaeology, new light can still be shed on other much-debated issues such as the relationship between lordship and the community in shaping landscape character (see Dyer 1985 and Harvey 1989 for previous discussions). Two recent studies in Somerset have also addressed the issue of whether it was landowners or the peasant communities on their manors who were the prime movers in shaping landscape character. In Shapwick, on the Polden Hills, a strong case is made for Glastonbury Abbey, and perhaps Abbot Dunstan, as having been instrumental in replanning the basic framework of this landscape (Gerrard with Aston 2007), while in extensive areas of marshland held by the bishops of Bath and Wells marked differences in landscape character within a few miles of each other suggest that it was local communities who decided whether to manage their newly won lands within the context of villages and open fields, or more dispersed settlement patterns and closes held in severalty (Rippon 2006). Even within areas that show evidence for estates having been sub-divided and their landscapes restructured through the creation of villages and open fields, the degree of variation in features such as the layout of settlements shows the significance of individual decision-making (Rippon 2008).

CURRENT DEBATES

Another recently developed technique is 'Historic Landscape Characterization' (HLC) which, in terms of the work carried out in almost all English counties, and the related form of characterization that was the Roberts and Wrathmell (2000) *Atlas of Rural Settlement in England* project, represents a major investment of public resources by English Heritage. The initiative is not, however, without its critics. HLC developed in the 1990s in both England (beginning in Cornwall: Herring 1998) and Wales (the Gwent Levels: Rippon 1996) as a way of understanding the processes that lay behind the creation of all areas of our countryside, and a similar process has been developed in Scotland where it is known as Historic Land-Use Assessment (Dixon 2007a). In all three regions, prescribed methodologies are followed by English Heritage, Historic Scotland and Cadw/The Countryside Council for Wales, and while it is important to remember that these HLCs are designed simply to inform planners and countryside managers of the historic time-depth present in our countryside, rather than addressing the academic community (for example, see Herring 2007; Lake 2007; Clarke *et al* 2004; Alfry 2007), significant discoveries have been made including previously unsuspected examples of medieval field systems still surviving in use in parts of Scotland (Dixon 2007a; 2007b). There are, however, problems in the way that some HLCs have been carried out — including the use of only modern map sources in some examples — and this has unfortunately led to considerable doubts about its research value (for example, see Austin 2007; Finch 2007; Williamson 2007). There is, however, more to characterization than these prescriptive schemes by governmental bodies, and the analysis of the earliest surviving map sources for a particular study area is clearly more rewarding. If we think instead of the broader idea of 'historic landscape analysis', that can include mapping and analysing layers of data such as patterns of landownership and occupancy, field- and place-names, vernacular architecture, and the results of archaeological survey and excavation, then characterizing settlement patterns and field systems is simply a further addition to the already diverse techniques of landscape archaeology (Rippon 2004; 2006; 2007b; Rippon *et al* 2009). The increasing use of computer packages is making such research increasingly straightforward, such as GIS, Kain and Oliver's (2002) mapping of ancient parish boundaries depicted on Tithe maps, and online resources such as Digimap (that includes a complete coverage of Ordnance Survey First Edition Six Inch maps) and some Historic Environment Records.

One problem with HLC is its almost complete reliance on morphology, most notably field boundary patterns, in reconstructing past patterns of land-use, but other layers of data can be added to this analysis to confirm or refute such hypotheses, including patterns of land ownership and land occupancy that can help identify areas of former open field that have been enclosed by agreement (eg Figure 11.5). Historic landscape analysis can even be used to integrate other strands of landscape research, such as the study of standing buildings, which have been used to confirm the antiquity of regional variation in settlement patterns mapped by Roberts and Wrathmell (eg Rippon 2006; 2007b; Rippon *et al* 2009). Indeed, the study of medieval buildings — both excavated and still standing — is a subject that has enormous potential for greater integration with research into the wider landscape (eg Gardiner 2007).

Historic Landscape Characterization was not the only issue being debated within landscape studies in 2007: far more significant doubts were being expressed over the past achievements and future direction of landscape archaeology as a whole. In his book *Ideas of Landscape* (2007), Matthew Johnson has examined the conceptual framework within which the British tradition of landscape archaeology has developed, appearing to argue that it is over empirical and lacking theoretical rigor. David Austin (2006, 193) has also recently commented on the still strongly empirical approach towards studying medieval rural settlement in Wales where 'in this pattern of explanation, humanity is either ignored — being seen as largely controlled by the systems — or is limited to the creators and controllers'. Johnson's apparent criticism of empirical research brought a swift response from Andrew Fleming (2007) whose plea 'Don't bin your boots' brought about an immediate and vigorous reply from Johnson (2007): 'Don't bin your brain'. Entertaining as such debates are, does such disagreement actually reflect some crisis within landscape archaeology? Johnson (2007, 1–2) is certainly right to observe that there is a clear divide between what can be regarded as a cultural geography approach, whose preoccupation is more theoretical and concerned with issues such as perception and the meaning of 'landscape', and the more empirical approach of 'traditional' landscape archaeology, historical geography and local history. It is true that some of the readers of *Landscape History*, the *Medieval Settlement Research Group Annual Report*, *Landscapes* and indeed *Medieval Archaeology* might struggle with the likes of Cosgrove's *Social*

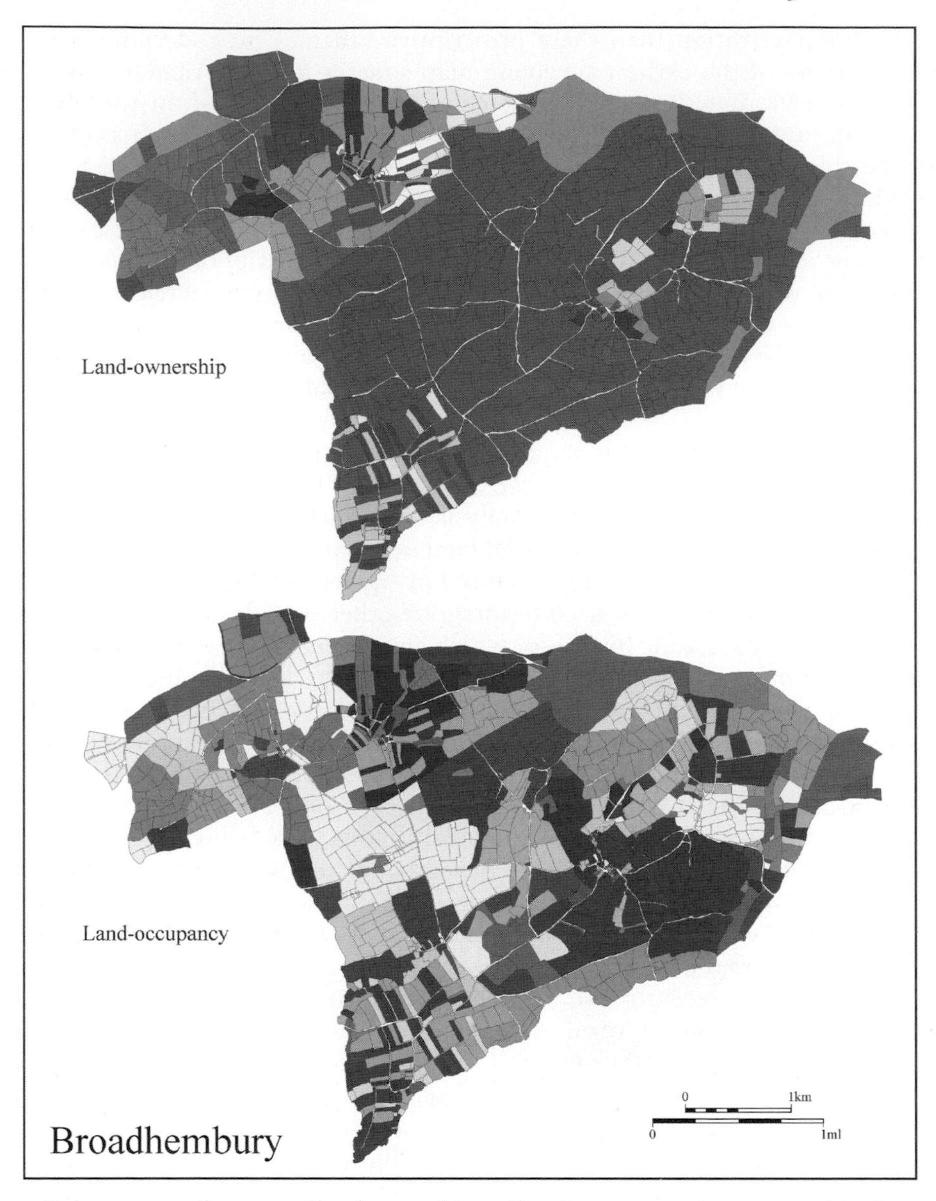

FIGURE 11.5. Patterns of landownership and land occupancy (ie tenements) in the parish of Broadhembury in east Devon. A characterization of this landscape based purely on morphology would suggest the presence of former open fields in the north and south-west of the parish. Such morphological hypotheses require testing with other data, and here such verification is provided by the highly fragmented patterns of landownership and land occupancy. Note how each open field was associated with a small hamlet and that most of the rest of the parish was dominated by closes held in severalty, a pattern typical of much of Devon. (Research and drawing by Richard Sandover)

Formation and Symbolic Landscape (1984), or Daniels's 'The political iconography of woodland in later Georgian England' (1988). But is Johnson (2007, 2) justified in dismissing the British tradition of landscape archaeology, historical geography and local history as remaining 'firmly in the grip of the most unreflective empiricism in which "theory" is a dirty word'? Theoretically incisive studies of the medieval landscape in Britain are relatively few and far between (eg Muir 1999; Holtorf and Williams 2006), in marked contrast to the emerging field of historical archaeology more globally (eg De Cunzo and Ernstein 2006; Pauls 2006), but need this concern us? In 50 years time, which books and papers will still be read: the discursive theoretical works of recent years, or the meticulous surveys of the English, Welsh and Scottish Royal Commissions, and major field-based programmes of research such as the Fenland Survey, many of which will record sites and landscapes that have long been destroyed?

Many readers will no doubt have reached a conclusion of their own, but if landscape research is to remain healthy we must try and reach a position where all these important works will still be valued in the future. Medieval archaeology has always been characterized by a multiplicity of special interest groups and this is not necessarily a bad thing: it is always good to enter a dialogue with colleagues who share a common interest. What is not healthy is the lack of communication with related disciplines such as the study of vernacular architecture, place-names and, yes, cultural geography. There is much in Ian Whyte's *Landscape History Since 1500* (2002) that should be of interest to landscape archaeologists and historians, yet his bibliography contains almost no reference to the work of 'traditional' landscape archaeology. Are geographers at fault for not embracing ideas and data from other disciplines, or is landscape archaeology at fault for not producing the sort of data and ideas that are of interest to anyone else? It is time for reflection, but the current debates such as these, and indeed the clear differences in philosophy between scholars with regards to the causes of regional variation in landscape character, should not be seen as a sign of a divided and declining discipline, but rather one that is facing up to the challenges of the future.

ACKNOWLEDGEMENTS

For their permission to reproduce illustrations I would like to thank Phillip Rahtz (Figure 11.3), Glenn Foard and David Hall (Figure 11.4), and Richard Sandover (Figure 11.5). I would also like to thank Piers Dixon, Della Hooke and Bob Silvester for their assistance with various sections of this paper and I am extremely grateful to David Austin, Oliver Creighton, Andrew Fleming, Mark Gardiner, Chris Gerrard, Chris Taylor and the editors for their comments on an earlier draft. All views expressed are, of course, those of the author.

BIBLIOGRAPHY

Abrams, L, 1996 *Anglo-Saxon Glastonbury: Church and Endowment*, Boydell Press, Woodbridge
Alfry, J, 2007 'Contexts for Historic Landscape Characterisation in Wales', *Landscapes* 8:2, 84–91
Allcroft, A H, 1908 *Earthwork of England: Prehistoric, Roman, Saxon, Danish, Norman, and Mediaeval*, Macmillan, London

Astill, G G, 1993 *Bordesley Abbey 3. A Medieval Industrial Complex and its Landscape: the Metalworking Watermills and Workshops of Bordesley Abbey*, Council for British Archaeology Research Report 92, York

Astill, G and Davies, W, 1997 *A Breton Landscape*, UCL Press, London

Aston, M, 1985 *Interpreting the Landscape: Landscape Archaeology in Local Studies*, Batsford, London

Aston, M, 2000 *Monastic Landscapes*, Tempus, Stroud

Aston, M and Rowley, T, 1974 *Landscape Archaeology: An Introduction to Fieldwork Techniques on Post-Roman Landscapes*, David and Charles, Newton Abbot

Atkinson, J A, Banks, I, and MacGregor, G, 2000a, *Townships to Farmsteads: Rural Settlement Studies in Scotland, England and Wales*, British Archaeological Reports 293, Oxford

Atkinson, J, 2003 'Late medieval bloomery sites: settlement and industry in the Scottish highlands', in Govan (ed) 2003, 35–42

Austin, D, 1978 'Excavations in Okehampton Park, Devon, 1976–78', *Proceedings of the Devon Archaeological Society* 36, 191–240

Austin, D, 2004 'Strata Florida and its landscape archaeology', *Archaeologia Cambrensis* 153, 192–201

Austin, D and Thomas, J, 1990 'The "proper study" of medieval archaeology: a case-study', in D Austin and L Alcock (eds), *From the Baltic to the Black Sea*, Unwin Hyman, London

Austin, D, 2006 'The future: discourse, objectives and directions', in Roberts (ed), 193–205

Austin, D, 2007 'Character or caricature? Concluding discussion', *Landscapes* 8:2, 92–107

Bailey, M, 1989 *A Margin Economy? East Anglian Breckland in the Later Middle Ages*, Cambridge University Press, Cambridge

Barker, G, 1995 *A Mediterranean Valley. Landscape Archaeology and Annales History in the Biferno Valley*, Leicester University Press, London

Barrett, J, Bradley, R, and Green, M, 1991 *Landscape, Monuments and Society: The Prehistory of Cranborne Chase*, Cambridge University Press, Cambridge

Bell, M, 1989 'Environmental archaeology as an index of continuity and change in the medieval landscape', in M Aston, D Austin and C Dyer (eds), *The Rural Settlements of Medieval England*, 269–286, Blackwells, Oxford

Benson, D and Miles, D, 1974 *The Upper Thames Valley: An Archaeological Survey of the River Gravels*, Oxford Archaeological Unit Survey 2, Oxford

Beresford, M, 1957 *History on the Ground*, Lutterworth Press, London

Beresford, M and Hurst, J, 1990 *The English Heritage Book of Wharram Percy*, English Heritage/ Batsford, London

Beresford, M and St Joseph, J K S, 1958 *Medieval England: An Aerial Survey*, Cambridge University Press, Cambridge

Bond, J, 2004 *Monastic Landscapes*, Tempus, Stroud

Bowden, M, 2005 *The Malvern Hills: An Ancient Landscape*, English Heritage, London

Bowen, H C, 1961 *Ancient Fields: A Tentative Analysis of Vanishing Earthworks and Landscapes*, The British Association for the Advancement of Science, London

Boyle, S, 2003 'Ben Lawers: an improvement-period landscape on Lochtayside, Perthshire', in Govan (ed) 2003, 17–30

Bradley, R, 1989 'Herbert Toms — a pioneer of analytical field survey', in M Bowden, D Mackay and P Topping (eds), *From Cornwall to Caithness: Some Aspects of British Field Archaeology. Papers Presented to Norman V. Quinnell*, 29–48, British Archaeological Reports 209, Oxford

Bradley, R, Entwistle, R, and Raymond, F, 1994 *Prehistoric Land Divisions on Salisbury Plain: The Work of the Wessex Linear Ditches Project*, English Heritage, London

Branch, N P, Burn, M, Green, C P, Silva, B, Swindle, G E and Turton, E, nd, 'Whittlewood Project: preliminary results of the environmental archaeological investigations' (http://ads.ahds.ac.uk/catalogue/archive/whittlewood_ahrb_220)

Branigan, K, 2005 *From Clan to Clearance: History and Archaeology on the Isle of Barra c.850–1850*, Oxbow Books, Oxford

Browne, D M and Hughes, S, 2003 *The Archaeology of the Welsh Uplands*, RCAHMW, Aberystwyth

Bonney, D, 1979 'Early Boundaries and Estates in Southern England', in P H Sawyer (ed), *English Medieval Settlement*, 41–51, Arnold, London

Brown, A E and Foard, G, 1998 'The Saxon landscape: a regional perspective', in P Everson and T Williamson (eds), *The Archaeology of Landscape*, 67–94, Manchester University Press, Manchester

Brown, I, 2004 *Discovering a Welsh Landscape: Archaeology and the Clwydian Hills*, Windgather Press, Macclesfield

Butler, L, 1971 'The study of deserted medieval settlements in Wales (to 1968)', in M Beresford and J Hurst (eds), *Deserted Medieval Villages*, 249–269, Lutterworth Press, London

Carley, J P, 1985 *The Chronicle of Glastonbury Abbey; An Edition, Translation and Study of John of Glastonbury's* Cronica sive Antiquitates Glastoniensis Ecclesie, Boydell, Woodbridge

Cessford, C, 2004 'The origins and early development of Chesterton', *Proceedings of the Cambridge Antiquarian Society* 93, 125–142

Cessford, C, 2005 'The manor of Hintona: the origins and development of Church End, Cherry Hinton', *Proceedings of the Cambridge Antiquarian Society* 94, 51–72

Chapman, H and Fenwick, H, 2002 'Contextualising previous excavation: the implications of applying GPS survey and GIS modelling techniques to Watton Priory, East Yorkshire', *Medieval Archaeology* 46, 81–90

Corcos, N, 2002 *The Affinities and Antecedents of Medieval Settlement: Topographical Perspectives from Three Somerset Hundreds*, British Archaeological Reports 337, Oxford

Crawford, O G S, 1953 *Archaeology in the Field*, Phoenix House, London

Crawford, O G S and Keiller, A, 1928 *Wessex from the Air*, Clarendon Press, Oxford

Creighton, O H, 2002 *Castles and Landscapes: Power, Community and Fortification in Medieval England*, Equinox, London

Creighton, O, 2009 *Designs Upon the Landscape: Elite Landscapes of the Middle Ages*, Boydell, Woodbridge

Croft, R A and Mynard, D C, 1993 *The Changing Landscape of Milton Keynes*, Buckinghamshire Archaeological Society Monograph Series 5, Aylesbury

Cunliffe, B W, 2000 *The Danebury Environs Programme: The Prehistory of a Wessex Landscape*, Oxford University Committee for Archaeology Monograph 48, Oxford

Darby, H C, 1940 *Medieval Fenland*, Cambridge University Press, Cambridge

Darby, H C, 1952 *The Domesday Geography of Eastern England*, Cambridge University Press, Cambridge

Darby, H C, 1977 *Domesday England*, Cambridge University Press, Cambridge

Darby, H C, 1983 *The Changing Fenland*, Cambridge University Press, Cambridge

Dark, P, 2000 *The Environment of Britain in the First Millennium ad*, Duckworth, London

Davison, A, 1990 *The Evolution of Settlement in Three Parishes in South-East Norfolk*, East Anglian Archaeology 49, Dereham

De Cunzo, L A and Ernstein, J H, 2006 'Landscapes, ideology and experience in historical archaeology', in D Hicks and M C Beaudry (eds), *The Cambridge Companion to Historical Archaeology*, 255–270, Cambridge University Press, Cambridge

Dixon, P, 2000 'Nuclear and dispersed medieval rural settlement in southern Scotland', in J Klápště (ed), *Ruralia III*, 187–200, Institute of Archaeology, Prague

Dixon, P, 2002 'The medieval peasant building in Scotland: the beginning and end of crucks', in J Klápště (ed), *Ruralia IV: The Rural House from the Migration Period to the Oldest Still Standing Buildings*, 252–272, Institute of Archaeology, Prague

Dixon, P, 2007a 'Conservation not reconstruction: Historic Land-Use Assessment (HLA), or characterising the historic landscape of Scotland', *Landscapes* 8:2, 72–83

Dixon, P, 2007b 'Reaching beyond the clearances: finding the medieval — based upon recent survey work by RCAHMS in Strath Don, Aberdeenshire', in Gardiner and Rippon (eds) 2007, 153–169

Dodgson, J M, 1966 'The significance of the distribution of the English place-name in *–ingas*, *–inga* in South-east England', *Medieval Archaeology* 10, 1–29

Dodgshon, R A, 2000 'Traditional highland field systems: their constraints and thresholds', in Atkinson *et al* (eds) 2000a, 109–116

Draper, S, 2006 *Landscape, Settlement and Society in Roman and Early Medieval Wiltshire*, British Archaeological Reports 419, Oxford

Drewett, P, 1982 *The Archaeology of Bullock Down, Eastbourne, East Sussex: The Development of a Landscape*, Sussex Archaeological Society Monograph 1, Lewes

Dyer, C, 1985 'Power and Conflict in the Medieval Village', in D Hooke (ed), *Medieval Villages*, 27–32, Oxford University Committee for Archaeology, Oxford

Eddison, J, 2000 *Romney Marsh: Survival on a Frontier*, Tempus, Stroud

Edwards, N, 1997a *Landscape and Settlement in Medieval Wales*, Oxbow monograph 81, Oxford

Edwards, N, 1997b 'Landscape and settlement in medieval Wales: an introduction', in N Edwards (ed), *Landscape and Settlement in Medieval Wales*, Oxbow monograph 81, 1–11, Oxford

Elton, C J, 1891 *Rentalia et Custumaria*, Somerset Records Society 5, Taunton

Fenton, A, 2000 'The adaptation of tools and techniques to ridge and furrow fields', in Atkinson *et al* (eds) 2000a, 67–72

Fleming, A, 1998 *Swaledale: Valley of the Wild River*, Edinburgh University Press, Edinburgh

Fleming, A and Ralph, N, 1982 'Medieval settlement and land use on Holne Moor, Dartmoor: the landscape evidence', *Medieval Archaeology* 26, 101–137

Finberg, H P R, 1951 *Tavistock Abbey. A Study in the Social and Economic History of Devon*, Cambridge University Press, Cambridge

Finch, J, 2007 '"Wider framed countries": Historic Landscape Characterisation in the Midland shires', *Landscapes* 8:2, 50–63

Foard, G, 1978 'Systematic fieldwalking and the investigation of Saxon settlement in Northamptonshire', *World Archaeology* 9, 357–374

Foard, G, 2001 'Medieval woodland, agriculture and industry in Rockingham Forest, Northamptonshire', *Medieval Archaeology* 41, 41–95

Foard, G, Hall, D and Partida, T, 2005 'Rockingham Forest, Northamptonshire: the evolution of a landscape', *Landscapes* 6:2, 1–29

Ford, S, 1987 *East Berkshire Archaeological Survey*, Berkshire County Council Department of Highways and Planning Occasional Paper 1, Reading

Fowler, P J, 1972 *Archaeology and the Landscape*, John Baker Ltd, London

Fowler, P J, 1975a *Recent Work in Rural Archaeology*, Adams and Dart, Bath

Fowler, P J, 1975b 'Continuity in the landscape: a summary of some local archaeology in Wiltshire, Somerset and Gloucestershire', in Fowler (ed) 1975a, 121–136

Fowler, P J, 1979 'Archaeology and the M4 and M5 Motorways, 1965–78', *Archaeological Journal* 136, 12–26

Fowler, P J, 2000 *Landscape Plotted and Pieced: Landscape History and Local Archaeology in Fyfield and Overton, Wiltshire*, Reports of the Research Committee of the Society of Antiquaries of London, London

Fox, A, 1939 'Early Welsh homesteads on Gelligaer Common, Glamorgan: excavations in 1938', *Archaeologia Cambrensis* 92, 247–268

Fox, A, 1958, 'A monastic homestead on Dean Moor, South Devon', *Medieval Archaeology* 2, 141–157

Fox, C, 1932 *The Personality of Britain*, National Museum of Wales, Cardiff

Fox, C and Raglan, Lord, 1951 *Monmouthshire Houses: A Study of Building Techniques and Smaller House-Plans in the Fifteenth to Seventeenth Centuries*, National Museum of Wales, Cardiff

Fox, H S A, 1996 *Seasonal Settlement*, University of Leicester Vaughan Papers 39, Leicester

Fox, H, 2001 *The Evolution of the Fishing Village: Landscape and Society Along the South Devon Coast, 1086–1550*, Leopard's Head Press, Oxford

Gaffney, V and Tingle, M, 1989 *The Maddle Farm Project: An Integrated Survey of Prehistoric and Roman Landscapes on the Berkshire Downs*, British Archaeological Reports 200, Oxford

Gardiner, M, 2007 'The origins and persistence of manor houses in England', in Gardiner and Rippon (eds) 2007, 170–182

Gardiner, M and Rippon, S (eds), 2007 *Medieval Landscapes: Landscape History After Hoskins, Volume 2*, Windgather Press, Macclesfield

Gelling, P S, 1961 'Medieval shielings in the Isle of Man', *Medieval Archaeology* 6–7, 156–172

Gerrard, C, 2003 *Medieval Archaeology: Understanding Traditions and Contemporary Approaches*, Routledge, London

Gerrard, C with Aston, M, 2007 *The Shapwick Project: A Rural Landscape Explored*, The Society for Medieval Archaeology Monograph 25, Maney Publishing, Leeds

Gilchrist, R, 1999 *Gender and Archaeology: Contesting the Past*, Routledge, London

Giles, K and Dyer, C (eds), 2005 *Town and Country in the Middle Ages: Contrasts, Contacts and Interconnections, 1100–1500*, Society for Medieval Archaeology Monograph 22, Maney Publishing, Leeds

Goodier, A, 1984 'The formation of boundaries in Anglo-Saxon England: a statistical study', *Medieval Archaeology* 28, 1–21

Govan, S (ed), 2003 *Medieval or Later Rural Settlement in Scotland: 10 Years On*, Edinburgh, Historic Scotland (http://www.molrs.org.uk/downloads/confproc.pdf)

Gray, H L, 1915 *English Field Systems*, Harvard University Press, Cambridge MA

Gregson, N, 1985 'The multiple estate model: some critical questions', *Journal of Historical Geography* 11:4, 339–351

Hall, D, 1982 *Medieval Fields*, Shire Archaeology, Aylesbury

Hall, D, 1996 *The Fenland Survey, Number 10: Cambridgeshire Survey, Isle of Ely and Wisbech*, East Anglian Archaeology 79, Cambridge

Halliday, S, 2003 'Rig-and-furrow', in Govan (ed) 2003, 69–81

Hamerow, H, 1993 *Excavations at Mucking, Volume 2: the Anglo-Saxon Settlement*, English Heritage, London

Hanson, L and Wickham, C (eds), 2000 *The Long Eighth Century: Production, Distribution and Demand*, Brill, Leiden

Harvey, P D A, 1981 *Medieval Gardens*, Batsford, London

Harvey, P D A, 1989 'Initiative and authority in settlement change', in M Aston, D Austin and C Dyer (eds), *The Rural Settlements of Medieval England*, 31–43, Basil Blackwell, Oxford

Hayes, P and Lane, T, 1992, *The Fenland Survey, Number 6: Lincolnshire Survey, The South West Fens*, East Anglian Archaeology 55, Sleaford

Herring, P, 1998 *Cornwall's Historic Landscape: Presenting a Method of Historic Landscape Character Assessment*, Cornwall Archaeological Unit, Truro

Herring, P, 2007 'Historic Landscape Characterisation in an ever changing Cornwall', *Landscapes* 8:2, 15–27

Hodgkinson, D, Huckerby, E, Middleton, R and Wells, C E, 2000 *The Lowland Wetlands of Cumbria*, Lancaster University Archaeological Unit, Lancaster

Holtorf, C and Williams, H, 2006 'Landscapes and memories', in D Hicks and M C Beaudry (eds), *The Cambridge Companion to Historical Archaeology*, 235–254, Cambridge University Press, Cambridge

Hooke, D, 1978 'Early Cotswold woodland', *Journal of Historical Geography* 4, 333–341

Hooke, D, 1981 *Anglo-Saxon Landscapes of the West Midlands. The Charter Evidence*, British Archaeological Reports 95, Oxford

Hooke, D, 1985 *The Anglo-Saxon Landscape: The Kingdom of the Hwicce*, Manchester University Press, Manchester

Hoskins, W G, 1952 'The making of the agrarian landscape', in W G Hoskins and H P R Finberg (eds), *Devonshire Studies*, 289–334, Jonathan Cape, London

Hoskins, W G, 1955 *The Making of the English Landscape*, Hodder and Stoughton, London

Hurst, J, 1985 'The Wharram research Project: problem orientation and strategy 1950–1990', in D Hooke (ed), *Medieval Villages*, 201–204, Oxford University Committee for Archaeology, Oxford

Johnson, M, 1993 *Housing Culture: Traditional Architecture in an English Landscape*, UCL Press, London

Johnson, M, 1996 *An Archaeology of Capitalism*, Basil Blackwell, Oxford

Johnson, M, 2002 *Behind the Castle Gate: From Medieval to Renaissance*, Routledge, London

Johnson, M, 2007 *Ideas of Landscape*, Blackwell Publishing, Oxford

Johnson, N, 1997 'An investigation into the locations of the royal courts of thirteenth-century Gwynedd', in Edwards (ed) 1997a, 55–70

Jones, G, 1972 'Post Roman Wales', in H P R Finberg (ed), *The Agrarian History of England and Wales 1(2), ad43–1042*, 281–382, Cambridge University Press, Cambridge

Jones, G R J, 1979 'Multiple estates and early settlement', in P H Sawyer (ed), *English Medieval Settlement*, 9–34, Edward Arnold, London

Jones, G R J, 1981 'Early customary tenures in Wales and open-field agriculture', in T Rowley (ed), *The Origins of Open Field Agriculture*, 202–225, Croom Helm, London

Jones, G R J, 1985 'Multiple estates perceived', *Journal of Historical Geography* 11:4, 339–351

Jones, R and Page, M, 2006 *Medieval Villages in an English Landscape*, Windgather Press, Macclesfield

Jope, M, 1972a 'Models in medieval studies', in D L Clarke (ed), *Models in Archaeology*, 963–990, Methuen and Co, London

Jope, M, 1972b 'The transmission of new ideas: archaeological evidence for implant and potential', *World Archaeology* 4, 368–374

Kain, R J P and Oliver R R, 2001 *Historic Parishes of England and Wales*, History Data Service, Colchester

Kelly, R, 1982 'The excavation of a medieval farmstead at Cefn Graeanog, Clynnog, Gwynedd', *Bulletin of the Board of Celtic Studies* 29, 859–908

Lake, J, 2007 'The English pays: approaches to understanding and characterising landscapes and places', *Landscapes* 8:2, 28–39

Lambourne, A, 2008 'A puzzle indeed: a study of the incidence and origins of regional variation within the historic landscape of southern England', unpublished PhD thesis, University of Exeter

Lane, T and Hayes, P, 1993 'Moving boundaries in the fens of south Lincolnshire', in J Gardiner (ed), *Flatlands and Wetlands*, 58–70, East Anglian Archaeology 50, Norwich
Leech, R, 1977 *The Upper Thames Valley in Gloucestershire and Wiltshire: An Archaeological Survey of the River Gravels*, Committee for Rescue Archaeology in Avon, Gloucestershire and Somerset Survey 4, Bristol
Leeds, E T, 1947 'A Saxon village at Sutton Courtenay, Berkshire: Third Report', *Archaeologia* 92, 79–94
Lelong, O, 2003 'Finding medieval (or later) rural settlement in the Highlands and islands: the case for optimism', in Govan (ed) 2003, 7–16
Lewis, C, 2007 'New avenues for the investigation of currently occupied medieval rural settlement: preliminary observations from the Higher Education Field Academy', *Medieval Archaeology* 51, 133–164
Lewis, C, Mitchell-Fox, P and Dyer, C, 1997 *Village, Hamlet and Field: Changing Medieval Settlements in Central England*, Manchester University Press, Manchester
Liddiard, R, 2000 *'Landscapes of Lordship': Norman Castles and the Countryside in Medieval Norfolk, 1066–1200*, British Archaeological Reports 309, Oxford
Liddiard, R, 2005 *Castles in Context: Power, Symbolism and Landscape, 1066–1500*, Windgather Press, Macclesfield
Liddiard, R, 2007 'Medieval designed landscapes: problems and possibilities', in Gardiner and Rippon (eds) 2007, 201–214
Linehan, C D, 1966 'Deserted sites and rabbit warrens on Dartmoor, Devon', *Medieval Archaeology* 10, 113–144
Longley, D 1997 'The royal courts of the welsh princes in Gwynedd, AD 400–1283', in Edwards (ed) 1997a, 41–54
Macinnes, L, 2003 'Medieval or later rural settlement in Scotland: 10 years on', in Govan (ed) 2003, 3–6
Moorhouse, S, 1979 'Documentary evidence for the landscape of the manor of Wakefield during the Middle Ages', *Landscape History* 1, 44–58
Morrison, A, 2000 'Scottish rural settlement studies: retrospect and prospect', in Atkinson *et al* (eds) 2000a, 2–9
Mortimer, R, 2000 'Village development and ceramic sequence: the Middle to Late Saxon village at Lordship Lane, Cottenham, Cambridgeshire', *Proceedings of the Cambridge Antiquarian Society* 39, 5–33
Muir, R, 1999 *Approaches to Landscape*, Macmillan, Basingstoke
Murphy, P, 1996 'The Anglo-Saxon landscape and rural economy: some results from sites in East Anglia and Essex', in J Rackham (ed), *Environment and Economy in Anglo-Saxon England*, 23–39, Council for British Archaeology Research Report 89, York
Murray, H K and Murray, J C, 1993 'Excavations at Rattray, Aberdeenshire. A Scottish Deserted Burgh', *Medieval Archaeology* 37, 109–218
Page, M and Jones, R, 2007 'Stability and instability in medieval village plans', in Gardiner and Rippon (eds) 2007, 139–152
Parry, S, 2006 *Raunds Area Survey: An Archaeological Study of the Landscape of Raunds, Northamptonshire 1985–94*, Oxbow Books, Oxford
Pauls, E P, 2006 'The place of space: architecture, landscape and social life', in M Hall and S W Silliman (eds), *Historical Archaeology (Blackwell Studies in Global Archaeology)*, 65–83, Blackwell Publishing, Oxford
Postan, M M, 1972 *The Medieval Economy and Society*, Penguin, London
Proudfoot, V B, 1960 'The economy of the Irish rath', *Medieval Archaeology* 4, 94–122
Rackham, O, 1986 *The History of the Countryside*, J M Dent and Sons, London

Rahtz, P, 1983 'Celtic society in Somerset A.D. 400–700', *Bulletin of the Board of Celtic Studies* 30, 176–200

Rahtz, P, Woodward, A, Burrow, I, Everton, A, Watts, L, Leach, P, Hirst, P, Fowler, P and Gardner, K, 1992, *Cadbury Congresbury 1968–73: A Late/Post-Roman Hilltop Settlement in Somerset*, British Archaeological Reports British Series 223, Oxford

RCAHMS, 1980 *Argyll. An Inventory of the Ancient Monuments, Volume 3, Mull, Tiree, Coll and Tiree (excluding the early medieval and later monuments of Iona)*, Royal Commission on the Ancient and Historical Monuments of Scotland, Edinburgh

RCAHMS, 1990 *North-East Perth: An Archaeological Landscape*, Her Majesty's Stationery Office/ Royal Commission on the Ancient and Historical Monuments of Scotland, Edinburgh

RCAHMS, 1994 *South-East Perth: An Archaeological Landscape*, Her Majesty's Stationery Office / Royal Commission on the Ancient and Historical Monuments of Scotland, Edinburgh

RCAHMS, 1997 *Eastern Dumfriesshire: An Archaeological Landscape*, The Stationery Office/ Royal Commission on the Ancient and Historical Monuments of Scotland, Edinburgh

RCAHMS, 2007 *In the Shadow of Bennachie: A Field Archaeology of Donside, Aberdeenshire*, Royal Commission on the Ancient and Historical Monuments of Scotland, Edinburgh

RCAHMW, 1982 *An Inventory of the Ancient Monuments in Glamorgan Volume III: Medieval Secular Monuments, Part III: Non-Defensive*, Royal Commission on the Ancient and Historical Monuments of Wales, Cardiff

RCAHMW, 1988 *An Inventory of the Ancient Monuments in Glamorgan Volume IV Part 2: Domestic Architecture from the Reformation to the Industrial Revolution; Farmhouses and Cottages*, Royal Commission on the Ancient and Historical Monuments of Wales, Cardiff

RCAHMW, 1997 *An Inventory of Ancient Monuments in Brecknock (Brycheiniog). The Prehistoric and Roman Monuments Part I: Later Prehistoric and Roman Monuments and Unenclosed Settlements to 1000 a.d.*, Royal Commission on the Ancient and Historical Monuments of Wales, Aberystwyth

RCHME, 1960 *A Matter of Time: Archaeological Survey of the River Gravels of England*, Royal Commission on the Historical Monuments of England, London

RCHME, 1972 *County of Cambridge Volume Two: North-East Cambridgeshire*, Her Majesty's Stationery Office, London

RCHME, 1982 *County of Northampton Archaeological Sites Volume Four: South-West*, Her Majesty's Stationery Office, London

Reynolds, A, 2002 'Burials, Boundaries and charters in Anglo-Saxon England: a reassessment', in S Lucy and A Reynolds (eds), *Burial in Early Medieval England and Wales*, London, Society for Medieval Archaeology Monograph 17, 171–194

Reynolds, A, 2003 'Boundaries and settlements in later sixth to eleventh century England', in D Griffiths, A Reynolds and S Semple (eds), *Boundaries in Early Medieval Britain*, 98–136, Anglo-Saxon Studies in Archaeology and History 12, Oxford

Richards, J, 1990 *The Stonehenge Environs Project*, English Heritage, London

Richardson, A 2005 *The Forest, Park and Palace of Clarendon, c. 1200–c. 1650: Reconstructing an Actual, Conceptual and Documented Wiltshire Landscape*, British Archaeological Reports 387, Oxford

Riley, H, 2006 *The Historic Landscape of the Quantock Hills*, English Heritage, London

Riley, H and Wilson-North, R, 2001 *The Field Archaeology of Exmoor*, English Heritage, London

Rippon, S, 1996 *The Gwent Levels: The Evolution of a Wetland Landscape*, Council for British Archaeology Research Report 105, York

Rippon, S, 1997 'Wetland reclamation on the Gwent Levels: dissecting a historic landscape', in N Edwards (ed), *Landscape and Settlement in Medieval Wales*, 13–30, Oxbow Books, Oxford

Rippon, S, 2000 *The Transformation of Coastal Wetlands*, Oxford University Press, Oxford

Rippon, S, 2004 '"Making the most of a bad situation"? Glastonbury Abbey and the exploitation of wetland resources in the Somerset Levels', *Medieval Archaeology* 48, 91–130

Rippon, S, 2006 *Landscape, Community and Colonisation: The North Somerset Levels During the 1st to 2nd Millennia ad*, Council for British Archaeology Research Report 152, York

Rippon, S, 2007a 'Emerging regional variation in historic landscape character: the possible significance of the "Long Eighth Century"', in M Gardiner and S Rippon (eds), *Medieval Landscapes*, 105–121, Windgather Press, Macclesfield

Rippon, S, 2007b 'Historic Landscape Characterisation: its role in contemporary British archaeology and landscape history', *Landscapes* 8:2, 1–15

Rippon, S, 2008 *Beyond the Medieval Village: The Diversification of Landscape Character in Southern Britain*, Oxford University Press, Oxford

Rippon, S J, Fyfe, R M and Brown, A G, 2006 'Beyond villages and open fields: the origins and development of a historic landscape characterised by dispersed settlement in South-West England', *Medieval Archaeology* 50, 31–70

Rippon, S, Claughton, P and Smart C, 2009 *Mining in a Medieval Landscape: The Royal Silver Mines of the Tamar Valley*, University of Exeter Press, Exeter

Rodwell, W, 1978 'Relict landscapes in Essex', in H C Bowen and P J Fowler (eds), *Early Land Allotment*, 89–98, British Archaeological Reports 48, Oxford

Roberts, B and Wrathmell, S, 2000 *An Atlas of Rural Settlement in England*, English Heritage, London

Roberts, B and Wrathmell, S, 2002 *Region and Place*, English Heritage, London

Roberts, K, 2006 *Lost Farmsteads: Deserted Rural Settlements in Wales*, Council for British Archaeology Research Report 148, York

Rogerson, A, Davison, A, Pritchard, D and Silvester, R, 1997 *Barton Bendish and Caldecote: Fieldwork in South-West Norfolk*, East Anglian Archaeology 80, Dereham

Seebohm, F, 1883 *The English Village Community*, Longman, London

Sharples, N and Parker Pearson, M, 1999 'Norse settlement in the Outer Hebrides', *Norwegian Archaeological Review* 31:1, 41–62

Shennan, S, 1985 *Experiments in the Collection and Analysis of Archaeological Survey Data: The East Hampshire Survey*, Department of Archaeology and Prehistory, University of Sheffield, Sheffield

Silvester, R J, 1988 *The Fenland Survey, Number 3: Norfolk Survey, Marshland and Nar Valley*, East Anglian Archaeology 45

Smith, P, 1988 *Houses of the Welsh Countryside, a Study in Historical Geography*, HMSO, London

Stacey, N E, 2001 *Surveys of the Estates of Glastonbury Abbey* c. *1135–1201*, Oxford, University Press for the British Academy, Oxford

Steedman, K, 1994 'Riby Crossroads', *Lincolnshire Archaeology and History* 28, 1–20

Suggett, R F, 2005 *Houses and History in the March of Wales*, Royal Commission on the Ancient and Historical Monuments of Wales, Aberystwyth

Taylor, A, 1994 'Field-work in Cambridgeshire: October 1993–September 1994', *Proceedings of the Cambridge Antiquarian Society* 83, 167–76

Taylor, C C, 1967 'Whiteparish: a study in the development of a forest-edge parish', *Wiltshire Archaeological and Natural History Magazine* 62, 79–102

Taylor, C, 1974 *Fieldwork in Medieval Archaeology*, Batsford, London

Taylor, C, 1975 'Roman settlements in the Nene Valley: the impact of recent archaeology', in Fowler (ed) 1975a, 106–120

Taylor, C, 1983 *Village and Farmstead: A History of Rural Settlement in England*, George Dent, London

Thompson, D and Yates, M, 2000 'Deserted rural settlement in Wales — a framework for study, a strategy for protection', in J Klápště (ed), *Ruralia III*, 37–45, Institute of Archaeology, Prague

Thompson, F H, 1960 'The deserted medieval village of Riseholme, near Lincoln', *Medieval Archaeology* 4, 95–108

Thorpe, H, 1949 'The village greens of County Durham', *Transactions of the Institute of British Geographers* 15, 155–180

Tingle, M, 1991 *The Vale of the While Horse: The Study of a Changing Landscape in the Clay Lowlands of Southern Britain from Prehistory to the Present*, British Archaeological Reports 218, Oxford

Tranter, M, Hawker, K, Rowley, J and Thompson, M (eds), 1999 *English Local History: The Leicester Approach. A Departmental Bibliography and History, 1948–1998*, Friends of the Centre for English Local History, Leicester

Turner, R, 2003 'The Ben Lawers Historic Landscape Project', in Govan (ed) 2003, 31–33

Van de Noort, R, 2004 *The Humber Wetlands: The Archaeology of a Dynamic Landscape*, Windgather Press, Macclesfield

Vinogradoff, P, 1892 *Villainage in England. Essays in English Medieval History*, Clarendon Press, Oxford

Wade-Martins, P, 1980 *Fieldwork and Excavation on Village Sites in Launditch Hundred, Norfolk*, East Anglian Archaeology 10, Dereham

Ward, A, 1997 'Transhumance and settlement on the Welsh uplands: a view from the Black Mountain', in Edwards (ed) 1997a, 97–112

Watkin, D A, 1947 *The Chartulary of Glastonbury Abbey* 1, Somerset Records Society 59, Taunton

Watkin, D A, 1952 *The Chartulary of Glastonbury Abbey* 2, Somerset Records Society 63, Taunton

Watkin, D A, 1956 *The Chartulary of Glastonbury Abbey* 3, Somerset Records Society 64, Taunton

Weaver, F W, 1910 *A Feodary of Glastonbury Abbey*, Somerset Records Society 26, Taunton

West, S E and McLaughlin, A, 1998 *Towards a Landscape History of Walsham le Willows, Suffolk*, East Anglian Archaeology 85, Ipswich

Whyte, I, 2002 *Landscape History Since 1500*, Reaktion Books, London

Whyte, I, 2000 'Historical geographical dimensions of medieval or later rural settlement in lowland Scotland', in Atkinson *et al* (eds) 2000a, 145–149

Wickham-Jones, C R, 2001 *The Landscape of Scotland*, Tempus, Stroud

Williamson, T, 2003 *Shaping Medieval Landscapes: Settlement, Society, Environment*, Windgather Press, Macclesfield

Williamson, T, 2006 *England's Landscape: East Anglia*, Collins/English Heritage, London

Williamson, T, 2007a 'The distribution of "woodland" and "champion" landscapes in medieval England', in Gardiner and Rippon (eds) 2007, 89–104

Williamson, T, 2007b 'Historic Landscape Characterisation: some queries', *Landscapes* 8:2, 64–71

CHAPTER 12
MEDIEVAL TOWNS AND URBANIZATION

By GRENVILLE ASTILL

This review takes a broad view of the impact of urban archaeology — paramount is the question, to what extent have we identified and understood the processes of urbanization that produced the distinctive urban character of medieval Britain? After a brief survey of the current state of knowledge, three major themes are addressed. First, in a reconsideration of the sequence and pace of urban development, it is argued that a scheme of continuous town growth is now an inappropriate way to interpret the evidence. Secondly, in assessing the character of medieval towns, we need to reinstate the importance of non-economic functions, and consider the extent to which, at certain stages in their development, towns may only have been used by particular social groups; and that this in turn may have limited the impact towns had on their surroundings. Thirdly, the relationship between town and country is reviewed in terms of the urban network and of exchange: the fluidity and dynamic in the workings of both need to be recognized because neither became formalized and fixed until relatively late in the Middle Ages. Finally, some potential themes for future research are suggested which are intended to exploit not only the economic but also the social and cultural potential of urban archaeology.

INTRODUCTION

Reviewing archaeological approaches to medieval towns and urbanization over the last 50 years is inevitably an impressionistic exercise, and in this case the wider issues dominate: more specific topics, such as housing, industry, trade, have been considered elsewhere relatively recently (eg Schofield and Vince 2005). While it could be said that too much time is still spent on data processing and description rather than providing archaeologically based syntheses, an 'archaeological approach' to towns may even seem inappropriate. And yet some would argue that a specific disciplinary analysis of towns is redundant when the urban problematic can be studied through an integrated approach, perhaps most recently demonstrated by the *Cambridge Urban History*, where archaeologists and historical geographers as well as historians provide overviews (Palliser 2000a). Nevertheless, as will become clear, it is archaeologists' long-standing relationships with historians which remain the dominant influence, with consequently less input from archaeologists and anthropologists who study the urban phenomenon cross-culturally, often in a more theoretically-informed way.

THE STATE OF PLAY — A VIEW

Historians' approaches to medieval towns have been hugely influential. Towns are now commonly accepted as part of the feudal world (rather than 'non-feudal islands') and so the relationship between town and country has become an important research goal for all (Hilton 1992). Our appreciation of the degree of urbanization has also increased. Whereas emphasis was previously on the legal and constitutional status of towns as boroughs, we now accept there were considerably more settlements of a diverse occupational character which had no such special status, but nevertheless contributed sufficiently to craft production and exchange to rank as part of the country's urban structure. The best evidence for these small-scale towns comes from 14th-century taxation records, especially the poll taxes, but it is assumed that such places had existed for at least a century before (Hilton 1975). Small towns probably had a population between 500 and 2000, and there were about 860 of them in Britain. Their recognition has thus given the British urban structure a very broad base — perhaps half of the urban population lived in small towns (C Dyer 2000, 508). It also means that a higher proportion of the population lived in towns. We are accustomed to thinking of 10% of the Domesday population living in towns, but by 1300 this had risen to 20%, which was maintained until the early 16th century (Holt 2000, 103–104; Palliser 2000d, 130).

The estimated size of the larger towns has also increased. By *c*1300 London had 80,000 people and Norwich 20,000; that this may have been the case earlier is suggested by some Domesday urban entries which are regarded as under-estimates. These revisions serve to emphasize not only London's clear dominance, but also that it was the only place in Britain that matched in size the major cities in Europe — another signal that the British urban structure was different from that of Europe (Holt 2000, 103, 83).[1]

The increase in medieval towns is of course a direct consequence of redefining them: occupational diversity has become the urban touchstone reflecting the dominant emphasis on the economic aspects of the town. However, attention has also been drawn to the social distinctiveness of towns: townspeople felt themselves to be different from outsiders, and this issue of identity takes us away from the modern taxonomic debate and could help us directly to address the concerns of medieval townspeople (eg Reynolds 1977, ix–x). FitzStephen's description of 1170s London concentrates on its social and religious, as opposed to its economic, life (C Dyer 2005, 315). And it may be a commonplace, but the debate about what a town was, or should be, is longstanding; it was integral to medieval town development, and so an element of the contested past and as such should continue to preoccupy us (Carver 1993, 1–5; Lilley 2002, 9–10, 21–25).

Urban historians' research themes have been recently summarized as: the extent of continuity in the post-Roman period; the nature of urban revival in the 8th to 10th centuries; feudalism and towns; the nature of urban communities; the role of women; the existence of urban oligarchy; and the extent of late medieval urban decline. The list is an historiographical and methodological comment on the practice of urban history: it reflects its cooperation with other disciplines, and contemporary concerns as well as those issues that first emerged in the 19th century (Palliser 2000b, 10; Reynolds 1992).

Those of the archaeologist betray a similar methodological and historical gestation, for example: post-Roman continuity; the issue of origins, which while relevant for most of the Middle Ages, has tended to concentrate on the pre-Conquest centuries; the physical expression of their vested interests in towns by particular groups in medieval society, both the secular and religious aristocracy; those who processed raw materials, manufactured commodities and traded them, and those who supervised and regulated them; and the spatial arrangements of towns, ranging from properties, buildings and backs, to streets and open spaces. The aim of reconstructing urban living conditions requires interdisciplinary cooperation, particularly with environmentalists, as does the concern to identify, characterize and provide a chronology for short- and long-term periods of urban change. Inevitably these topics are more descriptive and reflect the circumstances of data-retrieval. Most urban excavations have been development- rather than research-led, and this has been the case during the three phases of urban archaeological effort, from excavations prior to the post-war urban reconstruction (1946–*c* 1970) to the large-scale excavation of areas to be redeveloped in the cities, following the Winchester initiative, and further encouraged by developer funding (1970–80s). From 1990 (1994 in Scotland) and PPG16, the greater emphasis on preservation and mitigation strategies has resulted in a proliferation of small-scale evaluations, infrequently followed by larger-scale excavations (Schofield and Vince 2005, 1–20; Gerrard 2003, 94–99, 133–138, 185–186). We are still absorbing and processing (in some cases still waiting for) the data from the 1970–80s, and while the value of evaluations is still debated, the cumulative results have yet to be assessed for any one town. Despite calls for a research-led urban archaeology, most archaeological effort remains essentially a reaction to the destruction of urban deposits (eg Carver 1993, 1–18; Perring 2002, 92–134).

We are also still living with the legacy of an archaeological bias towards the large towns, even though half the urban population lived elsewhere. Despite two generations of urban assessments/'implications reports', small towns remain under-appreciated. Post-PPG16 has seen more archaeological attention paid to smaller towns, especially those in the Scottish Highlands, but the task of synthesizing the information remains. Small towns continue to be the most appropriate places for some urban research (Schofield and Vince 2005, 16; Astill 1985; Dyer 2003; Carver 1993, 78–83).

It is also in the smaller towns where we are most aware of the advances in topographic analysis. The simplistic plan analyses of entire towns, using the common classification of 'organic' and 'planted' towns (even the *Historic Towns Atlas* has not escaped criticism), has given way to a more detailed analysis of street, plot and building plans which has allowed the overall town plan to be interpreted as a sequence of 'plan units' giving us a much more sophisticated view of how towns changed and developed (Slater 2000, 106). This also allows us to recognize that there was a clear difference between urban aspiration (represented by the foundation of planned towns, for example) and actual urban achievement, and the probability that this latter process took a longer time. Regional patterns in town plans have been recognized, including the observation that boroughs often have a distinctive topography not shared by unchartered towns: this should encourage us to question long-held views and in this case to consider if boroughs were indeed distinctive, not only constitutionally but also in the nature of their urban fabric (eg Palliser *et al* 2000; Slater 2000; 2005; 2007). Some of the more theoretically informed work on towns stems from this research, as in the consideration of the non-economic factors that influenced the foundation and form of towns (eg Lilley 2002, 106–176; 2005).

Three major themes of archaeological concern are now presented: the sequence and pace of urban development; the character and social specificity of towns; and the relationship between town and country.

THE URBAN TRAJECTORY

Most discussions about urbanization are couched in terms of, first, a steady growth in the number of towns and, second, that each town becomes increasingly complex, as if in an evolutionary sequence — 'inexorable progress in English town life' (Carver 1987, 5).

This interpretation is also often apparent when the origins of towns are discussed: a 'proto-urban' phase is identified as if the inevitable outcome of this stage would be a town. There is thus a tendency in the literature to assume that the town is a natural 'climax' in the development of medieval settlement and that all discussions about urbanization should be predicated on this assumption. The exception to this 'steady growth' interpretation of urbanization occurs in the later Middle Ages with the debate about the role of the town in the 14th and 15th centuries (Astill 2000a; Lilley 2000; A Dyer 2000). The exception is significant because it underlines how much our interpretation of the urban sequence is dependent on demography, which, it is usually thought, featured continuous population growth from at least the 11th to the eve of the 14th century. The common interpretation is also partly explicable because our over-riding concern is to look at urban development, often over a long time span, and so we naturally concentrate on the successful cases. However, in any discussion about the rapid proliferation of new towns in the later 12th and 13th centuries, for example, we naturally acknowledge the potential for, and actual, urban failure in the face of too much local competition (eg Blair 2000, 264–270). Recent work on demographic trends might encourage us to think about towns in terms other than continuous growth: we might allow for times of stasis or even contraction;

instead towns might have experienced 'a veritable switchback from high investment to insidious blight from the tenth century to the twentieth' (Carver 1987, 59). That there might have been a delay in population growth until the last two decades of the 12th century, prefaced by at least a century of little and/or slow growth, should encourage us to re-examine the archaeological information (Langdon and Masschaele 2006).

THE CHARACTER OF MEDIEVAL TOWNS

Our preoccupation with continuous urban 'progress' might also be partially explained by our principal concern with the town as an economic entity. However, even if one disagrees with defining towns by using bundle criteria, it is important to remember that towns performed a variety of non-economic functions — to put it crudely, as centres of strategic importance or of political or secular or religious authority. A town's character, or indeed stage in its life-cycle (and it was a medieval conceit to portray the town as a body in need of protection), may depend on which of these particular attributes was dominant (eg the discussion in Carver 1993; Rosser 2000, 341). We are more prepared to accept these considerations during the formation of a town rather than when it has reached its maturity, but is this justifiable?

The importance of the town as a political and ideological statement is rarely emphasized. The theoretically informed debates about the development of the state as a complex social organization in other areas of archaeology and anthropology have had little impact on the study of medieval towns, partly because they have been regarded as inappropriate or expressed in terms that make their relevance to the Middle Ages difficult to appreciate. Historians' work on the importance of the monarchy in the development of the Anglo-Saxon state, and in particular the development of taxation, has been more influential (Campbell 1994; Hutcheson 2006). Royal occupation of the centres of old Roman towns, while not as currently popular as an ecclesiastical explanation for the revival of these towns as centres of authority, should not be discounted. Although still debated, most discussions about the origins and development of the emporia, for example, allow for royal involvement. Royal intervention is more clearly seen in the creation of the burhs in Wessex in the later 9th century (eg Palliser 2000c, 21–24; Scull 1997; Hinton 2000, 225–230). They were specifically sited for strategic purposes and stemmed, and then reversed, the Viking advance. The royal initiative was clearly militarily successful in a very short time, but what effect did the burhs have on their localities?

In the case of Mercia, fortification occurred at places that were already (or shortly to become) centres of county administration and taxation, and so were important tools for the exercise of royal power (Dyer and Slater 2000, 614–616). The process became more marked immediately after the Norman Conquest with the concentration of secular and religious power in one place and symbolized by the overwhelming constructions of castle and cathedral (Astill 2000b, 42–46). Once built into the structure of royal government, this urban relationship continued for the rest of the Middle Ages, and partly explains why British towns had less independence than their counterparts in Flanders, Germany or northern Italy. And unlike these regions, too, Britain had fewer towns with bishops as their lords — the king was the immediate lord of all the major towns (Palliser 2000d, 128–129). Royal interest in towns is occasionally recognized in archaeological interpretations, such as the effect of meetings of parliaments, councils or royal visits in York and Oxford and the reidentification of the Guildhall at Lincoln as Henry II's urban palace (Kemp and Graves 1996, 189–191; Dodd 2003, 59; Stocker 1991). We should, perhaps, bear this association more in mind, if only to acknowledge that such royal activity ensured a continued aristocratic interest and presence in towns.

One of the issues that continues to be debated is the extent to which, and for how long, the aristocracy was the initiator and the dominant consuming group (and therefore the driving force) in towns (it is curious that the 'agency' debate was confined to the countryside, and not carried into the towns. See Jones and Page 2006, 228–231 for a recent summary). On the one hand there are those who argue that the aristocracy was merely one of the many groups who had recourse to towns from the 8th century, and this mixed demand, articulated by the market, was present throughout the Middle Ages. Another view, reviving late 19th/early 20th-century work, sees the aristocracy (including the king) as being the essential prime mover in town creation and the sustaining influence for a considerable time, until the majority of the population had a need for centres of exchange and production, perhaps as late as the last two decades of the 12th century (eg Russo 1998; Astill 2000b). A town's impact on the countryside between the later 9th and 11th centuries may have been minimal. The aristocracy, with their scattered estates, could have used non-market exchange systems which potentially supported early medieval towns. The emporia and the subsidiary collection centres of *villae regales* and minsters, may, for example, have been supported by the surplus generated from estates and tribute. Similarly, the burhs with their garrisons could have been manned and victualled from the aristocracy's estates. That the aristocracy had a clear interest in the burhs is reflected in the grants of holdings — the 'urban manors' — and they also became royal agents — moneyers and borough reeves. The similarity of coin loss between 'thegnly' rural residences and the burhs, and that those two types of site were also the location for metalworking, particularly whitesmithing, suggests that the scale of such industry was more appropriate to a patron rather than a wider clientele that would be expected in fully developed towns. We should, then, consider whether it is possible to distinguish the effects of the different groups within the aristocracy on urbanization. In some towns, for example Worcester, thegnly interest in the city was waning by the later 11th century, also the time when some thegns were pursuing their own urban initiative by founding small boroughs (see Astill 2006 for a fuller discussion).

Aristocratic involvement is most obvious from the later 11th to 13th century in the surge of new towns, some of which failed from their over-provision. Recent work on towns in the context of colonization in south Wales and Ireland provides other reasons for arrested urban development. In late 12th-century Ireland, aristocratic town foundation formed part of the Norman colonization process, but many towns failed to make the transition from being a symbol of feudal overlordship, and therefore merely satisfying aristocratic demands, to acting as centres for the marketing of agricultural surpluses from the surrounding regions. By the later 13th century as much as 80% of the country still had no access to an urban and trading network, with the result that many towns failed during the later medieval contraction in the Irish agricultural economy (Clarke 2000).

In Wales, excavations have demonstrated the abandonment of burgages in Norman castle towns, probably as a result of attacks by the native Welsh, from the late 13th century. The ceramic evidence points to a very restricted trading area with no access to national or international commerce. Again, as with the Irish evidence, we have cases of faltering urbanization where contacts with the locality or beyond were not sufficiently developed to sustain continued urban growth (Murphy 2000). South Wales appears to have been similar with a relatively undeveloped urban structure. Much land was used for rough grazing and the local population had little use for currency or pottery. Marcher lords created the towns as part of a manorialized landscape, but again the towns failed to develop sufficiently to make themselves indispensable to the local population. A similar case has been made for the Edwardian castle towns from the later 13th century (Courtney 2005). While these different urban experiences are related to colonization, we should consider if there are other parts of the country that were not colonized but had similar urban experiences.

Who made use of the towns? We have already asked who initiated towns, but now need to consider whether their use changed after establishment to involve more groups. Over most of northern Europe the role of a secular authority appears to be a major stimulus, at least from the 9th century (Clarke and Ambrosiani 1991, 173–175). As mentioned above, the town could be seen as a political centre, and was developed as a means to disseminate an ideology and bureaucracy associated with a nascent state. In some cases, it might be argued that such settlements were superimposed on a landscape whose inhabitants had already devised a system of exchange which satisfied their social, economic and administrative needs. It was therefore a case of finding a way of integrating these 'royal' towns into a region in order to ensure their existence and purpose. Some towns may have remained a superficial part of the settlement and economic pattern until the early 13th century, as shown by the Welsh and Irish cases above. The question thus becomes: when did towns cease to be aristocratic preserves and become relevant for the majority of the population?

TOWN AND COUNTRY

How we should contextualize towns? The relationship between towns and the countryside is usually interpreted economically; it has already been suggested that such a relationship could change dramatically in a relatively short time. We should, however, consider alternative approaches. In other regions of Europe, for example, a distinction has been drawn between the process of town growth and that of urbanization. The town is seen as part of a developing power structure and it was therefore one means by which political control was exercised. It follows then that in such circumstances towns have to be seen in the context of how other central places develop that have an importance in that power structure. We cannot understand the genesis of towns without taking into account how the political — or indeed the economic — network was articulated in order to achieve this urbanization (eg Andersson 2003, 312–316).

In the later Saxon period, what we could call urban functions (when using bundle criteria) may well have been distributed among several settlements in the same region, none of which could be regarded as a fully-fledged town. In some areas, north Wiltshire for example, the religious and secular sites were in separate places at a distance from the economic centre (Astill 1991, 113). In some parts of the country these elements of an urban identity did not come together until after the Norman Conquest, as a result of political rather than economic fiat (Astill 2000b, 42–46). But was this process irreversible? In times of political or economic stress was there a possibility of urban functions fragmenting? This is certainly the case if we consider the changing patterns of the trading network (see below). It also means that it is important to investigate discontinuities in the urbanization process, and not always assume that the urban network came into being relatively early and remained fixed for most of the Middle Ages.

TOWN AND COUNTRY — THE URBAN NETWORK

In the 8th and 9th centuries the urban character of the country was determined by the emporia which were served by high-status sites, both secular and religious, which acted as collection centres for the onward transport of agricultural surpluses, giving a basic two-part exchange structure (Astill 2000b, 30–34). More recently this structure has expanded with the recognition of the 'productive sites' and potential beach market sites. The productive sites remain problematic, but they are often interpreted as fairs, many of which were attached to minsters or perhaps royal sites; in the latter case they may also have functioned as taxation centres (Pestell and Ulmschneider 2003; Hutcheson 2006, 74–92). This rudimentary exchange structure is different from that in contemporary Francia, one of the most commercially developed parts of Europe, where a three-level exchange network has been proposed. The most basic and longest-established were the estate centres, followed by the *portus*, that is the regional centres such as St Denis and Verdun which were mints, fairs and toll stations set in the major, north French, river valleys. At the estuaries of the rivers were the emporia, the least numerous element, but the most engaged with long-distance trade, and yet the shortest-lived. As yet, we do not seem to have evidence of *portus*-type settlements. The other main difference is that the Frankish structure continued, with the exception of the emporia, to influence the urban pattern for most of the Middle Ages (Verhulst 2000). In Britain the simpler structure seems to have been dismantled by the mid-9th century with the demise of the emporia and most of the productive sites and, while it is usually argued that minsters continued as exchange centres, we often have no evidence between their first documentary reference (usually 7th- or 8th-century) and when they became boroughs in the late 12th and 13th centuries (Blair 2000, 246–250; Astill 2000b, 27–30). Without the inland urban infrastructure that survived the emporia in Francia, it is possible that England had to develop a new exchange and urban framework after the 9th century.

That this was accomplished through royal initiative is normally assumed from the burh-building obligations developed in the Mercia of Offa and later in Wessex. While the dating of some Mercian fortifications is debated, for example the Hereford sequence, a similar situation exists in Wessex where many of the burh defences remain undated, except for the *terminus ante quem* of the Burghal Hidage (Hinton 2000, 222–225). The places listed in this document, most of which have been identified, were strategically sited and often on royal land: these included walled Roman towns and small-scale central places. In some cases, Somerset for example, burhs were located at a distance from the estate centres/central places, perhaps because they were strategically unsuitable. This reminds us that the Burghal Hidage is only a record of the defensive system at *c*914–918. The possibility that elements of the system could be abandoned according to changing military need should be borne in mind. The recommissioning of the South Cadbury and Old Sarum hillforts, or the Carisbrooke enclosure in the early 11th century, may signal that relocation of garrisons was more common than we have allowed for, and given the evidence of mints at some of these places, may argue that these changes had urban as well as military implications (Astill 2006, 240–243). The accepted division of the Burghal Hidage places into towns (or future towns) and forts, tends to emphasize the rigidity rather than the flexibility of the system and does not allow for the possibility (as with South Cadbury) that some of the forts may be embryonic towns (Biddle 1976, 124–127).

In this context the recent analysis of the urban network of the north-west is revealing. The importance of Chester for the region is clear, but the sites newly fortified by Aethelflaed, such as Eddisbury and Runcorn, seem to have been short-lived and replaced by others created by Edward the Elder — Thelwall, Manchester and Rhuddlan, the first of which remains unlocated (Higham 2007, 57–62).[2] While this might be interpreted as an indication of the economically undeveloped state of the north-west and the failure of some burhs to integrate into the local economy because they were not needed, it also points to the strategic flexibility that was necessary throughout the country at this time, which is difficult to disentangle because we have no successors to the Burghal Hidage. It nevertheless gives the impression that by the later 10th century (and perhaps considerably later) the urban network of the country had not become fixed.

In such regions, historical geographers often refer to a 'flat hierarchy' of towns suggesting a deviation from the norm in central place theory in the sense that there were lower-, middle- and upper-range places that articulated an exchange system. Such a hierarchical arrangement, with local, county and provincial centres, has been proposed on the basis of the AD 973–1066 coinage (Metcalf 1978). Central place theory has become the most influential way of conceptualizing the relationship between town and country. It has gained further credence from recent studies which demonstrate how trade was socially specific and hierarchically arranged and by the significant results of the London hinterland project (C Dyer 1989; Galloway 2000; 2005). It is thus important in outlining the economic relationships that sustained the core of the urban system. However, we also need to take into account the unstable elements that performed important short-term functions throughout the Middle Ages:

we have already referred to beach-markets and productive sites of the 8th and 9th centuries, but to these we must add the fairs, an important addition to the urban 'hierarchy' of the 12th and 13th centuries that mostly ceased a century later; similarly, we need to investigate those villages with markets. It might be time to consider if it were possible for a 'core' urban system to survive without additional, albeit short-lived, peripheral trading places, let alone the 'informal' trading that took place at a sub-institutional or group level (Gardiner 2007; C Dyer 1994).

By concentrating on the hierarchical nature of trade we are in danger of underestimating the importance of small-scale exchange systems for particular localities, systems which did not articulate with the higher-order centres, as in the Fens and in the coastal areas of the south-east. These networks have been described as 'dendritic' and offer an alternative to a hierarchical system (Spoerry 2005; Gardiner 2007). Such additional trading arrangements, with the under-recognized informal trade, blur the distinction between town and country. But we also need to investigate chronological change in these systems. Archaeologists should respond more to the debate concerning the extent to which the market was the dominant exchange system by *c*1300 and whether the influence of the towns on the general economy by then has been over-estimated (eg Britnell 2000). We must also remember that, while central place theory is a way of interpreting economic relationships, it does not necessarily help us interpret social or cultural relationships (below).

TOWN AND COUNTRY — EXCHANGE

As archaeologists we may not be sufficiently aware of the uncertainties about how commodities were exchanged. We rely to a great extent on ceramic distributions, such as that of Ipswich ware, which have made a big impact on our understanding of both exchange and urban catchments (Hinton 2005, 90–92). We have been less sure about using coinage, which is not necessarily surprising given that after over 30 years there is still no agreement whether the numismatic information for the pre-Conquest period is evidence for a highly monetized and market-based economy, described with modern-sounding, formalist, terms such as 'balance of payments deficit' or 'trade surplus', or indicates a more socially embedded system where transactions had little independent economic significance — the substantivist view (Blackburn 1991, 539). The huge fluctuations in the volume of coinage, such as the peak in sceatta use *c*700–750, were unsurpassed until at least the 1180s. Numismatists usually relate such trends common to northern Europe to the availability of silver, but they could also mask significantly different factors within particular countries which nevertheless produced a similar result (Blackburn 1993). Surely, such discussions should have a profound effect on how we appreciate the process of urbanization? One view is that a money economy did not exist in this country until the second half of the 13th century, in other words significantly later than all the periods of urban growth that have so far been identified. In this case a 'money economy' comprised a mutual interaction of the money supply, the bullion supply, a market economy, international trade, record-keeping, legal protection for debts and the transferability of debts

(Bolton 2004). While it would be impossible to evidence some of these aspects for earlier centuries, others could be used as important guides to levels of urbanization.

For example, one ongoing discussion is the extent to which burhs were performing urban functions from the 9th century. Those who argue for a short chronology of growth see the burhs as both forts and towns at the same time virtually from their creation. Others want to separate the urban and military functions and argue that there is little archaeological evidence for an urban character until the later 10th or 11th century. While it is difficult to get an impression of the activity of particular mints before the AD 973 reform, the similar pattern of coin loss between the burhs and excavated secular estate centres suggests that both types of site had a similar level of economic activity. Even Winchester and London had low levels of coin loss until the late 10th and early 11th century, when there is renewed evidence for long-distance trade in London. The rebuilding of defences, usually dated to the 11th century, at Wareham, Wallingford, Cricklade and Christchurch, is generally seen as a response to the renewed Scandinavian raids and settlement. However the refurbishment, for the first time in stone, could be read as an indication that these burhs were developing a new sense of identity that differentiated them from the countryside (Astill 2006).

The urban experience further north does not allow for a long period of development but rather shows intense activity from the later 9th century, reflected in the increased output from the Danelaw mints and Chester in particular (Astill 1991, 109–112). This emphasises how important it is to develop work on regional variation in town development, and perhaps return to such questions as the Scandinavian influence on towns. The relative urban activity between regions needs to be assessed, identifying periods where there was a more intensive blurring of the town/country division, and when there was a relative change in the activity of small compared to larger towns. This issue is particularly relevant for the 14th to 16th centuries and would allow a more significant archaeological contribution than simply trying to test the existence of a late medieval decline (Astill 2000a).

THE FUTURE?

One disadvantage of thinking in terms of town–country relations is to treat the elements as if they were in binary opposition; this fails to acknowledge similarities. For example, the current economic emphasis on urbanization tends to exaggerate the exchange and production aspects and consequently minimises a town's agricultural involvement. Many urban industries, of course, were based on rural surplus which it is often assumed was brought over some distance. It is, however, important to remember that the towns were often sustained by their own fields and commons that formed an important intermediary zone.[3] But British towns could not match the formalized and controlled inter-relationship some European cities had with their territory — the *contado* or *umland*. Yet the environmental work that has been most successful in demonstrating town–country relations should perhaps be re-evaluated so that some assessment of the towns' own agricultural resources could be made (Perring 2002, 34–46, 116–127). The social and economic distinctiveness of the

immediate surroundings of a town should receive more attention. Those urban churches whose parishes stretched into the extramural countryside would be worth study, perhaps in a similar way to those settlements surrounding towns which had an unusually high number of cottagers or small-holders in Domesday (Baker and Holt 1998, 209–213; Dyer 1985)). This immediate area seems to have been the main source of recruitment for a town to maintain its size — at least a third of the urban population in the later Middle Ages comprised first- or second-generation immigrants from local villages (Dobson 2000, 284). And it was these villages close to towns which appear to have been particularly vulnerable to shrinkage or even desertion in the 14th and 15th centuries (Palliser 1988, 18). Similarly the tendency for charitable institutions to concentrate in the peripheral areas, often at the very edge, of towns in pastoral and watery locations has most often been studied in terms of their liminality, but the social and bucolic distinctiveness of these zones would reward further investigation (Rawcliffe 2005).

Chronological variation in the intensity of urbanization — or, indeed, de-urbanization — also merits further study. The 11th century, for example, needs more archaeological attention, not only in terms of changes in the urban network but also in the extent to which the urban fabric was altered. The possibility of a revised demographic profile of the 12th century should also encourage us to re-examine the admittedly scant archaeological material for that century. Can we track any change in the relative intensity of industrial processes? Our appreciation of metalworking, for example, seems to be based more on by-products (in residual contexts which often indicate reuse) rather than the actual areas of the activity (Astill 1993, 272–273). Indeed, the whole issue of zoning of activities, or indeed the location of ethnic or religious groups within towns and how these changed through time, should be reopened (Holt 2000, 92–94; Hinton 2003). In this connection a more general enquiry into the evidence for relative and chronological change in the character of different parts of a town — and not just intramural and suburban areas — would be welcome — in the way that has been suggested for late-medieval Coventry, using a combination of archaeological and topographic evidence. This study is important because it looks at social as well as economic trends, in this case, for example, the marginalization of the poor (Lilley 2000).

Archaeologists should also be adept at looking at the cultural importance of towns. The role of towns in developing timber-framed buildings has recently received attention, as has the way an urban mentality influenced the development of forms of commemoration (Pearson 2005; Badham 2005). Detailed studies of aspects of material culture have again provided an alternative view to the economic, central-place, role of towns in showing that these settlements were part of a more general cultural province that extended over northern Europe (eg Hall 2001; Hall 2005). The potential for integrating the material culture of the household with the buildings remains largely unrealized.

There is also the related and fundamental need to investigate the religious life of the town. The impact of saints' cults and the town as pilgrimage centre should broaden our research horizons (eg Dobson 2000, 285–286). The work on burials within monasteries should be extended to the parish churches, in itself a neglected part of the urban archaeological scene, particularly as Britain was unusual in the extent of parochial provision within towns (Gilchrist and Sloane 2005; Tatton-Brown 1998; Barrow 2000, 134). Such churches might also yield evidence for the wide diversity of religious practice in late medieval towns (Rosser 2000, 349). The implications of change of location or indeed abandonment of religious institutions, as occurred in such towns as late medieval Newcastle or Norwich, need attention (Butler 1987, 169). And, perhaps most importantly, the aftermath of the Dissolution and its effect on the urban fabric was profound and can be seen in Chester; this is a theme which would bring the study of smaller and large towns together (Ward 1990).

Lastly, the town can be approached as a location where there were conflicting and contested identities. Towns were such heterogeneous places, and the potential for friction and open violence was always close to the surface. Cultural historians have made us aware of how much civic ritual and even dress codes were developed in order to contain and limit conflict (Rosser 1998). The examination of identity, as expressed for example in guild halls, could be extended to other urban buildings, including the parish church, and combined with an analysis of how particular groups moved through towns and used both buildings and the spaces in between on market days and festivals (Giles 2000; 2005).

This is an ambitious agenda, but its combination of social and cultural aims, as well as the economic, might exploit more fully the remarkable potential of the urban archaeological record.

NOTES

[1] A view first expressed by an Italian dignitary in *c*1497; Sneyd 1847, 42.

[2] Similar shifts are proposed in Devon and Wiltshire, but are mainly unsubstantiated: Astill 2006, 242.

[3] An example of why Tait's work (1936) is still important.

BIBLIOGRAPHY

Andersson, H, 2003 'Urbanisation', in K Helle (ed), *The Cambridge History of Scandinavia*, 1, 312–342, Cambridge University Press, Cambridge

Astill, G, 1985 'Archaeology and the smaller medieval town', *Urban History Yearbook*, 46–53

Astill, G, 1991 'Towns and town hierarchies in Saxon England', *Oxford Journal of Archaeology* 10, 95–117

Astill, G, 1993 'Metalworking at Bordesley and elsewhere: a review of the evidence', in G Astill, *A Medieval Industrial Complex and its Landcape: the Metalworking Watermills and Workshops of Bordesley Abbey*, 272–291, Council for British Archaeology Research Report 92, York

Astill, G, 2000a 'Archaeology and the late-medieval urban decline', in Slater (ed) 2000, 214–234

Astill, G, 2000b 'General survey 600–1300', in Palliser (ed) 2000a, 27–50

Astill, G, 2006 'Community, identity and the later Anglo-Saxon town: the case of southern England', in W Davies, G Halsall and A Reynolds (eds), *People and Space in the Middle Ages 300–1300*, 233–254, Brepols, Turnhout

Badham, S, 2005 'Evidence for the minor funerary monument industry 1100–1500', in Giles and Dyer (eds) 2005, 165–196

Baker, N, and Holt, R, 1998 'The origins of urban parish boundaries', in Slater and Rosser (eds) 1998, 209–235

Barrow, J, 2000 'Churches, education and literacy in towns', in Palliser (ed) 2000a, 127–152

Biddle, M, 1976 'Towns', in D Wilson (ed), *The Archaeology of Anglo-Saxon England*, 91–150, Methuen, London

Blackburn, M, 1991 'Money and coinage', in R Mckitterick (ed), *The New Cambridge Medieval History, Volume II c700–c900*, 538–559, Cambridge University Press, Cambridge

Blackburn, M, 1993 'Coin circulation in Germany during the early middle ages: the evidence of single-finds', in B Kluge (ed), *Fernhandel und Geldwirtschaft: Beitrage Zum Deutschen Mundzwesen*, 37–54, Sigmaringen, Mainz

Blair, J, 2000 'Small towns 600–1270', in Palliser (ed) 2000a, 245–272

Bolton, J, 2004 'What is money? What is a money economy? When did a money economy emerge in medieval England?', in D Wood (ed), *Medieval Money Matters*, 1–15, Oxbow, Oxford

Britnell, R, 2000 'Urban demand in the economy', in Galloway (ed) 2000, 1–22

Butler, L, 1987 'Medieval urban religious houses', in J Schofield and R Leech (eds), *Urban Archaeology in Britain*, 167–176, Council for British Archaeology, London

Campbell, J, 1994 'The late Anglo-Saxon state: a maximum view', *Proceedings of the British Academy* 87, 39–65

Carver, M, 1987 *Underneath English Towns*, Batsford, London

Carver, M, 1993 *Arguments in Stone. Archaeological Research and the European Town in the First Millennium*, Oxbow, Oxford

Clarke, H, 2000 'Decolonization and the dynamics of urban decline in Ireland, 1300–1550', in Slater (ed) 2000, 157–192

Clarke, H, and Ambrosiani, B, 1991 *Towns in the Viking Age*, Leicester University Press, Leicester

Courtney, P, 2005 'Urbanism and "feudalism" on the periphery: some thoughts from Marcher Wales', in Giles and Dyer (eds) 2005, 65–84

Dobson, B, 2000 'General Survey, 1300–1540' in Palliser (ed) 2000a, 273–290

Dodd, A, 2003 *Oxford before the University*, Oxford Archaeology, Oxford

Dyer, A, 2000 ' "Urban decline" in England, 1377–1525', in Slater (ed) 2000, 266–288

Dyer, C, 1985 'Towns and cottages in eleventh-century England', in H Mayr-Harting and R Moore (eds), *Studies in Medieval History Presented to R.H.C. Davis*, 91–106, Hambledon, London

Dyer, C, 1989 'The consumer and the market in the later middle ages', *Economic History Review* 42, 21–37

Dyer, C, 1994 'The hidden trade of the middle ages', in *Everyday Life in Medieval England*, 283–303, Hambledon, London

Dyer, C, 2000 'Small towns 1270–1540', in Palliser (ed) 2000a, 505–540

Dyer, C, 2003 'The archaeology of medieval small towns', *Medieval Archaeology* 47, 85–114

Dyer, C, 2005 'Conclusion', in Giles and Dyer (eds) 2005, 313–321

Dyer, C and Slater, T, 2000 'The midlands', in Palliser (ed) 2000a, 609–638

Galloway, J (ed), 2000 *Trade, Urban Hinterlands and Market Integration c1300–1600*, Centre for Metropolitan History, London

Galloway, J, 2000 'One market or many? London and the grain trade of England', in Galloway (ed) 2000, 23–42

Galloway, J, 2005 'Urban hinterlands in later medieval England', in Giles and Dyer (eds) 2005, 111–130

Gardiner, M, 2007 'Hythes, small ports and other landing places in later medieval England', in J Blair (ed), *Waterways and Canal-building in Medieval England*, 85–109, Oxford University Press, Oxford

Gardiner, M and Rippon, S (eds), 2007 *Medieval Landscapes*, Windgather, Macclesfield

Gerrard, C, 2003 *Medieval Archaeology. Understanding Traditions and Contemporary Approaches*, Routledge, London

Gilchrist, R and Sloane, B, 2005 *Requiem: The Medieval Monastic Cemetery in Britain*, Museum of London Archaeology Service, London

Giles, K, 2000 *An Archaeology of Social Identity: Guildhalls in York*, British Archaeological Reports 315, Oxford

Giles, K, 2005 'Public space in town and village', in Giles and Dyer (eds) 2005, 293–311

Giles, K and Dyer, C (eds), *Town and Country in the Middle Ages. Contrasts, Contacts and Interconnections, 1100–1500*, Society for Medieval Archaeology Monograph 22, Maney Publishing, Leeds

Hall, M, 2001 'An ivory knife handle from the High Street Perth Scotland: consuming ritual in a medieval burgh', *Medieval Archaeology* 45, 169–188

Hall, M. 2005 'Burgh mentalities: a town-in-the-country case study of Perth, Scotland', in Giles and Dyer (eds) 2005, 229–250

Higham, N, 2007 'Changing spaces: towns and their hinterlands in the north west, AD 900–1500', in Gardiner and Rippon (eds) 2007, 57–72

Hilton, R H, 1992 *English and French Towns in Feudal Society: a Comparative Study*, Cambridge University Press, Cambridge

Hilton, R H, 1985 'The small town as part of peasant society', in R H Hilton, *The English Peasantry in the Later Middle Ages*, 76–94, Oxford University Press, Oxford

Hinton, D, 2000 'The large towns 600–1300', in Palliser (ed) 2000a, 217–244

Hinton, D, 2003 'Medieval Anglo-Jewry: the archaeological evidence', in P Skinner (ed), *Jews in Medieval Britain*, 97–112, Boydell, Woodbridge

Hinton, D, 2005 *Gold and Gilt, Pots and Pins*, Oxford University Press, Oxford

Holt, R, 2000 'Society and population 600–1300', in Palliser (ed) 2000a, 79–104

Hutcheson, A, 2006 'The origins of King's Lynn? Control of wealth on the Wash prior to the Norman Conquest', *Medieval Archaeology* 50, 71–104

Jones, R and Page, M, 2006 *Medieval Villages in an English Landscape*, Windgather, Macclesfield

Kemp, R and Graves, P, 1996 *The Church and Gilbertine Priory of St Andrew, Fishergate*, Council for British Archaeology, York

Langdon, J and Masschaele, J, 2006 'Commercial activity and population growth in medieval England', *Past and Present* 190, 35–82

Lilley, K, 2000 'Decline or decay? Urban landscapes in late-medieval England', in Slater (ed) 2000, 235–265

Lilley, K, 2002 *Urban Life in the Middle Ages 1000–1450*, Palgrave, Basingstoke

Lilley, K, 2005 'Urban landscapes and their design: creating town from country in the middle ages', in Giles and Dyer (eds) 2005, 229–250

Metcalf, D, 1978 'The ranking of boroughs: numismatic evidence from the reign of Ethelred II', in D Hill (ed), *Ethelred the Unready*, 159–212, British Archaeological Reports 59, Oxford

Murphy, K, 2000 'The rise and fall of the medieval town in Wales', in Slater (ed) 2000, 193–213

Palliser, D, 1988 'Urban decay revisited', in J Thompson (ed), *Towns and Townspeople in the Fifteenth Century*, 1–21, Sutton, Stroud

Palliser, D, 2000a (ed), *The Cambridge Urban History of Britain*, 1, Cambridge University Press, Cambridge

Palliser, D, 2000b 'Introduction', in Palliser (ed), 2000a, 1–16

Palliser, D, 2000c 'The origins of British towns', in Palliser (ed) 2000a, 17–26

Palliser, D, 2000d 'Towns and the English state, 1066–1500', in J Maddicott and D Palliser (eds), *The Medieval State. Essays Presented to James Campbell*, 127–146, Hambledon, London

Palliser, D, Slater, T and Dennison P (eds), 2000 'The topography of towns 600–1300', in Palliser (ed) 2000a, 153–186

Pearson, S, 2005 'Rural and urban houses 1100–1500: "urban adaptation" reconsidered', in Giles and Dyer (eds) 2005, 43–64

Perring, D, 2002 *Town and Country in England: Frameworks for Archaeological Research*, Council for British Archaeology Research Report 134, York

Pestell, T and Ulmschneider, K, 2003 'Introduction', in T Pestell and K Ulmschneider (eds), *Markets in Early Medieval Europe: Trading and Productive Sites, 650–850*, 1–11, Windgather, Macclesfield

Rawcliffe, C, 2005 'The earthly and spiritual topography of suburban hospitals', in Giles and Dyer (eds) 2005, 251–274

Reynolds, S, 1977 *An Introduction to the History of English Medieval Towns*, Oxford University Press, Oxford

Reynolds, S, 1992 'The writing of medieval urban history in England', *Theoretische Geschiedensis* 19, 43–57

Rosser, G, 1998 'Conflict and political community in the medieval town', in Slater and Rosser (eds) 1998, 20–42

Rosser, G, 2000 'Urban culture and the church 1300–1540', in Palliser (ed) 2000a, 335–370

Russo, D, 1998 *Town Development in Early England, c400–950 AD*, Greenwood Press, Westport, CT

Schofield, J and Vince, A, 2005 *Medieval Towns: the Archaeology of British Towns in their European Setting*, Equinox, London

Scull, C, 1997 'Urban centres in pre-Viking England?', in J Hines (ed), *The Anglo-Saxons from Migration Period to the Eighth Century: An Ethnographic Perspective*, 269–310, Boydell, Woodbridge

Slater, T (ed), 2000 *Towns in Decline AD 100–1600*, Ashgate, Aldershot

Slater, T, 2000 'Understanding the landscape of towns', in D Hooke (ed), *Landscape: the Richest Historical Record*, 97–108, Society for Landscape Studies Supplementary Series 1

Slater, T, 2005 'Plan characteristics of small boroughs and market settlements: evidence from the midlands', in Giles and Dyer (eds) 2005, 23–42

Slater, T, 2007 'The landscape of medieval towns: Anglo-European comparisons', in Gardiner and Rippon (eds) 2007, 11–26

Slater, T and Rosser, G (eds), 1998 *The Church in the Medieval Town*, Ashgate, Aldershot

Sneyd, C (ed), 1847 *A relation or rather a true account of the island of England*, Camden Society Publications 37, J B Nichols and Son, London

Spoerry, P, 2005 'Town and country in the medieval Fenland', in Giles and Dyer (eds) 2005, 85–110

Stocker, D, 1991 *St Mary's Guildhall, Lincoln*, Council for British Archaeology, York

Tait, J, 1936 *The Medieval English Borough. Studies on its Origins and Constitutional History*, Manchester University Press, Manchester

Tatton-Brown, T, 1998 'Medieval parishes and parish churches in Canterbury', in Slater and Rosser (eds) 1998, 236–271

Verhulst, A, 2000 'Roman cities, *emporia* and new towns (sixth–ninth centuries)', in I Hansen and C Wickham (eds), *The Long Eighth Century*, 105–120, Brill, Leiden

Ward, S, 1990 *Excavations at Chester, the Lesser Medieval Religious Houses: Sites Investigated 1964–1983*, Grosvenor Museum, Chester

CHAPTER 13
HOUSING CULTURE: SCANDINAVIAN PERSPECTIVES

By Else Roesdahl

This article surveys traditions and recent trends in the study of housing culture in the Scandinavian countries, and discusses aspects based on selected recent research from Denmark, Norway, Sweden, Iceland and Greenland. Examples cover the period from the Viking Age to the late Middle Ages and are drawn from excavations, standing buildings, artefacts preserved in churches, building reconstructions (real and virtual), experimental work and contemporary pictorial representations. There were many different house types and the topics discussed include: function of rooms (social and practical); heating; the number of people in houses; regionality; identities, tradition and innovation; furniture, furnishing and children; and the impact of European ideas.

INTRODUCTION

Fifty years ago an article entitled 'Housing culture' would have been thought hardly a proper publication for the Society for Medieval Archaeology. The concept did not exist in our subject. But interest in what we today call housing culture is far from new. The first volume of the Society's journal, for example, had several articles on buildings and their social interpretation (1957). The same interest was present in Scandinavia at that time, and indeed at a much earlier date.

There is no exact definition of housing culture — the general idea being (in short) that houses can be 'read' as a mirror of aspects of society, as their physical appearance derives from the life lived in them. At the same time, housing culture structures that life. As Matthew Johnson wrote (1993, x): 'houses are seen as part of a material and symbolic framework for the everyday actions that created history'. The concept is of course linked to that of 'the archaeology of space', and to analytical methods like 'access analyses' and 'feature analyses' (see, for example, also Grenville 1997; Carelli 2001; Roesdahl and Scholkmann 2007). The theoretical apparatus, then, is fairly new and based on the considerable amount of data now available — with its possibilities of raising and sometimes answering complicated questions.

Fifty years ago and for a long time after, one of the great challenges in medieval archaeology was to produce data and chronologies. Many remember the time when it was extraordinarily interesting when an excavation revealed the plan of an entire building (not just a corner of it), while many of us have also seen the development from small confined digs to large-scale excavations of complete villages or parts of towns. We have also seen a revolution in the archaeology of standing buildings, and have followed the gradual development from interest in plans and construction methods of buildings, to house typologies, to a more general interest in their function, and to the function of individual rooms — taking into account *in situ* artefacts and ecofacts, and the context within the plot, the settlement structure and so on. Further, we have witnessed a revolution in the use of natural sciences — now so important in defining the function of rooms and much else.

The erection of many full-scale reconstructions of buildings has greatly helped our understanding of how such buildings actually functioned and were inhabited; or, indeed, how they were not lived in. The clutter of things seen in a photo from the 1970s (Figure 13.1) clearly does not show what the interior of a 9th-century Hedeby house originally looked like. Re-enactments can also show how a building might actually function in certain circumstances.

A unique opportunity to observe how a great hall functioned occurred in 1986 when the Queen of Denmark inaugurated the reconstruction of a 30m long-house at the Viking fortress of Fyrkat (Schmidt 1994, 61–66, 89–128, fig 43). In the 18m-long hall, the Queen was seated on a fine chair on one of the platforms, opposite the central fireplace, while the rest of us — more than a hundred people — sat on benches elsewhere on the platforms, according to rank. In front of everybody was a long narrow table. A meal was served by waiters moving freely on the vast floor space; a space which was later used by those who wanted to pay their respect to the Queen. Crossing the floor, they had conversations with her in full view of the assembly. It was like theatre — had there been performances by poets and acrobats, the illusion of a Viking feast would have been almost perfect. The design of a Viking hall is, indeed, splendidly suited to formal performances, and this particular hall is regularly used as a theatre space, with great success.

'SCANDINAVIAN' PERSPECTIVES

Despite the title of this article, I doubt if there are distinct Scandinavian perspectives. Each Scandinavian country (according to one definition Denmark, Norway and Sweden) has its own research tradition and agenda. Further, housing culture varied greatly within this vast area, which spans half of Europe's length from north to south. The climate varies, and there are mountainous regions as well as highlands and lowlands. It covers densely settled and (eventually) highly urbanized areas, as well as vast unpopulated tracts. Scandinavian societies were differently structured, and the natural resources, including building materials, differed enormously. Norway, for example, always had an abundance of good timber. Local traditions and foreign contacts also varied. And then there is also another Scandinavia — the Faroe Islands,

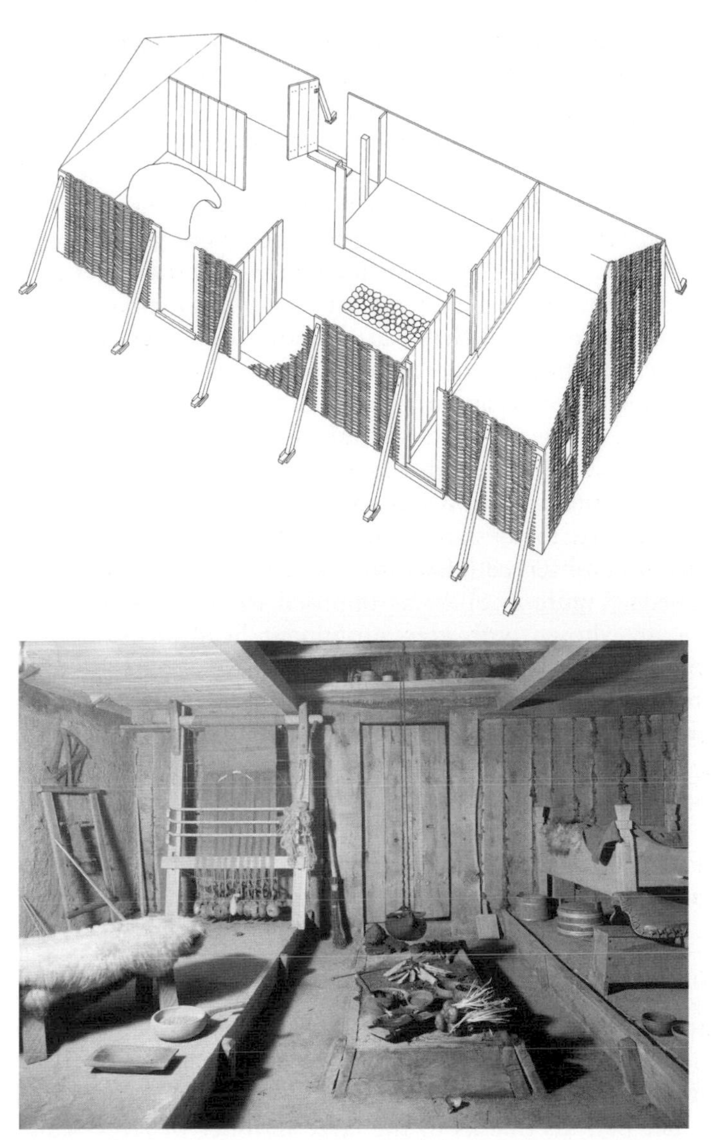

FIGURE 13.1 Above: reconstruction of a town house excavated at Hedeby, North Germany. Measuring 5m × 12m, it had walls of wattle and daub on a timber frame. The roof was supported by outer posts buttressed against the long walls. The house had a middle room with a hearth and wide platforms along the walls, and two gable rooms, one of which had a domed oven or stove. There were three outer doors. One gable had a small window. According to dendrochronology the house was built in AD 870 and repaired and slightly changed in 882. Below: the middle room of the full-scale reconstruction of the house at the Moesgaard Museum, with a selection of furniture and fittings. The bed, however, would almost certainly not have belonged to a house of this type and size, and most of the other objects hardly illustrate where such types were used. (Drawing courtesy of Archäologisches Landesmuseum, Schloss Gottorf, Schleswig; photograph courtesy of Moesgaard Photo/Media department, 1970s)

Iceland and Norse Greenland ('at the End of the World'), where entirely new settlements grew up in the late 9th and late 10th centuries. Finland in many respects had its own cultural characteristics and like the Faroes is not discussed here. The housing cultures reflect all this variety (cf Roesdahl and Scholkmann 2007).

But Scandinavia also shared some general similarities. First, unlike many other parts of Europe, there was no Roman building tradition, Scandinavia being far beyond the *limes*. Second, many housing features were gradually introduced from central and western Europe from the 12th century onwards, such as stone and brick buildings and modern heating systems (stoves, wall-fireplaces, and hypocausts), which allowed for heated, smokeless 'sitting rooms'. New types of household goods, as well as furniture and fittings were also introduced from there. We can hardly point to a single technological or design innovation of Scandinavian origin.

In some places, however, as in Iceland, there was a continued development of traditional house types — at least for some time (Stenberger 1943; see also below). Scandinavian ornamental tradition was sometimes continued on furniture (Roesdahl 2000) and, interestingly, the design of beds seems to follow particularly strong local traditions. It has been observed (Haastrup 2003, 216f) that Danish representations of late medieval beds (Figure 13.2) — as opposed to pictures of beds from south of Scandinavia — are shown with very prominent head-posts, even when a Danish picture is otherwise closely based on a European print. This love of prominent head-posts can probably be traced back to the 9th and 10th centuries, when such beds (with animal head-posts) are known from the Oseberg and Gokstad ship burials in southern Norway. But why did Scandinavian beds retain this old feature, whereas nearly everything else became European? It may be suggested that beds were particularly linked to concepts of family, tradition and identity — being the place where marriage was consummated, happy times were spent, and children conceived and born (Roesdahl 2002; 2003, 238).

SOURCES AND RESEARCH

Crucial to Scandinavia is the quality of the available sources, particularly those concerning medieval housing in the countryside. Such sources are scanty nearly everywhere after the 11th to 12th centuries. A great deal of evidence is available concerning earlier periods thanks to the large number of large-scale excavations of Iron-Age and Viking-Age farms and villages, although this evidence largely consists of information about plans, house-construction and settlement structure. Excavations of later medieval farmsteads in Denmark, Norway and Sweden are few (surveys in Hvass 1993; Porsmose 1993; Øye 2002, 276–294; Ekroll 2006, 85–98). A good recent example is a farm excavated at Tårnby, Sjælland, Denmark. Its development and elements of its housing culture could be traced from the 12th to the early 19th century (Svart Kristiansen 2005). It had been hoped to develop this work through renewed study of Axel Steensberg's extensive excavations of Danish farms and villages in the 1950s and 1960s, but this was not possible as their documentation is too ambiguous (Svart Kristiansen, forthcoming).

FIGURE 13.2 Mural in Sæby Church, North Jutland, Denmark, *c*1510. A man lies dying in a fine bed, the head and foot posts of which are adorned with rounded extensions, which seem to be a Scandinavian fashion. The man's soul is taken by the devil, while an angel sadly watches: the man and woman next to the bed are probably the widow and her lover. (Photograph: Else Roesdahl 2005)

Today the best Scandinavian, and probably the best European, evidence for housing culture on farms comes from Norse Greenland (although evidence from the early period is scarce). These farms were simply left to decay in the 14th and 15th century when the Greenland Norse disappeared — they probably sailed away or died. The collapsed turf walls and the permafrost ensured excellent conditions for the preservation of the abandoned buildings and the artefacts found there (Roussell 1941; Arneborg 1999; 2004).

We are far from being able to characterize the varied housing cultures of medieval Scandinavia. This is partly due to a lack of comprehensive research on the many scattered existing studies. But better data are needed. Fairly recent national and regional surveys have helped: articles on town houses in Sweden in their social perspective; on house structures, interior arrangements, and settlement patterns in a number of Scandinavian towns, and so on (eg *hikuin* 13, 1987; Thomasson 1997; Krongaard Kristensen 1999; Roesdahl 1999; Gläser 2001, 635–832). Further, in 2003 we published an anthology which dealt with topics of housing culture based on Danish material (Roesdahl 2003). Although written mainly by medieval archaeologists, it continued a strong Danish tradition of interdisciplinary cooperation, embracing contributions from students of prehistory, ethnology, history, art history, philology and architecture in discussing matters such as the role of family and household structure, concepts of private life, information from pictures and written sources, retrospective studies, and so on. This provides some basis for future work.

One urgent problem is the lack of a systematic terminology. In Scandinavia we have terms used only by archaeologists, others used by ethnologists, and a number of terms borrowed from Old Norse sources (which mainly relate to Iceland). Other terms are taken from a variety of Scandinavian law texts — while others are derived from English, German and French words. This causes much confusion.

SOME PERSPECTIVES: SELECT EXAMPLES

Functional partition of space in Viking Age houses

It has been known for a long time that the principal building of a Viking-Age farm normally had space for animals at one end, and a dwelling at the other, as for example at Vorbasse, Denmark. Further, it has also been known that the dwelling space was often subdivided and that one room had a central hearth (for example, Kaldal Mikkelsen 2003). Recently excavation and macrofossil analyses at Tæbring, Denmark, has shown that a room with a clay floor was used for food preparation (Figure 13.3); which is entirely logical, as this is often a messy activity (Mikkelsen, Moltsen and Sindbæk 2008).

This pattern has now been identified in a number of other places and has consequences for aspects of the housing culture: the number of people belonging to a

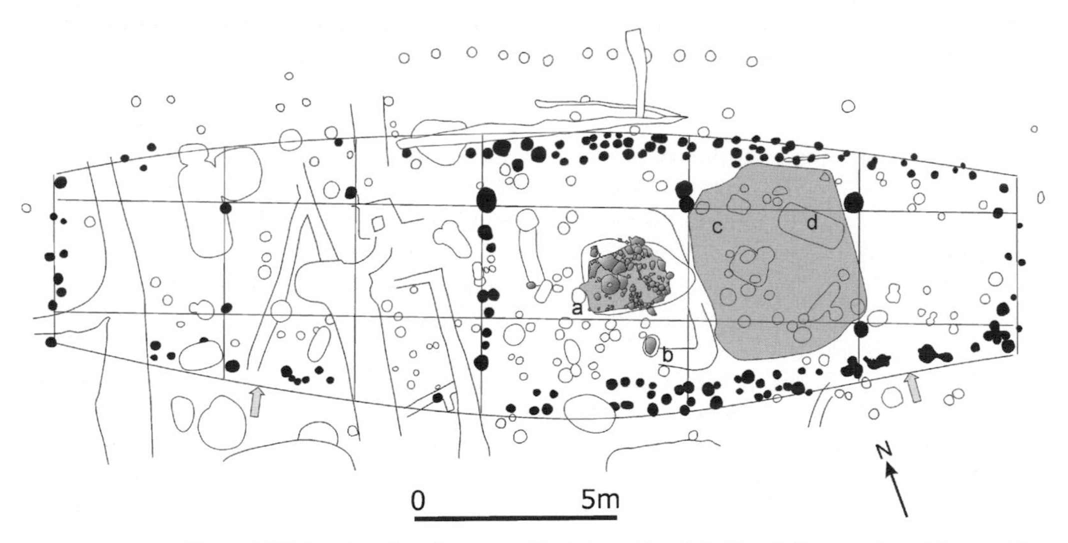

FIGURE 13.3 Plan of Viking Age farmhouse at Tæbring, North Jutland, Denmark, with several room divisions. Features interpreted as belonging to the building are marked in black. Entrances are indicated by arrows. The hearth in one room and the clay floor in the next room (used for food preparation) are shaded. a–d = find spots of a whetstone, two loom-weights and an arrowhead, respectively. (Drawing: Søren Sindbæk 2007)

household, their organization of the available space, and their degree of cleanliness. Indeed, from a functional point of view, considerable space would have been needed for many forms of food preparation and for food storage and, at aristocratic sites, for the preparation of big feasts with many guests. Strangely, this has rarely been fully realized. The Tæbring excavation further showed that there had been many outdoor activities of a domestic nature — a feature which was probably also common elsewhere.

In Iceland and Greenland there is a particularly strong tradition of extensive use of the natural sciences in archaeological investigations. This has produced results concerning the use of space within and outside houses from soil micromorphology, entomology, macrofossil analyses, zoology, and so on. In Reykjavík it has, for example, been shown that a 10th-century farmhouse was divided into many functional compartments (Figure 13.4). There was a central hearth, a raised platform on only one side, partitions around the entrance, separate spaces for storage, food preparation, crafts, and space for a few animals. This household is estimated to have consisted of only five to 10 people (Vésteinsson 2006; 2007) — far from the romanticized view of a large extended Viking family, but probably more realistic. The well-known Hedeby house (Schietzel 1984) (Figure 13.1) may have had a household of about the same size.

On heating and environmental conditions

In the Scandinavian winter efficient heating is of crucial importance, and various experiments, partly in full-scale reconstructions of buildings, have taken place in order to illuminate heating techniques and their effects on human beings. Such experiments may, at the same time, illuminate the function of certain elements of the house.

The Hedeby house (Figure 13.1) can be heated from its central hearth as well as by means of a dome-shaped stove/oven in one of the gable rooms. It appears that, when well fired, this stove/oven would keep the whole house warm for a long time and could be much more efficient than an open hearth. It also appears that while there is an unpleasant draught at floor level, the slightly raised platforms in the central room are comfortable areas of repose. These must be the places people spent their time working, sleeping and resting, while the floor would provide space for circulation, at the same time accommodating ashes and embers from the hearth, as well as other dirt, without risk (Roesdahl 1982, 110–113). This has consequences for concepts of the use of the interior of all houses with raised platforms and open hearths.

At Eketorp, on the island of Öland, Sweden, a group of young archaeologists once spent two weeks during winter in one of the reconstructed houses (of the period *c*400–650, when Eketorp was a fortified village). It was heated by an open hearth, and the effects of the heating methods and smoke on humans were studied. They began to suffer from a light smoke-poisoning — as was probably common in the past during hard winters when much time was spent indoors. It also became apparent that, because of the distribution of heat within the house, it was best to sleep about 1m above floor level where the temperature was comfortable and fairly stable. Interestingly, the tall beds known from the Oseberg and Gokstad burials would accommodate this (Herschend 1982). Related and well-documented experiments later took place at the Migration-period hall in Gene, northern Sweden and at the Lejre Experimental Centre in Denmark (Edblom 2004; Beck *et al* 2007).

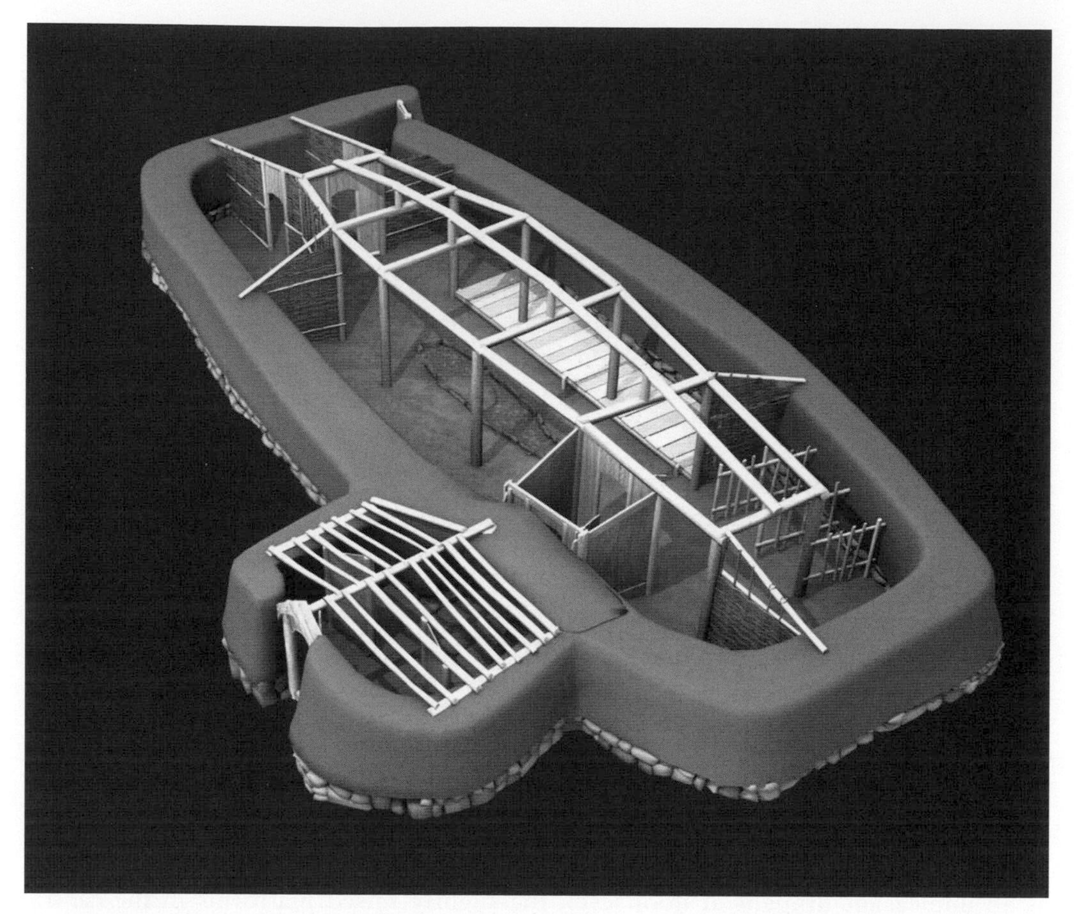

FIGURE 13.4 Digital reconstruction of a 17m-long, 10th-century farmhouse in Aðalstræti, Reykjavík, showing one interpretation of the use of space. The house was built on a timber frame covered with turf walls and had a long central hearth. Along one side was a wooden platform. Various activities, including food preparation had taken place along the other side of the room. A few animals were housed in the space to the right, but the actual byre was elsewhere. (© Gagarín)

But not all heating produced smoke. In Iceland, the natural hot and warm springs and pools were probably already used for baths and bathing by the early settlers. In the 13th century stone constructions were made in order to use these geo-thermal resources for bathing at the grand farm of Reykholt, probably by the chieftain and poet Snorri Sturluson. It has also been suggested that hot water might have been led into the house itself to provide some sort of central heating (Sveinbajrnardóttir 2005).

Recent research and test results further suggest that turf houses in North Norway and in the North Atlantic lands were deliberately built over the ruins of earlier turf houses. Over time this would develop into a settlement mound of highly organic soil; the houses would thus benefit from the natural heat produced by the humus. This contradicts traditional ideas that turf constructions and farm mounds were expressions of marginality and of a lack of timber. Instead, they probably demonstrate some awareness of a useful environmental system (Mook and Bertelsen 2007).

Settlers in Iceland

Icelandic archaeology is particularly concerned with 'beginnings', and in recent years intensive archaeological activity has produced crucial new information on how the incomers, arriving in the late 9th century, tackled the problems of settlement. It appears that all datable so-called 'hall-buildings' (over 20 have been excavated) are from the mid- to late 10th century or later, and are of typical Norse design. The incomers, once well established, probably wished to demonstrate a cultural unity and identity in the new land, as well as links to their origins. The beginnings seem, however, to have been humble (as in mid-west America in the 19th century). In some places it has been shown that the hall was preceded simply by a series of sunken-featured buildings (Vésteinsson 2004; 2006; 2007. For an alternative interpretation of the houses of the settlers, see Ólafsson 2008). Interestingly, this feature is not mentioned in the proud and somewhat later Icelandic literature!

Greenland farms

In Greenland (settled *c*985 from Iceland) the beginnings may have been as humble as in Iceland, but so far there is hardly any evidence to support such a statement. The earliest hall-buildings are of 11th-century date and, as in Iceland, typically Norse. A fine example is that from the Western Settlement, 15km from the inland ice, at a site called 'The Farm beneath the Sand'. It was excavated in the 1990s when threatened by heavy erosion by a river; indeed, some of the complex had already disappeared (Arneborg and Gulløv 1998, 7–95; Arneborg 1999; 2004; Berglund 2000).

The first house had typical Norse features — a central hearth and low platforms along the walls of the main room — probably (as in Iceland) a symbol of Norse identity in a new society. By way of a series of complicated changes this hall-building later developed into a so-called 'centralized farm' (Figure 13.5), where all buildings were concentrated into one huge structure, sharing walls and heat. The various 'buildings' each had their own roof and were connected by internal passages; external doors were few. This farm-type was particularly common to Greenland's Western Settlement and possibly specific to Greenland, although the richest farms seem not to have adopted it (on farms and types, see Roussell 1941; Andreasen 1981; Arneborg 1999; 2004).

At 'The Farm beneath the Sand', which was finally abandoned in the late 14th century, the function of many rooms could be determined. It was also shown that functions often changed: a barn might change into a store room or a living room, and back again. This feature has now been observed elsewhere and was probably quite common, as it was in Scandinavia proper in medieval and later times. It was further shown that the farm was not in continuous use — again a feature seen elsewhere (Arneborg, pers comm). All this points to general changes in the use of rooms and buildings during the life-time of a farm; it also shows that the situation of a farm in

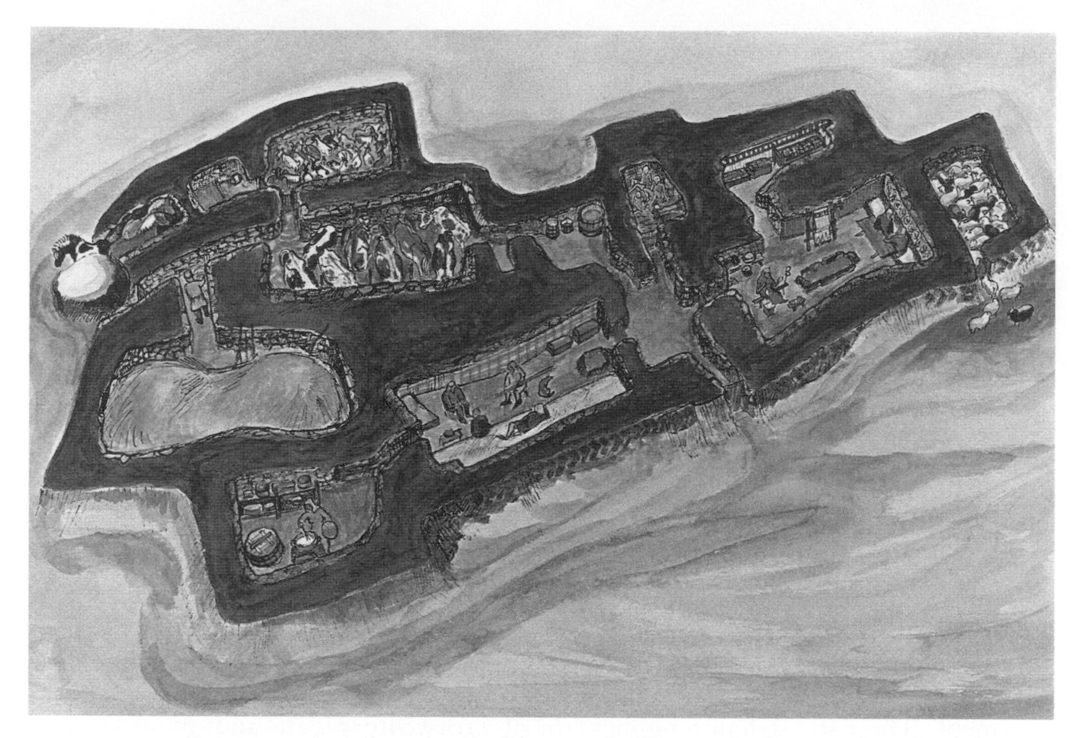

FIGURE 13.5 Reconstruction of a centralized farm at the Western Settlement, Greenland (V53c). A number of buildings with turf walls, each with its own roof, were concentrated into one huge structure. Most animals were in its north-western part, and the cows particularly were well protected against low temperatures. Other 'houses' were for human use. (Watercolour by Jens Rosing, after Rosing 1973)

Norse Greenland was not always stable. From this distant farm comes a series of exceptionally well-preserved artefacts — including a nearly complete loom, carefully decorated wooden objects and runic inscriptions — all signs of a distinctive Norse, as opposed to Inuit, culture.

Timbered houses in Norway — and identities

The town of Trondheim, Norway (the most northerly town in medieval Europe), would have had a very different housing culture. Large-scale excavations here and in other towns have revealed a large number of well-preserved timber buildings, on distinct plots, along streets, dated from *c* 1000 onwards (Figure 13.6) (Christophersen and Nordeide 1994; Ekroll 2006, 68–71, 113–130). On the basis of this massive evidence, questions of rural as distinct from urban identity have also been discussed, as well as the rise of a burgher identity in a country with few towns (Christophersen 1989; 2001).

The rich housing evidence from Norwegian towns is not yet fully researched, but it also appears to have crucial implications for the understanding of some fine farm-houses (some dated by dendrochronology), which were thought to reflect deep-rooted

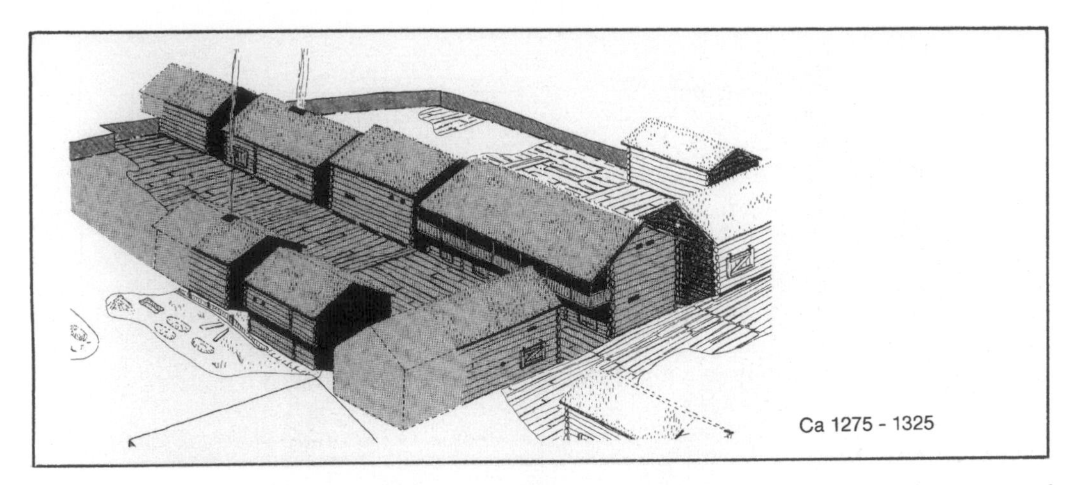

FIGURE 13.6 Plot structure with timbered town houses in medieval Trondheim. Reconstruction of one of the phases from the excavation at the Library Site, in the town centre. The buildings lining the street probably had shop-fronts. (after Christophersen and Nordeide 1994, fig 184)

national traditions. It has been pointed out, for example, that the so-called 'loft-houses' (Figure 13.7) must be based on the form of town houses, which in turn were inspired from abroad (Ekroll 2006, 52–53, 68–71, 93–99). So, sadly, no ancient Norwegian identity there!

Brick-built town houses in Denmark — and regional variety in a small country

The earliest remains of Danish brick houses are from the 13th century, while a fair number are known from the later Middle Ages; all are much rebuilt and restored (Krongaard Kristensen 1999; 2003). There is no evidence in modern Denmark of the Hanseatic *Dielenhaus* (and no good reason to suggest a 'Hansa identity'). Danish brick houses had different plan types, and the number of rooms increased here in the later Middle Ages, as elsewhere. There were spaces for a variety of purposes. Modern heating technology was introduced and, sometimes, an indoor toilet. Life became much more comfortable, and households would often be fairly small. But does this relate to developing wishes for 'privacy' and 'family life', as some would have it, or to developing desires for more comfort and international standards; or to both? Brick houses certainly provided stable physical frameworks for domestic life: room functions were not so easily changed, as they were in timber or turf houses which had to be regularly repaired or renewed. Did this new stability perhaps have consequences for a burgher mentality (eg Thomasson 1997; Roesdahl 1999; Poulsen 2003; Roesdahl and Scholkmann 2007)?

There appear to be some regional differences with regard to interior arrangements, particularly in the use of either stoves, or of wall-fireplaces: stoves were probably used mainly in eastern and northern Denmark, and fireplaces in western Denmark. This would accord with our knowledge of later Danish farmhouses, and with broader patterns in medieval Europe: stoves were mainly seen in central and north-eastern Europe (they originate in central Europe), and fireplaces in western

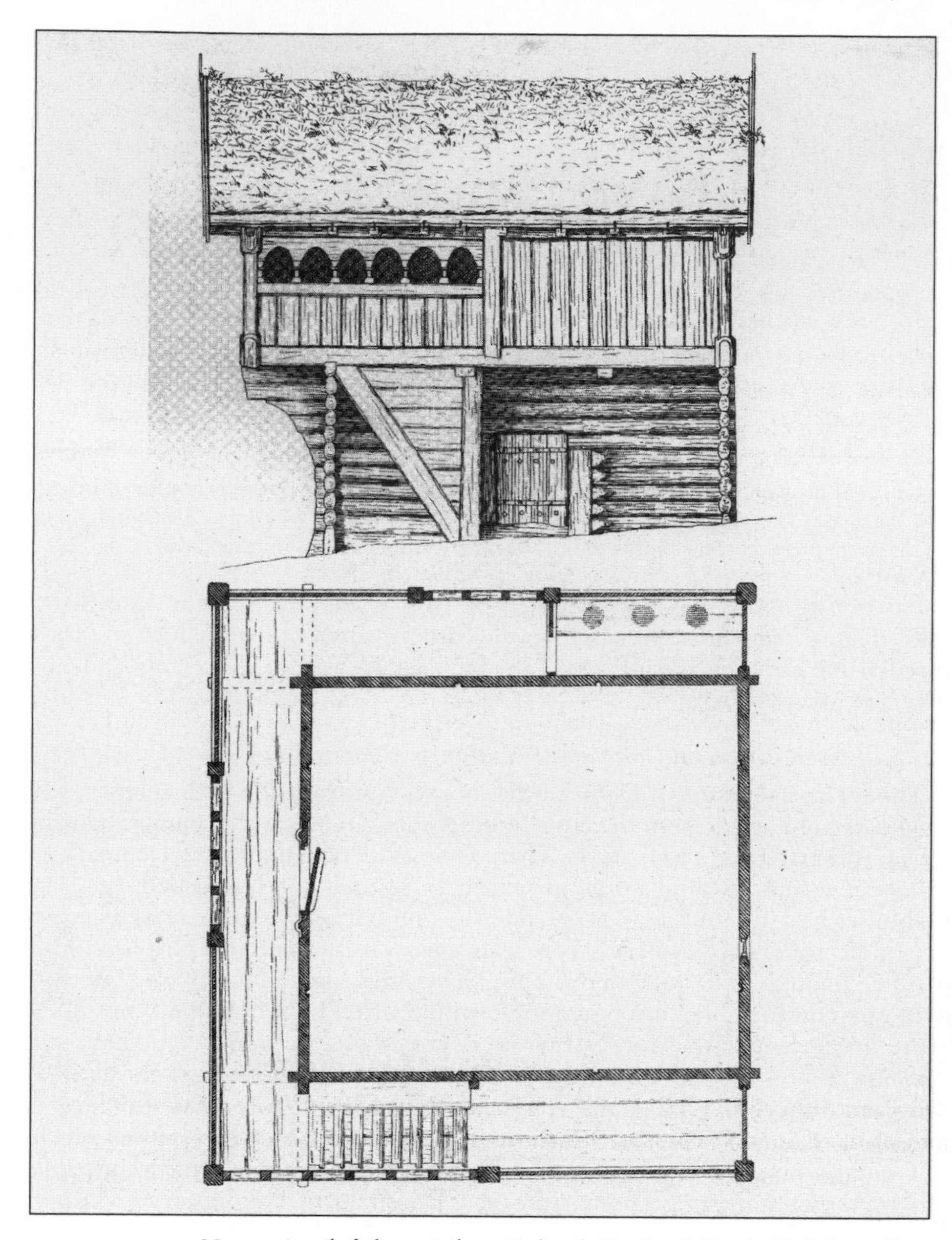

FIGURE 13.7 Norwegian 'loft-house', from Rolstad, Oppland, first half of the 14th century. This type of two- or three-storeyed building is preserved on some farms, but excavations show that earlier examples were in towns. Indeed, with its wider upper floor it seems designed for towns. This particular building had traces of benches along three walls of the windowless ground floor. The second floor had open galleries on three sides, with a three-seat latrine towards the rear. A door opens into a guest-room with traces of beds on three sides and a bench at the gable-end. (after Ekroll 2006, 95)

Europe (Krongaard Kristensen 1999; 2003; Stoklund 1969; general distribution map for stoves in Kristiansen 2003, fig 1).

Furnishing, and children

An important element of a housing culture lies in the furnishing of rooms, about which very little is known until the mid-15th century, when pictures of room interiors start to appear in some parts of Europe, but not yet in Scandinavia. Woodcuts from central and western Europe and some Flemish paintings are of particular interest to Scandinavia. To stimulate some discussion about the furnishing of late medieval sitting rooms in Danish towns, I have attempted a reconstruction (Figure 13.8).

It is based on the plan of a well-preserved and well-recorded late 15th-century brick-built town house in Kalundborg with a wall-fireplace (had there been a stove, the arrangements would have been different), and on 15th-century furniture and fittings known from Denmark and, in two cases, from western Europe. The

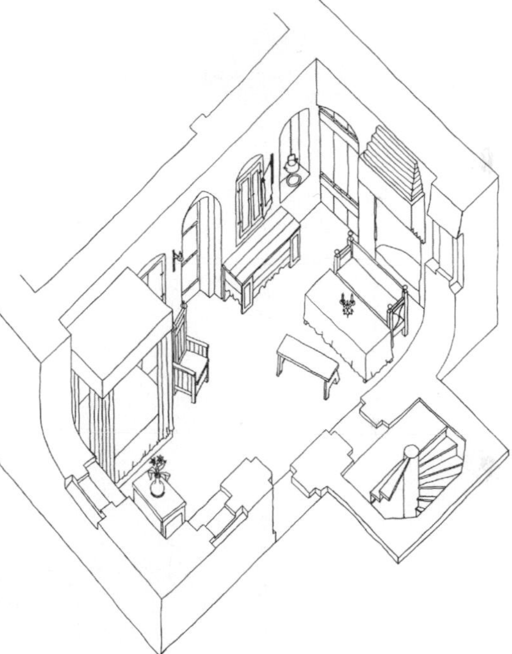

FIGURE 13.8 Left: brick-built house at Præstegade, Kalundborg, Denmark, seen from the yard, late 15th century. Probably the best-preserved medieval house in Denmark, it had two stories, a loft and a basement. The staircase-tower is reconstructed. The gable to the right shows traces of a lower side-building. The house was probably built by a priest. The ground-floor plan is unusual in that it is divided into a bigger room towards the yard and two smaller vaulted rooms towards the street. Right: suggested reconstruction of the interior of the larger room, which had a wall fireplace and several wall-niches. It was entered from the yard and had access to the side-building and to one of the smaller rooms. (Photograph: Else Roesdahl 2005; drawing by Heidi Maria Møller Nielsen, after Roesdahl 1999, 100)

arrangement of the furniture is based on the rather standard disposal seen in various west European pictures. One of these is the fine painting of the Annunciation by Robert Campin from Flanders, which is set in a burgher's sitting room, but which of course has symbolic elements (such as the white lily in the vase) (Roesdahl 1999; 2003). The reconstruction probably gives a pretty good idea of the appearance of a 'sitting room', or *stue*, of fairly wealthy late medieval Danish burghers, although it has been shown that this house, which has an unusual plan, probably belonged to a priest (on the house and its owner, see Krongaard Kristensen 2003, 172–174; 2007). Such rooms were furnished for comfort, and to show status and identity through the quality and ornament of the individual items.

In relation to this, attention should be drawn to the considerable corpus of early furniture dating from the 9th century and later from Norway and Sweden, which

FIGURE 13.9 Reconstruction (from the surviving back and side) of a child's chair from Lund, Skåne, Sweden, *c* 1050, with a doll. (Photograph: Annemarie Kruse 1992, Department of Medieval and Renaissance Archaeology, University of Aarhus)

derives from Viking burials and medieval churches. This material is little known in Europe, but provides information on cultural contacts, identities and much else, although more precise dates are often needed (Karlson 1928; Anker 1968; Roesdahl and Wilson 1992, cat nos 161–167, 561–566; Roesdahl 2002).

Special types of furniture relate to children, and such furniture seems to have been introduced into Scandinavia after *c* 1000, or at least became much more common at this time, which saw the introduction of Christianity. The same is true of toys. This may relate to new concepts of childhood, for which there is solid evidence. Archaeological remains of children's furniture are rarely found, but Danish finds include part of a cradle, two potty-stools and a chair (Roesdahl and Wilson 1992, cat nos 562, 566; Roesdahl 2003, 238–239, 243). As regards housing culture, a small chair (Figure 13.9) in which a toddler could be safely tucked to prevent it from crawling all over the floor and getting too close to the hearth, would surely ease the life of child-minders (the women).

FIGURE 13.10 Block print *c* 1475 by Hans Paur, Nuremberg. Twenty-four pictures of household equipment surround a young couple about to be married. The text above them explains the importance of the objects depicted and reminds us that they constitute only a tenth of what is necessary. The print is a visual variant of the detailed household poems and may have been meant as a didactic house ornament. The same types of objects would have been used in large parts of contemporary Scandinavia. (Photograph courtesy of Staatliche Graphische Sammlung, München)

CONCLUSIONS

We have come a long way in the study of housing cultures during the last half-century, both in Scandinavia and elsewhere. This field of study is promising and perspectives are manifold; there are many questions, some answers and a variety of ideas. Much remains to be done, but we can clearly see an increasingly strong 'Europeanization' of most aspects of housing culture. By the mid-15th century the housing culture of burghers would have had many features in common with housing cultures elsewhere in Europe north of the Alps. All the objects shown in a Nuremberg picture of *c*1475 (Figure 13.10) could probably be seen in many houses in contemporary Scandinavia, where a viewer would probably have a similar approach to the picture and its context. The scene portrayed belongs to the tradition of German *Hausratgedichte* (household poems) which spell out in versified detail the many practicalities needed before you marry (Assion 1981; Blosen 1993; 2003). Think, before you do it!

ACKNOWLEDGEMENTS

The author is most grateful to Jette Arneborg, Mette Svart Kristiansen, Søren M Sindbæk, and David M Wilson for discussion, comment and advice.

BIBLIOGRAPHY

Andreasen, C, 1981 'Langhus – ganghus – centraliseret gård', *hikuin* 7, 179–184 (English summary)

Anker, P, 1968 *Norske Møbler i fortid og nåtid*, Vestlandske Kunstindustrimuseum, Bergen, etc, Bergen, Oslo, Trondheim (English summary and captions)

Arneborg, J, 1999 'Nordboliv i Grønland', in Roesdahl (ed) 1999, 352–373

Arneborg, J, 2004 'Det europæiske landnam — Nordboerne i Grønland, 985–1450 e.v.t.', in H C Gulløv (ed), *Grønlands forhistorie*, 219–278, Gyldendal, København

Arneborg, J and Gulløv, H C (eds), 1998 *Man, Culture and Environment in Ancient Greenland*, Danish National Museum & Danish Polar Center, Copenhagen

Assion, P, 1981 'Hausratgedichte', in *Die deutsche Literatur des Mittelalters. Verfasserlexikon*, 2. Aufl. Bd. 3, 556–558, Walter de Gruyter, Berlin, New York

Beck, A S, Chrisdensen, L M, Ebsen, J, Larsen, R B, Larsen, D, Møller, N A, Rasmussen, T, Sørensen, L, Thafte, L, 2007 'Reconstruction — and then what? Climatic experiments in reconstructed Iron Age houses during winter', in M Rasmussen (ed), *Iron Age Houses in Flames. Testing House Reconstructions at Lejre*, 134–173, Studies in Technology and Culture 3, Historical-Archaeological Experimental Centre Lejre, Lejre

Berglund, J, 2000 'The farm beneath the sand', in W W Fitzhugh and E I Ward (eds), *Vikings. The North Atlantic Saga*, 295–303, Smithsonian Institution Press, Washington and London

Blosen, H, 1993 'Nürnberger Hausratgedichte: Hans Paur, Hans Folz, Hans Sachs — die beiden Ehen des Hans Sachs', in U Rautenberg (ed), *Über die Ehe. Von der Sachehe zur Liebesheirat. Eine Literaturausstellung in der Bibliothek Otto Schäfer, Scweinfurt*, 73–86, Schweinfurt

Blosen, H, 2003 'Senmiddelalderens tyske "Hausratgedichte"', in Roesdahl (ed) 2003, 283–292 (English summary)

Carelli, P, 2001 'Building practices and housing culture in medieval Lund: a brief survey', in Gläser (ed) 2001, 659–676

Christophersen, A, 1989 'Dwellings houses, workshops and storehouses. Functional aspects of the development of wooden urban buildings in Trondheim from c. AD 1000 to AD 1400', *Acta Archaeologica* 60, 101–129

Christophersen, A, 2001 'Bóndi, bæjarmaðr, burghere. Om folk, hus og fremveksten av urban identitet i norske byer ca 1000–1700', in A Andrén, L Ersgård and J Wienberg (eds), *Från stad till land. En medeltidsarkeologisk resa tillägnad Hans Andersson*, 51–62, Almqvist & Wiksell International, Stockholm

Christophersen, A and Nordeide, S, 1994 *Kaupangen ved Nidelva*, Riksantikvarens Skrifter nr 7, Trondheim (English summary)

Edblom, L, 2004 *Långhuset i Gene — teori och praktik i rekonstruktion* (Studia Archaeologica Universitatis Umensis 18), Umeå universitet, Umeå

Ekroll, Ø, 2006 *Ei anna historie — norsk mellomalder i arkeologisk lys*, Tapir akademisk forlag, Trondheim

Gläser, M (ed), 2001 *Lübecker Kolloquium zur Stadtarchäologie im Hanseraum* III. *Der Hausbau*, Hansestadt Lübeck, Lübeck

Grenville, J, 1997 *Medieval Housing*, Leicester University Press, London

Haastrup, U, 2003 'Interıørfremstillingeer i danske kalkmalerier — og forlæg', in Roesdahl (ed) 2003, 213–222 (English summary)

Herschend, F, 1982 'Att bo i den öppna spisen', *Fjölnir* 1:3, 66–83

hikuin 13, 1987. Middelalderlige stenhuse i danske og skånske købstæder, H Krongaard Kristensen and J Vellev (eds) (English summaries)

Hvass, S, 1993 'Settlement', in S Hvass and B Storgaard (eds), *Digging into the Past. 25 Years of Archaeology in Denmark*, 187–194, The Royal Society of Northern Antiquaries & Jutland Archaeological Society, Copenhagen

Johnson, M, 1993 *Housing Culture. Traditional Architecture in an English Landscape*, Smithsonian Institution Press, Washington, DC

Kaldal Mikkelsen, D, 2003 'Boligfunktioner i vikingetidens gårde', in Roesdahl (ed) 2003, 77–89 (English summary)

Karlson, W, 1928 *Studier i Sveriges medeltida möbelkunst*, Ph Lindstedts Universitetsbokhandel, Lund

Kristiansen, O, 2003 'Danske kakkelovne og deres billedprogrammer i 1. halvdel af 1500–tallet', in Roesdahl (ed) 2003, 259–282 (English summary)

Krongaard Kristensen, H, 1999 'Land, by og bygninger', in Roesdahl (ed) 1999, 55–81

Krongaard Kristensen, H, 2003 'Planløsninger i byernes stenhuse', in Roesdahl (ed) 2003, 169–192 (English summary)

Krongaard Kristensen, H, 2007 'Præstegadehuset i Kalundborg', *Årets gang på Kalundborg og Omegns Museum 2006*, 88–91

Mikkelsen, P, Moltsen, A S A and Sindbæk, S M, 2008 An archaeological and archaeobotanical study of three houses from Tæbring, north-western Denmark, AD 600–1100', *Acta Archaeologica* 79, 79–119

Mook, R and Bertelsen, R, 2007 'The possible advantage of living in turf houses on settlement mounds', *Acta Borealia* 24:1, 84–97

Ólafsson, G, 2008 'Ta din hall och gå — Med huset i släptåg', in C Paulsen and H Michelsen (eds), *Símunarbók. Heiðursrit til Símun V. Arge á 60 ára degnum*, 117–123, Faroe University Press, Tórshavn

Porsmose, E, 1993 'Rural settlement', in S Hvass and B Storgaard (eds), *Digging into the Past. 25 Years of Archaeology in Denmark*, 264–267, The Royal Society of Northern Antiquaries & Jutland Archaeological Society, Copenhagen

Poulsen, B, 2003 'Privatliv i middelalderens huse', in Roesdahl (ed) 2003, 31–45 (English summary)

Roesdahl, E, 1982 *Viking Age Denmark*, British Museum Publications, London

Roesdahl, E, 1999 'Boligernes indretning og udstyr', in Roesdahl (ed) 1999, 82–109

Roesdahl, E (ed), 1999 *Dagligliv i Danmarks middelalder — en arkæologisk kulturhistorie*, Gyldendal, København, 2nd edn, 2004, Aarhus Universitetsforlag, Århus

Roesdahl, E, 2002 'Danish Medieval furniture — regional or international?', in G Helmig, B Scholkmann and M Untermann (eds), *Centre · Region · Periphery. Medieval Europe Basel 2002* Vol 1, 218–220, Medieval Europe Basel, Hertingen

Roesdahl, E, 2003 'Møbler og indretning', in Roesdahl (ed) 2003, 223–246 (English summary)

Roesdahl, E (ed), 2003 *Bolig og familie i Danmarks middelalder*, Jysk Arkæologisk Selskab, Højbjerg (English summaries)

Roesdahl, E and Scholkmann, B, 2007 'Housing Culture', in J Graham-Campbell with M Valor (eds), *The Archaeology of Medieval Europe*. Vol 1. *Eighth to Twelfth Centuries AD*, 154–180, Aarhus University Press, Aarhus

Roesdahl, E and Wilson, D M (eds), 1992 *From Viking to Crusader. Scandinavia and Europe 800–1200*, Nordic Council of Ministers, Copenhagen

Rosing, J, 1973 *Ting og undere i Grønland*, Wormianum, Højberg

Roussell, Aa, 1941 *Farms and Churches in the Mediaeval Norse Settlements of Greenland*, Meddelelser om Grønland 89, København.

Schietzel, K, 1984 'Die Baubefunde in Haithabu', 'Dendrochronologische Gliederung der Baubefunde in Haithabu', in H Jankuhn, K Schietzel and H Reichstein (eds), *Archäologishe und naturwissenschaftliche Untersuchungen an ländlichen und frühstädtischen Siedlungen im deutschen Küstengebiet vom 5.Jahrhundert v. Chr. bis zum 11.Jahrhundert n. Chr.* Band 2. *Handelsplätze des frühen und hohen Mittelalters*, 135–158, 171–184, Deutsche Forschungsgemeinschaft, Bonn

Schmidt, H, 1994 *Building Customs in Viking Age Denmark*, Poul Kristensen, Herning

Stenberger, M (ed), 1943 *Forntida Gårdar i Island*, Munksgaard, København

Stoklund, B, 1969 *Bondegård og byggeskik før 1850*, Dansk historisk Fællesforening, København

Svart Kristiansen, M (ed), 2005 *Tårnby. Gård og landsby gennem 1000 år*, Jysk Arkæologisk Selskab, Højbjerg (English summaries and captions)

Svart Kristiansen, M, forthcoming 'Axel Steensbergs udgravning i Store Valby set med nutidens øjne. En analyse og dekonstruktion af de arkæologiske resultater', *Aarbøger for Nordisk Oldkyndighed og Historie* (English summary)

Sveinbjarnardóttir, G, 2005 'The use of geo-thermal resources at Reykholt in Borgarfjördur in the medieval period', in A Mortensen and S V Arge (eds), *Viking and Norse in the North Atlantic. Select Papers from the Proceedings of the Fourteenth Viking Congress, Tórshavn, 19–30 July 2001*, 208–216, Annales Societatis Scientiarum Færoensis Supplementum XLIV, Tórshavn

Thomasson, J, 1997 'Private life made public. One aspect of the emergence of the Burghers in Medieval Denmark', in H Andersson, P Carelli and L Ersgård (eds), *Visions of the Past. Trends and Traditions in Swedish Medieval Archaeology*, 697–728, Central Board of National Antiquities, Stockholm

Øye, I, 2002 'Landbruk under press 800–1350', in B Myhre and I Øye, *Norges landbrukshistorie* I, *4000 f. Kr.–1350 e. Kr. Jorda blir levevei*, 215– 414, Det norske samlaget, Oslo

Vésteinsson, O, 2004 'Icelandic farmhouse excavations. Field methods and site choice', *Archaeologica Islandica* 3, 71–100

Vésteinsson, O, 2006 'The building and its context', in B Sverrisdóttir (ed), *Reykjavík 871 ± 2. Landnámssýningin. The Settlement Exhibition*, 116–123, Reykjavík City Museum, Reykjavík

Vésteinsson, O, 2007 'The Icelandic house', in J Graham-Campbell with M Valor (eds), *The Archaeology of Medieval Europe*. Vol. 1. *Eighth to Twelfth Centuries AD*, 156, Aarhus University Press, Aarhus

CHAPTER 14
MATERIAL CONCERNS: NON-CERAMIC FINDS *c*1050–1500

By GEOFF EGAN

This paper looks at some broad developments and detailed changes and advances in dealing with and understanding non-ceramic finds from c1050 *to* c1500/50. *The main published resources are noted. Limitations and achievements are discussed and some possible future directions are indicated. Most categories of finds from the period have now been identified and their function defined at least at a basic level (a very few have had to be reclaimed from the Romanists or reinterpreted) and many have been researched in some depth. Developments across the traditional 1066 boundary need to be charted with a single narrative and the relatively few finds of 12th-century date particularly require more synthesis. Progress in the use of scientific techniques of analysis has been made with glassware and some metalwork, but further research beyond specific assemblages for the latter is limited (continual recycling of copper alloys may prove an insuperable complication), with pertinent questions still to be formulated. Such indications as there are suggest that marked regionality is evident in some everyday items like dress accessories in the earlier part of the period, but (in contrast with ceramics) this becomes less evident, with nationwide fashions the norm, though manufacture was probably undertaken in most towns. The Portable Antiquities Scheme has come to make an important contribution to the previously limited picture in rural areas. There remains a broad need for synthesis and use to be made of hidden gems in the grey literature.*

INTRODUCTION: RECEIVED WISDOM

The 50 years since the founding of the Society for Medieval Archaeology have seen sustained and very substantial advances in the study of later medieval material culture. There are several reasons for this. The profile of excavated assemblages from the period had previously been almost negligible. With the exception of the *London Museum Medieval Catalogue* (LMMC — Ward Perkins 1940) remarkably little by way of synthesis to help develop the subject had appeared in print since the pioneering efforts of antiquaries (for example, Syer Cuming 1851; 1855; 1858; 1862; 1863; 1867; 1868; 1869; 1870; 1878), often concerned with a single category of object, in the mid- to late 19th century. The LMMC, which deals almost exclusively with objects from London, stands out across Europe as the most successful of the early attempts at a synthesis primarily of excavated finds. Almost 70 years after its original publication it is the only academic volume to put so much of the subject matter into one set of covers (there were omissions and some of the dating has been tightened, but there are very few outright errors). John Ward Perkins travelled widely across northern Europe looking behind the scenes at major collections during its preparation. It remains in daily use (without textual revision) despite everything published over the intervening years and in demand as one of the principal places of first resort for researchers, which has ensured that it is still in print. On the Continent, a publication in 1933 on urban finds in Norway stands out as an even earlier synthesis, still of value, though it is not as comprehensively illustrated as later became the norm (Grieg 1933). In 1977 the first major finds publication to deal with a broad range of material culture categorized not by material, which had become the almost invariable tradition in the UK, but thematically by function (lighting equipment, dress accessories, etc) appeared (Baart *et al* 1977). It has many followers, particularly when dealing with large assemblages, but the basic criteria for categorization of finds remain a matter of individual preference.

This paper inevitably draws heavily in what follows on the writer's experiences, mainly in London, though a wider view has been attempted.

EXPANSION: THE RISE OF THE UNITS

The great expansion in staff numbers of those dealing full-time with finds from excavations was a consequence of the establishment of archaeological units in a number of major towns and areas through the 1970s. Plans for finds research were often on the grand scale — in the City of London the original aim was not only to publish everything, but to do this site by site in the order each was excavated — 'no excavation without publication'. This was laudable enough, and it took time to realize that it was completely impractical, and indeed that not every object recovered merited publication. In the event it was only the urban and some of the larger county units, especially those closely connected with museums, which developed an expertise in local non-ceramic finds. Compared with 10 years ago the number of full-time, in-house posts in this area is much diminished — a trend which continues. The smaller units bought in expertise from various consultants, and this looks set to continue.

SOME ACHIEVEMENTS OF THE PAST 50 YEARS

There are still difficulties with a 1066 Saxon/Norman divide: the use of the date 1050 as a nominal division is seen as more realistic in the present, very imperfect, state of knowledge of the precise dating of most changes in material culture around this time, despite the temptation to assign innovations to the influence of newly arrived

Normans. Approaches to the 'Cheapside Hoard' of unfinished pewter jewellery illustrate this, with some regarding it as the last of a Saxon tradition and others the start of a Norman one.[1] None of the related items of used jewellery more recently recovered in London provides a definitive answer (eg Egan 2007a, 350 fig 334). A few finds of Byzantine objects in England had until recently tended to be dismissed as deriving from recent collections. The discovery of a small number from deposits that were unquestionably medieval at Winchester and elsewhere now allows reassessment (Egan 2007b). Occasional 'loose' Byzantine finds elsewhere than from formally excavated strata are beginning to be seen as potential contemporary imports.

The recognition of the appropriate dating for some of the commonest later medieval objects, taken as read now, had still not been achieved just over four decades ago. As recently as the early 1960s it was possible for leading exponents to misinterpret some of the most common high-medieval buckle forms as Saxo-Norman items (eg Bu'Lock 1964, 25–5 and 22, fig 7, e–l).[2] An international survey of medieval buckles published in the early 1970s brought a more accurate appreciation of their chronology (Fingerlin 1971). It took large assemblages from urban excavations of the later 1970s and 1980s to establish the dating beyond question to the late 13th to early 15th centuries. A couple of discarded foundry assemblages have now shown how many of these familiar items were being produced by the same manufacturers, and the scale of mass production involved. A dozen oval and four rectangular standard designs for simple copper-alloy buckle frames have been identified as all potentially being produced together in the 14th century. Both foundry assemblages are from London, but similar if more restricted waste in York, Coventry, Dublin and continental centres from Toulouse in southern France, to Lund in Sweden, suggest that every city in western Europe might perhaps have produced a similar range (Egan 2007a, 463–464). A mould found discarded in a furnace in London demonstrates that 144 identical buckle frames (*c* 1kg of metal) were being cast together (Egan 2007a, 349). This was true mass production.

A broad picture for the use of lead/tin (pewter) in dress accessories is still emerging. It is already clear that from around 1050 decorative mounts, brooches and pins, often with green or yellow lead-glass stones, were available, probably into the 13th century (eg Egan and Pritchard 1991, 202–203, 256–257 and 274–275, nos 1094, 1344 and 1379, pls 4F and 6A; Egan 2007a, 319 fig 302 S9 and S23; 448–451). There seems to have been a hiatus or possibly just a period of low production for some reason for certain accessories (brooches in these metals continued to be manufactured, perhaps by new makers, who introduced a fresh tradition which continued separately from that of the other items). This was followed in the mid-14th century by a great expansion in the pewter repertoire, for the first time with buckles and strap-ends joining mounts, all in great variety in these metals (Egan and Pritchard 1991, buckles 102–106, mounts 190–205, strapends 149–154). These new products quickly gained great popularity, because of the ease with which they could be mass-produced with finely detailed decoration. The innovations seem to have begun before the Black Death, but subsequent economic conditions may well have fostered the market for such trinkets. It is difficult to point to any clearer archaeological evidence from urban assemblages of possible effects on material culture of this disaster, unless it may be in renewed ingenuity and diversification in the production of cheap goods of many kinds in the long-term.

A few received myths of dating have been set aside — copper-alloy mirror cases and the earliest thimbles have been reclaimed from the Roman period, and glass 'steeple' bottles (phials) together with most plain ivory combs are now seen as routine post-medieval items, while a much-cited group of lead crosses from a cemetery are now known to be of post-medieval date (Guildhall Museum Catalogue 1908, 61 no 109 and pl 24 no 1, mirror case described as a box; LMMC 1940, 291 and pl 88 no 1 comb — wrongly described as bone; LMMC 1940, 290 — cf Sloane and Watson 2005). A range of finds from Whitby Abbey originally published as Saxon is now seen as part of the common later medieval repertoire (Peers and Radford 1943).

In addition to the long-established standard works of first resort (the Guildhall Museum Catalogue 1908, the British Museum Medieval Catalogue 1924 and the LMMC) there are now a number of synthetic volumes on medieval finds in general, usually on urban assemblages, to help the generalist as well as the finds specialist seeking comparanda and other information. They are often parts of wider series or form single-volume reports on individual excavations, for example, on Colchester, Norwich, Southampton, Winchester, York, Dublin and Waterford (Crummy 1988; Margeson 1993; Platt and Coleman Smith 1975; Biddle 1990; Ottaway and Rogers 2002; Mould *et al* 2005; the *Medieval Dublin Excavations 1962–81* series B (the majority of these volumes cover a slightly earlier period than that considered here; for the most helpful from the present perspective, see Wallace 1988 and Halpin 2008), Hurley *et al* 1997; Bristol and Perth are yet to appear). Small towns are notoriously difficult in this regard. Ian and Alison Goodall have made a sustained, nationwide contribution, respectively on ironwork (eg I Goodall 1981, and in Biddle 1990) and non-ferrous metalwork (eg A Goodall 1981). There are, of course, also many volumes from Scandinavia and Russia to Iberia and Hungary covering comparable ranges of material on the Continent.

The influential seven thematic volumes of the *Medieval Finds from Excavations in London* series (Cowgill *et al* 1987; Grew and de Neergaard 1988; Egan and Pritchard 1991; Crowfoot *et al* 1992; Clark 1995; Egan 1998; Spencer 1998)[3] were born from the suggestion of Brian Spencer when viewing the first month's assemblage from the Swan Lane site recovered with the help of the local detectorists.[4] These relatively lavish publications (some single drawings of finely detailed leather knife scabbards individually took weeks to complete) could not with the resources currently available have been produced to the same standard today. This publication project was fortunate in its timing, its friends in high places within the Museum of London and in the archaeologists, mudlarks, researchers and illustrators, who combined to produce results that remain difficult to parallel in extent and scope in this subject. The range of pilgrim badges in the capital came as a revelation when they were first published (Spencer 1998). The volume in which they were presented built on those on collections in Norfolk and Salisbury (Spencer 1980 and 1990), as well as substantive contributions from the Continent, notably the Netherlands (*Rotterdam Papers* 1993 and 2001). Previously, the discovery of an ampulla was likely to appear at the end of the news on television, and excavated complete pilgrim badges stood a fair chance of being put on the front cover of an excavation report. They were seen as very special finds, and this remains in several ways true, but the recovery of literally thousands of the 14th/15th-century Becket-head badges mainly in London and Canterbury, but also much more widely, has given a new perspective on the mass consumption of these and other cheap religious trinkets (Spencer 2000, 322–324). This subject has subsequently expanded with monographs on individual cults and considerations of social, artistic and other aspects (eg Blick 2007).

The *Salisbury and South Wiltshire Museum Medieval Catalogues* series (Saunders and Saunders 1991; Saunders 2000 and forthcoming) are the only relevant English publications from the past 50 years that deal with an established museum collection (though much of the material included was acquired in the 1980s and 1990s). There are also some recent catalogues of generally upmarket material held in national museums, which are useful in their own right and for researching occasional finds of similar status (eg Stratford 1993; Lightbown 1992). The *Rotterdam Papers* series, several of which are devoted to non-ceramic medieval finds, have made an important contribution across much of north-west Europe on an international front (see those from the series listed in the bibliography). In addition to these main works there are a huge number of relevant books, and many papers in conference transactions and journals across Europe and beyond, not least those in the pages of The Society for Medieval Archaeology's journal *Medieval Archaeology* and its monograph series. The recent national surveys of medieval material culture presented as exhibitions have a significant lasting legacy in the lavishly illustrated catalogues of selected high-point objects with useful commentaries (Zarnecki *et al* 1984; Alexander and Binski 1987).

In the domestic sphere, the role of materials other than ceramics for vessels has become much clearer over the past 50 years. Observing the routine use of wooden vessels by the majority of medieval populations depends on relatively rare survivals in the ground of what escaped the ready fate of fuel for the fire, which means that this material is greatly under-represented in assemblages. There are now two general syntheses, both written by practitioners of turning: one focuses on finds from York but goes far beyond that, while the other is also national in scope and combines other insights with many attractive images of the grain of excavated vessels (Morris 2000; Wood 2005). The demise in the universal usage of treen tableware during the late medieval period into 16th century still needs to be charted in detail.

For medieval pewter, excavated finds from the past 50 years have been of the essence in reconstructing the range of wares in use from the 12th century to *c*1500 (Hornsby *et al* 1989). Apparently starting with a range of jewellery — brooches, decorative pinheads and mounts — in the late 11th century, the 1200s saw an expanded repertoire with household goods — candlesticks, mazer feet (for wooden bowls) and especially spoons (one London site produced over 30). This earliest domestic pewter (Egan 2000), all from the ground, has dense decoration in the form of panels of hatching, pellets, saltire crosses and arcs, covering the entire surface, and has therefore been called 'highly decorated'. These goods seem, with the exception of some of the jewellery which lasted into the post-medieval period, to have ceased to be fashionable in the early 14th century, when the plain wares familiar from more recent antiques came to the fore, after a brief period when the two categories were apparently both available. Just as the earliest pewter vessels appear to have been only part made of metal (with a wooden bowl: Egan 1998, 193–195, no 539), a similar phenomenon is evident for cast copper-alloy domestic vessels of the late 12th century, in which metal spouts were apparently attached to wooden-bodied jugs or ewers.[5] A recent study of cast, copper-alloy cooking vessels from the late medieval period and into the post-medieval era has drawn many strands together to produce a fresh picture of this industry and its products. It focuses on the West Country, drawing on excavated pieces, items from the saleroom/collecting ambit and including evidence from production sites and documents, all backed up by scientific analyses of the alloys used (Butler and Green 2003).

The study of medieval glass vessels has developed from the point where the material was barely recognized to have existed. It seems strange in retrospect that it was not better served earlier, but this was due to its property of readily fragmenting into sharp pieces and also its tendency of corroding to the point where the main features of its attractiveness, colour and translucency are partly or completely lost. With very few fragments known from prior to the 13th century, the gradual spread of this prestigious import within institutions and the homes of the rich in England came to be appreciated through the pioneering work of Harden (1972), but its true extent was demonstrated from survivals that include several complete vessels on the Continent. In particular the catalogues of exhibitions in Germany and France came as revelations to the majority of archaeologists (Baumgartner and Krueger 1987; Foy and Sennequier 1989). The Venetian enamelled beakers of the 14th century are among the most notable finds to have emerged (Clark 1983). Tyson's synthesis (2000), available for less than a decade, gives an indication of the extent of the range available in England, and was comprehensive when written. The number of new forms and variations that have emerged in the interim characterizes this as a young field of study, which is already significantly altered by the stimulation provided by the literature now available. English medieval domestic glassware still lacks its own exhibition, which would add significantly to what appears in these publications.

Knives are very diverse and, despite extensive study (Cowgill *et al* 1986; Biddle 1990, 835–861), fresh varieties continue to turn up. The study of decoration on scabbards has revealed several main traditions — surprisingly late intricate knotwork derived from Saxon motifs still being produced in the 14th century (ibid, 132–133, fig 86), overall stamping, pseudo-heraldry, manuscript-derived grotesques and scroll-work (including a fashion for strawberries (ibid, 136–137 and 160, figs 89 and 103 nos 418, 420 and 479). Archaeological finds of weaponry and armour have until very recently been a somewhat neglected subject. Individual finds have been reported on, but apart from arrowheads (eg Jessop 1996) there has been little attempt at synthesis. A new volume on finds from Dublin (Halpin 2008) will go some way to redressing this, but there is scope for further work on these subjects.

Assemblages from religious houses have come to be recognized as having a bias towards literacy as well as featuring items relating to health care, in addition to the more obvious religious paraphernalia (Cherry 1985; Egan 1997, 109, table 14). The humble bone stylus (no longer identified as a 'parchment pricker') is almost a type fossil of these institutions in the late medieval period.

A whole range of formerly obscure finds have been brought into the mainstream consciousness through the efforts of special-interest groups, like the Finds Research Group, whose Datasheets have provided a useful platform for making available work in progress, and the Historical Metallurgy Society, who have produced Guidelines on how to recognize and tackle production sites. Individuals have worked on specific categories of find with a wide range of papers in various outlets, though there are perhaps fewer monographs than might have been expected. MacGregor has made a lasting contribution to the study of objects made of skeletal materials (1985; MacGregor *et al* 1999). Other subjects tackled include children's toys (Forsyth and Egan 2005; Willemsen 1998), which have proved to be surprisingly varied from the 14th century onwards, and (for Norfolk) armorial pendants (Ashley 2002). Lead seals for traded textiles were one of many quality-control marks developed during the late medieval period by guilds and civic authorities on various goods including precious metals and pewterware. Several publications devoted to cloth seals from an English perspective have helped to tie down their date and origins (eg Egan 1995 and 2001; idem 2007a, 134). The scope for synthesis in other countries, appropriate for such a major internationally traded commodity, has yet to be exploited. From finds in England it is possible to trace textile consumption from 13th-century Flemish woollens and silks of Lucca, through the imported cloths of Brabant, to woollens from English looms from the late 1300s, with native textiles subsequently being supplemented by imports of linens and mixed cloths like those from Venice and St Gallen.

The relatively little known material culture of rural areas is gradually becoming better appreciated through excavations on the sites of medieval villages (Andrews and Milne 1979). The potential is indicated by Meols, regardless of any special reasons relating to trade there (Egan 2007c; Hume 1863); this was a fishing village on the Wirral, which did not even run to a parish church, and yet has a finds assemblage which matches that of any city in Britain (though it was retrieved in the mid-19th to early 20th centuries without formal excavation). It suggests that the few inhabitants fully partook in the complete range of material culture available through the later medieval period, including that relating to pilgrimage to the main centres in England and on the Continent, and the politics of the Wars of the Roses. The broad range of finds recovered more recently from archaeological investigations at Milton Keynes (Zeepvat and Tyrrell 1993; Mills *et al* 1995) gives support to this picture. It looks as if the wider implications of a broader and more varied material culture than had been expected for other rural areas are slowly being confirmed by the Portable Antiquities Scheme.[6] Its database of finds from other sources than formal excavation (largely metal detecting on the part of private individuals, whose potential cumulative contribution had long been widely ignored) is providing many valuable fresh insights (this all builds on previous outreach work, especially that in Norfolk). Overall, the picture of regional variation in material culture, so strongly evident in ceramic studies, seems not to be valid at least for metalwork after the Norman period. Instead, one is struck by the similarity of most categories of objects from the north to the south, the main differences being in the numbers of finds in the prosperous south and Yorkshire compared with the marked paucity in Cornwall, Wales, the north-west and Scotland outside the main towns. Beyond the land, the few later medieval shipwrecks investigated so far have provided disappointingly little by way of cargo assemblages to illustrate the vital trade in goods of all kinds and give further insights, but there is great potential here too (see Redknap 1997).

Some recent review publications provide very useful syntheses. One of the most stimulating, sustained current projects in Europe in later medieval archaeology is the continuing series of volumes arising from the Lübeck Colloquia on the urban archaeology of the Hanse. Each volume is on a different theme, with papers from over 30 archaeologists from former Hanse towns across the Baltic and North Sea regions (the volumes most pertinent to the present discussion are Gläser 1999; 2006; 2008). In Britain, David Hinton, with a working lifetime's experience of interpreting medieval material culture during a crucial period of the development of the subject, is the first to have taken advantage of the richness of the cumulative picture to write a reflective synthesis across the entire range (Hinton 1990 and 2005). Doubtless others will attempt to produce similar syntheses, based on more specific themes in neglected or fast developing areas.

CONCLUSIONS AND SOME POSSIBLE FUTURE TRENDS

There is a welcome and highly productive move towards using together evidence from all available sources to produce a fresh, fuller picture than anything that could possibly come from a single source in isolation. The clearest exemplars at this stage are the results derived from the Portable Antiquities Scheme, when its recorded finds are seen together with those excavated from datable sequences, and the recent work on copper-alloy cooking vessels (Butler and Green 2003). These constructive alliances, still anathema to some, are surely the way forward.

The importance of evidence for production of goods of all kinds has long been recognized. The pioneering volume compiled in 1981 has proved a valuable reference point over the years (Crossley 1981). It remains useful, although information on several industries has in part been superseded by the later volume on medieval English industries (Blair and Ramsay 1991; the latter book concentrates more on the artefacts than the processes, which received more emphasis in the earlier publication). It is unlikely now that at least the potential will not be recognized at an early stage of fieldwork if not before — something that could not be claimed 30 years ago.

In the international arena, the Lübeck Hanse volumes noted above will hopefully continue. An excellent idea originated by Jan Baart (former town archaeologist for Amsterdam) has not been so fortunate. The first volume of a projected series on specific finds, that dealing with thimbles, has been published (Langdijk and Boon 1999). It is almost exclusively concerned with finds from Amsterdam, but the idea led to negotiations for a second volume on spoons, which was to have a chapter by a selected team of specialists, one from each of half a dozen different countries, giving an account of the archaeological picture of these objects for their territory. Sadly, this project was not completed, but the potential remains for a series of detailed volumes, international in scope on material culture, if resources can be found. This is the kind of synthesis many aspire to produce from the mass of unpublished or sporadically noted 'grey-literature' finds in their stores, in a wider European setting. There seems to be little scope elsewhere for the kind of lavish, in-depth international surveys of surviving goods of particular categories published by the German *Bronzegeräte des Mittelalters* series (principally von Falke and Meyer 1983; Theuerkauff Liederwald 1988), which furnish invaluable visual guides from which occasional archaeological fragments and even rarer complete or near-complete finds of ornate, upmarket candlesticks, vessels, religious paraphernalia etc can be identified.

Inevitably, the subject retains the stimulation of many new variants of familiar objects, for example of dress accessories, constantly emerging to challenge the specialist, but now they are mainly within a datable framework. A few weak points remain: dating can probably be improved throughout the period, but there is a particular need for tightening for the 11th/early 12th centuries and the late 15th/early 16th centuries, and there is a relative paucity of metalwork assignable to the 12th century in particular (Steven Ashley, pers comm), which is in part responsible for the first of these areas of weak understanding. There is still scope for confusion in some areas where similar material crops up at two distinct periods — as with the revivals of globular pins, double-spiral pins, and hooked tags/clasps, each of which appear first in the late Saxon period and again with slight differences around the early 16th century — possibly a result of items half a millennium old and that had been found accidentally, inspiring jewellers in the late 1400s or early 1500s. The relative lack of finds assignable with confidence within the late 15th/early 16th century means there are several points that remain for clarification in the transition from 'gothic' to 'renaissance'-style in everyday material culture.

Several of the old major collections are slowly becoming available through both conventional publication and websites, but these valuable resources are still only partly known. It will probably be a long time before the complete archaeological medieval holdings of the British Museum and the Museum of London, for example, are fully available in the way that the Saxon-period objects in the Ashmolean Museum have become (eg MacGregor and Bolick 1993).

In contrast with the earlier part of the medieval period, the definition of different peoples (eg Saxon and Norman) from traits in material has not been a prominent issue for this more fully documented, arguably more settled era. Scientific analysis is increasingly being undertaken to try to group glassware, with some success, and metals, with useful results in defining the quality of knife and other iron blades in particular. The widespread use of non-ferrous metal alloys usually appropriate for the tasks intended is clear enough, but so far little immediately obvious progress is being made with the places of production of seemingly ubiquitous dress accessories, at least within the ambit of rescue archaeology. Repeated recycling over centuries of both copper and lead alloys seems to have resulted by the high medieval era in a 'dirty', much mixed stock of metals, and this seriously blurs the potential for defining geological origins of the raw materials and hence where in the country or beyond the various goods were probably made. The overall profile is difficult to categorize: there was little variation in alloys used for nationwide fashions. Isotopic studies may help to assign the origins of some lead and lead/tin wares. There may well be mileage here but perhaps it has yet to get the focus that will make these approaches productive.

It is still surprisingly difficult to give a full account rigorously century by century of material culture through the five centuries considered here. That remains for others to do, should they wish to take this approach at some time in the future. Following a period when the square-one road maps (basic identification, the range most likely to be encountered and at least basic dating) for most categories of finds in this period have become established, there is a diminution in the influence of any finds lobby at the crucial stages of project planning and fieldwork. After a single generation of expansion and at best relative stability for the study of material culture in rescue archaeology, a more limited remit is being imposed by other interests. The future for this interest is likely to be more diverse. It may be the universities and museum outreach programmes that will take up the baton that has been held by the units, though access from these routes to prime, newly excavated material may be limited. As ever, it is the cumulative filters of manner and location of discarding, survival in the ground, recovery from the ground, subsequent availability for study, and resources (not least the specialists) to allow adequate publication, that will determine how the study of medieval material culture will develop over the next 50 years.

ACKNOWLEDGEMENTS

Thanks for sustained help to Brian Spencer, Jan Baart, Marian Campbell, John Cherry, Helen Clarke, Jane Cowgill, Pyotr Gaidukov, David Hinton, Manfred Gläser, Nicholas Griffiths, Wiaard Krook, Penny MacConnoran, Arthur MacGregor, Jussi-Pekka Taavitsainen, members of the Society of Thames Mudlarks, the Finds Liaison Officers and those who have made finds available for recording by the Portable Antiquities Scheme.

NOTES

[1] This became particularly clear to the writer in comparing notes with Andrew Reynolds about the hoard. We had both come to the assemblage from our respective specialist periods. These basic assumptions inevitably colour each interpretation of the material. Dating objects by associated pottery (for which changes around this time are assigned to *c*1050) is hazardous. In the present state of knowledge nothing apart from some coins of the Conqueror could tie earlier items to the crucial 16 years 1050–66, but none of the relevant jewellery finds have this association without later issues too.

[2] Described there as 'heavily stylised zoomorphic forms' dated to the 9th to 12th centuries. Another instance appears in Wilson 1964, 109 — this was presumably followed by Hinton 1974, 25–26 and pl 8 no 20.

[3] 'The publication of the volumes of finds from recent excavations in London is arguably the greatest sustained achievement in British medieval archaeology in the last decade' (Gerrard 2003, 74).

[4] The Society of Thames Mudlarks was invited to come onto the excavation at Swan Lane to use their detecting skills to recover from the strata as many finds as possible for the Museum of London's archive to pass on to future generations. This highly controversial move was not made lightly, in fact several other more conventional means had been tried, but it had become clear that the archaeological workforce alone was not at that time capable of anything like as full finds recovery as detectors in the skilled hands of the Society's members. One of the most dismaying and difficult factors was the vociferous and fierce opposition of the then prime London exponent of waterfront archaeology insisting on the merits of 'structures only' recording on waterfront sites — ie the finds, which were seen in that quarter as reprehensible waste of precious resources, would be completely ignored. Fortunately, the unspeakable folly of the strange alliance prevailed (or perhaps was given enough rope to hang itself). These decisions may be judged by their results.

[5] Virtually identical examples of such spouts, closely datable from their contexts, have been excavated in Winchester and London (Biddle 1990, 957–958 no 3408; Egan 1998, 162 no 441).

[6] See the PAS Database. The Scheme does not cover Scotland, though arrangements there for *bona vacantia* mean that there is scope for comparison.

BIBLIOGRAPHY

Alexander, J and Binski, P, 1987 *Age of Chivalry: Art in Plantagenet England, 1200–1400*, Royal Academy of Arts, London

Andrews, D and Milne, G, 1979 *Wharram, A Study of a Settlement in the Yorkshire Wolds 1, Domestic Settlement 1, Areas 10 and 6*, Society for Medieval Archaeology Monograph 8, Leeds

Ashley, S, 2002 *Medieval Armorial Horse Furniture in Norfolk*, East Anglian Archaeology 101, Norfolk Museums Service, Gressenhall

Baart, J M, Krook, W and Lagerweij, A, 1977, *Opgravingen in Amsterdam*, Dienst der Publieke Werken/Amsterdams Historische Museum, Afdeing Archeologie, Fibula-van Dishoek, Haarlem

Baumgartner, E and Krueger, I, 1988 *Phönix aus Sand und Asche: Glas des Mittelalters*, Klinkhardt and Biermann, Munich

Biddle, M (ed), 1990 *Object and Economy in Medieval Winchester*, Winchester Studies 7.2, 2 vols, Oxford University Press, Oxford

Blair, J and Ramsay, N, 1991 *English Medieval Industries*, Hambledon, London

Blick, S (ed), 2007 *Beyond Pilgrim Badges: Essays in Honour of Brian Spencer*, Oxbow Books, Oxford

British Museum Medieval Catalogue, 1924 *British Museum A Guide to the Medieval Room*, British Museum, London

Bu'Lock, J D, 1960 'The Celtic, Saxon and Scandinavian settlement of Meols in Wirral', *Transactions of the Historical Society of Lancashire and Cheshire* 112, 1–28

Butler, R, and Green, C, 2003 *English Bronze Cooking Vessels and their Founders c1350–1830*, Roderick and Valentine Butler, Honiton

Cherry, J, 1985 *Some Ecclesiastical and Monastic Finds*, Finds Research Group 700–1700 Datasheet 2

Clark, J, 1983 'Medieval enamelled glass from London', *Medieval Archaeology* 27, 152–156

Clark, J, 1995 *The Medieval Horse and its Equipment*, Medieval Finds from Excavations in London 5, The Stationery Office, London

Cowgill, J, Griffiths, N and de Neergaard, M, 1987, *Knives and Scabbards*, Medieval Finds from Excavations in London 1, Her Majesty's Stationery Office, London

Crossley, D W (ed), 1981 *Medieval Industry*, Council for British Archaeology Research Report 74, London

Crowfoot, E, Staniland, K and Pritchard, F, 1992 *Textiles and Clothing*, Medieval Finds from Excavations in London 4, Her Majesty's Stationery Office, London

Crummy, N, 1988 *Post Roman Small Finds from Excavations in Colchester 1971–85*, Colchester Archaeological Report 5, Colchester Archaeological Trust Ltd, Colchester

Egan, G, 1997 'Non-ceramic finds', in C Thomas, B Sloane and C Philpott (eds), *Excavations at the Priory and Hospital of St Mary Spital, London*, 201–210, MOLAS Monograph 1, Museum of London, London

Egan, G, 1998 *The Medieval Household*, Medieval Finds from Excavations in London 6, The Stationery Office, London

Egan, G, 2000 'Butcher, baker, spoon- and candlestick maker? Some highly decorated medieval leadwares in Northern Europe', in D Kicken, A M Koldeweij and J R ter Molen (eds), *Lost and Found: Essays on Medieval Archaeology for H.J.E. van Beuningen*, 102–115, Rotterdam Papers 11, Rotterdam

Egan, G, 2007a various contributions, in D Bowsher, T Dyson, N Holder and I Howell, *The London Guildhall: An Archaeological History of a Neighbourhood from Early Medieval to Modern Times*, MOLAS Monograph 36, 2 vols, Museum of London, London

Egan, G, 2007b 'Byzantium in London? New archaeological evidence for 11th century links between England and the Byzantine world', in M Grünbart, E Kislinger, A Muthesius and D Stathakopoulos (eds), *Material Culture and Well-Being in Byzantium 400–1453*, 111–17, Veröffentlichungen zur Byzanzforschung 9, Österreichsche Akademie der Wissenschaften, Vienna

Egan, G, 2007c 'Later medieval non-ferrous metalwork and evidence for metalworking: AD 1050–1100 to 1500–50', in D Griffiths, R Philpott and G Egan, *Meols: The Archaeology of the North Wirral Coast: Discoveries and Observations in the 19th and 20th Centuries, with a Catalogue of Collections*, 77–188, Oxford University School of Archaeology Monograph 68, Institute of Archaeology, Oxford

Egan, G and Pritchard, F, 1991 *Dress Accessories*, Medieval Finds from Excavations in London 3, Her Majesty's Stationery Office, London

Fingerlin, I, 1971 *Gürtel des Hohen und Späten Mittelalters*, Kunstwissenshaftliche Studien 46, Deutscher Kunstverlag, Munich and Berlin

Forsyth, H and Egan, G, 2005 *Toys, Trifles and Trinkets*, Unicorn Press, Museum of London, London

Foy, D and Sennequier, G, 1989 *Á Travers le Verre du Moyen Âge á la Renaissance*, Musées et Monuments Départmentaux de la Seine-Maritime, Rouen

Gerrard, C, 2003 *Medieval Archaeology: Understanding Traditions and Contemporary Approaches*, Routledge, London

Gläser, M (ed), 1999 *Der Handel*, Kolloquium zur Stadtarchäologie im Hanseraum 2, Lübeck

Gläser, M (ed), 2006 *Das Handwerk*, Kolloquium zur Stadtarchäologie im Hanseraum 5, Lübeck

Gläser, M (ed), 2008 *Luxus und Lifestyle*, Kolloquium zur Stadtarchäologie im Hanseraum 6, Lübeck

Goodall, A R, 1981 'The medieval bronzesmith and his products', in Crossley (ed) 1981, 63–71

Goodall, I H, 1981 'The medieval smith and his products', in Crossley (ed) 1981, 51–62

Greig, S, 1933 *Middelalderske Byfund fra Bergen og Oslo*, Den Norske Videnskaps Akademi, Oslo

Grew, F and de Neergaard, M, 1988 *Shoes and Pattens*, Medieval Finds from Excavations in London 2, Her Majesty's Stationery Office, London

Guildhall Museum Catalogue 1908 *Catalogue of the Collection of London Antiquities in the Guildhall Museum, Library Committee of the Corporation of the City of London*, London (the 1905 edition is differently paginated)

Halpin, A, 2008 *Weapons and Warfare in Viking and Medieval Dublin*, Medieval Dublin Excavations 1962–81 series B 9, National Museum of Ireland, Dublin

Harden, D B, 1972 *Ancient Glass*, Royal Archaeological Institute, London

Hinton, D A, 1974 *A Catalogue of the Anglo-Saxon Ornamental Metalwork 700–1100*, Clarendon Press, Oxford

Hinton, D A, 1990 *Archaeology, Economy and Society: England from the Fifth to the Fifteenth Century*, Seaby, London

Hinton, D A, 2005 *Gold and Gilt, Pots and Pins: Possessions and People in Medieval Britain*, Oxford University Press, Oxford

Hornsby, P R G, Weinstein, R and Homer, R F, 1989 *Pewter, a Celebration of the Craft, 1200–1700*, Museum of London, London

Hume, A, 1863 *Ancient Meols: Or, some Account of the Antiquities Found near Dove Point on the Sea Coast of Cheshire*, privately printed, London

Hurley, M F, Scully, O M B and McCutcheon, S W J, 1997 *Late Viking Age and Medieval Waterford, Excavations 1986–1992*, Institute of Public Administration, Waterford

Jessop, O, 1996 'A new artefact typology for the study of medieval arrowheads', *Medieval Archaeology* 40, 192–205

Langedijk, C A and Boon, H F, 1999 *Vingerhoeden en Naairingen uit de Amsterdamse Bodem: Produktietechnieken vanaf de Late Middeleeuwen*, Archeologische Werkgemeenschap voor Nederland, Reeks 2, Amsterdam

Lightbown, R W, 1992 *Medieval European Jewellery, With a Catalogue of the Collection in the Victoria and Albert Museum*, Victoria and Albert Museum, London

MacGregor, A, 1985 *Bone, Antler, Ivory and Horn. The Technology of Skeletal Material since the Roman Period*, Croom Helm, London

MacGregor, A and Bolick, E, 1993 *Summary Catalogue of the Anglo-Saxon Collections (Non Ferrous Metals)*, British Archaeological Report 230, Oxford

MacGregor, A, Mainman, A J and Rogers, N S H, 1999 *Bone, Antler, Ivory and Horn from Anglo-Scandinavian and Medieval York*, The Archaeology of York, Craft, Industry and Everyday Life 17/12, Council for British Archaeology, York

Margeson, S M, 1993 *Norwich Households: The Medieval and Post Medieval Finds from Excavations by Norwich Survey 1971–1978*, East Anglian Archaeology 58, Gressenhall

Morris, C A, 2000 *Wood and Woodworking from Anglo-Scandinavian and Medieval York*, The Archaeology of York, Craft, Industry and Everyday Life 17/13, Council for British Archaeology, York

Mould, Q, Carlisle, I and Cameron, E, 2003 *Leather and Leatherworking from Anglo-Scandinavian and Medieval York*, The Archaeology of York: Craft, Industry and Everyday Life 17/16, Council for British Archaeology, York

Ottaway, P and Rogers, N, 2002 *Craft, Industry and Everyday Life, Medieval Finds from York*, The Archaeology of York, Craft, Industry and Everyday Life 17/15, Council for British Archaeology, York

Platt, C P S and Coleman Smith, R, 1975 *Excavations in Medieval Southampton 1953–69, 2 The Finds*, Leicester University Press, Leicester

Read, B, 1995 *History Beneath Our Feet*, Anglia Publishing, Ipswich (2nd edn)

Redknap, M (ed), 1997 *Artefacts from Wrecks*, Oxbow Monograph 84, Oxbow, Oxford

Rotterdam Papers: 1 Renaud, J G N (ed), 1968, A Contribution to Medieval Archaeology; 2 Renaud, J G N (ed), 1975 A Contribution to Medieval Archaeology; 4 Renaud, J G N (ed), 1982; 7 Carmiggelt, van A (ed), 1992 A Contribution to Medieval Archaeology; 8 van Beuningen, H J E and Koldeweij, A M (eds), 1993, *Heilig en Profaan: A Contribution to Medieval Archaeology*; 9 Henkes, H E, 1994, *Glass without Gloss:* A Contribution to Medieval and Post Medieval Archaeology; 10 Carmiggelt, A *et al*, 1999; 11 Kicken, D, Koldeweij, A M and ter Molen, J R (eds), 2000, *Lost and Found: Essays on Medieval Archaeology for H.J.E. van Beuningen*; 12 van Beuningen, H J E, Koldeweij, A M and Kicken, D (eds), 2001, *Heilig en Profaan* 2: A Contribution to Medieval Archaeology; all Rotterdam (Netherlands)

Peers, C and Radford, C A R, 1943 'The Saxon monastery of Whitby', *Archaeologia* 89, 27–88

Saunders, P and Saunders, E (eds), 1991 *Salisbury and South Wiltshire Museum Medieval Catalogue* 1, Salisbury and South Wiltshire Museum, Salisbury

Saunders, P (ed), 2001 *Salisbury and South Wiltshire Museum Medieval Catalogue* 3, Salisbury and South Wiltshire Museum, Salisbury

Saunders, P (ed), forthcoming *Salisbury and South Wiltshire Museum Medieval Catalogue* 4, Salisbury and South Wiltshire Museum, Salisbury

Sloane, B and Watson, B, 2005 'Crossed wires: The redating of a group of funerary lead crosses from Newgate', *Transactions of the London and Middlesex Archaeological Society* 55, 183–209

Spencer, B, 1980 *Medieval Pilgrim Badges from Norfolk*, Norfolk Museums Service, Norwich

Spencer, B, 1990 *Pilgrim Souvenirs and Secular Badges*, Salisbury and South Wiltshire Museum Medieval Catalogue 2, Salisbury and South Wiltshire Museum, Salisbury

Spencer, B, 1998 *Pilgrim Souvenirs and Secular Badges*, Medieval Finds from Excavations in London 7, The Stationery Office, London

Spencer, B, 2000 'Medieval pilgrim badges found at Canterbury, England', in D Kicken, A M Koldeweij and J R ter Molen (eds), *Lost and Found: Essays on Medieval Archaeology for H J E van Beuningen*, 316–327, Rotterdam Papers 11, Rotterdam

Stratford, N, 1993 *Catalogue of Medieval Enamels in the British Museum 2: Northern Romanesque Enamel*, British Museum Press, London

Syer Cuming, H, 1851 'On the horse shoes', *Journal of the British Archaeological Association* 6, 406–418

Syer Cuming, H, 1855 'On early English arrowheads', *Journal of the British Archaeological Association* 11, 142–144

Syer Cuming, H, 1858 'History of purses', *Journal of the British Archaeological Association* 14, 131–144

Syer Cuming, H, 1862 'On the Norman fermail', *Journal of the British Archaeological Association* 18, 227–231

Syer Cuming, H, 1863 'On signacula found in London', *Journal of the British Archaeological Association* 19, 94–100

Syer Cuming, H, 1867 'On signacula found in London', *Journal of the British Archaeological Association* 23, 327–333

Syer Cuming, H, 1868 'On signacula found in London', *Journal of the British Archaeological Association* 24, 219–230

Syer Cuming, H, 1869 'On early candlesticks of iron', *Journal of the British Archaeological Association* 25, 54–60

Syer Cuming, H, 1870 'Notes on a group of reliquaries', *Journal of the British Archaeological Association* 26, 270–280

Syer Cuming, H, 1878 'On stone moulds for religious signacula', *Journal of the British Archaeological Association* 34, 219–224

Theuerkauff-Liederwald, A-E, 1988 *Mittelalterliche Bronze- und Messingefässe: Eimer, Kannen, Lavabokassel*, Bronzegeräte des Mittelalters 4, Deutscher Verlag für Kunstwissenschaft, Berlin

Tyson, R, 2000 *Medieval Glass Vessels Found in England, c AD1200–1500*, Council for British Archaeology Research Report 124, London

von Falke, O and Meyer, E, 1983 *Romanische Leuchter und Gefässe: Giessgefässe der Gotik*, Bronzegeräte des Mittelalters 1, Deutscher Verlag für Kunstwissenschaft, Berlin (reprint of 1935 edn)

Wallace, P F (ed), 1988, *Medieval Dublin Excavations 1962–81*, Series B, Miscellany 1, National Museum of Ireland, Dublin

Ward Perkins, J B, 1940 *London Museum Medieval Catalogue*, Her Majesty's Stationery Office, London

Willemsen, A, 1998 *Kinder Delijt: Middeleeuws Speelgoed in de Nederlanden*, Nijmegse Kunsthistorische Studie 6, Nijmegen University Press, Nijmegen

Wilson, D M, 1964 *Anglo-Saxon Ornamental Metalwork, 700–1100, in the British Museum*, The British Museum, London

Wood, R, 2005 *The Wooden Bowl*, Stobart Davies Ltd, Ammanford

Zarnecki, G, Holt, J and Holland, T (eds), 1984 *English Romansque Art 1066–1200*, Weidenfeld and Nicolson, London

Zeepvat, R and Tyrrell, R, 1992 'The finds', in D C Mynard and R J Zeepvat (eds), *Excavations at Great Linford 1974–80*, 137–213, Buckinghamshire Archaeological Society Monograph 3, Aylesbury

WEBSITE

For the Portable Antiquities Scheme — http://www.finds.org.uk

PART IV

SCIENTIFIC PERSPECTIVES ON MEDIEVAL ARCHAEOLOGY

CHAPTER 15
HEALTH AND WELFARE IN MEDIEVAL ENGLAND: THE HUMAN SKELETAL REMAINS CONTEXTUALIZED

By CHARLOTTE ROBERTS

This paper presents a brief overview of the history of study of human remains from archaeological sites. This is developed into a thematic comparison of health and ill health in early and late medieval periods derived from 72 early medieval (mid-5th to mid-11th centuries AD*) and 63 later medieval (mid-11th to mid-16th centuries* AD*) funerary contexts in England, representing 7122 and 16,237 individual skeletons, respectively. The data presented suggest that populations would have been compromised by health problems during their daily lives. People living in the early medieval period in rural environments were healthier than those living in the later period. The latter's misfortunes were likely due mostly to the impact of urbanism. Air quality, hygiene and sanitation were poorer, the population denser, and housing was more crowded. Infectious disease load was higher, along with the amount of industry in towns and cities, and there was dietary deficiency and excess, while health care varied in provision and quality throughout the medieval period. Future prospects and developments are described, concluding that generally the infrastructure present within England for bioarchaeology to develop further is robust.*

INTRODUCTION

The study and interpretation of skeletal remains from archaeological contexts has a long history in England. It is only in the last 25 years or so, however, where there have been significant developments and changes in the discipline now more commonly known as bioarchaeology (Roberts 2006). The positive changes observed are the result of many factors which have changed, almost beyond recognition, the study of ill health in human remains from archaeological sites, better termed palaeopathology.

This paper aims to provide an overview of the state of health, and ill health, in medieval England, considering both early and later medieval periods, based on pooled data from a large number of cemetery sites. These data are mainly derived from a previously published book (Roberts and Cox 2003), but include more recent research. The emphasis here is on contextualizing the skeletal data, a feature that has taken some time to develop as routine practice in Britain. While exploring the impact of age at death and sex on poor health is now routinely practised in bioarchaeology, this has not always been a focus and thus much published (and unpublished) data on the evidence for disease lack this association. For this paper, it was not always possible to explore patterns with respect to age at death and biological sex; this is also the case for funerary contextual data. Additionally, and for brevity, the paper does not consider disease in cremated remains, due to the limited evidence available (McKinley 2000). To begin with, it is worth reflecting on bioarchaeology's development in Britain.

RECENT DEVELOPMENTS

There have been a number of key influences over the last 50 years or so regarding our knowledge and awareness of the health of our ancestors in England. Perhaps the most well-known practitioners are Don Brothwell (b 1934), Keith Manchester (b 1938) and the late Calvin Wells (d 1978). Their contributions are broad but their key books have been particularly influential, and remain so today (1981; 2005 — 3rd edition with Roberts 1964; respectively). Many more scholars, however, including younger researchers, have contributed to increasingly focused topics from the 1980s onwards, for example the late Trevor Anderson (developmental and carcinogenic problems), Megan Brickley (metabolic diseases such as rickets and scurvy, or vitamin D and C deficiency), Rebecca Gowland (the impact of plague on mortality), Simon Hillson and Dorothy Lunt (dental disease), Chris Knüsel (impact of activity on the skeleton), Louise Humphrey (impact of health on growth), Mary Lewis (the health of children), Simon Mays (many areas, but especially metabolic diseases such as osteoporosis, and infections such as tuberculosis), the late Juliet Rogers (joint disease), and Tony Waldron (on a variety of topics but especially emphasizing how to interpret data on disease). In recent years, additional contributions have been made by scholars working in biomolecular archaeology, most notably Abigail Bouwman, Terry Brown, Helen Donoghue, Mark Spigelman and Mike Taylor (ancient DNA analysis of tuberculosis, leprosy, venereal syphilis and malaria), and Mike Richards and Gundula Müldner on palaeodiet, the quality and quantity of which impacts on the burden of disease experienced by people today and would have in the past (see Müldner, this volume).

In contrast to today's bioarchaeologists, Wells was, and Manchester still is, a medical practitioner whose interests in archaeology were awakened locally through excavations of cemeteries in East Anglia and Yorkshire, respectively. Their paths into palaeopathology were guided by providing reports on skeletons from local excavations. Manchester went on to teach undergraduate and postgraduate students at the University of Bradford, thus igniting an interest in the wider archaeological community. Brothwell, a graduate in geology and zoology has, in the present writer's opinion, made the most substantial contribution to the development of palaeopathology in Britain. His publications range from seminal papers on population health in

Britain (eg 1961), to work on animal diseases (Baker and Brothwell 1980), the study of 'bog bodies' (Brothwell 1986), the impact of environment on health (Brothwell 1994), and research into specific diseases (Brothwell 2006). He remains a guiding light for bioarchaeology in Britain today. In recent years, with greater numbers of bioarchaeologists engaging in international conferences and publishing in international journals, Britain is fast establishing itself as a key contributor to the study of ill health in the past, using traditional and novel techniques of analysis, with its scholars producing globally used texts for both teaching and research (eg Cox and Mays 2000; Hillson 1996; Mays 1998; Pinhasi and Mays 2008; Roberts and Manchester 2005; Rogers and Waldron 1995; Waldron 1994).

Several key methodological advances have also shaped the more recent development of the discipline, most notably, perhaps, the introduction of standards for recording skeletal remains (Brickley and McKinley 2004). Previously, the standards produced by Buikstra and Ubelaker (1994) were most commonly used, and are still applied around the world. Their standards were a response to the threat of repatriation and reburial of skeletal remains of indigenous North Americans which prompted the need for systematic and standardized recording of such remains before they were lost to science. The ultimate aim was to ensure that all data were recorded in a standard way to facilitate comparison between skeletal assemblages. It is therefore heartening to see standards for recording of skeletal remains in Britain now that reburial is becoming more common (Ministry of Justice 2008).

Over the last 15 years guidance documents have been issued by a range of sectors regarding the law and burial archaeology (Garratt-Frost 1992), excavation and post-excavation treatment (McKinley and Roberts 1993), preparation of skeletal reports (English Heritage 2004), curation of human remains (Department for Culture, Media and Sport 2005), dealing with burials from sites within the jurisdiction of the Church of England (English Heritage and Church of England 2005), and from Scotland (Historic Scotland 1997), and Ireland (O'Sullivan *et al* 2002; O'Sullivan and Killgore 2003; Buckley *et al* 2004). These documents have been instrumental in informing bioarchaeologists and other interested parties about the various issues surrounding the study of human remains. The establishment of the British Association of Biological Anthropology and Osteoarchaeology in 1998 has also brought together bioarchaeologists working in a variety of fields, with the common goals of reconstructing past human behaviour, including exploring the impact of life on health (http://www.babao.org.uk). The Paleopathology Association, based in North America and founded in 1973, is also the key international group for many working in the field in Britain (http://www.paleopathology.org).

Finally, and mainly since the 1990s, one-year intensive masters courses on the study of human remains have been established at various universities in Britain. These courses mostly include palaeopathology in their curriculum; all have created a facility for training this and the next generation of bioarchaeologists. Until recently most physical anthropologists were employed in anthropology departments and focused on non-human primates and early hominines, but encouragingly there has been an increasing recognition of bioarchaeology's contribution to archaeology by a number of academic appointments in archaeology departments. Equally importantly, the introduction of PPG16 (Department of the Environment 1990) brought about a massive increase in the number of excavations in general, and cemeteries in particular, in advance of modern development. This development has generated a substantial number of skeletal assemblages, and in some cases involving very large numbers of skeletons (eg 10,516 at St Mary Spital, London — Connell *et al* in press; http://www.museumoflondon.org.uk/English/Collections/OnlineResources/CHB). This aspect has had the fortunate consequence of generating employment for many masters' graduates, and an increasing number of influential monographic publications (eg Drinkall and Foreman 1998; Fiorato *et al* 2007; Mays *et al* 2007; Connell *et al* in press). The overall effect has been to stimulate interest in bioarchaeology among the academic and contract archaeology communities, but especially among the general public via television programmes such as 'Meet the Ancestors', shown on BBC2 for several years. In terms of research, all of the above factors have influenced the range of studies of health and disease. There has been a gradual change of emphasis from case studies of individual skeletons to population based assessments of health focused on specific questions or hypotheses and using more novel techniques of analysis. Population studies, however, are still relatively rare compared to other parts of the world such as North America (see Mays 1997; in press). A matter of concern is that there needs to be an increase in placing data on health and disease in archaeological context if those data are to make any meaningful contribution to understanding the past (eg see Steckel and Rose 2002; Roberts and Cox 2003; Gowland and Knüsel 2006; Connell *et al* in press; Cohen and Crane-Kramer 2007). Those who doubt the value of the study of human remains in archaeology need only consider that archaeology can be defined as the study of past people. Human remains are the primary evidence for people and the closest we ever get to our ancestors.

WHAT DO WE KNOW ABOUT HEALTH IN BRITAIN?

Essentially, everybody experiences ill health today and would have in the past; thus, studying health is a unique way of understanding how people adapted to changing socio-economic and political environments through time, that is whether they experienced poor health and how that affected their ability to function in their communities. While people can adapt to change they may also initiate it, a factor which illustrates what it means to be human.

Recognition of bone changes as a result of disease comes in the form of either bone formation or destruction, or a combination of both in particular distribution patterns related to clinical knowledge (Roberts and Manchester 2005). It is not necessarily straightforward, however, to diagnose specific disease as the bone changes might represent several diseases, and the skeleton being examined may be fragmentary, thus compromising observation of distribution patterns. Skeletal data collected are usually presented as individual studies of skeletons with specific diseases, broad population studies of ill health in people buried at a particular site during a specific period, or studies of one disease both temporally and spatially; methodological papers focusing on disease are also of relevance (macroscopic, radiological, microscopic and biomolecular).

In some cases the data are placed into context to explain patterns observed, for example the impact on tuberculosis frequency of housing, population density, occupation, keeping animals, poverty and quality of diet. In other instances, there is little reference to context and the data are isolated as an example of a disease at a point in time in a specific place. Furthermore, when focusing on frequency of disease, one has to consider the impact of immune system strength of the people being analysed and their ability to fight disease (and show bone changes), and how representative the skeletal sample is of the living and dead population (Waldron 1994). A particular problem for interpretation of data, specifically for the later medieval period, is often the lack of high-resolution stratigraphic (or indeed radiocarbon) dating with which to trace fluctuations in disease over time within a given cemetery. Furthermore, the impact of marine-based diets on radiocarbon dates remains a continuing challenge (Bayliss *et al* 2004).

Presented here are a subset of data collected for the early and later medieval chapters of Roberts and Cox (2003), a subset meaning data on disease considered under particular themes which inform us about the impact of people's lives on their health. In addition, data from more recent studies are also incorporated. The data in Roberts and Cox (2003) derive from 72 early medieval (mid-5th to mid-11th centuries AD) and 63 later medieval (mid-11th to mid-16th centuries AD) funerary contexts in England, representing 7122 and 16,237 individual skeletons, respectively. The material was derived from published and unpublished works by a wide variety of authors completed over many years. Ideally, data would have been collected from the skeletons by one person using standardized methods. However, for obvious reasons, pooled data have been used in order to consider patterns of health in a large sample over long periods of time in a large geographic area.

Rather than consider evidence for disease in medieval England in categories such as 'infection', 'metabolic disease', and 'joint disease', in order to better contextualize the data, it is approached within three themes: 'living environment', 'economy and diet', and 'access to health care'. The data are divided into early (mid-5th to mid-11th centuries AD) and later medieval (mid-11th to mid-16th centuries AD) to explore general differences in health between the two periods, the first being at a time when people lived in more rural environments, and the second being a time when people were more urbanized. It should be noted that a greater number of urban cemeteries of the late medieval period have been excavated and their skeletal remains analysed, than rural cemeteries of the early medieval period; thus, the sample size for the latter is greater and may impact on the data available.

Living environment

It is well known that our interior (house) and exterior (outside the house) living environment contributes positively and negatively to our health status (eg see Bruce *et al* 2002; Namdeo *et al* 2005). Whether we live in urban or rural communities, coastal or inland areas, in the highlands or lowlands, in tropical, arctic or temperate climates, our environment will impact on the types of diseases we may experience.

Compounding the overall risk to health of these different environments is the work that we do (indoors or out?), the fuel we use for cooking, heating and travelling, and our innate immunity in these different environments. Teasing out which of many variables actually caused a health problem in any one environment is difficult in bioarchaeology, but it is possible to look overall at differences between people by focusing on disease that can be related to environment.

In order to determine whether air quality during the medieval period, both indoors and out, was such that it affected respiratory health, the frequency of sinusitis was explored. Sinusitis is an inflammation of the air-filled sinuses of the face which, in skeletal remains, can be recognized usually as bone formation (Figure 15.1); the sinuses comprise part of the upper respiratory system (Roberts 2007). Sinusitis may be caused by a number of factors, including allergies, air pollution and smoking, and it may be a complication of dental disease in the upper molar teeth and occur in people whose occupations generate particulate pollution, such as smelting metals, making pottery and mining (see Roberts and Cox 2003, 236–237, for an overview of possible occupations practised in the later medieval period). The frequency of maxillary sinusitis for skeletons from six early and six late medieval sites were considered: early: Norton, Cleveland (Jakob 2004), Bishopsmill School, Yorkshire (Bernofsky 2006), Spofforth, Yorkshire (Bernofsky 2006), Raunds, Northamptonshire (Roberts *et al* 1998), Castledyke, Barton-on-Humber, Lincolnshire (Jakob 2004), and Apple Down, Sussex (Jakob 2004); late: Wharram Percy (Lewis *et al* 1995), St Helen-on-the-Walls, York (Lewis *et al* 1995), Jewbury, York (Lilley *et al* 1994) and Fishergate House, York (Papapalekanos 2001), all in Yorkshire, Chichester, Sussex (Boocock *et al* 1995); with one post-medieval site for comparative purposes, Christ Church, Spitalfields, London (Roberts 2007). All the early medieval sites were rural in nature, while all the late sites were urban, apart from Wharram Percy.

Frequencies of sinusitis varied from 16% to 80% of individuals affected for the early period and 31% to 71.9% for the later period, with an overall higher rate

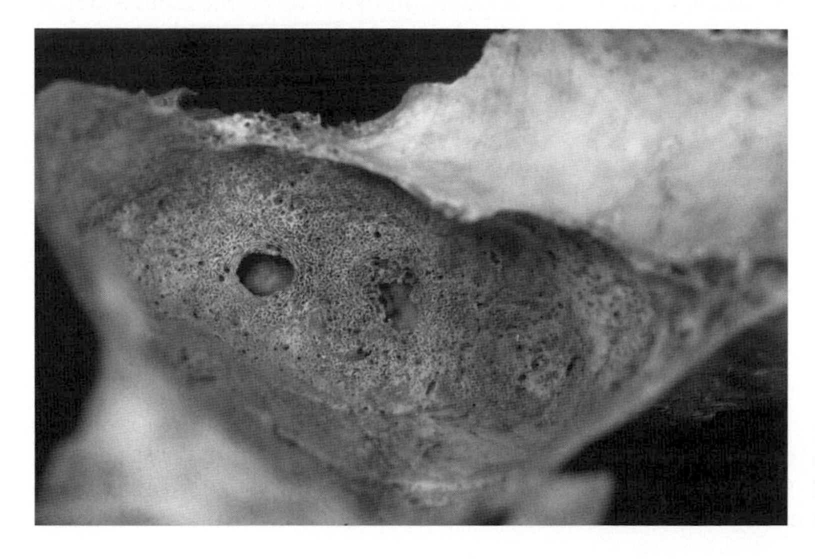

FIGURE 15.1 Example of sinusitis — new bone formed in maxillary sinus.

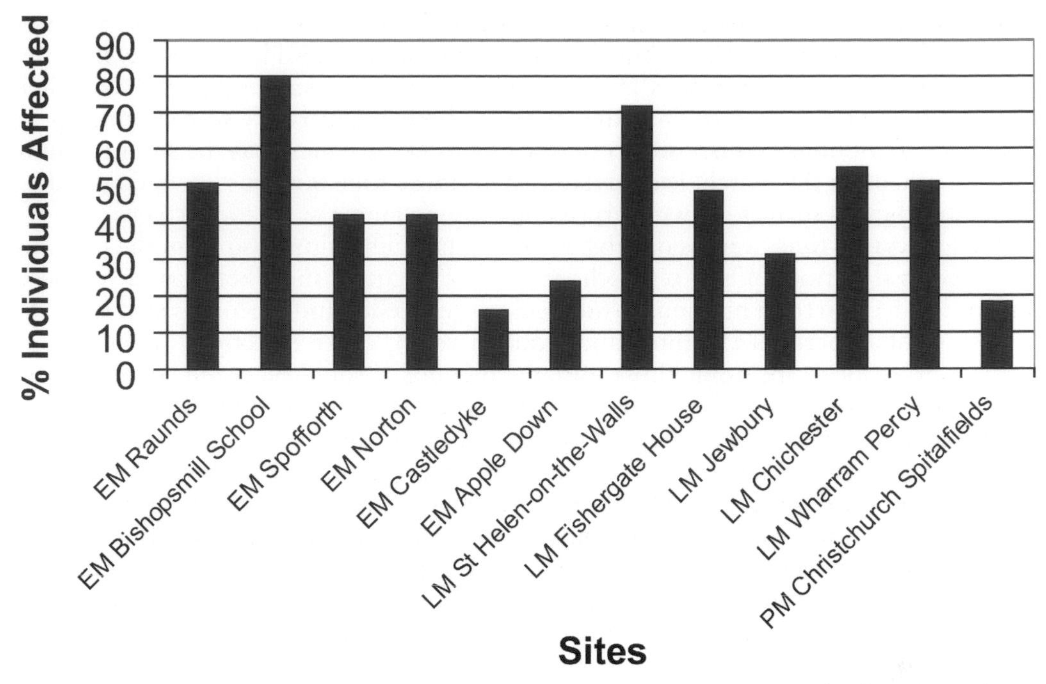

FIGURE 15.2 Frequency of sinusitis at early and later medieval sites in England (EM = early medieval; LM = late medieval; PM = post-medieval).

observed for the later sites (Figure 15.2). Factors which might contribute to this could include housing structure, higher population density and working in occupations which all affected air quality. Of interest is the high frequency at the Bishopsmill School site, contrary to the other sites; there is no obvious reason for this rate at this site but there is no available appropriate archaeological data to expand interpretation. At the later medieval sites, people buried at St Helen-on-the-Walls had the highest frequency and the males were especially severely affected; these data may reflect the intensively urban nature of the environment at the time in York, with closely packed housing, the perceived poverty of this population, and also the many industries being practised nearby in the Bedern district of the city. They may all have had their part to play in affecting air quality (brewing, tanning, lime-burning, etc). The lower frequency seen at Jewbury (Lilley *et al* 1994), although roughly contemporary with St Helen-on-the-Walls, may reflect the higher-status nature of this group of Jewish people and that they were, to a certain extent, protected from poor quality air by the very nature of their housing and the type of work they did. The frequency at the leprosy hospital of St James and St Mary Magdalene, Chichester, can be viewed as related to leprosy as this infectious disease predisposes people to sinusitis. The relatively high rate seen at Wharram Percy may reflect poor air quality due to pollen, animal dander and a general response to allergens. As a contrast, the post-medieval site of Christ Church, Spitalfields, gave an 18% frequency which is the lowest of all the sites; again, it is suggested that these middle-class people were protected from what was seen at the time to be a polluted environment in London (Molleson and Cox 1993). It is known, for example, that many of their houses were well ventilated and had chimneys, which dissipated the smoke from fires in a much more efficient way compared to earlier periods. It is also suggested that the (presumed) thatched roofs of early medieval houses may not have predisposed to smoky indoor environments as the smoke would dissipate through the thatch. People likely spent more time outdoors, too, engaged in agricultural tasks such as growing crops and keeping animals.

At the same time, lesions on ribs, reflecting lung infection, rise from the early to late medieval period. While research since 1984 suggests the likely cause of these lesions is infection from pulmonary tuberculosis (eg Kelley and Micozzi 1984; Roberts *et al* 1994; Lambert 2002; Santos and Roberts 2006), other infections (pneumonia, chronic bronchitis), including those initiated by poor air quality, could equally cause rib lesions. Thus, rib lesions caused by the same factors as sinusitis presented a common outcome for people living in towns. Poor air quality may also be explored through observing the effects of vitamin D deficiency on health in skeletal remains. This vitamin is formed in the skin but needs sunlight to manufacture it; it is necessary for the absorption of calcium and phosphorus in the diet so that the bones of the skeleton form correctly. If these processes are prevented through lack of sunlight then the bones are not mineralized, but soft and deformed (rickets in children and osteomalacia in adults). That people in both early and late medieval England show very little sign of vitamin D deficiency is seen in the general lack of skeletons with the recognizable bone changes, apart from prominent examples from late medieval Wharram Percy (Ortner and Mays 1998) and early medieval Jarrow (Anderson *et al* 2005).

There are also other clues in skeletal remains that belie quality of living environment of past populations. Eye sockets of skulls can develop small holes in their surfaces, termed by many as cribra orbitalia (Figure 15.3). These bony changes are believed to be the result most likely of increased pathogen load as a result of

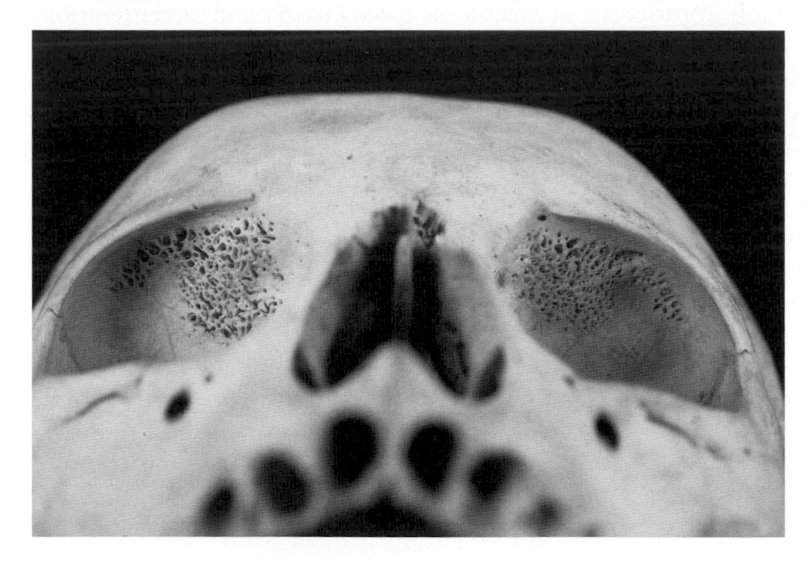

FIGURE 15.3 Example of cribra orbitalia — 'holes' in eye sockets.

infectious disease, although other diagnoses might include vitamin C deficiency (see Ortner 2003; Wapler *et al* 2003). Cribra orbitalia increases in frequency from the early to late medieval periods and suggests that the latter's urban living environment was 'less healthy' than its predecessor. Poor hygiene and sanitation may have predisposed people to more infectious disease and thus their body adapted to those circumstances. Essentially, if a person experiences infection, their body withholds iron from the pathogens causing the infection, resulting in iron deficiency, as seen in the holes in the orbits which indicate the red bone marrow working overtime to produce more red blood cells (Stuart-Macadam 1992). As Ortner (2008) points out, attributing anaemia to these lesions is risky unless there is other evidence to support the diagnosis.

There are other signs of infections increasing in the later medieval period. For example, skeletal evidence for tuberculosis (TB) sees an increase compared to the early medieval period (Roberts and Buikstra 2003). An infection resulting from specific human and other animal bacteria (*Mycobacterium tuberculosis* and *Mycobacterium bovis*, respectively), it is related to increased population density (the 'sneezing distance apart' is important for transmission of the bacteria from human to human via the lungs), and working with and ingesting infected products of animals such as cattle, pigs, and sheep. Contemporary historical evidence indicates that housing and population in urban situations was very dense (Dyer 1989). It is presently unknown whether the human or animal form of TB was most damaging for humans in medieval England, although ancient DNA analysis has isolated *M. tuberculosis* as causing TB at Wharram Percy (Mays *et al* 2001). Furthermore, little attention has been paid by zooarchaeologists to identifying TB in animal bones, although some (albeit debatable) evidence from Wharram Percy cattle ribs indicates that it may have been present there (Mays 2005). Leprosy, an infection caused by *Mycobacterium leprae*, also increases in the late medieval period (see Roberts 2002 for a summary of skeletal evidence, and Rawcliffe 2006 for an overview of leprosy in England). As this infection is also transmitted from human to human via the lungs, higher population density is necessary for its dispersal. Of interest is its decline in the 14th century AD in England, with a concurrent increase in tuberculosis (TB). This has been explained as likely due to the cross immunity induced by the bacteria (*Mycobacterium*) that cause the diseases. In effect, the TB bacterium is considered an earlier entity when compared to the leprosy bacterium and, with bacterial evolution, the leprosy bacterium saw a decrease in virulence. Thus, with biological competition, TB takes precedence over leprosy. Increasing exposure to TB during the height of urbanism in the late medieval period may have led to a degree of immunity to leprosy, thus reducing the chances of contracting leprosy (Manchester 1984; Leitman 1997).

Economy and diet

A well-balanced diet is essential for life, a strong immune system and a healthy body. Thus, the type of subsistence practised in the past was instrumental for providing people with food. Health therefore might have been affected by dietary deficiency, or even excess, and ultimately degeneration of the structure of the skeleton. In the medieval period, of course, the emphasis was on agriculture, although the collecting of wild plants and hunting wild animals was certainly not unknown and especially seen in rural society in the early medieval period. Along with settled communities and agriculture, health has been shown to decline in many studies of skeletal remains (eg Cohen and Crane Kramer 2007). For example, hunting and gathering can sustain small groups of people and provided a generally healthy, well-balanced and varied diet; people are also regularly mobile and therefore probably fitter than more sedentary farmers.

While there was very little evidence for specific dietary deficiency diseases such as a lack of vitamin C (scurvy) in both early and later periods, there was evidence for an increase in defects in the enamel of the teeth as time progressed. Enamel defects (or hypoplasias) can be seen in the teeth (Figure 15.4) and reflect stress during growth in childhood, the stress usually referring to dietary problems (Hillson 1996). A considerable increase overall of hypoplasia in the late period perhaps reflects increased population pressure on available resources and harvest failures in parts of the 13th, 14th and 15th centuries (Dyer 1989). Along with an increase in enamel defects, stature is also a reflection of quality and quantity of diet during the growth period. It declines from the early medieval period in both males and females, respectively (Figure 15.5). Males decline from 1.72m (5ft 6½in) to 1.71m (5ft 6in) and females decline from 1.61m (5ft 3in) to 1.59m (5ft 2in); while this decline does not appear large, it should be remembered that these are pooled average data from 996 male and 751 female early medieval skeletons and 8494 male and 7929 female late medieval skeletons from across England. Thus, the decline is clear, even from this large sample, and supports the enamel defect data for a likely dietary problem in the late medieval period.

Two examples of excess in the diet, especially in the late medieval period, can be seen in the increased frequency of dental caries and diffuse idiopathic skeletal hyperostosis (DISH). Caries (Figure 15.6) is an infectious disease of the teeth caused by a combination of carbohydrates (sugars) in the diet, plaque on the teeth (poor oral hygiene), and a lack of fluoride (Hillson 1996). Bacteria in plaque ferments sugars in the diet to produce acids that demineralize the tooth structure. Sugar was not

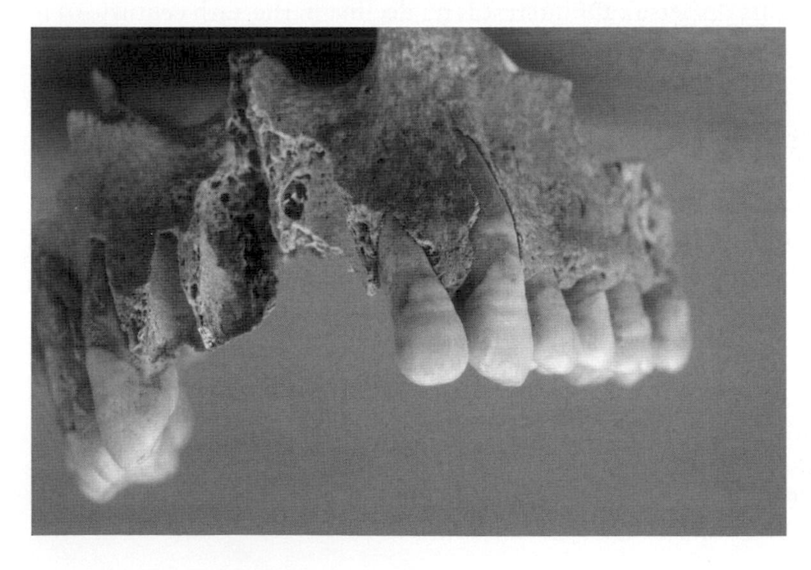

FIGURE 15.4 Example of enamel hypoplasia — lines, pits or grooves in the enamel of the teeth.

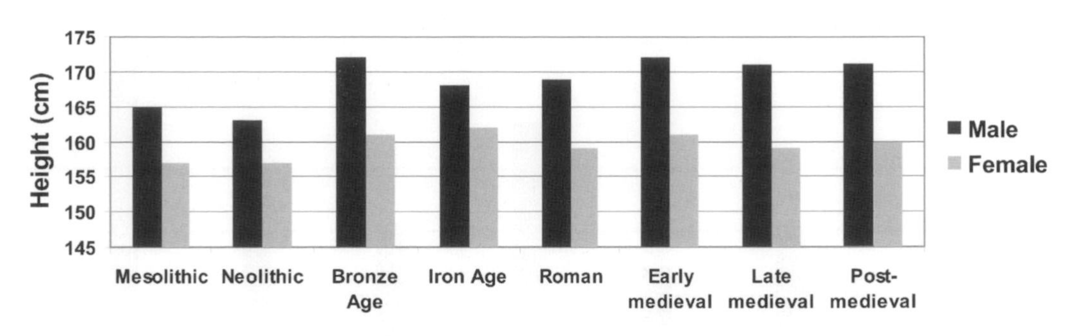

FIGURE 15.5 Stature through time in males and females in Britain.

FIGURE 15.6 Example of dental caries in a molar tooth. (Courtesy of Anwen Caffell)

introduced to England until the 12th century AD, which correlates with what is seen in caries rates, that is that they increase from the early to late medieval period (Figure 15.7). A more detailed study of regional caries rates in England showed that they also increased in both monastic and non-monastic sites from early to late periods (Caffell 2005); caries rates were lower in coastal sites overall which reflects the preventative nature of the high fluoride content of fish. DISH primarily affects the spine (Figure 15.8) and has been noted in monastic populations in England and elsewhere (see Rogers and Waldron 2001). In living populations DISH seems to have an association with Type II diabetes, obesity, older age and being male (see Resnick

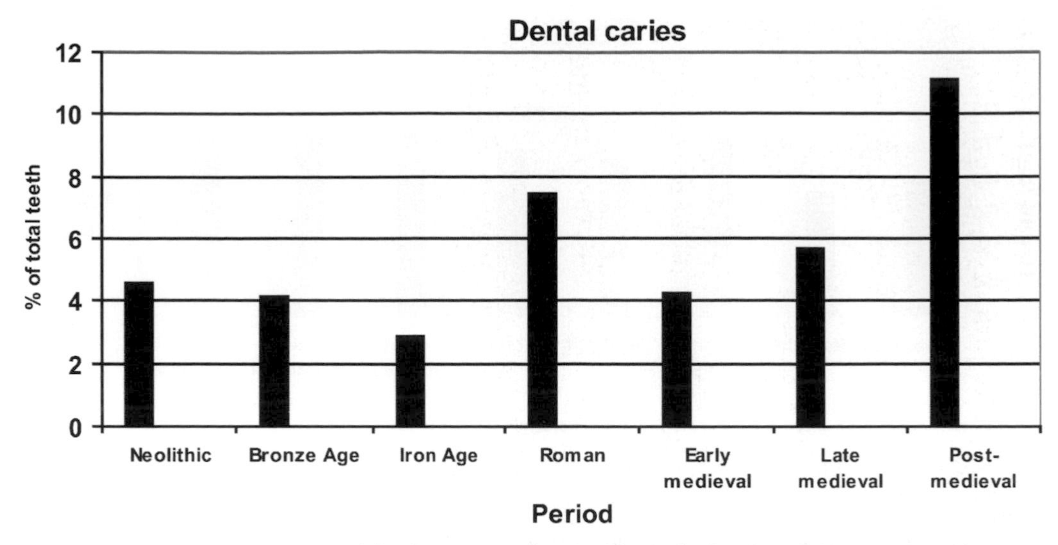

FIGURE 15.7 The frequency of caries through time in Britain.

1995). It has been suggested that it may be related to excess protein in the diet, amongst other components, and to the monks' diet, although DISH is found also in non-monastic groups in late medieval England. Current research is exploring the diet and hereditary hypotheses for DISH (Spencer 2008).

Access to health care

Everybody was unhealthy at some point in their lives during the early and late medieval periods, but what kind of health care did they access, if any? Today we live long enough for cancer and heart disease to take hold, and infant mortality has declined, but our length of life is determined by the availability of health care and better living conditions. There is much historical data for medical and surgical care in the medieval period (eg Porter 1997). In the late medieval period, for example, physicians, surgeons and bone setters are known and diagnosis of disease using urine, blood and faeces are described. Herbal remedies, cautery, bloodletting, bathing and specific diets were recommended as treatments. The most common evidence for treatment seen in skeletal remains is trepanation, but also amputation and dentistry, and wound dressings have been noted (see Roberts and Cox 2003 for an overview). There is also much evidence for the founding of hospitals especially in the late medieval period, both for people with general health problems but also for those with leprosy (Orme and Webster 1995).

Trepanation, or making a hole in the skull, was used to treat a number of complaints such as headache, epilepsy, migraine, and head injuries. Five types of trepanation (scraped, gouged, bored and sawed, square sawn, and drilled) have been observed in the bioarchaeological record reflecting materials available to be used as surgical implements. The scraped method appears quite common in Europe, and England in particular (Roberts and McKinley 2003). Here the majority of trepanations

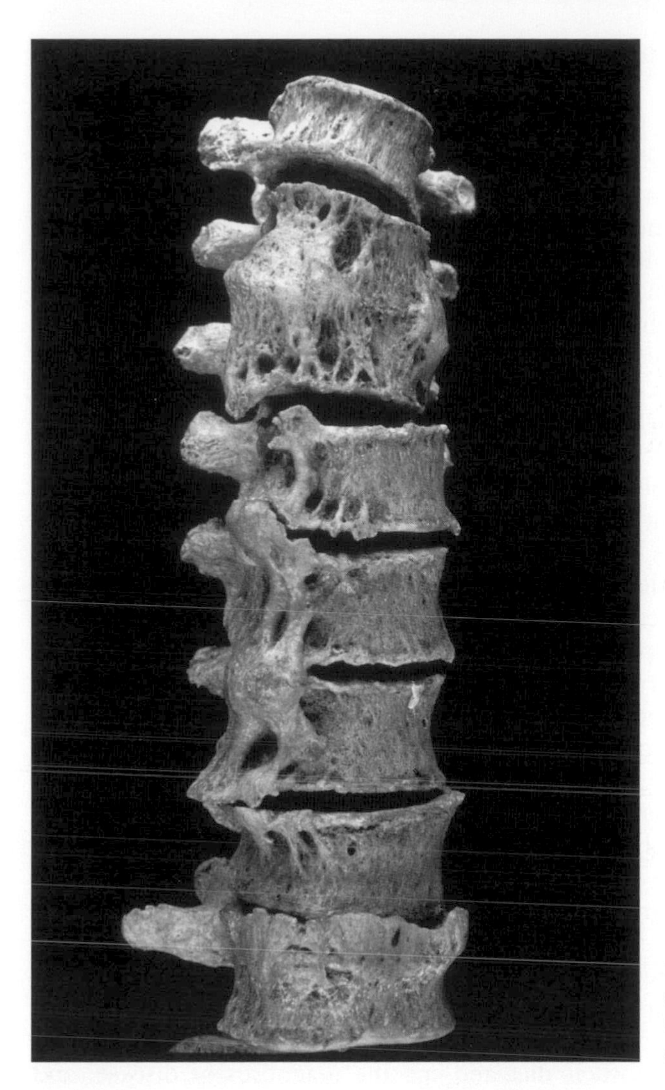

FIGURE 15.8 Example of DISH affecting the spine — new bone formation on the right side of the spine resulting in fusion.

come from the early medieval period and relatively few from the later period. Most of the skulls showed no reason for the operation but the vast majority were healed. Of particular interest was that most individuals derived from 'normal' funerary contexts for the period, indicating that people who had been trepanned were generally not treated differently to their peers through time.

Not all evidence for care and treatment in the medieval period will be visible on the skeleton and it remains difficult to determine whether early or late medieval people had better or worse access to care. All that can be said is that there is evidence for care in both periods, and that males, females, different status and age groups would likely have had access to different levels of care. Thus, inequality in provision of health care would have been evident as it is today.

CONCLUSIONS AND FUTURE PROSPECTS FOR HUMAN BIOARCHAEOLOGY IN BRITAIN

While this brief overview of health in medieval England has focused on certain conditions, it is clear from the data presented that populations would have been compromised by health problems during their daily lives. People living in the early medieval period in rural environments appear to have been healthier than those living in the later period. The latter's misfortunes were likely due mostly to the impact of urbanism, although the data from the skeletal remains from that time derives mostly from urban cemeteries. Air quality, hygiene and sanitation were poorer, and the population was denser, with housing being more crowded. Infectious disease load was higher, and along with the amount of industry in towns and cities there was dietary deficiency and excess, while health care varied in provision and quality throughout the medieval period. It should be remembered, however, that evidence for diseases from skeletal remains contain biases that must be accounted for, several of which are discussed above. Furthermore, only disease that affects the bones or teeth will be seen, unless DNA analysis has been used to detect ancient pathogens that had not impacted on the skeleton at death. Disease that only affects the soft tissues, such as plague and childhood diseases such as measles and chicken pox, will not be detected unless contemporary historical data is accessed (see Wood *et al* 1992 for an overview of the problems of inferring health from the skeleton).

Using large samples of skeletons produces an overview of health in the medieval period, but it also shows that there is much more to be learned. The medieval period was a time when there was a transition from small rural communities to urban societies where life was much more complex and potentially damaging to health. In the future more nuanced approaches to understanding health and answering specific questions/testing hypotheses are advocated with regional syntheses of medieval England being the focus, although similar approaches to health in Britain as a whole should be the ultimate goal. This will allow comparison of health between, for example, northern and southern regions, western and eastern regions, and coastal and inland areas, along with particular studies of health differences between, for example, the sexes, age groups, and statuses. Along with integrated biomolecular studies aimed at tracking the mobility of people, their diet and specific diagnoses of disease, and historical data analysis to flesh out the bones, multidisciplinary teams of researchers will undoubtedly change the face of what we know about health in medieval England. Of vital importance in this respect is the absolute need to record data in a standardized way so that comparative research can be done reliably. Particularly important too is the need for bioarchaeologists to work with other specialists to understand better the nature of other types of evidence that can be used for interpretation of the skeletal data. Additionally, working with contract archaeologists will identify what important questions need to be answered and how bioarchaeology can help.

There are, however, a number of developments needed in infrastructure to ensure that bioarchaeology flourishes as an integral part of archaeology. Establishing skeletal databases to provide information on the location and nature of skeletal collections available for study will allow these remains to be more effectively used.

Essentially, such information will help spread the handling load on an important archaeological resource, and encourage researchers to utilize skeletal collections outside of London more frequently, ultimately allowing bioarchaeologists to fill gaps in knowledge about health by understanding the nature of the resource better. A database saves valuable researchers' time searching for collections relevant to their questions. Access to grey literature is also essential so that important data become readily available in the public domain; 38% of the 311 site reports utilized for Roberts and Cox (2003) were unpublished.

Nevertheless, the future for bioarchaeology in Britain is potentially very bright. There are masters and PhD courses to provide training, many trained practitioners, a national organization (BABAO), large skeletal collections for analysis, standards for data recording, analytical facilities, and experienced specialists to conduct analyses beyond the basic macroscopic/visual stages of recording. 'The cloud on the horizon, which will probably not go away, is the reburial issue . . . there is good cause to review where our studies have got to and which aspects deserve our special research efforts before it is too late' (Brothwell 2000, 5). Brothwell's comments are very timely today and we need to heed his warning.

BIBLIOGRAPHY

Anderson, S, Wells, C and Birkett, D, 2005 'People and the environment. The human skeletal remains', in R Cramp (ed), *Monkwearmouth and Jarrow Monastic Sites. Volume* 2, 481–502, English Heritage, Swindon

Baker, J and Brothwell, D, 1980 *Animal Diseases in Archaeology*, Academic Press, London

Bayliss, A, Shepherd Popescu, E, Beavan-Athfield, N, Bronk Ramsey, C, Cook, G T and Locker, A, 2004 'The potential significance of dietary offsets for the interpretation of radiocarbon dates: an archaeological significant example from medieval Norwich', *Journal of Archaeological Science* 31, 563–575

Bernofsky, K S, 2006 'The effects of environment on respiratory health in early Medieval northeast England', unpublished University of Durham MSc dissertation

Boocock, P, Roberts, C A, Manchester, K, 1995 'Maxillary sinusitis in medieval Chichester', *American Journal of Physical Anthropology* 98, 483–495

Brickley, M and McKinley, J I (eds), 2004 *Guidelines to the Standards for Recording Human Remains*, Institute of Field Archaeologists Paper number 7, Reading

British Association of Biological Anthropology and Osteoarchaeology (http://www.babao.org.uk; accessed 21 October 2008)

Brothwell, D, 1961 'The palaeopathology of early British man: an essay on the problems of diagnosis and analysis', *Journal of the Royal Anthropological Institute* 91, 318–343

Brothwell, D, 1981 *Digging Up Bones*, Natural History Museum, London

Brothwell, D, 1986 *The Bog Man and the Archaeology of People*, British Museum Press, London

Brothwell, D, 1994 'On the possibility of urban-rural contrasts in human population paleobiology', in A R Hall and H K Kenward (eds), *Urban-rural Connexions: Perspectives from Environmental Archaeology*, 129–136, Oxbow Books, Oxford

Brothwell, D, 2000 'Studies on skeletal and dental variation: a view across two centuries', in M Cox and S Mays (eds), *Human Osteology in Archaeology and Forensic Science*, 1–5, Greenwich Medical Media, London

Brothwell, D, 2006 'North American treponematosis against the bigger world picture', in M L Powell and D C Cook (eds), *The Myth of Syphilis. The Natural History of Treponematosis in North America*, 481–496, University Press of Florida, Gainesville

Bruce N, Perez-Padilla, R and Albalak, R, 2002 *The Health Effects of Indoor Air Pollution Exposure in Developing Countries*, World Health Organisation, Geneva

Buckley, L, Murphy, E and Ó Donnabháin, B, 2004 *Treatment of Human Remains: Technical Paper for Archaeologists*, 2nd edn, Dublin, Institute of Archaeologists of Ireland, Dublin

Buikstra, J and Ubelaker, D, 1994 *Standards for Data Collection from Human Skeletal Remains*, Research Seminar Series 44, Fayetteville

Caffell, A C, 2005 'Dental caries in medieval Britain (c. 450–1540): temporal, geographic and contextual patterns', unpublished University of Durham PhD thesis

Cohen, M N and Crane Kramer, G (eds), 2007 *Ancient Health. Skeletal Indicators of Agricultural and Economic Intensification*, University Press of Florida, Gainesville

Connell, B, Gray Jones, A, Redfern, R and Walker, D (in press), *Spitalfields: a Bioarchaeological Study of Health and Disease from a Medieval London Cemetery. Archaeological Excavations at Spitalfields Market 1991–2007*, 3, Museum of London Archaeology Service, London

Cox, M and Mays, S (eds), 2000 *Human Osteology in Archaeology and Forensic Science*, Greenwich Medical Media, London

Department for Culture, Media and Sport, 2005 *Guidance for the Care of Human Remains in Museums*, Department for Culture, Media and Sport, London

Department of the Environment, 1990 *Planning Policy Guidance Note 16. Archaeology and Planning*, Her Majesty's Stationery Office, London

Drinkall, G and Foreman, M (eds), 1998 *The Anglo-Saxon Cemetery at Castledyke South, Barton on Humber*, Sheffield Excavations Report 6, Sheffield Academic Press, Sheffield

Dyer, C, 1989 *Standards of Living in the Middle Ages: Social Change in England c1200–1520*, Cambridge University Press, Cambridge

English Heritage, 2004 *Human Bones from Archaeological Sites. Guidelines for Producing Assessment Documents and Analytical Reports*, English Heritage in association with the British Association of Biological Anthropology and Osteoarchaeology, Swindon

English Heritage and Church of England, 2005 *Guidance for Best Practice for Treatment of Human Remains Excavated from Christian Burial Grounds in England*, English Heritage, London

Fiorato, V, Boylston, A and Knüsel, C (eds), 2007 *Blood Red Roses. The Archaeology of a Mass Grave from the Battle of Towton AD 1461*, 2nd edn, Oxbow Books, Oxford

Garratt-Frost, S, 1992 *The Law and Burial Archaeology*, Institute of Field Archaeologists Technical Paper 11, Institute of Field Archaeologists, Birmingham

Gowland, R and Knüsel, C (eds), 2006 *The Social Archaeology of Human Remains*, Oxbow, Oxford

Hillson, S, 1996 *Dental Anthropology*, Cambridge University Press, Cambridge

Historic Scotland, 1997 *The Treatment of Human Remains in Archaeology*, Historic Scotland Operational Policy Paper 5, Historic Scotland, Edinburgh

Jakob, B, 2004 'Prevalence and patterns of disease in early medieval populations: a comparison of skeletal samples from 5th–8th century AD Britain and Germany', unpublished University of Durham PhD thesis

Kelley, M A and Micozzi, M, 1984 'Rib lesions in pulmonary tuberculosis', *American Journal of Physical Anthropology* 65, 381–386

Lambert, P M, 2002 'Rib lesions in a prehistoric Puebloan sample from southwest Colorado', *American Journal of Physical Anthropology* 117, 281–292

Leitman, T, 1997 'Leprosy and tuberculosis: the epidemiological consequences of cross-immunity', *American Journal of Public Health* 87, 1923–1927

Lewis, M E, Roberts, C A and Manchester, K, 1995 'Comparative study of the prevalence of maxillary sinusitis in Later Medieval urban and rural populations in Northern England', *American Journal of Physical Anthropology* 98, 497–506

Lilley, J M, Stroud G, Brothwell D R and Williamson M H, 1994 *The Jewish Burial Ground and Jewbury*, The Archaeology of York 12/3, The medieval cemeteries, York Archaeological Trust and Council for British Archaeology, York

Manchester, K, 1984 'Tuberculosis and leprosy in antiquity', *Medical History* 28, 162–173

Mays, S (in press), 'Human osteoarchaeology in Britain 2001–2007: a bibliometric perspective', *International Journal of Osteoarchaeology*

Mays, S, 1997 'A perspective on human osteoarchaeology in Britain', *International Journal of Osteoarchaeology* 7, 600–604

Mays, S, 1998 *The Archaeology of Human Bones*, Routledge, London

Mays, S, 2005 'Tuberculosis as a zoonotic disease in antiquity', in J Davies, M Fabiš, I Mainland, M Richards and R Thomas (eds), *Diet and Health in Past Animal Populations. Current Research and Future Directions*. Proceedings of the 9th Conference of the International Council of Archaeozoology, Durham, 2002, 125–134, Oxbow, Oxford

Mays, S, Taylor, G M, Legge, A J, Young, D B and Turner-Walker, G, 2001 'Palaeopathological and biomolecular study of tuberculosis in a medieval skeletal collection from England', *American Journal of Physical Anthropology* 114, 298–311

Mays, S, Harding, C and Heighway, C, 2007 *The Churchyard. Wharram. A Study of Settlement on the Yorkshire Wolds XI*, York, University of York, York University Archaeological Publications 13, York

McKinley, J I, 2000 'The analysis of cremated bone', in M Cox and S Mays (eds), *Human Osteology in Archaeology and Forensic Science*, 403–421, Greenwich Medical Media, London

McKinley, J I and Roberts, C A, 1993 *Excavation and Post-Excavation Treatment of Cremated and Inhumed Remains*, Institute of Archaeologists Technical Paper Number 13, Birmingham

Ministry of Justice, 2008 *Burial Law and Archaeology*, Coroner's Unit, Steel House, Ministry of Justice, London

Molleson, T and Cox, M, 1993 *The Spitalfields Project. Volume 2 — The Anthropology. The Middling Sort*, Council for British Archaeology Research Report 86, York

Museum of London (http://www.museumoflondon.org.uk/English/Collections/OnlineResources/CHB; accessed 21 October 2008)

Nambdeo, A and Bell, M C, 2005 'Characteristics and health implications of fine and coarse particulates at roadside, urban background and rural sites in the UK', *Environmental International* 31:4, 565–573

Orme, N and Webster, M, 1995 *The English Hospital 1070–1570*, Yale University Press, New Haven

Ortner, D J, 2003 *Identification of Pathological Conditions in Human Skeletal Remains*, Academic Press, London

Ortner, D J, 2008 'Differential diagnosis of skeletal lesions in infectious disease', in Pinhasi and Mays (eds) 2008, 191–214

Ortner, D J and Mays, S, 1998 'Dry-bone manifestations of rickets in infancy and early childhood', *International Journal of Osteoarchaeology* 8, 45–55

O'Sullivan, J and Killgore, J, 2003 *Human Remains in Irish Archaeology*, The Heritage Council, Dublin

O'Sullivan, J, Hallisey, M and Roberts, J, 2002 *Human Remains in Irish Archaeology: Legal, Scientific, Planning and Ethical Implications*, The Heritage Council, Dublin

Paleopathology Association (http://www.paleopathology.org; accessed 21 October 2008)

Papapalekanos, A, 2003 'Living in an urban environment: lifestyle implications on a late medieval population from York with a focus on maxillary sinusitis', unpublished University of Durham MSc dissertation

Pinhasi, R and Mays, S (eds), 2008 *Advances in Human Palaeopathology*, John Wiley and Sons Ltd, New York

Porter, R, 1997 *The Greatest Benefit to Mankind: a Medical History of Humanity from Antiquity to the Present*, Harper Collins, London

Rawcliffe, C, 2006 *Leprosy in Medieval England*, Boydell Press, Woodbridge

Resnick, D, 1995 *Diagnosis of Bone and Joint Disorders*, Saunders, Edinburgh

Roberts, C A, 2002 'The antiquity of leprosy in Britain. The skeletal evidence', in C A Roberts, M E Lewis and K Manchester (eds), *The Past and Present of Leprosy. Archaeological, Historical, Palaeopathological and Clinical Approaches*, 213–222, British Archaeological Reports International Series 1054, Oxford

Roberts, C A, 2006 'A view from afar: bioarchaeology in Britain', in J Buikstra and L Beck (eds), *Bioarchaeology. Contextual Analysis of Human Remains*, 417–439, Elsevier, London

Roberts, C A, 2007 'A bioarchaeological study of maxillary sinusitis', *American Journal of Physical Anthropology*, 133, 792–807

Roberts, C A and Buikstra, J E, 2003 *The Bioarchaeology of Tuberculosis. A Global View of a Reemerging Disease*, University Press of Florida, Gainesville

Roberts, C A and Cox, M, 2003 *Health and Disease in Britain. From Prehistory to the Present Day*, Sutton Publishing, Stroud

Roberts, C A and Manchester, K, 2005 *The Archaeology of Disease*, 3rd edn, Sutton Publishing, Stroud

Roberts, C A and McKinley, J, 2003 'A review of trepanations in British antiquity focusing on funerary context to explain their occurrence', in R Arnott, S Finger and C U M Smith (eds), *Trepanation. History, Discovery, Theory*, 55–78, Swets and Zeitlinger Publishers, Lisse

Roberts, C A, Lucy, D and Manchester, K, 1994 'Inflammatory lesions of ribs: an analysis of the Terry Collection', *American Journal of Physical Anthropology* 95:2, 169–182

Roberts, C A, Lewis, M, Boocock, P, 1998 'Infectious disease, sex and gender: the complexity of it all', in A Grauer and P Stuart-Macadam (eds), *Sex and Gender in Palaeopathological Perspective*, 93–113, Cambridge University Press, Cambridge

Rogers, J and Waldron, T, 1995 *A Field Guide to Joint Disease in Archaeology*, Wiley, Chichester

Rogers, J and Waldron, T, 2001 'DISH and the monastic way of life', *International Journal of Osteoarchaeology* 11, 357–365

Santos, A L and Roberts, C A, 2006 'Anatomy of a serial killer: differential diagnosis of tuberculosis based on rib lesions of adult individuals from the Coimbra Identified Skeletal Collection, Portugal', *American Journal of Physical Anthropology* 130, 38–49

Spencer, R K, 2008 'Testing hypotheses about diffuse idiopathic skeletal hyperostosis (DISH) using stable isotope analysis and other methods', unpublished University of Durham PhD thesis

Steckel, R and Rose, J (eds), 2002 *The Backbone of History. Health and Nutrition in the Western Hemisphere*, Cambridge University Press, Cambridge

Stuart-Macadam, P, 1992 'Porotic hyperostosis: a new perspective', *American Journal of Physical Anthropology* 87, 39–47

Waldron, T, 1994 *Counting the Dead. The Epidemiology of Skeletal Populations*, Wiley, Chichester
Wapler, U, Crubézy, E and Schultz, M, 2003 'Is cribra orbitalia synonymous with anemia? Analysis and interpretation of cranial pathology in Sudan', *American Journal of Physical Anthropology* 123, 333–339
Wells, C, 1964 *Bones, Bodies and Disease*, Thames and Hudson, London
Wood, J W, Milner, G R, Harpending, H C and Weiss, K M, 1992 'The osteological paradox. Problems of inferring health from the skeleton', *Current Anthropology* 33, 343–370

CHAPTER 16
INVESTIGATING MEDIEVAL DIET AND SOCIETY BY STABLE ISOTOPE ANALYSIS OF HUMAN BONE

By Gundula Müldner

The study of human food consumption patterns is central, not only to questions of economy and subsistence but also to social organization and culture change. This paper introduces a relatively recent addition to the suite of techniques traditionally employed to study medieval foodways, carbon and nitrogen stable isotope analysis of bone collagen, to a non-specialist audience and reviews key case studies where isotope analysis was successfully used to investigate diachronic change and dietary variation between gender, age and social groups in the medieval periods. It is argued that although stable isotope data only give a very general picture of human diet, they provide significant new information that is not available from other methods. Stable isotope techniques can therefore be expected to make a significant contribution to medieval archaeology in the decades to come.

INTRODUCTION

The study of human use of food, its production, distribution and consumption together with regard to changes over time, is key not only for defining major economic trends but also for understanding social relations between groups and individuals who use food to shape, express and protect their identities (Gumerman 1997; Beardsworth and Keil 1997). Scholars of the medieval period have long engaged with questions of diet and nutrition, most prominently perhaps using them as reflections of everyday life and indicators of standards of living, as pioneered in the work of Fernand Braudel (1973) and Christopher Dyer (1998). More recently, and integrating with research in social and cultural anthropology, increasing attention has also been given to social perspectives on medieval foodways, with key themes in the development and enforcement of social hierarchies manifested in the restriction of access to food, for instance by the establishment of seigneurial control over fishing and hunting grounds (Hoffmann 1996; Marvin 2006), as well as in the construction of identities through active selection or avoidance of food. Important examples for the latter are the development of regional and national cuisines (Weiss Adamson 2002), the use of food to create not only community in individual faith groups but also their segregation from others, as is famously the case with the Jewish food laws and the Christian reaction to them (Roth 2003), as well as the prodigious fasting of religious women, which serves both as a means of empowerment and as expression of a distinctly female spirituality (Bynum 1987).

Although the study of medieval foodways is still dominated by historians, archaeologists have made significant contributions to this area over many decades, in particular through the study of animal bones or plant remains (see, for example, contributions in Woolgar *et al* 2006; Sykes, this volume). The purpose of this paper is to introduce a very recent addition to the suite of techniques employed to study medieval diet, stable isotope analysis of human skeletal remains. Although the dietary information available through this method is not as detailed as that obtainable through more traditional approaches, stable isotope analysis is no less valuable for archaeological investigations. It analyses the dietary intake of individuals and therefore offers a unique opportunity to study gender, age and social groups from a dietary perspective.

Compared to the task of other contributors to this volume who have surveyed decades of research in their field, delivering a review of the contribution isotope analysis has made to medieval archaeology so far should not be too onerous. Although the first applications of stable carbon isotope analysis to archaeological bone were published as long as 30 years ago (Vogel and van der Merwe 1977), the technique has been widely applied only for the last decade or so and interest in applications to material from the Middle Ages has been limited. As a result, the corpus of evidence that can be surveyed here is still relatively small and, with one or two exceptions, the available case studies illustrate mainly the significant potential of the method for addressing important research questions in the future. The chief aim of this paper is therefore to give an accessible introduction to the subject to non-specialists and to highlight, with examples, the key research themes suited to isotope analysis for dietary reconstruction.

'YOU ARE WHAT YOU EAT' — THE PRINCIPLES OF STABLE ISOTOPE ANALYSIS FOR DIETARY RECONSTRUCTION

All techniques that use chemical analyses in order to reconstruct diet from the skeleton essentially rely on the same basic principle, commonly referred to as 'You Are What You Eat'. According to this, our skeleton, like all body tissues, is formed and maintained from the basic molecular components of the food we consume. Significant dietary information is therefore encrypted in our bones and bone chemistry methods seek to identify ways that enable us to 'read' what is 'written' there. For this purpose, they focus on certain chemical 'signatures' that are characteristic of different types of food and which, if traced in skeletal tissue, allow inferences to be made about the diet consumed by the individual in question.

The best established and most widely applied bone chemistry method for reconstructing diet from the skeleton is currently stable isotope analysis of bone collagen. This technique owes much of its success to the fact that the substance it uses for analysis, bone collagen, is the same as that targeted for radiocarbon-dating of bone. Although it was not realized until the late 1970s that stable isotope data, which is produced as a 'by-product' of the C-14 dating process, yields dietary information (see van der Merwe and Vogel 1978), the long-standing (and well-funded) research that was aimed at improving radiocarbon dating has contributed immensely to our understanding of stable isotope analysis for dietary reconstruction and is therefore ultimately responsible for its success.

Isotopes are atoms of the same element but with slightly different atomic weights. Carbon, which is one of the key elements used in dietary reconstruction, has three different isotopes, C-12 (often written as ^{12}C) with an atomic mass of 12, as well as the 'heavier' isotopes C-13 (or ^{13}C) and C-14 (^{14}C). Unlike C-14 (radiocarbon), C-12 and C-13 are *stable*, which means that they do not decay radioactively over time. The stable carbon isotope composition of bone collagen, ie the ratio of C-13 to C-12 isotopes or $\delta^{13}C$ in a collagen sample (see captions Figure 16.1 for a detailed explanation of this and other terminology), therefore remains unchanged from the death of an organism until its analysis in the laboratory hundreds or possibly thousands of years later (Schwarcz and Schoeninger 1991).

The key to dietary reconstruction by stable isotope analysis is that different types of food can be characterized by different stable isotope 'signatures'. As illustrated in Figure 16.1 (which also serves as an example of how isotopic data are usually displayed), foods produced on the land usually have much lower carbon stable isotope ratios — that is, they contain fewer of the 'heavy' C-13 isotopes — than foods obtained from the sea. Nitrogen stable isotope ratios (referred to as $\delta^{15}N$ values, see captions Figure 16.1), increase in line with the trophic level of an organism. Carnivores, for example, have tissue $\delta^{15}N$ values that are three to five parts-per-thousand (‰) higher than those of the herbivores they are feeding on; marine mammals, which are at the top of a very long food chain, have $\delta^{15}N$ values that are several times higher (see Figure 16.1).

According to the 'You Are What You Eat' principle, the isotopic 'signatures' of different foodstuffs are incorporated in the bone collagen of a consumer. By comparing the stable isotope composition of an individual's bone collagen with typical values for foods available to them — which are usually obtained through analysis of animal remains from the same site and time-period — we can infer which of these foods formed major components of the diet of the individual (Mays 2000; see Figure 16.1).

Just like every other method of dietary reconstruction, stable isotope analysis has its limitations and it is very important to be aware of these, in order to correctly understand the information provided by isotopic data. It is obvious from the explanations above that stable isotopes reflect diet only in very general terms. In fact, the information that can be obtained refers almost exclusively to sources of dietary protein. Foods that contain little or no protein, such as fruit and vegetables, fats and oils or alcoholic drinks are as good as invisible in the isotopic signal, while the importance of high protein foods, such as meat or fish, in the diet will be over-emphasized (Ambrose 1993).

Stable isotope analysis is best suited for *distinguishing between* the consumption of foods from the land and from the sea. In areas where so-called C_4 plants are

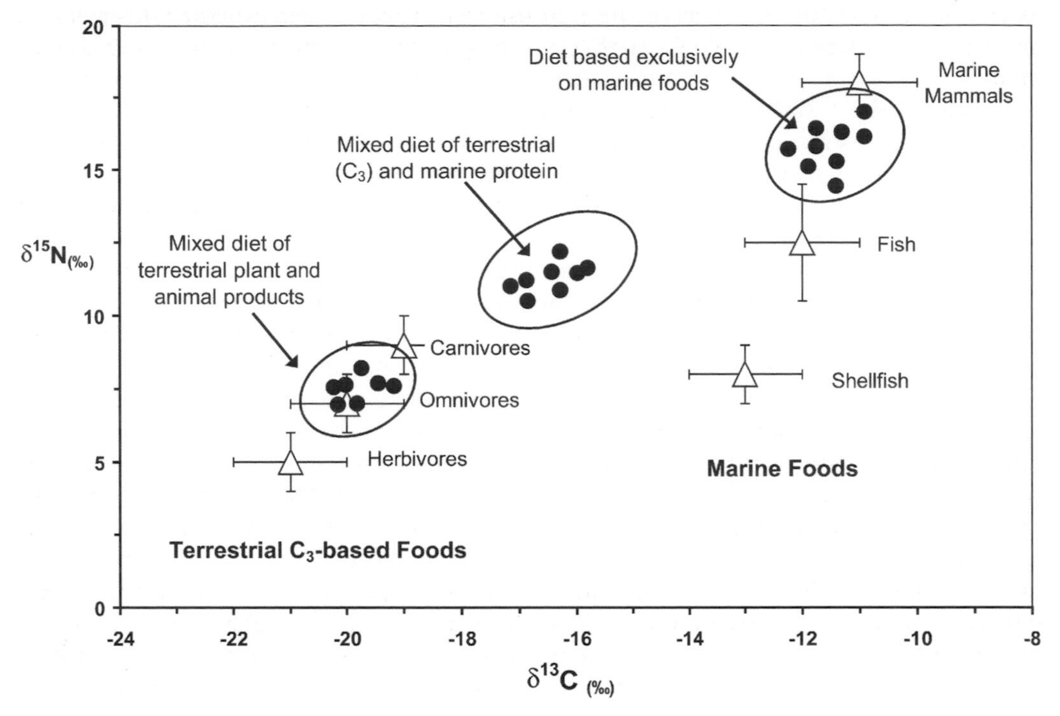

FIGURE 16.1 Typical stable isotope graph, displaying carbon stable isotope ratios ($\delta^{13}C$) on the horizontal and nitrogen stable isotope ratios ($\delta^{15}N$) on the vertical axis. The triangular symbols indicate characteristic bone collagen stable isotope values (± 1 standard deviation) for terrestrial and marine foodwebs in temperate Northwest Europe (after Richards 2000). Note the large difference in $\delta^{13}C$ between terrestrial and marine foods and the smaller difference in $\delta^{15}N$ values between animals of different trophic levels. The solid circles represent human isotope values as they might be obtained from European populations at different points in time. Their diet is inferred according to where they plot in relation to the animal bone data (see labels on graph).
Note on terminology: the stable carbon isotope composition of a given material is defined as the *ratio* of C-13 over C-12 isotopes ($^{13}C/^{12}C$). For technical reasons as well as for convenience, this is usually expressed as $\delta^{13}C$ (delta-13-C) which is the $^{13}C/^{12}C$ ratio but compared to the stable carbon isotope composition of an internationally agreed standard material. As most biological substances contain *less* C-13 isotopes than this standard (a carbonate rock formation of marine origin called V-PeeDeeBelemnite), their $\delta^{13}C$ values are usually negative. Stable isotope abundances are measured in parts-per-thousand or per mil (‰). An increase in $\delta^{13}C$ of 1‰, for example from −20 to −19‰, is therefore equivalent to one additional C-13 isotope per 1,000 carbon atoms. According to the same principle, the nitrogen stable isotope composition ($^{15}N/^{14}N$) is expressed as $\delta^{15}N$ (delta-15-N). The internationally agreed standard is the isotopic composition of atmospheric nitrogen or AIR. As most biological materials contain *more* ^{15}N than AIR, their $\delta^{15}N$ values are usually positive.

present, a group of plants which are adapted to warm and dry climates, their consumption (and the consumption of animals feeding on them) can also be differentiated from the reliance on other terrestrial (so-called C_3 plant-based) resources. This application has proved immensely important in many areas of the world, for instance for tracing the introduction of maize agriculture in the Americas (van der Merwe 1982), but has so far only been of limited use in European archaeology where plants are almost exclusively of the C_3 type (but see Mundee's (in press) work on medieval Spain).

Within the broad categories of foods from the land and the sea or C_3 and C_4 plant-based terrestrial foods, the resolution of the isotopic signal is rather poor. Nitrogen stable isotope ratios track trophic level and therefore reveal some information about the relative contributions of plant and animal products to the diet; however, they cannot differentiate between the consumption of different herbivore species, different cuts of meat, or even between meat and dairy products (Sealy 2001). Stable isotope analysis also registers only major dietary components. The method is not very sensitive to foods which constitute a small part of the diet. It has been estimated, for example, that an individual has to obtain around 20% of their total dietary protein from marine sources, before the analyst can be confident that they consumed marine foods at all (Hedges 2004). As a result, the dietary signals of most humans who consume protein from the same general sources and in similar quantities will be indistinguishable from another, even if their diets were in reality very diverse in terms of choice of food, preparation and manner of consumption. This strong 'levelling' effect of stable isotopes also has an advantage, however. Because the diet of most humans with access to the same resources appears isotopically the same, whenever there *are* significant differences between individuals in the isotope data, the dietary differences causing these must be *very* substantial and require explanation. The remainder of this paper will undertake to demonstrate how, despite its limitations, stable isotope analysis can be applied in medieval archaeology to great benefit.

STABLE ISOTOPE ANALYSIS AND MEDIEVAL ARCHAEOLOGY

Over the last 20 years, stable isotope analysis has been applied to early and later medieval skeletal remains from various European countries, including England (Mays 1997; Mays *et al* 2002; Privat *et al* 2002; Richards *et al* 2002; Bayliss *et al* 2004; Müldner and Richards 2005; 2007b; 2007a; Lakin in press), Scotland (Barrett *et al* 2000; 2001; Barrett and Richards 2005; Richards *et al* 2006; Müldner *et al* in press), France (Bocherens *et al* 1991; Herrscher *et al* 2001), Belgium (Ervynck *et al* 1999/2000; Polet and Katzenberg 2003; van Strydonck *et al* 2006), Germany (Schutkowski *et al* 1999; Dittmann and Grupe 2000; Schäuble 2006), Italy (Salamon *et al* 2007), Spain (Mundee in press), Greece (Bourbou and Richards 2007) and Scandinavia (Johansen *et al* 1986; Kosiba *et al* 2007; Linderholm *et al* 2008). This list is by no means exhaustive and it is likely that by the time the present contribution is in print a number of other studies will have appeared.

Many of the currently available publications are focused on individual sites or cemeteries. The number of individuals analysed, especially in the earlier studies, is often relatively small and reflects the difficulty, until fairly recently, of processing large numbers of samples. Although it is therefore too early to attempt generalizations from the available evidence, there are still some interesting parallels between isotope data from different sites and regions which may suggest the existence of general dietary trends. This paper introduces individual case studies best suited to highlighting the potential of stable isotope analysis for contributing to important research areas in the future. It should be noted that, to date, the largest corpus of medieval isotope data available has been produced on material from the British Isles.

Diachronic investigations into medieval diet

Human dietary habits are conservative and major dietary changes are therefore symptomatic of significant events or profound socio-cultural or economic changes affecting individuals or whole populations (Beardsworth and Keil 1997; Mintz and Du Bois 2002, 104). Taking a diachronic perspective in the study of food consumption patterns is therefore an extremely valuable approach and one which several medievalists have adopted using different methodologies (eg Mennell 1985; Dyer 1988; Sykes 2004).

Provided that environmental factors (which can be monitored through complementary analysis of animal bone) remain relatively even, stable isotope data-sets from different time-periods can be directly compared with each other, without most of the biases that complicate diachronic comparisons for other methods of dietary reconstruction (see Müldner and Richards 2006, 230). Diachronic investigations are therefore one of the key strengths of isotope analysis and, because of the affinity of the method to radiocarbon-dating, it is not surprising that the earliest stable isotope study involving human remains from the medieval periods took a long-term perspective. In the first application of stable isotope analysis for European archaeology, Tauber (1981) used evidence from carbon isotopes to argue that marine fish and sea foods lost their significance for human diet in Denmark after the Mesolithic and only rose to prominence again in the historical periods from around AD 1000. Although Tauber's far-reaching conclusions have often been dismissed on account of the small number of samples and the geographical bias in origin of the analysed individuals, his study was nevertheless seminal, as he realized the value of what is still the most fruitful application of stable isotope analysis in European archaeology: tracking the consumption of marine foods over time and within different populations. Given the criticism of Tauber's work, it is also ironic that, according to recent data, his main thesis of two major dietary transitions, at the end of the Mesolithic and again after AD 1000, may not have been far off the mark (see Richards *et al* 2003 and below).

Since Tauber, other projects have made use of stable isotopes to explore diachronic changes in diet in the historical periods (Arneborg *et al* 1999; Müldner and Richards 2007b; Salamon *et al* 2007). Possibly the most comprehensive long-term diachronic study to date, however, has been conducted by Barrett and colleagues (2000; 2001; Barrett and Richards 2005; Richards *et al* 2006), who combined a review of the fish bone evidence with stable isotope analysis and radiocarbon-dating of human bone, in order to trace the history of marine fish consumption in the Orkney Islands, off the North coast of Scotland, from the late Iron Age to the post-medieval period. One of the most surprising results of their investigation was that the late Iron Age ('Pictish') inhabitants of Orkney, despite being surrounded by ocean, did not rely on the sea for dietary staples: any contribution of marine foods to their diet was too small to register in the bone isotope signal and evidence from fishbone was also limited. It was only after the Norse colonization, in the 9th to 11th centuries, that more intensive use of marine resources was made, a trend which increased throughout the Viking Age but interestingly did not peak until much later, between the 11th and 14th centuries, when the stable isotope data shows that most individuals consumed marine fish on a regular basis, often in significant amounts (Barrett and Richards 2005).

Barrett and Richards (2005) offer several possible interpretations for the complex dietary patterns that emerge from Orkney. The increased consumption of marine foods after the Norse colonization almost certainly suggests the introduction of 'ethnic' Norwegian foodways to a culture that had previously focused their subsistence on the land. This interpretation is supported by the observation that some individuals in this time period, and particularly some of the males buried in 'Scandinavian' style (ie in boat graves and/or accompanied by grave goods) consumed more marine foods than others (Barrett *et al* 2001). The question of why the use of marine resources further intensified at and after the end of the Viking Age is more complex and possible interpretations are more varied. Those offered include the social emulation of the foodways of the Scandinavian lords, the conversion of Orkney to Christianity (prompting the adoption of Christian fasting practices) or the increasing involvement of the islands in the commercial production of fish for the European markets. More simply, this development may merely be the consequence of resource pressure following a rapid increase in the Orkney population (Barrett and Richards 2005).

As usual, the explanation that comes closest to the truth is probably one involving several, if not all, of the above factors (Barrett and Richards 2005). What this case study illustrates extremely well, however, is how studies of diachronic trends in diet are relevant not only within the framework of subsistence but can also contribute to questions of ethnicity, mobility, political, social and economic change. Stable isotope analysis with its capacity to provide information about the diet of individuals, was central to the investigation. Nevertheless, in order to counter a common stereotype about scientific data, it is important to note that it did not provide unambiguous answers. Stable isotope data may be generated by sophisticated analytical techniques; however, the patterns and trends observed within the data are open to different interpretations, just like any other form of archaeological evidence.

The increased appetite for marine fish which was observed in Orkney was merely part of a general trend towards increased consumption of sea fish across much of Northern and Central Europe from the 11th century onwards, marking a major dietary transition which was rooted in fundamental social and economic changes (see Enghoff 1999; 2000; Starkey *et al* 2000; Barrett *et al* 2004; Ervynck *et al* 2004). This phenomenon and the fact that even humans living far inland made sea fish an important part of their diet for several centuries, is the reason why stable isotope analysis for reconstructing diet is particularly valuable for investigating the medieval period. Tracing the contribution of sea fish to an otherwise terrestrial C_3-based diet is playing to one of the method's key strengths. The presence of fish on the medieval menu therefore greatly enhances the diagnostic power of the method and the number of potential applications. Focusing on only two basic food groups, marine and terrestrial, may seem limited in scope at first; however, as shall be shown in the remainder of this chapter, in the medieval period where fish had dual significance, not only as a sought-after source of animal protein which was not equally available to all groups of society, but also as a fasting food and sign of spiritual devotion, the capacity of stable isotope analysis to trace differences in fish consumption in medieval populations, can be successfully used to explore issues of gender, age and social status from a unique perspective.

Diet and social identity in the medieval period

Diet is intimately connected with social identity and numerous anthropological case studies have shown social factors such as age, gender, social group, ethnicity or religion to be at least as important in shaping personal food consumption as environmental aspects or individual taste (Mintz and Du Bois 2002; Beardsworth and Keil 1997; Counihan 1999). Stable isotope analysis allows us to correlate dietary information directly with anthropological and archaeological data specific to individuals, with age, sex or health status as inferred from osteological assessment of the skeleton or with social status and sometimes even ethnicity or religion, reflected in burial rites. Investigating past social structures by means of dietary variation is therefore another key application of isotope analysis in medieval archaeology.

Gender and age

Various case studies have explored gender and age in the medieval periods through stable isotope analysis and commented on isotopic differences — or the lack thereof — between males and females or individuals of different age groups (Dittmann and Grupe 2000; Herrscher *et al* 2001; Privat *et al* 2002; Richards *et al* 2002; Polet and Katzenberg 2003; Richards *et al* 2006; Müldner and Richards 2007a; Lakin in press).

One example where this approach came into its own is the investigation of the social dynamics of marine fish consumption in York from the Roman to the post-medieval period (Müldner 2005; see Müldner and Richards 2007b; 2007a). Consistent with the pan-Northern European trend discussed above, the York data-set illustrates a major change in diet, the introduction of marine fish as an important dietary staple after the Anglo-Saxon period. However, at one of the six cemeteries investigated for this project, the parish church of St Andrew, Fishergate, the investigators were fortunate to directly capture the transition. The earliest burials on the site date to the later 11th or early 12th century (Period 4b, see Kemp and Graves 1996), and the isotope data illustrate that the majority of the population still consumed the almost exclusively terrestrial diet that had been typical for York in the Anglo-Saxon period. Nevertheless, a small group of individuals breaks this pattern, exhibiting significantly higher carbon and nitrogen isotope ratios that indicate their diet included significant amounts of marine fish (Müldner and Richards 2007b). A closer look at the

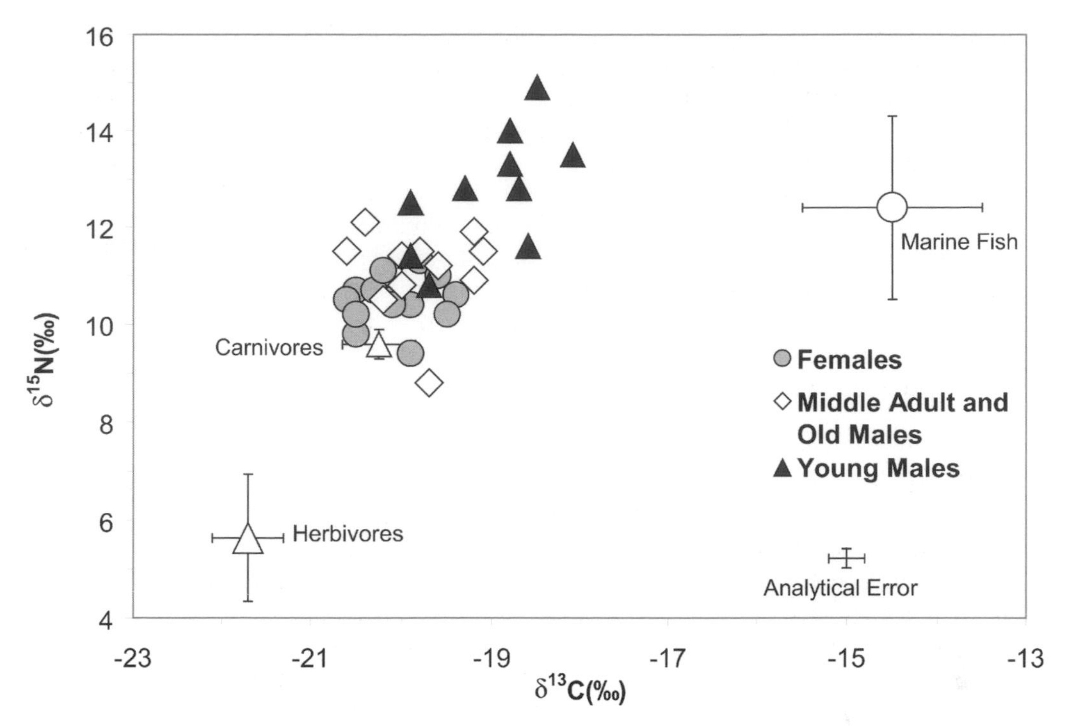

FIGURE 16.2 Human stable isotope data (after Müldner and Richards 2007b) from the parish church of St Andrew, Fishergate in York, Period 4b (dated mid-11th to mid-12th century) in comparison with animal bone data from York (error bars indicate 1 standard deviation). The human data plot somewhat higher than the carnivores (cats/dogs) and generally suggest a diet rich in animal products. Note the clear differences in data distribution between females, older and younger males which indicate very distinctive differences in their diet (see discussion in text).

demographic compositions of both groups, those that consumed fish on a regular basis and those that did not, revealed that these were not random (see Figure 16.2). Correlation of the isotopic data with osteological information on sex and age at death of the skeletons showed that it was the females in the population who had the most 'conservative' diet, with all data clustering tightly in a range that indicates a rather homogenous terrestrial diet consisting of plant and especially animal protein. Conversely, isotope data for the males show more variation and suggest greater variety in the type (or possibly the geographical origin?) of the foods they consumed, including some marine resources. A group of exclusively young males (age at death *c*18–28 years), however, displayed a clearly 'marine' signature, demonstrating that they consumed marine protein in considerable amounts and on a regular basis (Figure 16.2). Few data are available for the subsequent phase of the parish cemetery, Fishergate 4d, which can only be dated generally to the 12th century (Figure 16.3). Nevertheless, these are enough to show that any demographic differences in fish consumption no longer applied: the isotopic signal of several older males (age at death $> \sim 28$ years), and of at least one female, indicates that they had access to marine resources.

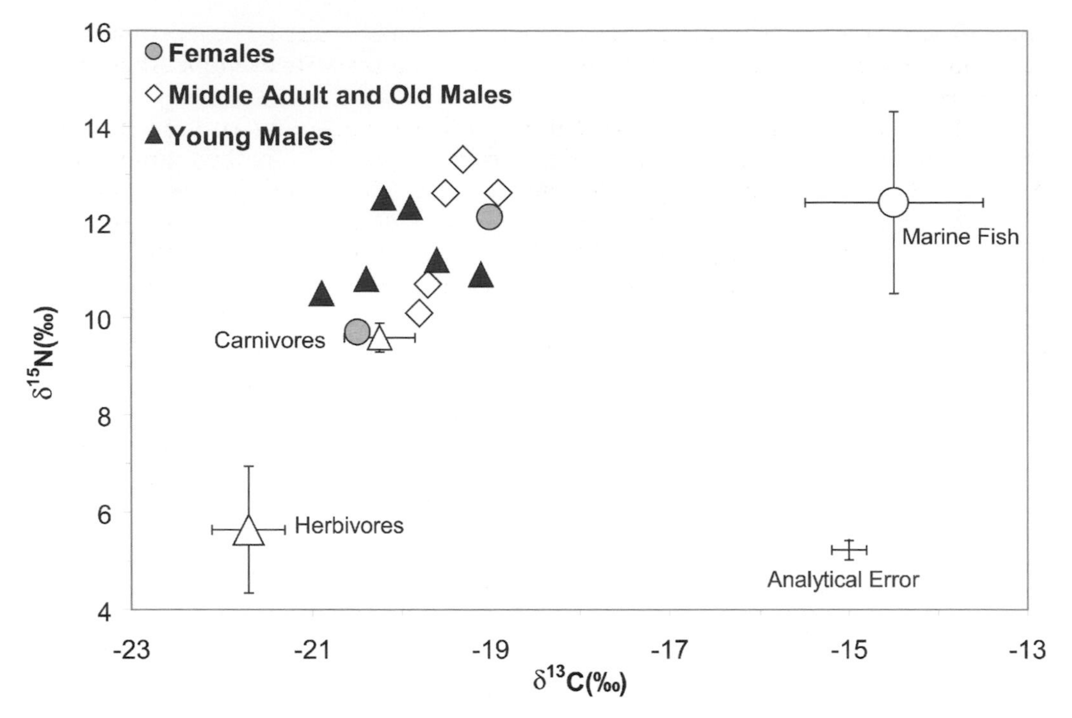

FIGURE 16.3 Human stable isotope data (after Müldner and Richards, 2007b) from St Andrew, Fishergate, Period 4d, dated 12th century (further details, see caption for Figure 16.2). Note that the differences between sex and age groups apparent in the previous period (Figure 16.2) are gone: several of the older males and one of the females now display relatively high carbon and nitrogen stable isotope values which suggest the consumption of marine protein.

The isotopic data from Fishergate offers a rare insight into the social dynamics of the major dietary change that occurred in York in the 11th and 12th centuries. Analysis of fishbone assemblages from York has shown that the import of marine fish and especially herring into York increased dramatically from around AD 1000, followed by larger off-shore species such as cod in the later 11th and 12th century (Barrett *et al* 2004; Harland 2008). The zooarchaeological data only provide indirect evidence for consumption, however, and it is the isotope data that can, in this case, demonstrate that the new staple was not equally available (or acceptable?) to all social groups until at least the 12th century. Greater mobility of the men, which allowed them access to a wider variety of foods, could be one explanation for the observed differences between males and females. In this context it may be significant that the place-name 'Fishergate', a combination of the Old English for 'fishermen' and Scandinavian/Old Norse for 'street', can be traced back to the 11th century, when we also know of the existence of a marine fish market at Foss Bridge, in close proximity to the site (Kemp and Graves 1996, 95–96). Hence it is likely that men directly engaged in the fishing industry were buried at the parish of St Andrew. Rather than a more conservative attitude of women towards a new dietary staple, it may therefore well be occupational differences between men, who spent much of their time out at sea, and the women who were engaged in more domestic tasks at home, that we see expressed in the isotopic record.

The site at Fishergate was converted to a Gilbertine priory in AD 1195; however, the monastic cemetery accommodated lay-burials, probably mainly drawn from York's middle classes, until the Dissolution in 1538 (Kemp and Graves 1996). The stable isotope data obtained from these illustrates that, by the 13th century, the dietary change in York was complete. In an almost complete reversal of the situation of 100 years earlier, sea fish was now an integral part of the diet of the vast majority of the population (see Müldner and Richards 2007b). Social and especially gender differences in fish consumption nevertheless persisted, although these too changed in how they were expressed. In contrast with the earlier phase of the parish cemetery, most females buried at the priory ate fish on a regular basis; nevertheless, on average they consumed less fish than the males, or rather, none of the females in the study consumed quite as much marine protein as some of the males (Figure 16.4).

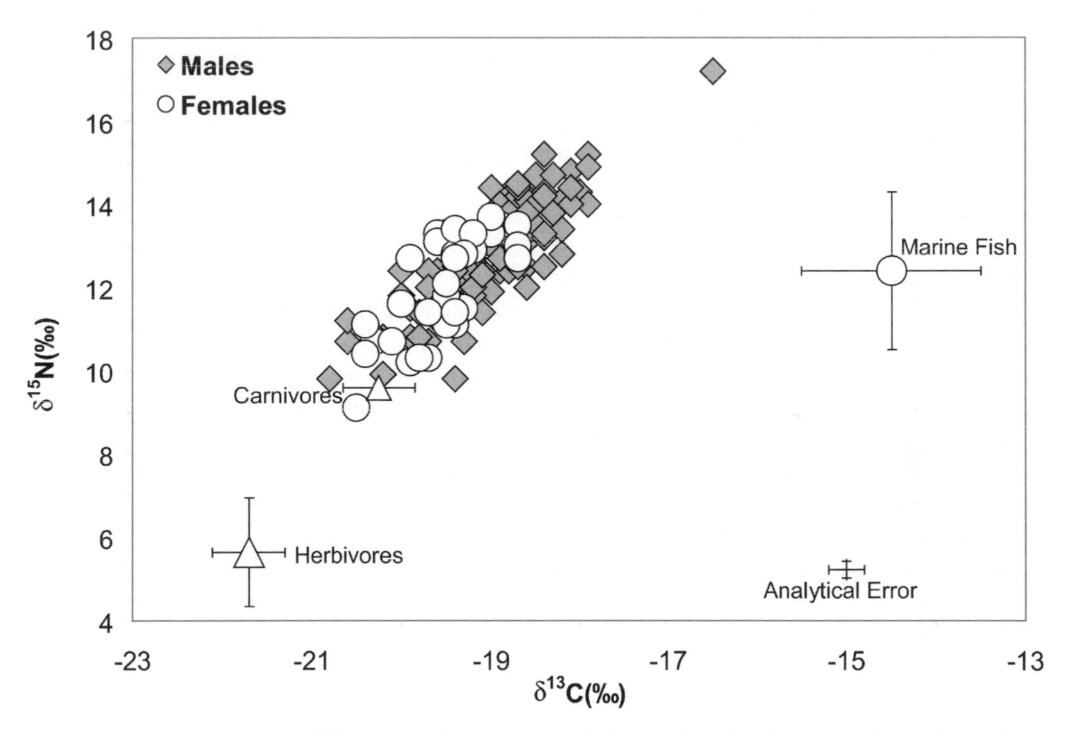

FIGURE 16.4 Human stable isotope data (after Müldner and Richards 2007a) for males and females from the Gilbertine priory of St Andrew Fishergate in York, dated 13th to early 16th century (further details, see caption for Figure 16.2). Carbon and nitrogen stable isotope ratios show a very good positive correlation and indicate that most individuals consumed significant amounts of marine foods. Note that the data for the two sexes mostly overlap but that a number of the males display significantly higher δ-values than any of the females, suggesting that they consumed significantly more marine fish.

The observation of male–female variation in later medieval diet may not seem surprising, given their different spheres and roles in society, but there is actually very little in the historical record to indicate that actual differences in food consumption should exist between the sexes. At first glance, the situation seems simple: later medieval dietetics, in the tradition of the theory of the four humours conceived in classical Antiquity, reasoned that because of differences in temperament between men and women, different foods were needed to balance their complexion and ensure their well-being. As men were usually considered 'hot' and 'dry', while women were thought of as 'cool' and 'moist' (Woolgar 2007), the consumption of fish, cold and moist itself, may not have been thought of as beneficial for the female temperament (although there appears to be little in the texts to say so explicitly; see Scully 1995). While this seems a straightforward explanation for the male–female differences observed at Fishergate, medieval dietary theory was much more complex than this. The dietary needs of an individual were assessed not only by taking into account their sex, but also age and lifestyle. At the same time, the humoral qualities that were attributed to different foods were dependent on various environmental factors and could also be significantly changed by different preparation methods, which were recommended to counteract the 'harmful' effects of certain dishes (Scully 1995, 40). Differences in the types of food advocated for men and women, which seem rather clear-cut at first, would therefore have been at the very least significantly blurred. In addition, it is generally unclear to what extent the majority of the population had access to or took note of this kind of 'scientific' advice in their everyday dietary choices. Where detailed historical records of dietary allowances for males and females exist, such as from the accounts of hospitals or monastic double-houses, differences in the allocations between men and women cannot usually be observed (Woolgar 2007).

The reason for the gender differences in diet at Fishergate must therefore be sought elsewhere, and it is worth remembering that fish in medieval diet had two different dimensions: a nutritional one as a source of animal protein, as well as a spiritual one as a fasting food, which could be consumed on the days when church law, drawing on the Rule of St Benedict, demanded abstinence from the flesh of quadrupeds (see Harvey 1993; Woolgar 2006). Women during pregnancy were exempt from fasting (Woolgar 2007); however, there are also numerous examples of religious women who fasted more fastidiously than men, refusing almost any food but bread and water and in extreme cases, even starving themselves to death (Bynum 1997). While it is tempting to see a connection between female spirituality expressed in women's attitude to food and the isotopic data, there is actually no evidence to suggest that the women in the sample were depriving themselves of food. The isotopic values of both males and females are suggestive of a diet rich in animal protein (although this may have come from either meat or dairy products). Data for the two sexes mostly overlap and comparison of male–female double burials from within the priory church suggest no measurable dietary differences between what presumably were husbands and wives living in the same household (Müldner and Richards 2007a). The question that needs to be asked is therefore perhaps not why the diet of the females contained less fish, but rather, who were the males that consumed fish in significantly greater quantities than their contemporaries?

Much has been written about feasting and conspicuous consumption in the medieval period and the large quantities of food consumed on these occasions (see, for example, Mead 1931; Dyer 1998; Woolgar 2001). It is likely that men, not being tied to the domestic sphere, had a greater part in these practices, just as it is a common anthropological observation that gender inequality and power relations are often expressed in differential access to food (Counihan 1997; Mintz and Du Bois 2002; see Hastorf 1991). More simply, however, it could also be that the gender differences observed in the Fishergate data-set are actually differences in diet between lay and monastic groups, as the isotope data for the males might be skewed towards a more marine diet by the presence of monks in the group (Müldner and Richards 2007a). Further isotopic studies of a variety of different sites — monasteries, nunneries and non-monastic cemeteries — are needed to validate these interpretations. Nevertheless, the discussion above demonstrates the fruitfulness of an isotopic approach to the investigation of gender in the medieval period.

Social status

Various isotopic studies have examined differences in social status from a dietary perspective, either by correlating isotopic evidence with grave goods (Schutkowski *et al* 1999; Privat *et al* 2002), or for the high and later medieval period, by contrasting different site types or burial locations (Herrscher *et al* 2002; Polet and Katzenberg 2003; Müldner and Richards 2005; 2007a). For the later periods, several studies have observed the kind of dietary variation that might be expected from the documentary sources, namely that high status individuals had access to a more varied diet rich in animal products, indicated in the isotopic data by the increased consumption of marine fish. For example, at the Cistercian house of Hulton Abbey (Staffordshire), Thorndyke (2005) found that males and females buried close to the altar of the church had consumed more marine protein than individuals interred further away, in the nave and north transept. Similarly, Müldner *et al* (in press) observed that the diet of a group of males from Whithorn Cathedral priory (Dumfries and Galloway, Scotland), which had been identified as bishops through contextual information, contained more marine fish than those of lower status individuals buried at the same site.

In other cases, patterns in the dietary data are less easily explained. At the Gilbertine priory at Fishergate in York, where the archaeological context allowed contrasting multiple burial locations within and outside the monastic buildings, the isotope evidence suggested no differences between individuals buried inside the priory church, in all likelihood high-status lay-benefactors, and those interred in the open cemetery to the south, which is assumed to hold the lowest status burials on site (Müldner and Richards 2007a). Similarly, once the bias due to the differences between male and female skeletons has been removed, there is no evidence that individuals buried in the presumed monastic cemetery east of the church consumed a different diet from the other males in the sample (ibid; but see Mays 1997). On the other hand, the analysis had several unexpected results, such as the observation that the diet of a number of individuals who had sustained severe blade-injuries around the time of death, and were buried in various different locations across the priory grounds, was very unusual compared to the great majority of the population. They had consumed either noticeably less or, in one case, very significantly more, marine fish (Figure 16.5).

The cemeteries at the Fishergate priory are unusual compared to other monastic sites because of the high frequency of sharp-force skeletal trauma recorded (see Stroud and Kemp 1993). Several scenarios have been considered, such as an ongoing feud involving benefactors of the priory, trial by combat or the existence of a hospital specialized in the treatment of battle trauma (Daniell 2001). The dietary evidence now strongly suggests that the individuals involved came from a very different social background to the canons, lay-benefactors, servants and workers that make up the majority of the burials. The explanation of a specialist hospital or even of an unrecorded tradition among the Gilbertines to care for and bury the victims of violent conflict therefore seems increasingly likely (Müldner and Richards 2007a).

The case of one of the blade-injured individuals is particularly intriguing. The individual represented by skeleton YFG5720 consumed not less, but significantly

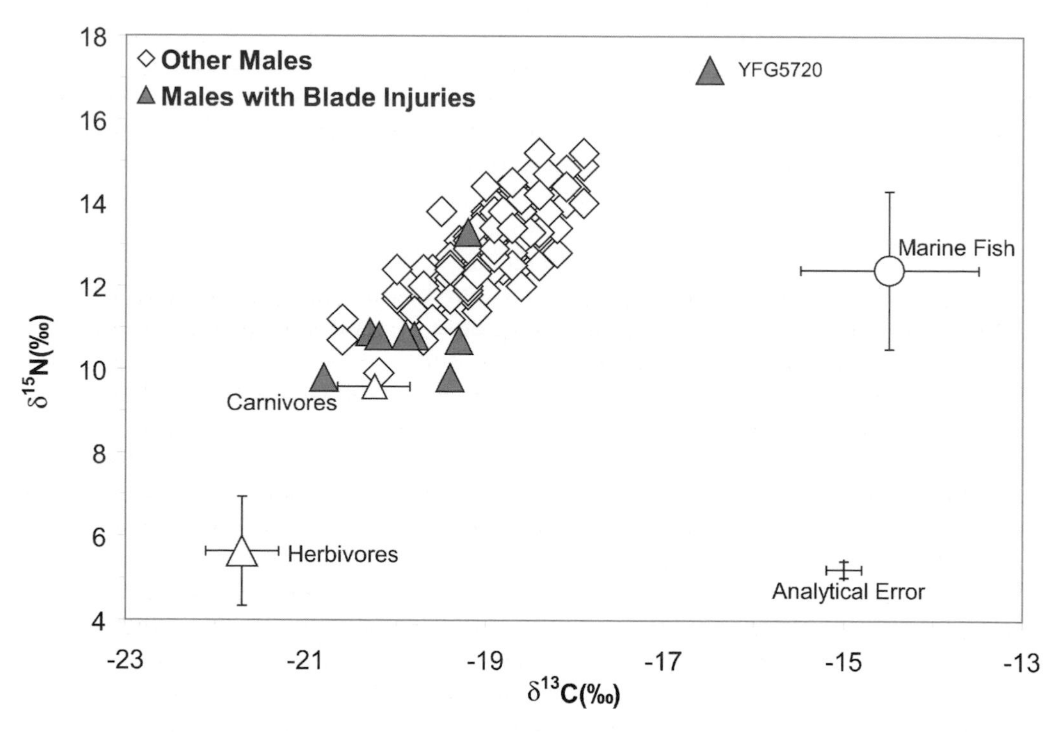

FIGURE 16.5 Human stable isotope data (after Müldner and Richards 2007a) for individuals with sharp force trauma sustained around the time of death in comparison with the remainder of the males from the Gilbertine Priory of St Andrew Fishergate in York (further details, see caption for Figure 16.2). Note that, with one exception, all individuals with blade-injuries consumed either significantly less or significantly more marine foods than the vast majority of the Fishergate population. The diet of one individual, YFG5720, is particularly unusual and so far without parallels in medieval data-sets from England (further discussion in text). Females were excluded from this comparison because of the male/female differences in the data-set.

more marine fish than any other man or woman buried at Fishergate; significantly more, in fact, than any other individual analysed from medieval England so far. He was buried in the priory's chapter-house, usually thought to be reserved for senior clerics or major benefactors (Gilchrist and Sloane 2005); however, as the excavators noted, the fact that he died of a severe injury to the back of his head, likely caused by a sword, was hardly consistent with a monastic lifestyle (see Stroud and Kemp 1993, 140). The extremely unusual dietary signal now further adds to this picture as it makes it highly unlikely that he shared his meals with the canons or even that he was prior of the house who kept a separate table. At the same time, as there are no similar values observed from medieval England so far, it is also difficult to see him as a regular lay benefactor who resided in the York area. Instead, it is much more conceivable that he was a migrant from abroad, perhaps from the fish-producing regions of Scandinavia or the North Atlantic, or, alternatively, if his burial location were to indicate a monastic background after all, a high-ranking cleric from a much wealthier institution than Fishergate (see Müldner and Richards 2007a).

These findings of dietary diversity at a monastic site like Fishergate are not only intriguing, as they hint at the diverse life-histories of individuals buried here, they also illustrate how isotopic evidence, although nominally restricted to giving information about diet, can make a significant contribution to the understanding of the spatial organization of medieval cemeteries and the functions of a site as a whole.

CONCLUSIONS

Carbon and nitrogen stable isotope analysis of bone collagen can only give very general information about human diet and its diagnostic range appears particularly limited when compared to the wealth of detail and subtle variation that is available through the study of texts, animal bones or plant remains. Nevertheless, the value of a method is not in how well it can reproduce knowledge that is already available through other sources, but in whether it can provide a new perspective and novel information which enables us to address important questions. This review has demonstrated that isotope analysis, despite its obvious limitations, has much to offer for the study of medieval diet and society.

Although stable isotope work on medieval populations has really only just begun, the examples presented here already highlight patterns of dietary variation — over time, between males and females, according to age and social groups at individual sites — which are deeply intriguing and would have been largely inaccessible by other methods. While some of the isotopic results can be easily reconciled with information from historical sources, others are more surprising. They suggest that not only the reality of social differences in medieval diet, but also the multitude of economic and cultural factors that caused them, were much more complex than we yet understand. Nevertheless, given that the data available at the moment are from a few sites only, it is likely that we have only just scratched the surface of the wealth of new information that could be obtained through the isotopic analysis of medieval cemetery populations. With methods and research questions being refined and new data being generated all the time, stable isotope analysis for medieval archaeology therefore promises to be an exciting field to be working in over the next few years.

Stable isotope analysis of bone for dietary reconstruction is still a relatively young technique. While its potential for contributing to our understanding of medieval diet and society is therefore yet to be fully realized, some key themes that seem particularly worth pursuing are briefly outlined here. Possibly the most promising area for further investigations is the question of gender differences in medieval diet, a subject which is notoriously difficult to approach by other archaeological methods but one where isotope analysis, with its capacity to target individuals, truly comes into its own. By contrasting males and females from different spheres of medieval society (monastic and secular, town and country, high and low status) and different stages of life (young and old), significant new information about gender roles and the life-experience of individuals may be gathered. These will have the potential to complement and inform medieval gender studies as a whole. Stable isotope data could also provide a fresh perspective on key debates on medieval subsistence, such as the impact of recurring famines and the Black Death on standards of living in later medieval town and country (see Dyer 1998). Ongoing investigations of East Smithfield Black Death cemetery in London, where survivors of the Great Famine of AD 1315–17 are buried, among others (Mueller *et al* 2008), should merely be the start to integrating bioarchaeological data on health and nutrition for this important period in European history. Finally, by extending the time frame to the post-medieval period, the impact of the Reformation on diet and particularly fasting practices (expressed in fish consumption) could be an extremely fruitful area of research. It would not only inform us about the repercussions for everyday life of a major socio-cultural upheaval but also better our understanding of key questions relating to the isotopic data for medieval diet by putting the evidence into its wider context (see Müldner and Richards 2007b).

With stable isotope analysis becoming easier to apply and a number of major projects currently under way, it may be hoped that a time when isotope analysis is as well established in medieval archaeology as, for instance, the study of plant or animal remains, is not too far off. In order to achieve this and to open a fruitful dialogue between medievalists and isotope analysts, the onus is on both sides, on the medieval archaeologists to take notice of what isotope analysis can offer but also on the archaeological scientists to communicate their results in an accessible way and to publish in journals and monographs that are read outside the scientific community. If this can be realized, then whoever undertakes to produce a similar review for the Society's 60th anniversary, will have much to write about.

BIBLIOGRAPHY

Ambrose, S H, 1993 'Isotopic analysis of paleodiets: methodological and interpretive considerations', in M K Sandford (ed), *Investigations of Ancient Human Tissue: Chemical Analyses in Anthropology*, 59–130, Gordon and Breach, Langthorne

Arneborg, J, Heinemeier, J, Lynnerup, N, Nielsen, H L, Rud, N and Sveinbjörnsdóttir, Á E, 1999 'Change of diet of the Greenland Vikings determined from stable carbon isotope analysis and ^{14}C dating of their bones', *Radiocarbon* 41, 157–168

Barrett, J H and Richards, M P, 2005 'Identity, gender, religion and economy: new isotope and radiocarbon evidence for marine resource intensification in early historic Orkney, Scotland, UK', *European Journal of Archaeology* 7, 249–271

Barrett, J H, Beukens, R P and Nicholson, R A, 2001 'Diet and ethnicity during the Viking colonization of northern Scotland: Evidence from fish bones and stable carbon isotopes', *Antiquity* 75, 145–154

Barrett, J H, Locker, A M and Roberts, C M, 2004 '"Dark Age Economics" revisited: the English fish bone evidence AD 600–1600', *Antiquity* 78, 618–636

Barrett, J, Beukens, R P, Simpson, I, Ashmore, P, Poaps, S and Huntley, J, 2000 'What was the Viking Age and when did it happen? A view from Orkney', *Norwegian Archaeological Review* 33, 1–36

Bayliss, A, Shepherd Popescu, E, Beavan-Athfield, N, Bronk Ramsey, C, Cook, G T and Locker, A, 2004 'The potential significance of dietary offsets for the interpretation of radiocarbon dates: an archaeologically significant example from medieval Norwich', *Journal of Archaeological Science* 31, 563–575

Beardsworth, A and Keil, T, 1997 *Sociology on the Menu: An Invitation to the Study of Food and Society*, Routledge, London and New York

Bocherens, H, Fizet, M, Mariotti, A, Olive, C, Bellon, G and Billiou, D, 1991 'Application de la Biogeochimie Isotopique (13C, 15N) a la Détermination du Régime Alimentaire des Populations Humaines et Animales durant les Périodes Antiques et Médiévale', *Archives des Sciences, Genève* 44, 329–340

Bourbou, C and Richards, M P, 2007 'The Middle Byzantine menu: palaeodietary information from Isotopic analysis of humans and fauna from Kastella, Crete', *International Journal of Osteoarchaeology* 17, 63–72

Braudel, F, 1973 *Capitalism and Material Life 1400–1800*, Harper and Row, New York

Bynum, C W, 1987 *Holy Feast and Holy Fast: The Religious Significance of Food to Medieval Women*, University of California Press, Berkeley and London

Bynum, C W, 1997 'Fast, feast, and flesh. The religious significance of food to medieval women', in C Counihan and P van Esterik (eds), *Food and Culture: A Reader*, 138–158, Routledge, New York and London

Counihan, C M, 1997 'Introduction — food and gender: identity and power', in C Counihan and S L Kaplan (eds), *Food and Gender: Identity and Power*, 1–10, Routledge, London and New York

Counihan, C, 1999 *The Anthropology of Food and Body: Gender, Meaning and Power*, Routledge, London and New York

Daniell, C, 2001 'Battle and trial: weapon injury burials of St Andrew's Church, Fishergate, York', *Medieval Archaeology* 45, 220–226

Dittman, K and Grupe, G, 2000 'Biochemical and palaeopathological investigations on weaning and infant mortality in the early Middle Ages', *Anthropologischer Anzeiger* 58, 345–355

Dyer, C, 1988 'Changes in diet in the Late Middle Ages: The case of harvest workers', *Agricultural History Review* 36, 21–37

Dyer, C, 1998 'Did the Peasants Really Starve in Medieval England?', in M Carlin and J T Rosenthal (eds), *Food and Eating in Medieval Europe*, 53–71, The Hambledon Press, London and Rio Grande

Dyer, C, 1998 *Standards of Living in the Later Middle Ages. Social Change in England c1200–1520*, rev edn, Cambridge University Press, Cambridge

Enghoff, I B, 1999 'Fishing in the Baltic region from the 5th century BC to the 16th century AD: evidence from fish bones', *Archaeofauna* 8, 41–85

Enghoff, I B, 2000 'Fishing in the southern North Sea region from the 1st to the 16th century AD: evidence from fish bones', *Archaeofauna* 9, 59–132

Ervynck, A, Strydonck, V and Boudin, M, 1999/2000 'Dieetreconstructie en herkomstbepaling op basis van de analyse van de stabiele isotopen 13C en 15N uit dierlijk en menselijk skeletmateriaal: een eerste verkennend onderzoek op middeleurwse vondsten uit Vlaanderen', *Archaeologie in Vlaanderen* 7, 131–140

Ervynck, A, Van Neer, W and Pieters, M, 2004 'How the north was won (and lost again): historical and archaeological data on the exploitation of the North Atlantic by the Flemish fishery', in R A Housley and G M Coles (eds), *Atlantic Connections and Adaptations: Economies, Environments and Subsistence in Lands Bordering the North Atlantic*, 230–239, Oxbow, Oxford

Gilchrist, R and Sloane, B, 2005 *Requiem: The Medieval Monastic Cemetery in Britain*, Museum of London Archaeology Service, London

Gumerman, G IV, 1997 'Food and complex societies', *Journal of Archaeological Method and Theory* 4, 105–139

Harland, J, 2008 'Using zooarchaeology to trace the origins of commercial fishing: A summary of the British evidence with particular emphasis on York', Paper presented at the Cod and Herring: The Archaeology and Early History of Intensive Fishing Conference, Westray, Orkney: 4–8 June, 2008

Harvey, B, 1993 *Living and Dying in England 1100–1540. The Monastic Experience*, Oxford University Press, Oxford and New York

Hastorf, C, 1991 'Gender, Space and Food in Prehistory', in Gero, J M and Conkey, M W (eds), *Engendering Archaeology: Women and Prehistory*, 132–159, Blackwell, Oxford and Cambridge, MA

Hedges, R E M and Reynard, L M, 2007 'Nitrogen isotopes and the trophic level of humans in archaeology', *Journal of Archaeological Science* 34, 1240–1251

Hedges, R E M, 2004 'Isotopes and red herrings: comments on Milner *et al.* and Lidén *et al.*' *Antiquity* 78, 34–37

Herrscher, E, Bocherens, H and Valentin, F, 2002 'Reconstitution des comportements alimentaires aux époques historiques en Europe à partir de l'analyse isotopique d'ossements humain', *Revue Belge de Philologie et d'Histoire* 80, 1403–1422

Herrscher, E, Bocherens, H, Valentin, F and Colardelle, R, 2001 'Comportements alimentaire au Moyen Âge à Grenoble: application de la biogéochimie isotopique à la nécropole Saint-Laurent (XIIIe–XVe siècles, Isère, France)', *Comptes Rendus de l'Académies des Sciences, Series III — Sciences de la Vie* 324, 479–487

Hoffmann, R C, 1996 'Economic development and aquatic ecosystems in medieval Europe', *American Historical Review* 101, 631–669

Johansen, O V, Gulliksen, S and Nydal, R, 1986 'δ13C and diet: analysis of Norwegian human skeletons', *Radiocarbon* 28, 754–761

Kemp, R L and Graves, C P, 1996 *The Church and Gilbertine Priory of St. Andrew, Fishergate*, The Archaeology of York, 11/2, Council for British Archaeology, York

Kosiba, S B, Tykot, R H and Carlsson, D, 2007 'Stable isotopes as indicators of change in the food procurement and food preference of Viking Age and Early Christian populations on Gotland (Sweden)', *Journal of Anthropological Archaeology* 26, 394–411

Lakin, K E, in press 'Medieval diet: evidence for a London signature?' in S Baker, M Allen, S Middle and K Poole (eds), *Food and Drink in Archaeology I: University of Nottingham Postgraduate Conference 2007*, Prospect, Totnes

Linderholm, A, Hedenstierna Jonson, C, Svensk, O and Lidén, K, 2008 'Diet and status in Birka: stable isotopes and grave goods compared', *Antiquity* 82, 446–461

Marvin, W P, 2006 *Hunting Law and Ritual in Medieval English Literature*, D S Brewer, Cambridge

Mays, S A, 1997 'Carbon stable isotope ratios in mediaeval and later human skeletons from northern England', *Journal of Archaeological Science* 24, 561–567

Mays, S A, Richards, M P and Fuller, B T, 2002 'Bone stable isotope evidence for infant feeding in mediaeval England', *Antiquity* 76, 654–656

Mays, S, 2000 'New directions in the analysis of stable isotopes in excavated bones and teeth', in M Cox and S Mays (eds), *Human Osteology in Archaeology and Forensic Science*, 425–438, Greenwich Medical Media, London

Mead, W E, 1931 *The English Medieval Feast*, Allen and Unwin, London

Mennell, S, 1985 *All Manners of Food: Eating and Taste in England and France from the Middle Ages to the Present*, Blackwell, Oxford

Mintz, S W and Du Bois, C M, 2002 'The anthropology of food and eating', *Annual Review of Anthropology* 31, 99–119

Mueller, V, Montgomery, J, Lee-Thorp, J A and White, W, 2008. '"The end of the world?" Famine, plague and climate change of 14th century London', Paper presented at the Third International Symposium of Biomolecular Archaeology, University of York, 14–17 September 2008

Müldner, G, Montgomery, J, Cook, G, Ellam, R, Gledhill, A and Lowe, C in press. 'Isotopes and individuals: diet and mobility among the medieval Bishops of Whithorn', *Antiquity*

Müldner, G and Richards, M P, 2005 'Fast or feast: reconstructing diet in later medieval England by stable isotope analysis', *Journal of Archaeological Science* 32, 39–48

Müldner, G and Richards, M P, 2006 'Diet in medieval England: the evidence from stable isotopes', in Woolgar *et al* (eds) 2006, 228–238

Müldner, G and Richards, M P, 2007a 'Diet and diversity at later medieval Fishergate: the isotopic evidence', *American Journal of Physical Anthropology* 134, 162–174

Müldner, G and Richards, M P, 2007b 'Stable isotope evidence for 1500 years of human diet at the city of York, UK', *American Journal of Physical Anthropology* 133, 682–697

Müldner, G, 2005 'Eboracum — Jorvik — York: A diachronic study of human diet in York by stable isotope analysis', unpublished thesis, University of Bradford PhD

Mundee, M, in press 'An isotopic approach to diet in Medieval Spain', in S Baker, A Grey, K Lakin, R Madgwick, K Poole and M Sandias (eds), *Food and Drink in Archaeology II: University of Nottingham Postgraduate Conference 2008*, Prospect, Totnes

Polet, C and Katzenberg, M A, 2003 'Reconstruction of the diet in a mediaeval monastic community from the coast of Belgium', *Journal of Archaeological Science* 30, 525–533

Privat, K L, O'Connell, T and Richards, M P, 2002 'Stable isotope analysis of human and faunal remains from the Anglo-Saxon cemetery at Berinsfield, Oxfordshire: dietary and social implications', *Journal of Archaeological Science* 29, 779–790

Richards, M P, Fuller, B T and Molleson, T I, 2006 'Stable isotope palaeodietary study of humans and fauna from the multi-period (Iron Age, Viking and Late Medieval) site of Newark Bay, Orkney', *Journal of Archaeological Science* 33, 122–131

Richards, M P, Mays, S and Fuller, B T, 2002 'Stable carbon and nitrogen isotope values of bone and teeth reflect weaning age at the medieval Wharram Percy Site, Yorkshire, UK', *American Journal of Physical Anthropology* 119, 205–210

Richards, M P, Price, T D and Koch, E, 2003 'Mesolithic and Neolithic subsistence in Denmark: new stable isotope data', *Current Anthropology* 44, 288–295

Richards, M, 2000 'Stable isotope analysis in archaeology: a short introduction', *The Archaeologist* 38, 19–20

Roth, N, 2003 'Laws relating to food use by Jews', in N Roth (ed), *Medieval Jewish Civilization: An Encyclopaedia*, 256–264, Routledge, New York and London

Salamon, M, Coppa, A, McCormick, M, Rubini, M, Vargiu, R and Tuross, N, 2007 'The consilience of historical and isotopic approaches in reconstructing the medieval Mediterranean diet', *Journal of Archaeological Science* 35, 1667–1672

Schäuble, A, 2006 'Ernährungsrekonstruktion dreier mittelalterlicher Bevölkerungen anhand der Analyse stabiler Isotope und Spurenelemente', PhD Thesis, Freie Universität Berlin, http://www.diss.fu-berlin.de/2006/1/ (accessed 12 July 2006)

Schutkowski, H, Herrmann, B, Wiedemann, F, Bocherens, H and Grupe, G, 1999 'Diet, status and decomposition at Weingarten: Trace element and isotope analyses on early mediaeval skeletal material', *Journal of Archaeological Science* 26, 675–685

Schwarcz, H P and Schoeninger, M J, 1991 'Stable isotope analyses in human nutritional ecology', *Yearbook of Physical Anthropology* 34, 283–321

Scully, T, 1995 *The Art of Cookery in the Middle Ages*, The Boydell Press, Woodbridge

Sealy, J, 2001 'Body tissue chemistry and palaeodiet', in D R Brothwell and A M Pollard (eds), *Handbook of Archaeological Science*, 269–279, John Wiley and Sons, Chichester

Starkey, D J, Reid, C and Ashcroft, N (eds), 2000 *England's Sea Fisheries. The Commercial Sea Fisheries of England and Wales since 1300*, Chatham Publishing, London

Stroud, G and Kemp, R L, 1993 *Cemeteries of the Church and Priory of St Andrew, Fishergate*, The Archaeology of York, 12/2, Council for British Archaeology, York

Sykes, N, 2004 'The dynamics of social status: wildfowl exploitations in England AD 410–1550', *Archaeological Journal* 161, 82–105

Tauber, H, 1981 '13C evidence for dietary habits of prehistoric man in Denmark', *Nature* 292, 332–333

Thorndyke, W, 2005 'Diet and diagenesis: Stable isotope analysis of remains from Hulton Abbey, Stoke-on-Trent', unpublished MSc dissertation, University of Reading

van der Merwe, N J and Vogel, J C, 1978 '13C content of human collagen as a measure of prehistoric diet in Woodland North America', *Nature* 276, 815–816

van der Merwe, N J, 1982 'Carbon isotopes, photosynthesis, and archaeology', *American Scientist* 70, 596–606

van Strydonck, M, Ervynck, A, Vandenbruaene, M and Boudin, M, 2006 *Relieken. Echt of vals?*, Davidsfonds, Leuven

Vogel, J C and van der Merwe, N J, 1977 'Isotopic evidence for early maize cultivation in New York State', *American Antiquity* 42, 238–242

Weiss Adamson, M (ed) 2002 *Regional Cuisines of Medieval Europe: A Book of Essays*, Routledge, London

Woolgar, C M, 2007. 'Does gender matter? The diet of women in late medieval England', Paper presented at the meeting of the Diet Group on 17 November 2007, Somerville College, Oxford

Woolgar, C, 2001 'Fast and feast: conspicuous consumption and the diet of the nobility in the fifteenth century', in M Hicks (ed), *Revolution and Consumption in Late Medieval England*, 7–25, Boydell, Woodbridge

Woolgar, C, 2006 'Group diets in late medieval England', in Woolgar *et al* (eds) 2006, 191–200

Woolgar, C, Serjeantson, D and Waldron, T (eds), 2006 *Food in Medieval England: History and Archaeology*, Oxford University Press, Oxford

CHAPTER 17
ANIMALS, THE BONES OF MEDIEVAL SOCIETY

By NAOMI SYKES

The importance of animals in medieval society cannot be overstated — they inhabited the landscape and minds of the population who utilized them for food, as economic commodities, raw materials and as symbols. The study of animal remains carries considerable potential to provide new insights into the medieval world but zooarchaeologists are often poor at communicating this possibility to the wider archaeological community. Here the development of medieval zooarchaeology is considered and a range of examples are presented to demonstrate the variety of questions that might be addressed profitably through the analysis of animal remains.

INTRODUCTION

When the Society for Medieval Archaeology was founded, the study of archaeological animal bones (zooarchaeology) was still to emerge as a distinct discipline. Yet medieval archaeologists were quick to realize the potential of animal bone analysis, as reflected by the Society's journal *Medieval Archaeology*, which began publishing zooarchaeological reports as early as its third volume (Jope 1959). The development of medieval zooarchaeology is charted well in the pages of the Journal. It shows how the earliest animal bone reports, such as that by Seddon *et al* (1964) on the remains from the 'Dark Age' settlement at Maxey, were little more than species lists that attracted only passing comment in the articles to which they were appended. Gradually new zooarchaeological methodologies were created, particularly during the 1970s and 1980s, allowing more ambitious analyses of site economy and animal husbandry regimes (eg Rackham 1979; Coy 1980). But it was not until the mid-1980s that zooarchaeological reports began to break out of the appendices. Gilchrist's (1988) study of animal bones from Dinas Powys in Wales is pivotal, being the first article in *Medieval Archaeology* to focus on zooarchaeology in its own right and showing how animal bone data might assist with the characterization of archaeological sites.

As zooarchaeological techniques became increasingly standardized and greater quantities of comparative data became available, specialists were able to look beyond individual sites and ask broader questions about medieval society. One of the first to achieve this was Clutton-Brock, whose study of early medieval animals was published in Wilson's (1976) edited volume on aspects of Anglo-Saxon England. This was followed later by Grant's (1988) comprehensive examination of animal resources in later medieval England, which considered not only traditional issues of animal husbandry and economy but also touched on the subjects of social identity and human–animal inter-relationships. These themes were developed from an international perspective by Salisbury (1994) in her book *The Beast Within*. Since these publications, innumerable animal bone studies have been undertaken both in Britain and on the Continent but, with a few exceptions (eg Albarella 1997; Baker and Clark 1993; Barrett *et al* 2004; Clavel 2001; Yvinec 1993; Ervynck 1997), analyses have remained conservative with specialists writing for each other rather than to advance knowledge of the medieval period. Lack of dialogue between zooarchaeologists, other medieval archaeologists and historians has recently been highlighted by O'Connor (2002, 14) in his review of medieval zooarchaeology in Europe: this article should be read for an overview of the main research trends of the last 30 years. I do not wish to rehearse O'Connor's arguments here; instead this paper will consider some of the approaches and recent works that have the potential to contribute greatly to mainstream discussions within medieval archaeology. It is not possible to provide a full account of all research currently being undertaken, so this chapter will concentrate instead on the British evidence and focus on one of the themes stressed within this volume: social identity. Before the issue of identity is explored in detail, a brief introduction to the methods of animal bone analyses is provided, illustrated with examples that highlight the benefits of zooarchaeology for understanding the medieval period, AD 450–1550.

APPROACHES IN MEDIEVAL ZOOARCHAEOLOGY: METHODS AND INTERPRETATIONS

It is easy to assume that techniques in medieval zooarchaeology have remained unchanged since the 1970s, but many new approaches have arisen and the rationale behind other traditional methods has altered. For instance, one of the primary aims of zooarchaeology has always been to determine which species are represented in an assemblage and in what frequency, but the interpretation of these basic data has gradually evolved. Originally, quantification was carried out with the aim of reconstructing diet and economy, in particular to determine whether communities based their subsistence on cattle, sheep/goats or pigs. Later it was recognized that the relative frequencies of the main domesticates could be used to help characterize medieval settlements: sheep/goat remains predominating on rural sites, urban assemblages generally containing higher percentages of cattle, with pigs being more abundant on religious and secular elite settlements (Figure 17.1 and see Grant 1988). The range of species within an assemblage has also been used to ascribe site character and function, most notably in the case of *wics*, whose unvaried assemblages are thought to reflect the inhabitant's lack of control over their provisions: it has been suggested that the elite maintained these trading settlements by redistributing the less desirable portions

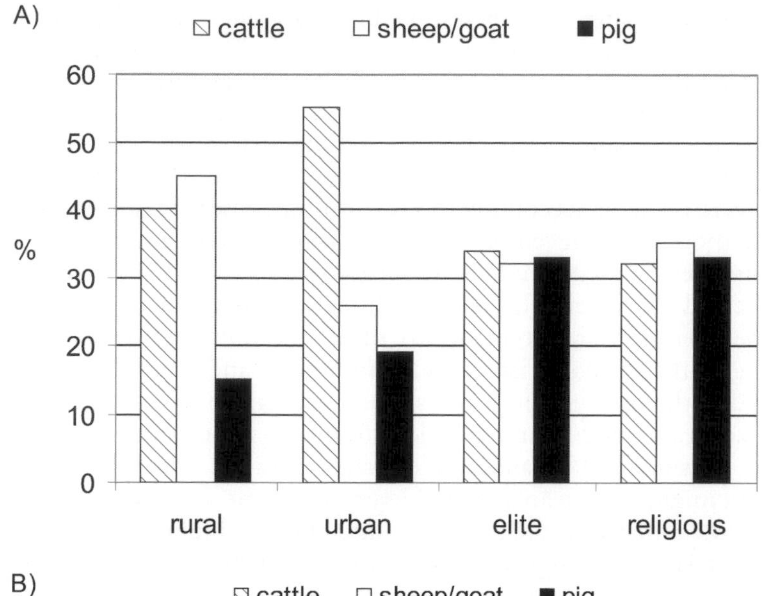

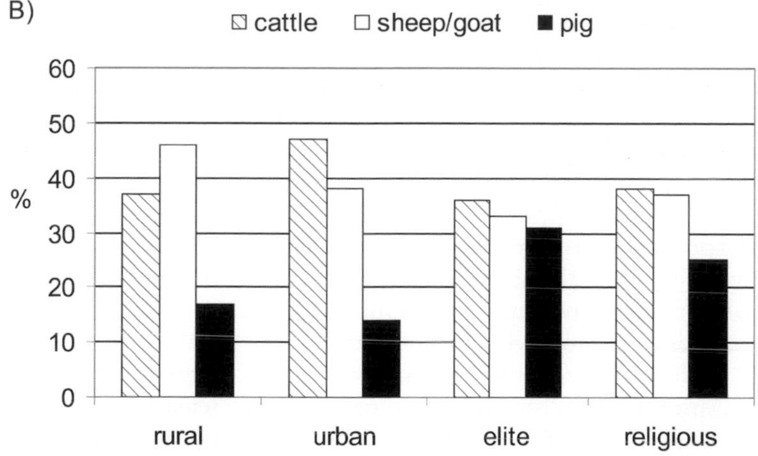

FIGURE 17.1 Relative frequencies of the main domesticates (according to NISP) shown, by sites type, for A) the pre-Conquest period and B) the post-Conquest period (for raw data, see Sykes 2007a).

of their food rents (Bourdillon 1994; O'Connor 2001). Conversely, the greater diversity of species represented in later medieval towns has been taken as evidence for the growth of commercialization and the increasing ability of urban consumers to demand and purchase a range of foodstuffs, especially poultry, fish and game (O'Connor 2001).

Recently, increasing attention has been given to the species least well represented in the archaeological record, because it is now recognized that the animals with which people interacted infrequently may actually have carried *more* social significance than those encountered on a daily basis. Anglo-Saxon and later medieval documents indicate that certain wild animals, such as deer, whales, porpoise, dolphin and large wildfowl (bittern, crane, swan and heron) were reserved for the upper echelons of society. Whilst these animals are poorly represented archaeologically, their remains are found almost exclusively on sites of high-status. Their presence is now a recognized marker of high-status settlement, reflecting the medieval elite's preoccupation with hunting, falconry and the consumption of game (Albarella and Thomas 2002; Dobney and Jaques 2002; Gardiner 1997; Sykes 2005; 2007; forthcoming). But the presence or absence of particular species can reflect much more than socio-economic status: it can also inform on the ideology of the consumer because in the medieval period not all animals were deemed acceptable foods for all members of society. On the basis of humoral theory it was believed that the temperament of an animal would be transferred to its consumer, so some animals were eaten preferentially or avoided, depending on their perceived character. This is exemplified well by the wild boar, the violent *bête noir*. On the Continent their remains are often found in high frequencies on settlements belonging to the secular aristocracy, who hunted and consumed these fierce animals to embolden themselves and increase their military prowess (Larioux 1988; Yvinec 1993). By contrast, wild boar are seldom found in assemblages deriving from religious houses, presumably because ecclesiastics avoided animals whose capture and consumption might induce an aggressive temperament. Instead, religious houses consistently yield the remains of roe deer, hare and crane in higher frequencies than is seen on any other site type — these animals were deemed to be meek in character, the roe deer in particular viewed as chaste and pious, and therefore fitting foods for men of the cloth (Yvinec 1993; Sykes 2007a).

Interpretations beyond 'what people ate' are provided by cull patterns, constructed from bone development and dental ageing data, which can indicate how animals were used prior to their slaughter. Such data have been used extensively to examine the economic and agricultural changes that occurred during the medieval period. For instance, the documented importance of England's wool trade was quickly validated by the earliest zooarchaeological studies, which found that most medieval sheep were maintained well into adulthood so that several wool-clips might be taken (eg Noddle 1975). The oldest sheep are found in assemblages dating between the late 14th and early 16th centuries, a period when wool prices were inflated as murrain destroyed many flocks; both improving markets and dropping sheep numbers encouraged farmers to maintain their surviving animals to at least three years (Figure 17.2; Grant 1988, 154). The later medieval period was also a time of changing cattle husbandry practices. Whereas the remains of cattle from early medieval sites tend to derive from adults slaughtered after serving for several years as plough animals, from the late 14th century onwards calf remains are represented in increasing numbers, suggesting a move towards a meat and dairy economy (Figure 17.3; Albarella 1997). Recently it has been recognized that such husbandry shifts are coincident with other changes observable in the zooarchaeological record, notably a significant increase in animal size, most probably attributable to selective breeding for greater meat weights. Traditionally it has been assumed that stock improvement did not occur until the so-called 'Agricultural Revolution' of the 18th/19th centuries; however, the animal bone data indicate that it began much earlier. Thomas has examined the situation using both traditional zooarchaeological methods (2005) and more novel palaeopathological approaches, in particular examining the incidence of weight-related joint disease (in press). He suggests that stock improvement was

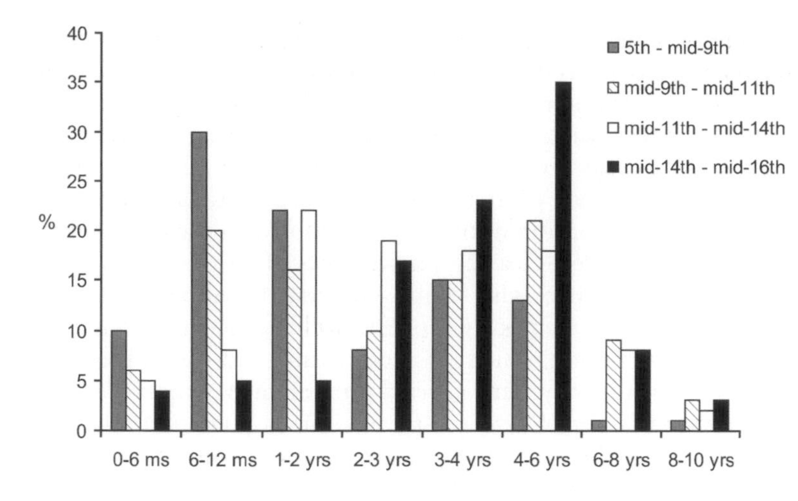

FIGURE 17.2 Temporal variation in the age of sheep/goat, shown as relative percentages of mandibles in each age group (for raw data, see Sykes 2006).

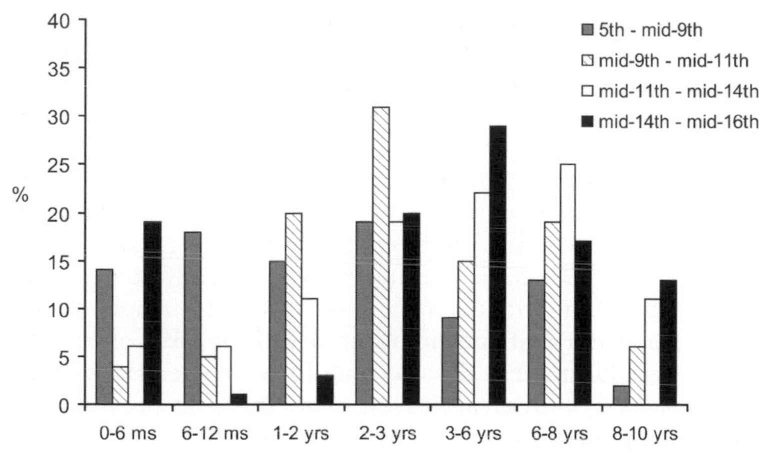

FIGURE 17.3 Temporal variation in the age of cattle, shown as relative percentages of mandibles in each age group (for raw data, see Sykes 2006).

amongst a suite of agricultural changes motivated by the social and economic upheaval that followed the Black Death (Thirsk 1997; Dyer 2005).

Age and size data can be particularly informative about inter-site relationships as well as providing an understanding of how animals were viewed and used to construct identity in the past. For instance, whilst it is often assumed that young and 'prime' aged animals — those producing tender meat — are universally favoured for consumption, zooarchaeological evidence suggests that this was not the case in the early medieval period. Studies of sheep/goat and cattle remains from Middle Anglo-Saxon sites of high status have shown that the animals consumed at these settlements were consistently the oldest available (Sykes 2006). At the elite site of Flixborough in Lincolnshire, the settlement was supplied with large numbers of 'elderly' animals whose meat, by modern standards, would be considered inedible (Dobney *et al* 2007, 141). However, the animals from this site were on average substantially larger than those from contemporary sites of lower status (Dobney *et al* 2007, 164). In this case it would seem that it was the size of the animal, rather than the tenderness of its meat, that made it desirable; bigger was clearly seen as better. This example highlights the problem of projecting modern perceptions of animals back onto the past.

The same point can be made by considering skeletal representation data. In zooarchaeology animal body part patterns are usually examined to determine whether a site was self-sufficient, as would be indicated by the equal presence of all anatomical elements, or if it was importing/exporting particular parts of the carcass. They can, however, provide more nuanced information about social actions. In terms of meat consumption, modern logic would suggest that the choice parts of an animal carcass are those bearing the most meat — the pelvis, femur, scapula, humerus, ribs and vertebrae — but these skeletal elements are poorly represented on elite sites dating to the Early and Middle Anglo-Saxon period where, instead, skulls and mandibles are more numerous, suggesting that heads may have carried greater cachet than meatier parts of the carcass. This pattern is true for domesticates but is particularly clear for deer assemblages. It could be argued that the pattern is due to preservation or recovery bias; however this can be discounted on the basis that, where present, deer assemblages from lower-status settlements tend to contain a higher proportion of meat-bearing elements (Sykes forthcoming). Taken together, the evidence suggests a situation whereby elite settlements periodically operated as butchery centres from where meat was redistributed to others on the estate. Such acts would have assisted with the creation of community, particularly when dealing with wild animals whose symbolism apparently exceeded that of domesticates. Indeed, Marvin (2006, 32) has suggested that the hunting of deer and the cutting up and sharing of venison bound together the arms-bearing men of the Middle Anglo-Saxon period, the importance of these acts perhaps explaining why, in *Beowulf*, Hrothgar saw it appropriate to name his great hall 'Heorot', the hart. Animal bone assemblages from Late Anglo-Saxon sites suggest a change in the treatment and consumption of venison. By contrast to Middle Anglo-Saxon assemblages, deer skeletal patterning for elite sites shows that all parts of the body are represented, with meat-bearing elements from the forelimb being particularly abundant. This suggests that venison was no longer being redistributed as a symbol of community but rather that the elite were consuming it as a marker of social difference; certainly the hunting and consumption of game as a form of social display fits with Senecal's (2001, 252) idea of 'thegnly culture'.

Skeletal representation patterns are often examined in conjunction with butchery marks in order to understand carcass-processing techniques. As yet there is no standard method for recording butchery marks and studies have generally been carried out on a site-by-site basis and so there is no large corpus of data for the period. Nevertheless, even at a superficial level of study, it is possible to detect some broad trends in butchery practices. Grant (1987) was the first to show how evidence from butchery marks could be used to pinpoint the rise of professional butchers. By studying multi-period assemblages, such as that from Portchester Castle in Hampshire, she was able to chart how practices changed through time: early medieval assemblages demonstrated seemingly haphazard disarticulation by knife, whereas remains dating from the 12th century onwards exhibited more consistent cleaver-based methods of carcass reduction. Included within this shift was a move towards the splitting of carcasses into equal sides, evidenced by the appearance of sagitally cleaved vertebrae.

Such butchery practices require suspension of the carcass, and it has been argued that, in the case of cattle, this could have been achieved only with the use of specialist equipment and purpose-built premises — the presence of cleaved vertebrae therefore indicates the presence of professional butchers.

Taking a more integrated approach to the study of medieval butchery, Seetah (2007) has stressed the importance of context and argued that cut and chop marks cannot be studied in isolation from the tools and, importantly, the process that created them. By combining these lines of enquiry he has demonstrated that the establishment of the Butchers' Guild (founded officially in the 1300s but almost certainly existing in some form prior to this) instigated a refinement in butchery style, facilitated by the production of new, specifically created butchery tools (Seetah 2007, 27). This emergence of artisan butchers would have enhanced meat as a symbol of social differentiation because there were now 'correct' methods, learnt by butchers over a seven-year apprenticeship, for the preparation of different animals. Subscription to these ideals and the consumption of meat prepared in the accepted fashion therefore demonstrated a person's social standing. Zooarchaeological evidence for butchery etiquette has been identified at a number of sites, particularly those of high status. The assemblage from Carisbrooke Castle on the Isle of Wight, for instance, contained a peacock foot bone exhibiting cut marks produced when the bird's toes were removed (Serjeantson 2006, 143). Another example, this time of a crane foot bone, was recovered from medieval Lincoln (Figure 17.4). Practically, it would have made more 'sense' simply to remove the entire lower leg, which carries no meat, rather than individually removing each toe, and it must be assumed that the butchery process was influenced by factors other than efficiency (O'Connor 2007, 7). Indeed, it seems probable that this unnecessarily complex method of carcass preparation was linked to the methods of 'dressing' game birds documented in later medieval recipe books (Furnivall 1868).

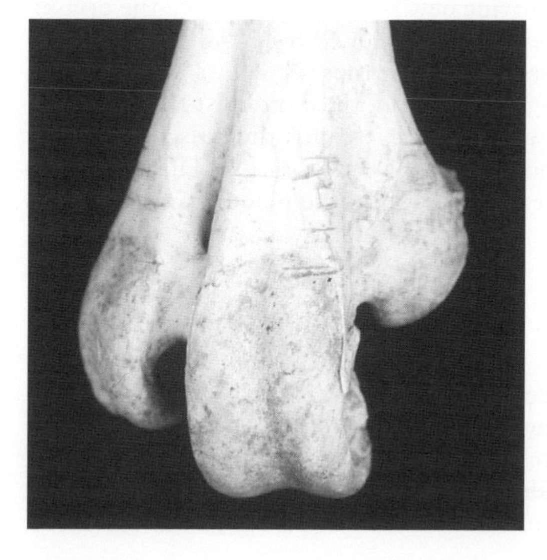

FIGURE 17.4 Medieval crane (*Grus grus*) tarsometatarsus from Flaxengate, Lincoln, showing fine cut marks on its distal end — evidence of dressing? (Photograph courtesy of T P O'Connor)

The above examples demonstrate how questions asked of zooarchaeological data have become increasingly ambitious over the last 50 years, even though the underlying methods of animal bone analysis have remained essentially unchanged. Within the last decade, however, new scientific techniques have come to the fore, pushing the boundaries of zooarchaeological analysis further still. Ancient DNA analysis of medieval animal remains is in its infancy but promising results are being produced: Edwards *et al*'s (2003) analysis of cattle from Viking Age Dublin indicated that the animals were probably native rather than stock imported by Scandinavian settlers. Also notable is the advent of isotope analysis for the reconstruction of diet and migration patterns, already a central research tool in the study of human remains (for principles and methods of analysis, see Müldner, this volume). Results from the analysis of human remains are often of direct relevance to understanding patterns of animal exploitation, as Barrett and Richards (2004) have shown in their study of fish consumption in Viking Age Orkney, but the benefits of analysing animal remains in their own right are now being recognized. For instance, by examining the strontium isotope compositions and concentrations in cattle, sheep and pig teeth, Evans *et al* (2007) were able to argue convincingly that two neighbouring Anglo-Saxon sites in the East Midlands — Empingham (6th–7th century) and Ketton (9th–12th century) — had very different animal husbandry regimes. According to the study, the cattle, sheep and pigs from Empingham demonstrated different and clearly defined isotopic signatures suggesting that the animals were closely managed: the three domesticates were kept in separate areas and their movements restricted. By contrast, the animals from Ketton had more diverse isotopic signatures with marked overlap between the species, indicating that they grazed together on a wider range of local soils. It is not made explicit in their work but Evans *et al*'s results appear consistent with a move from farming in severalty, whereby individual farmers took care to raise their own animals on their own land, to a situation of common field agriculture with farmers coming together to work fields and graze animals communally. If this is the case, these results clearly carry the potential to provide new insights concerning the origins of a farming regime that has been the subject of so much debate (eg Williamson 2003, 1–27; Jones and Page 2006, 92–95). To address this and other topical issues, however, it is not enough to consider the animal bones in isolation; the data must be integrated with wider archaeological research and with evidence from other disciplines and sources: history, cultural geography, iconography, the list goes on. The following section outlines the more dynamic interpretations that can be made if an integrated approach is adopted.

ZOOARCHAEOLOGY AND IDENTITY

As the examples above attest, it has long been recognized that animal bone studies can reveal much about medieval economies and husbandry regimes but now, by drawing on discussion from social anthropology (eg Mullin 1999), zooarchaeologists are beginning to realize that the investigation of human–animal relationships can provide insights into ideological phenomena — for instance, status, ethnic, religious or gender-based identity — often thought archaeologically intangible. To date, zooarchaeological studies of identity have focused on diet. This is unsurprising given that most animal bone assemblages represent food waste but it is also theoretically sound because eating is a very personal act, with food choices reflecting an individual's beliefs and ideals as well as social and cultural preferences (Miracle and Milner 2002; Twiss 2006).

Studies of socio-economic status have perhaps the longest tradition and 'vertebrate signatures' of elite consumption practices are now well documented (eg Grant 1988; 2002; Ashby 2002; Dobney and Jacques 2002). Within the last few years, however, researchers have been able to move beyond simply identifying markers of high-status diet. By viewing animal bone data diachronically and in conjunction with other sources of evidence it has been possible to explore how and, importantly why, social differentiation was communicated and maintained through consumption practices. A good example is provided by the work of Thomas (2007) who has suggested that the improved living standards of later medieval peasants, in particular their increased consumption of meat, encouraged the elite to eat greater quantities of game in an attempt to maintain social boundaries (Figure 17.5). Such studies of dietary dynamics are a welcome advance in medieval zooarchaeology, but it is perhaps too narrow to concentrate solely on meat consumption when identities are, and were, negotiated via a wide range of human–animal interactions. As Pluskowski (2007) has demonstrated, the elite of medieval western Europe engaged with wild and exotic animals in multifarious ways — by maintaining them alive within private parks, by hunting them, by using their body parts (furs and feathers) as objects of adornment or as trophies, and also by employing their images as heraldic devices — to create a socially distinct 'seigneurial culture'.

The flamboyancy and ubiquity of elite display has, for the later medieval period at least, left a mark in the zooarchaeological record that is clearly accessible for researchers to interpret. At the lower end of the social spectrum, however, there are

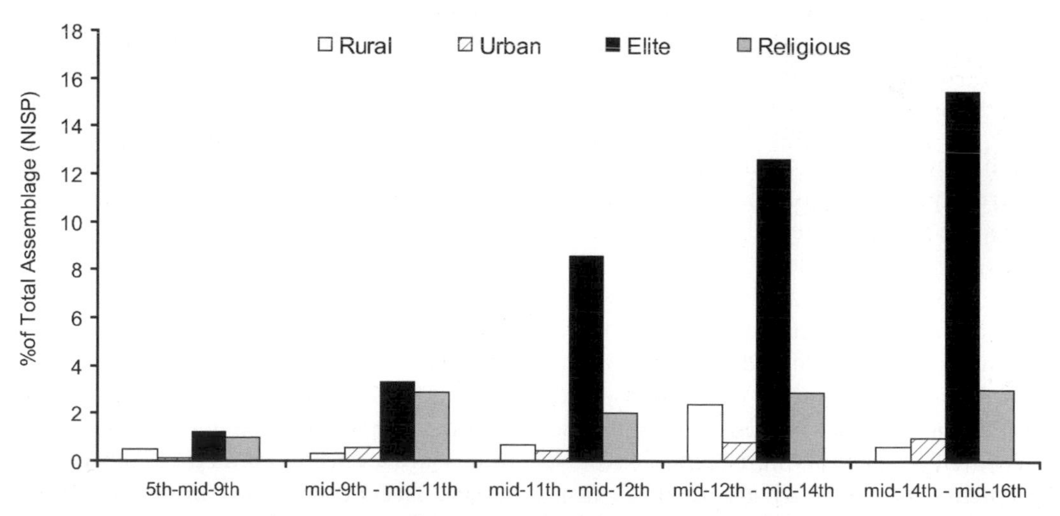

FIGURE 17.5 Temporal variation in the representation of wild mammals shown, by site type, as a percentage of total assemblages (excluding fish) (for raw data, see Sykes 2007a).

fewer clues and the task of examining social identity is more problematic. Yet, there is scope for using animal bone analysis to better understand peasant and urban identities. The representation of wild species would again seem to be the most profitable avenue to explore because, even for the lower classes, the acquisition, redistribution and consumption of game were social actions that allowed individuals to define themselves. There is ample evidence to suggest that members of the rural lower classes were active participants in aristocratic hunts, even being entitled to a share of the meat, which the zooarchaeological record suggests they took (Sykes 2007b). Without doubt, the framework of the medieval hunt was hierarchical and the peasants' place was at the bottom, but it was a place *within* a group — the hunt could actually facilitate social cohesion and foster feelings of group identity. Of course there were many individuals who were excluded from hunting or the group who practised it but, for them, poaching offered the opportunity for personal empowerment through the subversion of authority. Animal bone and historical evidence together suggest that poaching gangs operated from both rural and urban settings and, although their activities lacked the formal rituals of aristocratic hunting, they carried their own codes of conduct that cemented fraternity and bolstered identity in much the same way as the legitimate hunt (Birell 1996; Manning 1993; Sykes 2007b).

The third group within the idealized tripartite structure of medieval society was the ecclesiastics. Their well-known adoption of the rule of Saint Benedict, which forbade the consumption of four-legged terrestrial mammals, has meant that most zooarchaeological studies of medieval religious identity have concentrated on consumption practices, in particular examining how closely members of religious communities adhered to the rule: Ervynck (1997), for instance, has shown that animal bone assemblages from Belgian religious houses are very different to those from other site types, containing few mammalian remains but large quantities of fish. The prohibition against quadruped meat was not a biblical injunction, so presumably it was employed as a mechanism for social differentiation, abstemiousness being in stark contrast to the conspicuous consumption of the secular elite. Whilst a broad 'religious identity' may have been created through eating habits, the ecclesiastical community was not homogenous, there were many different orders. Unfortunately, in common with studies of monasticism based on human remains (see Mays 2006), there are currently insufficient animal bone data to allow the differences between orders, or between male and female houses, to be examined in detail; this would be a profitable area for future studies.

Most zooarchaeological investigations of group identity produce, at best, generalized interpretations because the animal bone deposits on which they are based cannot usually be linked to single events or individuals. One area in which progress towards understanding personal identities is being made is in bone artefact studies. Traditionally, worked bone is sent directly to finds specialists, bypassing the zooarchaeologists, but increasingly these specimens are being examined as important elements of medieval animal bone assemblages. Recent work on bone flutes has revealed that these instruments were more commonly associated with urban and elite sites, and that certain species were used by particular social groups: almost all flutes constructed of deer bone are found on elite settlements (Leaf 2007, 15). Similarly, Ashby's (2006) study of bone and antler combs from Viking Age Britain, which considered the means by which these personal possessions were produced, distributed and consumed, has shown that combs were not as homogenous as has often been suggested. Instead he argues that small-scale variations were important in the structuring and communication of identity. Analysis of combs from grave contexts has indicated that they played a role in expressions of elite social status, and it may also be possible to assign 'ethnicity' on the basis of the raw materials used in their construction; combs made of elk antler potentially indicating that the owner was from Scandinavia (Ashby 2006, 238–254).

Ethnicity is notoriously difficult to recognize archaeologically because it is fluid, situational and can be enmeshed with or obscured by many other forms of identity (Jones 1997). It has been shown repeatedly that there is not a fixed one-to-one relationship between ethnicity and material culture, so it is unsurprising that attempts to identify ethnic groups from simplistic studies of animal butchery or species presence/absence have been largely unsuccessful (Crabtree 1991). However, the medieval period, with its episodes of Anglo-Saxon migration, Viking colonization and Norman invasion, has great potential for investigations of ethnicity, and zoo-archaeologist are beginning to rise to the challenge. Barrett *et al* (2001) have suggested that the dramatic 9th-century uptake of offshore fishing observed at sites on Orkney and Shetland may reflect Norse ethnicity; the Picts being displaced, or at least their traditions replaced, by the colonizers who introduced their own maritime lifestyle and cuisine from Norway. Attempts to find similar patterns for Viking Age England have been less successful. Poole (in press) has intimated that some variations in animal bones assemblages from within and outside Danelaw could be linked to ethnic-based differences in attitudes to animals. For instance, he notes a much higher incidence of butchered horse bones in Danelaw areas, a pattern that could feasibly reflect Scandinavian traditions of horse consumption. In general, however, there is no obvious shift in animal exploitation coincident with either the period or area of Scandinavian occupation.

As an ideological phenomenon, ethnicity is easier to determine from the historical rather than archaeological record. This is clear from the dichotomous nature of the evidence for the Norman Conquest: there are numerous 11th- and 12th-century texts that describe the character and beliefs of the *Gens Normanorum* but, traditionally, Norman identity is seen as invisible archaeologically. Certainly material culture does not change dramatically at the point of 1066, but the same is not true for animal bone assemblages. The zooarchaeological record shows a very significant post-Conquest increase in wild animal representation on elite sites (Figure 17.5) as well as clear shifts in deer skeletal representation. I have suggested that these changes were brought by the Norman aristocracy who employed excessive hunting, forest law and exclusive Gallicized hunting rituals as mechanisms for asserting their ethnicity and legitimizing their rule over the defeated Saxon population (2007a). Hunting, with its references to warfare and male identity, would also have been symbolic of the Norman's ideals of martial prowess and masculinity.

The links between hunting and masculinity are well known and it is perhaps unsurprising that evidence for hunting became more apparent in a period of growing gender definition, when emphasis was being placed increasingly on machismo and military activity. But the exploitation of wild resources, if not hunting *per se*, could equally be a mechanism for the construction of female identity, particularly in the case of aristocratic women. By the 12th century falconry had become a well-known part of a young women's education; symbolic of this association was the use of the hawk on ladies' seals. It is interesting to note that the late 12th-century upsurge in iconography depicting women engaged in falconry, ferreting and bow and staple hunting coincides with a marked rise in the archaeological presence of wild birds, rabbits and fallow deer, the last caught principally through the bow and stable techniques (Sykes 2007c). To some extent the increased representation of these species can be attributed to the contemporary proliferation of parks, which were stocked with precisely these animals. However, it seems possible that these prey species were managed in parks specifically with women's leisure in mind. Considering that medieval courtly society placed great emphasis on the seclusion and enclosure of young aristocratic women (Gilchrist 1999, 142) it seems unlikely that they would have been encouraged to hunt or hawk within the open landscape. More probable is that it was within the confines of parks that ladies practised their arts without fear of uninvited observation.

CONCLUSION

Animal bone analysis has a great deal to offer medieval archaeology, providing not only analyses of animal husbandry, economy and diet but also new perspectives on old questions — such as the rise of commercialism, the origins of common field agriculture, the impact of Norman Conquest and the function of medieval parks — as well as offering insights into the social groups poorly documented in the historical records, such as the lives of the rural and urban poor. With the large amount of zooarchaeological data now available it is possible to draw interesting conclusions from even the smallest of animal bone assemblages. Unfortunately, this potential is seldom recognized beyond the zooarchaeological community. The fault here lies not with excavators and archaeological researchers but rather with zooarchaeologists themselves. Frequently, animal bone specialists make pleas for greater integration of their results, but such pleas are made in zooarchaeological literature. From an encouraging start in the 1980s it is now rare to see animal bone specialists publishing in mainstream journals or on issues that are central to the period. Indeed, it is interesting to note that some of the most important journal articles on medieval animals have been written by scholars who would not consider themselves to be zooarchaeologists (Gardiner 1997; Hamerow 2006). For these reasons I am delighted to have been able to contribute a chapter to this volume. It has been possible to provide only the most superficial overview of the zooarchaeological work that has been undertaken within the last 50 years; however, I hope that it is clear how much has and can be achieved through animal bone studies.

BIBLIOGRAPHY

Albarella, U, 1997 'Size, power and veal: zooarchaeological evidence for late medieval innovations', in de Boe and Verhaeghe (eds) 1997, 19–30

Albarella, U and Thomas, R, 2002 'They dined on crane: bird consumption, wildfowling and status in medieval England', *Acta Zoological Cracoviensia* 45, 23–38

Ashby, S P, 2002 'The role of zooarchaeology in the interpretation of socioeconomic status: a discussion with reference to medieval Europe', *Archaeological Review from Cambridge* 18, 37–60

Ashby, S P, 2006 'Time, Trade, and Identity: Bone and Antler Combs in Northern Britain c.AD700–1400', unpublished DPhil thesis, University of York

Baker, P and Clark, G, 1993 'Archaeolozoological evidence for medieval Italy: a critical review of the present state of research', *Archeologia Medievale* 20, 45–77

Barrett, J H, Beukens, R P and Nicholson, R A, 2001 'Diet and ethnicity during the Viking colonisation of northern Scotland: evidence from fish bones and stable carbon isotopes', *Antiquity* 75, 145–154

Barrett, J, Locker, A M and Roberts, C M, 2004 '"Dark Age Economics" revisited: the English fishbone evidence AD600–1600', *Antiquity* 78, 618–636

Barrett, J H and Richards, M P, 2004 'Identity, gender, religion and economy: new isotope and radiocarbon evidence for marine resource intensification in early historic Orkney, Scotland', *European Journal of Archaeology* 7:3, 249–271

Birell, J, 1996 'Peasant deer poachers in the medieval forest', in R Britnell and J Hatcher (eds), *Progress and Problems in Medieval England: Essays in Honour of Edward Miller*, 68–88, Cambridge University Press, Cambridge

de Boe, G and Verhaeghe, F (eds), 1997 *Environment and Subsistence in Medieval Europe: Papers of the 'Medieval Europe Brugge 1997' Conference Volume 9*, IAP Rapporten 9, Zellik

Bourdillon, J, 1994 'The animal provisioning of Saxon Southampton', in J Rackam (ed), *Environment and Economy in Anglo-Saxon England*, 120–125, Council for British Archaeology Research Report 89, York

Clavel, B, 2001 *L'animal dans l'alimentation Medievale et Moderne en France du Nord (XIIe–XVIIe siècles)*, Revue Archeologique de Picardie No Spécial 19

Clutton-Brock, J, 1976 'The animal resources', in D M Wilson (ed), *The Archaeology of Anglo-Saxon England*, 373–392, Cambridge University Press, Cambridge

Coy, J, 1980 'The animal bones', 41–51, in J Haslam, 'A Middle Saxon iron smelting site at Ramsbury, Wiltshire', *Medieval Archaeology* 24, 1–68

Crabtree, P, 1991 'Zooarchaeology and complex societies: some uses of faunal remains for the study of trade, social status and ethnicity', *Archaeological Method and Theory* 2, 155–205

Dobney, K and Jaques, D, 2002 'Avian signatures for identity and status in Anglo-Saxon England', *Acta Zoologica Cracoviensia* 45, 7–21

Dobney, K, Jacques, D, Barrett, J and Johnstone, C, 2007 *Farmers, Monks and Aristocrats: The Environmental Archaeology of Anglo-Saxon Flixborough*, Oxbow, Oxford

Dyer, C, 2005 *An Age of Transition? Economy and Society in the Later Middle Ages*, Oxford University Press, Oxford

Edwards, C J, Connellan, J, Wallace, P F, Park, S D E, McCormick, F M, Olsaker, I, Eythórsdóttir, E, MacHugh, D E, Bailey, J F and Bradley, D G, 2003 'Feasibility and utility of microsatellite markers in archaeological cattle remains from a Viking Age settlement in Dublin', *Animal Genetics* 34, 410–416

Ervynck, A, 1997 'Following the Rule? Fish and meat consumption in monastic communities in Flanders (Belgium)', in de Boe and Verhaeghe (eds) 1997, 67–81

Evans, J A, Tatham, S, Chenery, S R and Chenery, C A, 2007 'Anglo-Saxon animal husbandry techniques revealed through isotope and chemical variations in cattle teeth', *Applied Geochemistry* 22, 1994–2005
Furnivall, F J, 1868 *Early English Meals and Manners*, Oxford University Press, London
Gardiner, M, 1997 'The exploitation of sea-mammals in medieval England: bones and their social context', *Archaeological Journal* 154, 173–195
Gilchrist, R, 1988 'A reappraisal of Dinas Powys: local exchange and specialized livestock production in 5th- to 7th-century Wales', *Medieval Archaeology* 32, 50–62
Gilchrist, R, 1999 *Gender and Archaeology. Contesting the Past*, Routledge, London
Grant, A, 1987 'Some observations on butchery in England from the Iron Age to the medieval period', *Anthropozoologica* Premier Numéro Spécial, 53–57
Grant, A, 1988 'The animal resources', in G Astill and A Grant (eds), *The Countryside of Medieval England*, 149–197, Blackwell, Oxford
Grant, A, 2002 'Food, status and social hierarchy', in P Miracle and N Milner (eds), *Consuming Passions and Patterns of Consumption*, 17–23, McDonald Institute for Archaeological Research, Cambridge
Hamerow, H, 2006 '"Special Deposits" in Anglo-Saxon Settlements', *Medieval Archaeology* 50, 1–30
Jones, R and Page, M, 2006 *Medieval Villages in an English Landscape: Beginnings and Ends*, Windgather Press, Macclesfield
Jones, S, 1997 *The Archaeology of Ethnicity: Constructing Social Identities in the Past and Present*, Routledge, London
Jope, M, 1959 'The animal remains from Lismahon', 174–175, in D M Waterman 'Excavations at Lismahon, Co. Down', *Medieval Archaeology* 3, 139–176
Laurioux, B, 1988 'Le lièvre lubrique et la bête sanglante. Réflexions sur quelques interdits alimentaires du Haut Moyen Âge', *Anthropozoologica,* special number 2, 127–132
Leaf, H, 2007 'Medieval bone flutes in England', in Pluskowski (ed) 2007, 11–17
Manning, R B, 1993 *Hunters and Poachers: A Cultural and Social History of Unlawful Hunting in England 1485–1640*, Clarendon Press, Oxford
Marvin, W P, 2006 *Hunting Law and Ritual in Medieval English Literature*, Brewer, Cambridge
Mays, S, 2006 'The osteology of monasticism in medieval England', in R Gowland and C Knüsel (eds), *Social Archaeology of Funerary Remains*, 179–189, Oxbow, Oxford
Miracle, P and Milner, N, 2002 *Consuming Passions and Patterns of Consumption*, McDonald Institute for Archaeological Research, Cambridge
Mullin, M H, 1999 'Mirrors and windows: sociocultural studies of human-animal relationships', *Annual Review of Anthropology* 28, 201–224
Noddle, B, 1975 'A comparison of the animal bones from 8 medieval sites in southern Britain', in A T Clason (ed), *Archaeozoological Studies*, 248–260, North Holland Publishing, Amsterdam
O'Connor, T P, 2001 'On the interpretation of animal bone assemblages from *Wics*', in D Hill and R Cowie (eds), *Wics: The Early Medieval Trading Centres of Northern Europe*, 54–60, Sheffield Academic Press, Sheffield
O'Connor, T P, 2002 'Medieval zooarchaeology: what are we trying to do?', *Archaeological Review from Cambridge* 18, 3–21
O'Connor, T P, 2007 'Thinking about beastly bodies', in Pluskowski (ed) 2007, 1–10, Oxbow, Oxford
Pluskowski, A (ed), 2007 *Breaking and Shaping Beastly Bodies: Animals as Material Culture in the Middle Ages*, Oxbow, Oxford
Pluskowski, A, 2007 'Communicating through skin and bones: appropriating animal bodies in medieval western European seigneurial culture', in Pluskowski (ed) 2007, 32–51

Poole, K, in press 'Living and eating in Viking-Age towns and their hinterland', in S Baker, M Allen, S Middle and K Poole (eds), *Food and Drink in Archaeology 1*, Prospect Books, Totnes

Rackham, J, 1979 'The animal resources', 47–54, in M O H Carver, 'Three Saxo-Norman tenements in Durham City', *Medieval Archaeology* 23, 1–80

Salisbury, J E, 1994 *The Beast Within: Animals in the Middle Ages*, Routledge, London

Senecal, C, 2001 'Keeping up with the Godwinesons: in pursuit of aristocratic status in Late Anglo-Saxon England', *Anglo-Norman Studies* 23, 251–266

Seddon, D, Calvocoressi, D and Cooper, C with Higgs, E S, 1964 'Fauna', 69–71, in P V Addyman, 'A Dark Age settlement at Maxey, Northants', *Medieval Archaeology* 8, 20–73

Seetah, K, 2007 'The Middle Ages on the block: animals, guilds and meat in the medieval period', in Pluskowski (ed) 2007, 18–31

Serjeantson, D, 2006 'Birds as food and markers of status', in Woolgar *et al* (eds) 2006, 131–147

Sykes, N J, 2005 'The dynamics of status symbols: wildfowl exploitation in England AD 410–1550', *Archaeological Journal* 161, 82–105

Sykes, N J, 2006 'From *cu* and *sceap* to *beffe* and *motton*: the management, distribution and consumption of cattle and sheep in medieval England', in Woolgar *et al* (eds) 2006, 56–71

Sykes, N J, 2007a *The Norman Conquest: A Zooarchaeological Perspective*, Archaeopress, Oxford

Sykes, N J, 2007b 'Taking sides: the social life of venison in medieval England', in Pluskowski (ed) 2007, 150–161

Sykes, N J, 2007c 'Animal bones and animal parks', in R Liddiard (ed), *The Medieval Deer Park: New Perspectives*, 49–62, Windgather Press, Macclesfield

Sykes, N J, forthcoming 'Woods and the wild', in D Hinton and H Hamerow (eds), *A Handbook of Anglo-Saxon Archaeology*, Oxford University Press, Oxford

Thirsk, J, 1997 *Alternative Agriculture: A History from the Black Death to the Present Day*, Oxford University Press, Oxford

Thomas, R, 2005 'Zooarchaeology, improvement and the British Agricultural Revolution', *International Journal of Historical Archaeology* 9:2, 71–88

Thomas, R, 2007 'Maintaining social boundaries through the consumption of food in medieval England', in K Twiss (ed), *The Archaeology of Food and Identity*, 130–151, University of Southern Illinois Press, Carbondale

Thomas, R, in press 'Diachronic trends in lower limb pathologies in later medieval and post-medieval cattle from Britain', *Documenta Archaeobiologiae*

Twiss, K, 2006 *We Are What We Eat: Archaeology, Food, and Identity*, University of Southern Illinois Press, Carbondale

Williamson, T, 2003 *Shaping Medieval Landscapes. Settlement, Society, Environment*, Windgather Press, Macclesfield

Woolgar, C, Serjeantson, D and Waldron, T (eds), 2006 *Food in Medieval England: History and Archaeology*, Oxford University Press, Oxford

Yvinec, J-H, 1993 'La part du gibier dans l'alimentation du haut Moyen Âge', in J Desse and F Audouin-Rouzeau (eds), *Exploitation des Animaux Sauvages à Travers le Temps*, 491–504, Éditions A P D C A, Juan-les-Pins

CHAPTER 18
EMERGING FROM THE APPENDICES: THE CONTRIBUTIONS OF SCIENTIFIC EXAMINATION AND ANALYSIS TO MEDIEVAL ARCHAEOLOGY

By JUSTINE BAYLEY *and* JACQUI WATSON

This paper presents some of the benefits of using materials science and investigative conservation techniques in medieval archaeology. The examples illustrate the potential of the techniques, and also show how much the disciplines have developed over the past 50 years. What was once a curiosity can now be considered routine; and more practitioners are now available to carry out work of this type.

INTRODUCTION

Fifty years ago excavation reports of medieval sites were something of a rarity, and normally contained little or no information based on scientific investigations of either the site or the finds that came from it; there are many such examples in early volumes of *Medieval Archaeology*. From the 1960s a few reports had details of scientific investigations appended, for example species lists or identifications of materials, as in 'Appendix 7: Technical notes on iron-working at Dinas Powys' (Alcock 1963). These specialist reports became more common as time went on, but the information in them was seldom incorporated into the main text; the impression given was that the scientific investigations added little to the information in the excavation report, and so were provided but not utilized. The quality of the information then improved as the scientists developed an understanding of archaeological questions, and a new breed — the archaeological scientist or conservator — emerged from the shadows.

A range of techniques have since been developed, mainly in the scientific world but then customized to suit the rather different questions that archaeology poses. Of prime importance are various types of microscopy and chemical analysis. These techniques complement and expand on the observations that are conventionally made, providing a better, factual basis for statements. For example, the traces of 'wooden' handles seen on early medieval knife tangs are now known to be mainly horn, and 'bronze' objects have been shown to be made of a range of different copper alloys, each selected for their particular properties (see below).

A turning point came in 1983 when the Council for British Archaeology organized a conference, *The Archaeologist and the Laboratory*, which aimed at publicizing developments in archaeological science to an archaeological audience. The published papers (Phillips 1985) dealt with particular raw materials and the successes and limitations of their scientific investigation. Examples from sites of all periods were presented, and many archaeologists were persuaded that studies of these types should become the norm, rather than the exception, in any substantial excavation report. The reports of a wider range of archaeological scientists began to appear more frequently, initially still only in appendices, but increasingly their contributions became sections of the main text. Today their contributions are often incorporated into a multi-authored text which draws on all the available information; archaeological sciences are just some of the multiplicity of techniques with which archaeologists working in the 21st century should be familiar. However, this 'Brave New World' is not yet universal and scientists and conservators are sometimes marginalized alongside other specialists who write pottery and finds reports. Their work may be useful for dating the site, and for indicating its status and external linkages, but it is still often seen as subservient to the on-site features and structures and the interpretations that can be placed on them.

Rather than bemoan the fate of past scientific contributions to medieval archaeology, it is more instructive to consider the new information that scientific investigation of medieval artefacts and their manufacture has to offer. These techniques make substantial contributions to addressing social and economic questions at the core of medieval archaeology. They identify industrial processes and so help understand the organization of production; they also identify sources of raw materials and the provenance of finished objects. These types of information contribute to recognition of the social value of particular materials and their symbolic associations with individuals' status and activities — the possibilities are almost endless, as the examples below begin to demonstrate.

MATERIAL IDENTIFICATION

Metals

Fifty years ago metal objects were described as bronze, iron, lead or, more rarely, as pewter, without any real knowledge of their composition, and hence the properties of the metal. Tylecote (1962, 57) noted 'an almost complete absence of analytical information regarding Dark Age material', but went on to list average compositions for wrought and cast medieval copper-alloy objects, based on only a handful of analyses. Subsequent work has shown a more complex picture. We now know that a wide range of different copper alloys were used during the medieval period; there is usually a good correlation between composition and method of manufacture, and often with the function of the finished object. Wrought objects can only contain a maximum of a few per cent of lead, but castings often had far higher levels. Bayley (1991) has suggested a nomenclature to describe these metals, though other analysts have variations on this scheme (eg Mortimer 1991; Brownsword 1988).

In the early Anglo-Saxon period mixed copper alloys containing variable amounts of tin, zinc and lead were the norm in England (Blades *et al* 1989, fig 2; Mortimer 1991; Brownsword 1997) but in the Celtic West bronze (in the true sense of a copper-tin alloy) reigned supreme (Craddock *et al* 2001). From around the 10th century brass (the alloy of copper and zinc) reappeared in quantity, as can be seen in York (Bayley 1992a, 809) and Lincoln (White 1982), and in recent work in Dublin (Bayley in prep). The same pattern occurs in Scandinavia, where all of the bar ingots from Hedeby (Schleswig) are either brass or unalloyed copper, with or without some lead (Drescher, pers comm). Much of the Romanesque metalwork that has been analysed is lead-free copper with very low additions of tin and/or zinc (Oddy *et al* 1986) but this is because the only objects that could be definitely assigned to this period were the highly decorated pieces that are mainly mercury gilded and often enamelled — the applied decoration is the reason for the alloy choice. In the later medieval period there is now more data which show particular alloys are associated with specific classes of objects. Examples are the high-tin bronzes used for church bells because the hard metal had a good ringing tone (Bayley *et al* 1993); the zinc-rich copper alloys, brasses and gunmetals, used for dress accessories (Heyworth 1991) and aquamanilia (Barnet and Dandridge 2006, 56) because of their golden appearance; or the heavily leaded bronzes with significant amounts of antimony and/or arsenic, which were cheap and easy to cast, that were used for cauldrons and skillets (Dungworth and Nicholas 2004; Butler and Green 2003). Some objects, such as monumental 'brasses', have a name that assumes a composition — though even here analyses have shown that not all 'brasses' are truly brass, and that there is a gradual change in average compositions with time (Cameron 1974).

With 'iron' objects there is also considerable variation in composition. Some iron is almost pure (plain or wrought iron), but much contains significant amounts of either phosphorus (phosphoric iron) or carbon (steel and, at the end of the medieval period, cast iron). As with copper alloys, these iron alloys have different properties that were well understood by the smiths who turned the metals into objects. They would often combine more than one type of iron in a single object to get a combination of properties — the resilience but relative softness of plain iron mixed with the hardness of phosphoric iron or steel. Many knife blades are therefore composites, with steel cutting edges welded to plain iron backs (Wilthew 1987; McDonnell and Ottaway 1991; Blakelock and McDonnell 2007). The same combinations of different types of iron are also found in pattern-welded weapons which must be considered the apogee of the early medieval smiths' craft (Tylecote and Gilmour 1986). Warfare also led to the development of chain mail and sheet armour. Analytical investigations have demonstrated the range of qualities that were produced; the most beautiful did not necessarily provide the most effective protection (Williams 2003). Some ironwork was coated with non-ferrous metals, either tinning or brazing (eg Wilthew and Ottaway 1991), and a more decorative effect could be obtained by inlaying silver or brass, as in early Saxon buckles and belt plates (Evison 1955) or makers' marks in medieval knives (Beresford 1975).

Most medieval pilgrim badges have long been assumed to be made of pewter, and analytical programmes have confirmed this. What has also emerged from this work is that ampullae are not pewter, but pure tin (Spencer 1998, 11). Once the evidence for their manufacture is considered, the reason for this choice becomes clear. The ampullae were cast in two-piece stone moulds, like that found in Hereford (Shoesmith 1985, fig 14). The mould was assembled, the molten tin poured in and most of it tipped out, leaving behind a thin solid layer — an early example of slush casting. When the mould was taken apart, the hollow casting could be removed. The mould was a fine limestone so only a metal with a low melting point (tin or pewter) could be used, and because of the casting method, it had to solidify instantly, unlike pewter which usually solidifies over a range of temperature.

Glass

Scientific analyses have also thrown light on the composition of medieval glass, explaining its very variable state of preservation. In the Early Saxon period vessel glass had compositions that were a continuation of the late Roman tradition. The main flux used in glass-making was mineral soda, showing that the raw glass was produced in the eastern Mediterranean, though it is presumed it was re-melted and the vessels blown in northern Europe, and perhaps even in Britain — though no evidence of glass-blowing at this period is known here. Analytical work by Freestone *et al* (2008) has shown short-term fluctuations in composition which are interpreted as showing varying degrees of recycling and dilution of the glass stock by local raw materials, as trade with the Mediterranean became more difficult. Early window glass like that from Jarrow and Monkwearmouth is also soda glass and survives well (Brill 2006, 129). There is some evidence for soda-glass working later in the Saxon period (Bayley 2000a) with the best evidence coming from Glastonbury Abbey (Bayley 2000b).

Around the 10th century there is a major change in the composition of glass used to make windows and vessels right across northern Europe. The fluxes used to make the glass change to potash-rich ones, derived from terrestrial plant ashes. The problem is that this potash glass is far less durable than the earlier soda glass, which means that far less glass survives, and that which does is often badly decayed (Tyson 2000, 6).

Trinkets such as glass beads are frequent finds in pagan burials and are large and highly decorated (Guido 1999); variations in the composition of the glass, particularly the choice of colorants and opacifiers, can be used to demonstrate multiple sources and even to suggest areas of origin (Bayley 1987; 1999). In the 10th century a new type of glass, with origins in Russia and eastern Europe, appears in Britain. This is high-lead glass which was used mainly to make beads and rings. There is good evidence for the manufacture of objects from this glass in Britain (Bayley 2007; in press); although it appears to be a Viking introduction, it is found in southern England as well as in the Danelaw. Linen smoothers or slick stones are another type of glass object that appears around the 10th century, though they continue in use into the post-medieval period. Most are made of potash glass, but some have recently been shown to have a most unusual composition; they are made of glassy lead-smelting slag. The majority of these 'slag' smoothers come from France, and chemical and lead isotope analyses show the glass was most probably produced at Melle, near Poitiers, as a by-product of the rich Carolingian lead-silver mines there (Gratuze *et al* 2003). There are, however, outliers to the main distribution in Novgorod, Hedeby, York and Dublin; materials analysis has demonstrated the long-distance trade in these everyday objects.

Ceramics

Another group of materials that has benefited from scientific studies are ceramics. A variety of techniques can be used to identify the method of manufacture or the geographical origin of the clay (Barclay 2001). The appearance of pots and floor tiles, and the glazes found on them, can be explained by an understanding of the physical and chemical reactions that take place when they are fired; many examples can be found in Freestone and Gaimster's (1997) multi-period publication on world ceramic traditions.

One widely used technique is petrography: examining thin sections under a petrological microscope to identify the mineral temper, and hence the geology of the area that produced the pots or tiles. In Britain this technique was pioneered by David Peacock and early examples of its application to both English and Continental medieval ceramics appear in a collection of papers he edited (Peacock 1977). Petrography works best with relatively coarse fabrics that have not been fired at very high temperatures, and thus is more relevant to the early part of the medieval period (Vince 2005). From a national survey of over 6000 thin sections of medieval date it was possible to conclude that from the Middle to Late Saxon period onwards pottery production was carried out at a limited number of centres; the pots were traded, and the distances they moved remained similar until the 13th or 14th century (Vince 2005).

Chemical analysis can also provenance ceramics, and is usually most successful with fine-grained, homogenous fabrics (Barclay 2001, 16). Examples are the studies of Spanish and Italian maiolica by Hughes *et al* (Hughes 1991; Hughes *et al* 1977) which assigned pots to production areas.

Organic materials

Decay processes affect the range of artefacts that survive. Finds assemblages from waterlogged sites were thus a revelation — but not all periods are represented on waterlogged sites. For example, most Anglo-Saxon cemeteries that have been investigated were dry, so few of the organic artefacts survive intact and the only evidence for them is traces preserved in the corrosion on the metalwork.

It is possible to distinguish between most types of organic materials, even in the form of decorated objects, with the aid of a low-powered microscope or even a hand lens. The structure of these same materials can be more difficult to interpret when preserved in corrosion layers, especially those on iron objects, and under these circumstances wood and horn can be indistinguishable from bone and antler to the untrained eye. In some cases samples have to be taken and examined using a scanning electron microscope (SEM) to determine the material, and where possible the species of wood and fibres preserved (Watson *et al* 2008). After many years of examining the mineral preserved organic materials preserved on metalwork in Anglo-Saxon graves it is now possible to predict that horn is more likely to be used for knife handles and composite sword hilts rather than wood. There were preconceptions about the choice of wood species for items such as spears and shields. In early English texts spears are cited as being hafted with ash, which is mainly true (Figure 18.1), but there are also many examples of other species including willow, poplar, alder and hazel. In the case of shields, these were presumed to be made from lime, but far more are made from willow or poplar (Watson 1995). Figure 18.1 illustrates that some wood species were used just for a narrow range of applications, with only slight variations in different parts of England. Obviously some types of wood have inherent properties that make them ideal for a particular function, but in other cases the selection may point to workshops producing items such as caskets and copper alloy bound buckets.

Throughout the medieval period one of the most common artefacts to be found with burials or on settlement sites is a small knife for everyday use, and it seems that each individual had their own which was often customized to their owner's taste and pocket. This is particularly true of some of the scale tang knives dating from the 14th to 16th centuries, where the scales were usually made from wood, horn or bone but with some fine examples using ivory or shell (Cowgill *et al* 1987; Watson and Paynter 2001). As the blade and tang were made from iron, most of these materials are preserved in the iron corrosion and it can be difficult to recognize them without resorting to high-powered microscopy such as the SEM (Figures 18.2 and 18.3). Resins and varnishes can also be inferred from X-ray images and by finding glassy deposits within the wood structure in some examples (Figure 18.2). Many of these scale tang

	Oak	Ash	Willow Poplar	Lime	Alder	Hazel	Beech	Maple	Yew	Pine
Coffins	▲									
Grave structures	▲									
Beds		▲								
Shields			△	□	●					
Spear shafts		▲	■		●	●				
Vessels		□			□			△		
Buckets with copper alloy fittings								●	▲	●
Caskets		●					▲	■		

FIGURE 18.1 Woods used in Anglo-Saxon artefacts: ▲ over 50%; △ around 50%; ■ Around 30%; □ Around 25%. ● occasional examples.

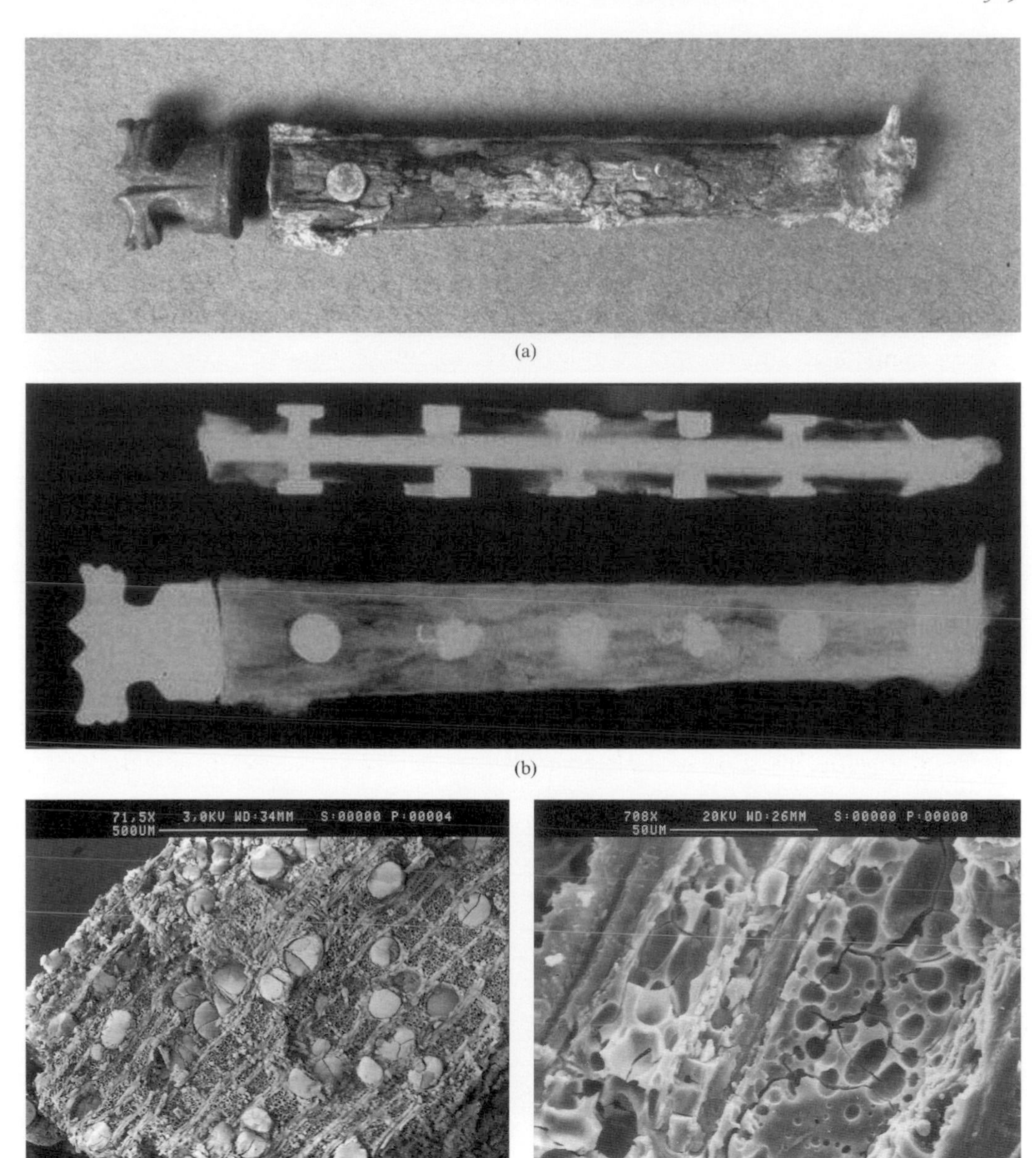

FIGURE 18.2 (a) Scale tang knife handle with wooden scales and copper alloy rivets and terminal; (b) X-radiograph showing two views of the handle; (c) SEM image showing pores in the wooden scale filled with a glassy material, probably a resin; (d) SEM image of resin or wax filling the wood structure.

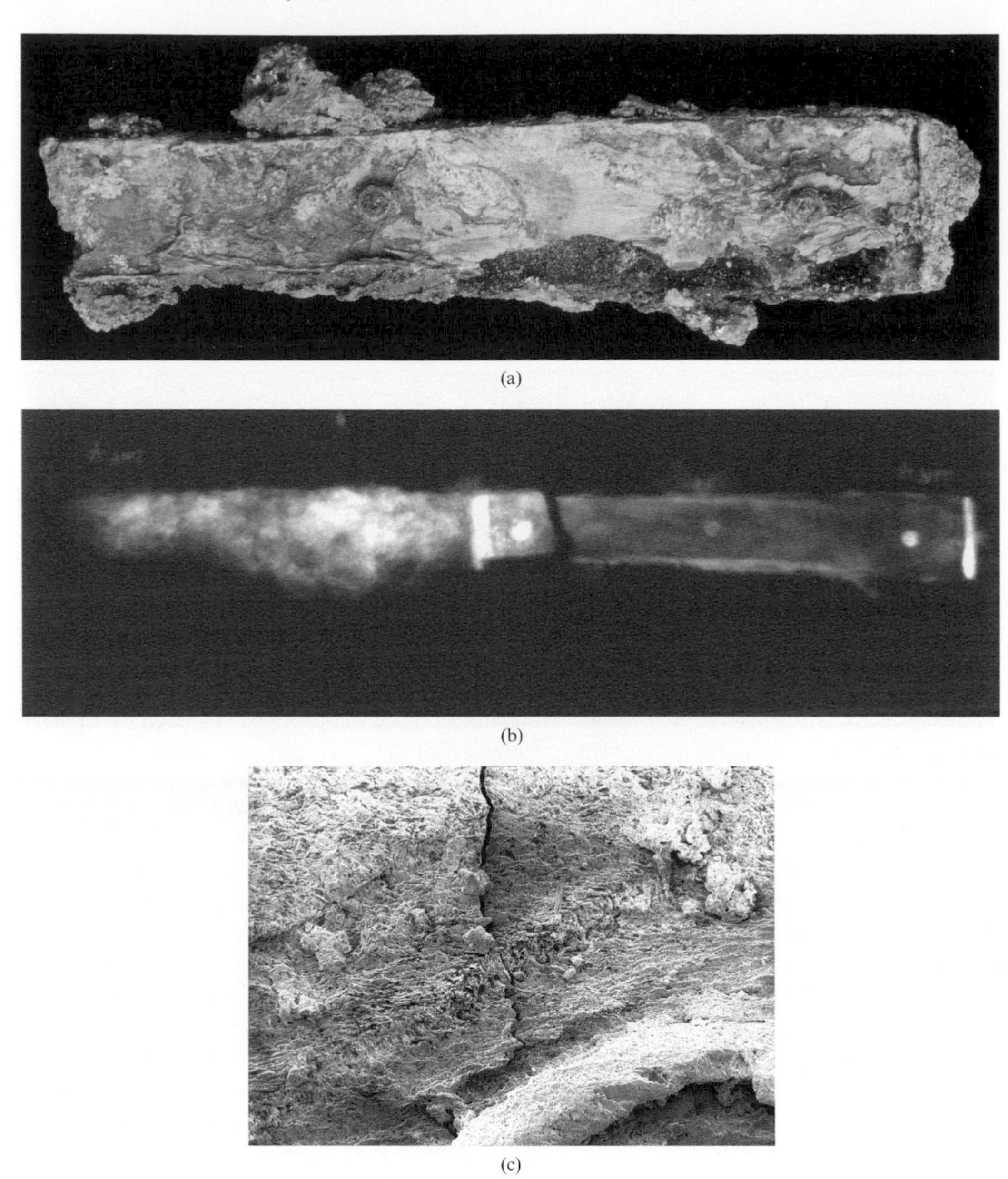

(a)

(b)

(c)

FIGURE 18.3 (a) Knife tang with traces of the organic scales preserved in the iron corrosion; (b) X-radiograph of the complete knife showing the non-ferrous metal rivets, end cap and shoulder plate; (c) SEM image of the organic material on the tang, whose structure is similar to weathered mother-of-pearl.

knives also have contrasting end caps, shoulder plates and decorative rivets made from brass or silver.

Some organic objects are only represented by traces within the corrosion layers on the remaining metal fittings — this is particularly important for clothes, containers and other personal items buried with inhumations. Organic materials preserved in this way can be grouped into three categories (Edwards 1989), and recognizing to which they belong is an important first step in the interpretation of fragmentary remains:

1. Organic components of metal artefacts, such as knife handles, sword hilts, spear shafts, shield boards, belt remains, purse remains, bucket staves, caskets and coffins.
2. Organic artefacts directly associated with metal objects, such as knife sheaths, sword scabbards and the remains of leather and textile purses preserved only on the metal objects they held.
3. Organic objects preserved by their proximity to metal objects, for example textiles from clothing, covers and containers; wood from coffins and other containers; plant materials; puparia and other insect remains; skin and bone.

Composite items, such as sword scabbards made from layers of fleece, wood and leather, can be very difficult to interpret where only small fragments are preserved in different areas along the length of the blade (Watson and Edwards 1990; Cameron 2000). Other objects such as antler combs can be reduced in acid soil conditions to just microscopic traces of antler remaining on the iron rivets that originally held the layers together.

ARTEFACT IDENTIFICATION AND RECONSTRUCTION OF ORGANIC OBJECTS

The routine scanning of assemblages of corroded metalwork, especially iron-work, by X-radiography has almost certainly resulted in the identification of more types of tools and personal items than had previously been recognized. In addition to revealing the outline of a corroded object, X-radiography will also indicate layers of information below the surface such as lock mechanisms which would otherwise be hidden from view unless the piece was broken open (Fell *et al* 2006).

Stereo X-radiography can be used to record complex groups of metalwork corroded together, without removing layers of corrosion containing preserved organic material, for example the leather and textile purses containing various small toilet items and amulets sometimes found associated with Anglo-Saxon female burials. An X-radiograph will show the individual pieces, but by taking a stereo pair of radio-graphs of a small block of soil containing the group it is often possible to see the exact relationship of the items within the block, so that the corrosion layers preserving the organic evidence can be left intact. A small group of toilet items wrapped in textile is illustrated in Figure 18.4, along with the X-radiograph showing that the block contains both copper alloy and iron pieces. By looking at a stereo pair of X-radiographs it was possible to work out how all the items related to one another to produce the reconstruction illustration.

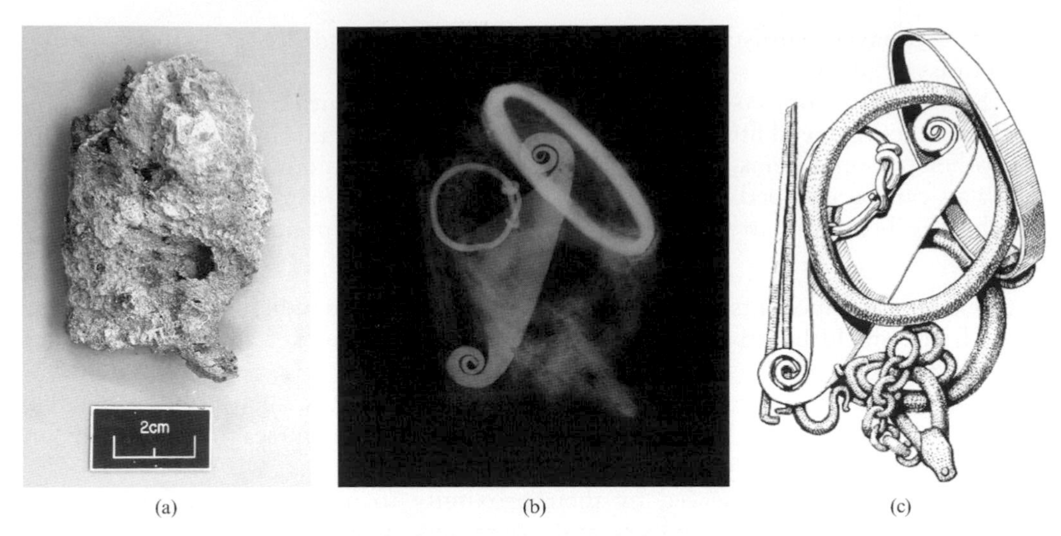

(a) (b) (c)

FIGURE 18.4 (a) Group of corroded metal objects wrapped in mineral-preserved textile; (b) X-radiograph of the same group; (c) illustration of the metalwork underneath the layers of textile.

As noted above, the presence of most organic artefacts in pagan graves are usually inferred from the remains preserved on metalwork or as soil stains, and this can be sufficient to identify the material and suggest the original form of the object. All that remains of many wooden bowls and small flasks is a small copper alloy rim mount or repair with a fragment of the wood, but this can be enough to identify the wood species, see if the grain orientation indicates if the piece has been lathe-turned, and produce a profile of the vessel. Two fragments of wood with copper alloy mounts were sufficient to produce the two alternative reconstruction profiles in Figure 18.5 of a small cup or bottle made from walnut (*Juglans* sp) found at Snape, Suffolk (Filmer-Sankey and Pestell 2001).

It is often possible to reconstruct how boxes with metal fittings were made (Watson 2000). One might think boxes were made from six wooden boards joined together with dowels or nails, but detailed studies have shown that there are differences in construction and form in different periods. Anglo-Saxon boxes fall into at least three groups:

1. Small box with a flat sliding lid; the metal fittings can include a handle and internal lock mechanism.
2. Rectangular box, with hinges, hasp, handle and often decorative corner brackets.
3. Small curved-lidded casket with hinges, hasp, handle, and often a small barrel padlock.

As well as having decorative metalwork on them, these boxes can also be decorated with carved designs like the example from Castledyke, North Humberside (Drinkall and Foreman 1998, 89), where remnants of a linear design on the lid were

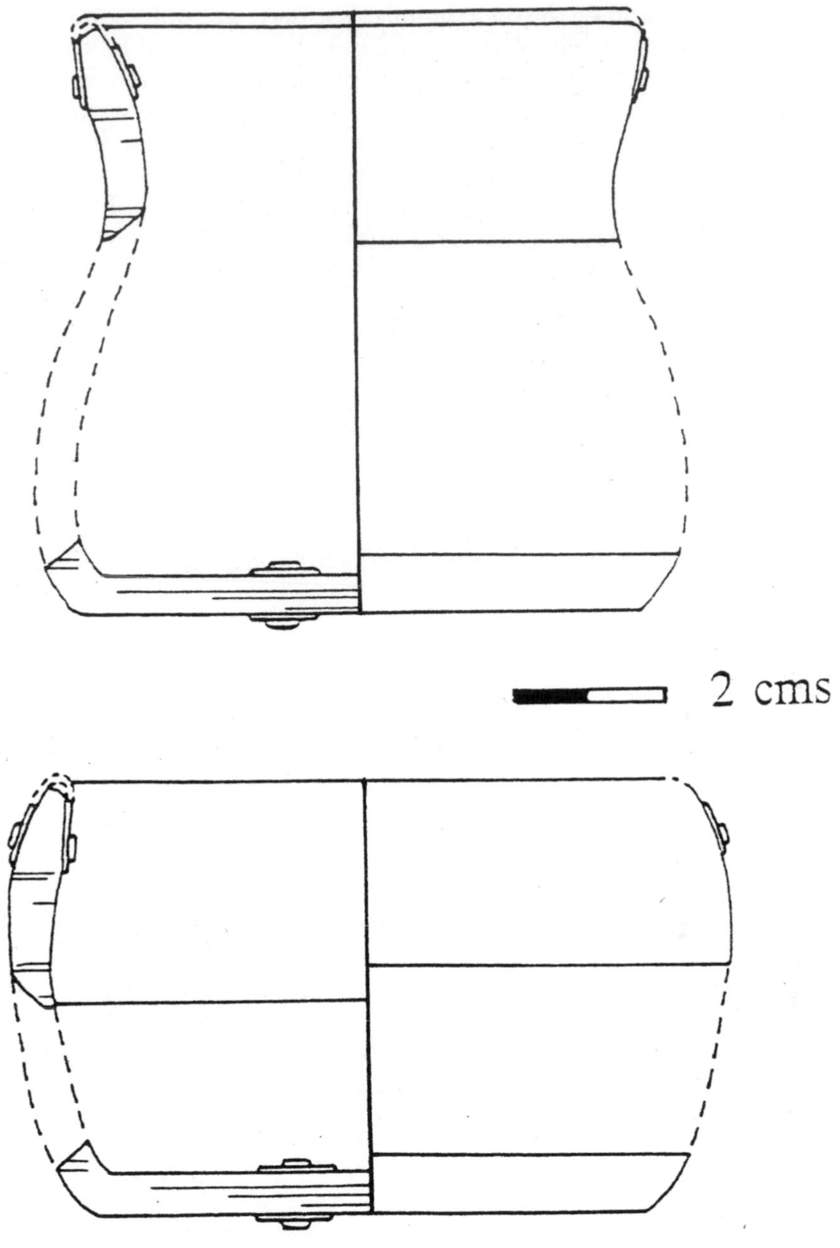

FIGURE 18.5 Two alternative profiles of a small cup or bottle made from walnut (*Juglans* sp.) reconstructed from traces of wood preserved on the metal fittings.

preserved in the corrosion of the drop handle; but these are only tantalizing hints of what may have been a very complex design. In the Viking period boxes appear to be long and thin in comparison to the Anglo-Saxon types, and were either rectangular with flat lids or trapezoid with curved lids, and both types were secured with metal strapping and locks (Arwidsson and Thorberg 1989). In later periods most of the evidence comes from extant examples such as the large chests found in churches which are heavily secured with iron bindings and complex locks. In addition to the reconstruction of boxes placed within graves it has also been possible to identify and study the construction of wooden chambers (Watson 2006a) and furniture, such as beds in 7th-century graves (Watson 2006b).

A great deal of work has been done on Anglo-Saxon costume (Walton-Rogers 2007) and much of this has been based on the fragments of textile preserved on brooches and dress accessories found in inhumations. The Anglian brooch in Figure 18.6 illustrates the different layers of textile and other organic materials that can be preserved by the combination of iron and copper corrosion originating from the pin and the brooch. In contrast, most of the evidence for later medieval costume comes from large waterlogged deposits in cities, particularly London; there are publications on footwear (Grew and de Neergaard 1988), clothing (Crowfoot *et al* 1992) and dress accessories (Egan and Pritchard 1991).

MANUFACTURING TECHNIQUES AND WORKSHOP ASSEMBLAGES

The technologies of material preparation or production and the manufacture of objects has changed little in the last couple of millennia — if the large-scale mechanized factories of the last two centuries are discounted. There are only a limited number of ways of turning raw materials into finished products, and most of these

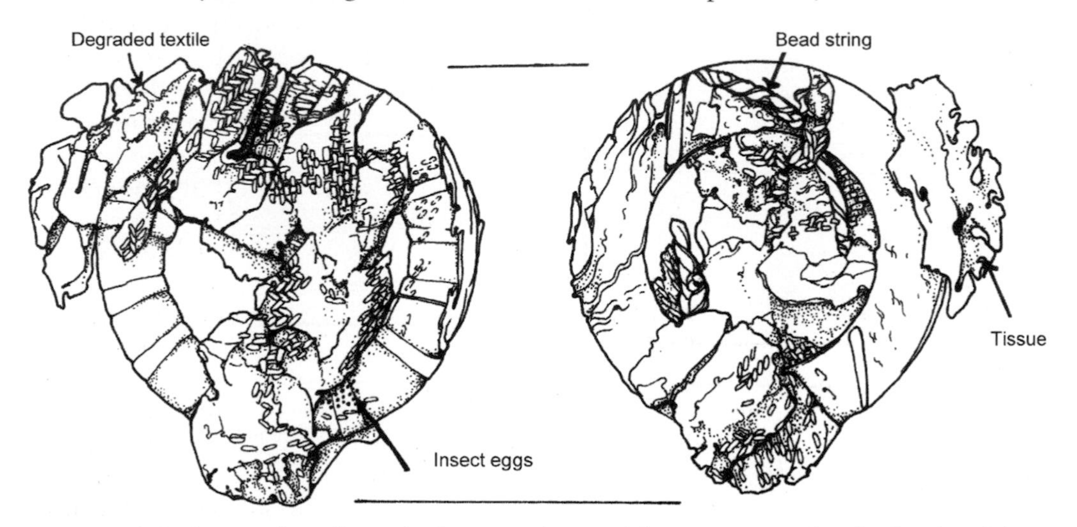

FIGURE 18.6 Layers of textiles and other organic materials were preserved on both sides of this annular brooch by the combination of iron and copper corrosion originating from the pin and the brooch.

were well known by early in the medieval period. The evidence we have comes from workshop debris and from objects themselves, where such things as casting flashes, tool marks and wear patterns can show how they were made or used. Scientific examination and analysis can add to the information derived from this evidence, and when combined with contemporary documentary sources can be powerful tools for understanding the techniques used in the past (eg Martinón-Torres and Rehren 2008).

Studying artefacts from any archaeological context can show how they were made, and analysis may be able to suggest sources for the raw materials used. However, only by identifying workshops and studying the debris associated with them can the full details of material production and its conversion into objects be determined. In many cases, especially where high temperature processes are involved, the use of scientific techniques expands the range of questions that can be asked and answered.

Clarke (1984, 129) began her survey of medieval craft and industry by saying: 'The crafts and industries which were the lifeblood of medieval England have generally been poorly served by the archaeologist, who has until recently shown a peculiar lack of interest in this most important aspect of medieval life'. At the same time Harvey (1983, 79) was bemoaning the lack of archaeological investigation of industrial sites as it could provide 'greater returns than any other work on the period's archaeology, simply because it fills such a gap in the written records'. It is not true craft and industry had been completely ignored prior to this time, though in the early days of the subject the publications were as likely to be in a scientific journal (eg Tylecote 1959) as in an archaeological one (eg Anstee and Biek 1961). A landmark publication was *Medieval Industry* (Crossley 1981), where the papers blended documentary and archaeological evidence, although a number of them dealt more with products than processes or workshops.

The problem with identifying workshops is that unless the process was large-scale or involved high temperatures, the features are usually almost indistinguishable from those found in domestic contexts. Even on sites like Coppergate, in York, where blacksmithing (Ottaway 1991), silver-working (Bayley 1992a) and wood-turning (Morris 2000) were practised on a considerable scale, it is only the distribution of portable finds that identifies the location of the manufacturing activity. The main industries where work places are readily identifiable are iron-smelting and glass-working, where furnace remains survive (eg Haslam *et al* 1980; Kenyon 1967), and potteries or tile works, where kilns are identified (Musty 1974), though the accompanying workshops are less often recorded (eg Bryant and Steane 1971; Drury and Pratt 1975). In the case of blacksmiths' forges, it is the distribution of hammerscale, a micro-slag, that can confirm the activity and locate it exactly within a building (Bayley *et al* 2001, fig 5; Jouttijärvi *et al* 2005, fig 27).

The main contribution of scientific techniques to the study of craft and industrial assemblages is the positive identification of specific processes. Many early reports mentioning ironworking interpret iron slags as evidence for smelting (converting ore into metal) even though iron-smithing (shaping metal into objects) is a far more common process. This type of misinterpretation can now easily be avoided as experience has shown smithing and smelting slags usually look very different (Bayley *et al* 2001), though sometimes scientific analysis will also be needed.

Crucibles are often identified by excavators or pottery specialists on the basis of their vitrified and highly coloured exteriors. Like any other pot, their form and fabric can indicate, at least approximately, their date and sometimes their place of manufacture (Bayley 1992b). However, only scientific analysis can determine the nature of the metal (or glass) being melted, or the process carried out in the vessel if it was not used for metal-melting (Bayley and Rehren 2007). Most of the crucibles from both the Coppergate site in York (Bayley 1992a) and from Chalk Lane in Northampton (Bayley 1981) were used for melting silver, rather than the copper alloys their red coloration had initially suggested. This, and the identification of a number of sherds as 'heating trays' or cupels, which were used to test the purity of precious metals, led to interpretations associating the metalworking with the 10th-century mints known to have operated in both towns.

Gold-working includes a number of different processes. Gold on metal-melting crucibles can be easily identified by eye, though the small size of the droplets may require magnification to make them visible. Parting, the separation of gold from silver, was described by Theophilus in the 12th century (Hawthorn and Smith 1979; Bayley 2008), but had not been identified in a medieval context until the finds from the Coppergate excavations were analysed (Bayley 1992a, 751–754); further examples are now known from other medieval sites. Mercury- or fire-gilding is a well-known decorative technique that became common in the late Roman period and continued until superseded by electroplating in the 19th century. The theory and practice of the technique is equally well known, though no specific archaeological evidence for it had been identified until recently. Now two mortars from Hamwic that were used for preparing gold-mercury amalgam have been identified on the basis of microscopic traces of gold which chemical analysis demonstrated were associated with the presence of mercury (Hook and Tite 1996; Bayley and Russel 2008).

OUTCOMES AND PROSPECTS FOR THE FUTURE

The examples given above demonstrate the range of contributions that materials science and investigative conservation have made to medieval archaeology. The scientific techniques have the potential to date objects, identify imports and traded materials or artefacts, understand the complexities of the technical processes used by medieval craftsmen, and indicate the quality and status of their products. Corroded metal objects can be identified by X-radiography and complex and organic objects reconstructed from surviving traces. Artefact studies have come a long way from the brief catalogues of old, and part of the reason for this is the increasing collation of information from many sources.

Archaeological science and investigative conservation should not operate in a vacuum but in full collaboration with other parts of the archaeological community. The relationship must be a symbiotic one, with scientific contributions being informed by the wider archaeological and historical context, and the results of these investigations feeding back into the mainstream. We should be striving to integrate our work fully into archaeology so the technical appendix becomes a thing of the past.

On the technical side, there is potential for the development of new scientific techniques, but making better use of existing techniques is more likely to be cost effective. However, with the increased miniaturization of scientific equipment it is already possible to get portable versions of some machines, and these are being routinely used by geologists and engineers in the field. If archaeologists and archaeological scientists did likewise, the laboratory could in effect move out to the excavation: complex burial groups could be X-rayed *in situ* before being carefully dismantled, and portable analytical equipment could be invaluable for interpreting industrial features and dumps of workshop debris in the field.

Most of the blank areas in our map of knowledge about the medieval period have the potential to be filled if the right sites were surveyed and excavated to the best possible standards in full collaboration with scientists and conservators using the most advanced of our current investigative techniques. However, many of the gaps remain because we cannot identify or locate the right site, or because we operate in a less than ideal world where resources of all sorts are limited. An awareness of these constraints is the first step towards remedying the situation.

Most important is to ensure that the developments of the past 50 years are available to all parts of the archaeological community. If all archaeologists — both those with curatorial responsibilities who set briefs for developer-funded projects, and those working in commercial units and academic departments — know what can be done, they are more likely to plan to use all appropriate techniques, with the result that more information will be extracted from those interventions that take place. Awareness, training and appreciation are thus fundamental to the continuing growth of scientific contributions to medieval archaeology.

BIBLIOGRAPHY

Alcock, L, 1963 *Dinas Powys: an Iron Age, Dark Age and Early Medieval Settlement in Glamorgan*, University of Wales Press, Cardiff

Anstee J W and Biek, L, 1961 'A study in pattern welding', *Medieval Archaeology* 5, 71–93

Arwidsson, G and Thorberg, H, 1989 'Kästen und schachteln', in G Arwidsson (ed), *Birka II:3 Systematische Analysen der Gräberfunde*, 113–121, Vitterhets Historie och Antikvitets Akademien, Stockholm

Barclay, K, 2001 *Scientific Analysis of Archaeological Ceramics: a Handbook of Resources*, Oxbow, Oxford

Barnet, P and Dandridge, P (eds), 2006 *Lions, Dragons, and Other Beasts: Aquamanilia of the Middle Ages, Vessels for Church and Table*, Yale University Press, New Haven and London

Bayley, J, 1981 'The metallurgical evidence', in J H Williams and M Shaw, 'Excavations in Chalk Lane, Northampton 1975–1978', *Northamptonshire Archaeology* 16, 87–135; 126 and fiche

Bayley, J, 1987 'Qualitative analyses of some of the beads', in V I Evison, *Dover: The Buckland Anglo-Saxon Cemetery*, 182–189, HBMCE, Archaeological Report 3, London

Bayley, J, 1991 'Alloy nomenclature', in G Egan and F Pritchard (eds), *Dress Accessories c.1150–c.1450. Medieval Finds from Excavations in London: 3*, 13–17, Her Majesty's Stationery Office, London

Bayley, J, 1992a *Non-ferrous Metalworking at 16–22 Coppergate*, Archaeology of York 17/7, Council for British Archaeology, London

Bayley, J, 1992b 'Metalworking ceramics', *Medieval Ceramics* 16, 3–10

Bayley, J, 1999 'Notes on the composition of coloured glass', in M Guido, *The Glass Beads of Anglo-Saxon England c.AD 400–700*, 89–93, Boydell Press, Woodbridge

Bayley, J, 2000a 'Glassworking in early medieval England', in J Price (ed), *Glass in Britain and Ireland AD 350–1100*, 137–142, British Museum Occasional Paper 127, London

Bayley, J, 2000b 'Saxon glassworking at Glastonbury Abbey', in J Price (ed), *Glass in Britain and Ireland AD 350–1100*, 161–188 and 204, British Museum Occasional Paper 127, London

Bayley, J, 2007 'Early medieval lead-rich glass trinkets', *Research News* 6, 24–25

Bayley, J, 2008 'Medieval precious metal refining: archaeology and contemporary texts compared', in M Martinón-Torres and T Rehren (eds), *Archaeology, History and Science: Integrating Approaches to Ancient Materials*, 131–150, Left Coast Press, Walnut Creek CA

Bayley, J, in press 'Early medieval lead-rich glass in the British Isles — a survey of the evidence', *Annales of the 17th Congress of l'Association Internationale pour l'Histoire du Verre, 2006*, Antwerp

Bayley, J, in prep *Metalworking in Viking Dublin*, Royal Irish Academy, Medieval Dublin Excavations Series, Dublin

Bayley, J, Bryant, R and Heighway, C, 1993 'A tenth-century bell-pit and bell-mould from St Oswald's Priory, Gloucester', *Medieval Archaeology* 37, 224–236

Bayley, J, Dungworth, D and Paynter, S, 2001 *Archaeometallurgy*, English Heritage, London

Bayley, J and Rehren, T, 2007 'Towards a functional and typological classification of crucibles', in S La Niece, D Hook and P Craddock (eds), *Metals and Mines: Studies in Archaeometallurgy*, 46–55, Archetype Publications, London

Bayley, J and Russel, A, 2008 'Making gold-mercury amalgam: the evidence for gilding from Southampton', *Antiquaries Journal* 88, 37–42

Beresford, G, 1975 *The Medieval Clay-Land Village: Excavations at Goltho and Barton Blount*, Monograph Series No 6, Society for Medieval Archaeology, London

Blades, N W, Bayley, J and Walsh, J N, 1991 'The ICPS analysis of ancient copper alloys', in P Budd, B Chapman, C Jackson, R Janaway, and B Ottaway (eds), *Archaeological Sciences 89*, 8–15, Oxbow Monograph 9, Oxford

Blakelock, E and McDonnell, G, 2007 'A review of metallographic analyses of early medieval knives', *Historical Metallurgy* 41:1, 40–56

Brownsword, R, 1988 *An Introduction to Base Metals and Their Alloys 1200–1700*, Finds Research Group 700–1700, Datasheet 8, Oxford

Brownsword, R, 1997 'Appendix 2: Analyses of the alloys of Anglo-Saxon great square-headed brooches', in J Hines, *A New Corpus of Anglo-Saxon Great Square-Headed Brooches*, 313–315, Boydell Press, Woodbridge

Bryant, G F and Steane, J M, 1971 'Excavations at the deserted medieval settlement at Lyveden. A third interim report', *Journal of Northampton Museums and Art Gallery* 9, 2–94

Butler, R and Green, C, 2003 *English Bronze Cooking Vessels and their Founders 1350–1830*, privately published, Honiton

Cameron, E, 2000 *Sheaths and Scabbards in England AD 400–1100*, British Archaeological Reports British Series 301, Oxford

Cameron, H K, 1974 'Technical aspects of medieval monumental brasses', *Archaeological Journal* 131, 215–237

Clarke, H, 1984 *The Archaeology of Medieval England*, British Museum Publications, London

Cowgill, J, de Neergaard, M and Griffiths, N, 1987 *Knives and Scabbards. Medieval Finds from Excavations in London: 1*, Her Majesty's Stationery Office, London

Craddock P T, Wallis, J M and Merkel, J F, 2001 'The rapid qualitative analysis of groups of metalwork: making a dream come true', in M Redknap, N Edwards, S Youngs, A Lane and J Knight (eds), *Pattern and Purpose in Insular Art*, 117–124, Oxbow, Oxford

Brill, R H, 2006 'Chemical analyses of some glasses from Jarrow and Wearmouth', in R Cramp, *Wearmouth and Jarrow Monastic Sites*, 126–147, English Heritage, Swindon

Crossley, D (ed), 1981 *Medieval Industry*, Council for British Archaeology Research Report 40, London

Crowfoot, E, Pritchard, F and Staniland, K, 1992 *Textile and Clothing. Medieval Finds from Excavations in London: 4*, Her Majesty's Stationery Office, London

Drinkall, G and Foreman, M, 1998 *The Anglo-Saxon Cemetery at Castledyke South, Barton-on-Humber*, Sheffield Excavation Reports 6, Sheffield Academic Press, Sheffield

Drury, P J and Pratt, G D, 1975 'A late 13th and early 14th-century tile factory at Danbury, Essex', *Medieval Archaeology* 19, 92–164

Dungworth, D and Nicholas M, 2004 'Caldarium? An antimony bronze used for medieval and post-medieval cast domestic vessels', *Historical Metallurgy* 38:1, 24–34

Edwards, G, 1989 'Guidelines for dealing with materials from sites where organic remains have been preserved by metal corrosion products', *Evidence Preserved in Corrosion Products: New Fields in Artifact Studies*, 3–7, UKIC Occasional Paper 8, London

Egan, G and Pritchard, F, 1991 *Dress Accessories. Medieval Finds from Excavations in London: 3*, Her Majesty's Stationery Office, London

Evison, V I, 1955 'Early Anglo-Saxon inlaid metalwork', *Antiquaries Journal* 35, 20–45

Fell, V, Mould, Q and White, R, 2006 *Guidelines on the X-radiography of Archaeological Metalwork*, English Heritage, Swindon

Filmer-Sankey, W and Pestell, T, 2001 *Snape Anglo-Saxon Cemetery: Excavations and Surveys 1824–1992*, East Anglian Archaeology 95, Suffolk County Council, Ipswich

Freestone, I and Gaimster, D (eds), 1997 *Pottery in the Making: World Ceramic Traditions*, British Museum Press, London

Freestone, I C, Hughes, M J and Stapleton, C P, 2008 'The composition and production of Anglo-Saxon glass', in V I Evison, *Catalogue of Anglo-Saxon glass in the British Museum*, 29–44, British Museum Press Research Publication 167, London

Gratuze, B, Foy, D, Lancelot, J and Tereygeol, F, 2003 'Les "lissoirs" carolingiens en verre au plomb: mise en évidence de la valorisation des scories issues du traitment des galènes argentifères de Melle (Deux Sèvres)', in D Foy and M-D Nenna (eds), *Echanges et commerce du verre dans le monde antique*, 101–107, Monographies Instrumentum 21, Monique Mergoil, Montagnac

Grew, F and de Neergaard, M, 1988 *Shoes and Pattens. Medieval Finds from Excavations in London: 2*, Her Majesty's Stationery Office, London

Guido, M, 1999 *The Glass Beads of Anglo-Saxon England c.AD 400–700*, Boydell Press, Woodbridge

Harvey, P D A, 1983 'English archaeology after the Conquest: a historian's view', in D A Hinton (ed), *25 Years of Medieval Archaeology*, 74–82, University of Sheffield Department of Prehistory and Archaeology, Sheffield

Haslam, J, Biek, L and Tylecote, R F, 1980 'A Middle Saxon iron smelting site at Ramsbury, Wiltshire', *Medieval Archaeology* 24, 1–68

Hawthorn, J G and Smith, C S, 1979 *Theophilus on Divers Arts*, Dover, New York

Heyworth, M, 1991 'Metallurgical analysis of dress accessories', in G Egan and F Pritchard (eds), *Dress Accessories c.1150–c.1450. Medieval Finds from Excavations in London: 3*, 387–395, Her Majesty's Stationery Office, London

Hook, D R and Tite, M S, 1996 'Report on three samples taken from the grinding mortar', in D A Hinton, *The Gold, Silver and Other Non-Ferrous Alloy Objects from Hamwic, and the Non-Ferrous Metalworking Evidence*, 80–81, Alan Sutton, Stroud

Hughes, M J, 1991 'Provenance studies of Spanish medieval tin-glazed pottery by neutron activation analysis', in P Budd, B Chapman, C Jackson, R Janaway and B Ottaway, (eds), *Archaeological Sciences 1989*, 54–68, Oxbow Monograph 9, Oxford

Hughes, M J, Blake, H, Hurst, J and Wilson, T, 1997 'Neutron activation analysis of Italian maiolica and other medieval Italian ceramics', in A Sinclair, E Slater and J Gowlett (eds), *Archaeological Sciences 1995*, 77–81, Oxbow Monograph 64, Oxford

Jouttijärvi, A, Thomsen, T and Moltsen, A S A, 2005 'Værkstedets funktion', in M Iversen, D E Robinson, J Hjermind and C Christensen (eds), *Viborg Søndersø 1018–1030: Arkæologi og naturvidenskab I et værkstedsområde fra vikingetid*, 297–320, Jysk Arkæologisk Selskab, Højbjerg

Kenyon, G H, 1967 *The Glass Industry of the Weald*, Leicester University Press, Leicester

Martinón-Torres, M and Rehren, T (eds), 2008 *Archaeology, History and Science: Integrating Approaches to Ancient Materials*, Left Coast Press, Walnut Creek CA

McDonnell, J G and Ottaway, P, 1991 'The smithing process', in P Ottaway, *Anglo-Scandinavian Ironwork from 16–22 Coppergate*, 480–486, Archaeology of York 17/6, Council for British Archaeology, London

Morris, C A, 2000 *Wood and Woodworking in Anglo-Scandinavian and Medieval York*, Archaeology of York 17/13, Council for British Archaeology, York

Mortimer, C, 1991 'A descriptive classification of early Anglo-Saxon copper-alloy compositions: towards a general typology of early medieval copper alloys', *Medieval Archaeology* 35, 104–107

Musty, J, 1974 'Medieval pottery kilns', in V I Evison, H Hodges and J G Hurst (eds), *Medieval Pottery from Excavations: Studies Presented to Gerald Clough Dunning*, 41–65, John Baker, London

Oddy, W A, La Niece, S and Stratford, N, 1986 *Romanesque Metalwork: Copper Alloys and Their Decoration*, British Museum Publications, London

Ottaway, P, 1991 *Anglo-Scandinavian Ironwork from 16–22 Coppergate*, Archaeology of York 17/6, Council for British Archaeology, London

Peacock, D P S (ed), 1977 *Pottery and Early Commerce: Characterization and Trade in Roman and Later Ceramics*, Academic Press, London

Phillips, P (ed), 1985 *The Archaeologist and the Laboratory*, Council for British Archaeology Research Report 58, London

Shoesmith, R, 1985 *Hereford City Excavations, Vol 3: The Finds*, Council for British Archaeology Research Report 56, London

Spencer, B, 1998 *Pilgrim Souvenirs and Secular Badges: Medieval Finds from Excavations in London: 7*, Stationery Office, Norwich

Tylecote, R F, 1959 'An early medieval iron-smelting site in Weardale', *Journal of the Iron and Steel Institute* 192, 26–34

Tylecote, R F, 1962 *Metallurgy in Archaeology: a Prehistory of Metallurgy in the British Isles*, Edward Arnold, London

Tylecote, R F and Gilmour, B J J, 1986 *The Metallography of Early Ferrous Edge Tools and Edged Weapons*, British Archaeological Reports 155, Oxford

Tyson, R, 2000 *Medieval Glass Vessels Found in England c AD 1200–1500*, Council for British Archaeology Research Report 121, York

Vince, A, 2005 'Ceramic petrology and the study of Anglo-Saxon and later medieval ceramics', *Medieval Archaeology* 49, 219–245

Walton–Rogers, P, 2007 *Cloth and Clothing in Early Anglo-Saxon England AD 450–700*, Council for British Archaeology Research Report 145, York

Watson, J, 1995 'Wood usage in Anglo-Saxon shields', *Anglo-Saxon Studies in Archaeology and History* 7, 35–48

Watson, J, 2000 'Wood', in D A Hinton, *A Smith in Lindsey. The Anglo-Saxon Grave at Tattershall Thorpe, Lincolnshire*, 86–93, Society for Medieval Archaeology Monograph Series 16, London

Watson, J, 2006a *Smythes Corner (Shrublands Quarry), Coddenham, Suffolk: The Identification of Organic Material Associated with Metalwork from the Anglo-Saxon Cemetery*, English Heritage Centre for Archaeology Report 27/2006, Portsmouth

Watson, J, 2006b *Smythes Corner (Shrublands Quarry), Coddenham, Suffolk: The Examination and Reconstruction of an Anglo-Saxon Bed Burial*, English Heritage Centre for Archaeology Report 60/2006, Portsmouth

Watson, J and Edwards, G, 1990 'Conservation of material from Anglo-Saxon cemeteries', in E Southworth (ed), *Anglo-Saxon Cemeteries: a Reappraisal*, 97–106, Alan Sutton, Stroud

Watson, J, Fell, V and Jones, J, 2008 *Investigative Conservation*, English Heritage, Swindon

Watson, J and Paynter, S 2001 *Examination of Metalwork from Castle Mall, Norwich*, English Heritage Centre for Archaeology Report 29/2001, Portsmouth

White, R 1982 'Non-ferrous metalworking on Flaxengate, Lincoln from the 9th–11th centuries', unpublished conservation diploma dissertation, Institute of Archaeology, University of London

Williams, A, 2003 *The Knight and the Blast Furnace. A History of the Metallurgy of Armour in the Middle Ages and the Early Modern Period*, Brill, Leiden

Wilthew, P, 1987 'Metallographic examination of medieval knives and shears', in J Cowgill, M de Neergaard and N Griffiths, *Knives and Scabbards: Medieval Finds from Excavations in London: 1*, 62–74, Her Majesty's Stationery Office, London

Wilthew, P and Ottaway, P, 1991 'Non-ferrous plating', in P Ottaway, *Anglo-Scandinavian Ironwork from 16–22 Coppergate*, 486–490, Archaeology of York 17/6, Council for British Archaeology, London

PART V

SOCIAL APPROACHES TO MEDIEVAL ARCHAEOLOGY

CHAPTER 19
MEDIEVAL ARCHAEOLOGY AND THEORY: A DISCIPLINARY LEAP OF FAITH

By ROBERTA GILCHRIST

This paper challenges the view that medieval archaeology has failed to engage with theory, exploring the impact over the last 25 years of processual and post-processual approaches. Trends are reviewed according to regional research traditions, chronological periods and research themes. It is concluded that processualism encouraged grand narratives on themes such as trade, the origins of towns and state formation, while the post-processual concern with agency and meaning has fostered study of social identity, gender, religious belief, sensory perception and spatial experience. It is argued that processualism created an artificial dichotomy between economic/scientific approaches on the one hand, and social/theoretical approaches on the other. The potential is discussed for medieval studies of embodiment, materiality, agency and phenomenology, and the case is made for greater engagement with the development of theory in the wider discipline, with the aim of achieving a more meaningful medieval archaeology.

INTRODUCTION

In 1982, the occasion of the Society's 25th anniversary prompted reflection on the discipline's relationship with archaeological theory. 'New Archaeology' had transformed the wider subject in the 1970s, and among its significant achievements was demonstration of the role played by explanatory philosophical frameworks in all aspects of archaeological data-collection and interpretation. Richard Hodges, in particular, called for medieval archaeologists to abandon their culture-historical paradigm, with its inclination to small-scale particularization. In its place, he advocated processual approaches based on systems theory and model-building, emphasizing the importance of internal and external processes in transforming societies (Hodges 1983). He challenged the comfortable, empirical stance of medieval archaeology and encouraged bigger and bolder questions — the medieval archaeologist as 'parachutist' rather than 'truffle-hunter' (Hodges 1989).[1] Twenty-five years later, and on the occasion of the Society's 50th anniversary, the time is ripe to revisit the relationship between medieval archaeology and theory. How has our discipline engaged with significant advances in archaeological thought since 1982? Has archaeological theory changed the way we interpret the Middle Ages?

THE LONG SHADOW OF PROCESSUALISM

The practice of medieval archaeology is sometimes characterized as anti- or a-theoretical, with exponents favouring allegedly 'common sense' or 'functionalist' approaches (Gerrard 2003, 173, 218). Matthew Johnson has commented on this tendency especially within medieval landscape archaeology: the inherent proposition is that archaeological features in the landscape are recorded objectively and therefore take on the status of facts that speak for themselves; the role of theory in mediating interpretation is rejected in favour of an empiricist position (Johnson 2007, 83). Johnson and others have demonstrated the extent to which apparently objective methods of archaeological data-collection are in fact socially constructed and 'deeply theoretical' (ibid, 93). For example, he notes that standard means of landscape recording — the hachured plan, the Ordnance Survey map and the aerial photograph — all present a bird's-eye view of the landscape from above. This prioritization of the plan view takes no account of how people in the past would have perceived and moved through the landscape; moreover, it fails to acknowledge the extent to which ostensibly objective methods of data-recording are selective, and imbued with modern value judgements. Archaeological observations are theory-laden, and intensely dependent on extended networks of theoretical claims and assumptions (Wylie 2002, 6).

It may be argued that the empiricist position in medieval archaeology was reinforced by the positivist methodologies of processualism, which perpetuate a separation of theory and data. Until the advent of New Archaeology in the 1970s, culture-history was the prevailing 'paradigm' in world archaeology, a tradition associated with the mapping of specific cultures and their influence, with no attempt to explain underlying meanings or trends in material culture.[2] Processualism constituted a 'scientific revolution' in archaeology, and has duly taken its place as the subject's prevailing paradigm.[3] New Archaeology appeared to offer a more objective, science-based method to the youthful discipline of medieval archaeology, one still struggling to come to terms with its parent discipline of history[4] (Gerrard 2003, 174). The hypothetico-deductive approach was first applied to medieval archaeology by Martyn Jope, entailing the testing of interpretations through quantification, mapping and modelling of data (Jope 1972). In summary, then, the term 'empiricism' has acquired two distinct meanings in medieval archaeology: the 'empiricist position' that archaeological data are facts that speak for themselves; and the positivist methods of data analysis that are associated with processualism.

The more ecological tenets of New Archaeology, developed by Eric Higgs at Cambridge in the 1960s, remain important today (eg Williamson 2003): the application of environmental and materials sciences helped to carve a distinctive niche for archaeology in medieval studies. Influenced by processualism, medieval archaeology has specialized in topics neglected by conventional documentary sources, including landscape, subsistence, diet, industry, technology, and the tenements and crofts of 'the common man'[5] of the medieval town and countryside. When the Society drew up its recommendations for research in 1987, greatest confidence for an archaeological contribution to medieval studies was in the realm of landscape economy and technology. For example, in relation to religious sites, it was proposed that ritual foci were no longer a priority; instead, we needed 'more information on the non-claustral areas of the Christian institutions, to examine their impact upon the economy and society of their surrounding region, and the investments made in agriculture and industry, both in the immediate area of the monastery and in its distant farms and granges' (SMA 1987, 4). Undoubtedly, this approach has advanced our understanding of monastic landscapes (see Bond 2004). Perhaps ironically, however, the period of the last 20 years has also seen some of the discipline's most important theoretical analyses directed specifically toward the ritual core of churches, cloisters and other religious sites (discussed below). In striving to consolidate its own identity within medieval studies, archaeology has tended to prioritize more economic enquiries, and to place greatest value on empirical evidence that appears more scientifically robust. An indirect legacy of processualism was the creation of an artificial dichotomy between economic/scientific approaches on the one hand, and social/theoretical approaches on the other.

Processualism impacted more overtly on early medieval archaeology (*c*6th to 10th centuries AD), an epoch relatively unfettered by documents. The comparative paucity of historical sources perhaps encourages more ambitious theoretical reflection on subjects such as early medieval state formation and the origins of feudalism (eg Randsborg 1980; 1991). The work of Richard Hodges was an exciting and radical departure, with *Dark Age Economics* (1982) addressing the origins of towns and long-distance trade networks. Its title signalled an alliance with the economic systems theory of Marshall Sahlins' *Stone Age Economics* (1974), proposing the thesis that trade networks in prestige goods were stimulated by political leaders such as Charlemagne and Offa, the medieval equivalents of Sahlins' tribal 'big-men'.[6] The explicit use of systems theory was short-lived in medieval archaeology, with the timing of Hodges' pioneering works coinciding almost precisely with the demise of processualism (in Britain, at least). Although seldom explicitly cited in interpretations today, processualism underpins much archaeological research on the role of politics and consumption in the formation of early medieval elites. For example, Martin Carver adopts the theme 'monumentality' as shorthand for investment in burial mounds, jewellery, churches, sculpture and illuminated manuscripts, which he regards as tangible fossils of the political language of early medieval Europe (Carver 2001).

THEORY IN MEDIEVAL ARCHAEOLOGY: THE LAST 25 YEARS

The influence of processualism in the wider subject of archaeology began to wane in the late 1970s and early 1980s, with challenges to the apparent objectivity of New Archaeology's methods, and calls for more anthropological approaches to interpretation. Ian Hodder was at the vanguard of these developments, experimenting with ethnoarchaeology and applying structuralist principles based on the premise that material culture is governed by grammatical rules similar to those of language (Hodder 1982a; 1982b). By the mid-1980s, cross-cultural approaches were beginning to be rejected in favour of contextual, historically grounded readings of archaeology, and a diversity of interpretative approaches drew inspiration from fields including anthropology, philosophy, feminism, Marxism and cognitive science. Together, these approaches are often termed 'post-processual'. As Matthew Johnson has emphasized, there is no unified post-processual paradigm, but common strands can be identified. Post-processualists take a social constructivist perspective in challenging scientific claims to unique and objective knowledge; they offer hermeneutic interpretations that focus on the meanings of material culture; and they stress agency, the active strategies of individuals to reproduce or transform their social contexts (Johnson 1999, 101–104). To what extent have these approaches influenced modes of interpretation in medieval archaeology?

By the early 1990s, some medievalists were calling for studies of agency and the active role of material culture in structuring social relations (Moreland 1991). But the engagement with post-processual theory has remained selective, with lines drawn according to geographical region, chronological periods and research themes. The appetite for archaeological theory can generally be seen to follow an Anglo-Scandinavian axis, and medieval archaeology is no exception in showing more rapid theoretical development in Nordic- and English-speaking areas. Medieval archaeology is commonly divided into at least two, and sometimes up to four, chronological sub-periods of early and later medieval; for example, in Germany, the period is divided into the Early Middle Ages (*c*450 to the 8th century), Carolingian/Ottonian (9th to 10th centuries), the High Middle Ages (*c*1000–1250) and the Late Middle Ages (*c*1250–1500). As previously noted, early medieval archaeology has tended to embrace theoretical perspectives more warmly. It is significant that medieval archaeologists in Scandinavia have been especially successful in integrating theory; here, the Viking period connects the late Iron Age to the early medieval period (beginning in the 11th century AD). Adoption of the *longue dureé*[7] merges Scandinavian prehistory seamlessly with the Middle Ages, promoting greater engagement with theoretical perspectives and yielding innovative work on topics such as cosmology, gender and childhood (eg Andrén *et al* 2006; Price 2002; Welinder 1998).

More generally, medieval archaeologists have accepted the post-processual principle that material culture plays an *active* role in creating and sustaining the social world. Theory is implicit in the discipline's move towards social archaeology, as evidenced by contributions to the journal *Medieval Archaeology*.[8] Explicitly theoretical articles are rare; for instance, David Hinton on 'closure theory' (1999), Howard Williams on monument reuse (1997) and Amanda Richardson on gender and space in the medieval English palace (2003). However, most issues of the journal now contain at least one empirical study which is broadly 'social', if not expressly theoretical (eg Dickinson 2005; Hamerow 2006; Clarke 2007).

The discipline of medieval archaeology has not developed a unifying or cohesive theoretical framework of its own, in contrast with some other chronological fields: notably the 'domestication' theme which has dominated post-processual Neolithic studies (Rowley-Conwy 2004), or the obsession of Roman theoretical archaeology with 'Romanization' (Hingley 2005). Theoretical contributions have developed largely within the confines of medieval archaeology's specialist or period groups (based on categories of monument or material), rather than through regular engagement with theory-building in the wider subject arena. The application of theory in medieval archaeology has remained highly contextual (or particularistic); this lack of interest in thematic theory-building may reflect the discipline's failure to acknowledge the political significance of interpretations of the Middle Ages to the present (see Biddick 1998). There have been occasional exceptions to this rule, for instance in the feminist development of global gender archaeology (Gilchrist 1999) and in debates about migrations and ethnicity (Härke 1998).

Respective specialist groups and research themes in medieval archaeology have varied in their responsiveness to post-processual theories. Perhaps most receptive has been the field of burial archaeology, which has demonstrated a profound shift of thinking from the assumption that grave goods directly reflect the possessions of the dead, to the premise that grave goods were used to make statements about the *social identity* of the deceased. Processualist applications to burial archaeology included efforts to score the value of grave goods and assess the territorial location of graves through Thiessen polygons (eg Arnold 1988). By the late 1980s, such approaches were abandoned in favour of studies exploring the constitution of identities through funerary display. Identity is understood to be historically contingent, dynamic, and operating along multiple social axes, such as class, gender, ethnicity, age and religious status; identity is experienced internally by the individual, and is at the same time employed by society in defining external categories. Early medieval burial archaeology has investigated aspects of identity including warriorhood (Härke 1990), gender (eg Halsall 1996; Stoodley 1999; Hadley 2004), age (Stoodley 2000), regionalism (Lucy 2000) and ethnicity (eg Härke 2007). Commemorative monuments have been discussed in the post-processual terms of material culture as text — ranging from runestones as family monuments that invoked memory through their collective reading (Andrén 2000), to the burials at Sutton Hoo as a form of poetry or theatre, funerary tableaux which served as compositions to memorialize the life of the deceased (Carver 1998). The rite of cremation has been conceptualized as a distinctively transformative technology with the power to alter identities and social relationships in death (Williams 2005; Gansum and Oestigaard 2004) (Figure 19.1). After 20 years of focus on the expression of social identity through early medieval funerary practices, there is currently a resurgence of interest in the role of emotion, religious belief and cosmology (eg Williams 2006; Kristoffersen and Oestigaard 2008; Hadley, this volume). Later medieval burial archaeology has taken longer to engage with theory, but recent studies have elucidated aspects of identity, memory, gender and agency (Williams 2003; Gilchrist and Sloane 2005; Gilchrist 2008).

A number of studies in buildings archaeology have drawn upon spatial theory to develop innovative readings of secular and religious architecture. Several have employed methods of formal spatial analysis based on the structuralist premise that, through patterns of physical access, space reproduces hierarchical social relations. The corresponding assumption is that space can be mapped in terms of a formal

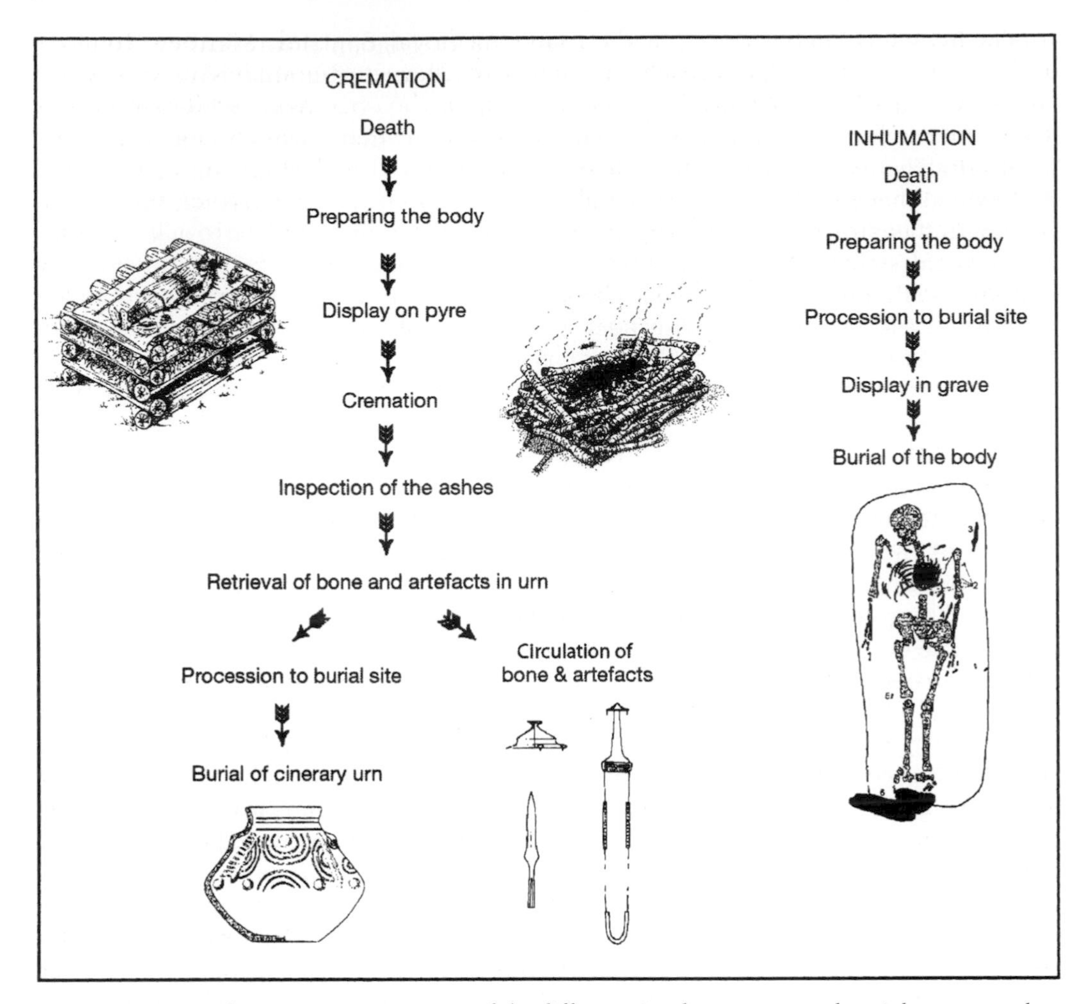

FIGURE 19.1 A schematic representation of the different ritual sequences and social processes that accompanied early Anglo-Saxon cremation and inhumation rites. Howard Williams used this illustration to emphasize the contrasting roles of these two mortuary technologies in managing the powerful mnemonic agency of weapons. (Reproduced with permission from Williams 2005)

grammar and read to infer past social relations (eg Fairclough 1992, based on Hillier and Hanson 1984). Applications of this approach to medieval material have tended to reject the cross-cultural assumptions of structuralism, and instead use the mapping method to explore specific historical questions. Formal spatial analysis can be criticized for its tendency to simplify the relationship between space and the expression of different types of social power; for its limitations in representing the culmination of numerous stratigraphic sequences as a single phase; and for its failure to address the sensory experience of space. Nevertheless, where these caveats are borne in mind, spatial analysis can be employed as a useful technique for comparative and problem-oriented analysis.

In his study of the rural house in later medieval England, Matthew Johnson rejected the typological approach that tends to characterize studies in vernacular architecture. Instead, he considered the meaning of the open hall to different groups in the household, discussing why this particular spatial format was pervasive and how it eventually changed with an increasing ideology of enclosure (Johnson 1993). Johnson's book on later medieval English castles (2002) moved further away from any method of formal or typological analysis to consider phenomenological readings of castles — a category of monuments that is more typically examined in terms of the diffusion of military technology. His phenomenological perspective emphasized castles as stage settings for social elites, with masculine identities expressed through architectural design, layout and landscapes.[9] Johnson's study contributed to the growing corpus of work on the symbolic and social dimensions of castles and their 'designed landscapes' (Dixon 1990; Everson 1996; Creighton 2002; Liddiard 2005; see Hansson, this volume).

The confrontation between processual and post-processual approaches in medieval archaeology has come to the fore in relation to the study of landscape and rural settlement. Johnson has critiqued landscape approaches for their intuitive, anti-theoretical foundations, while he describes the research agenda of medieval settlement studies — and in particular its quest for village origins — as a 'taphonomic retreat'. He argues that medieval landscape archaeology exhibits less and less confidence in its ability to make meaningful statements about the past, thereby reinforcing its position as an ancillary discipline to history (Johnson 2007, 117–119). He calls for more phenomenological studies that would reflect on how people moved across landscapes, and perspectives that would highlight agency, gender and the integration of religion within settlement studies — this *experiential* approach has been successfully demonstrated by Karin Altenberg (2003), in a comparative study of medieval marginality in southern Sweden and south-west England.

The initial reaction to Johnson's critique appears to reinforce the distance between theoretical and empirical medieval archaeology (see Rippon, this volume; Fleming 2007). Stephen Rippon's response is to restate the greater and more lasting value of meticulous empirical surveys over discursive theoretical works. Moreover, his assessment of medieval landscape archaeology sets up a tension between interpretations which privilege either social agency or environmental determinism as vectors of innovation and change. This is a false dichotomy which perpetuates the unfortunate split in medieval archaeology between economic/scientific and social/theoretical approaches. Throughout the social sciences there have been efforts to reconcile rigorous empirical approaches with social constructivist foundations (eg Latour 2005). For example, the study of prehistoric landscapes has been influenced by Tim Ingold's 'dwelling perspective', which integrates ecological and phenomenological approaches to consider how people inhabit and interact with their environment (Ingold 2000). Ingold actually selected a medieval example to elucidate his point that the landscape becomes a record of the lives and work of people in the past. However, rather than look to medieval archaeology for source material, he focused on a painting by Pieter Bruegel the Elder. *The Harvesters* (1565) depicts harvest-workers — men, women and children — resting from their labours beneath the shade of a tree;

this social scene is framed by the tower of the parish church and the panoramic view of the village and common fields in the distance. Ingold employs the painting as a device to reflect on 'being' in the medieval landscape, and to consider how the lifecycles of humans, plants, animals and monuments are woven into the texture and temporality of landscape (ibid, 198, 201–206).

MEDIEVAL MATERIAL CULTURE: *TABULA RASA*[10]

The last few decades have witnessed a shift from purely typological studies of medieval material culture to more thematic expositions. For example, pioneering work has clarified the material culture of everyday life, including objects from the household and children's toys. Toys from medieval Novgorod (Russia) and Turku (Finland) were made from wood, clay, leather and bone, while miniature household items and toy-weapons made of lead/tin have been recovered from later medieval English towns (Rybina 1992; Luoto 2007; Egan 1998). David Hinton has surveyed the artefacts that people used to express social affiliation and status, such as jewellery, drinking-vessels and tableware, to chronicle change from the 5th to the 15th century (Hinton 2005). He adopts the perspective of 'closure theory', which contends that a ranked society operates through competing groups which use material culture as one means of excluding others from membership. The material culture of dining has been considered more widely in terms of social etiquette and cultural preferences for certain table and kitchenwares (eg Brown 2005; Hadley 2005). A phenomenological analysis of these same materials has stressed the significance of sensual factors such as texture, colour and shape in the perception and use of everyday material culture (Cumberpatch 1997).

Post-colonial theory has begun to influence archaeological discussions of medieval migrations, for example in reconsiderations of the Viking expansion as a Scandinavian diaspora (Barrett 2008).[11] Controversially, Lotte Hedeager has reinterpreted the appearance of Germanic animal styles in Nordic art in the 5th and 6th centuries as evidence for the expansion of the Huns into Scandinavia (Hedeager 2007). Pottery has also been evaluated for its potential to address ethnic and cultural identity, for instance in David Gaimster's model of a proto-colonial, Hanseatic culture based on networks of mercantile exchange permeating from later medieval Germany (Gaimster 1999). This approach has recently been critiqued from the perspective of post-colonial theory, using a case study of medieval Turku to argue instead for local hybridity and interaction between German merchants and Finnish townspeople (Immonen 2007). Colonialism has also been addressed through animal bone studies, in Naomi Sykes' comparative analysis of assemblages from Norman England and northern France. She argues that Norman colonialization involved the intensification of hunting culture, with the plantation of parks and forests, increased exploitation of 'wild' species and the introduction of exotic species such as peafowl, rabbits and fallow deer (Sykes 2007). Isotopic analysis of human remains has also been harnessed to explore ethnic foodways: increased consumption of marine foods in Orkney has been linked to Norse colonization (Barrett and Richards 2005).

Contextual studies of medieval artefacts have made connections with wider discourses of popular culture and ritual practice. For example, Anders Andrén's reading of the iconography of Gotlandic picture stones (Sweden, AD 400–1100) links them with forms of narrative used also in the construction of ship burials and funerary rites. The stones were not grave markers but instead monuments placed on boundaries within the landscape. Those dating from *c*800–1100 were shaped like keyholes or mushrooms, and were decorated with a rich repertoire including ships, armed horsemen, women with drinking horns, battle scenes and animals. Andrén interprets the picture stones as 'doors' and links them with the symbolism of hearth and home, metaphoric representations which mediated between the worlds of the living and the dead (Andrén 1993). Mark Hall has traced the context of an ivory knife handle from 14th-century Perth, Scotland (Figure 19.2), demonstrating how a single artefact can illuminate an entire cultural milieu. He argues that this particular rendition of the Green Man, with foliage protruding from his ears, eyes and mouth, may allude to sins, or alternatively, to processes of rebirth and regeneration represented by the

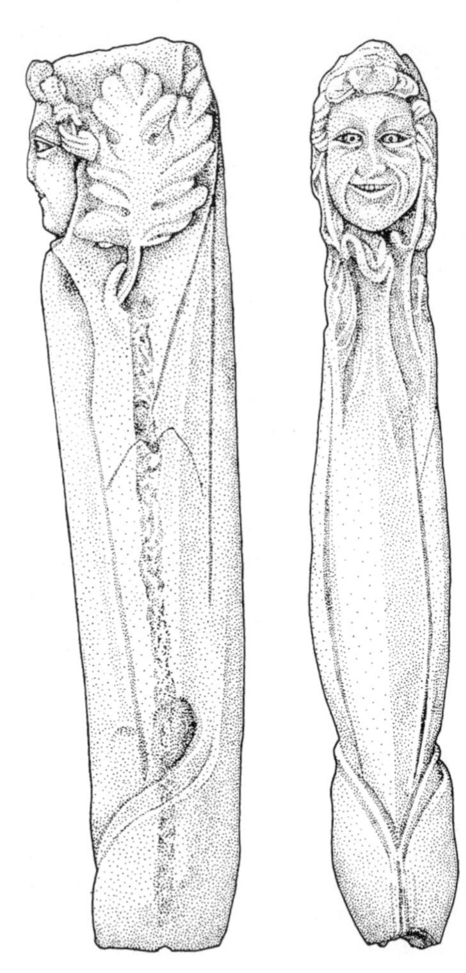

FIGURE 19.2 The Green Man ivory knife handle from Perth was made in the 14th century. Mark Hall has interpreted its iconography as having been connected with seasonal civic ritual such as May Day celebrations. (Reproduced with permission from Hall 2001)

emerging greenery. He suggests that this object is connected with the cultural imagery of religious and secular pageantry, and especially with the popular celebration of May festivities (Hall 2001).

In general, however, there has been little explicit theorization of medieval material culture in terms of identity or social practice. Discussion of the body and sexuality has been notably absent (although see Nøttveit 2006, for a discussion of the 13th-century 'ballock' dagger as a symbol of masculinity). This lacuna is in marked contrast with perspectives on embodiment that have been advanced in other areas of historical archaeology (eg Meskell and Joyce 2003), and with art-historical glosses on 'sexual' material culture such as medieval 'erotic' lead badges (Jones 2002, 248–273). This omission is particularly surprising, given the wealth of catalogued dress accessories from medieval settlements, and the thousands of actual bodies excavated as skeletons from medieval cemeteries. Osteological approaches tend to follow clinical models in assigning the age, sex and pathology of individuals in order to discuss general patterns of health and lifestyle in broad social groups. Although the specific historical contexts of health are explored, the social and experiential practices which create bodies tend to be neglected (Sofaer 2006). While the human body has yet to be theorized in medieval archaeology, zooarchaeologists have conceptualized animal bodies as material culture, exploring aspects of materiality, symbolism and human-animal interactions (eg Pluskowski 2007).

The approach of artefact biographies (after Kopytoff 1986) has been applied especially to medieval pictorial artefacts with complex life histories, such as sculpture (Stocker and Everson 1990), standing crosses (Moreland 1999) and Pictish symbol stones (Clarke 2007). Medieval archaeologists have been less eager to apply the themes of materiality and artefact agency that have characterized recent research on prehistoric material culture. 'Materiality' is often taken to refer to the quality of the object or 'thing', its 'thinginess', or more broadly to the 'socialness' of things. But materiality also takes account of how human sensory engagement with the material world of objects shapes cultural experience (eg Tilley 2006). The concept of artefact agency developed from the 'aesthetics' approach of Alfred Gell (1992),[12] which explores the appeal of objects in their historical context. The formal qualities of certain things are said to effect an 'enchantment' that can influence social action — and from this it is argued that artefacts possess some form of agency (Gosden 2001). It would be helpful if these debates distinguished more clearly between 'animate' and 'inanimate' agency: animate agents are able to '*do something*' or '*to act* intentionally', while inanimate agents, such as artefacts, have the potential '*to act on* other things' (Hacker 2007, 124, original italics). The agency of artefacts may not be intentional, but it has consequences nevertheless.

Tim Ingold has recently challenged these approaches by arguing that things are not active because they are imbued with agency, but because of the meanings of certain materials used in their production. He has called for greater attention to the properties of materials rather than the intrinsic materiality of objects (Ingold 2007). Medieval archaeologists are strongly placed to bring more robust discussions of causality to these debates. The historical framework contributes sophisticated insights to the meanings of materials and their perceived agency, for example the special properties of the relics of saints, healing gems, or the unicorn's horn (ie the narwhal's tusk: Pluskowski 2005). Within the framework of medieval rationality, the animate bones of saints are able to *do something* through divine agency, while the occult power of nature gave some inanimate objects and materials the inherent potential *to act on* other things. Inscriptions on medieval artefacts sometimes link them to the intentional agency of named individuals who made or commissioned them, such as the famous 9th-century Alfred Jewel (*Aelfred mec heht gewyrcan*, 'Alfred ordered me to be made'). In this case, Alfred's agency *to act* is personified through anthropomorphic representation: through a process of objectification, the agency of persons and things become entwined (Gell 1992; Tilley 2006, 63).

But we should also take inspiration from the imaginative approaches to materiality and meaning that prehistorians have developed. For example, interpretations of henge monuments have been influenced in recent years by concepts of the materiality of stone (Parker Pearson and Ramilisonina 1998). The argument is that henges were constructed in wood for ceremonial use by the living community and in stone to commemorate the dead. Stone monuments are understood to be the end-stage of a process of 'hardening' that is associated with the ancestral dead; the contrasting materials of timber and stone represent the metaphorical transformation of flesh to bone. We might apply similar insights to the 'great rebuilding' of parish churches *c*1050–1150, involving their translation from timber to stone. This process has been discussed variously in terms of chronology, technology, architectural style and cultural affiliation, but scant reflection has been given to the cultural meanings embodied by this massive replacement of materials. Until *c*950, only cathedrals and important monastic churches were likely to have been built of stone; many parish churches have their origins in the wooden chapels constructed by local lords and only gradually gained parochial status (Morris 1989, 165). It may be suggested that the translation from timber to stone represents a new cycle in the life of the parish church, one commemorated in materials of greater durability. Stone as a substance may have held the promise of spiritual eternity: its light-coloured hue and dense crystalline structure would have contrasted sharply with the dull, perishable timber used for the houses built and occupied by parishioners. These timber-framed dwellings were replaced generationally, while the masonry of the parish church would have symbolized the enduring permanence of the community of saints. The transition to stone in the 11th century was also bound up with the increasing influence of Rome in church affairs: stone was a 'petrine' material, referring literally and metaphorically to both rock (*Petrus*) and St Peter (D Stocker, pers comm). The materiality of parish churches was achieved through the reuse of Roman materials, by building in stone, and by adopting the Romanesque style — all of which evoked the Roman past and strengthened the contemporary connection to the papacy (Eaton 2000; Stocker and Everson 2006, 57).

PARISHES AND PARADIGMS: THE THEORIZATION OF CHURCH ARCHAEOLOGY?

I would like to look in more detail at the impact of theory on one branch of medieval archaeology over the past 25 years — and church archaeology may seem an unlikely candidate. The systematic recording and dating of church fabric commenced in the early 19th century, in association with repair programmes to cathedrals and churches and through the innovation especially of John Britton and Thomas Rickman. In contrast, the archaeological excavation of churches did not begin in earnest until the 1950s, with the clearance of bomb-damaged churches (Rodwell 1997). By the 1970s, genuine urgency drove the archaeological study of churches, spurred by contemporary concerns for their conservation. Dwindling congregations were resulting in redundancies and church closures, enabled by *The Pastoral Measure 1968*; due to the 'ecclesiastical exemption', these threatened monuments fell outside the protection of Ancient Monuments legislation (see Bianco 1993). Spearheaded by the Council for British Archaeology, the archaeological community was determined both to improve academic understanding of churches, and to provide adequate archaeological expertise to guide their conservation (Morris 1983). Church archaeology emerged from a conservation platform to develop specialist archaeological methods suited to the recording of sites that combine multi-period elements of standing fabric, subsurface deposits and complex burial sequences.

Throughout the 1980s and the early 1990s, the study of churches matured into a vibrant field of medieval archaeology (eg Blair and Pyrah 1996). In many regions of Europe, church archaeology has rewritten our understanding of the historical origins of the parish church (eg Zadora-Rio 2003; Kristjánsdóttir 2004; FitzPatrick and Gillespie 2006), and its place within the broader physical landscape and canvass of settlement (Morris 1989; Blair 2005; Turner 2006). But today the term 'church archaeology' is generally used to encompass a suite of specialist techniques, or to describe programmes of recording carried out on ecclesiastical sites (Rodwell 2005). In effect, church archaeology has evolved as a specialist methodology rather than as an interpretative approach or as a cohesive research framework. In contrasting the aims of medieval archaeologists and architectural historians, Eric Fernie observed that church archaeologists were more concerned with unravelling techniques of medieval construction, while architectural historians aimed to discern subtleties of '*meaning*' in ecclesiastical architecture (Fernie 1988; my italics). In his review of the global archaeology of Christianity, Paul Lane called for medieval church archaeologists to prioritize the '*meanings of religious spaces*' and to take theoretical guidance from prehistorians (Lane 2001, 159–161; my italics). In particular, he advocated the development of an 'archaeology of cult', focusing on material evidence for four themes: attention to the supernatural, emphasis on boundaries between the human and spirit worlds, the presencing of a deity, and the performance of acts of worship and offerings to the supernatural (after Renfew and Bahn 1991, 359).

Can we therefore conclude that church archaeology is all 'method' and no 'meaning'? To the contrary, in the study of religious sites over the last 20 years, medieval archaeologists have developed precisely the insights called for by Lane's proposed 'archaeology of cult'. Church space has been reconsidered in terms of social, temporal and cosmological meanings (eg Graves 1989; Andrén 1999; Gilchrist 1999, 83–87; Giles 2000a). Liturgy has been reassessed according to patterns of physical access and movement within and around churches, the way in which light and human sight interacted with the mass, and how the sound of bells connected the living with the dead (Graves 2000; Roffey 2007; Stocker and Everson 2006). Visual and sensory approaches have reinterpreted wall-paintings in the parish and monastic church (Giles 2007; Graves 2007). The burial and reuse of church fonts has been explored in terms of their status as 'special' artefacts, expressed through the selection of materials and decoration (Stocker 1997). The iconoclasm of the Reformation has been redefined within the framework of personhood, concluding that the attack on images of saints focused on particular parts of the body (Graves 2008).[13] The creation and maintenance of boundaries has been clarified especially in relation to monastic space, with gender examined as *habitus*[14] in the medieval nunnery (Gilchrist 1994), and the precinct of the monastic cathedral charted in terms of experiencing and inhabiting space (Gilchrist 2005, 236–257) (Figure 19.3). A Marxist analysis of space has focused on the exercise of power in the precinct of the archbishop's palace at Trondheim (Norway) (Saunders 2002) and material culture has been mapped to identify the 'soft spaces of pilgrimage' in the monastic precinct of a Norfolk cult centre (Pestell 2005). Guildhalls have been analysed from the perspective of structuration theory,[15] revealing the spatial paradox of an open space which symbolizes communal identity and fraternity, but which at the same time reinforces hierarchical divisions through corporate rituals (Giles 2000b). And medieval archaeologists have begun to integrate religion with studies of daily domestic life (as called for by Insoll 2004). For example, the persistence of folk beliefs can be discerned in the deliberate deposition of prehistoric lithics in medieval houses in northern Europe, ranging from Scotland to southern Sweden and Finland (eg Carelli 1997; Hall 2005).

On closer examination, 'church archaeology' has undergone a startling theoretical transformation. There has been no overarching manifesto (as called for by Lane 2001 or Insoll 2004) but the medieval archaeology of religion has seen a slow 'scientific revolution'. Moreover, its individual proponents have successfully integrated post-processual theory with rigorous empirical studies; the perceived divide between meticulous empirical scholarship and theoretical discourse has been dissolved by incremental degree. The reception of this body of work in the wider discipline is perhaps predictable — theoretical insights to medieval society are accepted only when the corpus of empirical evidence on which they are based has been thoroughly scrutinized in positivist terms. My own work on gender and medieval nunneries serves as one example: while welcomed by medieval historians and archaeological theorists, some monastic archaeologists were sceptical about gender (Coppack in Gilchrist *et al* 1996). When the patterns I proposed were eventually reassessed in purely positivist terms, the enduring value of a gendered perspective was conceded: nunneries really '*are* different' (Bond 2003, 86; original italics).

REFLECTIONS ON MEDIEVAL ARCHAEOLOGY AND THEORY

In conclusion, it is clear that over the past 25 years theory has changed the questions that we ask about the Middle Ages, and it has transformed some aspects of how we study medieval archaeology. Processualism encouraged grand narratives on themes such as trade, the origins of towns and state formation, while the post-processual concern with agency and meaning has fostered study of social identity,

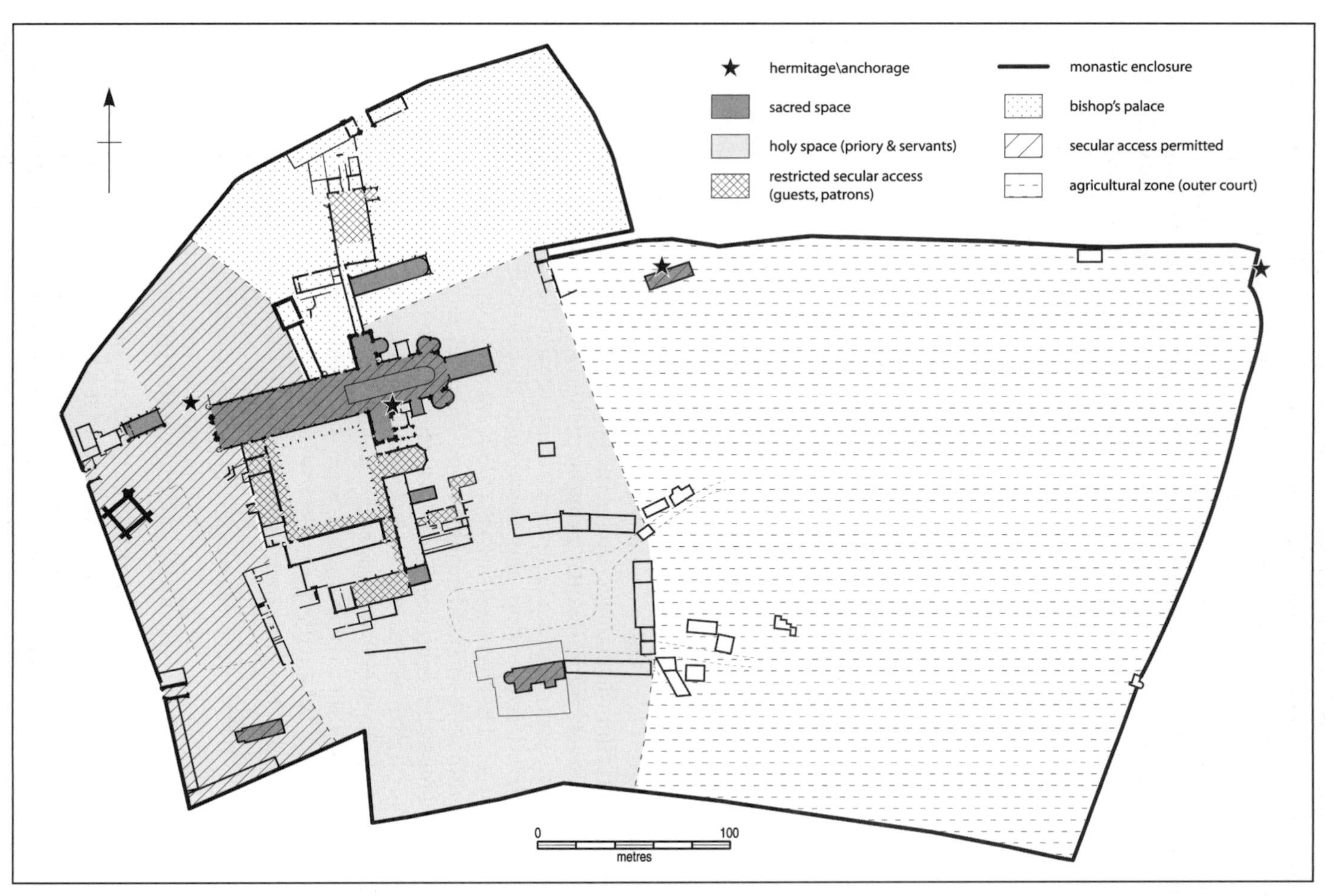

FIGURE 19.3 Norwich Cathedral: the mapping of sacred and social space in the precinct of a monastic cathedral, based on the construction and use of the built environment, including the sensory experience of moving through spatial zones, the control of boundaries and the manipulation of view-sheds. (Reproduced with permission from Gilchrist 2005)

gender, supernatural belief, sensory perception and spatial experience. Theoretical perspectives have burgeoned especially in the study of spiritual beliefs in north-west Europe — pagan, Christian, and the processes of conversion and hybridity bridging them (eg Andrén 2007; Hedeager 2001; Price 2002; Carver 2003; Gilchrist 2008). In contrast, relatively little theoretical interpretation has yet been directed towards Byzantine Christianity (eg Ousterhout 1991; James 2003; Clark 2007), or the Jewish and Islamic ritual spaces of medieval Europe. The development of post-processual approaches may partly explain the apparent shift in interest away from previously core topics such as urbanism, in favour of the fields of burial and buildings archaeology. Much of the theory in medieval archaeology over the past few decades has taken a spatial approach; for example, theoretical treatments of urbanism have shifted from economic to spatial and symbolic analyses (K D Lilley 2004; O'Keefe 2004). The tremendous theoretical potential of material culture has yet to be realized, particularly in addressing issues such as materiality and embodiment.

A survey of interpretative trends in church archaeology reveals a thriving enclave of post-processualism, packed with insights brought by theories of practice, phenomenology, gender and personhood, combined in studies that retain empirical integrity. This innovation is especially noteworthy given the neglect of religion by the broader field of post-processual archaeology (Insoll 2004, 77). Church archaeology has been much more responsive to new theoretical thinking than some others, particularly in contrast with research in medieval landscape and rural settlement. The nature of the data may account for some differences: ecclesiastical buildings and associated iconographic evidence hold rich potential for addressing meaning. However, this divergence also reflects contrasting attitudes in our confidence to address agency *via* the medium of material culture. The realm of religious belief is more obviously amenable to such approaches, but rare exceptions in medieval landscape archaeology have demonstrated the possibility of addressing agency and reconciling social and environmental approaches (eg Dyer 1990; Stocker and Everson 2006; POMLAS). The 'parachutist's' most daring leaps are sometimes made possible by years of 'truffle-hunting' sorties, gaining essential knowledge of the terrain.

Here, the salient point is that we cannot select *between* theoretical *or* empirical perspectives, nor is it easy to disentangle the tools for collecting and analysing archaeological data from the theoretical apparatuses that we use to interpret patterns in our evidence. New technologies such as Geographical Information Systems and Historic Landscape Characterization have aided empirical interrogation of the landscape (see Rippon, this volume), but their development has demanded a theoretical redefinition of the very concept of landscape itself. In particular, heritage managers have shifted from a definition of the landscape as a discrete physical and chronological entity, to a more conceptual perspective of landscape as a complex spatial and temporal matrix of perceptions (Florence Convention 2000, 1 and 7). Archaeologists may aim to achieve 'mitigated objectivity' — judging inferences made from archaeological evidence according to the degree of security of evidential claims (Wylie 2002, 177) — but ultimately all archaeological research is both empirical *and* theoretical.

The thesis that material culture is active and meaningful has accelerated the widespread growth of medieval social archaeology, but a stubborn rift has also been driven between approaches that can be grouped as social/theoretical *versus* economic/scientific. Medieval archaeology continues to privilege empirical (quantitative) evidence over social (qualitative) analysis, and to perpetuate the processualist tendency to perceive a distinction between data and theory. Excavation reports, building and field surveys, corpora of sculpture and artefacts are considered to possess more enduring value if reported without theoretical interpretation or social commentary. This attitude is changing in some sectors, for example the more thematic, integrated excavation reports published for London's medieval monasteries (eg Thomas *et al* 1997). Revolutions in archaeological publishing are likely to see increasing emphasis placed on interpretation in print media, with data archived electronically. This may provide an opportunity for more creative, interpretative approaches to the presentation of medieval archaeology, but it brings the danger of exacerbating the data/theory split.

Some aspects of early medieval archaeology continue to spar more enthusiastically with theory than their later medieval counterparts. Indeed, it might be argued that the internal periodization of medieval archaeology as a discipline inhibits more expansive theoretical and thematic experiment. To take just one example, later medieval burial archaeology has only recently begun to explore theoretical perspectives after 25 years of active theoretical research in the archaeology of early medieval burial. A range of issues would benefit from treatment across the *longue dureé* that bridges the early and later Middle Ages, including capitalism, technology, religious belief, memory, foodways and ideas about the body, with due regard to the temporality of events (Harding 2005). Within medieval studies, the archaeological perspective of 'deep time' may even lend a distinctive voice to medieval archaeology. We have much to benefit from closer integration within our own discipline, as well as drawing inspiration from outside.

The purpose of our subject is the writing of medieval history in its widest sense, with the result that many medieval archaeologists prioritize communication with other fields of medieval studies over contact with prehistory or other historical archaeologies.[16] More regular interaction with ideas current in prehistory can lend novel ideas to medieval archaeology — for example, 'structured deposition', a concept that has taken around 20 years to percolate from prehistoric, through Roman, to medieval archaeology (Hamerow 2006). And prehistorians could benefit equally from such an exchange: the conjoint use of historical and archaeological sources has produced some of the most convincing examples of post-processual interpretation. Indeed, it has been acknowledged that historical archaeology provides the most appropriate temporal resolution for the study of 'small-scale phenomena such as individual agency, inter-personal interactions and perception' (Bailey 2007, 201). The defeatist may argue that the daunting abundance, complexity and interdisciplinarity of medieval archaeology are challenge enough, without the expectation to keep abreast of archaeological theory. But these are precisely the disciplinary traits that offer fertile capacity for a more *meaningful medieval* archaeology. A mature discipline should have the ambition to combine empirical rigour with theoretical innovation, and the imagination to integrate historical, scientific and social perspectives. This is a leap of faith, and one of the most important challenges for the next 25 years of medieval archaeology.

ACKNOWLEDGEMENTS

I am grateful to David Stocker, Matthew Johnson and Andrew Reynolds for their helpful comments on an early draft of this article. The opinions expressed are those of the author.

NOTES

[1] Hodges was adopting the famous metaphor used by the eminent historian of the French Annales school, Emmanuel Le Roy Ladurie (b 1929), to distinguish between historians who are concerned exclusively with either the general (parachutists) or the particular (truffle-hunters).

[2] The roots of culture-history may be found in the 19th-century emergence of national archaeologies and their emphasis on ethnic groups (Trigger 1989, 174). Culture-history has remained the dominant approach of medieval archaeology in southern Europe, despite the differences created by respective Marxist and fascist regimes in the Balkans, Spain and Italy (see papers by Curta, Quirós Castillo, Augenti and Brogiolo, this volume).

[3] The term paradigm was adopted by the philosopher of science Thomas Kuhn to describe the established mode of scientific practice in a given discipline. Such traditions of 'normal science' are occasionally disrupted and transformed by episodes of 'scientific revolution': 'the successive transition from one paradigm to another via revolution is the usual developmental pattern of mature science' (Kuhn, quoted in Preston 2008, 21).

[4] For medieval archaeology's relationship to history, see discussions by Anders Andrén (1998, 25–36), Matthew Johnson (1999, 149–161) and John Moreland (2001).

[5] This was a favoured phrase of John Hurst, one of the founders of the Society for Medieval Archaeology, and it was also regularly employed by the landscape historian W G Hoskins.

[6] Hodges' proposition that up to the 9th century trade was stimulated exclusively by elites has since been challenged on empirical evidence: the recording of coins from metal-detecting suggests that trade was more widespread and promulgated via local markets and regional trading places, described by archaeologists as 'productive sites' (Ulmschneider 2000). Søren Sindbaek (2007) has rekindled this debate through the application of complex network theory, arguing that Viking long-distance trade was tightly connected by a small group of individuals working through a select network of sites.

[7] A term promoted by the Annales school of French history, which stresses the inter-relationship of long, medium and short timescales.

[8] The editorial policy is to encourage more discursive theoretical and synthetic pieces, and the officers of the Society regularly encourage postgraduate students to publish theoretical articles in the journal; despite these efforts (unjustified) suspicion lingers of a conservative editorial policy!

[9] See Gilchrist 1999, 109–145, for a gendered reading of the medieval castle from the perspective of elite female experience.

[10] *Tabula rasa* refers to the thesis that humans are born a blank slate, and that their knowledge is formed through specific cultural experiences and sensory perceptions of the material world.

[11] Diaspora studies focus on identity in communities dispersed amongst other peoples, to explore issues of migration, colonization and the cultural processes of hybridity and creolization. The concept originally referred to communities in forced exile (in particular the Jewish Diaspora and the Black Atlantic), but has been applied to the archaeological study of prehistoric, Roman, post-medieval (I Lilley 2004; van Dommelen 2006) and most recently, medieval communities (Bowles 2007; Immonen 2007).

[12] Gell employs the example of how the intricately carved prows of Trobriander canoes serve as psychological weapons to beguile Kula exchange partners. His discussion also refers to Salisbury Cathedral, but medieval archaeologists will be dismayed to hear that he was unimpressed by the monument itself, but enthralled instead by the 'technology of enchantment and the enchantment of technology' of the scaled matchstick model of the cathedral! (Gell 1992, 47).

[13] Personhood refers to the condition of being a person in a particular social context; personhood is created and maintained through relationships with other people but also with things, places, animals and spiritual beings (Fowler 2004, 7).

[14] Developed by the French sociologist Pierre Bourdieu (d 2002), the influential concept of *habitus* refers to the practical logic and sense of order that guides our knowledge of the world

(Bourdieu 1977). This unconscious 'learned ignorance' reproduces social relations but still allows for individual human agency that can promote change.

[15] Developed by the British sociologist Anthony Giddens (b 1938), structuration theory is based on the premise that social systems both result from human action and organize and reinforce human action. The 'duality of structure' has had considerable impact in archaeology; it acknowledges the interdependence of social structure and human agency, thus power is perceived to be enabling as well as constraining (Giddens 1984, 374).

[16] More pragmatic reasons may also be cited for improved communication. The panels of funding bodies and government research assessments for archaeology tend to be dominated by prehistorians — it would benefit medieval archaeologists to convey the significance of their research in terms that the wider subject will recognize.

BIBLIOGRAPHY

Altenberg, K, 2003 *Experiencing Landscapes. A Study of Space and Identity in Three Marginal Areas of Medieval Britain and Scandinavia*, Lund Studies in Medieval Archaeology 31, Lund

Andrén, A, 1993 'Doors to other worlds: Scandinavian death rituals in Gotlandic perspectives', *Journal of European Archaeology* 1, 33–56

Andrén, A, 1998 *Between Artifacts and Texts. Historical Archaeology in Global Perspective*, Plenum, London

Andrén, A, 1999 'Landscape and settlement as utopian space', in C Fabech and J Ringtved (eds), *Settlement and Landscape*, 383–393, Jutland Archaeological Society, Århus

Andrén, A, 2000 'Re-reading embodied texts — an interpretation of rune-stones', *Current Swedish Archaeology* 8, 7–32

Andrén, A, 2007 'Behind Heathendom. Archaeological studies of Old Norse religion', *Scottish Archaeological Review* 27, 105–138

Andrén, A, Jennbert, K, Raudvere C, (eds) 2006 *Old Norse Religion in Long-Term Perspectives*, Nordic Academic Press, Lund

Arnold, C J, 1988 *An Archaeology of the Early Anglo-Saxon Kingdoms*, Routledge, London

Bailey,G, 2007 'Time perspectives, palimpsests and the archaeology of time', *Journal of Anthropological Archaeology* 26, 198–223

Barrett J H, 208 'What caused the Viking Age?' *Antiquity* 82, 671–685

Barrett J H, and Richards, M P 2005, 'Identity, gender, religion and economy: new isotope and radiocarbon evidence for marine resource intensification in early historic Orkney, Scotland, UK', *European Journal of Archaeology* 7, 249–271

Bianco C, 1993 'Ecclesiastical buildings in use', in J Hunter and I Ralston (eds), *Archaeological Resource Management in the UK. An Introduction*, 89–99, Sutton, Stroud

Biddick, K, 1998, *The Shock of Medievalism*, Duke University Press, Durham NC

Blair, J, 2005 *The Church in Anglo–Saxon Society*, Oxford University Press, Oxford

Blair, J and Pyrah, C, (eds) 1996 *Church Archaeology: Research Directions for the Future*, Council for British Archaeology Research Report 104, York

Bond, C J, 2003 'English medieval nunneries: buildings, precincts, and estates', in D Wood (ed), *Women and Religion in Medieval England*, 46–90, Oxbow, Oxford

Bond, C J, 2004 *Monastic Landscapes*, Tempus, Stroud

Bourdieu, P, 1977 *Outline of a Theory of Practice*, Cambridge University Press, Cambridge

Bowles, C R, 2007 *Rebuilding the Britons. The Postcolonial Archaeology of Culture and Identity in the Late Antique Bristol Channel Region*, British Archaeological Reports 452, Oxford

Brown, D, 2005, 'Pottery and manners', in Carroll *et al* (eds) 2005, 87–99

Carelli, P, 1997 'Thunder and lightning, magical miracles. On the popular myth of thunderbolts and the presence of Stone Age artefacts in medieval deposits', in H Andersson, P Carelli and

L Ersgard (eds), *Visions of the Past. Trends and Traditions in Swedish Medieval Archaeology*, 393–417, Lund Studies in Medieval Archaeology 19, Lund

Carroll, M, Hadley, D M and Willmott, H (eds), 2005 *Consuming Passions. Dining from Antiquity to the Eighteenth Century*, Tempus, Stroud

Carver, M O H, 1998 *Sutton Hoo: Burial Ground of Kings?* University of Pennsylvania Press, London

Carver, M O H, 2001 'Why that? Why there? Why then? The politics of early medieval monumentality', in A Macgregor and H Hamerow (eds), *Image and Power in the Archaeology of Early Medieval Britain: Essays in Honour of Rosemary Cramp*, Oxbow, Oxford, 1–22

Carver, M O H (ed), 2003 *The Cross Goes North: Processes of Conversion in Northern Europe*, Boydell, Woodbridge

Clark, D L C, 2007 'Viewing the liturgy: a space syntax study of changing visibility and accessibility in the development of the Byzantine church in Jordan', *World Archaeology* 39:1, 84–104

Clarke, D V, 2007 'Reading the multiple lives of Pictish symbol stones', *Medieval Archaeology* 51, 19–39

Creighton, O H, 2002 *Castles and Landscape*, Continuum, London

Cumberpatch, C G, 1997 'Towards a phenomenological approach to the study of medieval pottery', in C G Cumberpatch and P W Blinkhorn (eds), *Not So Much a Pot, More a Way of Life*, 125–152, Oxbow, Oxford

Dickinson, T, 2005 'Symbols of protection: the significance of animal-ornamented shields in early Anglo-Saxon England', *Medieval Archaeology* 49, 109–163

Dixon, P, 1990 'The donjon of Knaresborough: the castle as theatre', *Château Gaillard* 14, 121–139

Dyer, C, 1990 'Dispersed settlements in medieval England. A case study of Pendock, Worcestershire', *Medieval Archaeology* 34, 97–121

Eaton, T, 2000 *Plundering the Past. Roman Stonework in Medieval Britain*, Tempus, Stroud

Egan, G, 1998 *The Medieval Household. Daily Living c1150–c1450. Medieval Finds from Excavations in London 6*, Museum of London, London

Everson, P, 1996 'Bodiam Castle, East Sussex: a castle and its designed landscape', *Château Gaillard* 17, 79–84

Fairclough, G, 1992 'Meaningful constructions — spatial and functional analysis of medieval buildings', *Antiquity* 66, 348–366

Fernie, E, 1988 'Contrasts in methodology and interpretation of medieval ecclesiastical architecture', *The Archaeological Journal* 145, 344–364

FitzPatrick, E and Gillespie, R (eds), 2006 *The Parish in Medieval and Early Modern Ireland. Community, Territory and Building*, Four Courts Press, Dublin

Fleming, A, 2007 'Don't bin your boots!', *Landscapes* 8:1, 85–99

Florence Convention http://www.coe.int/t/dg4/cultureheritage/Conventions/Landscape (accessed 4 September 2008)

Fowler, C, 2004 *The Archaeology of Personhood. An Anthropological Approach*, Routledge, London

Gaimster, D, 1999 'The Baltic ceramic market, c1200–1600: an archaeology of the Hansa', *Fennoscandia Archaeologica* 16, 59–69

Gansum, T and Oestigaard, T 2004, 'The ritual stratigraphy of monuments that matter', *European Journal of Archaeology* 7:1, 61–79

Gell, A, 1992 'The technology of enchantment and the enchantment of technology', in J Coote and A Shelton (eds), *Anthropology, Art and Aesthetics*, 40–63, Clarendon, Oxford

Gerrard, C, 2003 *Medieval Archaeology. Understanding Traditions and Contemporary Approaches*, Routledge, London

Giddens, A, 1984 *The Constitution of Society*, Polity Press, Cambridge
Gilchrist, R, 1994 *Gender and Material Culture: the Archaeology of Religious Women*, Routledge, London
Gilchrist, R, 1999 *Gender and Archaeology: Contesting the Past*, Routledge, London
Gilchrist, R, 2005 *Norwich Cathedral Close: the Evolution of the English Cathedral Landscape*, Boydell, Woodbridge
Gilchrist, R, 2008 'Magic for the dead? The archaeology of magic in later medieval burials', *Medieval Archaeology* 52, 1–41
Gilchrist, R, Dyer, C, Scott, E, Gero, J and Coppack, G, 1996 'Review feature: gender and material culture', *Cambridge Archaeological Journal* 6:1, 119–136
Gilchrist, R, and Sloane, B, 2005 *Requiem: the Medieval Monastic Cemetery in Britain*, Museum of London Archaeology Service Monograph, London
Giles, K, 2000a *An Archaeology of Social Identity. Guildhalls in York, c1350–1630*, British Archaeological Report 315, Oxford
Giles, K, 2000b 'Marking time? A 15th-century liturgical calendar in the wall paintings of Pickering parish church', *Church Archaeology* 4, 42–51
Giles, K, 2007 'Seeing and believing: visuality and space in pre-modern England', *World Archaeology* 39:1, 105–121
Gosden, C, 2001 'Making sense: archaeology and aesthetics', *World Archaeology* 33:2, 163–167
Graves, C P, 1989 'Social space in the English medieval parish church', *Economy and Society* 18, 297–322
Graves, C P, 2000 *The Form and Fabric of Belief: The Archaeology of Lay Experience in Medieval Norfolk and Devon*, British Archaeological Reports 311, Oxford
Graves, C P, 2007 'Sensing and believing: exploring worlds of difference in pre-modern England: a contribution to the debate opened by Kate Giles', *World Archaeology* 39:4, 515–531
Graves, C P, 2008 'From an archaeology of iconoclasm to an anthropology of the body. Images, punishment and personhood in England, 1500–1660', *Current Anthropology* 49:1, 35–57
Hacker, P M S, 2007 *Human Nature: the Categorical Framework*, Blackwell, Oxford
Hadley, D M, 2004 'Negotiating gender, family and status in Anglo-Saxon burial practices, *c*600–950', in L Brubaker and J M H Smith (eds), *Gender in the Early Medieval World. East and West, 300–900*, 301–323, Cambridge University Press, Cambridge
Hadley, D M, 2005 'Dining in disharmony in the Later Middle Ages', in Carroll *et al* (eds) 2005, 101–119
Hall, M A, 2001 'An ivory knife handle from the High Street, Perth, Scotland: consuming ritual in a medieval borough', *Medieval Archaeology* 45, 169–188
Hall, M A, 2005 'Burgh mentalities: a town-in-the-country case study of Perth, Scotland', in K Giles and C Dyer (eds), *Town and Country in the Middle Ages*, 211–228, Society for Medieval Archaeology Monograph 22, Maney Publishing, Leeds
Halsall, G, 1996 'Female status and power in early Merovingian central Austrasia: the burial evidence', *Early Medieval Europe* 5:1, 1–24
Hamerow, H, 2006 '"Special deposits" in Anglo-Saxon settlements', *Medieval Archaeology* 50, 1–30
Harding, J, 2005, 'Rethinking the great divide: long-term structural history and the temporality of event', *Norwegian Archaeological Review* 38:2, 88–101
Härke, H, 1990 'Warrior graves? The background of the Anglo-Saxon weapon burial rite', *Past and Present* 126, 22–43
Härke, H, 1998 'Archaeologists and migrations: a problem of attitude?', *Current Anthropology* 39:1, 19–45

Härke, H, 2007 'Ethnicity, "race" and migration in mortuary archaeology: an attempt at a short answer', in S Semple and H Williams (eds), *Early Medieval Mortuary Practices*, 12–18, Anglo-Saxon Studies in Archaeology and History 14, Oxford

Hedeager, L, 2001 'Asgard reconstructed? Gudme — a "central place" in the north', in M de Jong and F Theuws with C van Rhijn (eds), *Topographies of Power in the Early Middle Ages*, 467–507, Brill, Leiden

Hedeager, L, 2007 'Scandinavia and the Huns: an interdisciplinary approach to the migration era', *Norwegian Archaeological Review* 40:1, 42–58

Hillier, B, and Hanson, J, 1984 *The Social Logic of Space*, Cambridge University Press, Cambridge

Hingley, R, 2005 *Globalizing Roman Culture: Unity, Diversity, Empire*, Routledge, London

Hinton, D A, 1999 '"Closing" and the Later Middle Ages', *Medieval Archaeology* 43, 172–182

Hinton, D A, 2005 *Gold & Gilt, Pots & Pins. Possessions and People in Medieval Britain*, Oxford University Press, Oxford

Hodder, I, 1982a *Symbols in Action: Ethnoarchaeological Studies of Material Culture*, Cambridge University Press, Cambridge

Hodder, I, 1982b *The Present Past*, Batsford, London

Hodges, R, 1982 *Dark Age Economics: the Origins of Towns and Trade, AD 600–1000*, Duckworth, London

Hodges, R, 1983 'New approaches to medieval archaeology', in D A Hinton (ed), *25 Years of Medieval Archaeology*, 24–32, Department of Prehistory and Archaeology and the Society for Medieval Archaeology, Sheffield

Hodges, R, 1989, 'Parachutists and truffle-hunters: at the frontiers of archaeology and history', in M Aston, D A Austin and C Dyers (eds), *Rural Settlements of Medieval England: Studies Dedicated to Maurice Beresford and John Hurst*, 287–306, Blackwell, Oxford

Immonen, V, 2007 'Defining a culture: the meaning of *Hanseatic* in medieval Turku', *Antiquity* 81, 720–732

Ingold, T, 2007 'Materials against materiality', *Archaeological Dialogues* 14:1, 1–16

Ingold, T, 2000 'The temporality of landscape', in T Ingold, *The Perception of the Environment*, 189–208, Routledge, London

Insoll, T, 2004 *Archaeology, Religion, Ritual*, London, Routledge

James, L, 2003 'Colour and meaning in Byzantium', *Journal of Early Christian Studies* 11:2, 223–233

Johnson, M H, 1993 *Housing Culture. Traditional Architecture in an English Landscape*, University College London Press, London

Johnson, M H, 1999 *Archaeological Theory. An Introduction*, Blackwell, Oxford

Johnson, M H, 2002 *Behind the Castle Gate: from Medieval to Renaissance*, Routledge, London

Johnson, M H, 2007 *Ideas of Landscape*, Blackwell, Oxford

Jones, M, 2002 *The Secret Middle Ages. Discovering the Real Medieval World*, Sutton, Stroud

Jope, E M, 1972 'Models in medieval studies', in D L Clarke (ed), *Models in Archaeology*, 963–990, Methuen, London

Kopytoff, I, 1986 'The cultural biography of things: commodification as process', in A Appadurai (ed), *The Social Life of Things. Commodities in Cultural Perspective*, 64–91, Cambridge University Press, Cambridge

Kristjánsdóttir, S, 2004 *The Awakening of Christianity in Iceland*, University of Gothenburg Archaeological Thesis Series B No 31, Gothenburg

Kristoffersen, S and Oestigaard, T 2008, '"Death myths": performing rituals and variation in corpse treatment during the Migration Period in Norway', in F Fahlander and T Oestigaard (eds), *The Materiality of Death. Bodies, Burials, Beliefs*, 127–139, British Archaeological Report International Series 1768, Oxford

Lane, P, 2001 'The archaeology of Christianity in global perspective', in T Insoll (ed), *Archaeology and World Religion*, 148–181, Routledge, London

Latour, B, 2005 *Reassembling the Social: an Introduction to Actor-network Theory*, Oxford University Press, Oxford

Liddiard, R, 2005 *Castles in Context. Power, Symbolism and Landscape, 1066–1500*, Windgather Press, Oxford

Lilley, I, 2004 'Diaspora and identity in archaeology: moving beyond the Black Atlantic', in L Meskell and R W Preucel (eds), *A Companion to Social Archaeology*, 287–312, Blackwell, Oxford

Lilley, K D, 2004 'Cities of God? Medieval urban forms and their Christian symbolism', *Transactions of the Institute of British Geographers*, New Series 29, 296–313

Lucy, S, 2000 *The Anglo-Saxon Way of Death*, Sutton, Stroud

Luoto, K 2007 'Artefacts and enculturation — Examples of toy material from the medieval town of Turku', in V Immonen, M P Lempiäinen and U Rosendahl (eds), *Hortus novus. Fresh Approaches to Medieval Archaeology in Finland*, 10–20, Archaeologia Medii Aevi Finlandiae XIV

Meskell, L, and Joyce, R, 2003 *Embodied Lives. Figuring Ancient Maya and Egyptian Experience*, Routledge, London

Moreland, J, 1991 'Method and theory in medieval archaeology in the 1990s', *Archaeologia Medievale* 18, 7–42

Moreland, J, 1999 'The world(s) of the cross', *World Archaeology* 31:2, 194–213

Moreland, J, 2001 *Archaeology and Text*, Duckworth, London

Morris, R, 1983 *The Church in British Archaeology*, Council for British Archaeology Research Report 47, London

Morris, R, 1989 *Churches in the Landscape*, Phoenix, London

Nøttveit, O, 2006 'The kidney dagger as a symbol of masculine identity — the ballock dagger in the Scandinavian context', *Norwegian Archaeological Review* 39:2, 138–150

O'Keefe, T, 2004, 'Medieval towns, modern signs, identity inter-spaces: some reflections in historical archaeology', in E Casella and C Fowler (eds), *The Archaeology of Plural and Changing Identities: Beyond Identification*, 11–32, Springer, New York

Ousterhout, R, 1991 'The holy space. Architecture and the liturgy', in S Safran (ed), *Heaven on Earth. Art and the Church in Byzantium*, 81–120, University Park, Pennsylvania

Parker Pearson, M and Ramilisonina, 1998 'Stonehenge for the ancestors: the stones pass on the message', *Antiquity* 72, 308–326

Pestell, T, 2005 'Using material culture to define holy space: the Bromholm Project', in S Hamilton and A Spicer (eds), *Defining the Holy. Sacred Space in Medieval and Early Modern Europe*, 161–186, Ashgate, Aldershot

Pluskowski, A G, 2005 'Narwhals or unicorns? Exotic animals as material culture in medieval Europe', *European Journal of Archaeology* 7:3, 291–313

Pluskowski, A (ed), 2007 *Breaking and Shaping Beastly Bodies, Animals as Material Culture in the Middle Ages*, Oxbow, Oxford

POMLAS: Perceptions of Medieval Landscapes and Settlement http://www.britarch.ac.uk/msrg/pomlas.htm (accessed 25 July 2008)

Preston, J M, 2008 *Kuhn's 'The Structure of Scientific Revolutions'. A Reader's Guide*, Continuum, London

Price, N S, 2002 *The Viking Way. Religion and War in Late Iron Age Scandinavia*, Department of Archaeology and Ancient History, Uppsala

Randsborg, K, 1980 *The Viking Age in Denmark: the Formation of a State*, St Martin's Press, New York

Randsborg, K, 1991 *The First Millennium* AD *in Europe and the Mediterranean*, Cambridge University Press, Cambridge
Renfrew, C and Bahn, P, 1991 *Archaeology: Theories, Methods and Practice*, Thames and Hudson, London
Richardson, A, 2003 'Gender and space in English royal palaces *c*1160–*c*1547: a study in access analysis and imagery', *Medieval Archaeology* 47, 131–165
Rodwell, W, 1997 'Landmarks in Church Archaeology', *Church Archaeology* 1, 5–16
Rodwell, W, 2005 *The Archaeology of Churches*, Tempus, Stroud
Roffey, S, 2007 *The Medieval Chantry Chapel: an Archaeology*, Boydell, Woodbridge
Rowley-Conwy, P A, 2004 'How the West was lost: a reconsideration of agricultural origins in Britain, Ireland and southern Scandinavia', *Current Anthropology* 45, 83–113
Rybina, E A 1992 'Recent finds from Excavations in Novgorod', in *The Archaeology of Novgorod, Russia,* 160–192, Society for Medieval Archaeology Monograph 13, Lincoln
Sahlins, M, 1974 *Stone Age Economics*, Aldine, New York
Saunders, T, 2002 'Power relations and social space: a study of the late medieval archbishop's palace in Trondheim', *European Journal of Archaeology* 5:1, 89–111
Sindbaek, S M, 2007 'The small world of the Vikings: networks in early medieval communication and exchange', *Norwegian Archaeological Review* 40:1, 59–74
SMA, 1987 'Archaeology and the Middle Ages. Recommendations by the Society for Medieval Archaeology to the Historic Buildings and Monuments Commission for England', *Medieval Archaeology* 31, 1–12
Sofaer, J, 2006 *The Body as Material Culture*, Cambridge University Press, Cambridge
Stocker, D, 1997 '*Fons et origo*. The symbolic death, burial and resurrection of English font stones', *Church Archaeology* 1, 17–25
Stocker, D, and Everson, P, 1990 'Rubbish recycled: a study of the re-use of stone in Lincolnshire', in D Parsons (ed), *Stone Quarrying and Building in England* AD *43–1525*, 83–101, Phillimore, Chichester
Stocker, D and Everson, P, 2006 *Summoning St. Michael: Early Romanesque Towers in Lincolnshire*, Oxbow, Oxford
Stoodley, N, 1999 *The Spindle and the Spear*, British Archaeological Report 288, Oxford
Stoodley, N, 2000 'From the cradle to the grave: age organization and the early Anglo-Saxon burial rite', *World Archaeology* 31:3, 456–472
Sykes, N J, 2007 *The Norman Conquest: A Zooarchaeologial Perspective*, British Archaeological Report International Series 1656, Oxford
Thomas, C, Sloane, B and Phillpotts, C, 1997 *Excavations at the Priory and Hospital of St Mary Spital, London*, Museum of London Archaeology Service Monograph 1, London
Tilley, C, 2006 'Objectification', in Tilley *et al* (eds) 2006, 60–73
Tilley, C, Keane, W, Küchler, S, Rowlands, M and Spyer P (eds), 2006 *Handbook of Material Culture*, Sage, London
Trigger, B G, 1989 *A History of Archaeological Thought*, Cambridge University Press, Cambridge
Turner, S, 2006 *Making a Christian Landscape. The Countryside in Early Medieval Cornwall, Devon and Wessex*, Exeter University Press, Exeter
Ulmschneider, K, 2000 *Markets, Minsters, and Metal-Detectors*, British Archaeological Reports 307, Oxford
Van Dommelen, P 2006 'Colonial matters: material culture and postcolonial theory in colonial situations', in Tilley *et al* (eds) 2006, 104–124
Welinder, S, 1998 'The cultural construction of childhood in Scandinavia, 3500 BC–1350 AD', *Current Swedish Archaeology* 6, 185–204

Williams, H, 1997 'Ancient landscapes and the dead: the reuse of prehistoric and Roman monuments as early Anglo-Saxon burial sites', *Medieval Archaeology* 41, 1–32

Williams, H, 2003 'Remembering and forgetting the medieval dead', in H Williams (ed), *Archaeologies of Remembrance: Death and Memory in Past Societies*, 227–254, Plenum, New York

Williams, H, 2005 'Keeping the dead at arm's length: memory, weaponry and early medieval mortuary technologies', *Journal of Social Archaeology* 5:2, 253–275

Williams, H, 2006 *Death and Memory in Early Medieval Britain*, Cambridge University Press, Cambridge

Williamson, T, 2003 *Shaping Medieval Landscapes*, Windgather Press, Oxford

Wylie, A, 2002 *Thinking from Things. Essays in the Philosophy of Archaeology*, University of California Press, Berkeley

Zadora-Rio, E, 2003 'The making of churchyards and parish territories in the early-medieval landscape of France and England in the 7th–12th centuries: a reconsideration', *Medieval Archaeology* 47, 1–20

CHAPTER 20
MEANINGFUL LANDSCAPES: AN EARLY MEDIEVAL PERSPECTIVE

By ANDREW REYNOLDS

Landscape archaeology is often lauded as one of the more progressive developments in the recent study of the past. While it is difficult to disagree with this view in principle, questions must be asked regarding the extent to which the holistic study of medieval landscapes has been achieved. The realization that studying the interconnectedness and topographical setting of archaeological sites can provide fundamental insights into the organization of medieval landscapes is now well established; yet, as this paper argues, the fragmented study of the medieval period within archaeology, and a failure to promote interdisciplinarity in a positive light has resulted in an increasingly divergent study of the period. Plurality and multivocality with regard to interpretation and the nature of research questions posed are also considered, but the current way that archaeological specialisms are constituted has arguably resulted in the perpetuation of self-limiting research agendas. The final aim in this paper is to argue via three thematic case studies for a more holistic interdisciplinary approach as the way forward, framed by methodologies and theoretical approaches applied more widely in the social sciences.

INTRODUCTION

There remains a proliferation of increasingly specialized groups in the field of medieval archaeology, from long-established ones, such as the Medieval Settlement Research Group and the Castle Studies Group, to more recent formations, such as the Society for Church Archaeology: this list could be extended, considerably. Arguably, one of the most limiting features of the entire 'heritage business' in Britain, a criticism which can be extended to the environmental lobby as a whole, is its fragmented nature: special interests broken down to lowest common denominators render the whole almost completely powerless. The study of landscape archaeology, with which this paper is concerned, suffers because of such fragmentation. Too many people and special interest groups are failing to place their material or interests within wider frameworks, particularly overarching models of society explored more widely in the social sciences. In other words, one of the principal difficulties facing the construction of archaeological narratives presents itself before engagements with allied disciplines, such as history or anthropology, begin, namely a lack of dialogue within medieval archaeology.

A significant trend over the last decade has been the production of various guidelines, standards and research agendas, which have emanated from organizations across the board from the Medieval Pottery Research Group to the recent English Heritage-sponsored regional research frameworks, some of which have been published, with others in progress. While the aims and benefits of attempts to introduce 'standards' and baselines of current knowledge are obvious enough, regional research agendas vary greatly in terms of presentation, depth of research and foresight, to the extent that their overall value is rather questionable. A serious issue is just whose agenda is being presented? While research agendas provide a useful 'one-stop shop' for planning purposes or perhaps help to justify a research project, they rarely provide data or insights not already known to the audience that they are likely to reach. Guidelines and agendas must also be seen as part and parcel of the late 20th- and early 21st-century obsession with the verbiage of mission statements, protocols and procedures all ultimately produced in the quest for 'quality' and 'accountability'. While there may be benefits to such an approach, there is no doubt that conformity brings with it dullness — research managed by committee a stifling influence, endless protocol boots of lead.

A further matter of concern, which is central to the practice of medieval landscape archaeology, is interdisciplinarity. My own view, which is hardly an original observation, is that archaeology is by definition an interdisciplinary field of study, in common with so many other disciplines; yet medieval archaeology has often struggled with regard to defining its relationship with related fields. While there cannot be any doubt that for the greater part of its existence the agenda of medieval archaeology has been driven by paradigms constructed by historians, this is entirely the fault of archaeologists.

Movements in archaeology, particularly in the 1980s, attempted to set medieval archaeology free of the apparent 'tyranny of the historical record' (Alcock and Austin 1990). Yet much of this writing emanated from archaeologists working in prehistoric periods and others who chose to neglect the often intensely nuanced debates conducted among historians and which have now become so fashionable in prehistoric archaeology. Medieval archaeologists are often critical of their colleagues in history for their apparent 'kings and bishops' approach, but this does not do justice to the great volume of scholarly output which has engaged with a range of explicitly social and ideological themes, which should be viewed as fundamentally important comparative studies for research undertaken from an archaeological perspective. One thinks here, of the Annales School of French historians whose call for an interdisciplinary study of the past is as relevant now as it ever was (see, for example, the various studies in Bintliff 1991). Historians like Robert Bartlett, Wendy Davies, Eamon Duffy, Patrick Geary, Nicholas Howe and Barbara Rosenwein, among many others, have produced deeply thought-provoking work in fields where medieval archaeology can and should make a very strong contribution (Bartlett 2008; Davies 1988; Duffy 1992; 2006; Geary 1994; Howe 2008; Rosenwein 1999). Similarly, research collaborations between historians, archaeologists, linguists and others have also produced valuable and insightful results when focused on particular periods and themes (eg Ausenda 1995; Wood 1998; de Jong and Theuws 2001; Green and Siegmund 2003).

It remains a problem that those studying the Middle Ages through its material remains are resistant to engagements with written evidence and sometimes prefer instead to seek explanations from social anthropology without examining the full range of contemporary materials available for the study of a particular topic. A stimulating feature of working in a period with written records is that it is possible in certain circumstances, for example, to reveal the meaning of a formerly confusing text or a physical context for an otherwise unexplained image in a manuscript; surely a win-win situation for medieval studies as a whole, not a context for negative confrontation. The matter is much more complex than this, however, and stimulating discussions on the relationship between archaeology and text have been provided by Martin Carver and John Moreland, among others, to which reference should be sought (Carver 2002; Moreland 2006).

There was always going to be a clash with regard to theoretical approaches between prehistory and medieval archaeology, but it must be said that many of the interpretative claims made in prehistoric archaeology are likely to be just as wide of the mark as interpretations of materials from societies where explanatory frameworks have been determined by written evidence. I have often wondered what the intellectual position of later prehistoric archaeology in Britain would be like now had a Bronze Age *Beowulf* been discovered in an urn on Salisbury Plain in the 18th century. Soon after the discovery of the so-called Amesbury archer (an exceptionally wealthy 'Beaker' burial 5km south-east of Stonehenge), for example, it was a quickly proposed that the architect, 'lord' or 'king' of Stonehenge had been discovered (Fitzpatrick 2002a; 2002b); the application of medieval terminology is interesting here. While the status of that burial and its proximity to Stonehenge suggest the 'archer' was aware of and visited the site (oxygen isotope analysis of the remains of the man show he was originally from the Alps), the suggestion that he was its architect is as lacking in qualification as any of the linkages between textual reference and archaeological discovery made by medieval archaeologists, or indeed antiquaries of an earlier age. Moreover, a factor often neglected in prehistoric archaeology is that the interpretative frameworks applied therein are themselves entirely derived from written sources, be they reports on excavations, of ethnographic observation or a specific theoretical exposition, which can be equally as 'tyrannical' in their effect. The history of archaeological theory is itself characterized by the adoption of explanatory frameworks that become orthodox only to be regarded as virtually inadmissible following a short period of currency.

The potential for medieval archaeology to provide material culture signatures for societies whose mode of operation, be it economic, technological, religious or otherwise, is at least broadly known, has huge potential for comparative approaches between prehistoric and medieval societies, yet such work is hardly ever attempted, with Richard Bradley being one of the few prehistorians who has engaged in regular discourse with medievalists (Bradley 1980; 1987; 1993; 2006). One of the great benefits of such an approach is of course that comparisons can be made between societies who at least inhabited the same landscapes, albeit in different forms resulting from subsequent modifications.

Medieval archaeology has indeed been fairly criticized for its failure to theorize, but the flip side of the coin can be equally worrying in its lack of rigour. Cherry-picking of examples is easy within this kind of discussion, but it is a sobering reminder that prehistory is not quite so 'free' in terms how it is conceptualized and interpreted. This is not a debate that I wish to sustain here beyond making the point that an engagement with theory should ideally open up the mind rather than just lock it into another equally constraining paradigm.

Early medieval archaeology, besides the processual approaches adopted in Anglo-Saxon burial archaeology in the early 1980s, failed to pick up the lead set by Richard Hodges in his *Dark Age Economics* and related studies (Hodges 1982a; 1982b). Chris Arnold and Chris Scull remained pretty much the only writers to attempt to theorize early Anglo-Saxon social systems in their entirety with reference to archaeological and anthropological theory (Arnold 1982; 1988; Scull 1992; 1993), although the collected papers resulting from a 1984 Glasgow conference on early medieval power and politics was an important step forward in modes of approach (Driscoll and Nieke 1988). The first decade of the 21st century has witnessed a re-engagement with theorized approaches within early medieval archaeology, and more specifically landscape studies, with notable contributions from Stuart Brookes, Sarah Semple and Howard Williams, among others, who have each produced important new work that moves beyond traditional disciplinary boundaries and has established new directions and methodologies (Brookes 2007; Semple 2007; Williams 2006). Scandinavian medieval archaeology is in many respects at the forefront of the explicitly theorized study of the period, but lies beyond the scope of this paper: the impressive range of papers from a 2004 conference in Lund provides an illustration of the situation, with an earlier paper by Lotte Hedeager representing a particularly bold attempt to identify early medieval cosmology in the landscape (Andrén *et al* 2006; Hedeager 2001).

A number of influential studies, therefore, have revealed the undoubted necessity for medieval archaeology to engage explicitly with wider issues current within the social sciences and to explore their theoretical concerns and methodologies. As discussed by Roberta Gilchrist in this volume, the application of explicitly theorized approaches in medieval archaeology has been patchy with regard to topic and theme, and until very recently embraced more so by those working on aspects of the archaeology of the early Middle Ages than on the later part of the period, but even then only by a few scholars studying burial archaeology. There is now a new generation of archaeologists working on the later medieval period, among them Jon Finch, Kate Giles and Pam Graves, whose work has followed, at least in its desire to theorize, the lead set by Roberta Gilchrist and Matthew Johnson (Finch 2000; Giles 2000; Graves 2000; Gilchrist 1994; 1995; Johnson 1993).

Manifold expression is one of the most exciting aspects of academic discourse. In this vein the notion of multi-vocality is explored in the three case studies offered in this paper. This is a concept that has been approached in several ways and in different disciplines, Virtual reality studies in archaeology have attempted to reveal multiple experience of past environments via computer simulations and GIS analyses (cf Dawson *et al* 2007; Fitzjohn 2007), while the desire to find a voice in archaeological explanation for indigenous communities can also be considered under this general theme (see, for example, Cooney 1999; Strang 1999; Allison 1999). Multi-vocality has also been promoted to encourage interpretations that relate to gender and the human lifecycle and, more recently, to consider how archaeology is encountered in the field and how such knowledge is acquired (ie the way in which multiple actors engage in the process of gathering and interpreting field data) (Gilchrist 2004; Joyce 2002, 7, 56; 2004). In the case studies offered below, Joyce's (2002, 11) adoption of the philosopher Mikhail Bakhtin's (1984) definition of 'polyphony' as representing different voices with equal integrity is applied to multi-vocality, with one significant deviation. Joyce associates the term with the act of gathering and assembling archaeological data, while my application relates to the degree to which multi-vocal experiences of past populations can be accessed via a plural approach to source materials, an approach adopted by Lopiparo (2002, 73–74) with regard to the study of the prehistoric household, but using only archaeological evidence.

The discussion so far has taken a rather critical tone, but my aim has been to press home the view that the fragmented nature of the discipline must be overcome, that medieval archaeologists must freely engage with the debates of historians, and vice versa, and that the application of theory derived from the social sciences is vital if the relevance of the study of medieval society is to be appreciated above and beyond the Society for Medieval Archaeology and its membership.

LANDSCAPE ARCHAEOLOGY

Landscape archaeology has been reinvented several times. As far back as the 18th century the antiquary William Stukeley understood the importance of relating monuments to each other, appreciating aspects such as their landscape setting and quality of viewshed (Peterson 2003). Later antiquaries such as Greenwell working in the 19th century also expressed a sense of the character of the landscapes containing the monuments which were the focus of their interests (Greenwell 1877, 232–234). While Pitt Rivers set the standard for recording the immediate setting of field monuments, the likes of Major Allen, O G S Crawford and Sir Cyril Fox investigated archaeological landscapes in a way which had not been attempted before. They engaged with a series of themes and field remains which had largely escaped the attention of their forebears, and which, with several notable exceptions, have lain largely neglected since: one thinks here, for example, of the study of linear earthworks and roads and routeways (Pitt Rivers 1887–98; Crawford 1928; 1953; Fox 1955).

Later, in the 1970s and 1980s, a series of medieval landscape studies by Peter Fowler, Mick Aston and others built upon earlier approaches, and included forays with an explicitly theoretical bent, such as the application of Central Place Theory, while the theme of Roman to Anglo-Saxon continuity dominated much of the work of this period (Fowler 1972; 1975; Aston 1986). More recent developments have included among them the development of Historic Landscape Characterization (HLC), an ongoing process of mapping and describing the physical character of the English landscape, with analytical potential besides its principal purpose of providing a framework for landscape assessment for curators and other heritage managers (www.english-heritage.org.uk/server/show/nav.1293). At least in early medieval archaeology, the subtlety and breadth of approach demonstrated by the wider discipline's founders was never properly followed up; the development of the field has been greatly hampered by the increasing fragmentation noted at the outset of this paper.

The failure of medieval archaeologists in Britain to engage with theoretical approaches at the same pace and intensity as prehistorians is also partly due, ultimately, to the Roman occupation of Britain. While highlighting the many problems involved in back-projecting from later sources, Richard Bradley has recently discussed the benefits of being able to study the transition from prehistoric to medieval society in Scandinavia which was beyond the reach of the Roman world (Bradley 2006). While the degree of Roman influence upon Scandinavian culture is currently one of the most lively debates in that region (Hills 2007, 193), in Britain there can be little doubt that medieval societies have long been interpreted in the shadow of the Classical world, sometimes explicitly, more frequently implicitly, and by scholars with a Classical educational background. Such comparisons are not terribly useful for gauging the complexity of the early medieval world, for many of the measures by which complexity can be gauged in Classical societies are simply not applicable to early medieval ones. A prime field of study which highlights the overarching application of a Classical approach is the focus upon urban development as a measure of early medieval social complexity. A key feature of Anglo-Saxon society, for example, is the dispersed nature of social, economic and religious phenomena as the predominant mode of social organization throughout much of the period (Reynolds 1999). The theme of 'nucleation' has dominated settlement studies in Britain, both urban and rural, with the result that entire strata of settlement types have been neglected (Austin 1989). A combination, then, of both Classical and contemporary ideals of centralization as an indicator of complexity and civility can be seen to have affected both concepts of and approaches to understanding the early medieval period.

The most notable recent contribution to debating approaches to medieval landscapes is Matthew Johnson's book *Ideas of Landscape* (2007). A reading of this insightful and thought-provoking book prompts a desire to engage in much fuller terms with a series of the issues raised within. While this is not possible here, it is worth noting certain of Johnson's key observations and considering how the case-studies offered below relate to his appraisal of the practice and wider context of the study of the landscape archaeology of the medieval period. Johnson's major contention is that landscape archaeology as practised in Britain is firmly empirical in its approach and largely resistant to the kinds of theoretically informed enquiry and discourse encountered in other disciplines that engage with landscape, such as anthropology and geography (Johnson 2007, 1–2). Johnson places the origins of this difference of approach squarely with the English Romantic movement of the late 18th and 19th centuries, with the work of W G Hoskins providing the conduit by which such a world view became entrenched in landscape archaeology, particularly that concerned with the medieval period. Johnson calls for a series of much-needed lines of enquiry, framed within four crucial realizations: (1) in order to investigate the landscape it is necessary to escape the comfortable Romantic vision of the English countryside and (2) the social and cultural exclusivity inherent within such a view. A further important assertion is (3) that mobility, conflict and change require greater attention and, with such concepts in mind, that (4) multi-vocality must have a place in archaeological interpretation (ibid, 190–191).

To return to an earlier theme, a prime example of non-communication within the discipline is the almost total lack of discourse between 'burial' archaeologists and 'settlement' archaeologists and, in many respects, medieval landscape archaeology has been concerned almost entirely with the study of settlement patterns and field systems. Matthew Johnson briefly considers how religion in the landscape is a much-neglected topic and notes the potential limitations of interpretations of the role of religion and religious sites propagated by individuals of faith (ibid, 132). Perhaps as a result of the depth to which the medieval church was ingrained in society by the late Middle Ages, scholars have arguably over-emphasized the impact of Christianity on people's lives in earlier centuries. The decline of grave goods in Anglo-Saxon cemeteries of the 7th century was for many years attributed directly to changing religious belief (Boddington 1990), while a lively debate during the 1990s centred upon the degree to which the earliest monastic communities engaged with the wider world or were instead closed communities with little impact on the lives and culture of local people (Blair 1995; Cambridge and Rollason 1995). This is not the place to discuss the boundaries between organized religion, cult, superstition and folklore, but a nuanced approach to archaeology is revealing increasing evidence for behaviour of a ritualized character from a range of contexts from settlements to landscapes (Hamerow 2006; Semple 2007). Johnson's (2007, 133) assertion that 'the one thing all historic communities had was a church' cannot be applied to the first three Christian centuries (7th–10th) in Anglo-Saxon England, and while the emergence of parish churches in the late Saxon period may well reflect the emergence of new concepts of community in the landscape, a careful study of patterns of burial in the mid- to late Anglo-Saxon period reveals a complex geographical pattern of burial sites far more varied than that observed in the pre-Christian period (Reynolds 2002). One must therefore extend Johnson's approach to include not just a study of churches but of a range of further sites whose nature and location is likely to have been determined by ideological concerns, be they those of the Church or of local traditions. Semple's recent work on the landscape archaeology of pre-Christian cult sites brings together archaeology, place-names, topography and literary evidence in a way that provides a model for similar studies (Semple 2007).

With a few exceptions, burial archaeologists have failed to engage with the landscape context of their evidence, preferring instead to concentrate on the minutiae of material culture, in many cases focusing to a pitch way beyond the significance of the evidence. Ground-breaking work on the landscape context of Early Anglo-Saxon cemeteries was initiated by Sam Lucy (1998) working on East Yorkshire and by Howard Williams's (1999) study of high-status burial, while more recent studies have included further regional and topical considerations of early medieval burial evidence (Semple 2003; Reynolds 2002; 2008; 2009; Brookes 2007). It remains the case, however, that apart from Brookes's study of Kent there is still no quantified view, or extended discussion, of the fundamental relationships between Early and Middle Anglo-Saxon settlements and cemeteries. By contrast there are at least four classificatory frameworks alone for Kentish Early Anglo-Saxon burials, each based on complex artefact typologies, and very many catalogues of individual artefact types, wrist-clasps, beads, button brooches and so on from cemeteries across the country. While detailed material culture studies are of course very necessary, something is clearly wrong. How far have we really come if we know every detail of a certain class of pin or brooch, but next to nothing of the setting of the sites from which such material was recovered, or of the settlements that were inhabited by the populations of excavated cemeteries? From its beginnings, early medieval burial archaeology developed in increasingly myopic directions, while burial as a form of evidence capable of bringing a deeply meaningful texture to understandings of landscape never really came within the gravitational pull of mainstream landscape studies: there is barely a trace of burial archaeology in Johnson's *Ideas of Landscape*, yet such evidence can indeed provide a nuanced understanding of early medieval perceptions of landscape.

As sub-fields of medieval archaeology, settlement and burial archaeology have very different ideological foundations; the former in economic history, the latter in cultural historical approaches to ethnicity. The distinction is much less evident in later medieval archaeology where the study, for example, of monastic landscapes and 'mature' medieval rural settlements is well advanced. Burial may not feature explicitly in these latter two instances, but as cemeteries are features of both monastic houses and parish churches they enter the discourse of the later medieval settlement archaeologist by default. While not wishing to detract from the quality of the publications in question, however, the way in which medieval church and burial archaeology at Wharram Percy has been published if anything detracts from the holistic view, a situation also evident in the manner of publication of the church and churchyard at Raunds, Northamptonshire (Bell and Beresford 1987; Mays *et al* 2007; Boddington 1996). In both cases, church and cemetery are published separately from their associated settlements.

Theorized approaches to early medieval landscapes of settlement are almost entirely lacking, although aside from the work of Hodges and Arnold mentioned earlier in this paper, mention should be made of the various essays by Tom Saunders on towns and rural settlement (all too little referenced in discussions by other scholars) and Grenville Astill (Saunders 1990; 2000; 2001; Astill 1991; 1994). A major factor limiting a theorized archaeology of settlement has been the rather awkward way in which settlement archaeology has been studied. Quite unlike just about any other branch of medieval archaeology, the study of settlement development in the Anglo-Saxon period has not progressed from attempts to produce a seamless narrative for the emergence of the English village. I am not talking here about the very first attempts during the late 19th and earlier 20th centuries to talk about the origins of the English village on the basis of inferences drawn from written sources, but am instead referring purely to the way that archaeologists have approached the issue.

Settlement studies fall into two very distinct schools. The study of Early Anglo-Saxon settlements has been dominated by attempts to establish a settlement framework to accompany the far more abundant cemetery archaeology of the period and thus much has been written about settlement sites of the 5th to 7th centuries, mainly in terms of describing the range and form of buildings or overall settlement morphology (Hamerow 2002; Reynolds 2003). Much less attention has been given to the topographical setting of individual sites and how they relate to existing patterns of fields and trackways in the landscape, or to explaining the motivations which lay behind the orientations, viewsheds and inter-relationships between structures and groups of buildings. Working backwards in time from an initial concern with village desertion, the concerns of later medieval settlement archaeologists shifted to engage with the search for the origins of the medieval village. Work at Wharram Percy, Raunds and at a host of other sites appeared to reveal a late Saxon horizon for village formation, which appeared to concur with the evidence of 10th- and 11th-century charters for the division of the English landscape into what became medieval parishes. The matter is of course far more complex than this, but one major outcome of the development of the scholarly traditions just described is a yawning gap in understanding relating to the Middle Saxon period, where settlement related interests were, and still are, concentrated almost totally on the remains of monasteries, emporia and other exceptional settlements. There remains a very poorly understood (and largely ignored) archaeology of non-elite rural settlement of the 7th to 9th centuries, yet PhD theses concerning early Anglo-Saxon burial archaeology continue to roll out.

Wither early medieval landscape archaeology? The fragmented nature of research *within* sub-disciplines is clearly an issue with serious implications for a landscape approach, which by definition requires an understanding of long-term process. A further matter of importance, however, is the need for archaeologists to move beyond their traditional comfort zones and to engage fully with a whole host of topics and themes that will encourage more holistic considerations of the human habitation of landscape to be achieved. This paper now moves on to consider three themes fundamental to the study of human communities yet neglected by 'traditional' landscape archaeology in an early medieval setting, with an emphasis on interdisciplinarity and multi-vocal interpretations.

THREE CASE STUDIES AT THE 'FRINGE' OF LANDSCAPE ARCHAEOLOGY

Power and authority: beyond Sutton Hoo and Yeavering

Power and authority in the early medieval landscape are normally considered in terms of monumental constructions, burial mounds, imposing residences, sculpture, and so on, but a key mode of the exhibition of secular power within the early medieval landscape was the erection of gallows. Places of execution began to appear across the English landscape from as early as the later 7th or early 8th century and were a commonplace by the 10th century. Here as with the other case studies considered in this paper, multi-vocal interpretations can be offered and an important contribution made to a central concern of medieval historians, the nature of the emergence of judicial practice in early England. Furthermore, cross-cultural and cross-chronological comparisons made possible by anthropological studies allow the English evidence to be more securely interpreted. The details of this particular subject are considered elsewhere (Reynolds 2008; 2009), but a brief summary illustrates the point and can be related to many of the issues raised by Matthew Johnson and noted earlier in this paper.

Capital punishment is, to say the least, a highly emotive topic. Archaeological discoveries of execution cemeteries in combination with documentary evidence in the form of Anglo-Saxon charters, reveal that the sight of executed people hanging from gallows and decapitated heads stuck on poles were an everyday experience for both urban and rural dwellers in the Christian period in Anglo-Saxon England. What circumstances brought about the need for the exhibition of secular power in such a violent way? How was public execution perceived? How was the landscape used to display secular power? Many more questions can be posed of this material, but to address just these three makes the point. A study of the topographical setting of the four earliest execution sites (Cambridge, Staines, Sutton Hoo and Walkington Wold) shows that they all lay at the edges of major political entities during the later 7th and 8th centuries at major river crossings associated also with overland routes (Reynolds 2008) (Figure 20.1). Cambridge, Staines and Walkington Wold can be placed in a context of Mercian and Northumbrian territorial expansion as instruments of the consolidation of military conquest, while anthropological studies reveal that the use of violence in a highly controlled way is a consistent feature resulting from military conquest and the need for an expanding polity to impress its newly found dominance over occupied territory (Earle 1997). Gallows may have been read by some as an indicator of the protection offered by ruling authorities, by others as an oppressive and depressing reminder of decreasing social and personal rights, while children were very likely terrified. By the Late Anglo-Saxon period gallows had proliferated and it was evidently royal policy to exhibit the power of the regime in core territory rather than peripheral lands as had characterized the earliest phase of such activity. The location of places of execution in peripheral or liminal zones and the reuse of pre-existing barrows for such a purpose in a Christian context also has strong ideological connotations relating to concepts of wilderness and malevolence, which are revealed by recourse to Old English literature (Semple 2004; Reynolds 2009), and which bring a further layer of cultural texture to our appreciation of the early medieval landscape.

Introducing a landscape dimension to excavated execution sites thus facilitates a view of the reality of concepts and situations evident in prose, poetic and illustrative sources. To cite but one specific example, one of the major issues confronting students of manuscript illustrations is the degree to which a given artist is portraying the contemporary world or drawing upon earlier exemplars (Carver 1986). In the case of the late Saxon Harley Psalter (BL MS Harley 603), the majority of the many fine pen and ink drawings throughout the MS are copied directly from a Flemish MS of earlier 9th-century date, which is itself based on a lost, Late Antique antecedent (Hinks 1935, 115–116; Noel 1995). One of the benefits of being able to compare the English version, which is the work of perhaps half-a-dozen hands, is that innovations can be identified. One such innovation is a scene on folio 67 that depicts a mound, the outline of which is penned in a series of brush-like, bold lines which give a solid, unambiguous

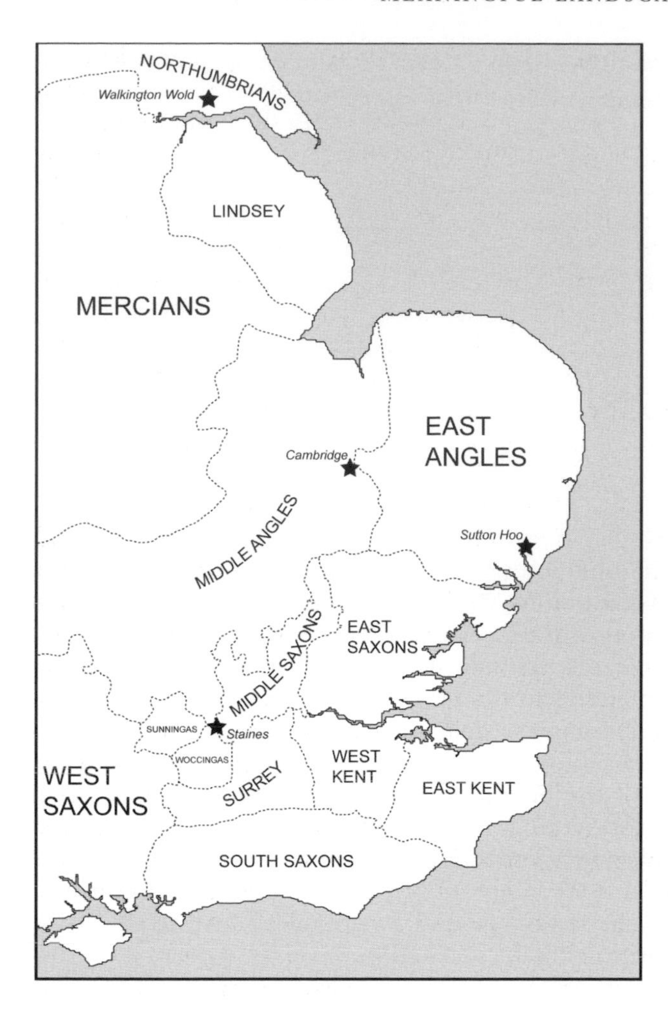

FIGURE 20.1 The relationships between execution cemeteries and kingdom boundaries in the later 7th and earlier 8th centuries (after Reynolds 2008).

impression of an artificial construction (Figure 20.2) (Semple 2004). Within the frame of the mound three headless corpses are depicted, but with a much lighter hand, indicating that they lay buried within. One of the bodies is face-down, the other two bent sharply backwards in a kneeling position. The heads are drawn in the firmer hand and one is depicted lying in a shallow hollow cut into the foot of the mound, the impression being that the heads are buried later than the bodies, if at all. Despite being an innovation, there is no way that a contemporary understanding of this image could have been achieved by anything other than a study of the archaeology of execution. Both the reuse of the mound and the range of body positions find precise parallels in excavated cemeteries, and there is little doubt that the artist who drew the scene would have been entirely familiar with the reality of what he was drawing. The Harley Psalter is one of the first English manuscripts to engage with the portrayal of landscape and it is fascinating that the artist in question appears to have drawn upon vivid personal experience in such an unambiguous way.

FIGURE 20.2 A torture scene and a mound containing decapitated corpses. (British Library MS Harley 603, f 67. © British Library Board. All Rights Reserved)

The study of execution provides an interesting ideological paradox between the apparent 'civilizing' influence of Christianity, with its emphasis on 'forgiveness', and the reality of the treatment of social outcasts. Archaeology reveals that individuals whose bodies were laid in the grave in ways indicative of 'otherness' were nevertheless buried within community cemeteries in the pre-Christian period, but exclusion expressed in the most powerful fashion is a clear feature from the conversion period onwards. My own view is that archaeological interpretations of society in the early medieval period must break free of the bonds of the comparative Judeo-Christian paradigm, whereby non-Christian societies are perceived as somehow less complex, less competent and ideologically barbaric. The topography and character of execution sites can be seen to encapsulate a wide range of social and ideological concerns expressed with clear reference to the landscape and to provide a case study of the interface between top-down imposition and local reaction.

Movement: archaeologies of journeying and travel

Landscape archaeology tends to deal with 'fixed' entities, settlements, farms, boundaries, fields, and so on, without considering the concomitant dynamics between such features and the complexity of the social networks that together they form. Indeed, two concepts that link all of the physical elements of the medieval landscape in one way or another are movement and boundedness, the latter of which we will return to shortly.

Travel and communication is a greatly neglected topic. While the former necessitates physically moving from one place to another, the latter can involve the transference of a message or command by sight or sound across the landscape. By combining archaeological, place-name and written evidence in a landscape context it is possible to reveal the subtlety of appreciation of topography by past populations. Recent research has revealed a layering of visual means of communicating across the landscape in the late Anglo-Saxon period in the context of military activity (Baker and Brookes in prep). Preliminary work on this topic has shown that visual lines of sight followed contemporary overland routes and that local networks operated alongside and within larger scale systems (Reynolds 1999, 92–96). A theme closely related to travel and communication is time, a concept that archaeologists only usually grapple with in regard to dating and sequence, although the topic is complex and multi-faceted (Lucas 2005). In a landscape context, there are many levels at which one might consider timescale from the cyclical passing of the agricultural year to the erratic and often unpredictable nature of the human lifecycle and its attendant tasks and roles. Understanding timescale as it would have applied in the past can be achieved to varying degrees according to the context in question. Plotting of major Anglo-Saxon beacon sites in southern England, for example, shows that only four fires were needed to convey a message from Totland Point on the Isle of Wight to the shire meeting-place and beacon site at Cuckhamsley on the Berkshire Downs (Hill and Sharpe 1996) (Figure 20.3). In ideal conditions and in a state of preparedness, a message could thus be sent from southern to central England in a very short time, perhaps well under half an hour. Journey times overland and by water initially appear straightforward to establish if the routes taken are known, but Norbert Ohler's excellent book on medieval travel makes it clear that mutli-vocality of experience is central to any discussion of journey times (Ohler 1989, 97–101) (Figure 20.4).

Travel thus invites plurality of interpretation for the archaeologist. At one level, the need for inter-connections between individual places can be drawn from textual sources that list specific types of settlements, for example, the Burghal Hidage, while

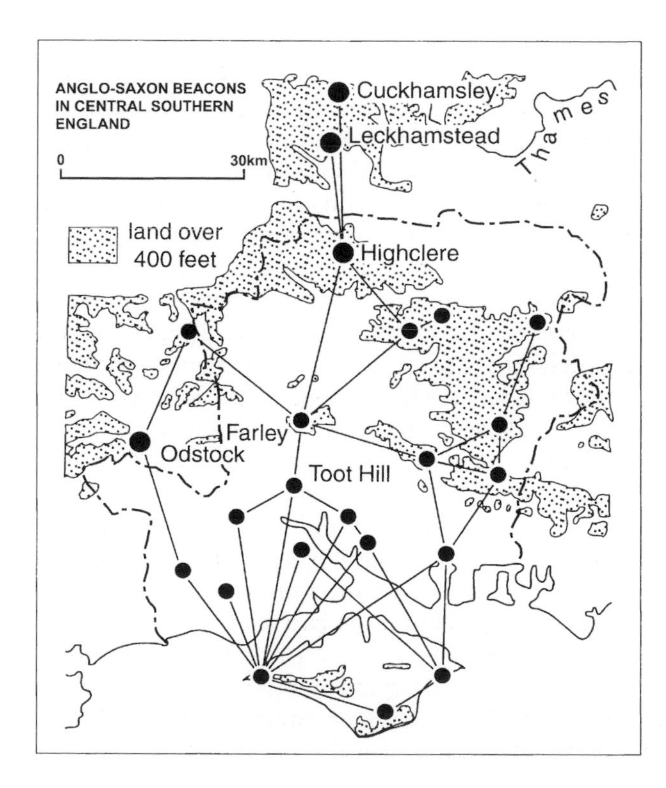

FIGURE 20.3 Major Anglo-Saxon beacon sites in southern England (after Hill and Sharpe 1996).

Traveller	Speed (mph)	Daily distance (miles)
Walker	2–4	15–25
Runner	6–7	30–40
Horse galloping	12–15	
'Average traveller' going slowly with followers and baggage train (eg merchants)		20–30
Able-bodied rider, in a hurry		30–40
Mounted couriers with change of horses		30–50
Mounted relay messengers in the Mongolian empire, 13th century (according to Marco Polo)		235
Relay runners in India, 14th century (according to Ibn Battuta)		190
Papal express messengers, 14th century (on level ground)		60
Papal express messengers, 14th century (in mountains)		30
Express messenger in France and Spain, 14th century		95–125
Inca relay runners	6	150
Mounted Spanish courier in 16th century South America		30

FIGURE 20.4 Estimated journey times (after Ohler 1989).

the extent of journeying can be reconstructed using documented itineraries, such as survive for certain Late Saxon kings, such as Eadwig and Edgar, or sources that relate to military campaigns, for example the movements of Viking armies described in *Anglo-Saxon Chronicle* entries, which relate not only point to point travel but on occasion actually refer to specific roads (Hill 1981, 82–92). From a purely archaeological perspective roads and routeways can be characterized as archaeological features, by width, by physical composition and definition, by an examination of the points or nodes that they connect or form. Study of the medieval landscape clearly reveals a ranking of routeways. Major highways, for example, (equivalent to modern A-roads) linked important settlements or towns, while villages and hamlets were often found set back from major routes and linked to each other by a network of 'B-roads' largely independent of major routes but often with settlements themselves on minor routes ('C-roads') facilitating access to upland pasture from individual settlements. The Avebury region provides a clear case study of just how such routes can be classified on the grounds of their archaeological manifestation in the landscape (Pollard and Reynolds 2002, 224–226, fig 103). Ranking of routeways according to their 'importance' is, of course, subjective and relative to the user; the shepherds 'A-road' will be another person's 'C-road'.

The actual experience of travel can be envisioned by bringing together a range of different forms of evidence. With regard to the Avebury area example just cited, it is clear that a long distance journey might be rather a lonely one, even though the traveller might pass close by very many settlements en route. Gallows were also frequently located alongside major routeways, often at bridges and other river crossings, leaving travellers in no doubt as to when they had crossed from one supra-local territory into another, or had reached the boundaries of a borough. In the latter case it is worth observing that the archaeological expression of the judicial authority of the Anglo-Saxon town is actually to be found in the countryside (Hayman and Reynolds 2005, 251). A particularly grim illustration of the nature of travel in late Anglo-Saxon Wessex is provided by the fact that no less than five Anglo-Saxon execution cemeteries have been excavated along the route of the highway linking Winchester with Old Sarum (Reynolds 2009), a distance of 22 miles which, at the walking speed of an able-bodied person, ensured a stark reminder of royal power every hour and a half or thereabouts. Apart from the settlement at Stockbridge, halfway between the two major settlements, not a single village lay on the route of the highway itself, all were and still are set off of the road.

Local communities also viewed elements of routeways in distinctive ways, particularly crossroads. Until recently crossroads burial was considered to be a late medieval or early post-medieval phenomenon in England (Halliday 1996). Archaeology, however, has revealed a series of excavated bodies buried at crossroads dated as early as the late 6th and 7th centuries. The most striking example is surely that revealed by the excavation in Kent of the intersection of the Pilgrim's Way, a major route linking east and west Kent, with the Roman road leading south from Rochester. Large-scale excavations uncovered the full extent of the road junction and showed the Pilgrim's way to be of at least Middle Anglo-Saxon date, while the burial of a woman aged 25–35 buried at the crossroads yielded a C14 date of AD 680–980 at 68% confidence (Booth *et al* forthcoming) (Figure 20.5). The crossroads also served as the meeting point of local parish and hundred boundaries. It is possible at this juncture to perhaps make a distinction relating to the experience of travel depending on whether the individual or party concerned were local or not. Locals may have especially feared a crossroads because of direct knowledge or local folklore, while foreigners might only have entertained the thought of the possible malevolence of such a spot on the basis of wider knowledge.

The experience of a journey will also have engaged the traveller with local landmarks and one example provided below again emphasizes multi-vocality with regard to interpretation. Running southeast to northwest along the foot and then up the northern scarp of the Pewsey Vale in Wiltshire is a green lane known from at least 1272 as Workway Drove (Gover *et al* 1939, 318). When travelling northwest along this route away from Pewsey towards Avebury the road takes a gentle turn to the north *c*3km before its junction with the Wessex Ridgeway, which at this point runs due south over the scarp and across the vale to Salisbury plain. At the point where the road turns north the imposing and unmistakable sight of the massive Neolithic long barrow known since at least the 18th century as Adam's Grave comes into view in the distance at the end of the track (Figure 20.6). To all intents and purposes Workway Drove (derived from Old English *(ge)weorc-weg* 'way or road by the earthwork', referring to either Adam's Grave or the adjacent Neolithic causewayed enclosure on Knap Hill) is clearly aligned on the barrow, in the manner of the way in which many

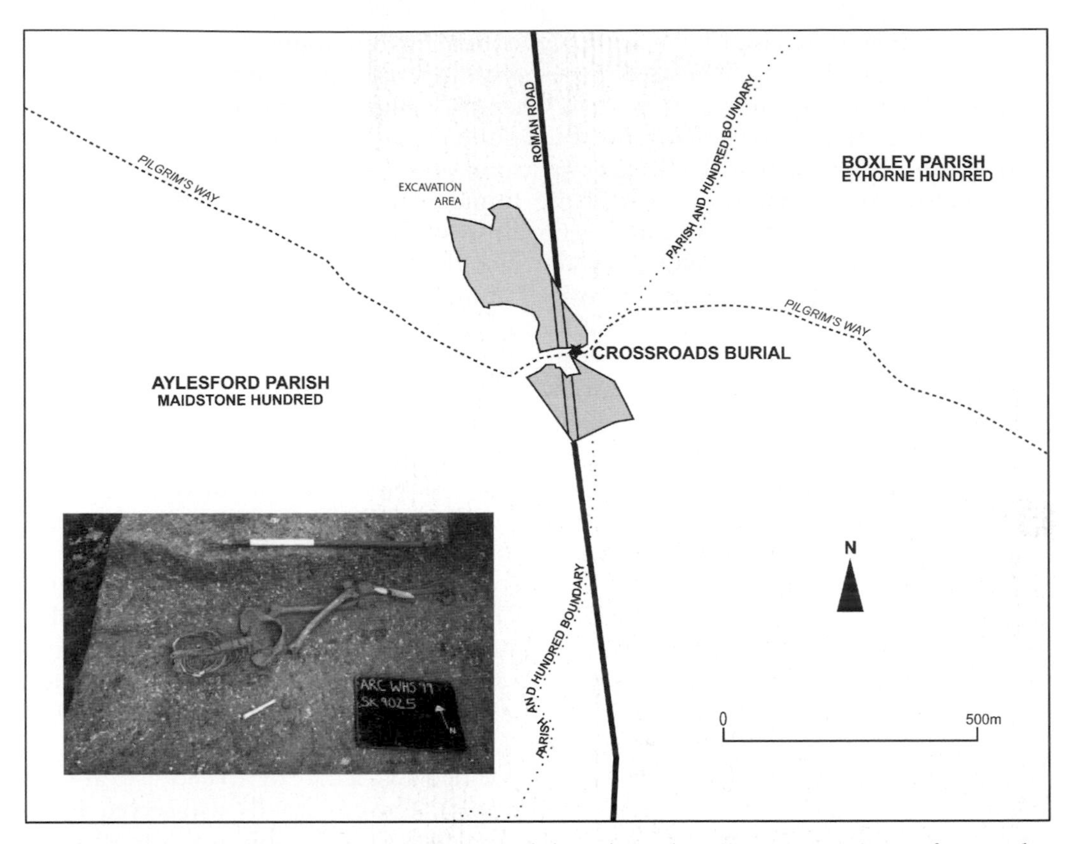

FIGURE 20.5 A Middle Anglo-Saxon crossroads burial at White Horse Stone, Kent (after Booth *et al* forthcoming).

Roman roads are aligned on both archaeological features and natural elements of the lansdscape, such as that between Bath (*Aquae Sulis*) and Mildenhall (*Cunetio*), which uses Silbury Hill as a marker between the southern spur of Calstone Down to the west and Overton Down to the east (Pollard and Reynolds 2002, 170).

To the foreigner, Adam's Grave will at least have appeared as a clear landmark, but to the local, the site of the monument will without doubt have been imbued with a strong sense of meaning. Both the *Anglo-Saxon Chronicle* and a local charter refer to the barrow as *wodnesbeorg*, 'Woden's Barrow' (*ASC* sa 592 and 716, S272, Gover *et al* 1939, 318). The fact that a major narrative source like the *Chronicle* refers to the barrow implies that the mound was a widely known landmark and a major waypoint in southern England: as previously noted, the Ridgeway passes immediately to the east of the mound. The *Chronicle* refers to battles fought at the site in 592 and 716, the name itself reveals either a pagan cultic or a West Saxon dynastic association, while the find of a 7th-century silver-gilt stud 'near' the barrow by a metal-detectorist may have been lost during combat or might even suggest the presence of a high-status burial placed in a sentinel-type position in common with other burials of this date in

FIGURE 20.6 A view of Adam's Grave (formerly Woden's barrow) looking north-west on the Workway Drove, Pewsey Vale, Wiltshire. (Photograph: author)

the region (Semple 2003; Reynolds and Langlands 2006, 32–34). The experience of travel through the locality, therefore, would have been highly nuanced and tempered according to the degree of one's knowledge of the place, which might be due to the short- or long-term transmission of local folklore, indirect knowledge provided by access to relevant written evidence or by chronological proximity to events which happened there. As noted above, wider concepts of barrow mounds having been perceived as malevolent places are evident from a range of sources (Semple 1998), both written and archaeological, and thus again the traveller might have experienced Woden's Barrow with trepidation even if completely ignorant of any direct biographical details of the mound.

Boundedness

A different kind of evidence links travel with boundedness, although the two concepts are not often related, the latter perhaps viewed as limiting the former.

Charter bounds, however, provide details of yet another form of journey, that of recording and, from the later medieval period, 'beating' the bounds of estates, while other early medieval ritualized journeys include the complex and arcane rituals of consecration of religious sites (Gittos 2002; Blair 2005, 486–489). Journeys, then, just in these two examples, can be seen to relate to circumstances beyond the straightforward requirement to travel between two points and to play a central role in the social rituals binding communities together as well as physically defining them or rendering certain spaces sacred. Although our primary evidence for the existence of boundary structures is textual, in the form of charter bounds and consecration rituals, there is a physical dimension to both which can be studied by the archaeologist and which facilitates bringing a significance and depth of understanding to the terminology, and therefore perception, of the Anglo-Saxon popular mindset.

Anglo-Saxon charters, largely the preserve of one of the most arcane fields of early medieval history, contain within them perhaps the most direct opportunity for gaining a nuanced understanding of the mental mapping of landscape in pre-Industrial society. In the main, charters are used to reconstruct the extent of landholdings of major institutions, their witness-lists reflecting the pecking order of Anglo-Saxon high society. Their boundary clauses relate directly to physical evidence, however, and present one of the most exciting interfaces between written and physical evidence in medieval studies. Early fieldworkers like Crawford engaged directly with the evidence of charter bounds, tracing the boundary marks of Anglo-Saxon charters in the field. Much of this early work, however, including the phenomenal output of G B Grundy, who worked from maps rather than directly with the landscape, was concerned with 'solving' boundary clauses rather than exploring the social meaning of the rich and varied terminology used by Anglo-Saxon surveyors to record parcels of land in a way that would make sense when recalled to local inhabitants not kings and bishops. This latter factor is evident partly in the fact that boundary clauses, at least from the later 9th century were written down in the vernacular, while other elements of land charters, preamble and witness list, were written in Latin.

A few selected excerpts from boundary clauses will suffice to illustrate the degree to which the landscape was imbued with meaning beyond the pragmatic requirement of describing boundaries for legal purposes. While considering the examples below, it is worth bearing in mind the annual journey undertaken at least from the post-Conquest period but probably earlier, by local people led by the parish priest around the bounds of local estates. Where documented in later times the standard practice was to involve children, usually boys, in the process of memorizing marks along the boundary route, commonly by pushing them down into animal burrows, dragging them through thorn bushes, banging their heads against stones or, in the case of boundaries running along the rivers to suspend them over the side of a boat and to dunk them at intervals head-first into the water (Hutton 1996, 277–294; Harte 2002). This was a pretty bad day out for any child, mentally and perhaps physically scarring, to the extent that the boundary of the community would be remembered.

Besides such direct physical engagement with boundaries, naming of markers as evidenced in charter bounds shows that they could be imbued with a meaning beyond literal description. While pragmatic boundary marks are the most common, one wonders how the assembled community of Chalke in Wiltshire would have understood *þar mon þane chiorl sloh for þan buccan*, 'the place where the ceorl [was] slain because of the goat', described in a boundary clause of 955, or the people of Witney, Oxfordshire the spot *ðær ða cnihtas licgað*, 'where the young men lie', recorded in a charter of 1044 (S1000). A forged charter for Taunton, but with pre-Conquest bounds, records an *ad quendam fraxinum quem imperiti sacrum vocant*, 'ash-tree which the ignorant call sacred' (S 311), while over 50 charters record 'heathen' and other burials (Blair 2005, 477, fn 277; Reynolds 2002). Such sites must have left a lasting impression on those processing around boundaries containing such marks and by this process the landscape was imbued with levels of meaning determined by a combination of knowledge regarding how the naming of individual marks came about and by contemporary cultural understanding of the significance of such names. Robert Bartlett's recent book on medieval conceptions of the natural and supernatural world prompts a reading of many of the situations he discusses in landscape terms (Bartlett 2008).

Can tenurial or social boundaries be identified without textual evidence? In the context of churchyards and the spatial division of church buildings, the answer is yes; with regard to territorial divisions in the wider landscape, the matter is more complicated, but, for example, in the Pewsey Vale many parish boundaries, certain of which are recorded in pre-Conquest charters, have a distinctive character. These latter boundaries are long and sinuous, they often exhibit short stretches of zigzag or step-like turns where they track around the limits of long ploughed out 'celtic' fields, and they selectively preserve earthworks of various kinds along their length. All of these features are absent from the internal field boundaries of the estates in question and thus it is possible in this case to model a truly archaeological characterization of boundaries of local tenurial significance.

Matthew Johnson (2007, 98) notes how boundaries 'condition and classify the documentary record'. For Johnson, the importance of boundary structures is not how 'scholars have engaged in complex and tortured arguments' about their antiquity, but the apparent certainty that 'many political and territorial boundaries have their origins in the Roman period' and that these boundaries 'often came to define civil and ecclesiastical administration, as well as the identity and self-perception of modern communities'. It must be said that it is by no means clear that Roman origins lay behind boundary structures, and that 'tortured arguments' are very necessary if we are to understand the circumstances by which human communities became bound by ideological, physical and legal structures as expressed in the range of contexts of delineation evident from the level of the household up to that of the kingdom: a process which can, and has, been observed through a series of readings of evidence from the purely archaeological to the interdisciplinary.

While understanding Johnson's weariness of intense debate, often revolving around well-trodden case studies literally at a parochial level, it is only when such detailed work is combined with wider anthropological readings of landscape that genuine advances in understanding of human behaviour through its expression in the physicality of landscape can be had. Close attention to the origins of the division of social space within the context of settlements, for example, reveals that the process begins in the late 6th century (Reynolds 2003), and thus prior to the influence of the Christian Church and its effects on modes of recording land-transactions and divisions, but also well before the period of the introduction of feudalism as a mode of social organization as traditionally understood.

Tom Saunders, following a revision of approach to concepts of feudalism by Susan Reynolds, suggests that its origins lie in the institution of lordship found in the written record from the 7th century. He concludes that its development can be observed in the changing nature of settlement space throughout the Anglo-Saxon period (Reynolds 1994, 2; Saunders 2000, 216–221). Saunders argues that the nucleated villages of the late Anglo-Saxon period and after also formed as a result of lordly action, and he cites Raunds and nearby West Cotton as case studies framed within a Marxist perspective (Saunders 2000, 218–223). Saunders's contention that the ordering of society according to Marxist principles can be read in the physical layout of Raunds and West Cotton is convincing and he provides a largely credible example of a link between evidence and explicit theoretical approach. Saunders also makes reference to Goltho, another 'classic' manorial site which he uses to bolster his case for placing feudal relationships at the core of nucleated settlement development. A careful reading of Goltho's archaeological sequence, however, reveals the existence of a large rectilinear settlement prior to the construction of the manorial complex (Reynolds 2003) (Figure 20.7). While Goltho may be a 'classic' manorial site, other explanatory frameworks must be sought for the origin of the planned mid- to late Anglo-Saxon settlement that precedes it (Reynolds forthcoming). It is worth making the point, however, that the search for a mono-causal explanation for the origins of the English village must now be abandoned. A refreshing debate indicating a change

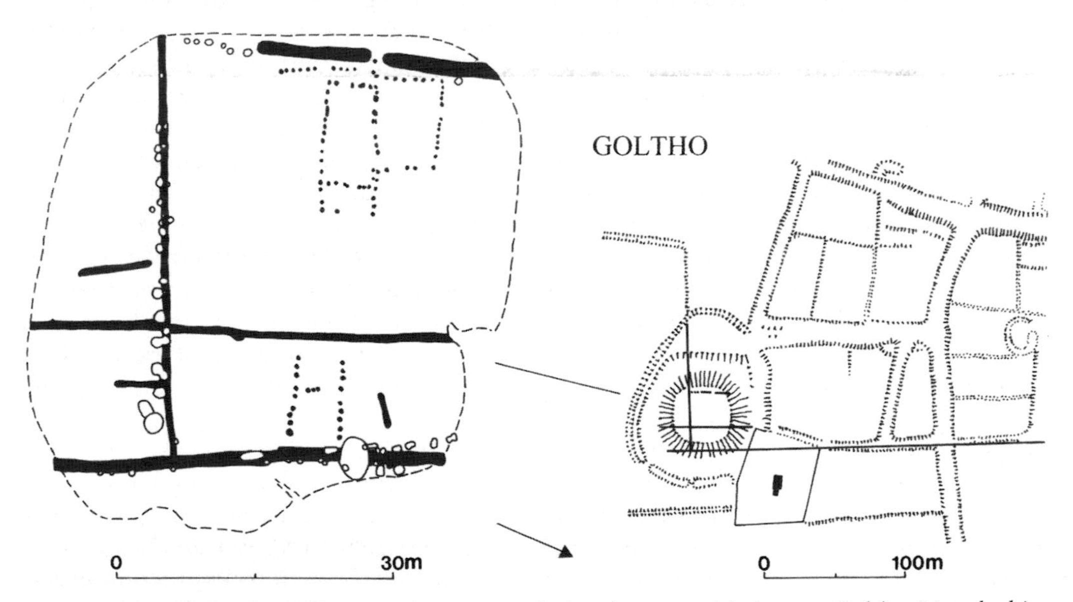

FIGURE 20.7 Planned rectilinear settlement pre-dating the manorial phase at Goltho, Lincolnshire (after Reynolds 2003).

of approach can be found in the recent synthesis of the results of the Whittlewood project (Jones and Page 2006).

Within archaeological debate, then, it is necessary to negotiate a path between empirical evidence, of which a careful high-definition reading is required, and theoretical approach.

DISCUSSION

The archaeology of judicial practice, travel and boundedness, in the terms in which they are considered above, are not found in museums, they feature only rarely in mainstream archaeological discourse as topics worthy of discussion and yet all three structured the meaning of early medieval landscapes from the level of momentary experience to that of the lifecycle. In a paper of this length it is only possible to present something of a rag-bag of examples, but what emerges is a series of themes that can be investigated in a wide range of situations. Plurality of experience is a key factor in engaging with landscape. Introducing concepts such as time and motion, fear and dread, familiar and exotic, political and religious, age and gender into landscape studies should ensure that the boundaries of current approaches are pushed forward to engage with a rehumanizing of the environment. Medieval archaeology can only really advance if it makes the most of the truly remarkable range of contexts and materials available to it and with a regard for intellectual problems relating to the development of human societies at a much broader level than is currently the case.

My point, then, has been to argue for a far more integrated study of medieval archaeology, where scholars are encouraged to engage with source materials beyond their traditional remit. While it is difficult enough for scholars to keep abreast of work in their respective fields, it is clear that conferences alone rarely engender genuine exchanges of approach. Moreover, unlike the medical sciences where the work of others must be acknowledged, it is a commonplace in the humanities for entire bodies of work key to a specific field to be simply ignored. Academic interchange is far better achieved via focused workshops, colloquia and field-based research projects where researchers with expertise in different fields gather to address common issues.

One area where methodological advance is crucial is in the explicit application of theory. While this if often done for the sake of it in PhD theses, to cause a fuss at TAG, or to justify reinventing the wheel, at the heart of the matter lies the point of it all. We can all go on attempting to model societal developments in various contexts nationally by applying the findings of individual excavations or even regional 'landscape' projects in blanket fashion, but project after project, especially in 'landscape archaeology' reveals the differences in human reactions to landscape not only from region to region but between and within individual settlements and communities. Rather than establishing the limit of what medieval archaeology can tell us, this situation instead identifies where anthropology steps in and where the cultural signatures of individual situations, be they subtle or overt, may be comparatively modelled within a framework of the broader understanding of the behaviour of human societies.

My hope is that medieval archaeology can grow up a little and that it will become a common-place for future generations to work comfortably with a wide range of source materials, seeking appropriate guidance and collaboration where required. The 'New Processualism' engendered by the rise of technology in methods of the capture of field data and its subsequent processing by increasingly powerful computational and mathematical modelling is tempered by the parallel development of a highly theorized critical literature (Wheatley and Gillings 2002; Conolly and Lake 2005), and in this way the contemporary advancement of methods and techniques is quite unlike that of previous generations, at least prior to the emergence of 'Old Processualism'. Methodological advance and the breaking down of disciplinary boundaries is the key to the future success of medieval archaeology.

In many ways, all who practise medieval archaeology, in whatever form, need to take a big step back from their particular field, ask why they are pursuing it, and think long and hard about the point of it all with regard to understanding the pattern and purpose of human action in long-term comparative perspective.

ACKNOWLEDGEMENTS

I am grateful to Stuart Brookes, Roberta Gilchrist and Sarah Semple for their helpful comments on earlier versions of this paper.

BIBLIOGRAPHY

Alcock, L and Austin, D (eds), 1990 *From the Baltic to the Black Sea: Studies in Medieval Archaeology*, Routledge, London

Allison, J, 1999 'Self-determination in cultural resource management: indigenous peoples' interpretation of history and of places and landscapes', in Ucko and Layton (eds) 1999, 264–283

Andrén, A, Jennbert, K and Raudvere, C (eds), 2006 *Old Norse Religion in Long-term Perspectives: Origins, Changes and Interactions*, Nordic Academic Press, Lund

Arnold, C, 1982 'Stress as a factor in social and economic change', in A C Renfrew and S Shennan (eds), *Ranking, Resource and Exchange*, 124–131, Cambridge University Press, Cambridge

Arnold, C, 1988 *An Archaeology of the Early Anglo-Saxon Kingdoms*, Routledge, London

Astill, G, 1991 'Towns and town hierarchies in Saxon England', *Oxford Journal of Archaeology* 10, 95–117

Astill, G, 1994 'Archaeological theory and the origins of English towns — a review', *Archaeologia Polona* 32, 27–71

Aston, M, 1986 'Post-Roman central places in Somerset', in E Grant (ed), *Central Places, Archaeology and History*, 49–77, University of Sheffield, Sheffield

Ausenda, G (ed), 1995 *After Empire: Towards an Ethnology of Europe's Barbarians*, The Boydell Press, Woodbridge

Austin, D, 1989 'The excavation of dispersed settlements in medieval Britain', in M Aston, D Austin and C Dyer (eds), *The Rural Settlements of Medieval England*, 231–246, Basil Blackwell, Oxford

Baker, J and Brookes, S, in prep *Beyond the Burghal Hidage: Anglo-Saxon Civil Defence in the Viking Age*

Bakhtin, M M (ed and trans C Emerson), 1984 *Problems of Dostoevsky's Poetics*, University of Minnesota Press, Minneapolis

Bartlett, R, 2008 *The Natural and the Supernatural in the Middle Ages*, Cambridge University Press, Cambridge

Bell, R D and Beresford, M W (eds), 1987 *Wharram: A Study of Settlement on the Yorkshire Wolds, 3: Wharram Percy: The Church of St Martin*, Society for Medieval Archaeology Monograph 11, London

Bintliff, J (ed), 1991 *The Annales School and Archaeology*, Leicester University Press, Leicester

Blair, J, 1995 'Ecclesiastical organisation and pastoral care in Anglo-Saxon England', *Early Medieval Europe* 4, 193–212

Blair, J, 2005 *The Church in Anglo-Saxon Society*, Oxford University Press, Oxford

Boddington, A, 1990 'Models of burial, settlement and worship: the final phase reviewed', in E Southworth (ed), *Anglo-Saxon Cemeteries, A Reappraisal*, 177–199, Alan Sutton Publishing, Stroud

Boddington, A, 1996 *Raunds Furnells: The Anglo-Saxon Church and Churchyard*, English Heritage, London

Glass, H, Garwood, P, Champion, T, Booth, P, Reynolds, A and Munby, J, 2009 *Tracks Through Time: The Archaeology of the Channel Tunnel Rail Link*, Oxford Archaeology, Oxford

Bradley, R, 1980 'Anglo-Saxon cemeteries: some suggestions for research', in P Rahtz, T Dickinson and L Watts (eds), *Anglo-Saxon Cemeteries 1979*, 171–178, British Archaeological Reports 82, Oxford

Bradley, R, 1987 'Time regained: the creation of continuity', *Journal of the British Archaeological Association* 140, 1–17

Bradley, R, 1993 *Altering the Earth*, Society of Antiquaries of Scotland, Edinburgh

Bradley, R, 2006 'Can archaeologists study prehistoric cosmology?', in Andrén *et al* (eds) 2006, 16–20

Brookes, S, 2007 *Economics and Social Change in Anglo-Saxon Kent* AD *400–900: Landscapes, Communities and Exchange*, British Archaeological Reports 431, Oxford

Cambridge, E and Rollason, D, 1995 'The pastoral organization of the Anglo-Saxon church: a review of the minster hypothesis', *Early Medieval Europe* 4, 87–104

Carver, M, 1986 'Contemporary artefacts illustrated in late Saxon manuscripts', *Archaeologia* 108, 117–145

Carver, M, 2002 'Marriages of true minds: archaeology with texts', in B Cunliffe, W Davies and C Renfrew (eds), *Archaeology: The Widening Debate*, 465–496, Oxford University Press, Oxford

Connolly, J and Lake, M, 2005 *Geographical Information Systems in Archaeology*, University Press Cambridge, Cambridge

Cooney, G, 1999 'Social landscapes in Irish prehistory', in Ucko and Layton (eds) 1999, 46–64

Crawford, O G S, 1928 *Wessex from the Air*, Clarendon Press, Oxford

Crawford, O G S, 1953 *Archaeology in the Field*, Phoenix House, London

Davies, W, 1988 *Small Worlds. The Village Community in Early Medieval Brittany*, Duckworth, London

Dawson, P, Levy, R, Gardner, D and Walls, M, 2007 'Simulating the behaviour of light inside Arctic dwellings: implications for assessing the role of vision in task performance', *World Archaeology* 39:1, 17–35

de Jong, M and Theuws, F (eds), 2001 *Topographies of Power in the Early Middle Ages*, Brill, Leiden/Boston/Cologne

Driscoll, S and Nieke, M (eds), 1988 *Power and Politics in Early Medieval Britain and Ireland*, Edinburgh University Press, Edinburgh

Duffy, E, 1992 *The Stripping of the Altars: Traditional Religion in England, c.1400–c.1580*, Yale University Press, New Haven/London

Duffy, E, 2006 *Marking the Hours: English People and their Prayers 1240–1570*, Yale University Press, New Haven/London

Earle, T, 1997 *How Chiefs Come to Power*, Stanford University Press, Stanford

Finch, J, 2000 *Church Monuments in Norfolk before 1850: an Archaeology of Commemoration*, British Archaeological Reports 317, Oxford

Fitzjohn, M, 2007 'Viewing places: GIS applications for examining the perception of space in the mountains of Sicily', *World Archaeology* 39:1, 36–50

Fitzpatrick, A, 2002a 'The Amesbury Archer: "King of Stonehenge"', *Past* 41, 1

Fitzpatrick, A, 2002b '"The Amesbury Archer": a well-furnished Early Bronze Age burial in southern England', *Antiquity* 76, 629–630

Fowler, P J (ed), 1972 *Archaeology and the Landscape: Essays for L. V. Grinsell*, John Baker, London

Fowler, P J (ed), 1975 *Recent Work in Rural Archaeology*, Moonraker Press, Bradford-on-Avon

Fox, C, 1955 *Offa's Dyke: A Field Survey of the Western Frontier-Works of Mercia in the Seventh and Eighth Centuries a.d.*, Oxford University Press, London

Geary, P, 1994 *Phantoms of Remembrance: Memory and Oblivion at the End of the First Millennium*, Princeton University Press, Princeton

Gilchrist, R, 1994 *Gender and Material Culture. The Archaeology of Religious Women*, Routledge, London

Gilchrist, R, 1995 *Contemplation and Action: The Other Monasticism*, Leicester University Press, London

Gilchrist, R, 2004 'Archaeology and the life course: a time and age for gender', in Meskell and Preucel (eds) 2004, 142–160

Giles, K, 2000 *An Archaeology of Social Identity: Guildhalls in York, c.1350–1630*, British Archaeological Reports 315, Oxford

Gittos, H, 2002 'Creating the sacred: Anglo-Saxon rites for consecrating cemeteries', in S Lucy and A Reynolds (eds), *Burial in Early Medieval England and Wales*, 195–208, Society for Medieval Archaeology Monograph 17, London

Gover, J E B, Mawer, A and Stenton, F M, 1939 *The Place-Names of Wiltshire*, Cambridge University Press, Cambridge

Graves, C P, 2000 *The Form and Fabric of Belief: an Archaeology of the Lay Experience of Religion in Medieval Norfolk and Devon*, British Archaeological Reports 311, Oxford

Green, D H and Siegmund, F (eds), 2003 *The Continental Saxons: An Ethnographic Persepective*, The Boydell Press, Woodbridge

Greenwell, W, 1877 *British Barrows: A Record of the Examination of Sepulchral Mounds in Various Parts of England*, Clarendon Press, Oxford

Halliday, R, 1996 'Wayside graves and crossroad burials', *Proceedings of the Cambridge Antiquarian Society* 84, 113–119

Hamerow, H, 2002 *Early Medieval Settlements: The Archaeology of Rural Communities in North-West Europe 400–900*, Oxford University Press, Oxford

Hamerow, H, 2006 '"Special deposits" in Anglo-Saxon settlements', *Medieval Archaeology* 50, 1–30

Harte, J, 2002 'Rethinking rogationtide', *Third Stone* 42, 29–35

Hayman, G and Reynolds, A, 2005 'A Saxon and Saxo-Norman execution cemetery at 42–54 London Road, Staines', *Archaeological Journal* 162, 115–157

Hedeager, L, 2001 'Asgard reconstructed? Gudme — a "central place" in the north', in de Jong and Theuws (eds) 2001, 467–507

Hill, D, 1981 *An Atlas of Anglo-Saxon England*, Basil Blackwell, Oxford

Hill, D and Sharpe, S, 1996 'An Anglo-Saxon beacon system', in A Rumble and D Mills (eds), *Names, Places and People: An Onomastic Miscellany in Memory of John McNeal Dodgson*, 157–165, Paul Watkins, Stamford

Hills, C M, 2007 'History and archaeology: the state of play in early medieval Europe', *Antiquity* 81, 191–200

Hinks, R, 1935 *Carolingian Art*, Sidgwick and Jackson, London

Hodges, R, 1982a *Dark Age Economics*, Duckworth, Stroud

Hodges, R, 1982b 'Method and theory in medieval archaeology', *Archaeologia Medievale* 8, 7–38

Howe, N, 2008 *Writing the Map of Anglo-Saxon England*, Yale University Press, New Haven and London

Hutton, R, 1996 *The Stations of the Sun*, Oxford University Press, Oxford

Johnson, M, 1993 *Housing Culture. Traditional Architecture in an English Landscape*, Smithsonian Institute Press, Washington DC

Johnson, M, 2007 *Ideas of Landscape*, Blackwell Publishing Ltd, Oxford

Jones, R and Page, M, 2006 *Medieval Villages in an English Landscape*, Windgather, Macclesfield

Joyce, R, 2002 *The Languages of Archaeology*, Blackwell Publishing, Oxford/Malden MA

Joyce, R, 2004 'Embodied subjectivity: gender, femininity, masculinity, sexuality', in Meskell and Preucel (eds) 2004, 82–95

Lopiparo, J, 2002 'A second voice: *crafting cosmos*', in Joyce 2002, 68–89

Lucas, G, 2005 *The Archaeology of Time*, Routledge, Abingdon

Lucy, S, 1998 *The Early Anglo-Saxon Cemeteries of East Yorkshire*, British Archaeological Reports 272, Oxford

Mays, S, Harding, C and Heighway, C, 2007 *Wharram: A Study of Settlement on the Yorkshire Wolds, 11: The Churchyard*, York University Archaeological Publications, York

Meskell, L and Preucel, R W (eds), 2004 *A Companion to Social Archaeology*, Blackwell Publishing, Oxford/Malden/Victoria

Moreland, J, 2006 'Archaeology and texts: subservience or enlightenment', *Annual Review of Anthropology* 35, 135–228

Noel, W, 1995 *The Harley Psalter*, Cambridge University Press, Cambridge

Ohler, N (trans C Hillier), 1989 *The Medieval Traveller*, The Boydell Press, Woodbridge

Peterson, R, 2003 'William Stukeley: an eighteenth-century phenomenologist?', *Antiquity* 77, 394–400

Pitt Rivers, Lieut Gen, 1887–98 *Excavations in Cranborne Chase*, 4 vols, privately printed

Pollard, J and Reynolds, A, 2002 *Avebury: The Biography of a Landscape*, Tempus, Stroud and Charleston SC

Reynolds, A, 1999 *Later Anglo-Saxon England: Life and Landscape*, Tempus, Stroud and Charleston SC

Reynolds, A, 2002 'Burials, boundaries and charters in Anglo-Saxon England: a reassessment', in S Lucy and A Reynolds (eds), *Burial in Early Medieval England and Wales*, 171–194, Society for Medieval Archaeology Monograph 17, London

Reynolds, A, 2003 'Boundaries and settlements in later sixth to eleventh century England', in D Griffiths, A Reynolds and S Semple (eds), *Boundaries in Early Medieval Britain*, 98–136, Anglo-Saxon Studies in Archaeology and History 12, Oxford

Reynolds, A, 2008 'The emergence of Anglo-Saxon judicial practice: the message of the gallows', *Anglo-Saxon* 2, 1–52

Reynolds, A, 2009 *Anglo-Saxon Deviant Burial Customs*, Oxford University Press, Oxford

Reynolds, A, forthcoming 'Debating scale and scale change in the English landscape: five case studies from the late Roman period into the Middle Ages', in J Escalona and A Reynolds (eds), *Scale and Scale Change in Early Medieval Western Europe*, Brepols, Turnhout

Reynolds, A and Langlands, A, 2006 'An early medieval frontier: a maximum view of Wansdyke', in W Davies, G Halsall and A Reynolds (eds), *People and Space in Early Medieval Europe, AD300–1300*, 13–42, Brepols, Turnhout

Reynolds, S, 1994 *Fiefs and Vassals: The Medieval Evidence Reinterpreted*, Clarendon Press, Oxford

Rodman, M C, 1992 'Empowering place: multilocality and multivocality', *American Anthropologist* 94, 640–656

Rosenwein, B, 1999 *Negotiating Space*, Cornell University Press, Ithaca

Saunders, T, 1990 'The feudal construction of space: power and domination in the nucleated village', in R Samson (ed), *The Social Archaeology of Houses*, 181–196, Cruithne, Glasgow

Saunders, T, 2000 'Class, space and "feudal" identities in early medieval England', in W O Frazer and A Tyrell (eds), *Social Identity in Early Medieval Britain*, 209–232, Leicester University Press, London and New York

Saunders, T, 2001 'Early medieval emporia and the tributary social function', in D Hill and R Cowie (eds), *Wics: The Early Medieval Trading Centres of Northern Europe*, 7–13, Sheffield Academic Press, Sheffield

Scull, C, 1992 'Before Sutton Hoo: structures of power and society in early East Anglia', in M Carver (ed), *The Age of Sutton Hoo*, 3–23, The Boydell Press, Woodbridge

Scull, C, 1993 'Archaeology, early Anglo-Saxon society and the origins of Anglo-Saxon kingdoms', *Anglo-Saxon Studies in Archaeology and History* 6, 65–82

Semple, S, 1998 'A fear of the past: the place of the prehistoric burial mound in the ideology of middle and later Anglo-Saxon England', *World Archaeology* 30:1, 109–126

Semple, S, 2003 'Burials and political boundaries in the Avebury region, North Wiltshire', in D Griffiths, A Reynolds and S Semple (eds), *Boundaries in Early Medieval Britain*, 72–91, Anglo-Saxon Studies in Archaeology and History 12, Oxford

Semple, S, 2004 'Illustrations of damnation in late Anglo-Saxon manuscripts', *Anglo-Saxon England* 32, 231–245

Semple, S, 2007 'Defining the OE *hearg*: a preliminary archaeological and topographic examination of *hearg* place names and their hinterlands', *Early Medieval Europe* 15:4, 364–385

Strang, V, 1999 'Competing perceptions of landscape in Kowanyama, North Queensland', in Ucko and Layton (eds) 1999, 206–218

Ucko, P and Layton, R (eds), 1999 *The Archaeology and Anthropology of Landscape: Shaping Your Landscape*, Routledge, London/New York

Wheatley, D and Gillings, M, 2002 *Spatial Technology and Archaeology: The Archaeological Applications of GIS*, Taylor and Francis, London/New York

Williams, H, 1999 'Placing the Dead: Investigating the Location of Wealthy Barrow Burials in Seventh Century England', in M Rundkvist (ed), *Grave Matters: Eight Studies of Burial Data from the first millennium AD from Crimea, Scandinavia and England*, 57–86, British Archaeological Reports International Series 781, Oxford

Williams, H, 2006 *Death and Memory in Early Medieval Britain*, Cambridge University Press, Cambridge

Wood, I (ed), 1998 *Franks and Alamanni in the Merovingian Period: An Ethnographic Persepective*, The Boydell Press, Woodbridge

WEBSITE

www.english-heritage.org.uk/server/show/nav.1293 (accessed 5 November 2008)

CHAPTER 21
THE MEDIEVAL ARISTOCRACY AND THE SOCIAL USE OF SPACE

By MARTIN HANSSON

This article discusses how the medieval aristocracy used space and landscape as valuable assets in the struggle to maintain and reproduce lordship. The concept of medieval feudal space is discussed as part of the ongoing debate on the significance of castles as military objects or status symbols. Furthermore, this paper calls for a broader view in the study of aristocratic landscapes. Instead of focusing only on settlements belonging to the higher nobility, fortified and unfortified residences and landscapes of the lesser nobility are also considered.

INTRODUCTION

The purpose of this article is to discuss how one group in medieval society, the aristocracy, used space and landscape to strengthen their position. The term aristocracy is used here in a broad sense to include members of the higher as well as lesser nobility.

There is a vast scholarly literature in archaeology and anthropology exploring how people used and created landscapes on several different levels, from purely economic to cognitive (Bender 1993; Ingold 1993; Knapp and Ashmore 1999). These studies have ranged from considering the landscape as a whole down to single settlements and monuments (Aston 1985; Samson 1990; Welinder 1992; Bradley 1993; Parker Pearson and Richards 1994; Tilley 1994). Common to these studies is an emphasis on the social importance of the landscape and the notion that space and its meanings are actively produced and reproduced by individuals. Since space and its meanings are created, space itself can become a medium for actors, individuals or a group, to emphasize and strengthen their own positions in society. Space therefore reflects power structures (Tilley 1994, 11). The archaeological concept of space that has evolved during recent decades is different from the concept of space within the natural sciences, where space is seen as a measure of objective attributes, such as area, shape, direction and distance. This concept of space does not consider that the experience of both time and space are culturally specific (Gosden 1994, 1; Altenberg 2003, 22).

Pre-modern concepts of visuality and space were arguably different from contemporary concepts. If that was the case, it questions the validity of many of the interpretations of spatial meaning that are made by archaeologist today. Such questions and their archaeological implications have been discussed by Kate Giles (Giles 2007). For the Middle Ages, 'seeing' was a form of perception that gave the beholder a sense of touching the object of vision. Seeing was a more embodied experience than it is today. In the same way, classical authors like Aristotle perceived space as an immobile container for human action. It was not until the late 14th century and after that the idea of space as something infinite and abstract emerged. The idea of space as a container for people, groups and objects gradually gave way to more modern notions of space as something that exists between people, groups and objects (Giles 2007, 107 and cited literature). Giles's discussion has been widened by Pamela Graves who questions how deeply into different strata of society medieval perceptions of space actually permeated (Graves 2007, 516). Did noblemen, priests and peasants have the same spatial understanding?

Acknowledging that the Middle Ages had different concepts of seeing and of space complicates our interpretation of medieval space, and questions the methods we use. Kate Giles argues that the methods often used for analysing space, for example the access analyses of Hillier and Hanson (1984), do not take the historicity of the concepts of space and seeing into consideration (Giles 2007, 109). Today, the view that space and landscape are objective and measurable dominates. Producing plans and maps, such as surveys of landscape elements, is a common archaeological method used to analyse archaeological problems. Plans and maps are thus used as a means to describe and analyse a historical context that itself very rarely used maps in this way, nor understood or perceived space in plan and map form (see Johnson 2007).

There is no simple solution to the problems of studying time and space in earlier societies. Karin Altenberg has stated that rather than regarding space as a factor that can be measured or quantified, or as a mirror passively reflecting human behaviour, we must consider the way in which space can be perceived by the people inhabiting a place. Accordingly, we should try to interpret the social meanings of specific contexts to be able to understand how and why people acted as they did (Altenberg 2003, 25). It is important to recognize that different strata of medieval society probably had various perceptions of space. A contextual analysis of the society in question is thus needed to cover the distance between now and then, while at the same time maintaining a critical eye on theory and method.

According to Harald Kleinschmidt, space during the Middle Ages was regarded as heterogeneous, qualitatively different and limited. Kleinschmidt recognizes that the spatial concept was tripartite: the space of daily experience, the space of regular communications, and the world. The space of daily experience is that where an individual or group performs daily activities. It should also be seen as a private space, a house, a room, a farm, where it was possible to have privacy. The space of daily experience is demarcated by boundaries, where trespass was a breach of the peace. Outside the space of daily experience, space can either be characterized as the space of daily experience of another individual or group, or as the space of regular communications, where one meets and interacts with friends, aliens or enemies. This is therefore a much more public space than the space of daily experience, since it is not owned by anyone in particular, despite being used by everyone. This type of public space was governed by the ruler, the lord, and its boundaries are normally invisible and very often defined as various administrative spaces. Both these types of spaces are related to action by individuals or groups, meaning that persons can know these spaces through their own experience. The third type of space, the world, was perceived as the universal terrestrial space, which could not be experienced by the individual, except from a theoretical point of view (Kleinschmidt 2000, 33).

FEUDAL SPACE

When discussing medieval space feudalism must be considered. Certain scholars argue that spatial relations were the basis for feudal society (Dodgshon 1987; Saunders 1990; 2000). The feudal system can be said to have made it easier for lords to control agrarian society by granting land in exchange for military service. Integrated in these grants of land were royal supremacy and jurisdiction (Bloch 1967; Brunner 1992). The classic feudal structure — with its intricate weave of monarchs, vassals and undervassals, all with hereditary fiefs and strong control over their villeins — developed in northern France and existed only in small parts of western Europe. In other areas similar circumstances prevailed, but here the feudal system appeared in many versions. Different varieties of feudalism have been identified for western and eastern Europe and Scandinavia (Gurevich 1979; Anderson 1974). Susan Reynolds has reassessed the concept of feudalism and argued that our image of feudalism is actually the result of studies of post-medieval sources and circumstances. According to Reynolds, the idea of medieval feudalism was developed during the 18th and 19th centuries (Reynolds 1994).

The concept of feudalism is nevertheless useful for characterizing the society that developed in western and northern Europe from the 10th century onwards. Feudal society can be defined in general terms as an agrarian society where power was based on the control of land and where certain groups were granted privileges and land in exchange for service. These privileges made it possible for certain groups, notably the kings, the Church and the aristocracy, to confiscate parts of the peasants' production, as taxation, tithes or rent (Hansson 2006, 33).

The feudal state was deeply integrated in the landscape, and can be defined by its use and definition of the landscape as a regulated space (Dodgshon 1987). The feudal system is as much a question of spatial as social relations; it is a system where specific territories were connected to specific rights and dues in the feudal hierarchy. On a macro-level this facilitated the spatial integration and administration of the state; on a micro-level, it was a way of confirming the spatial relations between lord and peasant. On this level space became a regulated, defined social space that determined the amount of rent, the number of days' labour and other dues that were connected with a specific space. The whole landscape was divided into a hierarchy of regulated social spaces, from the king's grant of a county to a baron, to the single lord's organization of manor and village (Dodgshon 1987, 185, Saunders 1990). The feudal lords' creation of planned, nucleated settlements dominated by the manor and the manorial church contributed to the formation of the feudal aristocracy. The social relationship between lord and peasant became constituted within bounded space (Saunders 2000, 221). This integration in the landscape also meant that feudal society had a firm local power base. Most social relationships were extremely localized and focused on one or several power centres in the landscape: the village, the manor, the monastery, the castle, the town and so on (Mann 1986, 376).

The territorialization of lordship and a feudal society based on different areas of regulated space also led to a hierarchy of spaces. Churches were, for example, God's house, which inevitably gave the church a certain social importance in the landscape. Different social spaces also existed inside the church, with the parishioners assembled in the nave, the lord in its western part and the priest performing the service partly secluded in the chancel. Similar different social spaces were present in monasteries, where most parts were closed to visitors, others only accessible for the monks and closed to the lay brothers (Gilchrist 1994; 1999, 83). Just as the internal space inside the church was divided into different social spaces, the same division and hierarchy of spaces can also be found in the landscape. A typical example is Castle Rising in Norfolk (Liddiard 2000, 53). Here we can find the aristocratic milieu inside the castle with its park, the tenants in the village, and the religious space in the priory.

THE DISCOVERY OF 'DESIGNED LANDSCAPES'

Since the 1980s a more social view has emerged of the castle and its importance in society and in the landscape. One of the first to acknowledge this was David Austin, who stressed the significance of the castle as a centre for military, administrative, social and symbolic power, and rejected the prevailing view of castles as isolated monuments in the landscape. Castles were instead just one of several elements in a complex web of social and economic relationships aimed at organizing the use of the landscape and its resources. Austin's extensive work at Barnard castle in northern England stands out as a model of how a single castle can be studied in a wider context (Austin 1984; 1998; 2007). The importance of the castle in the landscape has also been studied by Oliver Creighton, who has shown how the castle influenced settlements and landscape (Creighton 2002). So far this landscape approach to castles seems to have been mainly an English approach, although continental examples also can be found (de Waha 1986; Bult 1987; Hansson 2001; Nordin 2005).

The landscape approach to castles has led to one of the most interesting discoveries within British medieval archaeology during the last two decades: the recognition of so-called designed or ornamental landscapes surrounding castles. The existence of deer parks, orchards and gardens at castles have long been known in written sources, but not until recently have these features been identified and traced in the landscape. Thanks to extensive and careful fieldwork by the Royal Commission for Historical Monuments in England, a large number of designed landscapes consisting of gardens, deer parks, fishponds and artificially created lakes have been discovered. The landscape surrounding the castle was the place where much of aristocratic life took place: courtly love in the garden, hunting in the park, processional routes approaching the castle, tournaments and jousts, and so on. It was visible evidence of the power of the lord, showing contemporary visitors that he truly belonged to the aristocracy. Together with the castle itself, these surroundings were intended to impress visitors and create an aristocratic setting (Everson 1996a; 1996b; 1998; Everson and Williamson 1998; Liddiard 2000; Taylor 2000; Johnson 2002, 19; Creighton 2002, 72).

Among the best-known British examples of medieval ornamental landscapes are those at Bodiam Castle in East Sussex (Figure 21.1) and at Kenilworth Castle in Warwickshire. At both these places it has been possible to identify remains of gardens, processional walks and viewing platforms, but what has been most striking has been the importance of water and the substantial amount of labour required to create artificial lakes. Matthew Johnson has talked about the significance of 'watery landscapes' in aristocratic milieus, as an attempt by the aristocracy to make their social display look like a natural part of the landscape, and thereby timeless, and under no circumstances to be questioned (Johnson 2002, 53).

So far the discussion of medieval designed landscapes has mainly been a concern of English scholars, but there can be no doubt that the same type of landscapes also existed in other parts of Europe. A study by Anders Andrén has shown the presence of deer parks in medieval Denmark and that this phenomenon was probably much

FIGURE 21.1 Bodiam Castle, Sir Edward Dallyngrigge's late 14th-century castle is an excellent example of an individual putting his stamp on the landscape. It is also a castle in the centre of a scholarly debate. (Photograph: M Hansson)

more common than has previously been thought (Andrén 1997). Attempts have also been made to reconstruct designed landscapes surrounding Swedish residences (Hansson 2006, 156).

The discussion regarding designed landscapes and the social meanings of the castle has been closely connected to a major and ongoing discussion regarding how we should interpret castles. Castles have formed an important subject for historical, art-historical and archaeological research since the 19th century. During most of this period castle studies were usually concentrated on single sites: the origin of the individual castle, its different phases and dating and the castle's place and importance in the political process. At the same time, castle studies were mainly concerned with seeing the castle as a military structure. The scholarly view of the castle as a military object and the concentration on studying single settlements, especially larger castles built in stone that could be connected to kings and the higher nobility, is found all over Europe (Thompson 1987; 1991; Stocker 1992; Liddiard 2000; Mogren 1995). In the last 20 years, however, a broader view of the castle has emerged. Castles have started to be seen as symbols of power, whose military impression to a viewer has more to do with symbolism than actual military strength. Studies have also shown that careful planning and design were behind the layout and display of castles (Fairclough 1992; Andersson 1997; Dixon 1998). The castle's importance as a gendered space has also been studied and the castle has even been recognized as a theatre in a metaphorical sense (Dixon 1990; Gilchrist 1999, 109; Johnson 2002, 30).

In a series of often-quoted articles, Charles Coulson initiated the ongoing debate on the meaning of castles. Coulson emphasized the essential sociological functions of castles, often connected to the licence to crenellate that was given to a lord. These licences were used as a means of social expression and the crenellations that were actually built, according to Coulson, had little to do with actual military defence (Coulson 1979; 1982; see also 2003). Were castles mainly military objects built for war, or were they something else, symbols of aristocratic power? Central to this discussion has been Bodiam Castle in Sussex (Everson 1996a; 1996b; Johnson 2002, 19).

In his inspiring book *Behind the Castle Gate*, Matthew Johnson argues that the military view of castles is not wrong, but perhaps only part of the story. Many castles played important military roles, while others hardly ever saw military action (Johnson 2002, 4). Johnson argues that castles must be understood in their context and that there is no simple answer to the question of whether the castle was a military fortress or a social symbol. Castles were both, and much more. Johnson's analysis of Bodiam shows that the castle could be seen and understood in many ways; each visitor to Bodiam would have a different experience, according to their gender and social position (Johnson 2002, 29).

But Colin Platt has recently reasserted the interpretation of castles as profoundly military features. Castles were built for defence in periods of turmoil. Once again, Bodiam is at the centre of the debate, this time as an intrinsically military fortification built against French raiders, revolting peasants and hostile aristocratic enemies (Platt 2007). Platt criticizes several scholars for their lack of source criticism and for making unsubstantiated interpretations. According to Platt, archaeological theoreticians have prioritized the surviving buildings, while extant documents are neglected, which leads to misleading assumptions (Platt 2007, 98). Platt's article clearly highlights the differences in the two sides of this debate, a debate that perhaps to some extent is founded on different views of the value of material culture. Platt argues for a traditional archaeology dependent on written sources, while criticizing a more theoretically aware branch of medieval archaeology that relies on material culture and dares to question the value of documents.

Studies of designed landscapes have placed aristocratic culture within its landscape context. But this is only true for parts of the aristocracy, since most studies have concerned royal or baronial castles and landscapes. We lack studies regarding the spatial pattern and landscapes of the minor castles of the lesser nobility. Studies of designed landscapes often also lack a concrete connection between elements found in the landscape and a firm chronology (Creighton 2002, 83). Temporality in the landscape is neglected. The creation of designed landscapes was a process that needs to be taken into consideration. Another striking feature is that designed landscapes are often treated separately from the rest of the medieval landscape. There has been little connection between studies of how the aristocracy planned landscapes of production — villages, hamlets and fields — and the ornamental landscapes around their castles. To be able to reach a fuller understanding of how the aristocracy acted in space, these two sides of aristocratic planning and ordering of the landscape have to be integrated. Much of the debate concerning designed landscapes has neglected non-fortified residences. Focus is placed on the great castles, even if a mighty lord also had several non-fortified manors at his disposal. To study the aristocracy and the social use of space we must include other aristocratic places beside castles, from moated manor-houses to 'unfortified' manor-houses. A more holistic approach provides an alternative to the endless debate of whether castles are military forts or status symbols.

TOWARDS AN ARISTOCRATIC SPATIAL IDEOLOGY

One way forward could be to see how the aristocracy organized space and landscape on a European level. Is it possible to find any similarities in how aristocrats across western Europe organized the landscape around their residences and how they built their castles and residences? In a previous study of aristocratic residences in two different regions, I compared how residences in south Sweden and Norfolk were located in the landscape and their architectural layout (Hansson 2006). Despite the great differences in economy, social structure and so on between these two medieval societies, a significant number of common concepts or themes appear to have influenced how the aristocracy chose to organize space and landscape. Six themes were identified: War, History, Distance, Ordering, Religion, and Individuality.

War

One basic theme is connected to the nobleman's role as warrior. Being a mounted warrior was essential for a medieval aristocrat. This was the foundation for his existence and social position in society. The aristocracy were the 'bellatores', those who fought and protected society with divine sanction (Le Goff 1990, 255). Against this background it is not surprising to find martial elements in aristocratic landscapes and architecture. Moats and crenellated walls are as obvious in aristocratic architecture as warfare was in the life of the nobleman, regardless of whether the moat or crenellated wall in question had a military function. To maintain the position of the aristocracy in society, the presence of this type of military elements was crucial. Aristocratic residences with impressive military defences were built in the late Middle Ages, when the military role of the aristocracy on the battlefield was diminishing in comparison with mercenary foot soldiers and archers (Contamine 1989). To prevent this development from threatening the social position of the aristocracy, military elements were often promoted in aristocratic space and architecture in the late Middle Ages (Hansson 2006, 77). By acknowledging the profound martial dimension in the life of a nobleman, the discussion of whether castles are military or not becomes irrelevant. To some extent martial elements are almost always present at the place where an aristocrat resided.

History

Several studies have shown the importance of history and tradition for the formation of the aristocracy (Duby 1977; Crouch 2002). We also find an aristocratic predilection for places in the landscape that possessed an ancient connection to local lordship. Since the tradition and history of the place were intimately connected to lordship and dominion, this strengthened the dominion of the place in the present (Hansson 2006, 87). In Norfolk, the Normans chose to build new castles on the sites of previous Anglo-Saxon residences (Liddiard 2000). By connecting to old power structures, newly established lordship was strengthened (Creighton 2002, 70). The history of a place could come to determine the location, the duration and also the physical appearance of a residence (Hansson 2006, 100, 103).

Distance

It is evident that the aristocracy became more and more spatially isolated, both in the landscape and inside their residences. Through the architectural development of residences and castles, the nobleman and his family perpetuated increasingly more private rooms and halls, which facilitated private life on a different scale than previously (Blair 1993; Grenville 1997, 106; Hansson 2006, 121). In the landscape many residences moved from a position connected to a village and/or a church, to a much more isolated position. In other cases, evicting a nearby village created the isolated position. This process has often been connected to castle building and the need for a fortified residence, but it is more complex and should be connected to general social changes in medieval society. By isolating themselves in the landscape, in the residence, and in the church, the aristocracy became more unattainable, beyond the horizon of ordinary people. This both strengthened their social position and also worked as a means to prevent social change (Hansson 2006, 127).

Organizing

Several scholars have emphasized the role of the aristocracy in organizing the landscape from an economic and functional point of view, for example, by planning colonization and rearranging villages and fields (Taylor 1983; Saunders 2000). The last decade has also seen a number of studies that have focused on how the aristocracy organized a symbolic and aesthetically designed landscape surrounding their residences, as mentioned above. Studies of designed landscapes have very often concentrated exclusively on the symbolic landscape. But the functional and symbolic way of organizing the landscape should not be seen as opposites, rather as two sides of the same coin, both connected to aristocratic spatial ideology (Hansson 2006, 129). All over Europe there are examples of how the aristocracy to a greater or lesser degree, depending on local and regional circumstances, planned and organized landscapes, fields and villages. This impulse for planning had both economic-functional as well as symbolic grounds. In some cases, planning of the landscape could increase the income of a nobleman, but at the same time, rearranging the landscape was a clear expression of power, lordship and dominion over both people and nature.

Religion

A striking feature when studying aristocratic residences throughout Europe is the close spatial relationship between residence and church (Figure 21.2). There are many examples where the parish church is actually located in the courtyard of a residence. A religious dimension is almost always present in the spatial concept of the aristocracy. If a church is lacking from the vicinity of a residence, a minor chapel is often incorporated in the residence itself. Similar arrangements existed in almost all

FIGURE 21.2 Great Chalfield Manor with the church located on the partly moated platform of the residence. (Photograph: M Hansson)

castles across Europe. Regardless of economic and political status and power, the lord was always close to a place of worship (Hansson 2006, 161).

In a longer-term perspective, responsibility for religious affairs is something that was central to the concept of being lord. The lord was expected to fulfil the religious needs of the people (Sundqvist 2002). In this aspect, the connection between medieval lords and the church is a clear evolution from the time when religious cult took place inside the hall of the lord. Since churches started to be built, they have been closely linked to secular lords. It is actually possible to see the church as a specialized hall for religious purposes. In both the lordly hall and the church, space was divided into different social spheres, where access to specific areas depended on the social status of the individual. Apart from churches, the landscape surrounding aristocratic residences was filled with religious elements and institutions. Most obvious in this aspect were of course the family abbey, but also smaller features like dovecotes and gardens acted as religious symbols (Hansson 2006, 131, 170, 176).

Individuality

The Middle Ages witnessed the birth of individuality (Hansson 2006, 184). The aristocracy, as a means to strengthen the importance of their own family, promoted this individuality (Johnson 2000). By dressing in specific colours and using coats of arms it became very obvious for attendants at jousts and tournaments which nobleman was successful on the field. For the lesser nobility, the use of an aristocratic feature like the moat, was an efficient way to promote their personal position as belonging to the nobility. The moated sites so common over large parts of north-western Europe can be seen as remnants of the attempts and ambitions of single agents to establish themselves as noblemen. In this aspect the moat becomes a symbol for the owner's aristocratic ambitions. The fact that many moated sites never seem to have been in use at all, or only in use for a very short period of time, may suggest that they are remnants of the failed ambitions of single agents (Hansson 2006, 191).

Taken together, these six themes can be seen as an aristocratic spatial ideology, which was effected by individual agents. They chose where, how and when a residence was to be built or transformed and what type of aristocratic landscapes should be displayed. These agents also chose which aristocratic spatial themes they wanted to adjust: did they want to connect to perceived memory in the landscape, or did they want to emphasize their social position by distancing themselves in the landscape? There is a clear trend towards increasingly secluded residences where the aristocracy distanced themselves from the rest of society, starting in the 12th century in western Europe and in the 13th century in Scandinavia. But the many examples of medieval residences that remain integrated in villages, close to the church, show that many noblemen chose not to distance themselves in the landscape, but rather continued to emphasize the historical integration of the nobility in society. In both cases the nobleman adjusted to an overall aristocratic spatial ideology, but acted differently, perhaps due to different backgrounds and assumptions in economic and family history (Hansson 2006, 189). This discussion can be exemplified by two case studies, the first is situated in south-eastern Scania in medieval Denmark (modern Sweden), while the other can be found in Lincolnshire in England.

GLIMMINGEHUS

Glimmingehus is one example where several of the themes above can be found in both architecture and landscape (Figure 21.3). The castle was built by the knight Jens Holgersen Ulfstand, Lord High Admiral of Denmark and Provincial Governor of Gotland, a member of the higher aristocracy in Denmark (Ödman 1996; 1999; 2004). According to the inscription on a stone tablet over the entrance to the castle, Jens Holgersen laid the foundation stone to the castle in 1499. The castle replaced an earlier stone house that was demolished before the present house was built. It is a typical medieval castle on a platform demarcated by a moat, in a secluded position compared to the location of the medieval villages in the vicinity. The main building is a four-storey, rectangular stone building with thick walls with loopholes and tiny windows. The entrance and the internal staircase in the house are filled with defensive surprises for an intruding enemy, making it possible for the defenders to attack them at every floor level. Glimmingehus thus resembles a keep, where the defenders

FIGURE 21.3 Glimmingehus in Scania as it appears today. (Photograph: M Hansson)

theoretically could withdraw higher and higher up in the building while defending themselves (Olsen 1996, 111; Reisnert 1999).

Despite its highly developed internal defences, Glimmingehus is an old-fashioned castle for the late 15th century. The tall stone building was perhaps not suitable in a context where firearms were used, which was the case in Scandinavia at this time. Even more interesting is the fact that its likely architect, Adam van Düren from Westphalia, was also responsible for work on the cathedral in Lund at this time (Ödman 2004, 34). If he was the architect, he employed a style that did not correspond with his status as a modern Renaissance architect. Glimmingehus resembles a 14th-century castle more than a Renaissance palace of its time. It is evident that Glimmingehus was intentionally built to remind its owner and his noble visitors of their common chivalric past, when the knightly culture flourished, an interpretation further underscored by the reused stonework in the house (Figure 21.4). Almost all the stone sculpture and other figurative stone incorporated in windows and doors is of Gotlandic limestone. Many of the sculptures are also reused stones from the 13th and 14th centuries. Some of these worked stones could have come from a sacral milieu in churches, even if this cannot be established with certainty (Berggren 1999).

Glimmingehus in all its medieval glory is a place where the past is presented, not only in the building's architecture, but also in the reused sculptures inside the building. The whole planning and appearance of Glimmingehus, the martial defences and the reused stones, are more a reminder of the glorious chivalric culture of previous centuries. The castle was a statement about its founder, about an individual agent and his social context. Glimmingehus is thus a place where the themes of war, history and individuality are clearly present.

A close examination of the surrounding landscape shows that the castle was originally situated in a watery setting. In a 17th-century picture the residence is situated on an island in a lake. West of the residential platform was a separate platform called *Trädgårdsholmen*, 'Garden Islet'. Today, there are no visible traces of this former garden island and its date is unknown. Another remnant of the garden is perhaps the ornamented octagonal stone that today is mounted in a window niche. Originally the stone could have functioned as a top for a garden table (Hansson and Hansson 1997, 23). There are, however, remnants of a wall that originally made it possible to dam the water in the area and create a lake. A small-scale archaeological excavation has however dated this feature to the 17th century (Ödman 1999, 123), but the possibility cannot be excluded that the wall had an older predecessor. If that was the case, the watery setting of Glimmingehus was man-made and a Scandinavian version of the watery settings at Bodiam and Kenilworth Castles.

RAND

While Glimmingehus was a castle belonging to a person from the higher nobility, Rand in Lincolnshire, England, was a residence for noblemen of local importance from the late 12th to the middle of the 15th century. Thanks to the extensive field survey completed by the Royal Commission, an aristocratic landscape on a smaller

FIGURE 21.4 A late 13th-century doorway in the late 15th-century castle of Glimmingehus as an example of the reuse of history and the perpetuation of shared memory. (Photograph: Bengt Lundberg, Riksantikvarieämbetet)

scale can be traced (Everson *et al* 1991) (Figure 21.5). The manorial complex in Rand was situated in the north-western part of the medieval village, north-west of the church. The central part of the residence consists of a moated site with access from the centre of the south side, facing the village. South of the moat are four small fishponds. North-east of the moated residence is a long bank with an additional long mound at its south end and protected by a double hedgerow, perhaps a former rabbit warren. A linear ditch, parallel with the nearby stream, may have been a mill leat. South of the church is a large, circular embanked site with stone foundations, perhaps the site of the dovecote. The earthworks of the village hint at a planned origin for the settlement, with regular plots lying on either side of a hollow way running east–west (Everson *et al* 1991, 153).

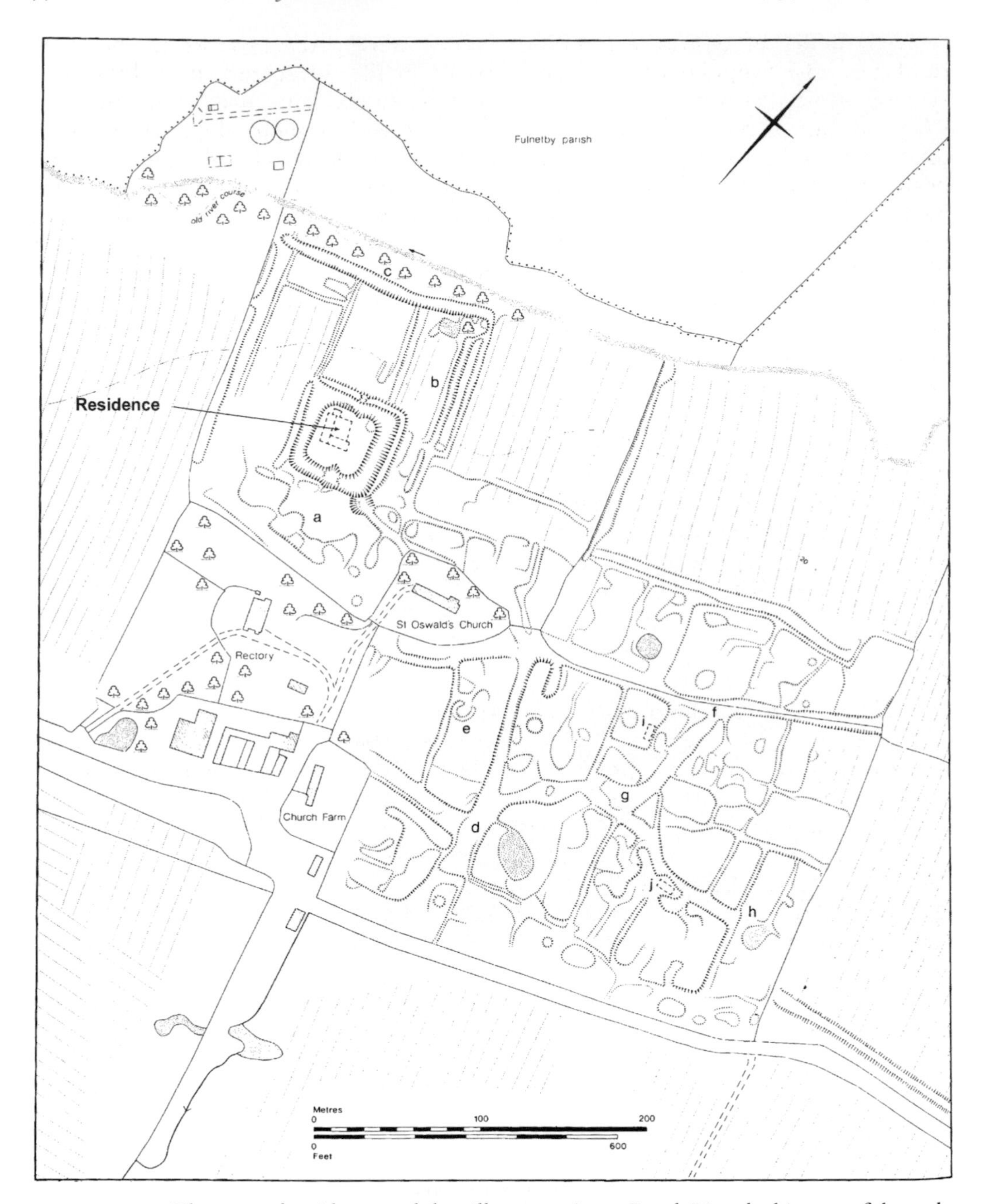

FIGURE 21.5 The moated residence and the village remains at Rand, Lincolnshire. a = fishpond, b = rabbit warren, c = mill leat, d = enclosure bank, e = dovecote (after Everson *et al* 1991, 154 fig 112). (Crown Copyright. NMR)

A number of typical aristocratic features were gathered close to the lordly residence. The fishponds, the rabbit warren and the dovecote can all be seen as symbols of an aristocratic life, just like the moated residence itself (Liddiard 2000, 58). The topography at Rand is rather flat, but with a slight slope to the north, towards a stream. Consequently, the residence is not in the usual visible and dominant position, but is lower than the village and the church. Against this topographical background, it is interesting to note that the dovecote was placed in the south-eastern part of the manorial enclosure, the part directly facing the village. The dovecote is likely to have been a fairly tall round, almost tower-like, stone building, distinctly visible and different from the buildings on the village plots. Placing the dovecote in a position where it had maximum visibility from the village was a clear symbolic act of manifesting the lordship of the village, a lordship that would otherwise have been less obvious, due to the somewhat secluded location of the residence on a slope. The lord of Rand thus used several aristocratic features to manifest his lordship and placed them in order to maximize their symbolic meaning.

As mentioned above, previous research has shown this type of designed landscape mainly connected to sites belonging to royalty or the upper nobility. But the example of Rand shows that designed landscapes on a smaller scale can also be found at residences belonging to the lesser nobility, and integrated with the landscape of production (Hansson 2006, 156).

CONCLUSION

There can be no doubt that the concept of space during the Middle Ages was embedded in social meanings. For the aristocracy space was a valuable asset in the struggle to maintain and reproduce lordship. The European aristocracy shared a common ideology about what it meant to be a nobleman and they used the landscape to strengthen their dominion. The ideology and the culture of the medieval European aristocracy can to some extent be equated with the chivalric culture that permeated the ruling classes during the Middle Ages. A nobleman balanced the role of the chivalric knight with the expectations of being a nobleman: by the way he dressed, behaved, acted, both in his daily routine and in exceptional circumstances (Duby 1977; Bengtsson 1999).

Another way to fulfil the aristocratic ideology was to recreate aristocratic culture in space and the landscape. By filling the space of daily routine with aristocratic elements, status was further underlined and could not be questioned. By controlling the landscape, the village and its people, the church and the priest, the aristocracy controlled the world.

BIBLIOGRAPHY

Altenberg, K, 2003 *Experiencing Landscapes. A Study of Space and Identity in Three Marginal Areas of Medieval Britain and Scandinavia*, Lund Studies in Medieval Archaeology 31, Almqvist & Wiksell International, Stockholm

Anderson, P, 1974 *Passages from Antiquity to Feudalism*, NLB, London

Andersson, H, Carelli, P and Ersgård, L (eds), 1997 *Visions of the Past: Trends and Traditions in Swedish Medieval Archaeology*, Lund Studies in Medieval Archaeology 19, Riksantikvarieämbetet, Arkeologiska undersökningar, Skrifter 24, Almqvist & Wiksell International, Stockholm

Andersson, A, 1997 'Spatial analysis in time: Hammershus Castle', in Andersson *et al* (eds), 1997, 645–670

Andrén, A, 1997 'Paradise Lost: Looking for Deer Parks in Medieval Denmark', in Andersson *et al* (eds), 1997, 469–490

Andrén, A, 1999 'Landscape and settlement as utopian space', in C Fabech and J Ringtved (eds), *Settlement and Landscape*, 383–393, Jutland Archaeological Society, Århus

Aston, M, 1985 *Interpreting the Landscape: Landscape Archaeology and Local History*, Batsford, London

Austin, D, 1984 'The castle and the landscape. Annual lecture to the Society of Landscape Studies, May 1984', *Landscape History* 6, 69–81

Austin, D, 1998 'Private and public. An archaeological consideration of things', in H Hundsbischler, G Jaritz and T Kühtreiber (eds), *Die Vielfalt der Dinge. Neue Wege zur Analyse mittelalterlicher Sachkultur*, 163–206, Verlag der Österr. Akademie der Wissenschaft, Wien

Austin, D, 2007 *Acts of Perception; Barnard Castle, Teesdale*, 2 vols, Architectural and Archaeological Society of Durham and Northumberland Monographs 6, Durham

Bender, B, 1993 'Landscape — meaning and action', in B Bender (ed), *Landscape Politics and Perspectives*, 1–17, Providence Berg, London

Bengtsson, H, 1999 *Den höviska kulturen i Norden: En konsthistorisk undersökning*, Kungl. Vitterhets Historie och Antikvitets Akademien. Stockholm.

Berggren, L, 1999 'Brottsplats Gotland', in *Glimmingehus 500 år: Tretton texter redigerade av Sten Åke Nilsson under medverkan av Annette Landen*, 59–66, Skånsk Senmedeltid och Renässans, Skrifter utgivna av Vetenskaps-Societeten i Lund 17, Lund University Press, Lund

Blair, J, 1993 'Hall and Chamber: English Domestic Planning 1000–1250', in G Meirion-Jones and M Jones (eds), *Manorial Domestic Buildings in England and Northern France*, 1–21, Occasional Papers, Society of Antiquaries of London 15, London

Bloch, M, 1967 *Feudal Society*. I–II *Social Classes and Political Organisation*, translated from the French by L A Manyon, foreword by M M Postan, 2nd edn, Routledge and Kegan Paul, London

Bradley, R, 1993 *Altering the Earth: The Origins of Monuments in Britain and Continental Europe*, Society of Antiquaries of Scotland, Edinburgh

Brunner, O, 1992 *Land and Lordship: Structures of Governance in Medieval Austria*, revd edn, University of Pennsylvania Press, Philadelphia

Bult, E J, 1987 'Moated sites in their economical and social context in Delfland', *Château Gaillard* 13, 21–39

Contamine, P, 1989 *War in the Middle Ages*, translated by Michael Jones, Basil Blackwell, Oxford

Coulson, C L H, 1979 'Structural symbolism in medieval castle architecture', *Journal of the British Archaeological Association* 132, 80–90

Coulson, C L H, 1982 'Hierarchism in conventual crenellation: an essay in the sociology and metaphysics of medieval fortification', *Medieval Archaeology* 26, 69–100

Coulson, C L H, 2003 *Castles in Medieval Society: Fortresses in England, France and Ireland in the Central Middle Ages*, Oxford University Press, Oxford

Creighton, O H, 2002 *Castles and Landscape*, Continuum, London

Crouch, D, 2002 'The historian, lineage and heraldry 1050–1250', in P Coss and M Keen (eds), *Heraldry, Pageantry and Social Display in Medieval England*, 17–37, The Boydell Press, Woodbridge

Dixon, P, 1990 'The donjon of Knaresborough: the castle as theatre', *Château Gaillard* 14, 121–139
Dixon, P, 1998 'Design in castle-building: the controlling of access to the lord', *Château Gaillard* 18, 47–57
Dodgshon, R, 1987 *The European Past: Social Evolution and Spatial Order*, Macmillan Education, Basingstoke
Duby, G, 1977 *The Chivalrous Society*, Edward Arnold, Berkeley and Los Angeles
Everson, P, 1996a 'Bodiam Castle, East Sussex: a fourteenth-century designed landscape', in D Morgan Evans, P Salway and D Thackray (eds), *'The Remains of Distant Times': Archaeology and the National Trust*, 66–72, Boydell for the Society of Antiquaries of London and the National Trust, London
Everson, P, 1996b 'Bodiam Castle, East Sussex: castle and its designed landscape', *Château Gaillard* 17, 79–84
Everson, P, 1998 '"Delightfully surrounded with woods and ponds": field evidence for medieval gardens in England', in P Pattison (ed), *There by Design: Field Archaeology in Parks and Gardens*, 32–38, British Archaeological Reports 267, Oxford
Everson, P and Williamson T, 1998 'Gardens and designed landscapes', in P Everson and T Williamson (eds), *The Archaeology of Landscape: Studies Presented to Christopher Taylor*, 139–165, Manchester University Press, Manchester and New York
Everson, P, Taylor, C C and Dunn, C J, 1991 *Change and Continuity: Rural Settlement in North-West Lincolnshire*, Her Majesty's Stationery Office, London
Fairclough, G, 1992 'Meaningful constructions — spatial and functional analysis of medieval buildings', *Antiquity* 66, 348–366
Gilchrist, R, 1994, *Gender and Material Culture. The Archaeology of Religious Women*, Routledge, London and New York
Gilchrist, R, 1999 *Gender and Archaeology: Contesting the Past*, Routledge, London and New York
Giles, K, 2007 'Seeing and believing: visuality and space in pre-modern England', *World Archaeology* 39:1, 105–121
Gosden, C, 1994 *Social Being and Time*, Blackwell, Oxford
Graves, P C, 2007 'Sensing and believing: exploring worlds of difference in pre-modern England: a contribution to the debate opened by Kate Giles', *World Archaeology* 39:4, 515–531
Grenville, J, 1997 *Medieval Housing*, Leicester University Press, London
Gurevich, A J, 1979 *Feodalismens uppkomst i Västeuropa*, Tiden, Stockholm
Hansson, M, 2001 'Rummet, herraväldet och residenset i Hultaby', in A Andrén, L Ersgård and J Wienberg (eds), *Från stad till land: En medeltidsarkeologisk resa tillägnad Hans Andersson*, 205–214, Lund Studies in Medieval Archaeology 29, Almqvist & Wiksell International, Stockholm
Hansson, M, 2006 *Aristocratic Landscape. The Spatial Ideology of the Medieval Aristocracy*, Lund Studies in Historical Archaeology 2, Almqvist & Wiksell International, Stockholm
Hansson, M and Hansson, B, 1997 *De skånska trädgårdarna och deras historia*, Signum, Lund
Hillier, W and Hanson, J, 1984 *The Social Logic of Space*, Cambridge University Press, Cambridge
Ingold, T, 1993 'The temporality of the landscape', *World Archaeology* 25:2, 152–174
Johnson, M, 2000 'Self-made men and the staging of agency', in M-A Dobres and J Robb (eds), *Agency in Archaeology*, 213–231, Routledge, London and New York
Johnson, M, 2002 *Behind the Castle Gate: From Medieval to Renaissance*, Routledge, London
Johnson, M H, 2007 *Ideas of Landscape*, Blackwell, Oxford
Kleinschmidt, H, 2000 *Understanding the Middle Ages: Transformation of Ideas and Attitudes in the Medieval World*, Boydell Press, Woodbridge

Knapp, A B and Ashmore, W, 1999 'Archaeological landscapes: constructed, conceptualised, ideational', in W Ashmore and A B Knapp (eds), *Archaeologies of Landscape. Contemporary Perspectives*, 1–30, Malden, Oxford

Le Goff, J, 1990 *Medieval Civilization 400–1500*, Basil Blackwell, Oxford

Liddiard, R, 2000 *'Landscapes of Lordship': Norman Castles and the Countryside in Medieval Norfolk, 1066–1200*, British Archaeological Reports 309, Oxford

Mann, M, 1986 *The Sources of Social Power. Vol. 1: A History of Power from the Beginning to a.d. 1760*, Cambridge University Press, Cambridge

Mogren, M, 1995 'Borgforskning förr och nu', in M Mogren and J Wienberg (eds), *Lindholmen: Medeltida riksborg i Skåne*, 24–30, Lund Studies in Medieval Archaeology 17, Almqvist & Wiksell International, Stockholm

Nordin, J M, 2005 *När makten blev synlig. Senmedeltid i södra Dalarna*, Stockholm Studies in Archaeology 36, Stockholm

Ödman, A, 1996 'Glimmingehus and Its Predecessor', in M Josephson and M Mogren (eds), *Castella Maris Baltici* II, 135–140, Sörmländska handlingar nr 49, Lund Studies in Medieval Archaeology 18, Södermanlands museum, Nyköping

Ödman, A, 1999 'De arkeologiska undersökningarna', in *Glimmingehus 500 år. Tretton texter redigerade av Sten Åke Nilsson under medverkan av Annette Landen*, 115–125, Skånsk Senmedeltid och Renässans, Skrifter utgivna av Vetenskaps-Societeten i Lund 17, Lund University Press, Lund

Ödman, A, 2004 *Glimmingehus*, Svenska Kulturminnen 7, Riksantikvarieämbetet, Stockholm

Olsen, R A, 1996, *Borge i Danmark*, 2nd edn, Fremad, Copenhagen

Parker Pearson, M and Richards, C, 1994 'Ordering the world: perceptions of architecture, space and time', in M Parker Pearson and C Richards (eds), *Architecture and Order: Approaches to Social Space*, 1–37, Routledge, London

Platt, C, 2007 'Revisionism in Castle Studies: A Caution', *Medieval Archaeology* 51, 83–102

Reisnert, A, 1999 'Försvaret', in *Glimmingehus 500 år: Tretton texter redigerade av Sten Åke Nilsson under medverkan av Annette Landen*. Skånsk Senmedeltid och Renässans, 97–107, Skrifter utgivna av Vetenskaps-Societeten i Lund 17, Lund

Reynolds, S, 1994 *Fiefs and Vassals: The Medieval Evidence Reinterpreted*, Oxford University Press, Oxford

Samson, R (ed), 1990 *The Social Archaeology of Houses*, Edinburgh University Press, Edinburgh

Saunders, T, 1990 'The feudal construction of spaces: power and domination in the nucleated village', in Samson (ed) 1990, 181–196

Saunders, T, 2000 'Class, space and "feudal" identities in early medieval England', in W O Frazer and A Tyrell (eds), *Social Identity in Early Medieval Britain*, 209–232, Leicester University Press, London and New York

Stocker, D, 1992 'The shadow of the general's armchair', *Archaeological Journal* 149, 415–420

Sundqvist, O, 2002 *Freyr's Offspring: Rulers and Religion in Ancient Svea Society*, Historia Religionum 21, Uppsala Universitet, Uppsala

Taylor, C, 1983 *Village and Farmstead: A History of Rural Settlement in England*, Philip, London

Taylor, C, 2000 'Medieval ornamental landscapes', *Landscapes* 1, 38–55

Thompson, M, 1987 *The Decline of the Castle*, Cambridge University Press, Cambridge

Thompson, M, 1991 *The Rise of the Castle*, Cambridge University Press, Cambridge

Tilley, C, 1994 *A Phenomenology of Landscape: Places, Paths and Monuments*, Berg, Oxford

de Waha, M, 1986 'Habitats "seigneuriaux" et paysage dans le Hainault médiéval', in M Bur (ed), *La Maison Forte au Moyen Âge*, 95–111, Éditions du CNRS, Paris

Welinder, S, 1992 *Människor och landskap*, Societas archaeologica Upsaliensis, Studentlitteratur, Uppsala

CHAPTER 22
MEDIEVAL IDENTITY ISSUES

By David A Hinton

Archaeologists of all periods have considered how people use the material culture available to them to construct different sorts of identity. For the early Middle Ages, ethnicity, kin and regionalism have long been foci of attention. Bigger political units then created new conditions: more awareness of social and economic division, with towns and the growth of commerce also having a role in altering social relationships. Race was always a factor, as the influence and treatment first of Jews and then of Flemings demonstrate; family remained important, although it was not the only support system. Distribution maps of different sorts of evidence do not correlate, suggesting that regional differences did not make for strongly localized identities. Sumptuary laws confirm the impression given by archaeological evidence that although 'closure' created identity shaped by a sense of personal place, social ambition was not precluded and was achieved by demonstration of access to resources.

INTRODUCTION

Words come and go; only Tania Dickinson (1983, 39) had the foresight to see 'identity' as an issue for the future in the volume of essays published to celebrate the 25th anniversary of the Society for Medieval Archaeology. During the 1990s, however, the word became sufficiently established to be the theme of the Society's annual conference in Glasgow in 1997. Archaeologists of all periods concerned with the challenges (not 'problems', I am told, for that word suggests fault in ourselves for not solving them; we now face 'challenges' and address 'issues') of recognizing the different ways in which people thought of themselves and how they were thought of, and of how 'Material culture can be seen to construct, maintain, control and transform social identities and relations' (Gilchrist 1994, 15). How can the social, economic, ethnic, religious, national, regional, kin, corporate, age or gender groups to which people belonged, or sought to belong, or were seen as belonging, or sought to avoid being seen as belonging, be identified in the archaeological record? And always for medievalists lurks the challenge of the extra information that documentary evidence provides and disguises about material culture.

Issues of identity and how it could be changed to adapt to new circumstances have been a focus of many recent studies (eg Díaz-Andreu *et al* 2005). For prehistorians, these discussions are usually rooted in the work of anthropologists' studies of stable societies operating outside modern industrial and commercial systems. Such analogies may be useful also for the early Middle Ages, particularly when gift-exchange systems or petty chieftainships seem to have dominated. Application of post-colonial theory to an examination of the nature of the identity that the leaders of south-western British societies assumed has shown how modern discourses can be worth considering (Bowles 2007). But the value of analogies with non-European societies diminishes as medieval people came to operate within commercial economic systems, wider political structures, an externally directed religion and social hierarchies governed by imposed law. Even when ancient tradition and custom were appealed to, they were malleable; in 1381, the townsmen of Corfe, Dorset, faced by a threat to their liberties from a customary produced by the castle's constable, had the extraordinary good fortune to find a customary of their own hidden away 'in a missal of the parish church', that had to be older because of its 'ancient writing' (*Cal Inq Misc* IV, no 147).

In her 1983 essay, Dickinson specified 'ethnic identity', a topic now back in discussion with a vengeance. In the first chapter of a book published in 1990, I deliberately omitted any mention of the Jutes, the third party in what seemed to me at the time the hugely over-discussed rationalization by Bede of the tribal origins of the English. That a few gold bracteates in Kent might have come from Denmark seemed far less important than how people used them after they had arrived, and that their eye-catching attractions should not be allowed to overshadow much more important challenges such as exploring the nature and strength of the economy (Hinton 1990, 16–17). The old debate was revived soon afterwards, however, first in argument over the numbers of migrants — A small elite rather than a mass movement? A few successful young males establishing themselves as dominant over cowered natives? — and then because of DNA analyses — could science prove that people in Kent had come from northern Denmark, where the Jutes were supposed to have originated? Admittedly even the most audacious geneticist has never claimed quite such precision, but this and other new factors have now to be taken into account (see Hills forthcoming for an overview). This is notwithstanding the scepticism of those of us who remember the discredited attempts to identify peoples by their skull shapes, usually associated with 1930s Nazi philosophy (eg Fetten 2002, 157–161), but in fact used long before that as a criterion for distinguishing British burials from 'Teutonic invaders', even by E T Leeds in his pioneering study of artefacts, principally metalwork, as a means of establishing ethnic identities, placing archaeology in the forefront (Leeds 1913, 24–25; for an appreciation of Leeds's great contribution, see MacGregor 2007).

The complexity of attaching identity labels to Anglo-Saxon metalwork has been highlighted by John Hines's recent work on great square-headed brooches. His classification reveals a chronology that runs from a small but widespread distribution at the start of the 6th century to one that is geographically restricted but considerably greater in numbers 75 years later (Hines 1997, esp 301–310). So what began as something of very high status to which the only identity that can be ascribed is 'elite' ends seemingly as a signal of allegiance to an area of eastern England, but one that is not very obviously linked to any one of the kingdoms that were then emerging, and only to a part of the region that Bede was not long afterwards to describe as settled by 'Angles'. It is, however, closely consonant with 6th-century Region 1 as defined by Penelope Walton Rogers on the basis of costume, insofar as it can be established by fabrics and fittings (2007, 232–233). But she considers factors such as British and Scandinavian influences to have been at work, just as Hines sees Scandinavian brooches behind the English great square-headed series (1997, 222–234). If Angles were a group who originated in the southern part of modern Denmark and north Germany, they had absorbed a very eclectic culture by Bede's day — even more so if they were really from Frisia (Bartholomew 2006, 25, in an argument depending on a complex word-play, which seems favoured by linguists (Denison and Hogg 2006, 9); although it appears less convincing than his proposal that Bede's Jutes were actually Eucii, from modern Flanders: 22–23).

The great square-headed brooches had a brief currency, replaced for equivalent social display by various forms of disc-brooch, most notably the 7th-century garnet-set composite type, of which the most spectacular continue to be found in Kent, but which have long been known in the upper Thames valley near Abingdon, and now also on the fringes of the *wic* sites at London and Ipswich, and near Norwich (Pinder 1995; Penn 2000, 45–49 and 76–82; Cowie 2001; also a new Kentish discovery reported in *British Archaeology*, 100 (May/June 2008), 6). Any thought that garnets were less admired in Wessex and Northumbria has had to be cast aside because of the fine pendant on the fringe of *Hamwic* and the objects from a cemetery near Redcar (Birbeck 2005, 53–71; *British Archaeology*, 100 (May/June 2008), 4). Even though the new Christian religion gave elites new devices in the shape of the cross and new tensions in their political confrontations, they did not use their wealth to show political allegiances, at least in any very obvious way. The Kentish forms of the sinuous animals that are called Style II are slightly different from those in other areas (Webster forthcoming), but seem unlikely to have been acknowledged by an onlooker as meaning more than differences between smiths and access to resources. Similarly, in the 8th century a 'Mercian' style can be seen, reflecting the rise to supremacy of the middle kingdom (Webster and Backhouse 1991, 193–253; Brown and Farr 2001), but not so markedly that it implies expression of ideas or values not current throughout England.

The later 8th- and 9th-century kings certainly sought to give themselves regal identity, as their coins show; the recent discovery of a gold one issued by Coenwulf of Mercia is a splendid example, as well as an indication of the importance of the *wic* at London (Williams and Bishop 2004). Although they had to claim descent from Woden, or at least to belong to a dynasty that was throne-worthy, the actual origins of many of these leaders are uncertain; where did Coenwulf, or Cadwalla and Ine of Wessex, really come from? They had to identify themselves with traditional power, but in reality family background was of decreasing importance, at least in the wide sense of kinship rather than paternity. New urban communities existed beyond the reach of claims to familial land and responsibilities. No inscriptions on objects and only three on dedication or memorial stones name the father of its owner or maker

(Okasha 1971, 87–88, 114–115: Kirkdale and Stratford Mortimer; Okasha 1983, 88–89: Canterbury. All are probably as late as the 11th century). This is in striking contrast to the British series.

The Anglo-Saxon kingdoms were short-lived, all but Wessex collapsing under Viking pressure. The extent to which in the late 9th and 10th centuries 'England' expressed itself differently from the 'Danelaw', or whether there was a composite 'Anglo-Scandinavian' culture with minor regional differences, will remain discussible (see Redmond 2007 for a recent summary), but increasing urbanism, manorialization and Cnut's settlement produced an 11th-century amalgam. Identity expression through objects became much less subtle; although bullion rings appear to have been worn, highly decorated objects almost disappear from the record, though a range of cheaper items is known. Duke William's Normans and Flemings violently added a new, French-speaking elite, but one that is difficult to trace in the direct archaeological record except in castles and possibly churches, although the short-term economic and long-term linguistic impact can be seen.

Following in William's wake was one small group of people whose self-expression was manifestly different from that of those around them. The Jews' financial success enabled them to administer their own cemeteries in the 12th century, and to construct their own places of ritual, the former outside towns because they were excluded, the latter either close to the cemeteries, or discreetly placed amongst the houses that were indistinguishable from the outside from those of gentile neighbours. Even when protected by kings the Jews had to be careful of themselves, but in the 13th century as that protection was withdrawn, their separateness became increasingly an issue. They were probably physically distinctive, as their costume, head-dress and body smell could make them stand out, but wearing badges as formal identifiers was forced upon them (Blair *et al* 2002; Hinton 2003). Awareness of different races remained strong even after the Jews' final expulsion in 1290; Scots and Welsh were placed under restriction in, or were excluded from, some English towns, and Flemish immigrants felt the force of indigenous nationalism from time to time (Barron 1995).

The Jews were town-based, but their 13th-century activities stretched into the countryside, as lenders of small sums to peasants (Mundill 1998). As the names of the villages and hamlets from which the peasants came to borrow money were carefully recorded by their Jewish creditors, they provide a record of marketing that can be usefully compared to medieval pottery distributions, as in Herefordshire, to which debtors came from all over the county, but in which the pottery that could be bought in the market mostly came from the west side of the River Wye (compare Vince 1977, fig 8 with Mundill 1998, fig 5).

When 12th-century and later pottery began to be seriously studied in the 1950s and 1960s (Rupert Bruce-Mitford's late 1930s work having been cut short by war: Mellor 1997, 67–68), one influence upon its students was the work of Sir Cyril Fox in seeking to establish the existence of cultural systems based on a highland/lowland division (Wheeler 1963, 2–4 for an appreciation of Fox's thinking). The *Festschrift* for him contains an essay in which E M Jope used distribution maps to argue that medieval England had 'regional cultures', recognizable at peasant level through different types of pottery vessel and of parish churches, and at elite level in the use of building stone and brick, despite 'underlying uniformity' (1963, esp 328). He did not quite find what he sought: 'distribution is not to be simply correlated with the variants of the rural economy', but he showed the way towards thinking about 'the many facets of medieval culture' (ibid, 350). He under-estimated the dynamism of the medieval economy, bemoaning the irruption in the 15th century of London's influence into the 'habitual contacts since prehistoric times up and down the NE–SW clay vale', an interpretation considerably nuanced by Maureen Mellor's work on the same area, showing how the Oxford market at its centre was supplied from many different directions even in the 12th and 13th centuries (1994, figs 35–36). Nevertheless, 'habitual contacts' and 'the complex chains and networks of circumstances' discussed in his final contribution to medieval studies (1972, 971) may be said to anticipate subsequent work on the concept of *habitus* (Giles 2000, 9–11; Hinton 2005, 4–5).

A different approach was taken in Fox's *Festschrift* by Stuart Rigold, writing on wealden houses (1963). Although he called them 'characteristic' of Kent and Sussex, he did not suggest that the south-east was therefore expressing a different identity, but that the buildings showed a difference between areas where free farmers predominated, and those in which the great ecclesiastical owners had their manors. Nowadays it might be said that the newly emerging independent yeomen were using their showy houses to express their identity as people independent of manorial subjection and control.

Rigold's distribution map of wealden houses showed a preponderance in the south-east, but with several outside it. At first glance more clearly linear is the 'cruck frontier', mapped by Nat Alcock (2002, fig 1). The origins of the long, curved timbers that support the roofs of many peasant farm-houses, suburban houses, barns and other structures at 'vernacular' or 'sub-manorial' level are still much debated, as is the extent to which carpenters or their patrons exercised choice over whether to use crucks rather than straight posts, so that the frontier was actually quite permeable (Alcock 2007). What remains true, however, is that the cruck-using zone conforms to no other. It cannot be explained by presence or absence of suitable trees — there are no crucks in the well-wooded Weald; by wealth — late medieval Somerset and Shropshire which have crucks were not poor; and certainly not by Celtic roots — crucks are frequent in the upper Thames valley, which was one of the first areas to experience Anglo-Saxon influence. The peasants who built themselves cruck houses may have chosen to follow a neighbour's lead, but were surely expressing their identities as being amongst the better off, not as cruck- rather than post-users; what mattered was that the timbers involved expense and could be admired from the outside.

Other lines across the medieval map include those that separate off a 'central zone' in which nucleated villages and open fields predominate (Gray 1915; Roberts and Wrathmell 2000). This is in part a refinement of Fox's highland and lowland zones, as dispersed settlement characterizes the former, but also the south-east, where wood-pasture, meadowland and marshland helped to create different regimes (Williamson 2003). Arable tied the peasantry down, and they probably had less chance to find opportunities for self-advancement, but how aware could they have been of distinctions between themselves and those who lived in the other 'provinces'? Quite probably no more and no less than they would have recognized the different patterns of speech and pronunciation that linguists tease out from documents produced in different parts of England, and which again have no obvious consistency with any different aspect of material culture — dialect can be used to create five regions, none of which conforms to the 'cruck frontier' or the 'central province' (Lass 1992, 35, map). Superficial search of the distribution maps of different word forms in a *Linguistic Atlas* does not reveal any that are clearly similar to any such produced by archaeologists (McIntosh *et al* 1986, 305–551). That atlas achieved so many distributions by comparing texts of unknown origin to those written in a particular place or area. It has led to claims, for instance, that trade links between the east Midlands and the north were influential in spreading particular words (Hogg 2006, 362–365); such links are not particularly strong in documentary evidence, but the well-known 13th-/14th-century knight-jug found in Nottingham came from Scarborough (McCarthy and Brooks 1988, 228), so provides some supporting archaeological evidence.

To be a town- rather than a country-dweller was a difference that people would have understood, and was expressed by medieval writers (Clarke 2006). Urban markets, however, drew in peasants who needed to raise cash to pay their rents, and whose younger children might have found work and lived there; in reality, barriers cannot have been great, although walls and gates made a great physical show of it for many bigger towns. Such places also used their seals to show their importance; usually they displayed an image of their principal church or saint, but walls and gates may have alluded to the licences that the towns had from the king, whose realm their strength helped to protect, as did the ships on many port seals. A few towns appropriated popular stories, to identify themselves with legendary heroes (Pedrick 1904; Rosser 1996). Rigold foreshadowed important work on towns as the inspiration for new house types and forms when he pointed out that wealden houses may have had urban prototypes (Rigold 1963, 353; Pearson 2005). Towns were probably always likely to be in the vanguard of ideas — as in the beginning of the abandonment late in the Middle Ages of one of the most prevalent building spaces, the open hall (eg Dymond 1998).

The open hall as social space was to be found in all but the lowliest housing, as well as in royal and aristocratic palaces and castles. Within it, everyone knew their place, knew their host and hostess, and knew how to behave. There is little direct evidence on how the space was used by the peasantry; the documents suggest that invitations to enter were made on formal occasions, but this impression may be exaggerated because they were recorded when marriage agreements were made or when insults led to court cases (Poos 1991, 84–86). Access analysis enables archaeologists to consider gendered space in the larger households (Richardson 2003); in the countryside, the house and garden were where peasant women spent most of their time, with the men more often out in the fields (Hanawalt 1986, 141–145 and 271 shows the locales of accidents and violence).

Access analysis can be used in the application of closure theory, a useful framework for investigating medieval society (Rigby 1995). Physical manifestations of closure can be seen at least from the late Saxon period in the way that rural tofts and crofts were demarcated by fences or ditches in open-field areas (Parry 2006, 129, for recent work in the Midlands on this). Contravention of someone's privacy by breaking into a homestead was particularly abhorred, and not by coincidence was the hue and cry raised by shouts of 'out, out' (Müller 2005). The hue and cry is an aspect of social responsibility within communities; responsibility for upkeep of churches is another. Late medieval village and parish guilds also show how family was far from the only obligation or source of help and protection (Hanawalt 1986, 262–265; Duffy 1992, 141–154; Graves 2000). A sense of family amongst lower social levels must have been enhanced, however, as surnames came to be hereditary rather than an expression of someone's occupation or place of origin, just as it had always existed amongst the aristocracy, who from the 12th century could express it visually in heraldry (Clark 2002; Woolgar 2006b, 183).

Money was raised for churches and the support of the poor by communal church-ales; increasing use of ale-houses excluded many, as of course did guild feasts (Martin 2001, 130–131). In towns, too, guilds were social institutions, through which their members could see themselves as masters, craftsmen, donors, sisters and brothers, their buildings structured to give them halls with high and low ends, chapels, and even hospital provision. For members of a guild the institution could be a substitute for a family, especially after 1349 when recurrent plague epidemics could so easily destroy a whole unit (Giles 2000). Members of the Church joined an institutional family, late medieval educational colleges providing a new one. But, as David Stocker has shown, religious institutional life was becoming less corporate, members seeking their own households within the close or quadrangle (2005). Provision of separate chambers became a requisite of elite residences, another expression of change in the meaning of communality, although the hall remained the focus for great occasions.

When Chaucer mocked the aspirations of the guildsmen and their wives in the Preface to *Canterbury Tales*, he drew attention to their clothes, belts, knives and purses, hinting that perhaps they were flouting the sumptuary laws that were designed to ensure that everyone dressed so that their identity as people of a particular social rank was instantly visible. The laws were not meant to fix people in the status into which they were born, as social mobility was well established (Maddern 2006), but were designed to ensure that those who could afford it should do their duty to the state and service to the king by paying tax and keeping a household appropriate to their rank. People were expected to use their purchasing power to show their status, but this could lead to dysfunction. The aristocracy issued liveries to their followers, which was harmless while cloth colours were not identified with a particular family; but badges like the Dunstable swan, emblem of the house of Lancaster, played their part in the Wars of the Roses (Cherry 1992, pl 34). Foodstuffs were also restricted by sumptuary legislation; the better range available to peasants and wage-earners from the 1370s was met by increase in aristocratic demand for even more exotic fare, as changes in the faunal remains show (Woolgar 2006a, 196–200).

Differences based on wealth, birth and ability — the last in theory always possible to exploit within the Church but increasingly in the late Middle Ages also by a career in the law — could lead to conflicts such as the Peasants' Revolt of 1381, an extreme expression of the underlying resentment that conflicting group interests engendered. People had many different group identities, as members of families, households, fraternities, regions and nations. Perhaps even more difficult for archaeologists than for anthropologists, however, is the question of people's sense of identity of themselves as individuals (Díaz-Andreu and Lucy 2005, 1–2; Rubin 2006; Johnson 1996, 204–206; see also Postles on names as 'personal identifiers': 2002, xv–xvi). The more frequent were tables, place settings, food served in portions and drink poured into small vessels for each diner, so people were made more aware of themselves as separate from those around them, though only in bowls and beakers does it show clearly in the physical record (Dyer 2005, 137 and 141–143; Hadley 2005). Hand-washing, especially at meals, a ritual in great households, also spread down the social scale, with pottery aquamaniles copying more expensive metal ones, although the reach of such refinements is not known (Woolgar 2006b, 133; Brown 2005, 90–91). Washing by the wealthy involved scented waters, and perfumes became increasingly a sign of status (Woolgar 2006b, 264–266). Washing, however, also brought purity, and Christian teaching stressed the individual's body and soul. Base-metal pilgrim badges showed affiliation to a different sort of family, the family of God and his saints (eg Spencer 1990). Rosary beads show the importance of individual prayer, some simply made of animal or fish bones (Stallibrass 2002). Even the most intense human experience may reveal itself in the most commonplace physical material.

Searching for salvation was one way in which medieval people came increasingly to see themselves as on an individual journey through life, the Lollards even asserting that the mediation of a priest was largely unnecessary (Tanner 1977, 10–12). Debate about the 'prime mover' of change — commerce, demography, climate, class conflict, chaos — focuses on economics (Hatcher and Bailey 2001 — Jope 1972 is a significant absentee from their bibliography), and is a useful reminder that theories other than social ones apply to the study of the Middle Ages, and that Fisher Price Index and Gresham's Law should be taken into account even by those who reject the substantivist position adopted at the start of this paper. Closure is criticized for not being explanatory of change (Hatcher and Bailey 2001, 197–200), but sets a context within which individual self-awareness could create ambition for self-advancement, an under-rated 'mover'. When aspiration could be allied to opportunity in the later Middle Ages, those who enjoyed enough good fortune were able to use the various forms of material culture available to them to mould themselves into new identities.

BIBLIOGRAPHY

Alcock, N W, 2002 'The distribution and dating of crucks and base crucks', *Vernacular Architecture* 33, 67–70

Alcock, N W, 2007 'A rejoinder', *Vernacular Architecture* 38, 11–14

Barron, C M, 1995 'Introduction: England and the Low Countries 1327–1477', 1–28, in C M Barron and N Saul (eds), *England and the Low Countries in the Late Middle Ages*, Sutton, Stroud

Birbeck, V, 2005 *The Origins of Mid-Saxon Southampton. Excavations at the Friends Provident St Mary's Stadium 1998–2000*, Wessex Archaeology, Salisbury

Blair, I, Hillaby, J, Howell, I, Sermon, R and Watson, B, 2002 'The discovery of two *mikva'ot* in London and a reinterpretation of the Bristol "*mikveh*"', *Jewish Historical Studies* 37, 15–40
Bowles, C R, 2007 *Rebuilding the Britons. The Postcolonial Archaeology of Culture and Identity in the Late Antique Bristol Channel Region*, British Archaeological Reports 452, Oxford
Brown, D, 2005 'Pottery and manners', in Carroll (ed) 2005, 87–99
Brown, M P and Farr, C A (eds), 2001 *Mercia: an Anglo-Saxon Kingdom in Europe*, Leicester University Press, London
Cal Inq Misc: *Calendar of Inquisitions Miscellaneous*, Her Majesty's Stationery Office, London
Carroll, M (ed), 2005 *Consuming Passions*, Tempus, Stroud
Cherry, J, 1992 *Medieval Craftsmen. Goldsmiths*, British Museum Press, London
Clark, C, 2002 'Socio-economic status and individual identity', in D Postles (ed), *Naming, Society and Regional Identity*, 101–121, Leopard's Head Press, Oxford
Clarke, C A M, 2006 *Literary Landscapes and the Idea of England, 700–1400*, D S Brewer, Woodbridge
Cowie, R, 2001 'Mercian London', in Brown and Farr (eds) 2001, 194–209
Crawford, S, Hamerow, H and Hinton, D A (eds), forthcoming *A Handbook of Anglo-Saxon Archaeology*, Oxford University Press, Oxford
Denison, D and Hogg, R (eds), 2006 *A History of the English Language*, Cambridge University Press, Cambridge
Denison, D and Hogg, R, 2006 'Overview', in Denison and Hogg (eds) 2006, 1–42
Díaz-Andreu, M, Lucy, S, Babić, S and Edwards, D N (eds), 2005 *The Archaeology of Identity. Approaches to Gender, Age, Status, Ethnicity and Religion*, Routledge, Abingdon
Dickinson, T M, 1983 'Anglo-Saxon archaeology: twenty-five years on', in D A Hinton (ed), *25 Years of Medieval Archaeology*, 33–43, Department of Prehistory and Archaeology, University of Sheffield, Sheffield
Duffy, E, 1992 *The Stripping of the Altars. Traditional Religion in England, c.1400–c.1580*, Yale University Press, New Haven
Dyer, C, 2005 *An Age of Transition? Economy and Society in England in the Later Middle Ages*, Clarendon Press, Oxford
Dymond, D, 1998 'Five building contracts from fifteenth-century Suffolk', *Antiquaries Journal* 78, 269–287
Fetten, F, 2002 'Archaeology and anthropology in Germany before 1945', in Härke, H (ed), *Archaeology, Ideology and Society, The German Experience*, 143–182, rev edn, Peter Lang, Frankfurt
Foster I LL and Alcock L (eds), 1963 *Culture and Environment. Essays to Sir Cyril Fox*, Routledge and Kegan Paul, London
Gilchrist, R, 1994 *Gender and Material Culture. The Archaeology of Religious Women*, Routledge, London
Giles, K, 2000 *An Archaeology of Social Identity: Guildhalls in York*, British Archaeological Reports 315, Oxford
Graves, C P, 2000 *The Form and Fabric of Belief. An Archaeology of Lay Experience of Religion in Medieval Norfolk and Devon*, British Archaeological Reports 311, Oxford
Gray, H L, 1915 *English Field Systems*, Harvard University Press, Cambridge MA
Hadley, D M, 2005 'Dining in disharmony in the later Middle Ages', in Carroll (ed) 2005, 101–119
Hanawalt, B A, 1986 *The Ties that Bound: Peasant Families in Medieval England*, Oxford University Press, Oxford
Hatcher, J and Bailey, M, 2001 *Modelling the Middle Ages. The History and Theory of England's Economic Development*, Oxford University Press, Oxford

Hills, C, forthcoming 'Overview: Anglo-Saxon identity: ethnicity, culture and genes', in Crawford *et al* (eds) forthcoming
Hines, J, 1997 *A New Corpus of Anglo-Saxon Great Square-Headed Brooches*, Boydell, Woodbridge
Hinton, D A, 1990 *Archaeology, Economy and Society. England from the Fifth to the Fifteenth Century*, Seaby, London
Hinton, D A, 2003 'Medieval Anglo-Jewry: the archaeological evidence', in P Skinner (ed), *Jews in Medieval Britain*, 97–101, Boydell, Woodbridge
Hinton, D A, 2005 *Gold and Gilt, Pots and Pins. Possessions and People in Medieval Britain*, Oxford University Press, Oxford
Hogg, R, 2006 'English in Britain', in Denison and Hogg (eds) 2006, 352–383
Horrox, R and Ormrod, W M (eds), 2006 *A Social History of England 1200–1500*, Cambridge University Press, Cambridge
Johnson, M, 1996 *An Archaeology of Capitalism*, Blackwell Publishers, Oxford
Jope, E M, 1963 'The regional cultures of medieval Britain', in Foster and Alcock (eds) 1963, 327–350
Jope, E M, 1972 'Models in medieval studies', in D L Clarke (ed), *Models in Archaeology*, 963–990, Methuen, London
Lass, R, 1992 'Phonology and morphology', in N Blake (ed), *The Cambridge History of the English Language*, 23–155, Cambridge University Press, Cambridge
Leeds, E T, 1913 *The Archaeology of the Anglo-Saxon Settlements*, Clarendon Press, Oxford
MacGregor, A, 2007 'E T Leeds and the formulation of an Anglo-Saxon archaeology of England', in M Henig and T J Smith (eds), Collectanea Antiqua*: Essays in Memory of Sonia Chadwick Hawkes*, 27–44, British Archaeological Reports International Series 1673, Oxford
Maddern, P C, 2006 'Social mobility', in Horrox and Ormrod (eds) 2006, 113–133
Martin, A L, 2001 'Old people, alcohol and identity in Europe, 1300–1700', in P Scholliers (ed), *Food, Drink and Identity. Cooking, Eating and Drinking in Europe since the Middle Ages*, 119–137, Berg, Oxford
McCarthy, M and Brooks, C M, 1988 *Medieval Pottery in Britain AD 900–1600*, Leicester University Press, Leicester
McIntosh, A, Samuels, M L and Benskin, M, 1986 *A Linguistic Atlas of Late Medieval English, Volume One, General Introduction, Index of Sources, Dot Maps*, Aberdeen University Press, Aberdeen
Mellor, M, 1994 'A synthesis of middle and late Saxon, medieval and early post-medieval pottery in the Oxford region', *Oxoniensia* 59, 17–218
Mellor, M, 1997 *Pots and People*, Ashmolean Museum Publications, Oxford
Müller, M, 2005 'Social control and the hue and cry in two fourteenth-century villages', *Journal of Medieval History* 31, 29–53
Mundill, R R, 1998 *England's Jewish Solution: Experiment and Expulsion, 1262–1290*, Cambridge University Press, Cambridge
Okasha, E, 1971 *Hand-List of Anglo-Saxon Non-Runic Inscriptions*, Cambridge University Press, Cambridge
Okasha, E, 1983 'A supplement to [Okasha 1971]', *Anglo-Saxon England* 11, 83–118
Parry, S, 2006 *Raunds Area Survey. An Archaeological Study of the Landscape of Raunds, Northamptonshire 1985–94*, Oxbow Books, Oxford
Pearson, S, 2005 'Rural and urban houses 1100–1500; "urban adaptation" reconsidered', in K Giles and C Dyer (eds), *Town and Country in the Middle Ages. Contrasts, Contacts and Interconnections 1100–1500*, 43–63, Society for Medieval Archaeology Monograph 22, Maney Publishing, Leeds

Pedrick, G, 1904 *Borough Seals of the Gothic Period*, J M Dent, London
Pinder, M, 1995 'Anglo-Saxon garnet cloisonné composite disc brooches: some aspects of their construction', *Journal of the British Archaeological Association* 148, 6–28
Poos, L R, 1991 *A Rural Society after the Black Death: Essex 1350–1525*, Cambridge University Press, Cambridge
Postles, D, 2002 'Introduction', in D Postles (ed), *Naming, Society and Regional Identity*, xv– xxiii, Leopard's Head Press, Oxford
Redmond, A Z, 2007 *Viking Burial in the North of England*, British Archaeological Reports 429, Oxford
Rigby, S H, 1995 *English Society in the Later Middle Ages*, Macmillan, Basingstoke
Rigold, S E, 1963 'Appendix: distribution of the "Wealden house"', in Foster and Alcock (eds) 1963, 351–354
Roberts, B K and Wrathmell, S, 2000 *An Atlas of Rural Settlement in England*, English Heritage, London
Rosser, G, 1996 'Myth, image and social process in the English medieval town', *Urban History* 23, 5–25
Rubin, M, 2006 'Identities', in Horrox and Ormrod (eds) 2006, 383–412
Spencer, B, 1990 *Pilgrim Souvenirs and Secular Badges*, Salisbury and South Wiltshire Museum Medieval Catalogue Part 2, Salisbury and South Wiltshire Museum, Salisbury
Stallibrass, S, 2002 *The Possible Use of Fish and Cattle Bones as Rosary Beads*, Finds Research Group 700–1700 Datasheet 29
Stocker, D, 2005 'The quest for one's own front door: housing the vicars choral at the English cathedrals', *Vernacular Architecture* 36, 15–31
Tanner, N (ed), 1977 *Heresy Trials in the Diocese of Norwich, 1428–31*, Camden 4th series 20, Royal Historical Society, London
Vince, A G, 1977 'The medieval and post-medieval ceramic industry of the Malvern region: the study of a ware and its distribution', in D P S Peacock (ed), *Pottery and Early Commerce*, 257–306, Academic Press, London
Walton Rogers, P, 2007 *Cloth and Clothing in Early Anglo-Saxon England, AD 450–700*, Council for British Archaeology Research Report 145, York
Webster, L, forthcoming 'Style: influences and chronology', in Crawford *et al* (eds) forthcoming
Webster, L and Backhouse, J (eds), 1991 *The Making of England. Anglo-Saxon Art and Culture AD 600–900*, British Museum Press, London
Wheeler, Sir Mortimer, 1963 'Homage to Sir Cyril Fox', in Foster and Alcock (eds) 1963, 1–6
Williams, G and Bishop, R, 2004 'Coenwulf, king of Mercia', *Current Archaeology* 194, 56–57
Williamson, T, 2003 *Shaping Medieval Landscapes. Settlement, Society, Environment*, Windgather Press, Macclesfield
Woolgar, C M, 2006a 'Group diets in late medieval England', in C M Woolgar, D Serjeantson and T Waldron (eds), *Food in Medieval England. Diet and Nutrition*, 191–200, Oxford University Press, Oxford
Woolgar, C M, 2006b *The Senses in Late Medieval England*, Yale University Press, New Haven

CHAPTER 23
BURIAL, BELIEF AND IDENTITY IN LATER ANGLO-SAXON ENGLAND

By D M HADLEY

This paper discusses the range of artefacts, including dress accessories, jewellery and coins, that have been recovered from burials of the later Anglo-Saxon period, c750–1100. These artefacts are rarely accorded much significance in excavation reports, perhaps because they occur in only small numbers, while the paucity of fully-published cemeteries of this date inhibits inter-site comparisons. The debate about the reasons for the decline of grave goods in graves over the course of the 7th and early 8th century has focussed on the influence of Christianity on the transformation of burial rites, yet there has been scant regard for the implications that this might have had for the emergence of new burial rituals, in which the deposition of artefacts might have continued to have been meaningful. This paper suggests that we need to consider the artefacts deposited in graves in similar fashion as indicators of ritual belief, and the amuletic quality of a variety of artefacts is discussed. It is also argued that some graves indicate that claims to status were expressed in graves, particularly in cases where clothed burial can be identified, but that this, too, derived from complex beliefs about anticipated fate in the afterlife.

INTRODUCTION

In recent years the funerary practices of the later Anglo-Saxon centuries, c750–1100, have at last begun to receive extended deliberation. The influences of religious belief on funerary provision have begun to be discussed, and attempts have been made to identify the extent to which funerary provision was related to the age, sex and social status of the deceased (Hadley 2000; 2008a; 2008b; Thompson 2002; 2004; Hadley and Buckberry 2005; Buckberry 2004; 2007; Cherryson 2005). This paper addresses a dimension of the later Anglo-Saxon funerary record that has still to receive significant attention: the placement of artefacts in the grave. The 7th century witnessed a decline in the range and frequency of grave goods deposited in burials, with many cemeteries of this date characterized by a high degree of unfurnished graves (Geake 1997), and by the early 8th century the furnished burial rite had essentially come to an end. Nonetheless, in cemeteries of the following centuries a small number of graves contain the remains of clothing, jewellery and other artefacts, such as coins, although site reports typically assign little significance to them. This is surprising since it is more than 25 years since Richard Morris (1983, 59–62) drew attention to this phenomenon. His survey of Anglo-Saxon graves accompanied by artefacts in or near churchyards was principally concerned with highlighting evidence to suggest that Christian cemeteries were founded close to existing furnished cemeteries, although he did allow for the possibility that 'the custom of depositing objects of a personal kind with burials was maintained for a time in Christian graveyards' (Morris 1983, 61). It is this observation that is pursued in the present paper.

THE DECLINE OF THE FURNISHED BURIAL RITE

Grave goods have traditionally been linked with paganism and their disappearance routinely ascribed to the influence of the Church (Hyslop 1963, 191–192; Meaney and Hawkes 1970, 53–54; Faull 1976, 232). However, this perspective has long sat uncomfortably alongside evidence that grave goods continued to be deposited, if in decreasing amounts, into the 8th century, and even after the traditional end date for the practice — *c*AD 730 — a restricted range of object types still occur (Geake 1997, 137–139, table 6.1). Audrey Meaney and Sonia Chadwick Hawkes (1970, 53–54) attempted to reconcile this apparent discrepancy by arguing that the presence of grave goods in the sparsely furnished 7th-century cemetery of Winnall II (Hampshire) 'was a custom the Church was at first prepared to wink at', but that the eventual disuse of grave goods was, nonetheless, a 'demonstration of the Church's success in combating one of the outward signs of heathenism'. Subsequently, however, the lack of ecclesiastical directives about burial has frequently been cited as reason to caution against assigning the decline of grave goods directly to the influence of Christianity (Bullough 1983, 186; Morris 1983, 50; Boddington 1990, 180–184; Hadley 1995, 147). Furthermore, following greater attention to anthropological parallels, it is now recognized that although religious belief undoubtedly informed aspects of funerary provision this does not necessarily mean that transformations in religious belief can be directly traced through alterations to funerary practices (Halsall 1995, 61–63).

Continental evidence also qualifies some of the assertions once routinely made, because furnished burials occur in and adjacent to churches in Frankia, while a similar decline there in the frequency of grave goods in the 7th century cannot be explained by reference to conversion to Christianity, which had long since happened in most regions (James 1992; Samson 1999, 122–125; Blair 2005, 240–241). Ross Samson (1999, 138–141) has suggested that increased ecclesiastical involvement in preparing the body for interment was decisive in transforming burial practices in the 7th and 8th centuries, and he draws on contemporary, mainly continental, written sources to argue that the shroud in which the deceased was wrapped echoed baptismal robes. In other words, it was not that the Church prohibited grave goods, but rather that it offered an alternative, simpler, mode of burial. The ostentatious austerity of monastic burial, which nonetheless sometimes involved dressing or wrapping the corpse in expensive fabrics (see below), was desired by royalty and the aristocracy from the later 7th century, and this doubtless in turn provided a model to which the wider lay community eventually aspired, as a means of expressing their membership of the Christian faithful (Samson 1999, 122–125, 134–136; Blair 2005, 233–234, 240).

Recent studies have tended to assign the transformation of burial practices over the course of the 7th century to social, economic and political factors. It has, for example, been argued that increasingly stratified societies emerged in the 7th century and that the smaller numbers of elaborate burials were now signifiers of social elites who drew on a similar repertoire of grave goods to display status, replacing the regionally-distinctive assemblages of earlier centuries (Stoodley 1999; Geake 1999; Hadley 2004, 303–304). The elite also appear to have begun investing their wealth in the building of churches and in the development of estates, while the taxation system introduced by the Church was arguably another factor in redirecting the expenditure of movable wealth away from the grave (Carver 1989, 157; 1999; Geake 1992, 91–92). However, while these were all important factors, the focus on socio-economic and political developments has effectively prohibited discussion of the spiritual dimension of funerary practices after the 7th century. Yet it is surely implausible that religious belief — however defined — played no part in informing burial rites, and, while it is unlikely that anyone would seriously dispute this, until recently it has been something of an unfashionable concept (for a review, see Hoggett 2007, 28–29).

CHRISTIAN ATTITUDES TO GRAVE GOODS

Although ecclesiastical pronouncements on appropriate forms of burial in later Anglo-Saxon England are sparse (Thompson 2002; 2004, 57–88), occasional references to furnished burial suggest that this rite was not regarded as being inherently pagan. The Anglo-Saxon poem *The Seafarer*, perhaps of the 8th century but which survives in the 10th-century *Exeter Book*, indicates that furnished burial would not assist in gaining atonement for sin from God, but it does not suggest that such a burial was specifically un-Christian: ‘Though he would strew the grave with gold, a brother for his kinsman, bury with the dead a mass of treasure, it will not work, nor can the soul which is full of sin preserve the gold before the fear of God’ (Gordon 1979, 45–46; Samson 1999, 131–132). Similarly, a late Anglo-Saxon homily reflects on the futility of the wealthy creating burial places of marble, adorned with gold ornaments set with gemstones, tapestries, spices and gold leaf, since ‘bitter death takes all that away’ (Napier 1967, 263; translation from Thompson 2004, 110). As Victoria Thompson (2004, 109–111) has recently observed, this is not perceived as a pagan practice, but rather as one with no advantage in a Christian context. In neither of these cases is it certain that the author is referring to the burial practices of their own times, for which there is no corresponding archaeological evidence, rather than to the practices of much earlier generations, nonetheless these sources provide valuable insights into contemporary attitudes to lavishly furnished burials (Thompson 2004, 111). In sum, Christian Anglo-Saxon commentators seem to have been less exercised than archaeologists about the prospect of grave goods in Christian burials!

Elaborate burial assemblages need not indicate pagan belief, but there are admittedly few examples of known Christians being afforded such funerary provision.

One important exception is St Cuthbert, bishop of Lindisfarne (d 687), who was famously buried in his priestly robes accompanied by a gold pectoral cross set with garnets, a paten, a gold chalice, an ivory comb enclosed in plates of silver, a Gospel book, scissors, a wooden travelling altar and expensive textiles, some of which were added when the body was translated in 698 or, certainly in the case of the rich textiles, during subsequent openings of the tomb (Coatsworth 1989; Muthesius 1989). A similar level of elaboration may be inferred from the account of the opening of the sepulchre of St Guthlac (d 714) a year after his death when his garments were said to have 'shone', suggesting that they may have been of a more elaborate fabric than the linen Abbess Ecgburh is recorded as having sent to shroud his body (Colgrave 1956, 147–161). Some archaeologists have attempted to distinguish between pagan furnished burial, interpreted as a rite that provided the deceased with artefacts for use in the next life, and Christian furnished burial, understood simply as clothed burial, but this distinction is belied by the burial of St Cuthbert; as has recently been argued by Victoria Thompson (2004, 33), the shoes he was wearing 'to meet Christ in', according to one of his *Lives*, have the hallmark of 'objects to be used in another life' (Gräslund 2000, 84).

Although it is generally hazardous to assign religious belief on the basis of funerary practices, it is, nonetheless, difficult to deny that some level of Christian influence is evident in certain 7th-century burials. For example, the burial excavated recently at Prittlewell (Essex) was lavishly furnished with hanging bowls, folding stool, sword, lyre, wooden buckets, bronze flagon, glass vessels and two gold foil crosses laid on the body (Blair 2007). This discovery has reignited debate about the supposed pagan associations of such so-called 'princely burials', with John Blair (2005, 53–54) arguing that the gold foil crosses are 'surely a clear statement of Christian affiliation'. Richly furnished 7th-century barrow burials have generally been regarded as pagan, and even as militantly pagan reactions to Christianity (van de Noort 1993; Carver 2001; 2002), but as Blair (2005, 230–233) observes both barrow burial and the contemporary practice of burial near to churches were 'a monumental expression of status', and may equally have been at home in a Christian milieu. Indeed, such burials sometimes reveal Christian influences in the form of overtly Christian artefacts, such as cross-shaped pendants and cruciform mounts on bowls, bags and, at Benty Grange (Derbyshire), a helmet, and it is possible that this represents part of the process of the Christianization of the pagan amuletic repertoire that had characterized graves of an earlier date (Blair 2005, 171–175, 230–232).

Indirect evidence for Christian influences occurs in the form of jewellery informed by Roman styles, such as linked pins, shorter necklaces with disc pendants, and annular and penannular brooches. As Helen Geake (1999) has argued, the increased Classical emphasis evident in 7th-century grave assemblages was inspired by the arrival of the Church, conveying Roman and Byzantine influences. This is not to say that such artefacts invariably occurred in the burials of Christians, and the classicizing influence can be found in regions yet to convert officially. Moreover, there are few secure examples from churchyards of furnished burials (for possible exceptions, see Blair 2005, 229, 237), let alone burials containing artefacts with Classical influences. Nonetheless, the Church was undoubtedly, as Geake (1999, 212) puts it, 'a political, spiritual and general all-round ideological force', bringing with it new ways of underpinning lordship and kingship, while the power of the Roman past and its heritage may also have proved attractive to the emergent Anglo-Saxon kingdoms.

'GRAVE GOODS' IN CHRISTIAN CEMETERIES

The foregoing review has established that grave goods appear not to have been regarded as inherently un-Christian. Nonetheless, there is no denying that after *c*AD 730 graves were comparatively less well-furnished than in earlier centuries, for which a variety of socio-economic and religious factors are responsible. Yet the oft-repeated assertion that Christian graves are, by their very nature, unfurnished needs to be qualified. There is evidence both for clothed burial and burial accompanied by artefacts that arguably made claims to status or possessed amuletic qualities. Furthermore, the traditional focus on the decline of 'grave goods' in the 7th century obscures the increased use of the various types of grave furnishings and linings in later graves, which evidently had ritual and symbolic resonances. This derives from an arbitrary archaeological distinction: as Victoria Thompson (2004, 108) has observed, 'it is unclear whether this division which defines some artefacts as grave-goods and others as "something else" is a dichotomy which would have been understood in the early medieval period'.

Dressing the body

Written sources detailing the death bed often imply that the body would be simply wrapped, presumably shrouded (Thompson 2004, 76–81), but the retrieval of dress accessories from later Anglo-Saxon graves suggests that the deceased were sometimes interred in their clothing (Figure 23.1). A representative sample includes the strap-ends found in graves at Bevis Grave, Bedhampton (Hampshire) (Rudkin 2001), Carlisle (Cumberland) (Redmond 2007, xxiv), Old Minster, Winchester (Biddle 1990, 498) and Barton-upon-Humber (Lincolnshire) (Waldron 2007, 165), silver hooked tags, of a type used to fasten garments, from a grave at Old Minster (Biddle 1990, 549), and two copper-alloy hooked tags from graves at Wearmouth (Durham) (Cramp *et al* 2006, 230, 233). Buckles, probably from belts, have been recovered from graves at Bevis Grave (Rudkin 2001), Barton-upon-Humber (Waldron 2007, 144), Great Hale (Lincolnshire) (Hadley and Buckberry 2001b), Carlisle (Redmond 2007, xxxiv), Old Minster (Biddle 1990, 512) and Christ Church Cathedral, Oxford (Boyle 2001, 355), while a trapezoidal copper-alloy plate dating to *c* 1000 found on the pelvis of a skeleton excavated at Waltham Abbey (Essex) appears to have been a belt mount (Huggins 1984). A 9th-century silver pin was found in another grave at Old Minster (Biddle 1990, 555), while at Caister-on-Sea (Norfolk) one grave produced a hairpin 'of Late Saxon type' (Darling and Gurney 1993, 252). These pins may also be indicative of clothed burial, although it is certainly possible that pins served to fasten shrouds, in particular those placed on the shoulder — as at Rivenhall (Essex) (Rodwell and Rodwell 1985, 80, 82) and Holton-le-Clay (Lincolnshire) (Sills 1982, 31, 40) — or on the pelvis — as at Sedgeford (Norfolk) (Davies and Hoggett 2001). It should also be noted that dress accessories of later Anglo-Saxon date are commonly

Site	Grave	Age and Sex	Date	Comments on dress-accessories found in grave	Source
St Peter's, Barton-upon-Humber (Lincolnshire)	Skeleton 822/ grave 1462	Adult	Phase E, *c*950–1150	Iron buckle	Waldron 2007, 144
	Skeleton 2322/ grave 5328	Male; 25–34 years		Copper-alloy strap-end	Waldron 2007, 165
Bevis Grave, Bedhampton (Hampshire)	Grave 5/ Skeleton 88	?Male; *c*50 years	Cemetery has produced radiocarbon dates and artefacts spanning the 7th to early 11th century	Iron buckle	Rudkin 2001
	Grave 19/ Skeleton	?Male; *c*45 years		Iron buckle just below waist	
	Grave 43/ Skeleton 61	Male; *c*45 years		Iron buckle to right of pelvis, iron pin adjacent to left elbow and iron ferrule with spike through it, thought to be attachment for a wooden object, perhaps a staff	
	Grave 12/ Skeleton 4	Female; *c*45 years	Dated to the 9th century on basis of strap-end	Bronze strap-end dating to the 9th century was found near the lower right leg	
	Grave 44/ Skeleton 41	?female; *c*40 years	Skeleton radiocarbon dated to AD 660–805	An iron knife and ring and an enamelled escutcheon plate were found together at the waist and had probably been in a leather bag, of which fragments survived; a bronze pin was located at the throat	Rudkin 2001; Cherryson 2005 (Appendix), 48
Caister-on-Sea (Norfolk)	Grave 90	—	Probably 9th or 10th century	Hairpin of 'late Saxon type'	Darling and Gurney 1993, 252
Carlisle Cathedral	Grave 251	—	Artefacts suggest late 9th to early 10th century	Copper-alloy buckle, and other artefacts including copper-alloy scale pan and ingot, iron knife and slate whetstone with silver suspension mount	Redmond 2007, xxiv
	Grave 242	—	Probably 10th century	Part of copper-alloy pin shank	
	Grave 269	—	Probably 10th century	Copper-alloy buckle and strap-end	
Great Hale (Lincolnshire)	—	Adult	Skeleton radiocarbon dated to AD 655–765	Iron buckle	Buckberry and Hadley 2001
Christ Church Cathedral Graveyard, Oxford	Skeleton 215/ grave 217	Adult; 40+ years	Radiocarbon dates suggest burial took place across the period from the 8th to 10th century	Copper-alloy buckle frame and pin recovered from the waist area	Boyle 2001, 341, 355
Repton (Derbyshire)	Grave 380	Female; 17–25 years	In an area of burial dating to the 10th century	Gold embroidered cuffs or gloves, accompanied by 3 spherical silver pendants or beads	Biddle and Kjølbye-Biddle 2001, 85–86

	Grave 387	Male; 17–20 years		Gold embroidered ribbon or braid running the length of the skeleton, suggesting that it decorated a cloak	Biddle and Kjølbye-Biddle 2001, 86
	Grave 94	Adult; 25–30 years		Tri-lobed leaf embroidered with gold thread on the chest	
Waltham Abbey (Essex)	—	Adult	No dating independent of belt mount	Trapezoidal copper-alloy mount or plate, perhaps from a belt, dating to the late 10th or early 11th century was found just above the pelvis	Huggins 1984, 175–176
Wearmouth (Co. Durham)	Grave 60/4	Adult	Late 7th to 9th century (ie the monastic phase of the cemetery)	Fragments of spirally twisted gold foil, dating to no earlier than the late 7th century, were found adjacent to the skull	Jones and Clogg 2006, 229–230
	Grave 67/7	?Male: 15–21 years		Copper-alloy hooked tag	Cramp *et al* 2006, 232
	Grave 67/14	Male; 35–45 years		Copper-alloy hooked tag	
Old Minster, Winchester (Hampshire)	Grave 673	Adult	Early to mid-9th century	Gold braid at base of skull	Biddle 1990, 469, 480
	Grave 82	Adult	Mid to late 9th century	Single gold thread on upper body	
	Grave 67	Adult		Gold braids from some sort of head covering around the skull; matching pair of silver hooked tags near the knees	Biddle 1990, 469, 480–481, 549
	Grave 717	Adult	Late 9th century	Gold braid around temples and down sides of skull to jaw, probably a cap or headband	Biddle 1990, 469, 481
	Grave 321	Adult	Mid-10th century	Copper-alloy strap-end	Biddle 1990, 498
	Grave 56	Adult	Early to mid-11th century	Copper-alloy buckle frame with silver pin	Biddle 1990, 512
	Grave 341	Adult	Early to mid-9th century	Silver pin	Biddle 1990, 555
New Minster, Winchester	Grave 664	Adult	Early 10th century	Fragments of gold thread between hands on pelvis	Biddle 1990, 481
York Minster	Grave 79	?Male; 12–15 years	Cemetery dates to between the 8th and 11th centuries	Gold thread	Phillips 1995, 91
	Grave 89	Two adult males		Gold thread	
	Grave 105	—		Dress pin	Phillips 1995, 92

FIGURE 23.1 Dress accessories in later Anglo-Saxon graves. This table includes only those examples in which the dress accessory appears to have a direct relationship with the body rather than simply being in the grave fill. Excluded from all three tables are burials certainly or probably of Scandinavian settlers, idendified as such on the basis of either stable isotope evidence or the very lavish furnishing of the burial. Also excluded are burials from execution cemeteries. Radiocarbon dates in these tables are cited at the 95% confidence level.

found in disturbed contexts in churchyards, and may often have derived from burials (Biddle 1965, 256, 262–264; Sills 1982, 40–41; Bassett 1982, 13; Hall 1994, 45).

Even in circumstances of good organic preservation, such as the waterlogged conditions encountered at Barton-upon-Humber (Waldron 2007, 26–27), clothing rarely survives. However, gold braiding or thread from clothing has been recovered from burials in Anglo-Saxon churchyards at Repton (Derbyshire) (Biddle and Kjølbye-Biddle 2001, 85–86), York Minster (Phillips 1995, 91), Old Minster, Winchester (Biddle 1990, 468–472) and Wearmouth (McNeil and Cramp 2005, 80; Jones and Clogg 2006, 229–230). In few of these burials were any metal dress accessories recovered, and it is salutary that without the survival of the gold adornment it would not in most cases have been possible to infer clothed burial. It is likely that many of these burials were of the laity, given their location in the respective cemeteries and the fact that some were of females.

Knives found in graves are another indication of clothed burial, as they were typically suspended from a belt at the waist. They are one of the most commonly occurring artefacts found in later Anglo-Saxon graves, continuing a tradition that emerged in the 7th century, when knives are the only surviving artefact in many graves (Geake 1997, *passim*; Härke 1989). Cemeteries radiocarbon dated to the 9th, 10th or 11th centuries that have produced burials with knives include those at Lewknor (Oxfordshire) (Chambers 1976), Chimney Farm, near Bampton (Oxfordshire) (Crawford 1989), Milton Keynes (Northamptonshire) (Parkhouse *et al* 1993), Swinegate, York (Hadley and Buckberry 2005, 138), Bevis Grave (Rudkin 2001) and at both Marine Parade and Westgate in Southampton (Hampshire) (Cherryson 2005 (Appendix), 69–70). Cemeteries in which knives are the only accompanying artefacts tend to be assigned to the 7th century, even though the types of knife concerned have been recovered from settlement contexts spanning the later Anglo-Saxon period (Chambers 1976, 83–84). It appears only to be in cemeteries that have yielded radiocarbon dates that a later date of deposition is entertained. Although the iron remnants of the knives are unprepossessing, their handles and the scabbards in which they were doubtless deposited may have been decorated (for later examples, see Cowgill *et al* 1987). Knives were multi-purpose artefacts used for work, food preparation, eating and even magical practices, with one later Anglo-Saxon charm advising a person to stick their knife into the required herb, leave overnight and then lay under the altar before consuming the remedy (Jolly 1985, 289). Knives were very closely associated with individuals during life, and in the grave may, thus, have possessed a mnemonic quality.

Items of jewellery occur occasionally in graves of the 8th to 11th centuries (Figure 23.2). At York Minster, for example, two graves contained a finger-ring (Phillips 1995, 90–91), as did two graves in a cemetery excavated within Norwich Castle bailey (Ayers 1985, 27), while a gold finger-ring dating to the 9th century had been placed next to the right arm of a skeleton buried near to the church of St Mary in Exeter (Devon) (Graham-Campbell 1982). An 11th-century gold ring was found with a skeleton in a stone coffin buried at St Aldate's Street, Oxford, gold rings of similar date were found in the churchyard at Hamsey (Sussex) and in association with human bones at Balmer (Sussex), respectively (Graham-Campbell 1988), and gold

Site	Grave	Age and Sex	Date	Comments on jewellery found in grave	Source
Balmer (Sussex)	—	—	No dating independent of the ring	Twisted gold ring of 10th to 12th-century date was first illustrated in 1824 around some finger bones	Graham-Campbell 1988, 266
Beverley Minster (Yorkshire)	—	—	Dendrochronological dating of a coffin suggests burial commenced in the 10th century	A willow wand and a glass bead	Johnson 2004, 12
St Mary's, Exeter (Devon)	Grave O.B.2	Adult	This phase of the cemetery is dated stratigraphically to the late 7th to 10th century	A gold finger-ring lay on the base of the grave adjacent to the upper right arm of the body	Graham-Campbell 1982
Jarrow (Co. Durham)	Grave 69/14	Male; 45–50 years	Belongs to the monastic phase of the cemetery, 7th to 9th century	Globular 'black' glass bead with white crossing trails and red and white *millefiori* poked eyes dates to 6th or 7th century, but the grave also contains fragments of an 8th-/9th-century crucible	Lowther 2005, 182; Cramp 2006, 259–260
Norwich, church excavated in the castle bailey	Grave 2178		Cemetery thought to date to the 11th century	Silver finger-ring found on the hand of the skeleton	Ayers 1985, 19, 27
	Grave 2092			Fragment of a silver finger-ring	
St Aldate's, Oxford	—	—	No dating independent of the ring	Gold finger-ring dating to the 11th century found with a skeleton in a stone coffin	Graham-Campbell 1988
Scarborough (Yorkshire)	—	Adult	Cemetery thought to date to the 8th to 11th centuries on basis of associated artefacts	Jet cross dated to the 9th century found on the chest of a burial	Rowntree 1931
Sedgeford (Suffolk)	—	Juvenile	Radiocarbon dates suggest the cemetery dates to between the late 7th and late 9th century	A single bead was reported in this grave	Davies and Hoggett 2001
Thwing (Yorkshire)	Grave 8	Female; 40–45 years	Radiocarbon dated to AD 789–992	An amber and glass bead were found at the neck and an iron knife was placed under the leg	Geake 1997, 159; Terry Manby, pers comm
St Martin's, Wallingford (Oxfordshire)	—	—	Cemetery is thought to date to the 10th or 11th century	Scallop shell pierced for suspension lay on the torso of one skeleton	Booth *et al* 2007, 267–268
York Minster	Grave 68	—	Cemetery dates to between the 8th and 11th centuries	Copper-alloy finger-ring	Phillips 1995, 90
	Grave 86	—		Silver finger-ring	Phillips 1995, 91

FIGURE 23.2 Jewellery in later Anglo-Saxon graves. This table includes only those examples in which the jewellery appears to have a direct relationship with the body rather than simply being in the grave fill.

rings were reportedly found in graves thought to date to the mid- to later Anglo-Saxon period in Barrow-upon-Humber (Lincolnshire) (White 1856, 687). These rings may have had amuletic functions, as has been suggested for the inclusion of finger-rings in early Anglo-Saxon collections of artefacts in waist bags in female graves (R White 1988, 149) and in some later medieval graves (Gilchrist 2008, 129, 136), and there is a long-standing tradition of gold rings being regarded as curative (Meaney 1981, 12). Rings were also highly prized personal possessions, capable of evoking powerful memories and associations (Whitelock 1930; van Houts 1999, 93–120). The importance of rings as heirlooms, and their capacity to be handed on across generations, prompts consideration of whether rings are of greater antiquity than the graves in which they are sometimes found; in which case we should be alert to the fact that the rings are typically the means by which the grave is dated. In any given case it is difficult to surmise what resonance a ring possessed, but it does suggest that as the corpse was being prepared for burial specific decisions were made to place the ring either on the body or next to it in the grave, implying that at that moment the life experiences, family and broader connections of the deceased were very firmly in mind. A small number of graves contained items that might plausibly be regarded as having been used in the preparation of the body for interment, which probably also had very personal associations with the deceased. For example, combs were deposited in graves at Heysham (Lancashire) (Potter and Andrews 1994, 124), Swaby (Lincolnshire) (Field 1993), Bevis Grave (Rudkin 2001) and the Ladykirk, Ripon (Yorkshire) (Hall and Whyman 1996, 127–128), while tweezers have been recovered from graves at Pontefract (Yorkshire) (Wilmott forthcoming), St Helen-on-the-Walls (Dawes and Magilton 1980, 15) and Norwich (Ayers 1985, 27).

While lavishly furnished burial was understood as offering no guarantee of safe passage into the afterlife, nonetheless, for some members of the lay and ecclesiastical elite the grave remained an arena for displays of status, doubtless deriving not only from social competition among the mourners, but also from complex ideologies about anticipated fate in the afterlife. The homilist Ælfric noted that the cloth in which the deceased was wrapped 'does not rise readily with the person' implying some of the laity anticipated that they would rise in the afterlife in whatever manner they were buried (Thompson 2004, 108). It is perhaps, then, not surprising to find evidence for clothed burial, occasionally very lavish, suggesting that some individuals were interred with an eye on maintaining their status in death. This notion is supported by 12th-century accounts of the opening of the tomb of Edward the Confessor indicating that he had been buried with his symbols of office (Barlow 1992, 152–153), and this was a practice that continued for royal burials into the later Middle Ages (Evans 2003). From *c*1100 medieval priests and bishops were often buried with their symbols of office, such as chalice and paten, and, in some cases at least, in their ecclesiastical robes (Gilchrist and Sloane 2005, 215), but there is little evidence about common practice between the time of St Cuthbert and the 12th century, although the *Regularis Concordia* indicates that a deceased monk should be dressed for burial in shirt, cowl, stockings and shoes (Symons 1953, 65). Crosses placed in graves, such as the 9th-century jet cross found on the breast of a skeleton from Scarborough (Yorkshire) (Rowntree 1931, 146–148) and a 10th- or 11th-century lead crucifix set with mother of pearl nails from the churchyard of St Martin's, Wallingford (Oxfordshire) (Booth *et al* 2007, 267–268), if not simply items of jewellery, are possible indications of priestly status.

Wealthier members of the laity also sought to maintain status in death through their patronage of the churches in which they expected to be interred (Thompson 2004, 8–25). Stone funerary monuments offered another medium in which elite status, as well as elements of belief, was articulated in a Christian context. Status was also expressed for some through burial in distinct locations, such as close to the church or prominent monuments within the churchyard (Stocker 2000; Stocker and Everson 2001; Hadley 2006, 258–262). Indeed, the link between manner of burial and anticipated fate in the afterlife was reinforced through the development of the concept of consecrated ground from the 7th century. Separate burial places for executed and excommunicated members of society simultaneously began to emerge, and in such cases evidence for clothed burial, combined with careless interment and multiple graves, was a sign of exclusion from the Christian community (Reynolds 1997).

The Church did not offer firm guidelines on appropriate forms of burial nor were expectations of the afterlife coherently articulated; in such circumstances it is perhaps not surprising that there should be diversity and experimentation as communities sought to negotiate both the transformation of the dead from one state to another and the passage of the soul (Thompson 2002). It can also be suggested that the memory of the deceased was an important factor in informing burial rites since the most commonly occurring artefacts in graves were closely associated with the deceased during life; the need 'to mediate relationships between living individuals and communities and the memory of the dead person' has been identified by Howard Williams (2006, 77) as an important motivating factor in earlier Anglo-Saxon burial tableaux, and it can now be suggested that this motivation persisted into later centuries.

Protective rituals

The protection of the corpse in the grave in the later Anglo-Saxon period has received much recent attention, arguably because, unlike what are perceived as 'grave goods', grave linings and furnishings are easier to incorporate into a securely Christian framework, and cannot be dismissed as the product of accidental loss. For example, Victoria Thompson (2002; 2004, 122–126) has recently suggested that the enclosed nature of later Anglo-Saxon graves may have derived from the contemporary concern with the grave as a place in which the body would decay and be subject to the ravages of worms, and from the recognition that the bodies of the most holy — saints — could be recognized by their incorruptibility. The placing of stones around parts of the body, especially the head, has been interpreted as a demonstration of care and compassion in protecting the corpse (Figure 23.3) (Boddington 1996, 48, 69; Thompson 2004, 118). At Barton good organic preservation revealed that the stones on either side of the skull in one grave supported an organic grass-filled pillow; it is a rare reminder of what is otherwise missing in the archaeological record (Waldron 2007, 26–27; see also Boddington 1996, 37). The provision of a layer of charcoal, either above or below the corpse, is a characteristic feature of later Anglo-Saxon cemeteries, although of variable frequency. The potential symbolic qualities of this charcoal are

FIGURE 23.3 Stone-lined graves from Fillingham (Lincolnshire), dating to the 10th to early 11th century. The skeleton on the left has stones packed in the mouth and an oval-shaped stone placed over each eye socket.

multiple: it has been linked with the 'sackcloth and ashes' of the monastic burial rite (Daniell 1997, 158–159); with the purifying rituals of the Ash Wednesday ceremonies (Thompson 2004, 118–122); and with notions of cleanliness, humility and eternity, due to its perceived indestructible qualities (Kjølbye-Biddle 1992, 231). It has also been suggested that ecclesiastical influences can be identified in the use of coffins with locks, which may reflect the literary and visual association with death of St Peter, who was symbolized by keys (Thompson 2004, 125–126, 129–131). The presence of clench nails in graves at Barton (Rodwell and Rodwell 1982, 291), York Minster (Phillips 1995, 85–86) and Caister-on-Sea (Darling and Gurney 1993, 52–53, 253–254) has suggested the reuse of ship timbers, which rather than simply being a functional act, may have carried symbolic associations with a journey. Scandinavian influence may be discerned, but it should be noted that in Scandinavia burials incorporating diverse modes of transport increased in the wake of conversion and were evidently absorbed into Christian ideology (Staecker 2003). Discussion of the enclosed nature of later Anglo-Saxon burials has largely been divorced from analysis of other forms of grave inclusion and the broader debate about the significance of the disappearance of the more extensive tradition of grave goods in the earlier Anglo-Saxon period. The latter debate is predicated on the basis that grave goods were unnecessary, if not downright incongruous, in a Christian context, yet recent discussion of grave linings and the enclosure of the body reveals that later Anglo-Saxon grave had numerous inclusions, and that these were redolent with symbolic meaning.

Discussion of natural materials in burials has similarly emphasized their symbolic associations. The placing of white quartz pebbles in graves is particularly common in

Ireland, both in prehistory and later, but early medieval examples from further east have been recorded at Barnstaple (Devon) (Miles 1986), Wearmouth (McNeil and Cramp 2005, 89), Llandough (Glamorgan) (Holbrook and Thomas 2005, 35–37), Whithorn (Dumfriesshire) (Hill 1997, 172) and Kellington (Yorks) (Mytum 1993). The precise significance of these pebbles is unclear, but folkloric accounts point to their symbolic association with purity, and their capacity to serve as 'lucky charms' or as 'an admission ticket to the other world'. Frequently cited in such discussions is the statement from the Book of Revelation (II: 17) that 'To him that overcometh . . . I will give a white stone, and in the stone a new name written, which no man knoweth save that he receiveth it' (Lebour 1913–14; Hill 1997, 173; Daniell 1997, 165; Holbrook and Thomas 2005, 37; Gilchrist 2008, 138–139). Elsewhere stones of various types were placed in the mouths of individuals at St Nicholas Shambles, London (W White 1988, 24), Raunds, where the male concerned had a shortened left humerus and shortened and atrophied right femur (Boddington 1996, 42), and Fillingham (Lincolnshire), where one individual also had stones placed in the eye-sockets (Figure 23.3) (Buckberry and Hadley 2001, 15–16). The association of such stones with the parts of the body blessed by a priest during the final moments of life, and the emphasis in late Anglo-Saxon service books on closing the eyes and binding the mouth (Thompson 2004, 76–82), suggest that the stones represent an extension of the protective rituals of the death-bed.

Good organic preservation encountered during excavation at Barton-upon-Humber (Waldron 2007, 12), the Guildhall site, London (Bateman 1997, 119) and at Beverley (Johnson 2004, 12) has permitted the identification of rods of hazel or willow in graves. These have been variously interpreted as symbolic of pilgrimage or of the Resurrection, since it has been observed that hazel and willow are both trees that 'if coppiced regularly, become effectively eternal' (Bateman 1997, 119; Daniell 1997, 167). More recently, however, Roberta Gilchrist (2008, 126–128) has suggested that wooden rods, which also occur in later medieval graves, may have been associated with protective charms, as the wood from which they were made was recognized as having curative properties, while a staff is invoked in an 11th-century journeying charm (Grendon 1909, 176–179).

The possibility that Christian graves might contain items with amuletic significance has scarcely been entertained, but the presence of coins in graves is highly suggestive (Figure 23.4). A 1st-century Roman coin found adjacent to the skull of an infant burial in a cemetery dating to the 8th century at The Booths, Pontefract (Yorkshire) was highly worn and, in a rare example of discussion of the significance of such a find, Tony Wilmott (forthcoming) has suggested that this indicates its 'possible use as an amulet'. Support for the claim that Roman coins might have a meaningful role in later Anglo-Saxon funerary practices comes from the cemetery excavated at Staple Gardens in Winchester, in which burial commenced *c*AD 900 and ended in the mid-11th century according to radiocarbon dating (Kipling and Scobie 1990; Cherryson 2005 (Appendix), 89–90). In this cemetery at least 11 graves contained Roman coins deliberately deposited in various locations including on the pelvis, on the abdomen, in the hand, on the shoulder or, in one case, on the forehead (Scobie, pers comm). Roman coins placed on the body or within a coffin have also

Site	Grave	Age and Sex	Date	Comments	Source
St Peter's, Barton-upon-Humber (Lincolnshire)	Skeleton 1180/ grave 3548	Child; 6 years	Phase E, *c*950–1150	Roman coin on left shoulder	Waldron 2007, 28, 149
Caister-on-Sea (Norfolk)	Grave 14	Adult	Cemetery dated to late 8th to early 11th century on basis of associated artefacts	Coin of King Ecgbert of Wessex (*c*828–839) beneath the skull	Darling and Gurney 1993, 252
Bath Abbey (Somerset)	—	—	Burial dated on the basis of the coins	A hoard of *c*40 coins was found in 1755 in a grave near Bath Abbey. One report states that the coins were in a stone coffin, but another records that they were 'under the occiput of a skeleton . . . in a wooden box'. The hoard has been dated to AD 950–955	Blunt and Pagan 1975, 19–24
Honedon (Suffolk)	—	—	Burial dated on the basis of the coins	Between 200 and 300 coins were reportedly found in a grave near a skull. On the basis of records of 24 coins for which detailed records are available a date of *c*953 has been suggested	Blunt and Pagan, 1975, 28
Kintbury (Berkshire)	—	—	Burial dated on the basis of the coins	A hoard discovered in 1761 was reportedly under a skull in the churchyard. It consisted of *c*50 coins, dated on the basis of those that survive, or of which detailed records exist, to 957–960	Blunt and Pagan 1975, 25–28
Pontefract, The Booths (Yorkshire)	Grave 228	—	Radiocarbon dates from this phase centre on the 8th century	Sestertius of Domitian (AD 81–96), worn smooth on both sides, was found at the head end of the grave	Wilmott forthcoming
St Mary, Reading (Berkshire)	—	—	Burial dated on the basis of the coins	At least 11 coins of the 860s/870s found 'in a coffin' in the churchyard	Blackburn and Pagan 1986, 302
Wharram Percy (Yorkshire)	Grave V56	—	Burial radiocarbon dated to AD 1000–1280	Coin dates to *c*841–849/50	Mays *et al* 2007, 194, 303
Staple Gardens, Winchester (Hampshire)	Grave 208	Child; 6–8 years	Radiocarbon dating suggests the cemetery dates to the 10th–11th centuries	Roman coin in right hand	Scobie, pers comm
	Grave 225	Male; 45+		Three Roman coins above right pelvis and femur, associated with brown stain interpreted as a purse	
	Grave 228	Male; 45+		Roman coin above spine in area of abdomen	
	Grave 233	Male; adult		Roman coin below pelvis on right side	
	Grave 274	Male; adult		Roman coin found on rib-cage	
	Grave 293	Female; adult		Two Roman coins in right hand	
	Grave 331	?Female; 25–35 years		Roman coin placed on forehead	

	Grave 393	Infant		Two Roman coins in right hand	
	Grave 541	Male; 35–45 years		Roman coin on sternum	
	Grave 327	Male; 35–45 years	Radiocarbon dated to AD 780–990	Roman coin on right shoulder-blade	
	Grave 203	Female; 17–25 years	Radiocarbon dated to AD 988–1018	By right elbow	
St Helen-on-the-Walls, York	Grave 5168	Adolescent; *c*.15 years	Unlikely to be earlier than the 11th century	Coin dates to AD 852–874	Dawes and Magilton 1980, 15
York Minster	Grave 65	?male; adult	Cemetery dates to between the 8th and 11th centuries	Coin dates to AD 841–848. The burial was in a wooden chest	Phillips 1995, 90
	Grave 79	?Male; 12–15 years		Coin dates to AD 352. The burial was in a wooden chest	Phillips 1995, 91
	Grave 81	?Male; mature adult		Coin dates to AD 841–848. The burial was in a wooden chest	

FIGURE 23.4 Coins in later Anglo-Saxon graves.

been identified at Barton-upon-Humber (Waldron 2007, 28) and York Minster (Phillips 1995, 91). Although Roman coins may sometimes have been retrieved during grave digging, it is also entirely possible that they had been curated over a long period of time before being committed to the grave. Relevant in this respect is the fact that three coins found resting on the right pelvis of the male buried in grave 225 at Staple Gardens were associated with a brown organic stain that has been interpreted as representing the remains of a purse (Scobie, pers comm), implying that they had been carried around in life. Significantly, the location and context of their deposition mirrors the placing of amulets in bags suspended from the waist in 7th-century graves, a practice that has been associated with female healers or 'cunning women' (Meaney 1981; 1989; Geake 1997, 98–99). Later this association with females seems to have diminished, as does the disproportionate association of Roman coins with female graves, but the carrying of amulets in waist bags evidently continued (R White 1988, 99; Gilchrist 2008, 139–144).

It has long been recognized that Roman artefacts commonly occur in earlier Anglo-Saxon graves (R White 1988; Eckardt and Williams 2003), but the continuation of this practice into the later Anglo-Saxon period has largely escaped comment. The image of the emperor on Roman coins may have carried Christian connotations given its very clear association with Rome, the centre of early medieval Christianity. The amuletic associations of the image of the emperor is recorded on the continent in the early Middle Ages, and is suggested in earlier Anglo-Saxon England by evidence for the wearing of Roman coins as a component of necklaces or in bag collections (R White 1988, 101; Maguire 1997; Leahy 2006). Furthermore, Hella Eckardt and Howard Williams (2003) have argued that the association between Roman artefacts and prehistoric artefacts and fossils in early Anglo-Saxon graves indicates that their very antiquity was valued, perhaps for apotropaic purposes, while Roberta Gilchrist (2008, 144) has drawn attention to the association of antique artefacts, including those of Roman provenance, with medieval natural magic. The material remains of the Roman past were certainly desirable from the 7th century. The influence of Roman styles on jewellery in 7th-century burials has already been highlighted and the reuse of Roman sarcophagi for the interment of Christians is known from both written sources and the archaeological record. Most famously a Roman sarcophagus was acquired for the interment of St Æthelthryth in 695 at Ely (Cambridgeshire) (Colgrave and Mynors 1969, 366–368), while a recent analysis by David Stocker (2007, 271–281) of three grave covers from 11th-century burials at Wharram Percy (Yorkshire) has revealed that they were reused Roman sarcophagi lids. Although the source of the Roman sarcophagi is uncertain they were certainly not from the immediate vicinity, and Stocker suggests that these sarcophagi may have been acquired to make a political point (Stocker 2007, 281–284). If they were from York, it was, perhaps, an attempt to make a link with the archbishop; indeed, there is evidence that in the earlier 10th century Roman monuments were supplied from the vicinity of York for use as funerary monuments at churches in Lincolnshire, at a time when the archbishop's control appears to have extended south of the Humber (Stocker 2000). Alternatively, Stocker (2007, 284–285) suggests, the acquisition of Roman sarcophagi lids from a temple or villa complex near to Wharram may have been making a statement about the status of the manorial elite, by linking them with earlier generations of landholders in the vicinity. In sum, the Roman past had an enduring appeal in Anglo-Saxon England, and it is within this context that the deposition of Roman coins must be understood, with their amuletic, antique and Christian associations.

Anglo-Saxon coins are common finds when digging modern graves in churchyards (Morris 1983, 61) and — even taking into account the fact that churchyards were locations for a wide range of activities including commercial transactions (Sawyer 1986) — it is probable that some of these derive from graves. This deduction is supported by a small number of excavated graves that have produced coins. Examples include burials containing a single 9th-century coin excavated at Caister-on-Sea (Darling and Gurney 1993, 252), where the coin was found beneath the skull, and York Minster, where they appear to have been within wooden chests in two graves (Phillips 1995, 90–91). In some cases Anglo-Saxon coins were of some antiquity when deposited: a burial dating to no earlier than the 11th century contained a 9th-century coin at both St Helen-on-the Walls, York (Dawes and Magilton 1980, 15) and Wharram Percy (Yorkshire) (Mays *et al* 2007, 303). Single coins are prone to be dismissed as accidental inclusions, but groups of coins cannot be explained away in this fashion. In the churchyard at Kintbury (Berkshire) *c* 50 mid-10th-century Anglo-Saxon coins were found under the skull of a burial (Blunt and Pagan 1975, 25–28), while a group of late 9th-century silver pennies were excavated in a grave in the churchyard at St Mary, Reading (Berkshire) (Blackburn and Pagan 1986, 294, 302). A group of *c* 40 coins was found in a grave at Bath, probably dating to the 950s (Blunt and Pagan 1975, 18–24), and a similar date has been suggested on the basis of the few surviving coins from a reported deposit of 200–300 coins found near the skull in a grave at Honedon (Suffolk) (Blunt and Pagan 1975, 28). Although not necessarily all from graves, it is notable that there are many recorded coin hoards from churchyards, including those from Lower Dunsforth (Yorkshire) (dating to the late 9th century) (Reynolds 1975), Amesbury (Wiltshire) (early 10th century) (Robinson 1984), Constantine (Cornwall) (early 11th century) (Blackburn and Pagan 1986, 306), Rougham (Suffolk) (early 11th century) (Warren 1858–63), St John's, Chester (early 10th century) (Mack 1967) and Betham (Westmorland) (mid-11th century) (Blackburn and Pagan 1986, 308).

Hoarding is typically interpreted as a security measure during turbulent times, and the known hoards certainly peak during the period of Scandinavian raiding in the later 9th and early 10th century (Blackburn and Pagan 1986), yet hoards from graves and churchyards span the later Anglo-Saxon period. Moreover, the disruptive nature of grave digging renders churchyards a less than sound choice for safe-keeping of hoarded wealth, while the intention of retrieving coins from beneath the skull of a rotting corpse is surely a sufficiently strange notion that it ought to prompt us to consider alternative explanations for the deposition of coins in graves. In some cases it is probably indicative of Scandinavian ritual practices. The skeletal remains from a burial at Repton that included five silver Anglo-Saxon pennies and a gold ring have been subject to stable isotope analysis, which confirmed that this individual spent their early years in Scandinavia (Biddle and Kjølbye-Biddle 2001; Budd *et al* 2004), while a burial accompanied by late 9th-century coins at Leigh-on-Sea (Essex) is also likely to be that of a Scandinavian given the simultaneous deposition of a horse and sword (Blackburn and Pagan 1986, 302; Graham-Campbell 2001, 114). However, the deposition of coins in graves occurs across the country, not only in areas of Scandinavian settlement, and it is a practice that continues at a low level into the later Middle Ages (Gilchrist 2008, 133–135). The recent recognition of the continuing importance of ritual deposition through the Anglo-Saxon centuries and beyond provides a relevant context. David Stocker and Paul Everson (2003) have recently discussed the array of later Anglo-Saxon and medieval finds, including weapons and jewellery, from the River Witham in Lincolnshire, suggesting that these were deliberately deposited, not simply lost, in a river valley that long had a sacred character, being the location of a notable cluster of Anglo-Saxon and later medieval religious communities. In this context, the possibility that coins were placed both in graves and churchyards as some form of votive deposit appears entirely plausible.

The deposition of coins in graves continues into the later Middle Ages, when the votive dimension is reinforced by the fact that some of the coins were folded, which as Roberta Gilchrist (2008, 135) has recently argued, may have been part of a magic rite; ethnographic evidence suggests that the folding of artefacts was integral to preserving their magical powers. The amuletic quality of coins was enhanced by their circular form, which is a feature of many amulets (Meaney 1981, 222; Merrifield 1987, 91; Hinton 2005, 159; Gilchrist 2008, 135). Coins were certainly not purely a medium of exchange for the Anglo-Saxons, and were, for example, incorporated into items of jewellery, apparently as amulets (Leahy 2006).

The importance of the deposition of artefacts with amuletic qualities in earlier Anglo-Saxon cemeteries has long been recognized, but the possibility that this practice persisted has seemingly not been entertained. Given that this has practice has recently been detailed in later medieval burial rites, the need to take seriously this dimension of the earliest generations of churchyard burial is imperative (Gilchrist 2008). At Jarrow (Durham) two graves contained a single polychrome glass bead; these date to the 6th to 7th century, but one of these graves also included a fragment of a crucible dating to the 8th or 9th century, which may indicate that the bead had been curated for some time before deposition (Lowther 2005, 182). Beads have also been found in a late 10th-century grave from Beverley (Johnson 2004, 12), a 9th- or 10th-century grave from Thwing (Yorkshire) (Geake 1997, 159) and a grave dating to somewhere between the late 7th and late 9th century at Sedgeford (Davies and Hoggett 2001), and since beads have a traditional association with protecting against the 'evil eye' they may be another example of a later Anglo-Saxon amulet (Meaney 1981, 193, 213–215, 272; Gilchrist 2008, 149). The tusk of a boar is also widely recognized as possessing amuletic qualities, and examples have been found in graves in Anglo-Saxon churchyards at Wearmouth (McNeil and Cramp 2005, 80) and St Oswald's, Gloucester (Heighway and Bryant 1999, 202, 214). The pierced scallop shell from a burial at St Martin's, Wallingford, is indicative of pilgrimage and was perhaps also imbued with apotropaic powers given its association with a cult centre (Booth *et al* 2007, 268).

CONCLUSIONS

Although Richard Morris (1983, 59–62) long ago flagged the possibility that graves continued to contain artefacts into the later Anglo-Saxon period, the extent and significance of this practice is still scarcely appreciated. In part this is because of the lack of a comprehensive survey to compare with the many corpuses of earlier and mid-Anglo-Saxon burial practices (eg Geake 1997), but equally significant is the widespread reluctance of archaeologists to accept that deliberate deposition of artefacts occurred in Christian cemeteries. We have come to accept that natural landscapes, earlier cult sites and such pagan practices as the use of magic and charms continued to be meaningful after they were Christianized in the mid–later Anglo-Saxon period (Pluskowski and Patrick 2003; Blair 2005, 171–175), and it is surely now time to admit that as the grave was Christianized it, too, continued to resonate with symbolic meaning.

ACKNOWLEDGEMENTS

I am grateful to the editors and to Annia Cherryson for feedback on an earlier draft of this paper. I would like to thank Graham Scobie, Tony Wilmott and Terry Manby for providing information on their unpublished sites, and Annia Cherryson and Jo Buckberry for permission to cite their unpublished theses.

BIBLIOGRAPHY

Ayers, B, 1985 *Excavations Within the North-East Bailey of Norwich Castle*, East Anglian Archaeology 28, Norfolk Museums Service, Gressenhall

Barlow, F, 1992 *The Life of King Edward who Rests at Westminster*, 2nd edn, Oxford University Press, Oxford

Bassett, S R, 1982 *Saffron Walden: Excavations and Research, 1972–80*, Council for British Archaeology Research Report 45, Chelmsford

Bateman, N, 1997 'The early 11th to mid 12th-century graveyard at Guildhall, City of London', in de Boe and Verhaeghe (eds) 1997, 115–120

Biddle, M, 1965 'Excavations at Winchester 1964, third interim report', *Antiquaries Journal* 45, 230–264

Biddle, M, 1990 *Object and Economy in Medieval Winchester, Vol ii*, Clarendon Press, Oxford

Biddle, M and Kjølbye-Biddle, B, 2001 'Repton and the "great heathen army", 873–4', in Graham-Campbell *et al* (eds) 2001, 45–96

Blackburn, M A S and Pagan, H, 1986 'A revised check-list of coin hoards from the British Isles, *c*.500–1100', in M A S Blackburn (ed), *Anglo-Saxon Monetary History*, 291–313, Leicester University Press, Leicester

Blair, I, 2007 'Prittlewell prince', *Current Archaeology*, 207, 8–11

Blair, J, 2005 *The Church in Anglo-Saxon England*, Oxford University Press, Oxford

Blunt, C E and Pagan, H E, 1975 'Three tenth-century hoards: Bath (1755), Kintbury (1761), Threadneedle Street (before 1924)', *British Numismatic Journal* 45, 19–32

Boddington, A, 1990 'Models of burial, settlement and worship: the final phase reviewed', in E Southworth (ed), *Anglo-Saxon Cemeteries: a Reappraisal*, 177–199, Sutton, Stroud

Boddington, A, 1996 *Raunds Furnells: the Anglo-Saxon Church and Churchyard*, English Heritage, London

Bonner, G, Rollason, D and Stancliffe, C (eds), 1989 *St Cuthbert, his Cult and his Community*, Boydell, Woodbridge

Booth, P, Dodd, A, Robinson, M and Smith, A, 2007 *Thames Through Time. The Archaeology of the Gravel Terraces of the Upper and Middle Thames. The Early Historical Period: AD 1–1000*, Oxford University School of Archaeology, Oxford

Boyle, A, 2001 'Excavations in Christ Church Cathedral graveyard', *Oxoniensia* 66, 337–68

Buckberry, J L, 2004 'A social and anthropological analysis of conversion period and later Anglo-Saxon Cemeteries in Lincolnshire and Yorkshire', unpublished PhD thesis, University of Sheffield

Buckberry, J L, 2007 'On sacred ground: social identity and churchyard burial in Lincolnshire and Yorkshire, c.700–1100', in Semple and Williams (eds) 2007, 117–29

Buckberry, J L and Hadley, D M, 2001 'Fieldwork at Chapel Lane, Fillingham', *Lincolnshire History and Archaeology* 36, 11–18

Budd, P, Millard, A, Chenery, C, Lucy, S and Roberts, C, 2004 'Investigating population movement by stable isotope analysis: a report from Britain', *Antiquity* 78, 127–141

Bullough, D, 1983 'Burial, community and belief in the early medieval West', in P Wormald (ed), *Ideal and Reality in Frankish and Anglo-Saxon Society*, 177–201, Blackwell, Oxford

Carver, M, 1989 'Kingship and material culture in early Anglo-Saxon East Anglia', in S R Bassett (ed), *The Origins of Anglo-Saxon Kingdoms*, 141–158, Leicester University Press, Leicester

Carver, M, 1999 'Cemetery and society at Sutton Hoo: five awkward questions and four contradictory questions', in C Karkov, K Wickham-Crowley and B Young (eds), *Spaces of the Living and the Dead: an Archaeological Dialogue*, 1–14, Oxbow, Oxford

Carver, M, 2001 'Why that? Why there? Why then? The politics of early medieval monumentality', in H Hamerow and A MacGregor (eds), *Image and Power in the Archaeology of Early Medieval Britain*, 1–22, Oxbow, Oxford

Carver, M, 2002 'Reflections on the meanings of monumental barrows in Anglo-Saxon England', in Lucy and Reynolds (eds) 2002, 132–143

Carver, M (ed), 2003 *The Cross Goes North: Processes of Conversion in Northern Europe, AD 300–1300*, York Medieval Press, Woodbridge

Chambers, R A, 1976 'The cemetery site at Beacon Hill, near Lewknor, Oxon. 1972 (M40 site 12): an inventory of the inhumations and a re-appraisal', *Oxoniensia* 41, 77–85

Cherryson, A K, 2005 'In the Shadow of the Church: Burial Practices in the Wessex Heartlands, c.600–1100', unpublished PhD thesis, University of Sheffield

Coatsworth, E, 1989 'The pectoral cross and portable altar from the tomb of St Cuthbert', in Bonner, Rollason and Stancliffe (eds) 1989, 287–301

Colgrave, B, 1956 *Felix's Life of St Guthlac*, Cambridge University Press, Cambridge

Cowgill, J, de Neergaard, M and Griffiths, N, 1987 *Knives and Scabbards. Medieval Finds from Excavations in London*, Her Majesty's Stationery Office, London

Cramp, R (ed), 2005 *Wearmouth and Jarrow Monastic Sites, Volume 1*, English Heritage, Swindon

Cramp, R (ed), 2006 *Wearmouth and Jarrow Monastic Sites, Volume 2*, English Heritage, Swindon

Cramp, R, 2006 'Bangles, beads and glass objects', in Cramp (ed) 2006, 258–267

Cramp, R, Cherry, J and Lowther, P, 2006 'Copper alloy and silver', in Cramp (ed) 2006, 230–257

Crawford, S, 1989 'The Anglo-Saxon cemetery at Chimney, Oxfordshire', *Oxoniensia* 54, 45–56

Daniell, C, 1997 *Death and Burial in Medieval England, 1066–1550*, Routledge, London

Darling, M J and Gurney, D, 1993 *Caister-on-Sea: Excavations by Charles Green 1951–55*, East Anglian Archaeology 60, Norfolk Museums Service, Gressenhall

Davies, G and Hoggett, R, 2001 'Sedgeford Historical and Archaeological Research Project', unpublished report

Dawes, J D and Magilton, J R, 1980 *The Cemetery of St Helen-on-the-Walls, Aldwark*, The Archaeology of York 12, London

de Boe, G and Verhaeghe, H (eds), 1997 *Death and Burial in Medieval Europe*, Instituut voor het Archeologisch Patrimonium, Zellik

Dickinson, T and Griffiths, D (eds), 1999 *The Making of Kingdoms*, Anglo-Saxon Studies in Archaeology and History 12, Oxford

Eckardt, H and Williams, H, 2003 'Objects without a past? The use of Roman objects in early Anglo-Saxon graves', in H Williams (ed), *Archaeologies of Remembrance. Death and Memory in Past Societies*, 141–170, Kluwer, New York

Evans, M, 2003 *The Death of Kings: Royal Deaths in Medieval England*, Hambledon, London

Faull, M, 1976 'The location and relationship of the Sancton Anglo-Saxon cemeteries', *Antiquaries Journal* 56, 227–233

Field, N, 1993 'A possible Saxon cemetery at Swaby', *Lincolnshire History and Archaeology* 28, 45–46

Geake, H, 1992 'Burial practice in seventh- and eighth-century England', in M Carver (ed), *The Age of Sutton Hoo*, 83–94, Boydell, Woodbridge

Geake, H, 1997 *The Use of Grave-Goods in Conversion-Period England, c.600–c.850*, British Archaeological Reports 261, Oxford

Geake, H, 1999 'Invisible kingdoms: the use of grave-goods in seventh-century England', in Dickinson and Griffiths (eds) 1999, 203–215

Gilchrist, R, 2008 'Magic for the dead? The archaeology of magic in later medieval burials', *Medieval Archaeology* 52, 119–159

Gilchrist, R and Sloane, B, 2005 *Requiem: the Medieval Monastic Cemetery*, English Heritage, London

Gordon, I L, 1979 *The Seafarer*, 2nd edn, Exeter University Press, Exeter

Graham-Campbell, J, 1982 'A middle-Saxon gold finger-ring from the Cathedral Close, Exeter', *Antiquaries Journal* 62, 366–367

Graham-Campbell, J, 1988 'The gold finger-ring from a burial in St Aldate's St, Oxford', *Oxoniensia* 53, 263–266

Graham-Campbell, J, Hall, R, Jesch, J and Parsons, D (eds), 2001 *Vikings and the Danelaw: Select Papers from the Proceedings of the Thirteenth Viking Congress*, Oxbow, Oxford

Graham-Campbell, J, 2001 'Pagan Scandinavian burial in the central and southern Danelaw', in Graham-Campbell *et al* (eds) 2001, 105–123

Gräslund, A-S, 2000 'The conversion of Scandinavia — a sudden event or a gradual process?', in A Pluskowski (ed), *Early Medieval Religion*, Archaeological Review from Cambridge 17:2, 83–98

Grendon, F, 1909 'The Anglo-Saxon charms', *Journal of American Folklore* 22, 105–237

Hadley, D M, 1995 'The historical context of the inhumation cemetery at Bromfield, Shropshire', *Transactions of the Shropshire Historical and Archaeological Society* 70, 145–155

Hadley, D M, 2000 'Burial practices in the northern Danelaw, c.650–1100', *Northern History* 36, 199–216

Hadley, D M, 2004 'Gender and burial practices in England, c.650–900', in L Brubaker and J M H Smith (eds), *Gender in the Early Medieval World: East and West, 300–900*, 301–323, Cambridge University Press, Cambridge

Hadley, D M, 2006 *The Vikings in England: Settlement, Society and Culture*, Manchester University Press, Manchester

Hadley, D M, 2009a in press 'Engendering the grave in later Anglo-Saxon England', in G McCafferty, S Terendy and M Smekal (eds), *Proceedings of the 2004 Chacmool Conference*, University of Calgary Press, Calgary

Hadley, D M, 2009b in press 'Burying the socially and physically distinctive in later Anglo-Saxon England', in J L Buckberry and A K Cherryson (eds), *Later Anglo-Saxon Burial, c.650 to 1100AD*, Oxbow, Oxford

Hadley, D M and Buckberry, J L, 2001 'Great Hale', *Lincolnshire History and Archaeology* 36, 59

Hadley, D M and Buckberry, J L, 2005 'Caring for the dead in later Anglo-Saxon England', in F Tinti (ed), *Pastoral Care in Late Anglo-Saxon England*, 121–147, Boydell, Woodbridge

Hall, R A, 1994 *Viking Age York*, Batsford, London

Hall, R A and Whyman, M, 1996 'Settlement and monasticism at Ripon, North Yorkshire, from the 7th to 11th centuries A.D.', *Medieval Archaeology* 40, 62–150

Halsall, G, 1995 *Early Medieval Cemeteries: an Introduction to Burial Archaeology in the Post-Roman West*, Cruithne, Glasgow

Härke, H, 1989 'Knives in early Saxon burials: blade length and age at death', *Medieval Archaeology* 33, 144–148

Heighway, C and Bryant, R, 1999 *The Golden Minster. The Anglo-Saxon Minster and Later Medieval Priory of St Oswald at Gloucester*, Council for British Archaeology Research Report 117, York

Hill, P, 1997 *Whithorn and St Ninian: The Excavation of a Monastic Town*, Sutton, Stroud

Hinton, D, 2005 *Gold and Gilt, Pots and Pins. Possessions and People in Medieval Britain*, Oxford University Press, Oxford

Hoggett, J, 2007 'Charting conversion: burial as a barometer or belief?', in Semple and Williams (eds) 2007, 28–35

Holbrook, N and Thomas, A, 2005 'An early-medieval monastic cemetery at Llandough, Glamorgan: excavations in 1994', *Medieval Archaeology* 49, 1–92

Huggins, P J, 1984 'A note on a Viking-style plate from Waltham Abbey, Essex and its implications for a disputed late-Viking building', *Archaeological Journal* 141, 175–181

Hyslop, M, 1963 'Two Anglo-Saxon cemeteries at Chamberlains Barn, Leighton Buzzard, Bedfordshire', *Archaeological Journal* 110, 161–200

James, E, 1989 'Burial and status in the early medieval West', *Transactions of the Royal Historical Society* 39, 23–40

Johnson, M, 2004 'Beverley Minster', *Yorkshire Archaeology Today* 6, 12

Jolly, K, 1985 'Anglo-Saxon charms in the context of a Christian world view', *Journal of Medieval History* 11, 279–293

Jones, J and Clogg, P, 2006 'Examination and analysis of the gold foil', in Cramp (ed) 2006, 229–230

Kipling, R and Scobie, G, 1990 'Staple Gardens 1989', *Winchester Museums Service Newsletter* 6, 8–9

Kjølbye-Biddle, B, 1992 'The disposal of the Winchester dead over 2000 years', in S Bassett (ed), *Death in Towns: Urban Responses to the Dying and the Dead*, 210–247, Leicester University Press, Leicester

Leahy, K, 2006 'Anglo-Saxon coin brooches', in B Cook, G Williams and M Archibald (eds), *Coinage and History in the North Sea World, cAD500–1250*, 267–285, Brill, Leiden

Lebour, N, 1913–14 'White quartz pebbles and their archaeological significance', *Transactions of the Dumfriesshire and Galloway Natural History and Antiquarian Society* 2, 121–134

Lowther, P, 2005 'The Jarrow pre-Norman burial ground', in Cramp (ed) 2005, 173–186

Lucy, S and Reynolds, A (eds), 2002 *Burial in Early Medieval England and Wales*, Society for Medieval Archaeology Monograph 17, London

McNeil, S and Cramp, R, 2005 'The Wearmouth Anglo-Saxon cemetery', in Cramp (ed) 2005, 77–90

Mack, R P, 1967 'St John's church, Chester, hoard of 1862', *British Numismatic Journal* 36, 36–39

Maguire, H, 1997 'Magic and money in the early Middle Ages', *Speculum* 72:4, 1037–54
Mays, S, Harding, C and Heighway, C, 2007 *Wharram: a Study of Settlement on the Yorkshire Wolds. Vol. 11, The Churchyard*, University of York, York
Meaney, A L, 1981 *Anglo-Saxon Amulets and Curing Stones*, British Archaeological Research Reports 96, Oxford
Meaney, A L, 1989 'Women, witchcraft and magic in Anglo-Saxon England', in D Scragg (ed), *Superstition and Popular Medicine in Anglo-Saxon England*, 9–40, Manchester University Press, Manchester
Meaney, A L and Hawkes, S C, 1970 *Two Anglo-Saxon Cemeteries at Winnall, Winchester, Hampshire*, Society for Medieval Archaeology Monograph 4, London
Merrifield, R, 1987 *The Archaeology of Ritual and Magic*, Batsford, London
Miles, T J, 1986 'The excavation of a Saxon cemetery and part of the Norman castle at North Walk, Barnstaple', *Proceedings of the Devon Archaeological Society* 44, 59–84
Morris, R K, 1983 *The Church in British Archaeology*, Council for British Archaeology Research Report 47, London
Muthesius, A, 1989 'Silks and saints: the rider and peacock silks from the relics of St Cuthbert', in Bonner *et al* (eds) 1989, 343–366
Mytum, H, 1993 'Kellington church', *Current Archaeology* 133, 15–17
Napier, A S, 1967 *Wulfstan: Sammlung der ihm zugeschriebenen Homilien nebst Untersuchungen über ihre Echtheit*, revd edn, 1st pub 1883, Max Niehans Verlag, Zürich
Parkhouse, J, Roseff, R and Short, J, 1993 'A late Saxon cemetery at Milton Keynes village', *Records of Buckinghamshire* 38, 199–221
Phillips, D, 1995 'The pre-Norman cemetery', in D Phillips and B Heywood (eds), *Excavations at York Minster, Vol. 1, From Roman Fortress to Norman Cathedral*, 75–92, HMSO, London
Pluskowski, A and Patrick, P, 2003 '"How do you pray to God?" Fragmentation and variety in early medieval Christianity', in Carver (ed) 2003, 29–55
Potter, T W and Andrews, R D, 1994 'Excavation and survey at St Patrick's chapel and St Peter's church, Heysham, Lancs', *Antiquaries Journal* 74, 55–134
Redmond, A, 2007 *Viking Burial in the North of England*, British Archaeological Research Reports 429, Oxford
Reynolds, A, 1997 'The definition and ideology of Anglo-Saxon execution sites and cemeteries', in de Boe and Verhaeghe (eds) 1997, 33–41
Reynolds, K M, 1975 *The History of Lower Dunsforth*, Aldborough
Robinson, P H, 1984 'Saxon coins of Edward the Elder from St. Mary's churchyard, Amesbury', *Numismatic Chronicle*, 198–201
Rodwell, W and Rodwell, K, 1982 'St Peter's church, Barton-upon-Humber: excavation and structural study, 1978–81', *Antiquaries Journal* 62, 283–315
Rodwell, W and Rodwell, K, 1985 *Rivenhall: Investigations of a Villa, Church, and Village, 50–1977*, Council for British Archaeology Research Report 55, London
Rowntree, A, 1931 *The History of Scarborough*, J M Dent and Sons, London
Rudkin, D J, 2001 'Excavations at Bevis's Grave, Camp Down, Bedhampton, Hants.', unpublished report
Samson, R, 1999 'The Church lends a hand', in J Downes and T Pollard (eds), *The Loved Body's Corruption*, 120–144, Cruithne, Glasgow
Sawyer, P H, 1986 'Early fairs and markets in England and Scandinavia', in B L Anderson and A J H Latham (eds), *The Market in History*, 59–77, Croom Helm, London
Semple, S and Williams, H (eds), 2007 *Early Medieval Mortuary Practices*, Anglo-Saxon Studies in Archaeology and History 14, Oxford University Committee for Archaeology, Oxford
Sills, J, 1982 'St Peter's church, Holton-le-Clay', *Lincolnshire History and Archaeology* 17, 29–42

Staecker, J, 2003 'The cross goes north: Christian symbols and Scandinavian women', in Carver (ed) 2003, 463–482

Stocker, D, 2000 'Monuments and merchants: irregularities in the distribution of stone sculpture in Lincolnshire and Yorkshire in the tenth century', in D M Hadley and J D Richards (eds), *Cultures in Contact: Scandinavian Settlement in England in the Ninth and Tenth Centuries*, 179–212, Brepols, Turnhout

Stocker, D, 2007 'Pre-Conquest stonework — the early graveyard in context', in Mays *et al* (eds) 2007, 271–287

Stocker, D and Everson, P, 2001 'Five towns funerals: decoding diversity in Danelaw stone sculpture', in Graham-Campbell *et al* (eds) 2001, 223–243

Stocker, D and Everson, P, 2003 'The straight and narrow way: fenland causeways and the conversion of the landscape in the Witham valley, Lincolnshire', in Carver (ed) 2003, 271–288

Stoodley, N, 1999 'Burial rites, gender and the creation of kingdoms: the evidence from seventh-century Wessex', in Dickinson and D Griffiths (eds) 1999, 99–107

Symons, T, 1953 *The Monastic Agreement of the Monks and Nuns of the English Nation*, Nelson, London

Thompson, V, 2002 'Constructing salvation: a homiletic and penitential context for late Anglo-Saxon burial practice', in Lucy and Reynolds (eds) 2002, 229–240

Thompson, V, 2004 *Dying and Death in Later Anglo-Saxon England*, Boydell, Woodbridge

van de Noort, R, 1993 'The context of early medieval barrows in western Europe', *Antiquity* 67, 66–73

van Houts, E 1999 *Memory and Gender in Medieval Europe, 900–1200*, Macmillan, Basingstoke

Waldron, T, 2007 *St Peter's, Barton-upon-Humber, Lincolnshire. Vol. 2, The Human Remains*, Oxbow, Oxford

Warren, J, 1858–63 'Antiquities found in churchyards', *East Anglian Notes and Queries* 1, 437

White, R, 1988 *Roman and Celtic Objects from Anglo-Saxon Graves*, British Archaeological Research Report 191, Oxford

White, W, 1856 *History, Gazetteer, and Directory of Lincolnshire*, Independent Office, Sheffield

White, W, 1988 *Skeletal Remains from the Cemetery of St Nicholas Shambles, City of London*, MOLAS, London

Whitelock, D, 1930 *Anglo-Saxon Wills*, Cambridge University Press, Cambridge

Williams, H, 2006 *Death and Memory in Early Medieval Britain*, Cambridge University Press, Cambridge

Wilmott, T, forthcoming 'An Anglo-Saxon church and its cemetery: excavation in The Booths, 1985–86'

CHAPTER 24
MAKING THE PAST PRESENT: CINEMATIC NARRATIVES OF THE MIDDLE AGES

By MARK A HALL

By the eagerness of the human mind things which are obscure are more easily believed.
Tacitus (*History*, 1.22)

Probable impossibilities are to be preferred to improbable possibilities.
Aristotle (*Poetics*, 24.1460a)

This paper offers a broad overview of the cinematic portrayal of the medieval past, particularly by narrative-based, popular film culture. Within that overview it identifies and focuses on some key themes, namely, monasticism, cultural biography, historical veracity and the contemporary context (encompassing the depiction of archaeologists and surviving medieval material culture). Whilst noting that there are problems with a narrative approach, the paper urges medievalists to engage more fully with such films as part of the wider debate on the relevance, manipulation and appropriation of the past.

INTRODUCTION

Within the confines of a short paper I hope to achieve an overview of how cinema has depicted the medieval past and a closer examination of some particular themes[1] supporting the broader social perspectives of this volume: the monastic experience (both as a retreat from the world and as a point of political engagement and corruption), the question of cultural biography and material culture (examining in particular the symbolic roles of the Bayeux tapestry and the Lewis chessmen), a Beowulf case-study (to illuminate questions of veracity and appropriation) and the linked questions of how (medieval) archaeologists and the survival of medieval culture are depicted. In a volume that marks the 50th anniversary of the Society for Medieval Archaeology and so 50 years of diverse, interdisciplinary practice, this essay is intended to also reflect the wider popularity of things medieval. Cinematically this was well underway before the foundation of the Society and its trajectory is recorded in the opening theme that follows this introduction. The available space also means that whilst I am aware that films are part of a wider commercial, consuming culture (see, for example, Marshall 2007), I will only make cursory reference to some of those other aspects.[2] Such films comprise one of the arenas where so-called popular culture and public archaeology interface in acts of public and private contestation and consumption, and negotiate their relationships to the past and present. Films are bound up with perceived meanings of reality and life and how the past is constantly in flux with the present: consumed, reused and appropriated to help define the future. Films are both part of this dialogue and (semi-)detached observers of it. It is not so much that films portraying a medieval past deliberately get it wrong; they are more focused on contemporary fears and anxieties. This can translate into a philosophical concern with the idea of whether art can be both part of life and an observer of it. This is no better demonstrated than by perhaps the finest cinematic excursion into the medieval, *Andrei Roublev* (USSR 1966) which charts the life of the renowned, eponymous icon painter and in doing so demonstrates that the artist is not detached as an observer but integral, whether it be Roublev or the director, Tarkovsky, in making a film about Roublev (Le Fanu 1987; Tarkovsky 1986). There is an analogy here for archaeology generally as both observer of and participant in the world — the dramatically moral and political actions of fictional archaeologist Indiana Jones (see below) can be seen reflected in the comparatively recent phenomenon of what Jeremy Sabloff (2008) has christened 'action archaeology', solving contemporary world problems through the application of archaeological knowledge.

A lack of historical veracity often runs rampant in many medieval-set escapades and generally arouses panic and alarm (at least from many academics). It would be easy to be sidetracked into cataloguing a plethora of woeful inaccuracies, particularly for the likes of the incompetent *Beowulf* (US 1998), *Robin Hood Prince of Thieves* (US 1991), *King Arthur* (US 2005), *The Viking Queen* (UK 1967) and *Attila the Hun* (US 2001). But this would become dull, and instead I have adopted an approach that accepts that veracity is an issue but not one to be overly dwelt on. The main focus of this paper is a variety of films (of varying artistic merit and archaeological/historical veracity) that can raise questions about how and why the medieval past is refashioned for other than obvious commercial imperatives. The frequently decried *A Knight's Tale* (US 2001) uses the medieval past to mirror our own times, making it a film in very marked contrast to the Czech masterpiece *Markéta Lazarová* (1968). The latter consciously sought to avoid anything approaching contemporary people in historical costumes; indeed, to try and achieve psychological exactness the actors and crew were made to live in a forest for two years, dressed in rags (Hames 2000). In *A Knight's Tale* the medieval past wears raiment of the modern world, both literally (including the cut of the costumes) and metaphorically. Thus, the tournament becomes a world championship sport by which a lowly man can make his name and win glory. It is nothing less than the American capitalist dream fuelled by the rebellion of rock music. Its inescapable flaw is that it makes then and now essentially the same and does not allow for a sense of 'other' about the past (cf Muir 2005, 11). It does put forward a cogent view of its own, based on research which it chooses to interpret non-academically. This is compellingly performed by its central cast of actors, notably Heath Ledger as the knight and Paul Bettany as Chaucer (who is obviously the inspiration for the title and the film posits itself as an account of six months in his life which are not historically accounted for). One may dislike how it chooses to deploy the past, but it is more than the lazy nonsense-soups listed above, which fail to define, create, challenge or otherwise stimulate thought about cultural categories (Krasniewicz 2006, 12–14). Both *A Knight's Tale* and its contemporary *Timeline* (US 2003, see below) may not be historically or archaeologically true, but in redefining medieval culture they are engaging with the debate about original meanings and the changing nature of cultural history, in turn a reflection of the multi-temporality of existence: future, present and past constantly interlinking (Holtorf 2002). Thus, present-day film-makers can treat the medieval period as an artefact and give it new meanings to reflect contemporary concerns; just as a Bronze Age arrowhead can be seen to have one set of meanings in the Bronze Age (principally to do with hunting and killing) and at least one distinct meaning in the medieval period as a found piece of apotropaic elf-shot (Hall 2005, 213).

It is also worth pointing out that a concern with authenticity and historical exactitude has rarely been a concern of artistic and cultural pursuits. It is absent, for example, from the works of Shakespeare, whose historical plays were written in a continuum of Tudor and Stuart politics and propaganda, and were always contemporarily rather than historically costumed. In a more contemporary setting, the historical veracity of James Bond is not really the issue; what is, is his vicarious acting-out of the desires of Britain's post-war society to uphold the rationale of British interest/empire (Winder 2006). The collective Bond oeuvre of novels and films form a modern example of a well-attested (but not exclusive) medieval phenomenon, the retelling of tales (Brewer 1997). An acute consequence of the Enlightenment for Western culture is the assumption that there should be no gap between words and what they represent and that the objective correspondence between the two is the principal focus for language (Brewer 1997, 15). But it was not and is not always so:

> the truth that language might have is not limited to ... objective materialist fact. As Gurevich remarks of medieval monastic forged charters, made as it were in good faith, because they expressed what ought to be true: 'The function of documents was to express the highest truth — justice in the ideal meaning of the term — and not simply record chance facts.' Such an attitude of mind is not intrinsically ridiculous. Language has larger uses than materialistically verifiable description — for example expression (which may include internal incompatible desires) and persuasion. (Brewer 1997, 15, and quoting Gurevich 1985, 177)

It is something of a double-irony that in the Middle Ages the Bible was rarely, if ever, taken literally as a book of verifiable facts, in sharp contrast with our supposed more rational world in which Christian fundamentalists can only see the Bible as a book of facts, perhaps in part because of the widely recognized notion fostered by science that truth equals facts. Following its invention in the late 19th century, cinema rapidly made itself and was made by audiences the narrative medium of visual mass consumption (a role it now shares with television and the internet). Cinema is a voracious reteller of tales and its voracity has endorsed the credulity of human belief. As Terry Eagleton (2004, 4) has observed: 'Human existence is at least as much about fantasy and desires as it is about truth and reason'. The consequence is a profusion of imagined realities, given credence through narrative construction. They can rarely be separated from the reality of life as lived because they deeply inform the latter and mould it (for example, the cult of saints in the medieval period).[3]

This paper is not intended as a paean to narrative which clearly has its dangers, principally a tendency to progress to a neatly resolved ending, something which links to a wider sense of time as a linear progression, also a cultural construct (see, for example, Latour 1993; Whitrow 1988; and Lucas 2005). The dramatic satisfactions of this approach can be such that many of us expect to find them repeated in our own lives (in professional circles alone it has been reinvented as CPD, Career Professional Development, for example), though in reality narrative is perhaps more surreal than real. It is certainly an embedded cultural reflex and so something to which we can all respond: surely then, archaeologists (medieval or otherwise) should consider deploying narrative frameworks as a valid strategy to help communicate the human past.

FROM ESMERALDA TO THE LAST LEGION: REVIEWING THE MAIN TRENDS

Medieval costume epic is almost as old as cinema itself. Victor Hugo's neo-gothic literary re-imagining of medieval Paris, *The Hunchback of Notre Dame*, was filmed as early as 1906, with the title *Esmeralda*, closely followed by other film adaptations of the same novel, Fritz Lang's filming of the *Niebelungenlied* in the mid-1920s and several adaptations of Mark Twain's *A Connecticut Yankee in the Court of King Arthur*. The impact of World War II brought four of the most enduring cinematic imaginings of our medieval past — *The Hunchback of Notre Dame* (US), *The Adventures of Robin Hood* (US), *Alexander Nevsky* (USSR) (all 1939) and *Henry V* (UK 1944). The last three are paramount examples of successful medieval forays, in part due to their fusion of the medieval with the contemporary context in which they were filmed (in both the USA and the USSR) — successfully propagandizing the moral need to resist Hitler's expansionist aggression. Still, it was not until the 1950s that things really took off, with a veritable explosion of medieval costume epics: *Ivanhoe*, *The Vikings*, *The Knights of the Round Table*, *The Virgin Spring*, *The Seventh Seal*, *The Court Jester*, *The Seven Samurai* and innumerable Robin Hoods. It would be easy to put this down to the quest by studios for box office receipts that the safe, colourful heroic past could provide, especially with what had by then become the widespread use of colour film stock. But there are other factors at play, including a collective, social desire to leave behind war-time austerity and a growing interest in and study of the medieval past (of which the foundation of the Society for Medieval Archaeology in 1957 was, of course, symptomatic). This found expression in other fields of culture, including Angus Wilson's 1956 novel *Anglo-Saxon Attitudes*. This 'medieval momentum' was successfully maintained into the 1960s with the likes of *The War Lord*, *El Cid*, *Siege of the Saxons*, *Lancelot and Guinevere*, *Camelot*, *Taras Bulba*, *Alfred the Great* and perhaps the film that remains the finest cinematic expression of the medieval world, Andrei Tarkovsky's *Andrei Roublev*, and in particular the magnificent bell-casting sequence, in which a young apprentice has to cast his first bell or feel the bite of the sword that has killed his master. In its fusion of formal aesthetics, realism and inner poetic it opens an acute window on the world it depicts that feels as if we have literally stepped through a mirror.

There was something of a tailing off in the 1970s and 1980s as society shifted focus away from 1960s liberalism, though these years still managed to produce some key masterpieces, most notably Bresson's *Lancelot du Lac*, Tavernier's *La Passion Béatrice*, Gaup's *Pathfinder*, Vigne's *The Return of Martin Guerre*, *Monty Python and the Holy Grail* and Ward's *Navigator: A Medieval Odyssey*. The last is a standout movie in which Ward's apocalyptic vision of the Black Death and its arrival in a remote Cumbrian mining community successfully links 14th-century Cumbria with modern-day New Zealand. All of these in some sense ran counter to the prevailing culture and used their perceptive medieval recreations to question a complacent nostalgia about the past. They are not typical of their decades and the 1980s in particular went down something of a cul-de-sac with the stereotypical Dark Age influenced sword-and-sorcery epics defined by *Conan the Barbarian* (derived from the original R E Howard pre-World War II stories, later adapted into comic book form). The interest in more mainstream medievalism resumed in the 1990s and continues in our present decade, though with no noticeable qualitative improvement, despite advances in special effects and period detailing. Certainly the finest achievement of the 1990s is *The Hour of the Pig* (UK/FR 1993) a perceptive, bawdy, well-conceived evocation of the medieval world-view as other to our own (revolving around the trial of a pig for murder in a remote French village).

Undoubtedly the most consistent thread to cinema's appropriation of the Middle Ages (usually via literature and pulp fiction) is its resolute reliance on certain mythologized characters, in particular King Arthur (closely followed by Robin Hood and then probably Joan of Arc). Virtually every decade has produced two or three versions, generally of dubious artistic merit but useful barometers on their times of production rather than the period of Arthur. Of the two most recent (leaving aside the contemporary Grail fantasy *The Da Vinci Code*), *King Arthur* (US 2005) claims to be an accurate reflection of current archaeological thinking on Arthur but proves to be woefully inadequate as both popular exposition and popular narrative. Set in the late 5th century, *The Last Legion* (UK/IT *et al* 2006) is by no means a masterpiece but does have a narrative integrity, tied to the familiar academic theme of the inheritance of Rome. It offers the viewer a myth about the origin of Excalibur, with the sword made in Britannia for Julius Caesar and the Julian bloodline. *King Arthur*, in particular, demonstrates a wider point that if you take all these films together there is no readily apparent upward curve of improving representation. Films not only reflect the concerns of the times in which they are made but the varying ignorances and economic exigencies of their makers.

NAMING THE ROSE: IN AND BEYOND THE MONASTIC CLOISTER

The filmed monastic space (whatever its gender distinction) encompasses several dimensions or contexts. There are those films which seek to reconfigure a medieval narrative in which the monastery/nunnery plays a pivotal or significant supporting role. Chief amongst them are *The Adventures of Robin Hood*, *The Name of the Rose*, *Markéta Lazarová*, *Andrei Roublev* and *Ivanhoe*. These fictionalized accounts of medieval monasticism are characterized by compunction to subvert or question a notion of medieval spirituality and expose its human failings. This is at its most human and realistic in the film about the 14th-century master of icon painting, *Andrei Roublev* (Figure 24.1). The wanderings of Roublev and his fallings-out with fellow Russian orthodox monks are central to the film's exploration of the role (observer or participant?) of the artist in society. This also questions the role of monks: should they be entirely separate from society or fully engaged with it? This serves, too, as a metaphor for Andrei Tarkovsky's — the film's director — perception of his role and his control by communist state hierarchies. Hollywood's Robin Hood gives us the

FIGURE 24.1 *Andrei Rublev* (USSR 1966): sometimes a picture is worth a thousand words, as with this brilliantly composed image which speaks of the monk as spiritual and social agent through the practice of art. The environment strikingly evokes Novgorod. (Source: BFI)

narrative contrast of Friar Tuck, the gluttonous preaching friar, fighting against injustice and the political machinations and greed of the 'Bishop of the Black Canons' (sumptuously dressed in purple robes and a cardinal's hat). *The Name of the Rose* (based on Umberto Eco's novel) is centred on male monasticism and is able to contrive a portrait that, whilst leaning towards corruption, also dramatizes diversity of belief at an individual and group level, making a case for orthodoxy as contested territory. It also dramatizes the paradox of medieval monasteries as gatekeepers of knowledge — on one side of the door preserving the wisdom of the text through copying, on the other preventing wider access even to the point of destroying 'dangerous' texts.[4] *Markéta Lazarová* combines both male and female monasticism with a rather inept, wandering preacher (a holy fool metaphor), whose principal attachment appears to be to his companion sheep, contrasted with a Carmelite nunnery of cruel and compassionless women (and implicitly antithetical to human love and motherhood). This strict, authoritarianism may have something to do with the film being made in Communist Czechoslovakia and towing the party-line on religion. The tone was much softer in the 1931 novel on which the film was based, by Vladislav Vančura (Slododová 2000).

Perhaps the most compelling film portrait of medieval monasticism as narrative is the 1950 Italian work *Francesco Giullare Di Dio* (*Francis, Jester of God*), which skilfully imparts a spiritual dimension to the rejection of wealth and the embracing of poverty by Francis and his early disciples. Their simple, rude, transient, unenclosed dwelling huts and church would leave barely a discernible trace in the archaeological record. The film's realism was assisted by employing non-professional actors (including Franciscan monks) and emphasizes the rejection of materialism and violence in a warm, earthy manner. It includes a final scene in which Francis's brothers all spin around until collapsing giddy, the direction each is pointing to in their prone positions then becomes the direction each must travel on their preaching journeys — a brilliant visual evocation of the spirit breathing where it will, but also of one aspect of medieval divination. The structure of the film also skilfully evokes its medieval source material: a series of episodes is each preceded by its own inter-title captioning the sequence, rather like the medieval combination of word and image in any number of tableaux and sequential paintings of saints' lives.

My focus in this paper is commercial, narrative cinema, but there is at least one documentary portrait of monasticism which we should take account of, *Die Grosse Stille* (*Into Great Silence*, GY 2004). This is a record of the mother-house of the Carthusian order, Grande Chartreuse, founded in 1084, and perched, eyrie-like, high in the Chartreuse Mountains north of Grenoble, France. Clearly, this is not an attempt to narrate a medieval story but it is about a medieval establishment and its continuation in our own times. It is carefully structured so as to capture the cyclical rhythm of monastic time and routine, its seclusion and silence. Like the lives of the monks, it is largely free of dialogue. The monastery has survived by following this cyclical time (pulsing with medieval echoes) rather than historical time. It has never been entirely immune from history — it was closed by the State between 1901–40, and its architecture spans the centuries rather than being frozen in the 11th century. In the routines of monastic life one can also see laid out the great medieval debates about the balance of work and prayer, of speech and silence, and of play. Once a week the monks are allowed beyond the walls for recreational walking and talking, and the scene where they improvise a snow slide is redolent with Thomas Aquinas's endorsement of play (Hall forthcoming). There is also a single scene which captures the brothers in rare conversation: they talk about hand-washing as a ritual and how it is practised differently elsewhere, or not at all; and they debate whether the rituals are empty, or if there is an error, whether it is in the mind, not the action. This feels like a timeless debate, one had since the foundation of the monastery. At times the film achieves a transcendent quality where it no longer just represents the monastery but feels as though it has become the monastery, a sort of filmic skeuomorph. The film also forms a useful contrast with another documentary, *Temenos* (UK/FR 1998), which is concerned not with the insular, conventual space but the holy place in the world and the roots of sacredness.

I have explored in some detail elsewhere (Hall 2006a) the cinematic depiction of the cult of saints and here I will focus briefly on elements of how we can see through films medieval cultural traits evolving and changing in later times. The film trajectory of St Joan of Arc mirrors the persistent trait of medieval Christianity in proclaiming saints that were not officially recognized in Rome[5] — it took nearly 500 years for the church to canonize Joan (see, for example, Airlie 2001, 166–168; Lerner 1996, 54–59; and Hall 2006a). The magic lantern of cinema is almost the ideal artistic medium for depicting miracles, as it is for exposing them. The framework of belief-suspended that it can create gives faith a convincing, real-world reality. This has never been more brilliantly achieved for a depiction of the medieval past than by Ingmar Bergman in *The Seventh Seal* (SWE 1957), structured as a film essay on the Dance Macabre and the devastating impact of the Black Death. It boasts a sequence which is both riveting and haunting: a vision of the Virgin Mary as Queen of Heaven, gliding across the ground through the early morning mist, beside a camp of travellers. Several other films incorporate the continuing practice of the cult of saints as a part of their fabric but space is at a premium and so I will deal with only one, *Manon des Sources* (FR 1986). Set in 1920s rural Provence, it depicts a diversely practised faith incorporating orthodox piety and sympathetic magic. The medieval parish church is ever present but not always central. When a frequently absent congregation returns to the church because of a desperate drought, their priest castigates them and then leads them in a procession with the holy relics, to try and induce God to restore their water. As the wronged party and someone perceived to be innocent, Manon is asked to join the procession and she does. Various holy banners are carried and also a canopied stretcher on which sits a painted bust or head reliquary, presumably of the village's patron saint. They process around the fountain, singing hymns and when the water resumes all presume/perceive a miracle (though the atheist mayor sees only coincidence). In reality, an hour or so earlier, Manon and her fiancé had unblocked the spring. The link between faith and water is further defined by Manon's surrogate parents, an elderly couple (tinkers) who establish a spring-side grotto that includes a small shrine to the Virgin — a small, blue painted statue of Mary, set amidst straw and with several candles lit about her. It represents a robust, demanding faith, akin to magic in its results orientation. The film contrasts this with the more secular, sympathetic love-magic of the character Ugolin, which is bloody, futile and ends in his suicide.

BEDKNOBS, BROOMSTICKS AND THE PHILOSOPHERS' STONES: CULTURAL BIOGRAPHY OR OBJECTS BIG AND SMALL

Cultural biography is a key area of academic discourse that finds a ready home in film culture, if not in all its rich complexity. The main aim of cultural biography is to explore the whole and changing range of human relationships invested in material culture: it is about charting the social life of things, to coin the title from one of the founding texts of this field of enquiry (Appadurai 1986). In its narrative application, cultural biography is no stranger to the cinema screen (as to other fictive cultures, see, for example, Terry Pratchett's *The Fifth Elephant*). Both *The Yellow Rolls Royce* (UK 1964) and *The Red Violin* (CAN/IT 1998) centre their stories on a chronological progression of owners of, respectively, a car and a violin and how they influence the lives of their various owners. Though limited by their linear chronologies and the fairly static identities of their chosen items of material culture they still address the question of life-cycles so fundamental to cultural biography (see Lucas 2005, 96–97, who notes that this aspect has been part of archaeological theory since the 1950s). The cinema frame can contribute to cultural biography at a wider level with respect to our subject, in recording how our concepts of the medieval period change. Thus many of the films discussed in this paper, however variable in quality, still offer insights into how the Middle Ages are and have been perceived and appropriated; if you like, how they have been forced out of their old clothes of academic, originary meanings into new, rather gaudy garb, reflecting non-academic taste. They also demonstrate, through their appropriations, the life-cycle focus of cultural biography.

One of the most engaging biographies of medieval material culture is Carola Hicks's *The Bayeux Tapestry, The Life Story of a Masterpiece* (2006), which is neither confined to the medieval period nor to the origins of the Tapestry, but tracks how it has been interpreted, analysed and appropriated down to our own times. It includes a short chapter on both its filmic depictions and its theoretical modelling as a proto-film (Hicks 2006, 262). In terms of commercial cinema, the Tapestry is commonly deployed as a generic medieval object that audiences will recognize and is often presented with varying degrees of humour and affection (Hicks 2006, 265). Hicks identifies five films that deploy the Tapestry: *The Vikings* (US 1958), *Becket* (US 1964), *Bedknobs and Broomsticks* (US 1971), *Robin Hood Prince of Thieves* (US 1990) and *Hamlet* (US 1990). *The Vikings*, *Bedknobs and Broomsticks* and *Robin Hood Prince of Thieves* all adapt the Tapestry for their opening credit sequence, echoing its framing structure as a framing device. It analogizes, respectively: Viking raids on Britain, well before the time of the Tapestry; resistance to Nazi invasion at Hastings during World War II (having the effect of reversing the outcome of the first Battle of Hastings, the second battle is fought by a bewitched 'army of the dead');[6] and the return of Robin from the Crusades. *Becket*, *Robin Hood* and *Hamlet* all deploy the Tapestry within their dramas, indicating the oft-presumed female context of production. In *Robin Hood*, Maid Marian is seen making the Tapestry; in *Becket*,

Matilda (granddaughter of William and mother of Henry II) and Eleanor of Aquitaine work on it together; and in *Hamlet*, Ophelia and her ladies work on it in her bedchamber in Elsinore (with the various portions being worked correctly laced onto frames; Hicks 2006, 267). But this cinematic trend appears to have started with *El Cid* (US 1961), in which Queen Urrica visits El Cid's beloved Charmaine in her secluded nunnery, where she is working alone on the Tapestry in her guest apartment. A section (scene 53) is laid out on a frame, both ends rolled up, with a pattern-scroll at hand. The association with royal ladies (if not the production context) is also taken up by the medieval-fantasy *Dragonheart* (US 1996), in which the queen's bedspread is designed in line with the marginalia of the Tapestry. There are at least three further cinematic appropriations of the Tapestry — one of them is the earliest I have been able to identify, *The Court Jester* (US 1955), in which Danny Kaye hilariously satirizes Robin Hood and the notion of chivalry. The main hall of the king's castle in Dover has its entrance flanked by two massive, floor-to-ceiling tapestries (apparently cotton prints): one a scene of mounted knights engaging with foot-soldiers, that does not precisely correlate to a Tapestry scene, and the other copying scene 44, where William is shown sitting with Odo and Robert. The second is set in 1183, *The Lion in Winter* (UK 1968), and in it various castles in England and France belonging to the feuding Angevin family have rooms decorated with Tapestry-inspired hangings (rather than direct copies of scenes). None of the films show an awareness of the ecclesiastical link via Odo to Bayeux and the Tapestry's life as a relic in its cathedral. The third film, *Is Paris Burning?* (FR/US 1966), covers a much later episode in the Tapestry's biography — its near theft by the Nazis as part of their retreat from Paris during World War II (on which see Hicks 2006, 210–247).

These films, though largely inaccurate in their depiction of techniques, do engage with the notion of royal ladies organizing production and to a valid context of display in royal halls. They convey authenticity without full accuracy, which is of course the point. Within royal and high noble circles of the 12th and 13th centuries the Tapestry was so well known, indeed was not stylistically unique, that it (or they) could have been used as a model for copying. The Tapestry, wherever deployed, is clearly meant to be recognized by most of its audience as a touchstone of the medieval period. This is confirmed by its most recent film appearance, the contemporary existential comedy *I ♡ Huckabees* (US/GY/UK 2004). The scene in question was deleted from the final release but is available on the DVD release. It is set in the living room of the story's existential detectives where several books lie scattered on the carpet around the coffee table, including a briefly glimpsed copy of a large tome on the Tapestry (probably David Wilson's 2004), an indication of broad-ranging intellectual interests.[7]

My second example is a group of connected objects rather than a single item, namely, the so-called Lewis chessmen. While they might more properly be called the Lewis gaming hoard (Caldwell *et al* forthcoming), it remains true that the hoard is widely understood and recognized as a chess set. As such it is deployed as a readily recognizable symbol of elite play and intellectual pretension. It is part of the appropriate 12th-century setting of both *Becket* and *The Lion in Winter*. In the former, King Louis of France plays chess against one of his nobles using red and white Lewis-style pieces with the addition of castle-style rook pieces (presumably because they would be more readily understood as such by the audience). In the latter, the pieces are black and white and played by Philip II of France and Geoffrey Plantagenet as they plot the demise of Henry II. The pieces are randomly laid on the board, clearly only to be glimpsed as a metaphor (rather than a meaningful game) for power-politics. To make the kings more distinctive they are given very elaborate, high-backed thrones and there are minor variations to several of the other pieces; traits they appear to have borrowed from the earliest film depiction of the pieces I have found, *The Seventh Seal* (1957) (Figure 24.2). In this film, though, they reflect a different concern, the overriding power of death. The pieces play their part in an accurate rendition of the medieval concept of Death as a chess player, one whose victory is always assured and a concept that was part of the wider metaphor of the Dance Macabre (Hall 2009). It shows the pieces as black and white (we only have white pieces) but this — together with the film's stylistic departure from the Lewis pieces, its interpretation of the warders as pawns and their a-chronology — are all valid choices for dramatic, symbolic communication. Outside a medieval context, the French film *Le Bossu* (1959) includes a scene where two 18th-century noblemen

FIGURE 24.2 *The Seventh Seal* (SWD 1957): a knight plays chess with death — using some Lewis-inspired pieces. (Source: BFI)

engage in a game using Lewis-style pieces: its medieval origin is not the issue here, but signifying the game and its elite social status is. Its most recent deployment is in the medieval-gothic fantasy adventure *Harry Potter and the Philosopher's Stone* (US 2001) where Lewis-style pieces (again in red and white) are used by Harry and his friend Ron to play 'Wizards' Chess', where the pieces are moved by voice command and physically strike each other when capturing. The use of medieval chess pieces in post-medieval and parallel world contexts reminds us that although it is essentially a medieval game, it is not fossilized as such. It is a significant example of a long-lasting legacy from the medieval period, a legacy acknowledged by a long list of films that depict chess either as the centre of attention or as a supporting, powerful symbol.

BEOWULF: THE MONSTERS AND THE FANTASISTS

In November 2007 cinema screens across Britain were suddenly alive with a striking reimagining of Beowulf, variously shown in 2-D and digital 3-D versions. It has its flaws but it is a notable mirror of Western society's contemporary obsession with sex and the fear of death. For *Beowulf*, demonic sex in particular is made the narrative fulcrum of the story, as signalled by the film's poster-tag: 'Face your Demons'. The history of the cinematic interpretation of *Beowulf* is chronologically long but with comparatively few entries. The earliest I know of is a 1920s' Danish film. It is then fairly quiet until the last 30 years or so, when there has been something of a flurry of adaptations, namely: *Grendel, Grendel, Grendel* (Australia 1981, animated adaptation of John Gardiner's novel, reviewed in Hall 2005), *Beowulf* (UK 1998, animated), *Beowulf* (US/GY 1998 — it has to be said, an utterly unforgivable piece of nonsense), *The 13th Warrior* (US 1999, a partial adaptation), *Beowulf and Grendel* (US 2005), *Wrath of Gods* (US 2007, a documentary on the making of *Beowulf and Grendel*) and *Beowulf Prince of the Geats* (US 2007; notable for its controversial casting of a black actor as Beowulf, Nokes 2008). The 2007 version is particularly notable for its creation of the three monsters. The poem is primarily concerned with combating external evil, aptly summed up by Heaney (1999, xii) as:

> Three struggles in which the preternatural force-for-evil of the hero's enemies comes springing at him in demonic shapes . . . in three archetypal sites of fear: the barricaded night house; the infested underwater current; and the reptile haunted rocks of a wilderness.

The film has more interior concerns, mainly achieved through a dose of narrative-simplifying sex, which ironically leads to some unintentionally hilarious coyness about showing Beowulf's penis when he fights naked. There are several plot changes as a consequence.

Hrothgar is depicted as a drunken, guilt-ridden old man kicked out of the marriage bed by his young queen, Wealtheow. He has lain with the water-demon to gain his power and Grendel is their offspring. Beowulf also succumbs to this temptation, and so Hrothgar names him his successor and then commits suicide. Beowulf marries Wealtheow and rules in Heorot. Fifty years later he must fight his offspring from the demon, a golden-skinned man able to transform into a dragon. Dying, he names Wiglaf his successor and Grendel's mother comes to seduce him, the cycle of temptation set to begin again. These changes serve to simplify and humanize the story, and paradoxically bring the monsters to the fore. Grendel is a giant figure of repulsion — deformed, gouged, self-harmed, with raw, exposed flesh and inhuman strength, something that could have been hybridized from the imaginations of Blake, Goya and Bacon (Figure 24.3). He does, though, elicit a spark of sympathy heightened by being the son of Hrothgar. His mother is the very definition of voluptuousness and seduction and the dragon is a fabulous creation — fearsome, cruel, vengeful, brutal and deadly. They serve to underline the frailty of the human condition, destined to fall, to succumb to temptation.

The film is somewhat less interesting for the physical world it tries to evoke, a flawed attempt betraying only a limited grasp of cultural context, be it material culture, architecture or its pagan-Christian interface. The latter does strike a reasonable tone of conversion-process but trips itself up by explicitly setting it in the early 6th century ('AD 507'), blurring the fusion of heroic ideal and Christianity, where the *Beowulf* poet's skill kept a clear and reinforcing distinction. The material culture context is highly implausible, for it mixes a whole range of 7th- to 12th-century objects and is determinedly Viking (rather than Germanic) in outlook. Thus we see Heorot's walls draped with Baldishel inspired tapestries (Norway, *c*AD 1200), Hrothgar using a copy of the Cammin casket (*c*AD 1000), with red velvet lining, a copy of a 9th-century Tatting ware jug to pour mead and copies of the 10th-century Jelling cup to drink out of. Additionally, dialogue exchanges mention Vinland, Iceland and the Orkneys. Architecturally Heorot looks splendid, but it is unaccountably overshadowed by a huge stone tower, linked to stone battlements that enclose the site, none of which makes any sense for the 6th century. This inaccurate use of material culture left me with something of a quandary, because in terms of the

FIGURE 24.3 *Beowulf* (US 2007): Grendel, a 6th-century nightmare? (Source: BFI and copyright Warner Brothers)

functions they perform they are more or less correct or believable. Does this matter? The anachronistic combination of objects and contexts has never been a bar to creative story telling. Objects have long histories of reappropriations, reuses and repurposes. Indeed, it applies beyond material culture. Words, for example, can often acquire new meanings. This happens, for example, in early Christian Anglo-Saxon poetry (Bazelmans 1999, 72, fn 14). It has been suggested that the author of *Beowulf* was involved in this Christian transformation of the traditional *Ars Poetica* — 'It is ... possible that in his representations of the actions and speech of his pagan characters he was "playing" with both the old and new meanings of words' (Bazelmans 1999, 73). Is it in any sense valid, then, to see the film's transformation of early medieval material culture as a parallel act of creative grammar?[8] Finally, another *Beowulf*-related retelling or reconstituting is worth noting. It is one that the film plays down in eschewing the poem's politics, namely the manifestation of the 'urwarrior-king' as the refounder king: kings who prove their legitimacy by fighting wild beasts and saving important cities from evil/chaos. This has strong resonances in the 8th century, including Al-Mansur's Baghdad, Pippin's Aachen and Constantine V's Constantinople, with a literary parallel in *Beowulf*, his deeds and his restoration of Heorot (Stoclet 2005). Unintentionally, the film does touch on this with a powerful scene in which Beowulf reopens Heorot, a striking contrast with the grandeur of the more considered refounding of Minas Tirith (a parallel Aachen) by its returned, refounder king, Aragon, in *The Lord of the Rings: The Return of the King* (US/NZ/GY 2003).

IN BRUGES AND NAPLES: ARCHAEOLOGISTS AND THE CONTEMPORARY CONTEXT

The contemporary relevance of the pursuit of the medieval past is documented to some extent by the pseudo-medievalism of such films as *The Da Vinci Code* (US 2006) (Hall 2005c) and *National Treasure* (US 2004) (Hall 2006b), but far more rewarding is *Indiana Jones and the Last Crusade* (US 1989), still fantasy but with a solid foundation. It manages to pull off the trick of archaeologist as adventurer because of its meaningfully exaggerated real historical context — the 1930s Nazi collecting drive to acquire medieval relics and other artefacts. This aspect also forms an effective backdrop (with the relics including the spear of Longinus) to the comicbook-inspired *Hellboy* (US 2004). In both films the perceived supernatural power of these relics is matter-of-factly accepted but in a way that is appropriate to the narrative arc of their respective films and not as duplicitous artifice. The modern, contemporary context of engagement with the medieval past through the practice of archaeology and education is only seen in a handful of films. Indian Jones is, of course, an archaeologist and all four films in which he appears show him engaged in fieldwork, collecting artefacts for the university museum and teaching undergraduates. Somewhat more realism is brought to bear in the post-war Ealing comedy *Passport to Pimlico* (UK 1949), in which Margaret Rutherford plays a venerably eccentric local historian who identifies as 15th-century Burgundian the treasure and documents uncovered by an unexploded bomb going off. This enables Pimlico to legally and politically redefine its identity — a consummate film essay in nested identity, triggered by material culture long before it was fashionable in academic circles. Towards the end of the war, Powell and Pressburger gave us one of their great portraits of war-time life in England with *A Canterbury Tale* (UK 1944), which deliberately evoked Chaucer's original but very much focused on contemporary war-time Britain. Set predominantly in a small town near Canterbury (though the cathedral does get its turn), its local JP and museum curator uses Roman and medieval antiquities to teach soldiers stationed near the town about local history. Twelve months later, Powell and Pressburger gave us *I Know Where I'm Going* (UK 1945), filmed on the Scottish West Coast island of Mull. It graphically demonstrates how the Western Isles' identity is suffused by its medieval past. The landscape of medieval ruins (particularly Moy Castle) is redolent with contemporary meaning expressed through stories — including a Viking tale of a Norse prince who must brave the whirlpool of Corryvreckan to win the hand of the daughter of the Lord of the Isles (further reified in a painting of a Viking ship in the whirlpool, hanging in the local post office), and the curse of the MacNeil Lord of Kiloran if he crosses the threshold of Moy Castle. There is fantasy here, but it is tangible and relevant. The Viking legend celebrated in the film seems evidently a part of the real-life that Powell and Pressburger sought to capture for their film, and need not have been of any great antiquity. It could have been inspired by the excavation of a Viking boat burial at Kiloran Bay, Colonsay in 1882 and 1883 (for which see Graham-Campbell and Batey 1998, 118–122).

The importance of communicating and understanding the medieval past is unexpectedly promoted in the serial-killer fable *Seven*, in which police research includes the library-based reading of several medieval (particularly religious) texts to get a handle on the killer. Most of us would find more familiar the founding inspiration of *Timeline*, a hilariously bonkers time-travel adventure in which a group of archaeologists find themselves in the middle of the Hundred Years War. The basic premise of *Timeline* is too silly to rehearse, but think of a giant fax machine that works through time as well as space and can send people, not just paper. Thus a group of archaeologists working on a site in France are sent back through time to the site they have been excavating in the present. In 1357 it is a thriving village, monastery and castle, about to be the scene of a protracted engagement between the French and the English in the Hundred Years War. To survive, the archaeologists must fully engage with their past (which is now their present) including combat and death, in a socially inclusive way (their dress is 'designer peasant'). One of the archaeologists achieves ultimate glory by remaining in the past (it is his future), leaving his colleagues to return to their future present and excavate his tomb 600 years later (it reads 'born 1971, died 1382'). Its politics are very much those of today. The reason why a profusion of Scottish archaeologists are working on a French site soon becomes clear: so that the 14th-century English commander can identify them as allies of the French and glibly remark both on their working together and how the English are at war with everybody (and winning). The clear demarcation of accents — Glaswegian Scots, upper-class English and Franglais — provides a clear sense of narrative distinction but side-steps the medieval reality of large numbers of the English and Anglo-

Scottish aristocrats being of (Norman) French stock. It also suits the Hollywood convention of the English as being the bad guy (especially in historical dramas), whilst American movies have rarely fallen out of love with France or Scotland. The look of the site under excavation is good, with its discrete areas of operation and state of the art equipment, and there is a key short speech by one of the archaeologists about the motivating desire of finding out about what happened in the past. But it then falls down on its generally unrealistic portrait of teacher-student relations and its indulgence in the hoary old stereotype of studying the past as a means of escaping the present. Commercial culture never misses an opportunity to undermine the role of the expert and here they go one better by having an expert undermine himself, by choosing to remain in the past. It certainly forms a marked contrast to two more down-to-earth deployments of the medieval monastic ruins of Yorkshire. *Kes* (UK 1970) is adapted from Barry Hines novel *A Kestrel for a Knave*, a title which immediately evokes a medieval social hierarchy which it seeks to subvert, through a working-class Barnsley lad owning and training a kestrel. Its Barnsley setting encompasses the ruins of Monk Bretton Priory. It is here that the boy sees kestrels nesting high on the church tower, which he scales to steal an egg. The school he attends is close by, but no reference to the priory remains is ever made. By contrast, *The History Boys* (UK 2006, adapted by Alan Bennett from his play) has a strong emphasis on the teaching and learning of medieval history. We see in particular the classroom teaching of the dissolution of the monasteries backed up by a field trip to Fountains Abbey. It effectively demonstrates the value of studying the medieval past and sets this in the wider debate about the purpose of education — should it be for itself (its intrinsic worth — not a popular concept these days) or because of its relevance and application to other purposes and to passing exams?[9]

Two final films deserve examination in telling contemporary stories firmly rooted in a surviving medieval material culture and atmosphere. *Viaggio in Italia* (IT/FR 1953) is set in and around Naples and Pompeii and records an actual Marian procession: its miracle cure plays a key role as an actual miracle and as a symbol of the central couple's inner healing. The film takes great pains to capture a real social backdrop. Throughout the film, Ingrid Bergman's character visits a number of museums and archaeological sites, which allow her to make a bridge between now and then. One of the sites she visits is that of the temple of the Cumaean Sibyl and cult of Apollo, led by an elderly male guide who tells her of the sibyl's association with young lovers and ecstatic prophesies. This visit, along with that to the Christian catacombs in Naples and the enforced participation in the Marian procession, creates a sub-text in the film about the continuity and evolution of 'popular' religious cult practice or syncretism. This accords with more academic understandings of cultic continuity and appropriation. It has been noted, for example, that the close association between the sibyl and Rome led early Christians to consult her in their quest for evidence from pagan sources for the truth of Christian beliefs (Hornblower and Spawforth 1999, 1401). This can be seen as a reflection of a deeply rooted psychological response that can be paralleled in medieval attitudes, a way of wrapping-up continuity within change. *In Bruges* (US/UK/GY 2007) is a very dark comedy, set in Bruges, about hitmen, tourism and purgatory. It makes use of its Bruges setting in two ways: as a tourist destination and as a metaphysical setting for the film's moral discourse (Figure 24.4). Virtually every frame of the film shows the old medieval town as an integral backdrop, either in panorama or detail. Several trips are made to the 13th-century founded bell-tower, we see close-ups of the 12th-century founded Sint-Jonshaspitaal, the late 16th-century De Halve Maan Brewery and the 15th-century Gruuthuse Museum; the hitmen, Ken and Ray, visit the Basilica of the Holy Blood, where Ken touches the holy relic but is unable to persuade Ray to do so, and they also visit the Groeninge Museum. There, they reflect in particular on Bosch's *Last Judgement*, considering the nature of hell and purgatory and whether they still believe in their childhood faith. Their eyes also linger on David's 1498 painting of *The Judgement of Cambyses*, in which a corrupt judge is publicly skinned. Thus we are given a cross-section of the medieval past that draws tourists to Bruges; indeed, we are made surrogate tourists, all the more so as the film questions the purpose of this tourism. It recognizes its uplifting qualities (its 'fairytale' appearance included) but

FIGURE 24.4 *In Bruges* (US/GY/UK 2008): The Church of Our Lady and St John's Hospital — existential angst and moral metaphor in medieval and modern Bruges. (Source: BFI and copyright Universal)

also reflects that stimulation and moral improvement through education are not assured, doing so both vociferously in Ray's rejection of Bruges as a 'shit hole' and of history generally as 'just a load of stuff that has already happened'. The violent nature of the film's principal characters, added to the seemingly tourist trappings of Bruges, forms the platform on which the film builds its metaphysical discourse on morality, redemption, death and the roles of violence. The conjunction of location and dialogue throughout suggests that Bruges may in fact be a very medieval purgatory, at least for Ray (though it also provides redemptive release for Ken). As Ray's body is lifted into an ambulance we hear the voice-over of his thoughts musing that, for him, hell would be the rest of eternity spent in Bruges.

DISCUSSION

In commenting on the many historical/archaeological failings of *Braveheart* (US 1995), Watson (1998) is surely right to say that film narratives are there as an elective choice, as are the narratives of history and archaeology. In the end, the point is not to force a choice one way or the other but to have a debate between alternatives: a debate in which it is for archaeology and history to stand their ground and make their case, but not to be overly dismayed if they are not chosen, and not to tilt at the windmills of narrative invention. The latter rarely desires to officially rewrite history, so much as to create successful drama to which an audience (always a diverse rather than a uniform body) is perceived as being able to more readily relate. It is dangerous to assume that audiences soak-up such narratives sponge-like and without questioning (though it is sometimes self-evident from conversation that some audience members do simply accept them as accurate and official accounts of the past). The narrativization of the past can be positively embraced by archaeology to great effect, as witnessed, for example, by the special issue of the journal *Historical Archaeology* (vol 32). This focused on the role of archaeologists as storytellers, with a range of case studies from America bracketed by two discussions (Praetzellis 1998, 1–3; Deetz 1998, 94–96) which cogently present the interpretation and communication advantages of a narrative approach. For my own part, I can only testify that as a teenage boy if I had not seen *The Adventures of Robin Hood*, *The Sea Hawk*, *The Warlord*, *Seven Samurai*, *El Cid*, *The Vikings* and *Ivanhoe*, I would not have been passionately inspired to find out what really happened. The published conversation between film director John Sayles and professor of history, John Foner, critically observed that even if a director finds that the known history is actually a better story (in terms of interest and complexity), it does not stop the search for fresh perspective or a visceral, page-turning compulsion, balanced by an assumption on the part of film-makers that the audience will not believe everything they see (a fundamental but often forgotten prerequisite to watching any movie). As Sayles observed, 'If historical accuracy were the thing people went to the movies for, historians would be the vice-presidents of studios' (Foner and Sayles 1996, 22).

Films are a particular example of imagined realities, and imagined realities have been an ever-present part of the human drive to explain and adapt through narrative constructions. The same wellspring produced the creative drives for mythopoesis, invention, and material culture. Archaeological and historical explanations have grown and sought their own path, influenced mostly by an honestly meant desire to be objective. The paradox has grown as a consequence of the fantasy/truth split. On the one hand invention and mythopoesis are part of the human condition and so infuse material culture and the archaeological record. The cult of saints and the associated cult of heroes is a prime example: thus in the 12th century the abbey of Landevennec (Finistere, Brittany), under the patronage of local secular potentates, had a new chapel built dedicated to King Gradlon, a fictitious first ancestor and king of Avalon. He was given a reality in stone, mortar and worship.[10] On the other hand, in a contemporary context we require an objective separation between archaeological, scientific, fact-centred analysis of reality and narrative desires. It can be hard to separate fact from fiction when fiction is a fact of existence. Telling stories also gives the individual a greater freedom to think (albeit sometimes corrosively) where as the perceived fixity of academic discourse does not invite that same freedom for many. It is the freedom to think, to hold that possibility of knowing that is to be cherished. At its best it can encourage a dialogue between past, present and future. Film can help to stimulate the debate and communicate it to a wider audience. A compelling recent example is *Stardust* (US/UK 2007) which imaginatively appropriates elements of myth, legend, history and science to tell a new story around old magic. It counter-points, in a 19th-century context, rational science with folk-belief and experience, setting up its fairy realm as a parallel world beyond a magical boundary manifest as a dry stone wall (an archaeological artefact symbolizing the magical quality of investigating the past). This fairy realm is portrayed as a medieval world and includes a high, mountain-top castle and palace (a metaphor for vertical, social stratification) and a walled town on the plain below. The material culture, including dress and other technologies, is clearly medieval and it is also a place where magic works. The chief protagonists and 'star-crossed' lovers are Tristan and Yvaine and represent a re-working of the Romance of Tristan and Isolde, with Yvaine being a fallen star in human form. This celestial shape-shifting evokes an older stratum of belief that saw meteors and shooting stars as deities and the vestiges of their coming to earth as sacred.[11] Equally important in this context is *Pan's Labyrinth* (US/SP/MEX 2006), which is set during the civil war of Franco's Spain and skilfully reinforces elements of Spain's medieval past (including ruins and folk beliefs) as part of the fabric of a fairytale about political resistance. The past — with an emphasis on its medieval elements — reconnects the girl at the heart of the story with a truer, non-Fascist Spain and helps her to mature into an adult. The animated Japanese fantasy *Spirited Away* (2001) also centres on a young girl protagonist who is drawn into a world of largely medieval folk belief that socially strengthens her and helps her to come of age. Though in part prompted by anxieties about childhood being swamped by technology and consumerism, it is not simplistically against change. It deploys very high tech-nology animation to reinvigorate traditional beliefs for a new audience, confirming how, though we may think of them as medieval, they are in fact 'evolving rather than set in stone. They are alive and continue to stay alive, morphing with the times' (Reider 2005, 21).

Perhaps archaeologists and historians should write more narrative constructions, but should these form part of their analysis of the past? We need to be aware of our own and our audiences' desires to know all and to subvert the past to an ideal reality, but we should not produce myths in lieu of not knowing. We should not feel threatened by the range of alternative readings produced by writers and film-makers, or indeed, the audience. Such debates are an essential element of reception studies, which several related disciplines have critically embraced to their benefit (eg the Classical Reception Studies Network). In recent years classical pasts portrayed in the cinema have been well served by books exploring individual films in a collaborative, interdisciplinary way that encompasses historical, archaeological and film perspectives, two notable examples being *Gladiator* and *Spartacus* (Winkler 2005 and 2007 respectively). The time is surely ripe for an interdisciplinary analysis of the key films that explore and reinvent the medieval world. If there are those readers who remain unconvinced of the need for medieval archaeology to engage with other ways of encountering the past, then I hope that this paper might begin to persuade them otherwise. Film is essentially a mechanism of magic, a sleight of hand, a mirror that reflects what we might have been and what we could be. Whether its depictions of the medieval past run counter to, parallel to, or are interwoven with those of medieval archaeology, they engage with audiences and they tell stories. Only the fabled ostrich would keep its head in the sand and refuse to listen.

NOTES

[1] This paper has had a long gestation and I am grateful to the Society for Medieval Archaeology for the opportunity to try out ideas in my contributions exploring popular culture (especially movies) and medievalism in the Society's Newsletter. I am particularly grateful for the encouragement and support of Sally Foster, Roberta Gilchrist and Gabor Thomas. A special thank you goes to my daughter, Eleanor, who steadfastly held, in the way that only teenagers can, to the value of certain films as story and entertainment (with no prerequisite to believe in them) rather than as lessons in history and archaeology.

[2] One relatively overlooked area of appropriated medievalism is that of comics. Various entries in March's 2006 *The Marvel Encyclopedia*, including the Gods of Asgard, Warriors, Three, Valkyrie, Thor, Loki, Balder the Brave, Fenris, Enchantress, Black Knight, Arabian Knight, Morgan Le Fay and Excalibur, give an indication of the range of borrowings.

[3] I have explored elsewhere the question of invented reality with respect to the medieval past (Hall 2008) and see also Lowenthal 1998 and Taschen 2007, for a survey of fantasy worlds made concrete in our own (several of them influenced by eccentric perceptions of the medieval).

[4] *The Name of the Rose* is useful in another respect: demonstrating the subjective nature of film analysis and appreciation. It has been both lauded as a triumph and dismissed as a disaster by two eminent medieval historians: Cantor (1992, 441) takes the triumphal view ('better than the book in my judgement') and Airlie (2001, 163) the disaster view ('a lumbering failure'). They equally disagree on *The Seventh Seal* ('Bergman's masterpiece' and 'it has not worn well', respectively) and yet both agree on the brilliance of *The Navigator* and *Alexander Nevsky*.

[5] For example, St William of Perth (Hall 2005b, 80; Crook 2006, 126), St Guinnefort (Schmitt 1983) and St John Schorn (Spencer 1998, 192–195).

[6] Lack of space precludes a discussion of ghosts but the medieval phenomenon of the 'army of the dead' (Schmitt 1998, 93–122), and ghosts generally bears fruitful comparison with a whole range of films situating them in new contexts, including *Return of the Evil Dead* (SP 1973), *Ghost Breakers* (US 1940), *Ghostbusters I* and *II* (US 1984 and 1989), *Ghost* (US 1990), *Scooby Doo 2* (US 2004), *High Plains Drifter* (US 1972), *Rashomon* (JAP 1951), *Kwaidan* (JAP 1964) and *Lord of the Rings: Return of the King* (US, NZ/GY 2003).

[7] I am not concerned here with TV (whilst recognizing it is part of the wider cultural context) but note must be made of the cult animated science-fiction satire *Futurama*. Season 4 includes a typically brilliant episode (16) entitled 'Three Hundred Big Boys', in which the treasure of the conquered Spiderians is put on display and

includes a large silk tapestry, woven by the Spiderians as they fought, and lost, their Hastings against the conquering Earthians. It is a delightful satire on the Tapestry and its being woven by the losing side.

[8] This speculation has, if not dismissed out of hand, ramifications for the rational, scientific categorization of culture; see Hall 2008.

[9] Education as life-long learning is demonstrably argued for in the specific context of the aftermath of World War I, by the film *A Month in the Country* (UK 1987). This charts the story of two British ex-soldiers in the same Yorkshire village, one there to uncover the white-washed medieval Doom painting on the parish church's chancel arch, and the other to excavate a medieval grave. The story gives archaeology a status pivotal in an individual's thinking of things out (about the past and in the present), as friendship-forming and as antithetical to war.

[10] This is not a lone reflex in the medieval period and it is also evident in portable material culture: in 1191 King Richard of England presented to Tancred of Sicily the sword Excalibur 'and the legend was brought to life', thus demonstrating how 'precious symbols of the past become objects which one could touch and admire or give as gifts' (Schnapp 1996, 98), and they also served as practical manifestations of psychological desires 'to magnify our power, enhance our well-being and extend our memory into the future' (Csikszentnihalyi 1993, 28). Objects which today, in hindsight, are too easily dismissed as simple fakery and chicanery in fact usefully objectified boundaries between religion, magic, myth and science and constitute crucial, 'material evidence for the imaginary universe inhabited by the human mind' (Jones 1990, 79).

[11] The meteor crater at Kaali, Estonia, for example, has accrued a long history as a sacred lake (Rasmussen *et al* 2000). The 5th-century AD impact in Abruzzo, Italy, came at a time of Christian conversion and, falling during a pagan festival, was exploited to aid that conversion (Santilli *et al* 2003). What seems like one of the film's most fantastic elements — a ship that sails the clouds, farming lightning, can readily be seen to be inspired by the sky-ships of the 9th-century weather magicians or *tempestarii*, charlatans roundly condemned by Archbishop Agobard of Lyons (Halsall 2001).

BIBLIOGRAPHY

Airlie, S, 2001 'Strange eventful histories: the Middle Ages in the cinema', in P Linehan and J L Nelson (eds), *The Medieval World*, 163–183, Routledge, London

Appadurai, A (ed), 1986 *The Social Life of Things. Commodities in Cultural Perspective*, Cambridge University Press, Cambridge

Bazelmans, J, 1999 *By Weapons Made Worthy — Lords, Retainers and Their Relationship in Beowulf*, Amsterdam University Press, Amsterdam

Brewer, D, 1997 'Retellings', in T Hahn and A Lupack (eds), *Retelling Tales Essays in Honour of Russell Peck*, 9–34, Cambridge University Press, Cambridge

Cantor, N F, 1991 *Inventing the Middle Ages*, Cambridge University Press, Cambridge

Carnes, M C (ed), 1996 *Past Imperfect. History According to the Movies*, Cassell, London

Classical Reception Studies Network online at http://www2.open.ac.uk/ClassicalStudies/GreekPlays/crsn/index.shtml (accessed 23 July 2008)

Crook, J, 2006 'The medieval shrines of Rochester Cathedral', in T Ayers and T Tatton-Brown (eds), *Medieval Art, Architecture and Archaeology at Rochester*, 114–129, Maney Publishing, Leeds

Csikszentnihalyii, M, 1993 'Why we need things', in S Lubar and W P Kingary (eds), *History From Things Essays On Material Culture*, 20–29, Smithsonian Institution Press, Washington

Deetz, C, 1998 'Discussion: Archaeologists as Storytellers', *Historical Archaeology* 32:1, 94–96

Eagleton, T, 2004 *After Theory*, Penguin, London

Foner, E and Sayles, J, 1996 'A Conversation between Eric Foner and John Sayles', in Carnes (ed) 1996, 11–30

Graham-Campbell, J and Batey, C E, 1998 *Vikings in Scotland. An Archaeological Survey*, Edinburgh University Press, Edinburgh

Gurevich, A J, 1985 *Categories of Medieval Culture*, Routledge, London

Hall, M A, 2005a 'Burgh mentalities: a town-in-the-country case study of Perth, Scotland', in K Giles and C Dyer (eds), *Town and Country in the Middle Ages. Contrasts, Contacts and Interconnections 1100–1500*, 211–228, Society for Medieval Archaeology Monograph 23, Maney Publishing, Leeds

Hall, M A, 2005b 'Of holy men and heroes: the cult of saints in medieval Perthshire', *The Innes Review* 56:1, 60–87

Hall, M A, 2005c 'Material culture, narrative and getting it wrong: three views of the medieval past', *Medieval Archaeology Newsletter* 32, 8–11

Hall, M A, 2006a 'Cinema Paradiso: Re-picturing the Medieval Cult of Saints', *Peregrinations* 2:1, 40–54. http://peregrinations.kenyon.edu/

Hall, M A, 2006b 'More Medieval Movie Madness', *Society for Medieval Archaeology Newsletter* 35, 7–10

Hall, M A, 2008 'Speculum Fantasia – Middle –Earth and Discworld as Mirrors of Medieval Europe', *European Journal of Archaeology Blog* (http://eje.e-a-a.org), mounted 16 January 2008

Hall, M A, 2009 'Where the abbot carries dice: gaming-board misericords in context', in E C Block (ed), *Profane Imagery in Marginal Arts of the Middle Ages*, Profane Arts of the Middle Ages 1, Brepols, Turnhout, 63–81

Hall, M A, forthcoming 'Playtime: The Material Culture of Gaming in Medieval Scotland', in T Cowan and L Henderson (eds), *Everyday Life in Scotland Volume 1 (Medieval)*, Edinburgh

Halsall, P, 2001 'Medieval sourcebook: Agobard of Lyons (9th century): on hail and thunder', online at http://www.fordham.edu/halsall/source/Agobard-OnHailandThunder.html (accessed 21 June 2008)

Hames, P, 2000 'In the shadow of the werewolf — František Vláčils *Markéta Lazarová's* revival in the UK', *Central Europe Review* 2:35 (16 October 2000), online at http://www.ce.review.org/00/35/kinoeye35_hames.hyml (accessed 12 September 2007)

Harty, K J, 1997 *The Reel Middle Ages, American, Western and Eastern European, Middle Eastern and Asian Films About Medieval Europe*, McFarland & Co, Jefferson, North Carolina

Heaney, S, 1999 *Beowulf A New Translation*, Faber and Faber, London

Hicks, C, 2006 *The Bayeux Tapestry The Life Story of a Masterpiece*, Chatto & Windus, London

Holtorf, C, 2002 'Notes on the life history of a pot sherd', *Journal of Material Culture* 7:1, 49–71

Hornblower, S and Spawforth, A (eds), 1999 *The Oxford Classical Dictionary*, Clarendon Press, Oxford

Jones, M (ed), 1990 *Fake? The Art of Deception*, British Museum Press, London

Krasniewicz, L, 2006 '"Round up the usual suspects" anthropology goes to the movies', *Expedition* 48:1, 8–14

Latour, B, 1993 *We Have Never Been Modern*, translated by Catherine Porter, Harvard University Press, Cambridge MS

Le Fanu, M, 1987 *The Cinema of Andrei Tarkovsky*, British Film Institute, London

Lerner, G, 1996 'Joan of Arc: Three Films', in Carnes (ed) 1996, 54–59

Lowenthal, D, 1998 'Fabricating heritage', *History and Memory* 10:1, 1–16, online at http://www.iupress.indiana.edu/journals/history/ham10-1.html (accessed 4 July 2008)

Lucas, G, 2005 *The Archaeology of Time*, Routledge, London

March, D (ed), 2006 *The Marvel Encyclopedia*, Dorling Kindersley, London

Marshall, D W (ed), 2007 *Mass Market Medieval Essays on the Middle Ages in Popular Culture*, McFarland & Co, Jefferson NC and London

Muir, E, 2005 *Ritual in Early Modern Europe*, 2nd edn, Cambridge University Press, Cambridge

Nokes, R S, 2008 'Beowulf: Prince of the Geats, Nazis, and Odinists', *Old English Newsletter* 41.3 26–32

Praetzellis, A, 1998 'Introduction: why every archaeologist should tell stories once in a while', *Historical Archaeology* 32:1, 1–3
Pratchett, T, 1999 *The Fifth Elephant*, Corgi, London
Rasmussen, K L, Aaby, B and Gwozdz, R, 2000 'The age of the Kaalijärv meteorite craters', *Meteoritics and Planetary Science* 35:6, 1067–71
Reider, N T, 2005 '*Spirited Away*: film of the fantastic and evolving Japanese folk symbols', *Film Criticism* 29:3, 4–27, online at http://www.corneredangel.com/amwess/papers/spirited_away.pdf (accessed 26 July 2008)
Sabloff, J, 2008 *Archaeology Matters. Action Archaeology in the Modern World*, Left Coast Press, Walnut Creek, CA
Santilli, R, Ormö, J, Rossi, A P and Komatsu, G, 2003 'A catastrophe remembered: a meteorite impact of the fifth century AD in the Abruzzo, central Italy', *Antiquity* 77, 313–320
Schmitt, J C, 1983 *The Holy Greyhound: St Guinnefort Healer of Children Since the 13th Century*, Cambridge University Press, Cambridge and Paris
Schmitt, J C, 1998 *Ghosts in the Middle Ages, the Living and the Dead in Medieval Society*, Chicago University Press, Chicago
Schnapp, A, 1996 *The Discovery of the Past. The Origins of Archaeology*, British Museum Press, London
Slobodova, Z, 2000 'Is that the best you can do?', *Central Europe Review* 2:42, online at http://www.ce.review.org/00/35/kinoeye42_slobodova.html (accessed 12 September 2007)
Spencer, B, 1998 *Pilgrim Souvenirs and Secular Badges*, Museum of London, London
Stoclet, A J, 2005 'From Baghdad to *Beowulf*: eulogising "Imperial" capitals east and west in the mid-eighth century', *Proceedings of the Royal Irish Academy* 105C:4, 151–195
Tarkovsky, A, 1986 *Sculpting in Time. Reflections on the Cinema*, Bodley Head, London
Taschen, A (ed), 2007 *Fantasy Worlds*, Taschen, Köln
Watson, F, 1998 'Braveheart: more than just pulp fiction?', in J Arnold, K Davies and S Ditchford (eds), *History and Heritage — Consuming the Past in Contemporary Culture*, 129–140, Donhead, Shaftsbury
Whitrow, G J, 1988 *Time in History*, Oxford University Press, Oxford
Wilson, D M, 2004 *The Bayeux Tapestry*, Thames and Hudson, London
Winder, S, 2006 *The Man Who Saved Britain*, Picador, London

INDEX